lonely planet

Ecuador & the Galápagos Islands

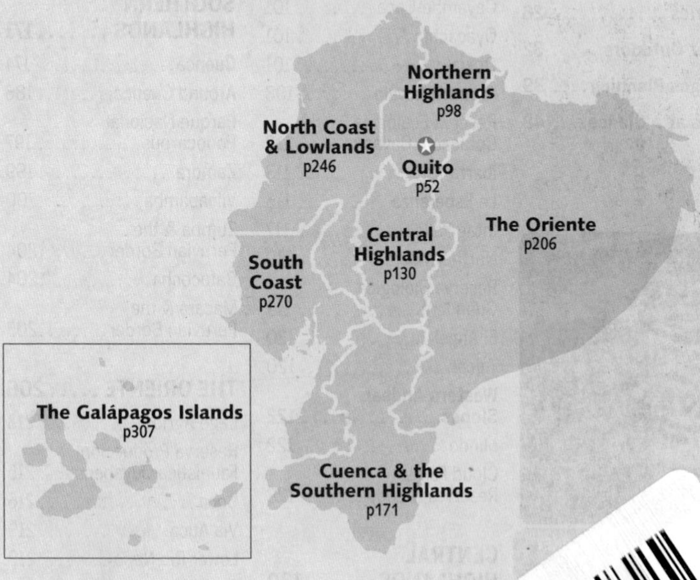

Northern Highlands
p98

North Coast & Lowlands
p246

Quito
p52

The Oriente
p206

Central Highlands
p130

South Coast
p270

The Galápagos Islands
p307

Cuenca & the Southern Highlands
p171

Isabel Albiston, Jade Bremner, Brian Kluepfel,
MaSovaida Morgan, Wendy Yanagihara

PLAN YOUR TRIP

BARNA TANKO/SHUTTERSTOCK ©

OTAVALO CRAFTS MARKET P104

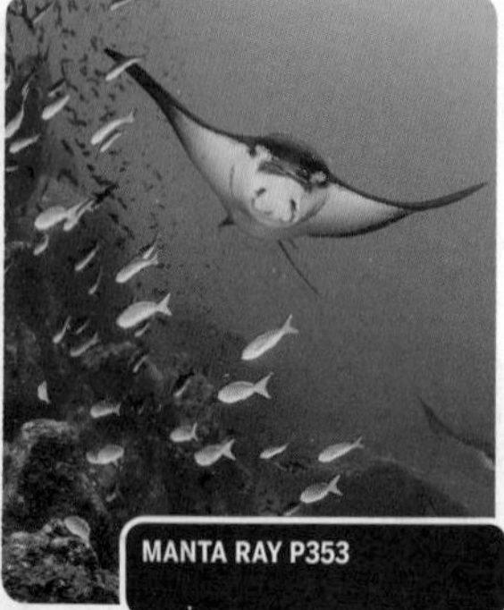

WILDESTANIMAL/SHUTTERSTOCK ©

MANTA RAY P353

ON THE ROAD

Contents

UNDERSTAND

SURVIVAL GUIDE

SPECIAL FEATURES

Welcome to Ecuador

Postcard-pretty colonial centers, Kichwa villages, Amazonian rainforest and the breathtaking heights of the Andes – a dazzling array of wonders is squeezed into this compact country.

Cultural Splendor

The historic centers of Quito and Cuenca are lined with photogenic plazas, 17th-century churches and monasteries, and beautifully restored mansions. Wandering the streets amid architectural treasures from Spanish colonial days is a fine way to delve into the past. Beyond the cities, the Ecuadorian landscape unfolds in all its startling variety. There are Andean villages renowned for their colorful textiles and sprawling markets, Afro-Ecuadorian towns where days end fresh seafood and memorable sunsets, and remote settlements in the Amazon where shamans still harvest the traditional rainforest medicines of their ancestors.

Andean Adventure

Setting off on a hike in the Andes can seem like stepping into a fairy tale: a patchwork of small villages, gurgling brooks and rolling fields and maybe a condor slowly wheeling overhead. You don't have to scale a mountain to enjoy the Andes. These verdant landscapes make a fine backdrop for mountain biking, horseback riding or hiking from village to village. Ecuador's other landscapes offer equally alluring adventures, from surfing off the Pacific coast to white-water rafting rivers along the banks of the Oriente.

Wildlife-Watching

The famous Galápagos Islands, with their volcanic, otherworldly landscapes, are a magnet for wildlife lovers. Here, you can get up close and personal with massive lumbering tortoises, scurrying marine iguanas (the world's only seagoing lizard), doe-eyed sea lions, prancing blue-footed boobies and a host of other unusual species both on land and sea. The Amazon rainforest offers a vastly different wildlife-watching experience. Set out on the rivers and forested trails in search of monkeys, sloths, toucans and river dolphins. Some lodges also have canopy towers offering magnificent views.

Sublime Scenery

After days of Ecuadorian adventures, there are many places where you can go to relax amid awe-inspiring scenery. Head to the highlands to recharge at a historic hacienda, or find Zen-like beauty at a cloud-forest lodge near Mindo. There are peaceful, timeless mountain villages like Vilcabamba and picturesque former gold-mining towns such as Zaruma that offer a perfect antidote to modern life. And for a coastal getaway, you'll have plenty of options, from tiny end-of-the-road settlements like Ayampe and Olón to charming towns on the Galápagos, with great beaches and magnificent sunsets.

Why I Love Ecuador

By Isabel Albiston, Writer

Ecuador is a compact country, but its size is one of its greatest appeals. From lush Amazonian jungle, to snow-capped volcanoes, to the sandy beaches and relaxed rhythms of the coast, to the sublimely beautiful Galápagos Islands, there is such diversity to be found within Ecuador's borders that you might feel you need never travel elsewhere again. The country's hospitable people and delicious and varied cuisine are yet another plus for this wonderful place. No wonder, then, that just seven months after my first visit I returned for more. One trip to Ecuador is never enough.

For more about our writers, see p415

Above: Inti Raymi festivities, Pujili

Ecuador & the Galápagos Islands

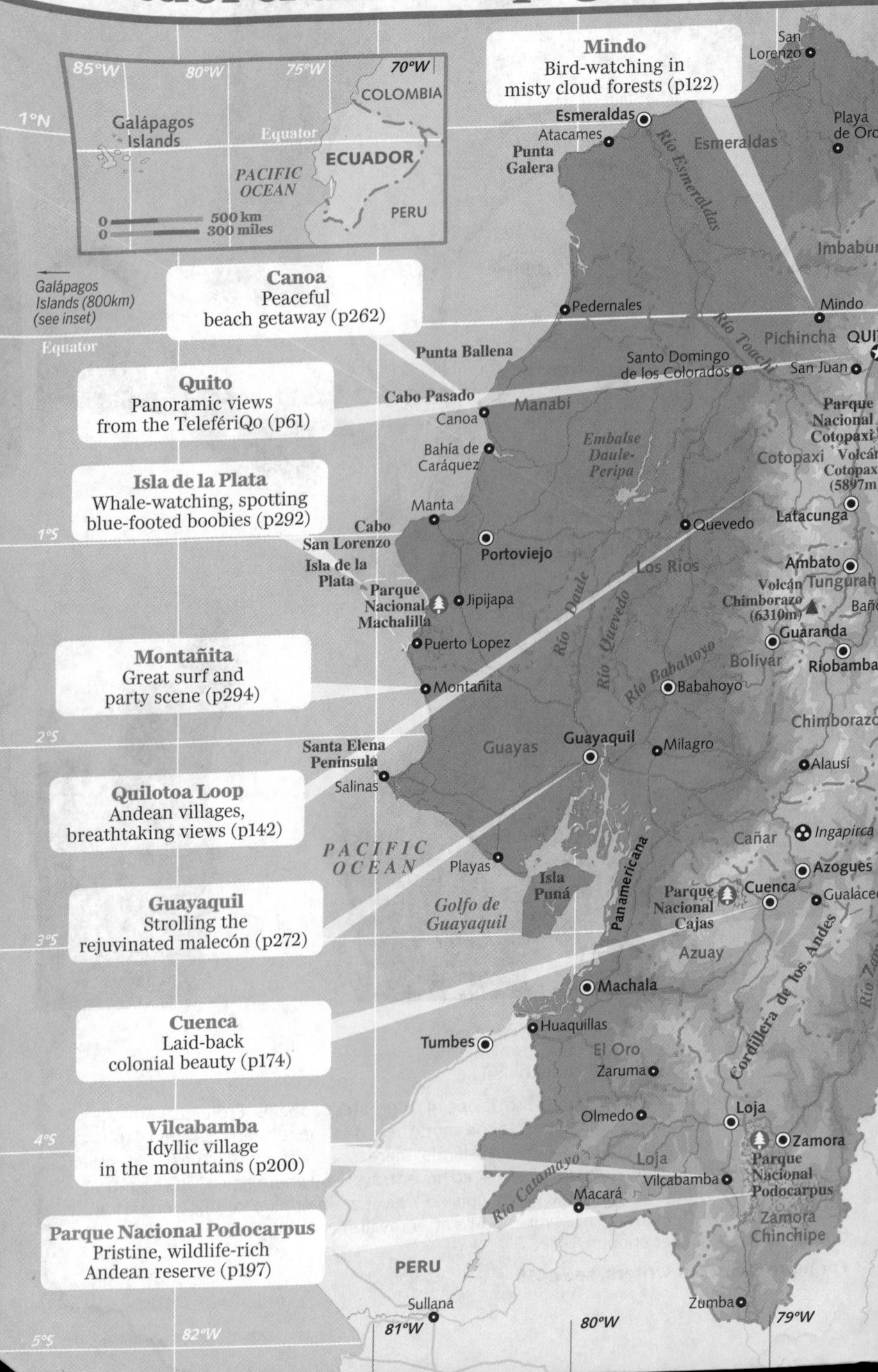

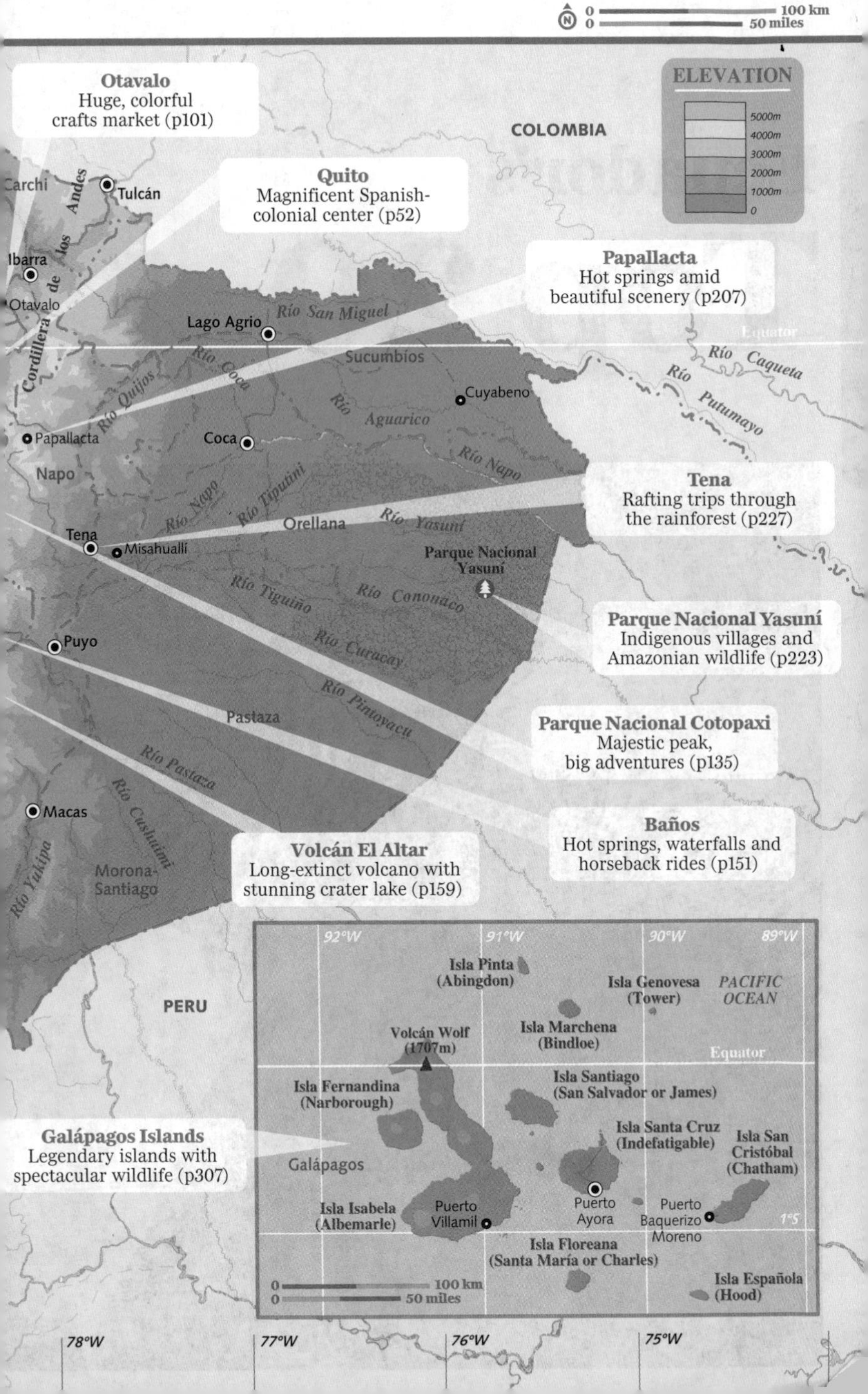

0 100 km
0 50 miles

ELEVATION
5000m
4000m
3000m
2000m
1000m
0

COLOMBIA

Otavalo
Huge, colorful crafts market (p101)

Quito
Magnificent Spanish-colonial center (p52)

Papallacta
Hot springs amid beautiful scenery (p207)

Tena
Rafting trips through the rainforest (p227)

Parque Nacional Yasuní
Indigenous villages and Amazonian wildlife (p223)

Parque Nacional Cotopaxi
Majestic peak, big adventures (p135)

Baños
Hot springs, waterfalls and horseback rides (p151)

Volcán El Altar
Long-extinct volcano with stunning crater lake (p159)

Galápagos Islands
Legendary islands with spectacular wildlife (p307)

Carchi
Tulcán
Cordillera de los Andes
Ibarra
Otavalo
Lago Agrio
Río San Miguel
Equator
Río Caqueta
Río Putumayo
Sucumbíos
Río Coca
Río Quijos
Río Aguarico
Cuyabeno
Papallacta
Coca
Río Napo
Napo
Río Tiputini
Orellana
Río Yasuní
Tena
Misahuallí
Parque Nacional Yasuní
Río Tiguiño
Río Cononaco
Puyo
Río Curacay
Río Pintoyacu
Pastaza
Río Pastaza
Macas
Río Cushuimi
Río Yukipa
Morona-Santiago
PERU

92°W
91°W
90°W
89°W
Isla Pinta (Abingdon)
Isla Genovesa (Tower)
PACIFIC OCEAN
Isla Marchena (Bindloe)
Volcán Wolf (1707m)
Equator
Isla Fernandina (Narborough)
Isla Santiago (San Salvador or James)
Isla Santa Cruz (Indefatigable)
Isla San Cristóbal (Chatham)
Galápagos
Isla Isabela (Albemarle)
Puerto Villamil
Puerto Ayora
Puerto Baquerizo Moreno
1°S
Isla Floreana (Santa María or Charles)
Isla Española (Hood)
0 100 km
0 50 miles

78°W
77°W
76°W
75°W

Ecuador's Top 20

1

Iguana-Spotting in the Galápagos

1 There aren't many places that can beat the Galápagos Islands (p307) for close encounters of the prehistoric kind. Rather than scurrying away when approached, the unique lizard species of iguanas found throughout the archipelago go about their slow-moving business with little concern for the clicking cameras. The dark gray or black marine iguanas pile on top of one another like a messy pyramid of cheerleaders basking in the sun, while the imposing yellow land iguanas nibble on cactus plants for sustenance.

Quito Old Town

2 A Spanish-colonial stunner, Quito's vibrant Centro Histórico (p54) is packed with elaborate churches and old-time monasteries (some were centuries in the making), people-packed plazas and looming bell towers. History lurks around every corner of this well-preserved center. Delve into the past by stepping off the cobblestones and entering beautifully maintained museums, historic mansions and jaw-dropping sanctuaries. Afterwards, have a meal in an old-world restaurant or join the festivities on lively La Ronda street before retiring to one of the many charming guesthouses in the neighborhood.

Below: Iglesia y Convento de San Francisco (p59)

FOTOGRIN/SHUTTERSTOCK ©

2

PHILIP LEE HARVEY/LONELY PLANET ©

ECUADORPOSTALES/SHUTTERSTOCK ©

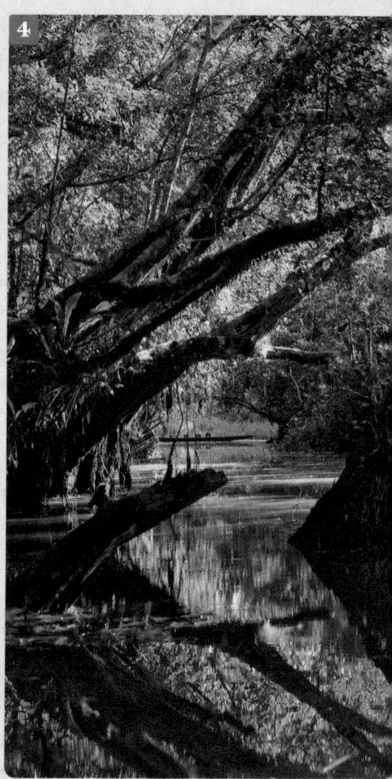

Parque Nacional Cotopaxi

3 Home to Ecuador's best known volcano, Parque Nacional Cotopaxi (p135) offers quick adventures from the capital with million-dollar views and great mountainside lodging options. Climbing the 5897m peak of Volcán Cotopaxi (pictured: p135) will no doubt be a highlight for the lucky few who make it to the top. Otherwise, you can skip the crampons and ice-axes, opting instead for life-affirming snapshots from the edge, or hikes, bikes and horseback rides around high Andean lakes and up to nearby volcanic peaks.

Parque Nacional Yasuní

4 This vast tract of protected rainforest (p223) contains a dazzling biodiversity matched almost nowhere else on earth. Excitement-filled canoe trips through tiny overgrown creeks and hikes across the jungle floor with experienced guides reveal all manner of flowers, plants and creatures, many of which you won't have heard of before, let alone have seen in real life, while several populations of indigenous peoples continue to resist contact with the outside world here. This natural wonder remains, at present, unspoiled.

Cuenca

5 The fairy-tale colonial center of Cuenca (p174) is a Unesco World Heritage Site that's been charming visitors since the 16th century. While the cobblestone streets, polychrome building fronts and well-preserved cathedral will have you snapping a photo on nearly every corner, it's the town's laid-back feel, friendly locals and bohemian spirit that will truly fill your heart. Top that off with great nightlife, plenty of museums and galleries, and some of Ecuador's best eateries, and there's no doubting why this is the top highlight. Above right: Catedral de la Inmaculada Concepción (p175)

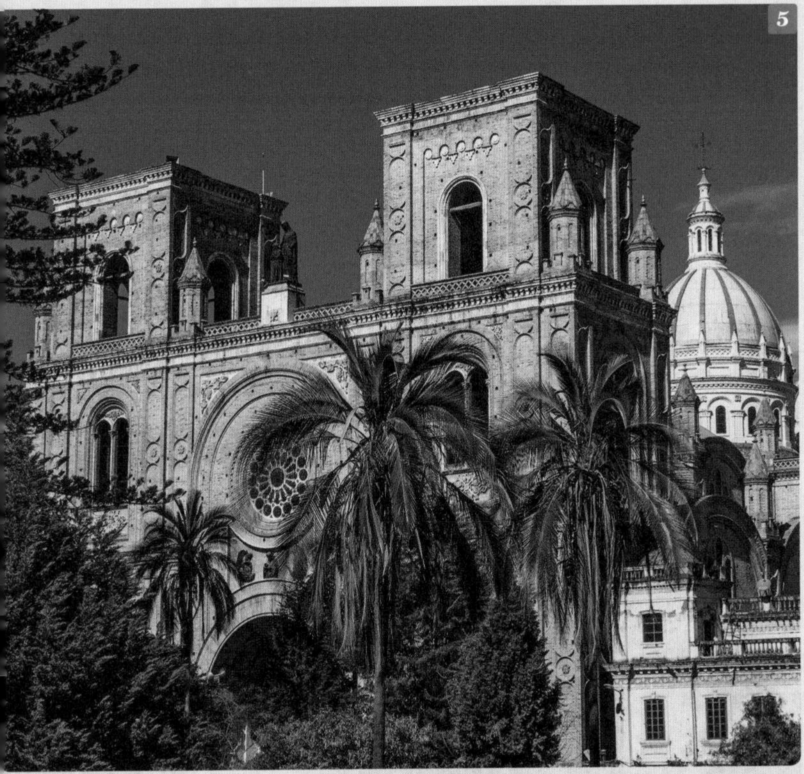

Beaches of the Northwest Coast

6 Think Ecuador isn't the place for sun and sand? Well think again, because the northwest of the country is packed with fishing villages, resort towns, surfer hangouts and pristine areas of golden sand. One of the best places for a sunny getaway is Canoa (p262), where you'll find a long beach backed by cliffs, and some excellent surf. When the sun goes down, Canoa's lively eating and drinking spots make the perfect ending to a day spent frolicking among the waves.

FOTOGRIN/SHUTTERSTOCK ©

Quilotoa Loop

7 Adventure begins at 3000m along the popular Quilotoa Loop (p142), a rough travelers' route that takes you through indigenous villages and painters' colonies to a deep-blue crater lake and into the heart of Ecuador's central highlands. The best thing about the loop is that you can custom-build your adventure to fit your needs. Want to volunteer in a sustainable agriculture project? No problem. Or would you like to hike from village to village on forgotten trails? Yep, they've got that, too.

Soaking in the Steaming Waters of Papallacta

8 The beautifully maintained public baths just outside the Andean village of Papallacta (p207) offer one of Ecuador's best natural highs: move between baths of thermally heated water surrounded by mountains all around, swim in the fantastic pool, enjoy a bracing jump into the icy plunge pool and then get right back into those steaming baths. It's even more magical at night, when you can lie back and watch the stars come out in the giant black sky above.

7

8

PAULWOLF/GETTY IMAGES ©

ALL CANADA PHOTOS/ALAMY STOCK PHOTO ©

Riding the TelefériQo

9 Proving there's more than one way to summit the Andean peaks, the TeleférіQo (p61) whisks you up by aerial tram to breathtaking heights (4100m) over Quito. In a city of sublime views, Cruz Loma offers the finest of all – assuming you go on a clear day. Here, Quito spreads out across the Andean valley, with majestic peaks (including Cotopaxi) visible in the distance. At the top, you can extend the adventure by hiking (or taking a horseback ride) to the 4680m summit of Rucu Pichincha.

Whale-Watching off Isla de la Plata

10 In terms of sheer awe-inspiring natural power, experiencing firsthand the breaching of a humpback whale is hard to equal. From June to September every year nearly 1000 of these majestic creatures migrate to the waters off the coast of Ecuador. The prime base for organizing boat trips, during which you might also spot dolphins and killer, pilot and beaked whales, is the fishing town of Puerto López (p288); you can also arrange trips in Salinas.

Parque Nacional Podocarpus

11 Down by the Peruvian border, Parque Nacional Podocarpus (p197) is one of the southern highlands' least-visited reserves. With elevations ranging from 900m to 3600m, Podocarpus is home to an amazing array of plant and animal life. There are an estimated 3000 plant species (many not found elsewhere in the world). For bird lovers, an astounding 600 unique types of feathered friends await. Top that off with trails, highland lakes and sweeping views, and you have one of Ecuador's most unique offbeat attractions.

Above right: Paradise tanager

12

13

Climbing El Altar

12 Climbers are spoiled for choice with the range of volcanoes and mountains in Ecuador, but El Altar (p159) is considered by many to be the country's most picturesque and fascinating peak. At 5319m, this long-extinct volcano in the Parque Nacional Sangay is the country's fifth-highest mountain. It's a challenging, technical climb to the top, but a more manageable, two-day hike takes you over the Collanes plain to the stunning and atmospheric jade-colored Laguna Amarilla at 4300m, surrounded by nine craggy peaks.

Vilcabamba

13 The air in Vilcabamba (p200) just feels right – not too hot, not too cold – giving this southern highlands draw a mystical quality that many travelers find inescapable. Perhaps that's why you'll find more foreigner-owned businesses here than almost anywhere else in Ecuador. And who can blame them? The hiking is great, there's a national park nearby for backwoods adventures on horseback and mountain bike, and the pitch-perfect spa resorts will cater to your every need, whim and desire.

Surfing at Montañita

14 A dependable year-round beach break and a welcoming community of experienced surfers and mellow dread-locked travelers make this coastal village (p294) an ideal stop to ride some waves. Beginners unafraid to take a little pounding and swallow some salt water can easily find willing locals for lessons, and there are smaller breaks north of here in Olón. Even if you're not looking to get air on gnarly overheads, watching the exploits from the beach while stunning sunsets provide the backdrop is not a bad alternative.

Punta Suárez

15 Looking over the dramatic cliffs on the western tip of Isla Española (p334) is like standing at the edge of the known world. Wide-open sea stretches to the horizon and a spectacular blowhole erupts rhythmically in the foreground. Waved albatrosses and their fluffy young nest in the bushes, and tiny finches hop along the rocky path. Nazca and blue-footed boobies (pictured) gather along the precipice, and red-billed tropicbirds and Galápagos hawks soar over the ledge in beautiful displays of aerial virtuosity.

16

17

JUAN CARLOS VINDAS/GETTY IMAGES ©

18

Hiking & Bird-Watching in Mindo

16 Word is out about this friendly town set amid gorgeous cloud forest in a dramatic valley between Quito and the Pacific coast. While Mindo (p122) may no longer be an off-the-beaten-track destination, its twin attractions – world-class bird-watching and wonderful hiking scenery – remain as dazzling as ever. The biodiversity means that birdwatchers can spend days with a village guide seeing a variety of avian life, while walkers explore the nearby waterfalls, thick cloud forest and soaring cliffs. Above: Crested quetzal

Guayaquil's Malecón

17 There's nowhere more emblematic of Guayaquil's rejuvenation and civic pride than its riverside promenade (p272). It's a parade of couples, office workers and strolling families. This once neglected and maligned waterfront now combines the often conflicting virtues of a park and town plaza. Historic monuments abut landscaped gardens, a top-flight museum and art-house movie theater are only a short walk from a contemporary kids' playground, and outdoor restaurants and cafes looking out on the river make downtown seem far away.

Baños

18 Caught between the Andes and the Amazon in a magical little valley complete with its own waterfall and numerous natural springs, Baños (p151) is an adrenaline junkie's paradise. Gearheads and naturalists alike will love the mountain-bike descent down to the remote outpost of Puyo in the Amazon Basin. For paddlers, there are a handful of white-water trips and flat-water floats. It's also the most popular backpacker spot in the central highlands, meaning that, for better or worse, you'll never be alone in Baños.

White-Water Rafting near Tena

19 Take to the waters around Tena (p227) for some of South America's top rafting and kayaking, where rivers churn through tropical valleys and canyons, and serve up some memorable one-day to week-long adventures. Experienced Tena outfitters school you in the art of paddling and get you out on everything from lazy rainforest meanders to gargantuan Class V white-water thrills, where you'll be camping out in the jungle in between stints of getting gloriously wet.

Local Crafts at Otavalo Market

20 Every Saturday the world seems to converge on the bustling indigenous town of Otavalo (p101) in the Andes, where a huge market (which goes on in a rather redacted form every other day of the week) spreads out from the Plaza de Ponchos throughout town. The choice is enormous, the quality changeable and the crowds can be a drag, but you'll find some incredible bargains here among the brightly colored rugs, traditional crafts, clothing, striking folk art and quality straw hats.

Need to Know

For more information, see Survival Guide (p381)

Currency
US dollar ($)

Language
Spanish

Visas
Visitors from most countries don't need visas for stays of less than 90 days. Residents from a handful of African and Asian countries (including China) require visas.

Money
The official currency is the US dollar. Aside from euros, Peruvian soles and Colombian nuevos soles, it's difficult to change foreign currencies in Ecuador.

Cell Phones
Cell (mobile) numbers are preceded by 09. Bring your phone and purchase a SIM card (called a 'chip', costing $5 to $10) from a local network. Add credit at convenience stores and supermarkets.

Time
Ecuador Time (GMT/UTC minus five hours), Galápagos Time (GMT/UTC minus six hours)

When to Go

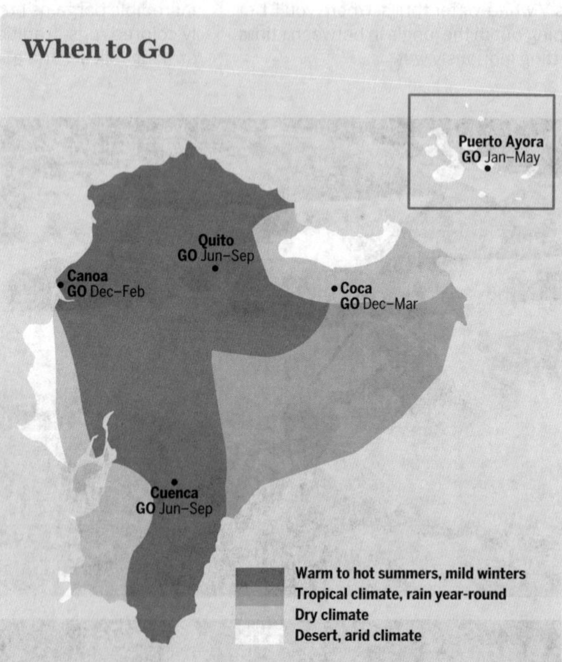

High Season
(Jun-Sep)

➡ Sunny, clear days in the highlands; less rain in the Oriente.

➡ December to April is high season on the coast: expect warm temperatures and periodic showers.

➡ January to May is high season in the Galápagos.

Shoulder
(Oct-Nov)

➡ Cooler temperatures, more showers (usually sun in the morning and rain in the afternoon) in the highlands.

Low Season
(Dec-May)

➡ Cooler, rainier days in the highlands.

➡ June to December is low season in the Galápagos, with cooler, drier weather and rougher seas.

➡ Low season is April to July in the Oriente, when heavy rains are common.

Useful Websites

Lonely Planet (www.lonelyplanet.com) Destination information, hotel bookings, travel forum, photos.

Ministry of Tourism Ecuador (http://ecuador.travel) Handy overviews of highlights, cuisine and travel tips countrywide.

Latin American Network Information Center (http://lanic.utexas.edu/la/ecuador) Scores of useful links about everything Ecuadorian.

Important Numbers

To call any regular number, dial the area code, followed by the seven-digit number.

Ambulance	☎131
Directory Assistance	☎104
Emergency (major cities only)	☎911
Fire	☎102
Police	☎101

Exchange Rates

Australia	A$1	US$0.78
Canada	C$1	US$0.79
Europe	€1	US$1.18
Japan	¥100	US$0.88
New Zealand	NZ$1	US$0.70
UK	UK£1	US$1.32

For current exchange rates see www.xe.com.

Daily Costs

Budget: Less than $40

- Budget guesthouses: $15–20 per person
- Set lunches: $2.50–3.50
- One-day bike rental for trip from Baños to Puyo: $10

Midrange: $40–100

- Double room in midrange hotel: $40–90
- Dinner for two in a good restaurant: $20–30
- Climbing, cycling and bird-watching tours: $60–80
- Jungle lodges: from $175 for four days

Top end: More than $100

- Galápagos tour: from $300
- Top Amazon lodges: around $400
- Haciendas on Cotopaxi: from $100

Opening Hours

Opening hours are provided when they differ from the following standard hours:

Restaurants 10:30am to 11pm Monday to Saturday

Bars 6pm to midnight Monday to Thursday, to 2am Friday and Saturday

Shops 9am to 7pm Monday to Friday, 9am to noon Saturday

Banks 8am to 2pm or 4pm Monday to Friday

Post offices 8am to 6pm Monday to Friday, 8am to 1pm Saturday

Telephone call centers 8am to 10pm daily

Arriving in Ecuador & the Galápagos Islands

Aeropuerto Internacional Mariscal Sucre (Quito) The capital's airport is about 38km east of the city center. Taxis charge $22 to $30 to town, or take a shuttle bus ($8) to central Quito.

Aeropuerto José Joaquín de Olmedo (Guayaquil) Taxis to downtown cost around $5. A Metrovia bus stops in front of the airport and runs downtown ($0.30).

Getting Around

Ecuador has an efficient public transportation system, and because of its small size you can usually get to most places fairly easily.

Air Apart from the Galápagos Islands, flights from Quito also serve several destinations on the mainland, none of which last much more than an hour.

Boat In the Galápagos and the Oriente, boat travel is not only practical and/or necessary, but also part of these regions' attractions.

Bus Long-distance buses cover most of the country, with smaller local buses and shared taxis or trucks serving smaller villages.

For much more on **getting around**, see p392

If You Like...

Colonial Splendor

Ecuador has a treasure chest of architectural wonders, with magnificent churches, cathedrals and convents looming above photogenic plazas – some of which date back to the 16th century.

Quito Step inside the atmospheric churches, house museums and colonial-art galleries of the Old Town. (p52)

Cuenca Soaring bell towers loom over cobblestone streets and a gurgling river down below. (p174)

Loja Picturesque colonial center with centuries-old streets and plazas that are being given a major makeover. (p191)

Dramatic Scenery

Home to dramatic mountain peaks, misty cloud forests, Amazonian verdure and the otherworldly Galápagos Islands, Ecuador has countless places to stop and savor the scenery.

Laguna Quilotoa This topaz lake set deep in a volcanic crater is a magnificent setting for hiking. (p143)

San Rafael Falls Ringed by rainforest, Ecuador's highest falls are well worth a detour. (p211)

Lagunas de Mojanda At eagle's-nest heights, these alpine lakes glimmer like jewels way up high in the northern highlands. (p109)

Parque Nacional Cotopaxi Climb, hike or simply savor the view of Volcán Cotopaxi. (p135)

Isla Isabela (Albemarle) Gaze out over Darwin Lake or Volcán Sierra Negra on Isla Isabela. (p326)

Parque Nacional Sumaco Napo Galeras Jungle, cloud forest and *páramo* (high-altitude Andean grasslands) packed into unforgettable treks and remote ecolodges. (p226)

Outdoor Adventures

Adrenaline junkies can get their fix in this wild and wondrous Andean nation, where snowcapped peaks, rushing rivers and pounding surf provide the perfect backdrop to a long day's adventuring.

Ziplining Blaze through the canopy at high speed on several exhilarating ziplines. (p123)

White-water rafting White-knuckle rides, with something for everyone – Class III to Class V. (p154)

Mountain biking Race down the flanks of 6310m-high Chimborazo – best arranged in Riobamba. (p165)

Surfing You'll find decent surf breaks all along the coast, especially Canoa and Montañita. (p263)

Craft Markets

Leave plenty of extra space in your bags, or plan on buying an extra one while you're here: Ecuador is a fantastic place for market lovers.

Otavalo This sprawling market is a must for first-time visitors. (p101)

Guamote Taking place on Thursdays, this is one of the most authentic markets in the central highlands. (p169)

Mercado Artesanal La Mariscal Daily market in Quito with a decent selection of clothes and handicrafts and a great place to pick up souvenirs. (p91)

Saquisilí Bustling with mostly local shoppers, this Thursday market is a fascinating slice of highlands life. (p147)

Gualaceo, Chordeleg & Sígsig A trio of small towns hosting charming Sunday markets where local artisans sell their fine works. (p188)

Top: Loja (p191)

Bottom: Volcán Chimborazo (p162)

Wildlife Encounters

An astounding variety of animals have made their home in Ecuador's rainforests and cloud forests, high-altitude grasslands and tropical dry forests and on its islands.

The Galápagos Home to creatures so tame, you'll practically trip over all the sea lions you see. (p307)

Bird-watching With more than 600 recorded bird species in the area, the cloud forests outside Mindo are a mecca for birders. (p124)

Amazonian jungle lodges Spy monkeys, toucans, caiman, river dolphins and more from one of a handful of jungle lodges in the pristine Lower Río Napo. (p219)

Parque Nacional Podocarpus This massive but little-known park is home to tapirs, bears and nearly 600 bird species. (p197)

Climbing, Hiking & Trekking

Strap on crampons and make your way up a 5000m volcano, blaze through endangered forests or plot a route between villages in the highlands. Whether you're out for a short day's hike or a multiday trek, Ecuador has you covered.

Quilotoa Scenic highland hiking from Quilotoa to Chugchilán to Isinliví, overnighting at simple village guesthouses. (p142)

Cotopaxi Only about one in two succeed in summiting this massive volcano, one of Ecuador's most popular climbs. (p135)

Camino del Inca This three-day, 40km hike to Ingapirca follows the original Incan royal road. (p189)

Parque Nacional Machalilla Great day and overnight hikes at this coastal national park near Puerto López. (p290)

Chimborazo Climb to the summit to reach the closest point on Earth to the sun. (p162)

El Altar Hike to the spectacular gem-colored crater lake. (p159)

Pre-Columbian History

Ecuador has seen thousands of years of human habitation, with the ancestors of today's indigenous peoples living in every corner of the country.

Casa del Alabado Atmospheric museum showcasing pre-Columbian works of art and exploring the mystical side of ancient beliefs. (p59)

Ingapirca See Inca stonemasonry up close at Ecuador's best-preserved archaeological site. (p188)

Agua Blanca Guides lead tours around a fascinating archaeological museum and nearby ruins. (p291)

Beaches

Although not known for its shoreline, Ecuador does have some pretty beaches, plus charming seaside villages where you can unwind and get away from it all after a few hard days of traveling.

Los Frailes Dazzling white-sand beach close to several short hiking trails. (p292)

Tortuga Bay Awe-inspiring stretch of sand with a calm lagoon nearby. (p311)

Canoa Laid-back seaside town with a beach at its back door. (p262)

Montañita Youthful, surf-loving town with fine waves and buzzing nightlife. (p294)

The North Coast For end-of-the-road getaways, plan a beachside stay in Mompiche or Same. (p260)

La Lobería Rise early for an unforgettable view over this sea-lion-loved point on Floreana. (p321)

Indigenous Culture

With more than three million indigenous people hailing from at least a dozen distinct groups, the country offers numerous ways to interact with native Ecuadorian culture.

Tsáchila Gain an understanding about the traditions and beliefs of the 3000-strong Tsáchila community. (p248)

Shuar Visit traditional Shuar villages, where you can stay overnight and learn about traditional lifestyles in the rainforest. (p241)

Saraguro A wonderful spot to immerse yourself in a Kichwa-speaking indigenous community. (p190)

Guamote Inti Sisa runs an early childhood education program and offers awesome community tours. (p169)

Salinas Discover an example of successful community tourism in a high-altitude setting. (p161)

Month by Month

TOP EVENTS

Carnaval, February

Semana Santa, March

Inti Raymi, June

Fiesta de la Mamá Negra, September

Fiestas de Quito, December

February

Cooler, wetter days are common in the capital and the highlands, while dry, sunny skies rule the Oriente. Blazing sunshine mixed with heavy downpours is common along the coast.

Carnaval

Held during the last few days before Ash Wednesday, Carnaval is celebrated with water fights – sometimes dousing passers-by with all manner of suspect liquids. Guaranda is famous for its Carnaval, with dances and parades. (p161)

Fiesta de Frutas y Flores

Held in Ambato, the fruit and flower festival coincides with Carnaval and features fruit and flower shows, bullfights, parades and late-night dancing in the streets. Unlike in other parts of Ecuador, water-throwing here is banned. (p149)

March

The highlands' rainy season is still in full swing (running roughly from October to May), but March is a fine time to visit to beat the crowds. Expect plenty of sunshine in the Oriente, and be prepared for storms and sunshine along the coast.

Fiesta del Durazno

In the southern highlands, the small village of Gualaceo showcases one of its finest fruits – the peach – during an annual harvest festival on March 4. You'll find flowers, crafts and live music. (p188)

Semana Santa

Beginning the week before Easter Sunday (in late March or early April), Semana Santa (Holy Week) is celebrated with religious processions throughout the country. The Good Friday procession in Quito, with its purple-robed penitents, is a particularly colorful event. (p72)

April

The highlands continue to have the rainy season pattern of morning sunshine and afternoon showers; the Oriente and coast remain generally sunny but with periodic rainstorms.

Founding Day, Cuenca

The anniversary of Cuenca's founding runs over several days near April 12 and is one of the biggest events in the southern highlands. Locals celebrate with live bands, parades and fireworks-laced floats, while food stalls along the river draw daytime crowds. (p179)

Independence Battle of Tapi

Riobamba's biggest night out, April 21, revolves around the historic 1822 battle. Expect an agricultural fair, with the usual highland events: street parades, dancing and plenty of traditional food and drink.

May

The highlands head toward the dry season with fewer

showers and sunnier days, while rain picks up in the Oriente. On the Galápagos Islands, the warm and wet season (January to June) prevails, with warmer days and some periodic showers.

Chonta Festival

Held during the last week in May in Macas, the Chonta Festival is the most important Shuar celebration of the year. It culminates in a dance to help ferment the *chicha* (a fermented corn or yuca drink). (p243)

Corpus Christi

This religious feast day combines with a traditional harvest fiesta in many highland towns, and features processions and street dancing. Good fests are in Cuenca and Salasaca. It takes place in late May or early June. (p180)

June

The highlands' dry season coincides with Ecuador's peak season, when more North Americans visit the country. It's generally rainy in the Oriente, and cool and dry in the Galápagos (with rougher seas through August).

Inti Raymi

This millennia-old indigenous celebration of the summer solstice and harvest is celebrated throughout Ecuador's northern highlands, including Otavalo, where it is combined with celebrations of St John the Baptist (on June 24) and Saints Peter and Paul (on June 29).

Top: Semana Santa (p72), Quito

Bottom: Carnaval (p179), Cuenca

July

Clear, sunny highland skies make this an excellent time to visit, while rain is more prevalent in the Oriente. The Galápagos and the coast remain dry and cool (though sometimes overcast).

Founding of Guayaquil

Street dancing, fireworks and processions are all part of the celebration on the nights leading up to the anniversary of Guayaquil's founding (July 25). Along with the national holiday on July 24 (Simón Bolívar's birthday), the city closes down and celebrates with abandon. (p279)

August

It's still warm and dry in the sierra, while the Oriente sees a brief respite from the heavy rains. It's a busier time to visit, with holidaying North American and European visitors.

Fiestas de San Lorenzo

Head to the north Afro-Ecuadorian outpost of San Lorenzo to shake your money maker to the tribal beats of marimba and salsa. It happens on August 10. (p251)

La Virgen del Cisne

In the southern highlands, thousands of pilgrims take part each year on August 15 in the extraordinary 70km procession to Loja carrying the Virgen del Cisne (Virgin of the Swan). (p194)

September

The highlands remain sunny and clear, while a mix of rain and heat marks the Oriente. September is a lively time to visit, with important traditional fests under way.

Feria Mundial del Banano

In the third week of September, Machala celebrates its favorite yellow fruit with music, parades and fireworks. One of the biggest events is a beauty pageant to select the Reina del Banano (the Banana Queen). (p302)

Fiesta de la Mamá Negra

Latacunga hosts one of the highlands' most famous celebrations, in honor of La Virgen de las Mercedes. La Mamá Negra, played by a man dressed as a black woman, pays tribute to the 19th-century liberation of African slaves. There is a second celebration in early November. (p139)

Fiesta del Yamor

Imbabura province's biggest festival celebrates the fall equinox and Colla Raimi (festival of the moon) with bullfights, dancing, cockfights, partying, feasts and lots of *yamor* (a nonalcoholic drink made from seven varieties of corn). (p104)

October

You'll find fewer tourists and slightly lower prices in October. The seas are rougher at this time in the Galápagos; but it also means you can sometimes score good deals.

Independence Day

This massive holiday (October 9) fetes Guayaquil's independence from Spain, and it's a festive time to be in the tropical city. Folks flood the center for parades, concerts, street parties and fireworks. (p279)

December

Despite the cooler temperatures and rainier skies in the highlands, December to mid-January brings a fair number of holidaying North Americans and Europeans to Ecuador.

End-of-Year Celebrations

Parades and dances starting on December 28 culminate on New Year's Eve with the burning of life-size effigies in the streets, plus fireworks. You'll see the most celebrating in Quito and Guayaquil (particularly along the Malecón). (p73)

Fiesta de Baños

December 16 is Baños' best-loved day for party-minded folk. An assortment of street fests, concerts and abundant eating and drinking mark the event. (p155)

Fiestas de Quito

Quito's biggest bash is a much-anticipated event, with bullfights, parades and street dances throughout the first week of December. Open-air stages all across town fill the capital with music. (p72)

Itineraries

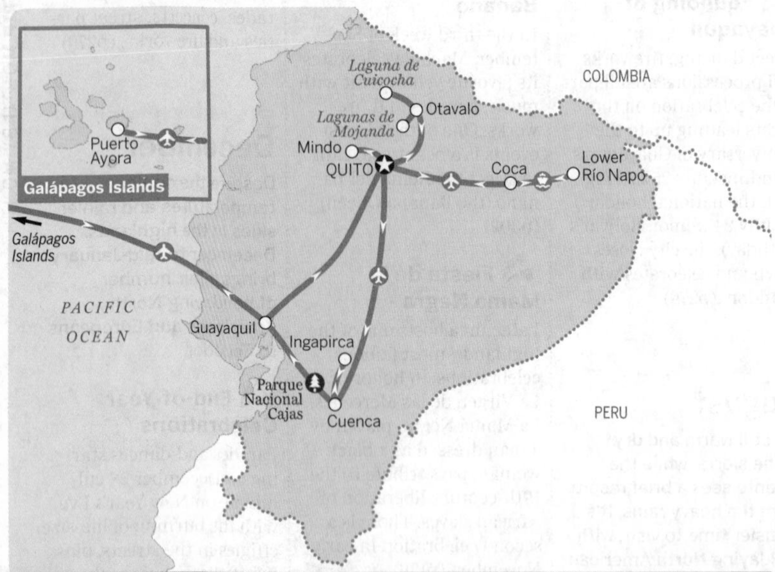

Best of Ecuador

Colonial treasures, cloud forests, rainforests, teeming markets and wondrous wildlife are all on the menu of this action-packed journey around Ecuador.

Begin the trip in **Quito**. Spend two days soaking up the architectural gems of the Old Town, then go 2½ hours north to **Otavalo** for its famous market (best on Saturdays). Spend the night there and squeeze in a hike out to the stunning lakes **Laguna de Cuicocha** or **Lagunas de Mojanda**. On the fourth day, go west (via Quito) to the lush cloud forests of **Mindo**. Overnight in a riverside or mountaintop lodge, then return to Quito for a flight to **Cuenca**, the colonial jewel of the south. Spend two days exploring 500-year-old churches and visiting the fairy tale-like setting of **Parque Nacional Cajas**, 30km to the west. If time allows, visit the Inca ruins of **Ingapirca** before continuing to **Guayaquil** for a flight to the **Galápagos**. Spend four days there, wildlife-watching and island-hopping. For the final part of the Ecuadorian adventure, fly back to Guayaquil and onward to **Coca** (via Quito), gateway to the Amazon. Spend three nights at a jungle lodge on the **Lower Río Napo**, one of the best places to marvel at Ecuador's Amazonian wildlife.

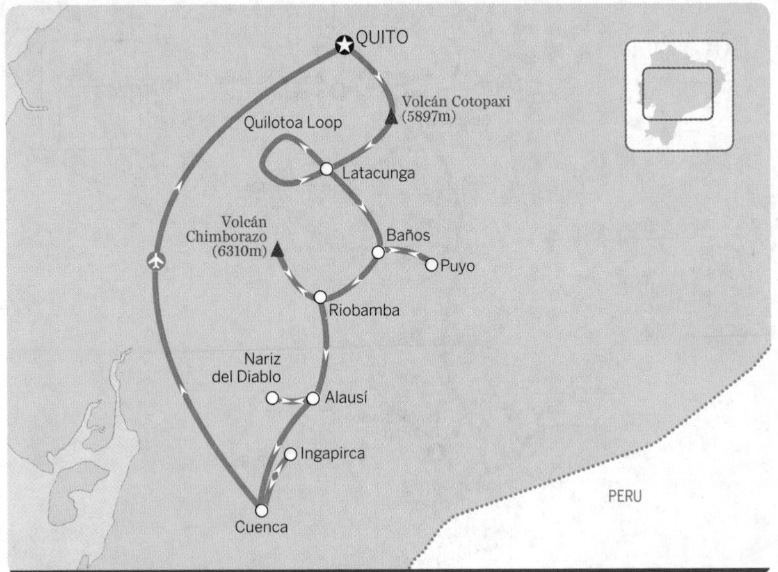

Exploring the Andes

Traveling along the spine of the Andes, you'll take in sublime alpine scenery, laid-back villages and a mix of colonial and pre-Columbian wonders. Opportunities for hiking, trekking, mountain biking and climbing are superb.

Start the highland adventure in **Quito**, where you can acclimatize to the altitude while exploring one of South America's most fascinating capitals. After two nights in the city, head south for a night or two in a historic hacienda on the flanks of **Volcán Cotopaxi**, where you can horseback ride and hike; avid climbers can tackle one of Ecuador's iconic peaks. Around day four, travel south to **Latacunga** and journey into the mountainous landscape of the **Quilotoa Loop**. This is a great place to hike between high-up indigenous villages, staying in simple guesthouses along the way.

After two days spent in the clouds near Quilotoa, head to a slightly lower elevation and the delightful subtropical town of **Baños**, where you can soak in natural spring baths, book into a charming inn with views, and take a fabulous downhill bike ride past refreshing waterfalls to **Puyo** in the Oriente. After Baños, move on to **Riobamba**, an ideal base for setting out on a high-adrenaline mountain-bike ride or hike around **Volcán Chimborazo**. From Riobamba take a bus to **Alausí**, then take a train ride on the famed **Nariz del Diablo**, with its dramatic views of Chimborazo, El Altar, Laguna de Colta and other vistas dotting the Avenue of the Volcanoes. Returning to Alausí, continue by bus to the marvelous colonial city of **Cuenca**. There, enjoy a few days taking in the colonial churches, peaceful plazas and the idyllic river setting before striking out for the Inca ruins of **Ingapirca**. You can visit by bus, organized day trip, or on a more challenging three-day hike along the Camino del Inca (Inca Trail), with gear and guides available in Cuenca. Afterwards, make your way back to Quito for a final night out (Zazu is a good choice, followed by drinks and dancing at La Juliana) and a big send-off to the great Andean experience.

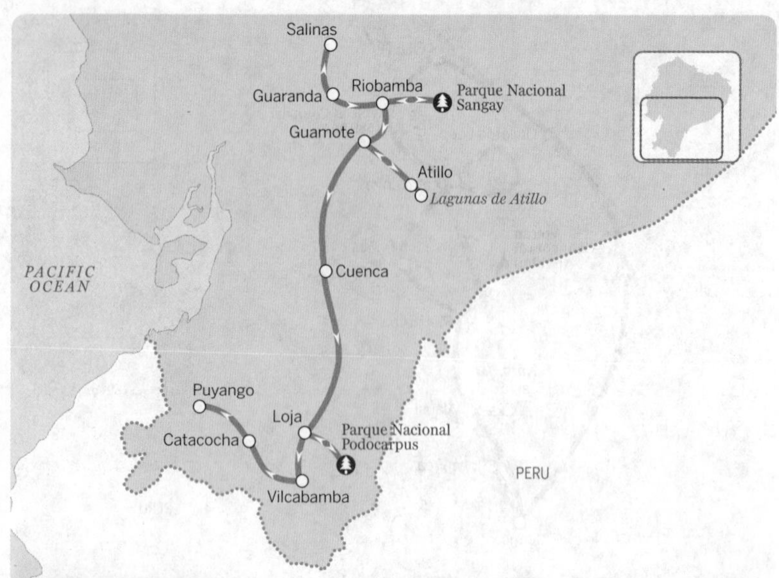

Southern Ecuador

Heading south from Quito, you'll soon find yourself in bustling market towns, remote indigenous villages and pristine national parks far from the touring crowds.

Start your journey in the gateway town of **Riobamba**, a rather workaday mid-sized settlement that's at its liveliest during its Saturday market. From here, take a detour west to **Guaranda**, a scenic town that's the gateway up to **Salinas**, a fascinating and charming country village where you can visit cooperatives producing chocolate, cheese, mushrooms and wool products; or you can just take a walk or horseback ride through the pretty countryside. Stay overnight in the village before heading back through Riobamba and continuing east to **Parque Nacional Sangay**, a setting of magnificent volcanoes and diverse flora and fauna. Head back to Riobamba then south to the lovely Kichwa town of **Guamote**. Spend the night in the cozy community-run Inti Sisa, which is also a good place to arrange horseback rides or hikes in the pristine countryside. If possible, try to time your visit for Thursday, when a massive indigenous market takes over the town.

After Guamote, travel south to **Atillo** for a couple of days of spectacular hiking around the crystalline **Lagunas de Atillo**. Afterwards, head back to Guamote, then south to **Cuenca**. After days of rugged traveling, pamper yourself with a stay in one of the city's many fine guesthouses and a meal at one of its eclectic eateries. Recharged and refreshed, continue south to **Loja**, where you can sample one of the city's specialties, *cuy* (guinea pig) – or, if you don't fancy that, try its famous corn- and plantain-based delicacies.

From Loja head east to the **Parque Nacional Podocarpus**, a massive park that's home to astounding biodiversity and offers hikes through mesmerizing landscapes of *páramo* (high-altitude Andean grasslands) and cloud forest. Afterwards, go back through Loja and continue south to **Vilcabamba**. This pretty village offers some fine walks, cycling and horseback rides, although it's also a perfect spot to simply enjoy the peaceful scenery. Next work your way down the western side of the Andes to **Catacocha**, a charming, little-visited highland town. Spend a day here, then head to **Puyango** to visit one of South America's largest petrified forests.

Top: Ingapirca (p188)

Bottom: Riobamba Cathedral (p164)

NORADOA/SHUTTERSTOCK ©

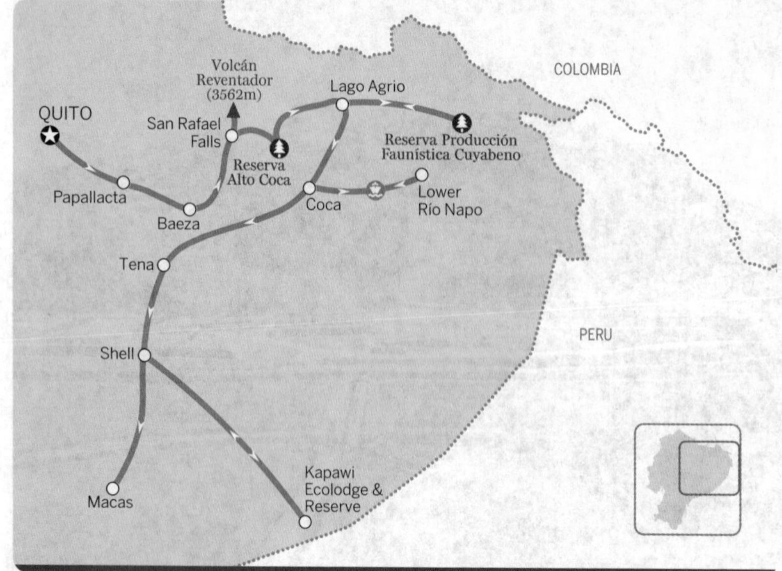

3 WEEKS Adventure in the Oriente

The Oriente is Ecuador's slice of the Amazon, one of the world's most biologically diverse regions. For adventurers, wildlife lovers and budding anthropologists, there's much to discover here, from indigenous reserves to jungle lodges with an incredible array of plant and animal life.

Start in **Quito**; pre-book jungle lodges you plan to stay at and load up on any needed supplies, then catch a bus southeast to **Papallacta**, a sparkling complex of thermal baths with magnificent mountain views on a clear day. With both high-end and budget options, this is a fine place to overnight before continuing east to **Baeza**, a pleasant base for hiking, biking, rafting, bird-watching and other activities. From there, go north to the thundering drama of photogenic **San Rafael Falls** – Ecuador's highest falls. For spectacular views of nearby **Volcán Reventador** in action, make the hike up to the **Reserva Alto Coca**, a remote cloud-forest reserve with great hiking and bird-watching, plus rustic cabins with striking views of the volcano.

Continue on to the gritty oil town of **Lago Agrio**; from here, head out to the **Reserva de Producción Faunística Cuyabeno** – a spectacular rainforest reserve packed with biodiversity. Spend a few days at the recommended Cuyabeno Lodge then travel back to Lago Agrio and on to **Coca**, another tiny river settlement turned oil boom town. Take a stroll along the river, then hook up with a jungle guide (best arranged beforehand in Quito) for a trip out to the **Lower Río Napo**, home to some of Ecuador's finest jungle lodges. Here you'll find superb wildlife-watching on hikes, canoe rides or climbs to the top of the jungle canopy.

Get your fill of piranha fishing, caiman-spotting and bird-watching, then head back to Coca and down to **Tena**. This river town is an ideal spot to gain a different perspective on the rainforest: namely, by rushing past on a white-water rafting trip through spectacular Class IV rapids. If time allows, you can tack on a trip to the less-visited southern Oriente, via **Macas**. The Achuar-run **Kapawi Ecolodge & Reserve** (reachable by chartered aircraft from **Shell**) is a wonderfully remote piece of Amazonia.

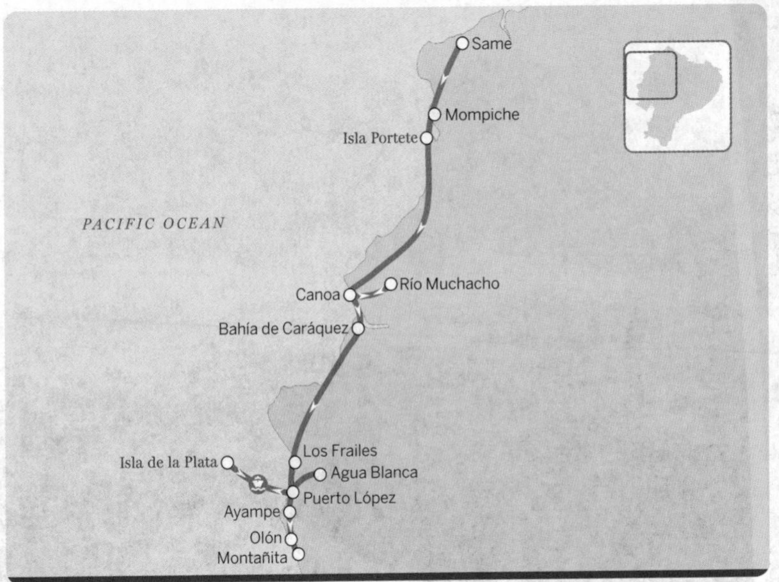

Surf & Sun

Ecuador's charming coastal villages and attractive beaches draw a wide mix of travelers, including sun-seekers, surfers and seafood lovers.

Start in the laid-back beach spots near **Same** (*sah*-may) and the Corredor Turistico Galera-San Francisco on the north coast. After the long journey from Quito, book into a beachfront cabaña (cabin), walk on the beach, and get your fill of seafood. On day two, catch a bus down to **Mompiche**, a beloved haunt for surfers and paradise-seekers alike with a long brown-sugar beach, big waves and a fun traveler scene that still hasn't become overrun. Take a whale-watching day trip from here or visit the far-off island paradise of **Isla Portete** before continuing south.

Next up is **Canoa**, a slow-moving beach town with a long sandy stretch backed by forested cliffs. Canoa invites lingering: you can take surf lessons, study Spanish and ride horses or cycle to deserted beaches nearby. There are some fine beachfront guesthouses and decent restaurants. While in Canoa, leave time for a visit to the **Río Muchacho**, a working organic farm, at which you can take a tour, stay overnight and enjoy the fantastic food grown right on-site.

On day six, continue south to **Bahía de Caráquez**, where you can explore mangroves, look for frigate birds and take an ecocity tour. Spend the night, then continue on day seven to **Puerto López** (you'll probably have to transfer at Manta). This sleepy town is the gateway to the **Isla de la Plata**, a fine place to see blue-footed boobies if you're not heading to the Galápagos. In season (mid-June to early October), there's also good whale-watching. Other area attractions include the stunning beach of **Los Frailes**, the indigenous community of **Agua Blanca**, and surrounding rainforest with memorable hiking and horseback riding.

Spend your last two days in **Montañita**, a surf town with a serious party vibe. If you're looking for something more mellow, stop instead in **Ayampe** or **Olón**.

Parque Nacional Cotopaxi (p13

Plan Your Trip

Ecuador Outdoors

Ecuador has a vast range of adventures, and its compact size makes it possible to combine a number of activities in a short time. You can go bird-watching in misty cloud forests, hike amid Andean peaks and snorkel with abundant sea life off the Galápagos Islands. There's also excellent surfing, mountain biking and rafting.

Best Outdoor Adventures

Best Climb

The majestic heights of Volcán Cotopaxi (5897m) provide a fantastic view for those fit enough to make the summit.

Best Trek

The multiday Camino del Inca follows the Inca royal road for 40km to the striking ruins of Ingapirca.

Best Bird-Watching

The biologically diverse cloud forest of Mindo is home to hundreds of colorful species.

Best Mountain-Biking Trip

Descend 61km from the crisp highlands town of Baños to steamy Puyo in the Amazon.

Best White-Water Rafting

In the Oriente, both Tena and Macas offer fantastic full- and multiday rafting trips past jungle-clad scenery.

Best Surfing

Montañita, Mompiche and Canoa on the mainland offer good breaks, while Isla San Cristóbal on the Galápagos has more challenging waves.

Hiking

The opportunities for hiking are practically limitless. Stunning scenery is a guarantee wherever you go, with snow-covered peaks, cloud forests and verdant lowland jungle setting the stage for hiking and wildlife-watching. Most of the best independent hiking is in the national parks.

Top Destinations

Parque Nacional Cotopaxi (p135) This 330-sq-km national park is home to the snowcapped peak of the active Volcán Cotopaxi, Ecuador's second-highest point (5897m). There are great opportunities for hiking here and in the surrounding countryside, but few established trails so you'll need to blaze your own. Just be sure to stay safe.

Parque Nacional Cajas (p186) Amid the picturesque *páramo* (high-altitude Andean grasslands), there are a number of trails (some better signed than others), which take in great views of pretty alpine lakes. Be prepared for rain (the driest months are August to January).

Quilotoa Loop (p142) Near the dramatic topaz crater lake of Quilotoa, there are some excellent hikes, including village-to-village trips and a few shortcuts through high-altitude canyons. One excellent DIY route goes from Quilotoa to Isinliví, overnighting in Chugchilán along the way.

Parque Nacional Podocarpus (p197) Across lush tropical lowlands and chilly, mountainous highlands, Podocarpus offers several memorable hikes, including a day hike through cloud forest and a multiday hike to Andean lakes.

Parque Nacional Machalilla (p290) The country's only coastal national park covers 400 sq km, with trails through tropical dry forest as well as cloud forest. The park also includes Isla de la Plata, which has several loop hiking trails and has been called 'the poor man's Galápagos' because of its wildlife, which includes red-footed boobies.

Camino del Inca (p189) For a fascinating journey along part of the royal road that linked Cuzco (Peru) to Quito, take the Inca trail to the archaeological site of Ingapirca; it's a popular 40km hike that most travelers do in three days.

Bird-Watching

Nowhere else in the world has such incredible avian diversity been crammed into such a small country. Some 1600 species, including a number of unique species, have been spotted in mainland Ecuador and on the Galápagos. Scope is one of the biggest challenges for bird-watchers – with rainforest, cloud forest and islands all offering allure.

Cloud Forest

One recommended place to start exploring is just north of Quito. The cloud forests outside of **Mindo** are a bird-watcher's paradise. Highlights include the Andean cock-of-the-rock, scaled fruiteater, and golden-headed and crested quetzals. More than 400 bird species have been recorded in the region, and you'll find excellent guides and lodges here.

Amazon

An excellent destination is the lower **Río Napo** region of the Amazon, where more than 600 bird species have been logged. Some of Ecuador's best jungle lodges are in this area, some with their own canopy towers and biologist guides.

Galápagos Islands

The Galápagos Islands have their own feathery appeal, owing to their 28 endemic species that have evolved in extraordinary ways. Isla Santa Cruz boasts the highest bird count overall, and it's a good place to begin to find the 13 species of Darwin's finches. Various large species are easily seen around Puerto Ayora harbor, including blue-footed boobies, magnificent frigate birds and lava herons.

Mountaineering

The towering Andes sweeping through Ecuador set the stage for serious adventure. The country has 10 peaks over 5000m, eight of which are in the central highlands. This is where you'll find Ecuador's most impressive summits. Keep in mind that many of Ecuador's most impressive peaks are volcanoes, and their status can change quickly. Some are climbable one year and not the next. Those looking to climb a peak where no equipment is required might consider **Volcán Imbabura** (4609m) in the northern highlands. It's a challenging and highly rewarding climb just outside of Ibarra.

OTHER GREAT BIRD-WATCHING SITES

- Parque Nacional Cajas (p186)
- Parque Nacional Podocarpus (p197)
- Jorupe Reserve (p205)
- Bosque Protector Cerro Blanco (p287)
- Reserva Ecológica Manglares Churute (p301)

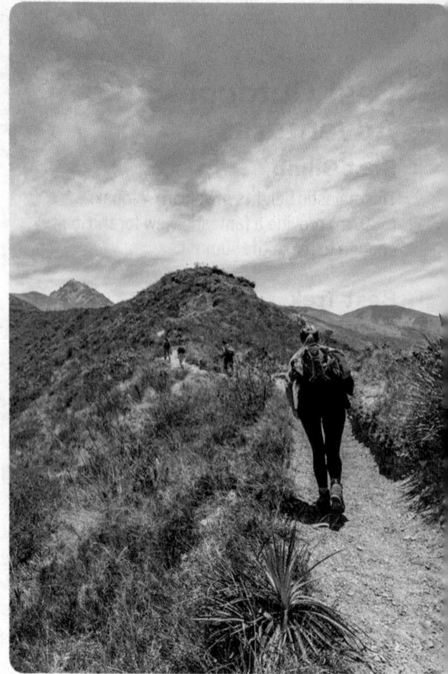

Laguna de Cuicocha (p112)

Climbing Essentials

Mountaineers will require standard snow and ice gear: rope, crampons, ice axe, high-altitude sun protection and cold-weather clothing as a minimum. Unless you are very experienced, hiring a guide from Quito or Riobamba is recommended. The weather can turn bad quickly in the Andes, and even experienced climbers have been killed. Several agencies offer both rental gear and guides: expect to pay about $250 per person for a two-day climb up a major peak. The best guides have a card accrediting them to the Ecuadorian Mountain Guides Association (ASEGUIM).

You can climb year-round, but the best months are considered to be June to August and December to February.

Major Peaks

Volcán Chimborazo (p162) Ecuador's highest peak is an extinct volcano that tops at 6263m. It's a relatively straightforward climb for experienced climbers, but ice-climbing gear is essential. From the climbing refuge, most climbers opt for the Normal Route, which takes eight to 10 hours to the summit and two to four on the return.

Darwin's finch (p347), Galápagos Islands

Riobamba is the best place for arranging a guided hike, hiring equipment and unwinding when the climb is done.

Volcán Cotopaxi (p135) The country's second-highest peak is an active volcano and one of the most popular summits in the Andes for serious climbers. Cotopaxi can be climbed in one long day from the climbers' refuge, but people usually allow two days. Climbers must acclimatize for several days before attempting an ascent. Lodges in and around Cotopaxi are great for acclimatization.

Ilinizas (p134) The jagged sawtooth peak of Iliniza Sur (5248m) is Ecuador's sixth-highest peak and one of the country's most difficult climbs. It's suitable only for experienced climbers. Iliniza Norte (5126m), on the other hand, is a rough scramble and can be climbed by acclimatized, experienced hikers. The small village of El Chaupi is a good base for acclimatizing climbers and hikers, with a handful of simple but pleasant guesthouses.

Volcán El Altar (p159) This long-extinct 5319m volcano is widely considered the most beautiful and most technical of Ecuador's mountains. December to March is the best time to visit this area. In July and August El Altar is frequently shrouded in clouds.

Mountain Biking

There are some excellent spots for mountain biking, especially the adrenaline-charged downhills on the flanks of **Cotopaxi** and **Chimborazo**. The best mountain-biking operators (with the best bikes, guides and equipment) can be found in Quito and Riobamba.

Also awash in midrange mountain bikes is **Baños**, thanks to the popular and excellent downhill ride (by road) to Puyo. Nicknamed 'La Ruta de las Cascadas' (Highway of the Waterfalls), it follows the Río Pastaza canyon, dropping steadily from the highlands town of Baños at 1800m to the jungle settlement of Puyo at 950m. It's a 61km ride, with some refreshing dips in waterfalls along the way.

Diving & Snorkeling

The **Galápagos Islands** are among the world's great dive destinations, offering dramatic underwater wildlife: sharks, rays, turtles, penguins, sea lions, moray

FOTOGRIN/SHUTTERSTOCK ©

Surfing, Montañita (p294)

eels, sea horses, fish of many kinds and, if you're very lucky, dolphins or even whales. Conditions are difficult for beginners, with strong currents and cold water temperatures. There are dive operators based in **Puerto Ayora** and **Puerto Baquerizo Moreno**.

Experienced divers with deep pockets can opt for a week's tour aboard a dive-dedicated boat, stopping at the aquatic hot spots around the archipelago. Those looking for less commitment can arrange two-tank dives for a day. The Galápagos is also a good place for snorkeling as the marine life doesn't often require great depths to access.

On the mainland, you can arrange dive trips with operators in **Puerto López** and **Montañita**. The sea bottom here mixes rock with coral reef patches and sand. Aquatic life includes angelfish, trumpet fish, puffer fish, morays, parrot fish, manta rays, guitar rays and white-tip sharks.

The water temperature is around 22°C (72°F) from January to April and about 18°C (64°F) the rest of the year; operators rent wet suits if you don't want to bring your own.

Surfing

Ecuador isn't a huge surf destination but has some excellent breaks if you know where to go. The season is generally November to April, with peak months in January and February. Localism is generally minimal; Ecuadorians and foreigners mix it up pretty peacefully.

The classic mainland break is **Montañita**, a fast, powerful reef-break that can cough up some of the mainland's best barrels. The break is best from December to May, when swells of 2m to 3m are common. It also has some tolerable beach-breaks nearby. Near Muisne, in Esmeraldas province, **Mompiche** is a world-class left point-break offering rides of up to 500m on top days. **Canoa** is a fun spot for left and right beach-breaks, if only because the town here is a great little hangout and the beach is beautiful.

In the Galápagos, Isla San Cristóbal is home to three world-class reef-breaks, all near the town of **Puerto Baquerizo Moreno**. They're extremely fast and best for experienced surfers. The high price of getting there keeps the crowds down. Optimal surf season on the islands is December to May. **Isla Isabela** also has some nice breaks near Puerto Villamil.

White-Water Rafting

Ecuador boasts world-class river rafting and kayaking year-round. Some of the rivers offer up to 100km of continuous Class III to Class IV white water before flattening out to flow toward the Pacific on one side of the Andes and into the Amazon Basin on the other. Wherever you go, the best time for rafting is from October to February.

Ecuador's river-guide association is called Asociación de Guías de Águas Rápidas del Ecuador (AGAR; Ecuadorian White-Water Guides Association). We recommend only reputable companies. When shopping around for an outfit, make sure it has decent life jackets, professional guides, first-aid kits and throw bags. Some outfitters also offer wet-suit rental on several of the longer runs (recommended).

Top: Ziplining, Baños (p151)

Bottom: Green sea turtle (p350), Galápagos Islands

ALTERNATIVE ADVENTURES

Ecuador has much more than volcanoes and rainforests up its sleeve. Valleys, caves, rivers and the proximity of the continental shelf all create opportunities for uncommon adventures.

Caving Located on the eastern slopes of the Andes, the Cueva de los Tayos (Cave of the Oil Birds) provides a fascinating wonderland for cave lovers. The journey starts with a 70m descent into the caves.

Tubing While some prefer kayaks and rafts, in Mindo you can jostle down the rocky Río Mindo, bottom securely planted in a rubber inner tube. A guide pushes you along.

Ziplining Baños and Mindo both have impressive ziplines where you can blaze over the forested canopy.

Whale-watching During the annual migration of humpback whales (June to September), numerous boat operators along the coast offer whale-watching tours, especially from Puerto López and Mompiche.

Canyoning & Puenting A favorite Baños-based activity, canyoning involves rappelling (abseiling) down waterfalls, swimming in rivers and taking short hikes through canyons. Daredevils can also go 'puenting', a kind of bungee-style bridge-jumping.

Top Rafting Spots

Tena This is Ecuador's de facto white-water capital, with the nearby upper Río Napo (Class III+) and the Río Misahuallí (Class IV+) among the country's best-known rivers.

Macas Further south, the Río Upano (Class III to IV+) near Macas is excellent for multiday trips and outrageous jungle scenery, including the spectacular stretch along the Namangosa Gorge, where more than a dozen waterfalls plummet into the river.

Río Blanco On the western slopes of the Andes, about 2½ hours west of Quito, the Río Blanco (Class III to IV) is a year-round possibility and a favorite day trip from the capital, with wildest conditions from February to about June. There is approximately 200km of maneuverable white water here, including the challenging Upper Blanco. There are several Class II to III runs for complete beginners and families near Quito as well.

El Chaco On the eastern slopes of the Andes, El Chaco is the gateway to the Río Quijos, a Class IV to V river with verdant scenery.

Río Pastaza & Río Patate These are two of the country's most popular rivers due to their proximity to the tourist mecca of Baños. The Patate, unfortunately, remains very polluted.

Horseback Riding

Ecuador has some great horseback-riding opportunities, especially in the highlands. Unfortunately, many of the horses used in tourist hikes are not properly looked after. There are, however, some agencies that take proper care of their animals, and they're worth seeking out, even though they charge more for tours. Haciendas throughout the highlands generally use good horses and offer some of the best opportunities for riding. **Vilcabamba** offers some fine rides in the surrounding mountains. Trips range from a few hours to three days. **Baños** is also a good place to sign up for a casual half- or full-day ride.

Another fine place for riding is at the **Reserva Geobotánica Pululahua** near Quito. Located inside a volcanic crater, this reserve boasts cloud forests and a fascinating microclimate. You can arrange full- or multiday horseback rides from there.

An expensive but reputable company is RideAndes (www.rideandes.com). It offers day tours, multiday tours and custom-made tours for both experienced and inexperienced riders.

A small boat ferries passengers to shore

Plan Your Trip

Galápagos Planning

There's much to consider before setting off for the islands: weather and seasons, land-based tours versus cruises, picking an itinerary, and money-saving strategies. Independent travelers can visit the island on their own, taking inter-island boats and staying in hotels – though you won't see as much wildlife or scenery.

Best Outdoor Adventures

Best Snorkeling

Devil's Crown off Floreana

Los Túneles off Isabela

Best Bird-Watching

Punta Suárez on Española

Isla Genovesa

Best Diving

Isla Wolf

Isla Darwin

Gordon Rocks off Santa Cruz

Best Hiking

Volcán Alcedo and Volcán Sierra Negra on Isabela

Cerro Crocker on Santa Cruz

Best Mountain Biking

San Cristóbal highlands

Santa Cruz highlands

Best Sunbathing

Tortuga Bay outside Puerto Ayora

Cerro Brujo on San Cristóbal

Best Surfing

Puerto Baquerizo Moreno

Isla Isabela

Best Scenery

Isla Bartolomé

Isla Rábida

Post Office Bay on Floreana

When to Go

There really isn't a bad time to visit. However, there are several factors to keep in mind in determining when to go. The islands have two distinct seasons, though the tourism high season is generally December to April, and July to August.

Warm & Wet Season (January to May) Generally sunny and warm (average air temperature is 25°C) with strong but short periods of rain. Coincides with vacation periods in the USA such as Christmas and Easter, which means more boats and more groups. The hottest month is March (average 31°C) and water temperatures average 25°C from February to April. Flowers bloom, bringing more color to the landscape; sea turtles nest; and many bird species mate.

Cool & Dry Season (June to December) Often known as the *garúa* for the misty precipitation that affects the highlands. While the air temperature is pleasant (average 22°C), the water is colder (18°C to 20°C) as a result of the dominant Humboldt Current, and the seas can be rough during overnight passages between islands. There are somewhat fewer visitors; however, it's also the season preferred by divers (6mm to 7mm wetsuits with hoods are worn). Penguin encounters are more common, waved albatrosses arrive on Española and blue-footed boobies mate.

Types of Tours

There are basically three kinds of tours in the Galápagos: the most common and most recommended are boat-based trips with nights spent aboard – this is because of their relatively low environmental impact and the exposure to a variety of wildlife and geography. There are also day trips returning to the same island each night, and hotel-based trips staying on different islands.

Boat Tours

Most visitors tour the Galápagos on boat tours, sleeping aboard the boat. Tours can last from three days to three weeks, although five- to eight-day tours are the most common. It's difficult to do the Galápagos justice on a tour lasting less than a week, but five days is just acceptable. If you want to visit the outlying islands of Isabela and Fernandina, a cruise of eight days or more is recommended. On the first day of a tour, you arrive from the mainland by air before lunchtime, so this is really only half a day in the Galápagos, and on the last day, you have to be at the airport in the morning. Thus, a five-day tour gives only three full days in the islands.

Itineraries

You can find boats to go to almost any island, although it takes more time to reach the outlying ones. Boats have fixed itineraries, so think ahead if you want a tour that visits a specific island. Make sure the tour doesn't include more than one night or half a day in either Puerto Ayora or Puerto Baquerizo Moreno, since you can always tack on a few days at the beginning or end on your own.

The daily itinerary on almost all boats includes taking a morning *panga* (small boat used to ferry passengers from a larger boat to shore) to a site on land to observe birds and other wildlife, followed by snorkeling nearby. Lunch and snacks are served while the boat motors to another island or site for a similar combination in the afternoon. There's usually a few hours of time to rest or socialize before dinner, and there's a pre- or post-meal briefing of the next day's schedule. While the standardized routine may irk those accustomed to the flexibility of independent travel, it's exceedingly comforting to have everything planned out – in the end, it's a surprisingly tiring trip.

Boat Types

Tour boats range from small yachts to large cruise ships. By far the most common type is the motor sailer (a medium-sized motorboat), which carries between eight and 20 passengers.

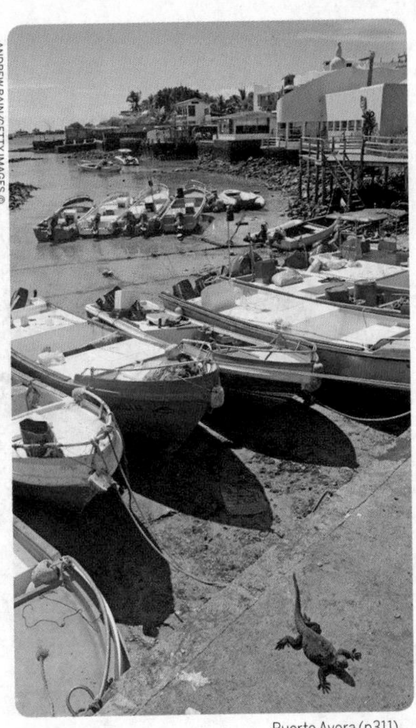

Puerto Ayora (p311)

Tipping

On cruises, it's customary to tip the crew and guide at the end of the trip. Some tour operators advise a 50-50 split; others give more to the crew than to the guide. How much to tip is very much a personal decision, but here are some general guidelines:

For basic and superior class cruises, \$14 to \$20 per passenger per day is about the norm; on first-class and luxury boats,

DIY GALÁPAGOS

If you don't have the funds for a cruise or simply don't wish to go on an organized tour, you can still have a rewarding experience on the islands. There are four inhabited islands (Santa Cruz, San Cristóbal, Isabela and Floreana) that offer lodging covering all price points. Inter-island boats travel daily between neighboring islands (though crossings can be rough). And from the main towns, you can head out on excursions on foot or by bike (aside from Floreana). You can also take day tours to sites for snorkeling, wildlife-watching and guided walks (prices range from \$95 to \$250, depending on the type of tour and distance traveled).

The downside to a DIY trip of this type is that you will only be able to visit limited sites; many of the most impressive parts of the Galápagos are simply unreachable by day trip from these towns. However, some travelers find that the sense of freedom (you set your own schedule and go where you want to go) – not to mention the more affordable price tag – amply makes up for the drawbacks.

Pinnacle Rock, Isla Bartolomé (p333)

$18 to $28 per passenger per day is fairly standard. The total amount per passenger per day should be split between guide and crew.

Hotel-Based Tours

These tours go from island to island, and you sleep in hotels on three or four different islands: Santa Cruz, San Cristóbal, Isabela and Floreana. Tours typically last five days and four nights and cost $600 to more than $1800 per person, plus airfare and park fee. Several of the travel agencies in Puerto Ayora and Puerto Baquerizo Moreno book these – Red Mangrove Aventura Lodge (p316) in Puerto Ayora; **Tropiceo** (in the US 1800-207-8615; www.destinationecuador.com), a tour agency based in Quito; and Galakiwi (p323) are recommended for these trips.

The problem with most tour companies is that they use a mix of boats, hotels and guides, so the quality of all three is difficult to guarantee and there's little consistency from one trip to the next. The camaraderie between guests and guides that adds to the enjoyment of Galápagos boat trips is lost when there's often a new guide for every stop.

Day Tours

Boat-based day trips depart from either Puerto Ayora or Puerto Baquerizo Moreno. Several hours are spent sailing to and from the day's visitor sites, so only a few central islands are feasible destinations. Some trips may involve visiting sites on other parts of Isla Santa Cruz or Isla San Cristóbal.

One of the downsides of this kind of tour is that there is no chance of visiting the islands early or late in the day. The cheapest boats may be slow and overcrowded; their visits may be too brief; the guides may be poorly informed; and the crew may be lacking an adequate conservationist attitude. Nevertheless, day trips are useful if your time and budget are extremely limited.

Companies in Puerto Ayora and Puerto Baquerizo Moreno charge $95 to $200 per person per day, depending on the destination on offer and the quality of the boat and guides.

Galápagos sea lions, Isla Española (p334)

Booking Your Trip

Most visitors arrange tours before arriving at the islands. You can do this in your home country (it tends to be more expensive, but it's efficient), or you can arrange something in Quito, Guayaquil or Cuenca. Booking in Ecuador is generally cheaper, but you sometimes have to wait several days or weeks during the high season (which could eat into your traveling time). One other word of caution if planning a Galápagos trip while in Ecuador – the default security protocols of some banks and credit-card companies make it difficult to pay for such relatively large amounts without hassle while you're abroad.

Shopping for a Smooth Sail

There are six boats (*Celebrity Xpedition, Explorer II, Endeavour, Galápagos Legend, Santa Cruz II* and *Silver Galapagos*) that carry up to 98 passengers each, and six boats (*Isabela II, Coral I & II, Celebrity Xperience, La Pinta* and *Islander*) that carry up to 48 passengers each; all are considered luxury or first-class ships. The majority of the other 75 or so boats or yachts carry fewer than 20 people. There are also several catamarans. Groups that book far in advance are often able to negotiate prices that are just as good as last-minute rates. Almost every boat operator charges 15% to 20% less in the low season.

The airfare, $100 park fee and bottled drinks are not included in fare quotes. Boats are divided roughly into the following categories (prices per day except for live-aboards):

Tourist-class yachts (tourist superior or standard tourist) $450 to $520

First-class yachts $520 to $750

Luxury ships from $750

To avoid disappointment, the following questions should always be asked before booking:

Is the guide a freelancer? Guides affiliated with one company or boat are more likely to feel responsible for their passengers' satisfaction and less likely to take a *laissez faire* approach to complaints.

What is the itinerary? Refer to the map and text of the Galápagos Islands chapter to understand the wildlife and activities common at each site. Joining boats that spend half-days in Puerto

WHAT TO TAKE

- binoculars
- good SLR or digital camera (the higher the zoom, the better)
- GoPro camera (for underwater shots)
- small backpack
- wide-brimmed hat
- sunglasses
- light cotton clothing
- sturdy hiking shoes or boots
- rain jacket
- light sweater
- flip-flops (thongs/jandals)
- swimming gear
- motion-sickness pills
- cash for park fee and cruise-staff tips
- refillable water bottle

ROLAND FANKHAUSER/500PX ©

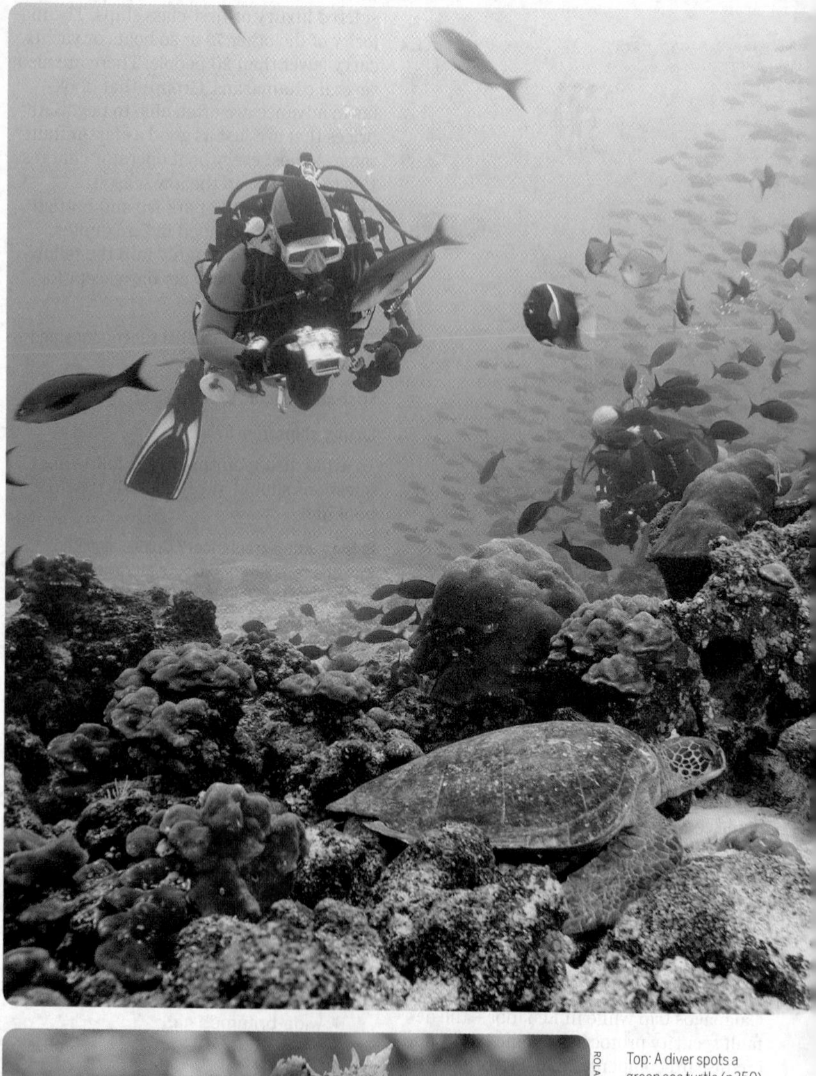

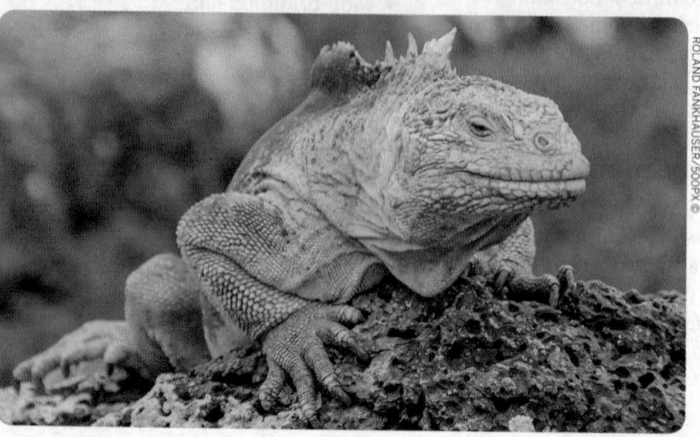

Top: A diver spots a green sea turtle (p350)
Bottom: Land iguana (p350)

LIVE-ABOARD DIVING TOURS

Not surprisingly for a place with an underwater habitat resembling a well-stocked aquarium, scuba diving in the Galápagos is world class. The conditions aren't suitable for beginners because of strong currents, sometimes cloudy visibility and cold temperatures. When the water is warm (January to March), there's not much of a current, so it's also a little murky; from July to October there's better visibility, but the water is colder. Besides an array of tropical fish, there are plenty of whale sharks, hammerheads, manta rays and even sea horses to be seen.

Standard overnight boat tours are not allowed to offer scuba diving as an option. Only six boats are currently available for diving: *Galápagos Sky*, *Galápagos Master*, *Galápagos Aggressor III*, *Nortada*, *Astrea* and *Humboldt Explorer*. Because there are so few options, these boats are usually booked as far as six months in advance. The cost of one week on a live-aboard ranges from $4000 to $5900 and includes up to four or five dives a day, plus stops at some visitor sites on land.

Most live-aboard boats go to Wolf and Darwin, northwest of the major islands, where there's a large number of different species of sharks. July is the best month to dive with whale sharks, but they're around from May to October.

The majority of divers take day trips from either Puerto Ayora or Puerto Baquerizo Moreno.

Ayora, Puerto Baquerizo Moreno and/or Puerto Villamil might seem like too much civilization.

Is snorkeling equipment in my size guaranteed? Masks, snorkels and fins are generally supplied; however, some boats may lack enough fins and wetsuits in certain sizes for all passengers.

What's the refund policy? Read the fine print and clarify how much money you can get back in case of a mechanical breakdown or other unforeseen circumstance that results in the cancellation or alteration of your trip.

How would you rate the food? This can be difficult to determine since chefs come and go and some agencies may be less than forthcoming in assessing their own product. Nevertheless, it's worth asking ahead of time if this is an important issue for you.

One bed or two? Couples be warned: all the boats have a limited number of cabins with matrimonial beds. Unless you reserve early, you may be stuck with two narrow single beds.

It's quite common for boats and companies to receive favorable reviews from some people and unfavorable reviews from others. Expectations and standards differ and sometimes things go wrong on one trip but smoothly on another. The quality of your sailing experience will depend on a few things, including the chemistry between you and your fellow passengers; the smaller the boat, the more important it is that you get along. However, the larger boats with more passengers can feel impersonal, and the trip and islands may lose some of their unique aura.

There are a number of boats and companies that are worth checking out.

Adventure Life (☎800-344-6118 in the US; www.adventure-life.com) Books a wide selection of boats in all categories.

Columbus Travel (☎02-255-7699 in Quito, 877-436-7512 in the US; www.columbusecuador.com) Excellent customer service; can book a range of boats depending on budget and dates of travel.

Detour Destinations (☎866-386-4168 in the US; www.detourdestinations.com) Multisport trips for active types, including stand-up paddleboard excursions in the islands.

Ecoventura (☎02-283-9390, 800-633-7972 in the US; www.ecoventura.com) One of the pioneers in conservation and sustainable tourism. All of its four boats (five in 2019), including its diving live-aboards, are highly recommended.

Ecuador Adventure (☎888-234-3413 in the US & Canada; www.neotropicexpeditions.ec) Specializes in hotel-based and multisport tours including hiking, mountain biking and kayaking.

Galapagos Odyssey (☎02-286-0355; www.yachtgalapagosodyssey.com) This luxurious 16-passenger yacht includes a Jacuzzi.

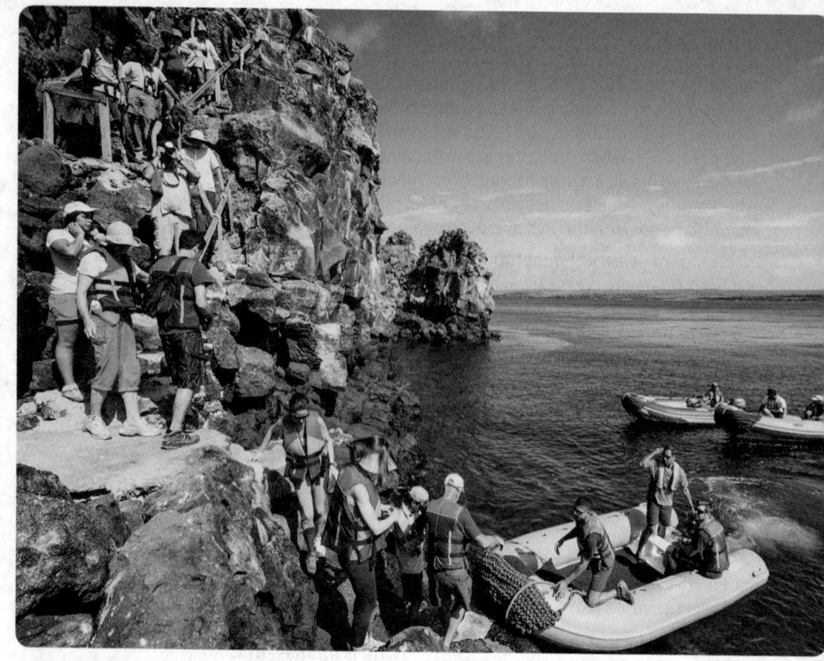

Boarding a *panga*, Isla Genovesa (p335)

Happy Gringo Travel (☎02-512-3486, in UK 800-051-7125, in the US & Canada 800-269-0216; www.happygringo.com) Excellent agency that books a wide range of boats, plus offers last-minute deals.

Lindblad Expeditions National Geographic (☎800-397-3348 in the US; www.expeditions.com) Offers *National Geographic Islander* (48 passenger) and *Endeavour* (96 passenger) yachts.

Metropolitan Touring (☎02-298-8312, 888-572-0166 in the US; www.metropolitan-touring.com) Affiliated with the Finch Bay Hotel in Puerto Ayora; books the luxury yachts *La Pinta* and *Isabela II*.

Natural Habitat Adventures (☎800-543-8917 in the US; www.nathab.com) Offers a 10-day tour, cruising long distances on a catamaran and then exploring the nooks and crannies by kayak – one of the only tours of its kind.

Row Adventures (☎800-451-6034 in the US; www.rowadventures.com) Luxury camping and kayaking tours.

Zenith Travel (☎02-252-9993; www.galapagosgay.com; cnr Juan Leon Mera N24-264 & Luis Cordero, Quito) Specializes in gay and lesbian tours.

Local Bookings

Most people arrive in the islands with a prearranged tour, although it's usually cheaper to arrange a tour in Puerto Ayora or Puerto Baquerizo Moreno. As a general rule, the cheaper boats are more available for booking once you're in the Galápagos. Don't fly to the Galápagos counting on getting a really good boat for less money. Arranging a tour from the Galápagos can take several days – sometimes a week or more – and is therefore not a good option if you have limited time.

The most important thing is to find a good captain and an enthusiastic naturalist guide. You should be able to meet both and inspect the boat before booking. Agreeing on a quality itinerary is also paramount. For last-minute four-day and eight-day tours, expect to pay at least $800 and $1600.

Dangers & Annoyances

There are some common pitfalls and hassles with Galápagos boat tours. It's

Onboard dining area

sometimes the case that the cheaper the trip, the more likely you are to experience problems. That's not to say that costlier boats are glitch-free, but the companies are often more attentive and quick to respond to complaints.

Some of the recurring complaints involve last-minute changes of boat (which the contractual small print allows), cancellations if there aren't enough passengers, poor crew, lack of bottled drinks, changes in the itinerary, mechanical breakdowns, insufficient and poor-quality snorkeling gear, hidden charges ($5 to $10 per day for wet suits is common), bad smells, bug infestations and overbooking.

Passengers share cabins and are sometimes not guaranteed that their cabinmates will be of the same gender. Always ask to see a photograph or layout of the boat, including those of the cabins, before booking.

It's frustrating but not uncommon to discover that shipmates have paid substantially less than you for the same services, especially if you've booked abroad and they've arranged things locally and at the last minute – there's little recourse, so it's best not to ask and to simply enjoy the trip.

When things go wrong, a refund is difficult to obtain. If you have a problem, report it to the *capitanía* (port captain) in Puerto Ayora and contact the agency where you booked the boat. You should also report problems (in person or by email) to the **Cámara de Turismo** (Tourist Information Office; Map p312; Av Darwin near Av 12 de Febrero; ⌚8am-12:30pm & 2:30-6pm) in Puerto Ayora, which keeps a database of complaints to share with agencies and tourists.

There are occasional reports of crew members of tourist boats (and, more commonly, small fishing boats) illegally fishing and killing wildlife. Complaints of this kind should be reported to the Natural Reserve office, a green building just to the left of the information booth at the entrance to the Charles Darwin Research Station in Puerto Ayora.

With all the boats cruising the islands, it's easy to forget that these are remote, inhospitable and dangerous places to be marooned. Seventeen people have disappeared since 1990 – most were found alive, though a few have died after straying from the designated paths.

Regions at a Glance

Quito

Scenery
Art & Architecture
Nightlife

City Panoramas

At 2850m and flanked by a massive volcano named Pichincha, this Andean city does not lack for breathtaking views. There are scores of great places to admire the panorama, whether at a rooftop restaurant in the old town, at a lush park or from the ridges of Pichincha itself (catch the TeleféridQo).

Convents & Monasteries

Quito's old town is a magnificent Unesco World Heritage Site of baroque churches, cobblestone streets, picturesque plazas and sun-baked Spanish colonial roofs. You can wander the cloisters of 16th-century monasteries, gaze at masterpieces of the Escuela Quiteña and ponder pre-Colombian carvings at fine museums.

Dining, Drinking & Dancing

Quito offers a wide array of temptations: tangy ceviche, tender *corvina* (sea bass), rich *seco de chivo* (goat stew), plus global flavors from Italy, Peru, Japan and beyond. Afterwards, you can work off those calories at a *salsateca* (nightclub) or go bar-hopping in the Mariscal.

p52

Northern Highlands

Bird-Watching
Scenery
Shopping

Cloud Forest Birds

One of Ecuador's most diverse regions for birdlife, the northern highlands is a mecca for bird-watchers, who particularly love the cloud forest reserves near Mindo for the sheer variety of avian life.

Volcanic Peaks

The soaring peaks of the Andes make for some of the country's best scenery: the snow-topped Volcán Cotacachi, the stunning views from the Panamericana as you head north, and the mesmerizing Lagunas de Mojanda near Otavalo should not be missed.

Artisan Crafts

Otavalo's massive clothing and handicrafts market is a feast for the eyes: colorfully woven textiles, tagua (vegetable ivory) carvings, primitivist folkloric paintings and alpaca blankets, scarves and shawls in every color of the rainbow. For leather goods of all sorts, don't miss Cotacachi.

p98

Central Highlands

Scenery
Culture
Outdoor Adventure

Avenue of the Volcanoes

There's a snapshot on nearly every corner. The spine of South America has glacier-capped volcanoes and high-altitude grasslands, precipitous canyons that rush white water down to the Amazon, and centuries-old haciendas cut from Incan stone.

Indigenous Communities

In the heart of the Andes, age-old cultural traditions remain a mainstay of everyday life. Culturally curious visitors will be rewarded with vibrant festivals, thriving crafts markets and remote indigenous villages, plus excellent museums in Ambato and Riobamba.

Climbing, Biking & Rafting

For adventure at full throttle, head just about anywhere in the central highlands. There are volcanoes to be climbed, rivers to be rafted, bridges to be jumped off and mountains to be cycled down.

p130

Cuenca & the Southern Highlands

Art & Architecture
Outdoor Adventure
Cuisine

Colonial Wonders

The colonial city of Cuenca is a veritable open-air museum with amazing architecture, historic center and plenty of artsy folks to get you in the mood.

Backcountry Adventures

Several national parks in the region provide intrepid explorers with splendid vistas, wildlife encounters and adventures aplenty. It takes some effort to truly get into the backcountry here, making the views, animal sightings and journey back all the more rewarding.

Gourmet Guinea Pig

The south serves up some of Ecuador's best-loved dishes, from Cuenca's magnificent *fanesca* (bean-and-codfish soup), served during Holy Week, to Loja's corn-loving delicacies of tamales, *quimbolitos* (corn dumplings) and *humitas* (like tamales), served anytime. For the avant-garde foodie, there's always *cuy* (roast guinea pig).

p171

The Oriente

Wildlife-Watching
Outdoor Adventure
Culture

Jungle Wildlife

Caimans, sloths, anacondas, howler monkeys, parrots...these are just some of the amazing creatures you can expect to see while staying at a jungle lodge deep in Ecuador's dense rainforest. You can even swim (safely) with piranhas.

River Adventures

If being deep in the rainforest isn't adventurous enough for you, then the Oriente has no shortage of additional thrills to offer: white-water rafting, kayaking, tubing, climbing and horseback riding.

Boat-Building & Gold Panning

Sensitively organized community visits to indigenous villages can be a great means of cultural interaction, and hugely enjoyable. Learn how to cook, trap animals, build boats, pan for gold and prepare traditional meals.

p206

North Coast & Lowlands

Beach Towns
Cuisine
Ecotourism

Catching Waves

The north coast has some enchanting laid-back beach towns, from sleepy Same to captivating Canoa, with great surf spots (especially forest-ringed Mompiche) along the coast.

Coconuts & Ceviche

Cocina manabita and *cocina esmeraldeña* are considered two of the best cuisines in Ecuador, which makes the north coast a great place to sample the spicy, coconut-infused local cooking. Don't miss the country's best ceviche in Esmeraldas province.

Community Tourism

This area boasts some worthwhile community-run ecotourism destinations, including Playa de Oro jungle reserve and the wildlife-rich Reserva Biológica Bilsa. Other highlights include exploring mangrove forests around Muisne, learning about organic farming at the Río Muchacho Organic Farm and taking an ecocity tour in Bahía de Caráquez.

p246

South Coast

Wildlife-Watching
Beaches
Cuisine

Whale-Spotting

Migrating humpback whales share the waters with pods of porpoises, and first-rate birdlife can be observed in several nature reserves and the coastal mountain-range cloud forests.

White-Sand Beaches

The Santa Elena Peninsula has strings of resort towns for *guayaquileños,* lined with condominiums and soft white sand. North of here, all the way to Puerto López, beachfront villages with kilometer after kilometer of beach-breaks beckon, especially at Montañita, Olón and Ayampe.

Fresh Seafood

The region's long coastline means freshly caught seafood is in plentiful supply. Piles of shellfish, ceviche, *cazuela* (seafood stew) and lobster are on the menu of even the most casual eateries. Guayaquil's culinary scene is a showcase for Ecuador's best restaurants.

p270

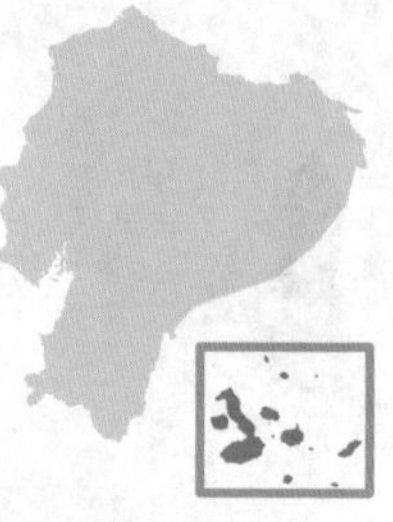

The Galápagos Islands

Wildlife-Watching
Snorkeling & Diving
Scenery

Reptiles & Blue-Footed Boobies

Get up close and personal with prehistoric-looking reptiles and a menagerie of birdlife, from vast colonies of endemic seabirds, mating albatrosses and flightless cormorants to tiny mockingbirds and ever-vigilant birds of prey.

Sea Lions & Sea Creatures

The variety of aquatic life is astounding. You can snorkel with sea turtles, rays, sharks, tropical fish, frolicking sea lions, speedy penguins and algae-crunching marine iguanas. Divers have spectacular options and memorable sites. It is best for intermediate-level divers and above.

Volcanic Landscapes

The Galápagos chain is an archipelago of volcanic islands; its scenic drama comes in the form of massive fumaroles, fantastic rocky escarpments, misty highlands and gorgeous beaches (with white, red, black, and gold sand).

p307

On the Road

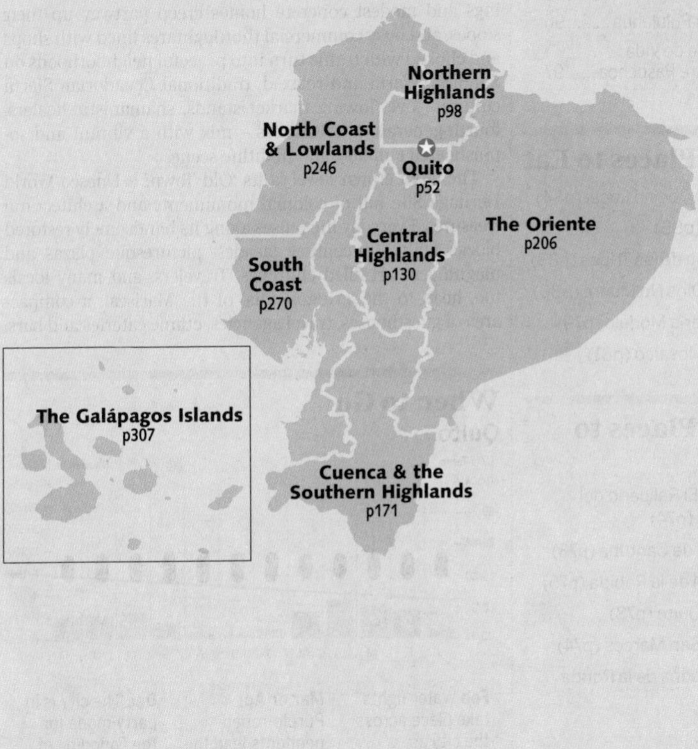

North Coast & Lowlands
p246

Northern Highlands
p98

Quito
p52

Central Highlands
p130

The Oriente
p206

South Coast
p270

The Galápagos Islands
p307

Cuenca & the Southern Highlands
p171

Quito

☎02 / POP 1.6 MILLION / ELEV 2800M

Includes ➡

Best Places to Eat

➡ UKRO Cocina Local (p84)
➡ Zazu (p85)
➡ Parque de las Tripas (p83)
➡ Café Dios No Muere (p80)
➡ Cafetería Modelo (p79)
➡ Café Mosaico (p81)

Best Places to Stay

➡ Hotel El Relicario del Carmen (p74)
➡ Portal de Cantuña (p73)
➡ Hostal de la Rábida (p75)
➡ BoutiQuito (p78)
➡ Casa San Marcos (p74)
➡ La Casona de la Ronda (p74)

Why Go?

A capital city high in the Andes, Quito is dramatically situated, squeezed between mountain peaks whose greenery is concealed by the afternoon mist. Modern apartment buildings and modest concrete homes creep partway up their slopes, and busy commercial thoroughfares lined with shops and choked with traffic turn into peaceful neighborhoods on Sundays. Warm and relaxed, traditional Ecuadorian Sierra culture – overflowing market stands, shamanistic healers, fourth-generation hatmakers – mix with a vibrant and sophisticated culinary and nightlife scene.

The city's crown jewel is its 'Old Town,' a Unesco World Heritage Site full of colonial monuments and architectural treasures. Everyday life pulses along its handsomely restored blocks with 17th-century facades, picturesque plazas and magnificent art-filled churches. Travelers, and many locals too, head to the 'gringolandia' of the Mariscal, a compact area of guesthouses, travel agencies, ethnic eateries and bars.

When to Go

Quito

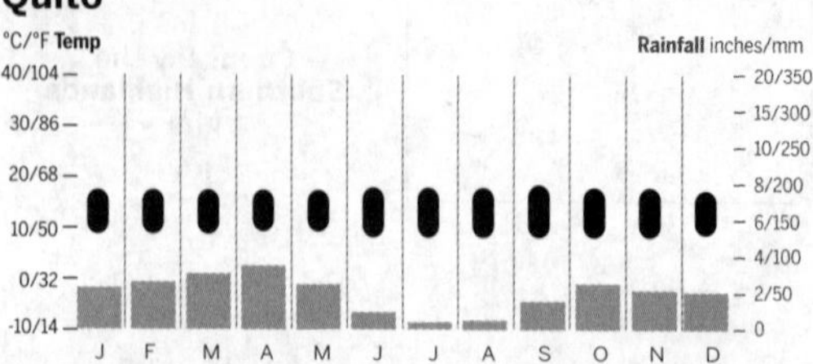

Feb Water fights take place across the city as *quiteños* celebrate Carnaval.

Mar or Apr Purple-robed penitents lead the Semana Santa processions.

Dec The city is in party mode for the Founding of Quito Festival.

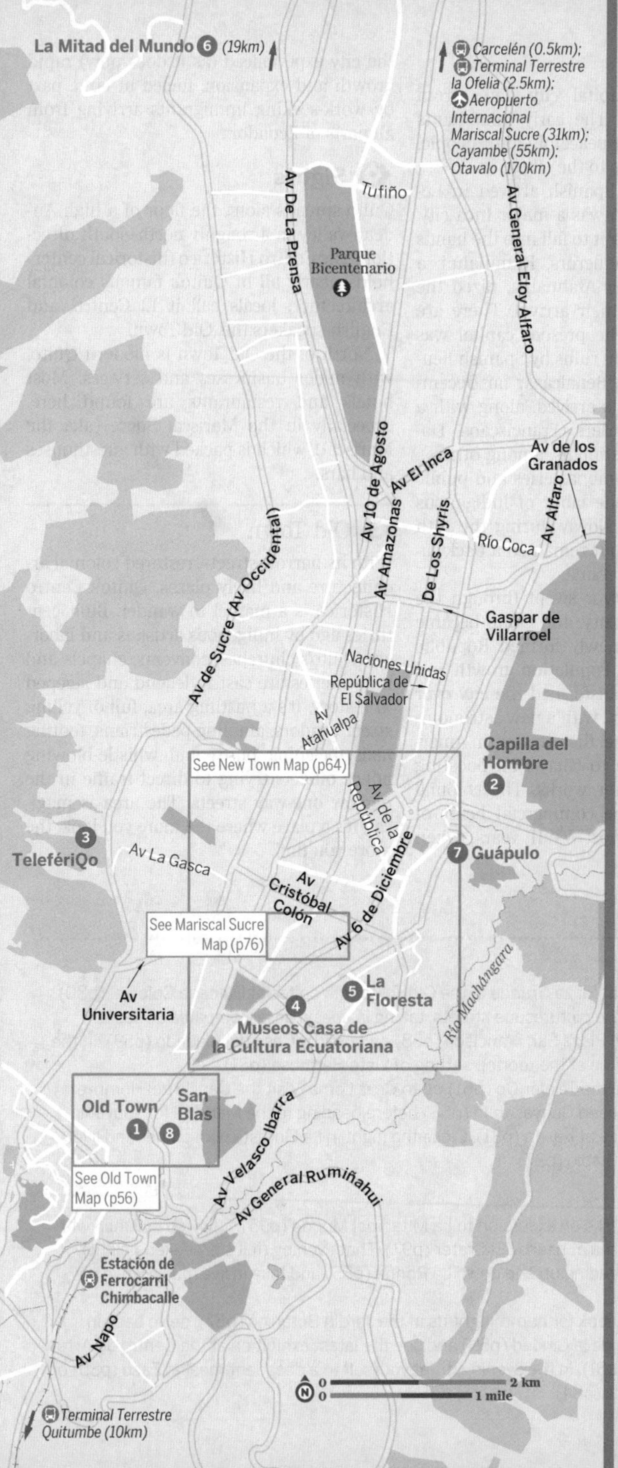

Quito Highlights

1 Old Town (p54) Exploring the cobblestone streets that crisscross one of South America's finest colonial centers.

2 Capilla del Hombre (p63) Gazing at Oswaldo Guayasamín's monumental paintings and visiting his treasure-filled home.

3 TeleféríQo (p61) Riding an aerial tram up Volcán Pichincha for magnificent views over the Andean capital.

4 Museos Casa de la Cultura Ecuatoriana (p63) Admiring works by Ecuador's finest artists in the newly renovated museum.

5 La Floresta (p83) Sampling street food and strolling between cafes along the neighborhood's tree-lined streets.

6 La Mitad del Mundo (p95) Getting close to earth's belly button at the kitschy museums surrounding the monument to the equator.

7 Guápulo (p86) Sipping *canelazo* while savoring the views in one of the bohemian neighborhood bars.

8 Craft Beer (p85) Tasting local *cerveza artesanal* in the cluster of brew bars in San Blas.

History

The site of the capital city dates from pre-Hispanic times. The early inhabitants of the area were the peaceful Quitu people, who gave their name to the city.

By the time the Spanish arrived in Ecuador in 1526, Quito was a major Inca city. Rather than allowing it to fall into the hands of the Spanish conquerors, Rumiñahui, a general of Inca ruler Atahualpa, razed the city shortly before their arrival. There are no Inca remains. The present capital was founded on top of the ruins by Spanish lieutenant Sebastián de Benalcázar on December 6, 1534. Colonists arrived, along with a host of religious orders (Franciscans, Dominicans and Augustinians, among others), and built churches, monasteries and public works, often with the labor of indigenous people. Quito grew slowly during the 17th and 18th centuries but remained a backwater in comparison to Lima.

Revolutionary fervor swept through the city in the 19th century, and Quito became the capital of the newly formed Republic of Ecuador in 1830. Population growth and building projects transformed the city over the following century, with a new astronomical observatory (the first in South America), a key rail line to Guayaquil boosting commerce, and other works. The colonial center remained the commercial heart of the city until the post-WWII years, when the city experienced (as it does now) rapid growth and expansion, fueled in large part by work-seeking immigrants arriving from all parts of Ecuador.

Sights

Quito spreads along the floor of a high Andean valley in a roughly north–south direction. The Centro Histórico (historical center) holds nearly all of Quito's famous colonial architecture; locals call it El Centro, and English-speakers the 'Old Town.'

North of the Old Town is modern Quito, with major businesses and services. Most hotels and restaurants are found here, especially in the Mariscal Sucre (aka the Mariscal), which is packed with guesthouses and bars.

Old Town

With its narrow streets, restored colonial architecture and lively plazas, Quito's Centro Histórico is a marvel to wander. Built centuries ago by indigenous artisans and laborers, Quito's churches, convents, chapels and monasteries are cast in legend and steeped in history. It's a bustling area, full of yelling street vendors, ambling pedestrians, tooting taxis, belching buses and whistle-blowing police officers trying to direct traffic in the narrow one-way streets. The area is magical; it's a place where the more you look, the more you find.

QUITO IN...

Two Days

Start your day off at Plaza Grande in the Old Town with coffee at Dulceria Colonial (p80). From there, stroll the picturesque streets, taking in Iglesia de la Compañía de Jesús (p56), the sights in Plaza San Francisco (p58) and nearby Casa del Alabado (p59). In the evening, drink or dine at the rooftop setting of Vista Hermosa (p81).

On day two, ride the TelefériQo (p61) up to Cruz Loma. Visit the Capilla del Hombre (p63) and Casa Museo Guayasamín (p63) before heading to the Mariscal for souvenir shopping and coffee at Kallari (p81). Close the night in La Floresta with dinner and live music at El Pobre Diablo (p87).

Four Days

On your third day take an excursion to La Mitad del Mundo (p95), followed by lunch with a stunning panorama at nearby El Crater (p97). That evening (if it's a weekend night), join the crowds parading up and down La Ronda (p85) and take in live music while having a drink or meal.

On the last day, look for hummingbirds in the Jardín Botánico (p67), delve back in time at the Museo de la Ciudad (p59) and see the latest exhibition at the Centro de Arte Contemporáneo (p61). In the evening, treat yourself to a decadent meal at Zazu (p85) or UKRO Cocina Local (p84).

DON'T MISS

PLAZA GRANDE

While wandering around colonial Quito, you'll probably pass through the **Plaza Grande** (Map p56) several times. Its benches are great for soaking up the Andean morning sun and watching the bustle all around. On Monday, the changing of the guards takes place on the plaza at 11am.

On the northeast side of the plaza, the **Palacio Arzobispal** (Archbishop's Palace; Map p56; Chile), a former archbishop's palace, is now a colonnaded row of small shops and restaurants.

The low white building on the northwestern side of Plaza Grande is **Palacio de Gobierno** (Carondelet Palace; Map p56; www.presidencia.gob.ec/palacio-de-gobierno; cnr Espejo & García Moreno, Plaza Grande; guided tours 9am-6pm Tue-Fri, to 8pm Sat, to 9pm Sun), the seat of the Ecuadorian presidency. Visitors can enter by joining a free guided tour in Spanish and English which leave every 20 minutes; bring photo ID to the ticket office on Espejo to reserve a space. The President lives and works here, so sightseeing is limited to rooms that are not in use.

Inside the palace, the tour begins in the excellent new **Museo de la Presidencia**, with exhibits celebrating Ecuador's history, human rights and social justice themes and the country's biodiversity, and also displays of some of the 11,000 official gifts received by former President Rafael Correa. On the tour of the palace you'll see Andalusian patios (where bullfighting once took place), the cabinet room, banquet room, balcony and Presidents' room, where the portraits of Ecuador's constitutional presidents are displayed. At the staircase, don't miss Guayasamin's brilliantly hued mosaic depicting Francisco de Orellana's descent of the Amazon.

On Plaza Grande's southwest side stands Quito's **Catedral Metropolitana** (Map p56; 02-257-0371; Plaza Grande; cathedral adult/child $3/2, cathedral & dome (adults only) $6; 9am-5pm Mon-Sat). Although not the most ornate of the Old Town's churches, it has some fascinating works by artists from the Quito School and houses the tomb of independence hero Antonio José de Sucre. Behind the main altar is a plaque marking where President Gabriel García Moreno died on August 6, 1875; after being slashed with a machete outside the Palacio del Gobierno, he was carried, dying, to the cathedral.

Don't miss the painting of the Last Supper, with Christ and disciples feasting on *cuy* (guinea pig), and a nativity painting that features a llama and a horse peering over the newborn Jesus. Admission includes a free guided tour in Spanish and entry to the small Cathedral museum. For an extra $3 you can climb up a narrow spiral staircase and onto the cathedral's domed roof; the views are impressive but there is some clambering along narrow ledges involved.

Just off Plaza Grande, the beautifully restored **Centro Cultural Metropolitano** (Map p56; cnr Moreno & Espejo; galleries 9am-4pm Mon-Fri, to 1pm Sat, patio 9am-5pm Mon-Sat, 10am-4pm Sun) houses the municipal library and lecture rooms, and hosts temporary art exhibitions.

The location is rich in history: it is supposedly the site of one of Inca ruler Atahualpa's palaces; a Jesuit school from 1597 to 1767; an army barracks after the expulsion of the Jesuits in the late 1700s; and in 1809 the site at which royalist forces held a group of revolutionaries, before murdering them a year later.

Churches are open daily (usually until 6pm), but are crowded with worshippers on Sunday. They regularly close between 1pm and 3pm for lunch.

The heart of the Old Town is the Plaza Grande, a picturesque, palm-fringed square surrounded by historic buildings and bustling with everyday life.

'**La Ronda**' – a completely restored narrow cobblestone lane lined with postcard-perfect 17th-century buildings housing festive restaurants, bars and colorful shops – comes alive on Friday and Saturday nights when *canelazo* (aguardiente with hot cider and cinnamon) vendors keep the crowds nice and warm and live music spills outdoors. Placards along the walls describe (in Spanish) some of the street's history and the artists, writers and political figures who once resided here. This should not be missed.

Old Town

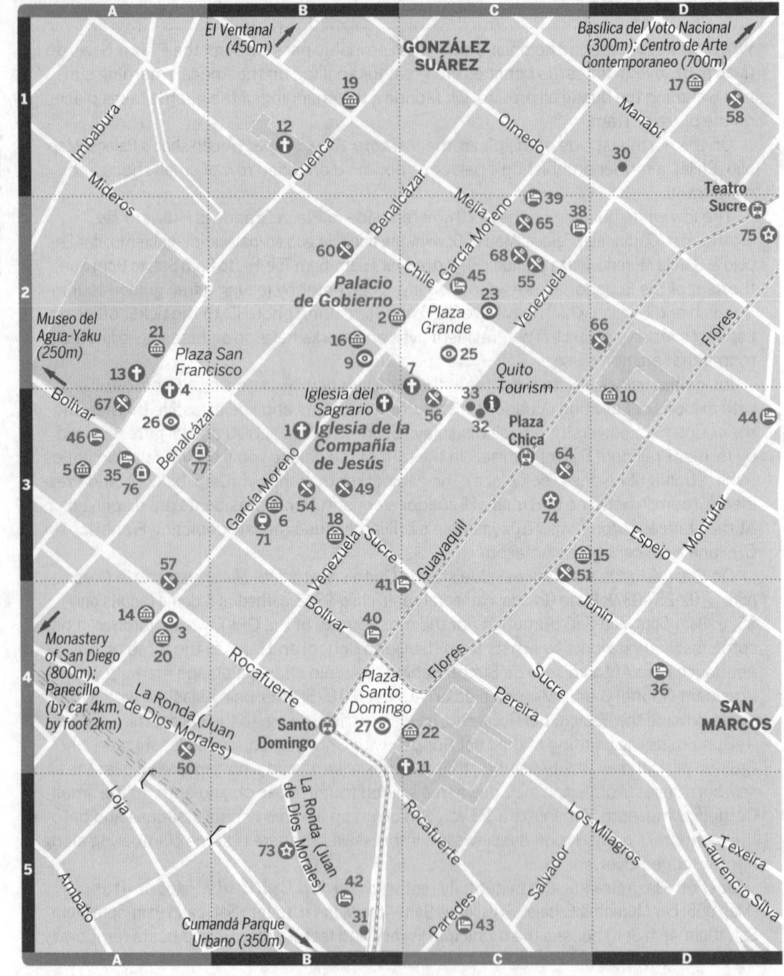

★Iglesia de la Compañía de Jesús CHURCH

(Map p56; www.fundacioniglesiadelacompania.org.ec; García Moreno & Sucre; adult/student $5/2.50; ⏲9:30am-6pm Mon-Thu, to 5:30pm Fri, to 4pm Sat, 12:30-4pm Sun) Capped by green-and-gold domes, La Compañía de Jesús is Quito's most ornate church and a standout among the baroque splendors of Old Town. Free guided tours in English or Spanish highlight the church's unique features, including its Moorish elements, perfect symmetry (right down to the *trompe l'oeil* staircase at the rear), symbolic elements (bright-red walls are a reminder of Christ's blood) and its syncretism (Ecuadorian plants and indigenous faces are hidden along the pillars).

Construction on this marvelously gilded Jesuit church began in 1605 but wasn't completed for another 160 years; the main altarpiece alone took 20 years (former president Gabriel García Moreno is buried here). The made-in-the-USA organ is circa 1889. Check out the chiaroscuro-style series of paintings called the *16 Prophets* by Nicolás Javier de Goribar and the large canvas *Hell and Final Judgement* from 1879 – it's still a mystery what happened to the original, painted

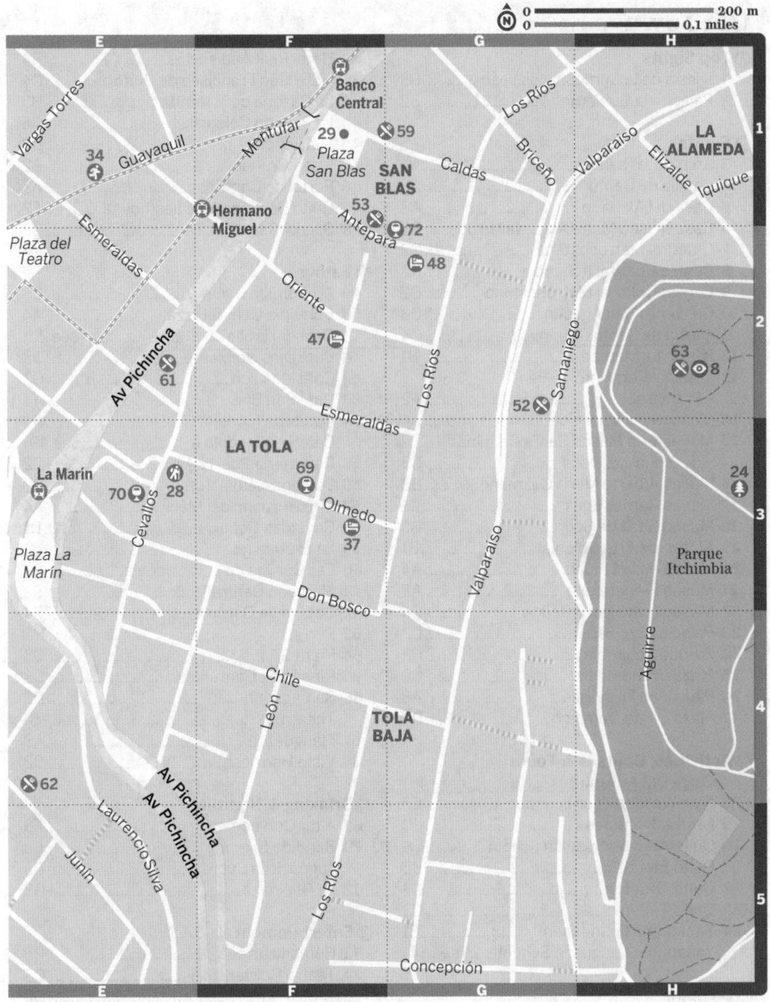

by Hermano Hernando de la Cruz in 1620. *Quiteños* (people from Quito) proudly call it the most beautiful church in the country, and it's easy to see why.

Casa Museo María Augusta Urrutía MUSEUM
(Map p56; ☎02-258-0103; www.fmdj.org; Moreno N2-60 near Bolívar; $2; ⏱10am-6pm Tue-Fri, 9:30am-5:30pm Sat & Sun) Of Quito's house museums, this is the one not to miss: it's a splendidly preserved, 19th-century home that was once the abode of the city's best-loved philanthropist, María Augusta Urrutía, and it's packed with period furnishings, stained-glass windows and European artwork. Free guided tours in Spanish and English.

Museo Casa de Sucre MUSEUM
(Map p56; Venezuela 573 near Sucre; ⏱9am-4pm Tue-Sun, last admission 3:30pm) FREE The beautifully restored former home of Mariscal Antonio José de Sucre, the hero of Ecuadorian independence, is now a small museum full of early-19th-century furniture. The museum offers free guided tours in Spanish.

Old Town

Top Sights
1 Iglesia de la Compañía de Jesús B3
2 Palacio de Gobierno B2

Sights
3 Arco de la Reina A4
4 Capilla de Cantuña A3
5 Casa del Alabado A3
6 Casa Museo María Augusta Urrutía B3
7 Catedral Metropolitana C2
8 Centro Cultural Itchimbia H2
9 Centro Cultural Metropolitano B2
10 Convento San Agustín D3
11 Iglesia de Santo Domingo C4
12 Iglesia La Merced B1
13 Iglesia y Convento de San Francisco A2
14 Monasterio Museo del Carmen Alto A4
15 Monasterio Museo Santa Catalina de Siena C3
16 Museo Alberto Mena Caamaño B2
17 Museo Camilo Egas D1
18 Museo Casa de Sucre B3
19 Museo de Arte Colonial B1
20 Museo de la Ciudad A4
21 Museo Franciscano A2
22 Museo Fray Pedro Bedón C4
23 Palacio Arzobispal C2
24 Parque Itchimbia H3
25 Plaza Grande C2
26 Plaza San Francisco A3
27 Plaza Santo Domingo B4

Activities, Courses & Tours
CarpeDM Adventures .... (see 48)
28 Free Walking Tour Ecuador E3
29 Latin Adventures F1
30 Quito Antiguo Spanish School D1
31 Quito Eterno B5
32 Quito Tour Bus C3
33 Quito Turismo C3
34 Yanapuma Foundation E1
Yanapuma Language School .... (see 34)

Sleeping
35 Casa Gangotena A3
36 Casa San Marcos D4
37 Colonial House F3
38 Hotel El Relicario del Carmen C2
39 Hotel Patio Andaluz C2
40 Hotel Real Audiencia B4
41 Hotel San Francisco de Quito C4
42 La Casona de la Ronda B5
43 La Posada Colonial C5
44 Mia Leticia D3
45 Plaza Grande C2
46 Portal de Cantuña A3
47 Quito Backpacker Guesthouse F2
48 Secret Garden G2

Eating
49 Ari Comida Sana B3
50 Bohemia Cafe & Pizza A4
Café del Fraile .... (see 23)
51 Café Dios No Muere C3
52 Café Mosaico G2
53 Café San Blas F1
54 Cafetería Modelo B3
Cafetería Modelo II .... (see 49)
55 Cevicheria Puerto Azul C2
56 Dulceria Colonial C3
57 El Kukurucho del Maní A4
58 Govindas Gopal D1
59 La Exquita G1
60 Las Cuevas de Luís Candela B2
61 Mercado Central E2
62 Octava de Corpus E4
63 Pim's H2
64 Pizza SA C3
65 Rincón de Cantuña C2
66 San Agustín D2
Theatrum .... (see 75)
67 Tianguez A3
68 Vista Hermosa C2

Drinking & Nightlife
69 Altar Cervecería F3
70 Bandido Brewing E3
71 Jugos de la Sucre B3
72 La Oficina G2

Entertainment
73 Humanizarte B5
74 Teatro Bolívar C3
75 Teatro Sucre D2

Shopping
76 ARIU A3
77 Homero Ortega P & Hijos A3
Tianguez .... (see 67)

Displays include the household shopping list for Simón Bolívar's visit in June 1822, including 50 rabbits, 16 cow tongues and eight very fat pigs.

Museo Alberto Mena Caamaño MUSEUM
(Map p56; Espejo near García Moreno; adult/child $1.50/0.50; 9am-5pm Mon-Sat, 10am-4pm Sun) Get a glimpse of Quito's early colonial history through wax figures depicting the city's key events, including the massacre of August 2, 1810 when some 200 independence-seeking *quiteños* (people from Quito) were executed.

Plaza San Francisco PLAZA
(Map p56) Walking from the old town's narrow colonial streets into this open plaza reveals one of the finest sights in all of Ecua-

dor: a sweeping cobblestone plaza backed by the mountainous backdrop of Volcán Pichincha, and the long, whitewashed walls and twin bell towers of Ecuador's oldest church.

Iglesia y Convento de San Francisco CONVENT

(Map p56; Cuenca near Sucre; ⌚7-11am & 3-6pm Mon-Thu, 7-11am Fri-Sun) **FREE** Construction of the convent, the city's largest colonial structure, began only a few weeks after the founding of Quito in 1534, but wasn't finished for another 70 years. Although much of the church has been rebuilt because of earthquake damage, some is original. The **chapel of Señor Jesús del Gran Poder**, to the right of the main altar, has original tile work. The **main altar** itself is a spectacular example of baroque carving, while much of the roof shows Moorish influences.

The founder was the Franciscan missionary Joedco Ricke, credited with being the first man to sow wheat in Ecuador.

Museo Franciscano MUSEUM

(Museo Fray Pedro Gocial; Map p56; www.museofraypedrogocial.com; Cuenca 477 near Sucre; adult/child $2.50/0.50; ⌚9am-5:30pm Mon-Sat, to 12:30pm Sun) Sitting to the right of the Iglesia de San Francisco's main entrance, and within the Convent of St Francis, this museum contains some of the church's finest artwork including paintings, sculpture and 16th-century furniture, some of which is fantastically wrought and inlaid with thousands of pieces of mother-of-pearl. The admission fee includes a guided tour in English or Spanish.

Good guides will point out Mudejar (Moorish) representations of the eight planets revolving around the sun in the ceiling, and will explain how the light shines through the rear window during the solstices, lighting up the main altar. They'll also demonstrate an odd confessional technique, where two people standing in separate corners can hear each other while whispering into the walls.

Capilla de Cantuña CHAPEL

(Map p56; ☎02-228-1124; Cuenca near Bolívar; ⌚7-8am Tue & Thu, 8-9am Sun) **FREE** The Cantuña Chapel houses a small art collection from the Quito School. It's shrouded in one of Quito's most famous legends, that of the indigenous builder Cantuña, who supposedly sold his soul so the devil would help him complete the church on time. Just before midnight on the day of his deadline, Cantuña removed a single stone from the structure, meaning the church was never completed. He duped the devil and saved his soul.

Casa del Alabado MUSEUM

(Map p56; ☎02-228-0940; www.alabado.org; Cuenca N1-41 near Bolívar; $4; ⌚9:30am-5:30pm) Housed in an elegant colonial-era home, the privately owned Casa del Alabado has contemporary-style displays and showcases an impressive collection of pre-Columbian artifacts. Thematically organized around subjects such as shamans and the afterlife, explanations in English and Spanish (audio guides are available) explore the indigenous beliefs represented by the finely crafted ceramic pieces and jewelry.

Museo de la Ciudad MUSEUM

(Map p56; ☎02-228-3883; www.museociudadquito.gob.ec; García Moreno S1-47 near Rocafuerte; adult/child $3/1; ⌚9:30am-4:30pm Tue-Sun) This first-rate museum depicts daily life in Quito through the centuries, with displays including dioramas, model indigenous homes and colonial kitchens. The 1563 building itself (a former hospital) is a work of art. There are also a number of temporary exhibitions. Free entry on the last Sunday of the month.

The museum is located just past the 18th-century arch, **Arco de la Reina** (Map p56; cnr García Moreno & Rocafuerte), built to give shelter to churchgoers.

Monasterio Museo del Carmen Alto MUSEUM

(Map p56; ☎02-228-1513; García Moreno S1-47 near Rocafuerte; adult/student/child $3/2/1; ⌚9:30am-5:30pm Wed-Sun, last entry 4:30pm) The Monasterio Museo del Carmen Alto, built in 1653 and still home to an order of 20 Carmelite nuns, now houses an interesting museum. Exhibits explore the daily routines of the nuns who made their lives here, including Marianita de Jesus (1618–1645), Quito's patron saint. The whitewashed two-story building surrounds a sun-filled inner courtyard, and several rooms contain emotive, religiously themed paintings. Free tours in Spanish; tours in English $4.

The cloistered nuns who live in the monastery stay busy producing some of Quito's tastiest traditional sweets. A top pick is the *limones desamargados* (literally 'de-soured lemons'), made by hollowing out tiny lemons and filling them with a sweetened-milk concoction. Purchase them at the small shop near the museum exit, where you can also

WHAT'S NEW

➡ The relaxing of Ecuador's brewing laws has seen new craft beer producers and microbreweries pop up, including Altar Cervecería (p86), La Oficina (p85) and Santa Rosa Cerveza Artesanal (p86).

➡ The Palacio de Gobierno (Presidential palace; p55) houses a new museum containing the official gifts received by former President Rafael Correa, along with other interesting exhibitions. See it on a free guided tour of the Presidential palace.

➡ Quito's network of ciclovías – pathways dedicated solely to bicycle traffic – has been expanded.

➡ The newly renovated Museos Casa de la Cultura Ecuatoriana (p63) houses a modern art collection, musical instrument museum and an excellent ethnography museum with state-of-the-art exhibits.

➡ Teatro Bolívar (p90), one of the city's most illustrious and important theaters, has reopened. The art deco building has been in various stages of restoration since it was badly damaged by a fire in 1999.

➡ Bookworms won't want to miss the Librería del Fondo Carlos Fuentes (p90), a fabulous bookstore with regular readings and cultural events housed in the former mansion of ex-President Galo Plaza Lasso.

➡ The innovative new restaurant UKRO Cocina Local (p84) is worth checking out for its fresh take on traditional Ecuadorian cuisine.

buy traditional baked goods, aromatic waters for nerves and insomnia, bee pollen, honey and bottles of full-strength *mistela* (anise-flavored liqueur).

Plaza Santo Domingo PLAZA

(Map p56) Plaza Santo Domingo, near the southwest end of Calle Guayaquil, is a regular haunt for street performers. Locals fill the plaza to watch pouting clowns and amateur magicians do their stuff. The plaza is beautiful in the evening, when the domes of the 17th-century **Iglesia de Santo Domingo** (Map p56; cnr Flores & Rocafuerte; ⏲7am-1pm & 5-7pm) FREE, on the southeast side of the plaza, are floodlit.

The church is worth a look inside for the Moorish ceiling, the wood carvings and the silver throne in the main altar. It must have been an inspiring place to study philosophy when the Colegio Mayor de San Fernando was housed here during colonial times. Next door, the **Museo Fray Pedro Bedón** (Convento Santo Domingo; Map p56; adult/child $3/1; ⏲9am-1:30pm & 2:30-5pm Mon-Fri, 9am-2pm Sat) has a pretty garden cloister and a fine assortment of colonial religious art.

Monasterio Museo Santa Catalina de Siena MUSEUM

(Map p56; Espejo 779 near Flores; adult/child $2.50/1; ⏲9am-4pm Mon-Fri, to 12:30pm Sat) Guided tours (in Spanish) of the museum at this fully functioning Dominican monastery, founded in 1592, take in 18th-century religious paintings, some of which are downright gruesome. To this day, the nuns here have only one hour each day to talk to each other or watch TV. But they make all sorts of natural products (shampoos, wine, hand cream and more), which you can purchase from a rotating door that keeps the nuns hidden.

Convento San Agustín MUSEUM

(Museo Miguel de Santiago; Map p56; cnr Chile & Guayaquil; adult/child $2/1; ⏲9am-12:30pm & 2-5pm Mon-Fri, 9am-12:30pm Sat) This monastery is a fine example of 17th-century architecture, with unusual Moorish arches decorated with hundreds of golden pineapples. Many of the heroes of the battles for Ecuador's independence are buried in the crypt here, and it is the site of the signing of the Independence Act of August 16, 1809. Entrance includes a guided tour in English or Spanish.

The museum also contains several important works by Miguel de Santiago, a leading artist of the Quito School.

Basílica del Voto Nacional CHURCH

(cnr Venezuela & Carchi; church/tower $1/2; ⏲9am-4pm) On a hill in the northeastern part of the Old Town looms this massive Gothic church, built over several decades beginning in 1892. Rather than gargoyles, however, turtles and iguanas protrude from the church's side. The highlight is the basilica's **towers**, which you can climb if you have the nerve – the ascent requires crossing a rickety wooden plank inside the main roof and climbing steep stairs and ladders (with solid handrails) to the top.

Centro de Arte Contemporáneo MUSEUM
(CAC; www.centrodeartecontemporaneo.gob.ec; Dávila & Venezuela; ⏲10:30am-5:30pm Tue-Fri, 9:30am-5:30pm Sat & Sun) FREE Inside a beautifully restored former military hospital, this excellent museum showcases cutting-edge multimedia exhibits as well as top modern-art shows that travel to the city.

There's a good cafe (p86) on site.

Iglesia La Merced CHURCH
(Map p56; cnr Cuenca & Chile; ⏲7-11:30am & 3-6pm) FREE This 18th-century church boasts the highest tower in colonial Quito and a wealth of fascinating art, including paintings that show volcanoes erupting over the church roofs of the city and the capital covered with ashes.

Legend says that the tower, the only unblessed part of the church, is possessed by the devil. Supposedly the only person strong enough to resist the devil was a bell-ringer

QUITO FROM ON HIGH: THE CITY'S BEST VIEWPOINTS

TelefériQo (Av Occidental near Av La Gasca; adult/child $8.50/6.50; ⏲9am-8pm Tue-Thu, 8am-8pm Fri-Mon) For spectacular views over Quito's mountainous landscape, hop aboard this sky tram that takes passengers on a 2.5km ride (10 minutes) up the flanks of Volcán Pichincha to the top of Cruz Loma. Once you're at the top (a mere 4100m), you can hike to the summit of Rucu Pichincha (4680m), a 4km (five-hour) round-trip – you should ask about the safety situation before attempting the climb, and bring warm clothes. You'll need to start walking before 11am.

Don't attempt the trip to Rucu Pichincha until you've acclimatized in Quito for a couple of days, and go with a qualified guide. You can also hire horses ($15 per hour), which are about 500m from the upper station (follow signs to *'paseos a caballo'*). Try to visit in the morning, when the views here are best; the clouds usually roll in by noon. A taxi here costs about $5 from the Mariscal.

Vulqano Park (☎02-222-2733; www.vulqanopark.com; rides $1.50-2.50; ⏲10am-8:30pm), a children's amusement park, is at the base station.

El Panecillo (General Melchor Aymerich; $1; ⏲9am-1:30pm & 2:30-5pm Mon-Fri) Topped by a 41m tall aluminum mosaic statue of La Virgen de Quito (Virgin of Quito; completed in 1976), with a crown of stars, angelic wings and a chained dragon, the hill to the south of Old Town called El Panecillo (the Little Loaf of Bread) is a major Quito landmark. From the summit there are marvelous views of the sprawling city and the surrounding volcanoes. Climb steps up to the base of the Virgin statue for an even loftier outlook.

The best time for volcano views (particularly in the rainy season) is early morning, before the clouds roll in. It's possible to walk via the stairs at the end of Calle García Moreno, but the neighborhood dogs can be a problem and muggings have occurred. A taxi from the Old Town is a better way to go.

Cima de la Libertad (Av de los Libertadores; adult/child $1/0.25; ⏲9am-5:30pm) Up the flanks of Volcán Pichincha, this monument offers one of the finest views of the city. It was built at the site of the May 1822 Batalla de Pichincha (Battle of Pichincha), led by Mariscal Antonio José de Sucre, a decisive battle in the struggle for independence from Spain. There is also a military museum and a tiled mural by Eduardo Kingman. It's best to take a taxi to the site, which lies roughly 3km west of Plaza Grande.

Mirador de Guápulo (Map p64; Calle Larrea) The views from the lookout platform are magnificent: on a clear day, you can see Volcán Cayambe and Cerro Puntas as well as the upscale suburb of Cumbayá (there are several good restaurants and bars in the main plaza there).

Look for the statue of Francisco de Orellana depicting the Spaniard looking down into the valley, marking the beginning of his epic journey from Quito to the Atlantic – the first descent of the Amazon River by a European.

named Ceferino, and no one has dared enter the tower since he died in 1810.

Museo de Arte Colonial MUSEUM
(Map p56; Mejía Oe6-132 near Cuenca; 9am-5pm Tue-Sat) FREE This museum, in a handsomely restored 17th-century building, houses an excellent collection of colonial art. On display are famous sculptures and paintings of the Quito School, including the works of Miguel de Santiago, Manuel Chili (the indigenous artist known as Caspicara) and Bernardo de Legarda.

Museo Camilo Egas MUSEUM
(Map p56; Venezuela 1302 near Esmeraldas; 8am-5pm Tue-Fri, to 4pm Sat) FREE Inside a restored colonial home, there is a small but iconic collection of work by painter Camilo Egas (1899–1962), Ecuador's first *indigenista* (indigenous movement) painter. One of the galleries showcases temporary exhibitions by contemporary painters.

Parque Itchimbia PARK
(Map p56; 5am-6pm) Sitting high on a hill above the Old Town, this grassy park boasts magnificent views of the city, running and cycle tracks and a children's playground. It's the perfect spot to spread out a picnic lunch, soak up the sun and take in the panorama. It's a steep climb up here from the San Blas neighborhood; walk up Elizalde, from where steps lead up to the park.

The park's centerpiece is the **Centro Cultural Itchimbia** (Map p56; www.facebook.com/ItchimbiaCentroCultural; hours vary), a large glass-and-iron building modeled after the city's original Mercado Santa Clara, which hosts regular art exhibitions and cultural events.

Museo del Agua-Yaku MUSEUM
(02-251-1100; www.yakumuseoagua.gob.ec; El Placer Oe11-271; adult/student/child $3/2/1; 9am-5:30pm Tue-Sun) Housed in a stunning modern glass building on the lower slopes of Pichincha, at the site of the city's first water distribution tanks, this museum tells the story of the city's relationship to the most vital resource through interactive exhibits that are good for kids.

There are outdoor fountains, gardens with fabulous views of the city, and a terrace cafe.

Convento de San Diego MUSEUM
(Museo Padre Almeida; cnr Farfán & Chimborazo; adult/child $3/1; 10am-1pm & 2-5pm Mon-Sat, 10am-2pm Sun) Overlooking the Old Town, this beautiful 17th-century Franciscan convent sits in a quiet courtyard behind thick walls. Inside, you'll find outstanding colonial works from both the Quito and Cusco Schools, including one of Quito's finest pulpits, carved by the notable indigenous wood-carver Juan Bautista Menacho.

There's also a fascinating 18th-century painting by Miguel de Santiago of the Last Supper. The oddest piece of work here is an unidentified painting by Hieronymus Bosch,

QUITO FOR CHILDREN

There's plenty to keep the kiddies happy in Quito. Parque La Carolina (p67) is a good place to start: you can pedal around the lake in a paddleboat, or take in the natural history museum or the Vivarium (p67), where the snakes, turtles and lizards will surely interest and/or frighten them. Nearby, the Jardín Botánico (p67) has a hands-on area for kids. The park is also home to the **Mundo Juvenil** (Map p64; 02-224-4314; www.mundojuvenil.org; cnr Av de los Shyris & Pasaje Rumipamba, Parque La Carolina; adult/child $5/3.50; 9am-4:30pm Mon-Fri, 11am-4:30pm Sat & Sun), with a tiny planetarium, kids' shows and changing exhibits.

At the base of the TeleféríQo there's an amusement park, Vulqano Park (p61), complete with bumper cars and other rides.

Housed in a former textile factory south of Old Town, **Museo Interactivo de Ciencia** (02-266-6061; www.museo-ciencia.gob.ec; Sincholagua near Maldonado, Chimbacalle; adult/child $3/1; 9am-5:30pm Wed-Sun;) has loads of hands-on exhibits to keep all ages engaged, from toddlers to tweens.

Built on the lower slopes of Pichincha and at the site of the city's first water distribution tanks, Museo del Agua-Yaku tells the story of the city's relationship to the most vital resource through interactive exhibits good for kids.

Tourist-oriented babysitting services are difficult to find in Quito unless you're staying at one of the city's top-end hotels, in which case the hotel will arrange for a sitter.

titled *Passage from this Life to Eternity*: no one can explain how it got here. At the end of the tour, you can climb narrow stairs to the bell tower and walk along the rooftop.

New Town

★Casa Museo Guayasamín MUSEUM

(www.guayasamin.org; Calvache E18-94 & Chávez, Bellavista; adult/child $8/4, incl Capilla del Hombre; 10am-5pm) In the former home of the legendary painter Oswaldo Guayasamín (1919–99), this wonderful museum houses the most complete collection of the artist's work. Guayasamín was also an avid collector, and the museum displays his outstanding collection of pre-Columbian ceramic, bone and metal pieces. Admission includes entry to the Capilla del Hombre gallery.

The pieces are arranged by theme – bowls, fertility figurines, burial masks etc – and in the geometric designs and muted color schemes you can see the influence on Guayasamín's work.

The museum also houses Guayasamín's collection of religious art, including works by highly skilled indigenous artists from the Escuela Quiteña; there's even a collection of bloody crucifixes (although Guayasamín was agnostic, he incorporated tortured, Christ-like images in his own work).

Guayasamín is buried alongside his friend, the writer Jorge Enrique Adoum, under a pine tree near the house.

★Capilla del Hombre GALLERY

(Chapel of Man; www.guayasamin.org; Calvache E18-94 & Chávez, Bellavista; adult/child $8/4, incl Casa Museo Guayasamín; 10am-5pm) Next to the Casa Museo Guayasamín stands one of the most important works of art in South America, Guayasamín's **Capilla del Hombre**. The fruit of Guayasamín's greatest vision, this giant monument-cum-museum is a tribute to humankind, to the suffering of Latin America's indigenous poor and to the undying hope for something better. It's a moving place and the tours (in English, French and Spanish, included in the price) are highly recommended. Admission includes entrance to the Casa Museo.

★Museos Casa de la Cultura Ecuatoriana MUSEUM

(Map p64; 02-222-1006; www.casadelacultura.gob.ec; cnr Av Patria & Av 12 de Octubre; 9am-5pm Tue-Sat) FREE Newly reopened following a full-scale makeover, Museos Casa de la Cultura encompasses three museums in a single bright, modern space. The expansive **Museo de Arte Moderna** (Modern Art Museum) features canvases by some of Ecuador's most famous artists, including Oswaldo Guayasamín, Eduardo Kingman and Camilo Egas, while the **Museo de Instrumentos Musicales** houses a curious collection of musical instruments. The excellent new **Museo Etnográfico** (Ethnography Museum) has interesting exhibits highlighting the spiritual beliefs, lifestyle and festivals of Ecuador's indigenous peoples.

Museo Nacional MUSEUM

(Map p64; cnr Av Patria & Av 12 de Octubre; 8:30am-4:30pm Tue-Fri, 10am-4pm Sat & Sun) FREE Located in the circular, glass-plated, landmark building of the Casa de la Cultura is one of the country's largest collections of Ecuadorian art, with magnificent works of pre-Hispanic and colonial religious art. At research time the museum had been closed for two years after plans for a state-of-the-art refurbishment stalled somewhere in the depths of government bureaucracy.

The museum collection includes more than 1000 ceramic pieces dating from 12,000 BC to AD 1534, a magnificent radiating, golden sun mask, and masterful works from the Quito School. Archaeological exhibits include arrowheads from Ecuador's first nomadic hunter-gatherers, the Valdivia culture (Ecuador's first settled agriculturalists) and the Inca. Highlights are 'whistle bottles' from the Chorrera culture, figures showing skull deformation practiced by the Machalilla culture, wild serpent bowls from the Jama-Coaque, ceramic representations of *tzantzas* (shrunken heads), 'coin axes' from the Milagro-Quevedo culture and the famous ceremonial stone chairs of the Manteños.

Parque El Ejido PARK

(Map p64) Northeast of La Alameda, the pleasant, tree-filled Parque El Ejido is a popular spot for impromptu games of soccer and volleyball. The park teems with activity on weekends, when open-air art shows are held along Avenida Patria. Just inside the north end of the park, artisans and crafts vendors set up stalls and turn the sidewalks into a handicrafts market.

National Assembly NOTABLE BUILDING

(Asamblea Nacional; Map p64; 02-399-1488, for guided tours 09-917-8416; www.asambleanacional.gob.ec; Montalvo near Av 6 de Diciembre) Sitting between Parque Alameda and Parque

New Town

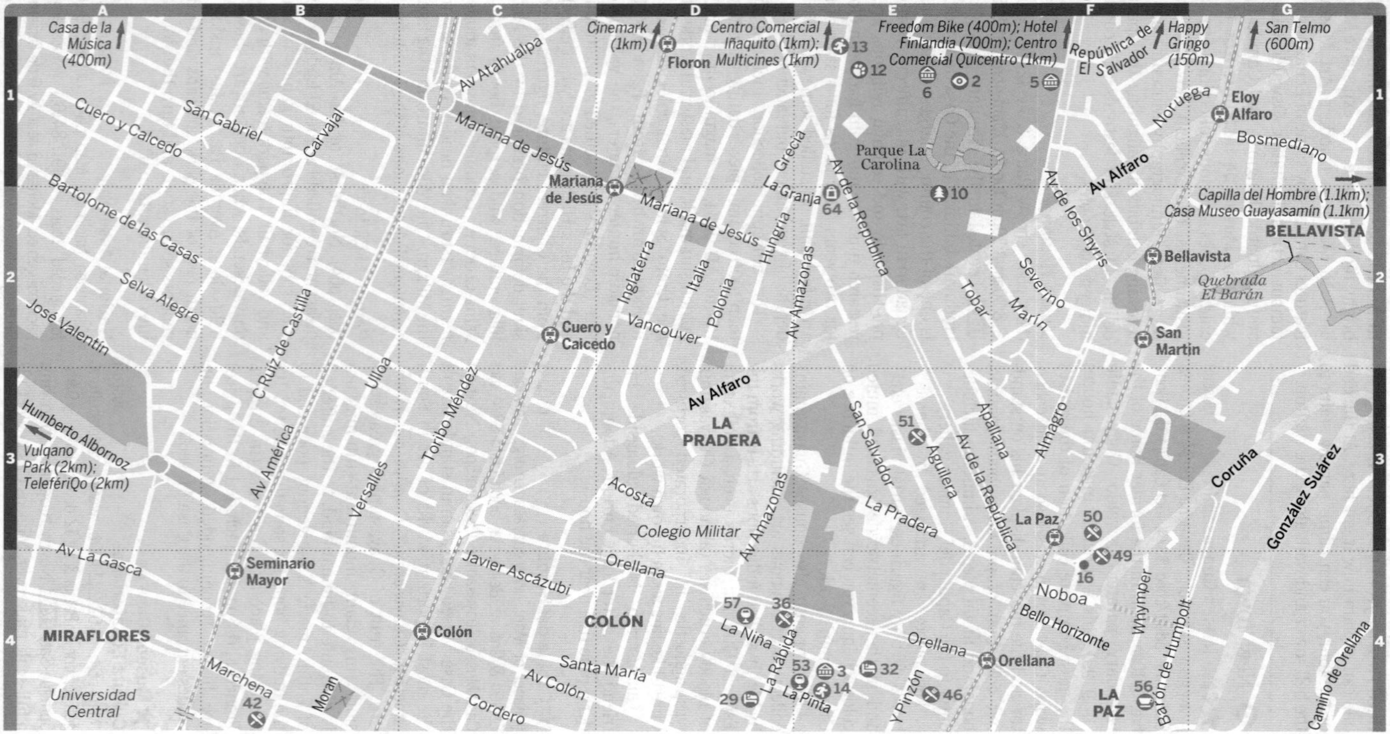

0 500 m
0 0.25 miles
Casa de la Música (400m)
Cinemark (1km)
Floron
Centro Comercial Iñaquito (1km); Multicines (1km)
Freedom Bike (400m); Hotel Finlandia (700m); Centro Comercial Quicentro (1km)
República de El Salvador
Happy Gringo (150m)
San Telmo (600m)
Av Atahualpa
Cuero y Calcedo
San Gabriel
Carvajal
Mariana de Jesús
Mariana de Jesús
Parque La Carolina
Grecia
La Granja
Av de la República
Av de los Shyris
Av Alfaro
Noruega
Eloy Alfaro
Bosmediano
Capilla del Hombre (1.1km); Casa Museo Guayasamín (1.1km)
BELLAVISTA
Bellavista
Quebrada El Barán
San Martin
Bartolome de las Casas
Selva Alegre
José Valentín
Hungria
Inglaterra
Italia
Polonia
Av Amazonas
Vancouver
Cuero y Caicedo
Severino
Marín
Tobar
C Ruiz de Castilla
Ulloa
Toribo Méndez
Av Alfaro
LA PRADERA
San Salvador
Aguilera
Apallana
Av de la República
Almagro
Coruña
González Suárez
Humberto Albornoz
Vulqano Park (2km); TelefériQo (2km)
Av América
Versalles
Acosta
Colegio Militar
Av Amazonas
La Pradera
La Paz
Av La Gasca
Seminario Mayor
Javier Ascázubi
Orellana
Noboa
Bello Horizonte
Whymper
Barón de Humbolt
MIRAFLORES
Colón
COLÓN
La Niña
La Rábida
Orellana
Orellana
Marchena
Santa María
Av Colón
La Pinta
Y Pinzón
LA PAZ
Camino de Orellana
Universidad Central
Moran
Cordero
1 2 3 4 5 6 10 12 13 14 16 29 32 36 42 46 49 50 51 53 56 57 64
A B C D E F G

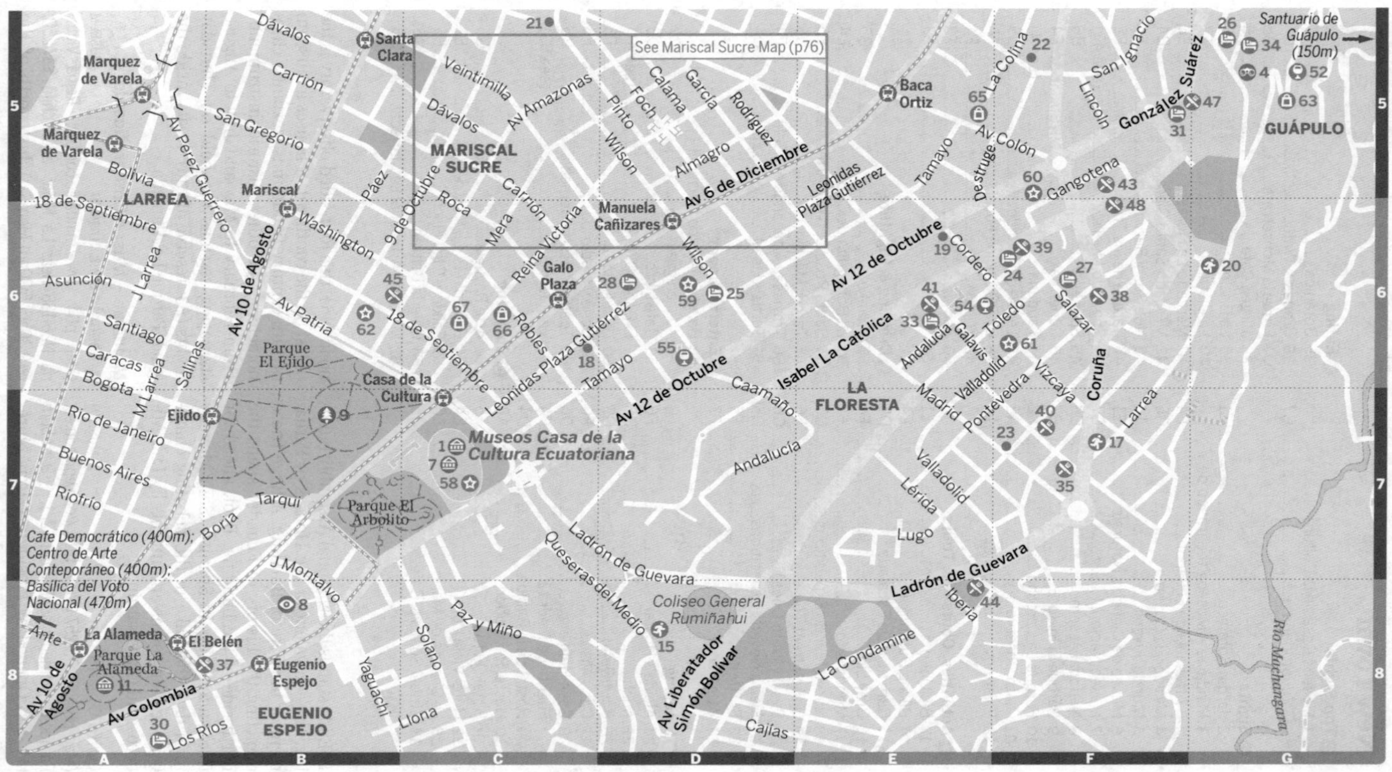
Dávalos
Santa Clara
21
See Mariscal Sucre Map (p76)
Veintimilla
Av Amazonas
Dávalos
Calama
García
Foch
Pinto
Rodríguez
Wilson
Almagro
MARISCAL SUCRE
Carrión
Roca
Mera
9 de Octubre
Reina Victoria
Manuela Cañizares
Av 6 de Diciembre
Leonidas Plaza Gutiérrez
Baca Ortiz
Tamayo
Destruge
La Colina
Av Colón
Lincoln
San Ignacio
González Suárez
Santuario de Guápulo (150m)
GUÁPULO
Gangotena
Marquez de Varela
Marquez de Varela
Carrión
San Gregorio
Av Perez Guerrero
Bolivia
LARREA
18 de Septiembre
Mariscal
Washington
Páez
Av 10 de Agosto
Asunción
J Larrea
Santiago
Caracas
Bogota
M Larrea
Salinas
Rio de Janeiro
Buenos Aires
Riofrío
Ejido
Av Patria
Parque El Ejido
18 de Septiembre
Robles
Galo Plaza
Wilson
Leonidas Plaza Gutiérrez
Tamayo
Casa de la Cultura
Av 12 de Octubre
Cordero
Isabel La Católica
Caamaño
LA FLORESTA
Andalucia
Galavis
Toledo
Salazar
Valladolid
Pontevedra
Vizcaya
Madrid
Coruña
Larrea
Museos Casa de la Cultura Ecuatoriana
Andalucía
Valladolid
Lérida
Lugo
Tarqui
Parque El Arbolito
Borja
Cafe Democrático (400m); Centro de Arte Conteporáneo (400m); Basílica del Voto Nacional (470m)
J Montalvo
Ladrón de Guevara
Queseras del Medio
Coliseo General Rumiñahui
Ladrón de Guevara
Iberia
Paz y Miño
Solano
Ante
La Alameda
El Belén
Parque La Alameda
Eugenio Espejo
Av 10 de Agosto
Av Colombia
Los Ríos
EUGENIO ESPEJO
Yaguachi
Llona
Av Liberatador Simón Bolívar
La Condamine
Cajías
Río Machangara
A
B
C
D
E
F
G
5
6
7
8

New Town

Top Sights
1 Museos Casa de la Cultura Ecuatoriana C7

Sights
2 Jardín Botánico E1
3 Mindalae – Museo Etnográfico de Artesanía de Ecuador E4
4 Mirador de Guápulo G5
5 Mundo Juvenil F1
6 Museo de Ciencias Naturales E1
7 Museo Nacional C7
8 National Assembly B8
9 Parque El Ejido B7
10 Parque La Carolina E2
11 Quito Observatory A8
12 Vivarium E1

Activities, Courses & Tours
13 BiciQuito E1
14 Biking Dutchman E4
15 Complejo De Escalada D8
16 Gray Line F4
17 Mono Dedo F7
18 Nuevo Mundo Expeditions C6
19 Quito Street Tours E6
20 Reserva Alto Coca G6
21 Sierra Nevada Expeditions C5
22 Surtrek F5
23 Vida Verde F7

Sleeping
24 Aleida's Hostal F6
25 Anahi D6
26 BoutiQuito G5
27 Casa Aliso F6
28 Casa Helbling D6
Fuente de Piedra 1 .... (see 25)
29 Hostal de la Rábida D4
30 Hostel Revolution A8
31 Hotel Quito F5
32 Hotel Vieja Cuba E4
33 La Casona de Mario E6
34 Stubel Suites & Café G5

Eating
35 Botánica F7
36 Crepes & Waffles D4
37 Frutería Monserrate B8
38 Jürgen Cafe F6
39 La Briciola F6
40 La Cleta F7
41 Mercado La Floresta E6
42 Mercado Santa Clara B4
43 Noe Sushi Bar F5
44 Parque de las Tripas E8
Segundo Muelle .... (see 43)
45 Spanes B6
46 Supermaxi E4
Tandana .... (see 4)
47 Techo del Mundo G5
48 UKRO Cocina Local F6
49 Z(inc) F4
50 Zao F3
51 Zazu E3

Drinking & Nightlife
52 Ananké G5
53 La Bodeguita de Cuba E4
54 Santa Rosa Cerveza Artesanal E6
55 Tercer Milenio D6
56 Traviesas Artesanos del Cafe F4
57 Turtle's Head D4

Entertainment
58 Ballet Folklórico Nacional Jacchigua C7
59 Café Libro D6
El Pobre Diablo .... (see 41)
60 La Juliana F5
61 Ocho y Medio F6
62 Teatro Patio de Comedías B6
Varadero .... (see 53)

Shopping
63 Arte Rayuela G5
64 El Jardín E2
65 Folklore Olga Fisch E5
66 Galería Beltrán C6
67 Mercado Artesanal La Mariscal C6

El Ejido stands the National Assembly building, the equivalent of the Houses of Parliament or the Capitol Building. A huge frieze depicting the history of Ecuador spans the north side of the building. Book ahead for free guided tours in Spanish (8am Monday to Friday) that take in the debating chambers, session rooms and murals by Luis Mideros and Guayasamín.

Quito Observatory MUSEUM

(Map p64; 02-257-0765; http://oaq.epn.edu.ec; Parque La Alameda; adult/child $2/1; 9am-5pm Mon-Sat) Opened by President García Moreno in 1864, this four-sided observatory is the oldest on the continent. It houses a museum of 19th-century pendulums, sextants, chronometers and other historic instruments. From February to May and July to August, stargazing sessions are held on Thursday nights ($3; reserve ahead). It sits inside the small Parque La Alameda.

Mindalae – Museo Etnográfico de Artesanía de Ecuador MUSEUM

(Map p64; www.mindalae.com.ec; Reina Victoria N26-166 near La Niña; adult/child $3/1.50; 9:30am-5:30pm Mon-Sat) Just north of the

Mariscal, this worthwhile museum has displays on the spiritual beliefs and practices, artwork, clothing and utensils of Ecuador's indigenous people. Start at the top with the fifth-floor shamanism exhibition and make your way down via the spiral staircase at the center of the unusual curved building. It's run by the fair-trade organization Fundación Sinchi Sacha, and there's an excellent shop selling indigenous crafts from across Ecuador.

Parque La Carolina PARK
(Map p64) North of the Mariscal lies expansive Parque La Carolina. The attractively landscaped park fills on weekends with families who come out for paddleboats, soccer and volleyball games, and to exercise along the bike paths.

Jardín Botánico GARDENS
(Map p64; www.jardinbotanicoquito.com; Parque La Carolina; adult/child $3.50/2; ⏲8am-4:45pm Mon-Fri, 9am-4:45pm Sat & Sun) Parque La Carolina's most popular attraction is this peacefully set botanical garden with native habitats covering *páramo* (high-altitude Andean grasslands), cloud forest, wetlands and other areas, plus an *orquideario* (orchid greenhouse), ethnobotanical garden (exploring the plants used by indigenous groups) and Amazonian greenhouse. There's also a kids' play/discovery area, a new Japanese garden and a collection of more than 100 bonsai trees.

Vivarium ZOO
(Map p64; www.vivarium.org.ec; Av Amazonas 3008, Parque La Carolina; adult/child $3.75/1.75; ⏲9am-1pm & 1:30-5:30pm Tue-Sun) Provide fodder for your jungle fears with a visit to the Vivarium, home to 40 species of reptiles and amphibians including snakes, iguanas, turtles, frogs and caimans. It's a herpetological research and education center, and the staff periodically give close demonstrations with one of the snakes.

Museo de Ciencias Naturales MUSEUM
(Map p64; Parque La Carolina; adult/child $2/0.60; ⏲8am-4:45pm) To further acquaint yourself with Ecuador's flora and fauna, head to the curious natural-history museum inside the Instituto Nacional de Bioversidad in Parque La Carolina. Contemplating the thousands of dead insects and arachnids on display is a good way to rile your nerves before a trip to the Oriente.

Santuario de Guápulo CHURCH
(Plaza de Guápulo; adult/child $2/1; ⏲8am-noon & 2-6pm Mon-Fri) In an elegant square in Guápulo stands the neighborhood's centerpiece, the 17th-century Santuario de Guápulo. It has an excellent collection of Quito School art and sculpture, and a stunning 18th-century pulpit carved by master wood-carver Juan Bautista Menacho.

Activities

Those seeking a bit more adventure can spend the day rock-climbing, hiking and cycling – all within city limits.

Old Town's old bus terminal has been converted into **Cumandá Parque Urbano** (☎02-257-3645; www.facebook.com/quitocumanda; Av 24 de Mayo; ⏲7am-8pm Tue-Fri, 8am-6pm Sat & Sun) , a sparkling, covered sports complex with a volleyball court, a soccer pitch, a climbing wall, yoga studios and several small swimming pools. Those not interested in getting their heart rate up can take in the art exhibitions, film screenings, live music and other cultural events that are now held here.

Cycling

Local mountain-biking companies rent bikes and offer excellent tours, including one-day rides through the *páramo* (high-altitude Andean grasslands) of Parque Nacional Cotopaxi as well as downhill descents, trips incorporating a stop at Papallacta hot springs, and two-day trips to Cotopaxi and Chimborazo and to Cotopaxi and Quilotoa. Single-day trips cost about $60. It's best to compare prices and trips before committing to a particular operator.

Biking Dutchman CYCLING
(Map p64; ☎02-256-8323; www.bikingdutchman.com; La Pinta E-731 near Reina Victoria; 1-day tours from $59; ⏲office 9:30am-5:30pm Mon-Fri) Ecuador's pioneer mountain-biking operator has good bikes and guides and an outstanding reputation, and it offers one- to eight-day tours.

Arie's Bike Company CYCLING
(☎02-238-5712; www.ariesbikecompany.com) Owned by a Dutch-Ecuadorian couple, Arie's organizes multiday mountain-biking trips throughout Ecuador.

BiciQuito CYCLING
(Map p64; ☎02-395-2300; www.biciquito.gob.ec; Av Amazonas N33-299 near Inglaterra, 1st fl, Agencia Metropolitana de Tránsito; ⏲7am-7pm

Mon-Fri, 8am-3pm Sat & Sun) The city's bike-share program is free of charge but you'll need to register at the Agencia Metropolitana de Tránsito on Avenida Amazonas with a completed application form (downloaded from the website) and a color photocopy of your passport photo ID page and your Ecuador entry stamp. Once you're registered you can pick up a bike from any of the rental stations.

Bikes are sturdy to say the least.

Retro Bici Club CYCLING
(☎099-502-9088; www.facebook.com/RetroBiciClub; Av Lasso N47-76 near Albeniz) Serious cyclists who repair, restore and rent bicycles for city riding. City cycling tours are also available.

Climbing

Mono Dedo CLIMBING
(Map p64; ☎02-290-4496; www.monodedoecuador.com; Larrea N24-36 near Coruña; $3-4; ⊙11am-9pm Mon-Fri, 10am-1pm Sat) A highly recommended full-service indoor climbing gym with expert instructors. It runs all manner of trips throughout Ecuador.

Complejo De Escalada CLIMBING
(Map p64; ☎02-250-8463; Queseras del Medio, La Vicentina; ⊙9am-7:30pm Mon-Fri, to 4pm Sat & Sun) An outdoor 25m-high climbing facility with more than a dozen routes on the main walls. Located across from Coliseo General Rumiñahui in the Vicentina neighborhood.

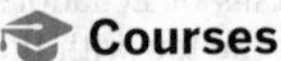

Courses

Ecuador is a great place to study Spanish, with homestays, organized activities and volunteer opportunities typically on offer.

Quito is also a good spot to hone (or learn) those salsa moves.

Language

Yanapuma Language School LANGUAGE
(Map p56; ☎02-228-7084; www.yanapumaspanish.org; Guayaquil N9-59 near Oriente) This excellent foundation-run school is located in the heart of the Old Town in an old building with a light-filled courtyard. Profits from the conversation-focused lessons go to the foundation (p390), which supports sustainable development in indigenous communities.

Vida Verde LANGUAGE
(Map p64; ☎02-252-4333; www.vidaverde.com; Madrid E13-137 near Lugo, La Floresta) A recommended Ecuadorian-owned school in an airy and bright converted home with a kitchen, lounge and small lending library. It can also arrange for travel and study in the rainforest (near Tena or Coca) and on the coast (at Puerto López and at Rio Muchacho Organic Farm near Canoa). Ten percent of profits go to environmental and social projects in Ecuador.

CLIMBING VOLCÁN PICHINCHA

Quito's closest volcano is Pichincha, looming over the western side of the city. The volcano has two main summits – the closer, dormant **Rucu Pichincha** (4680m) and the higher **Guagua Pichincha** (4794m), which is active and is monitored by volcanologists. A major eruption in 1660 covered Quito in 40cm of ash; there were three minor eruptions in the 19th century. A few puffs of smoke occurred in 1981, but in 1999 the volcano rumbled into serious action, coughing up an 18km-high mushroom cloud and blanketing the city in ash.

Climbing either of the summits is strenuous but technically straightforward, and no special equipment is required. **Rucu Pichincha** can be climbed from the top of the **TelefériQo** (p61), from where it takes three to 3½ hours to the summit. Weather conditions, however, can pose a problem. Once heavy fog rolls in it's easy to lose your way, so it's best to go with a guide. Check the forecast before heading out and have a mobile phone on you in case you need assistance. Several tour companies, including High Summits (p71), offer guided trips.

Climbing the smoking **Guagua Pichincha** is a longer undertaking. It is accessible from the village of Lloa, located southeast of Quito. From the village, it's possible to reach the **refugio** (Hikers' Refuge; dm $20) by road (you'll need a four-wheel drive), or it's about eight hours by foot. It is then a short but strenuous hike from the refugio to the summit. Reaching the summit will take you two days if you walk from Lloa. Check with a mountaineering agency in Quito about this trip; a recommended local guide for this trip is **Joaquín Andino** (☎099-993-3015; joaquin.andino@hotmail.com).

Simon Bolivar LANGUAGE
(Map p76; ☎02-254-4558; www.simon-bolivar.com; Foch E9-20 near Av 6 de Diciembre) This school, with another in Cuenca, offers individual classes ($8 per hour) in an attractive outdoor lounge space in a professional-looking building in the Mariscal. A $35 registration fee covers coffee, tea, snacks, internet and activities such as salsa classes and soccer. Group lessons ($5.50 per hour) are only available for true beginners.

Quito Antiguo Spanish School LANGUAGE
(Map p56; ☎02-228-8454; www.quitoantiguospanish.com; Venezuela 1129) Housed in an old (and somewhat run-down) building in the Old Town, Quito Antiguo offers a range of study options, a variety of excursions, inexpensive apartment rentals and homestays.

Colourful Ecuador LANGUAGE
(Map p76; ☎02-223-1595; www.colourfulecuador.com; García E6-15 near Mera) Group and private conversation-based Spanish classes held in a beautiful old building with wood floors, a garden in front and a great lounge space in back on a busy Mariscal street. Volunteer programs (for a fee) are offered for projects in the Galápagos, Quito and the coast.

Dance

Academia Salsa & Merengue DANCING
(Map p76; ☎02-222-0427; www.facebook.com/tropicaldancing; Foch E4-256 near Av Amazonas; private/group lessons per hour $10/8; ⏲10am-8pm Mon-Fri) Run by Sylvia Garcia, a pro dancer with several decades of experience, this place offers lessons in a wide variety of styles.

Ritmo Salvaje DANCING
(Map p76; ☎02-290-3852; García E5-45; ⏲10am-8pm Mon-Fri) This small, well-liked dance space offers a free introductory lesson on Thursday nights at 8pm. It becomes a popular salsa spot on Friday and Saturday nights.

Ritmo Tropical DANCING
(Map p76; ☎02-255-7094; www.ritmotropicalsalsa.com; Av Amazonas N24-155 near Calama; private/group lessons $10/6; ⏲9am-8pm Mon-Fri) Offers capoeira in addition to its very popular salsa classes.

Candeias DANCING
(☎09-9852-9776; www.candeiasecuador.com; Isla Isabela & Río Coca, Gimnasio Challenge) One of Ecuador's top capoeira schools, Candeias offers regular group classes. Check online for the schedule.

LOCAL KNOWLEDGE

FREE-WHEELING IN QUITO

Every Sunday, the entire length of Avenida Amazonas and most of the Old Town closes to cars (from 9am to 2pm) as thousands of cyclists take to the street for the weekly **ciclopaseo**. The entire ride (some 30km), which you can cycle part or all of, stretches past the old airport, through the Old Town and into the southern reaches of Quito. It's a marvelous way to experience the city. Bikes can be hired along the way for $3 an hour.

Another good place for cyclists to check out is the bicycle-loving cafe La Cleta (p84).

☞ Tours

Quito is one of the easiest places in Ecuador to arrange a guided tour, be it a Galápagos cruise, mountain-climbing, Amazon lodge, biking tour or white-water rafting. Itineraries ranging from one day to several weeks can be customized for small groups. Many agencies offer standard tours to nearby places such as Mitad del Mundo, Pululahua and further afield to Otavalo, Mindo, Cotopaxi and Baños. Be sure to stop by on weekdays (many offices close on weekends), and for longer trips it's worth trying to meet your guides in advance.

CarpeDM Adventures TOURS
(Map p56; ☎02-295-4713; www.carpedm.ca; Antepara E4-70 near Los Rios) CarpeDM earns high marks for its affordable prices and wide range of tours, though it's the excellent service that makes this agency, run by the friendly, reliable and knowledgeable Paul Parreno, stand out from many others. Day trips to Cotapaxi, Otavalo and Mindo for those short on time.

The office is in the Secret Garden Hostel in the San Blas neighborhood.

Happy Gringo TOURS
(☎02-512-3486; www.happygringo.com; Aldaz N34-155 near Portugal, Edificio Catalina Plaza, 2nd fl; ⏲9am-6pm Mon-Fri) A British- and Dutch-owned company catering to a mid-range market, Happy Gringo can organize week- to month-long customized itineraries

City Walk
Old Town

START PLAZA GRANDE
END PARQUE LA ALAMEDA
LENGTH 3KM; FOUR HOURS

This walk meanders along the cobblestone streets of the Old Town, passing 18th-century churches and picturesque plazas.

Start at the lively 1 **Plaza Grande** (p55), with its shoeshine boys, singsong vendors and well-worn benches. After checking out the 2 **Palacio de Gobierno** (p55; and changing of the guards on Monday), head inside the 3 **cathedral** (p55) for a look at paintings from the Quito School. Head down García Moreno to 4 **La Compañía de Jesús** (p56), Quito's most staggering church. Then walk northwest along Sucre to the impressive 5 **Plaza and Monastery of San Francisco** (p58), with majestic Pichincha visible behind it on a clear day.

From the plaza, cut down Bolívar and turn right on García Moreno. Pass under the arch at Rocafuerte to the 6 **Museo de la Ciudad** (p59), an excellent place to learn about Quito's development. Continue on García Moreno toward the historic street of 7 **La Ronda**, which is lined with colonial balconied houses, galleries and shops. Come evening, live music makes this the liveliest place in the Old Town. From La Ronda, turn left onto Guayaquil, and you'll pass the 8 **Plaza and Church of Santo Domingo** (p60), its 17th-century domes making a nice backdrop to yet another picturesque snapshot.

From the Plaza Santo Domingo, head north along Flores to the attractive 9 **Plaza del Teatro** and peek inside the theater foyer to see what's on while you're in town. From here, walk north to Esmeraldas and turn left, then right at Venezuela and continue north to the looming 10 **Basílica del Voto Nacional** (p60). Climb to the top of the clock tower for superb views over the Old Town. From the church, walk east along Caldas to busy Guayaquil. Glimpse the pretty 11 **Plaza San Blas** before continuing on to the 12 **Parque La Alameda** and the handsomely restored 13 **Quito Observatory** (p66), where you can peruse 19th-century instruments and return by night for a look at the (often fog-shrouded) sky.

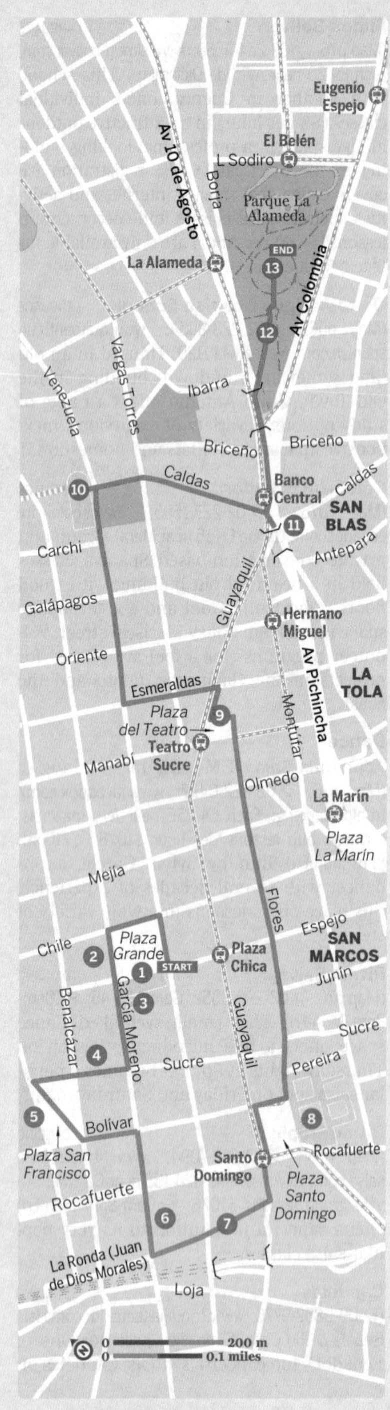

throughout the country, from the Galápagos to the Amazon. Professionally run with English-speaking guides and private drivers available, it's one of the best all-around tour companies in the city.

Quito Street Tours WALKING
(Map p64; ☎099-886-0539; www.quitostreettours.com; ⏲10:30am & 5:30pm daily) FREE Offers a daily three-hour walking tour of La Floresta and evening tours of Guápulo, focusing on street art and local culture. Tours are free but tips are expected. Reserve online in advance.

Gulliver TOURS
(Map p76; ☎02-252-9297; www.gulliver.com.ec; Foch E-738 near Reina Victoria; ⏲8:30am-5:30pm Mon-Fri) Gulliver is a well-regarded operator offering hiking, climbing, mountain-biking and horseback-riding trips in the Andes. Excellent prices, daily departures.

Zenith Travel TOURS
(Map p76; ☎02-252-9993; www.zenithecuador.com; Mera N24-264 near Cordero) This gay-friendly agency has a full spectrum of tours, including city tours, Otavalo market, Cotopaxi, the Amazon and the Galápagos.

Condor Trekk ADVENTURE
(Map p76; ☎02-222-6004; https://condortrekkexpeditions.com/; Reina Victoria N24-295 near Cordero; ⏲9:30am-6pm Mon-Fri, to noon Sat & Sun) Condor Trekk is a reputable climbing operator offering single- and multiday guided climbs up most of Ecuador's peaks.

Eos Ecuador TOURS
(Map p76; ☎02-601-3560; www.eosecuador.travel; Av Amazonas N24-66 near Pinto) Eos offers a full range of climbing, trekking, Galápagos and Amazon trips, in addition to stays in community-oriented tourism initiatives.

Nuevo Mundo Expeditions BOATING
(Map p64; ☎02-450-5412; www.nuevomundoexpeditions.com; Roca N21-293 near Gutierrez; ⏲9am-5:30am Mon-Fri) Professional outfit with top-end tours and guides. Organizes a range of trips including four- to five-day Río Napo cruises aboard its comfy *Manatee Amazon Explorer*.

Sierra Nevada Expeditions ADVENTURE
(Map p64; ☎02-255-3658; http://sierranevada.ec; Pinto E4-152 near Cordero) Long in the business, Sierra Nevada offers river-rafting and climbing trips. Owner Freddy Ramirez is well established and a very reputable mountain guide.

Quito Turismo WALKING
(Map p56; ☎02-299-3300; www.quito-turismo.gob.ec; Venezuela near Espejo; tours per person $8.50-16.50; ⏲9:30am, 10am & 11am Mon-Sat) Operating out of the Quito Tourism (p92) office just off Plaza Grande, this company offers a variety of guided walks in Old Town in English, Spanish, French and Italian. Book in advance.

Free Walking Tour Ecuador WALKING
(Map p56; www.freewalkingtourecuador.com; Cevallos N6-78 near Olmedo) Local Ecuadorian guides give twice-daily (except Sunday) tours beginning at 10:30am and 2:30pm from the Community Hostel in Old Town. Free, but tips expected.

High Summits TOUR
(Map p76; ☎02-290-5503; www.highsummits.com; Pinto E5-29 near Mera, 2nd fl) Company with long experience organizing climbing trips around Ecuador. English-, French- and German-speaking guides, all certified members of the ASEGUIM (Ecuadorian Association of Mountain Guides).

Tren Crucero RAIL
(Train of Wonders; ☎1-800-873-637; www.trenecuador.com; adult/child $1,650/1,485; ⏲Tue-Fri) Four-day, four-night luxury train tour from Quito Chimbacalle station via the Avenue of Volcanoes and the Devil's Nose to Guayaquil.

Safari Tours TOURS
(☎02-255-2505; www.safari.com.ec) Safari Tours has an excellent reputation and it has been around a long time. It offers all range of tours and trips, from volcano climbs and jungle excursions to local jeep tours and personalized off-the-beaten-track expeditions. Call or book online.

Quito Eterno WALKING
(Map p56; ☎02-228-9506; www.quitoeterno.org; La Ronda 989) Walking tours with costumed guides who highlight lesser-known aspects of Old Town's history and sights.

Latin Adventures TOURS
(Map p56; ☎02-316-1568; www.latinadventures.ec; Caldas E1-38 near Cevallos, Plaza San Blas) This outfit offers many tours, with a particular focus on experiencing indigenous cultures – in Santo Domingo, the Oriente and elsewhere in Ecuador.

Freedom Bike TOURS
(☎02-250-4339; www.freedombikerental.com; Finlandia N35-06 near Suecia) Offers guided motorcycle tours (both on- and off-road) ranging from four to 12 days with a bilingual guide. You can also do a self-guided tour, with a programmed GPS. Also offers motorcycle rental.

Quito Tour Bus BUS
(Map p56; ☎02-243-5458; www.quitotourbus.com; Quito Tourism Office; adult/child $15/7.50; ⊙8:30am-4pm Sun-Thu, to 7pm Fri & Sat) Operated by the city tourism authority, these double-decker hop-on hop-off bus tours stop at 12 key locations, including La Compañía, the Basílica, Parque La Carolina, El Panecillo and the TelefériQo. You can purchase tickets and pick up a schedule at the Quito Tourism (p92) office in the Old Town or on the bus.

Quito Tour Bus also runs daily trips to La Mitad del Mundo and the Pululahua volcano crater viewpoint from 11am to 7pm (adult/child $30/20, includes bus, guide and entrances to all attractions).

Tierra de Fuego TOURS
(Map p76; ☎02-250-1418; www.ecuadortierradefuego.com; Av Amazonas N23-23 near Veintimilla) Specializes in Quito day tours and Galápagos trips.

Surtrek TOURS
(Map p64; ☎02-250-0660; www.surtrek.com; San Ignacio E10-114 near Caamaño; ⊙9am-6pm Mon-Fri) Top-end company with years of experience in hiking and climbing. Personalized tours are available. Surtrek also offers island-hopping Galápagos tours.

> **ANDEAN HIGH**
>
> Did the hotel stairs make you breathless? Is your head spinning or achy? Having trouble sleeping? If so, you're probably suffering the mild symptoms of altitude sickness, which will disappear after a day or two. Quito's elevation of about 2850m can certainly have this effect if you've just arrived from sea level. To minimize symptoms, take things easy upon arrival, eat light and lay off the cigarettes and alcohol. For alleviating symptoms, some swear by the benefits of *té de coca* (coca-leaf tea), which some cafes, such as Tianguez (p81), have on hand.

Tropic TOURS
(☎02-240-8741; www.tropiceco.com; Pasaje Melo OE1-37 near Av Lasso; 🐾) Long-standing agency offering numerous three- to six-day tours to the Oriente, the Andes and cloud forests.

Neotropic Turis TOURS
(☎02-292-6153; www.neotropicturis.com; Los Shyris N36-188 near Naciones Unidas; ⊙8:30am-1pm & 2-5:30pm Mon-Fri) Neotropic runs the wonderful Cuyabeno Lodge in the Reserva de Producción Faunística Cuyabeno.

Gray Line TOUR
(Map p64; ☎02-394-8520; https://graylineecuador.com/; Rivet E3-54 near Orton, Edificio Mokai, 7th fl) A franchise of the US-based company. It handles Quito city tours (from $33) and day trips to Otavalo ($65) as well as multiday trips to Cotopaxi and beyond. Also offers shared airport transfers to and from Quito hotels ($9 per person one-way).

Festivals & Events

Carnaval CARNIVAL
(www.quitocultura.info; ⊙Feb) Held the weekend before Ash Wednesday, Carnaval is celebrated by intense water fights across the city – no one is spared.

Semana Santa RELIGIOUS
(Holy Week; ⊙Mar or Apr) Colorful religious processions are held during Easter Week, the most spectacular being the procession of *cucuruchos* (male penitents wearing purple robes and conical masks) and *verónicas* (their female purple-clad equivalents) on Good Friday.

Founding of Quito Festival CITY FESTIVAL
(⊙early Dec) Quito's biggest annual festival, on December 6, commemorates the founding of the city by the Spanish. The festivities, however, start two weeks earlier with street parties, parades and live music in the build-up to the main event.

In late November, Quito chooses a queen, and the evenings are dominated by colorful *chivas* (open-sided buses) maneuvering through the streets, packed with dancing revelers. In the week leading up to the big day, bullfights are held at the Plaza de Toros, located about 2km north of Parque La Carolina on Avenida Amazonas, and flamenco dancing is staged throughout town. Momentum builds as the day draws near, with DJs and popular local bands taking to open-air stages set up all over town. Business in Quito comes to a near standstill on December 5, when everyone comes out to party.

New Year's Eve NEW YEAR
(Dec 31) As throughout Ecuador, Quito's residents ring in the new year by burning elaborate, life-sized puppets in the streets at midnight, launching explosives into the sky and otherwise throwing general public safety to the wind.

Sleeping

Most travelers tend to stay near the Mariscal, which is packed with guesthouses and hostels. The quieter neighborhood of La Floresta is a pleasant alternative and it begins only a few blocks away. There's a good range of accommodations in the Old Town (including the city's best top-end hotels), which offer easy access to its museums, churches and other sights. A lack of nightlife is the downside.

There are several hostels in the Old Town neighborhood of San Blas, an ordinary, working-class area that you'll need to taxi to and from at night.

International chains, including Marriott, Best Western, Swissôtel and Hilton, are well represented throughout the city.

Old Town

La Posada Colonial GUESTHOUSE $
(Map p56; 02-228-2859; www.laposadacolonial.com; Paredes S1-49 near Rocafuerte; r with shared/private bathroom per person $10/12; @) A no-brainer for those looking for low-key, low-budget non-hostel accommodations in the Old Town. It's even within stumbling distance of La Ronda. The rooms have high ceilings and wood floors, and most have several beds, making it good value for groups. Bathrooms, however, are compact. It has a small rooftop with good views and a kitchen for guests' use.

Secret Garden HOSTEL $
(Map p56; 02-295-6704; www.secretgardenquito.com; Antepara E4-60 near Los Ríos, San Blas; dm $10-12, d $38, without bathroom $28; @) This perennially popular hostel has an undeniably social vibe, and wallflowers or those seeking privacy will want to head elsewhere. Long-term travelers getting by on bartending jobs in Quito and others on the South America circuit swap stories over a beer on the rooftop terrace with magical views over Old Town. You'll also find simple but clean wood-floor rooms.

Steep flights of stairs head up to the roof, which also doubles as reception. It has nightly dinners (mains $4.50), Spanish lessons, volunteer opportunities, regular events (including quiz nights, Aussie-style barbecues) and CarpeDM, a first-rate tour agency on-site.

Hostel Revolution GUESTHOUSE $
(Map p64; 02-254-6458; www.hostelrevolutionquito.com; Los Ríos N13-11 near Castro; dm/d/tr $9/23/30; @) For an escape from the Mariscal circus, this friendly hostel is an excellent, laid-back option with comfy rooms, shared kitchen, terrace with views and colorful bar/lounge where you can meet other travelers. Just a block uphill from Parque La Alameda.

Quito Backpacker Guesthouse GUESTHOUSE $
(Map p56; 02-257-0459; www.quitobackpackerguesthouse.com; Oriente E3-108 near Léon, San Blas; dm/s/d incl breakfast $10/22/27;) A good choice for those seeking hostel prices with a family-run guesthouse vibe, this large converted colonial home in the San Blas neighborhood has several floors of spacious, high-ceilinged, wood-floor rooms; kitchens on every floor; and a rooftop terrace with views of Old Town.

There's table tennis, a pool table, a barbecue and a movie-screening area up on the roof.

Colonial House HOSTEL $
(Map p56; 02-316-1810; www.colonialhousequito.com; Olmedo E-432 near Los Ríos; dm $10, r $25, without bathroom $20; @) The facade might be colonial but inside, this guesthouse is rather haphazardly designed. There's a messy backyard garden with hammocks, a barbecue and pet rabbits, where you can camp or work out with weights (these might be centuries old). The guestrooms are variously shaped as well as variously appealing, though all have (sloping) wood floors.

The vibe is bohemian and easygoing, and there's a guest kitchen, games room and several comfy common areas. Another plus is free coffee, grown on the owner's family farm.

★**Portal de Cantuña** BOUTIQUE HOTEL $$
(Map p56; 02-228-2276; www.portaldecantunaquito.com; Bolívar OE6-105 near Cuenca; r incl

breakfast $88;) Hidden down an alleyway, this beautifully restored mid-19th-century building once housed an order of nuns. No doubt they would have been distracted by the charming stained-glass window covering the inner courtyard, the gold leaf and baroque decorations, and an overall feeling of warmth and comfort. Wi-fi generally only available in lobby area.

Hotel San Francisco de Quito HOTEL $$
(Map p56; 02-228-7758; www.sanfranciscodequito.com.ec; Sucre Oe3-17 near Guayaquil; s/d incl breakfast $45/73; @) No exaggerating, stepping through the medieval-looking doorway into the bright, plant-filled inner courtyard of this historic hotel is like being transported back to another century. Specifically, to 1698 when the bones of this house were originally built. There's a variety of differently configured and sized rooms, though all are wood-floored and have cozy furnishings.

Because it's a colonial building, most rooms lack windows, but doors open onto a balcony ringing the enchanting interior patio with a stone fountain as its centerpiece. Several others, part of a small annex, adjoin a charming little outdoor sitting area. A basic breakfast is served in a vaulted, brick-walled dining area on the ground floor.

Mia Leticia HOTEL $$
(Map p56; 02-295-1980; www.mialeticia.com; Montúfar N5-91 near Mejía; s/d/tr incl breakfast $35/55/75; @) The interior is less stately than its colonial-style exterior and the covered atrium is kept dim. However, the surrounding simple wood-floored rooms have large windows that provide plenty of light (ask for one that faces the street), though the bathrooms could use some work. The hotel is located on a small, busy plaza fronting Avenida Pichincha, Old Town's major thoroughfare.

★Hotel El Relicario del Carmen GUESTHOUSE $$$
(Map p56; 02-228-9120; www.hotelrelicariodelcarmen.com; Venezuela 1041 near Olmedo; s/d/ste incl breakfast $110/140/168; @) This delightful 18-room guesthouse is set in a converted colonial mansion sprinkled with colorful paintings and stained-glass windows. Rooms are even sweeter, with polished wood floors and beamed ceilings (but small bathrooms); most face an interior courtyard.

★Casa San Marcos BOUTIQUE HOTEL $$$
(Map p56; 02-228-1811; www.casasanmarcos.com; Junín E1-36 & Montúfar; r incl breakfast $120-300;) This beautifully restored colonial mansion has just six rooms, which are set with antique furnishings, 18th- and 19th-century oil paintings and luxurious fittings. There's also an art gallery and antiques shop here, and a breakfast room with picturesque views of El Panecillo.

La Casona de la Ronda BOUTIQUE HOTEL $$$
(Map p56; 02-228-7501; www.lacasonadelaronda.com; La Ronda OE1-160 near Guayaquil; r incl breakfast $177-270) In a beautiful house dating from 1738 located right on La Ronda, this boutique hotel oozes class. Rooms have shiny hardwood floors, huge beds and bathrooms with rain showers; some have small private patios. There's a cozy living room with a wood-burning stove and a pretty covered patio with plants and a specially commissioned mural of the tree of life.

Casa Gangotena HOTEL $$$
(Map p56; 02-400-8000; www.casagangotena.com; Bolívar Oe6-41 near Cuenca; r incl breakfast from $550; @) Overlooking Plaza San Francisco, Casa Gangotena offers some of Quito's finest accommodation, with first-rate service and elegantly designed rooms set in a beautifully restored mansion that blends art nouveau with contemporary modernism. Common areas include a wood-paneled library, covered patio and roof terrace. The plaza-view rooms have marble columns framing the windows and king-sized bed.

Plaza Grande HOTEL $$$
(Map p56; 02-251-0777; www.plazagrandequito.com; cnr García Moreno & Chile; ste from $500; @) One of Quito's finest hotels, the Plaza Grande offers 15 gorgeously decorated rooms (all suites) with carved-wood details, chandeliers and marble bathrooms with Jacuzzi tubs. Some rooms have small balconies overlooking the square. There's also a small spa and two restaurants, and the service is world-class.

Hotel Patio Andaluz HOTEL $$$
(Map p56; 02-228-0830; www.hotelpatioandaluz.com; García Moreno N6-52 near Olmedo; d/ste incl breakfast $361/423; @) Inside a remodeled 16th-century home, the plush rooms of this elegant hotel have interior balconies and thick walls. Beautiful woodwork fills the rooms and common areas, service is top-notch and a peaceful air pervades the

place. There's a top restaurant, the **Rincón de Cantuña** (Map p56; mains $15-28; ⏰6:30am-10:30pm), serving Spanish and Ecuadorian cuisine in the covered courtyard.

Hotel Real Audiencia HOTEL $$$
(Map p56; ☎02-295-0590; www.realaudiencia.com; Bolívar Oe3-18 near Guayaquil; s/d incl breakfast $70/97; @📶) Offering a more standard hotel stay than other Old Town lodgings, rooms at the Real Audiencia have faux wood floors, soundproof glass and nice modern bathrooms with rainwater showers. The front desk staff is professional and slightly formal, and there's a top-floor restaurant with views.

La Mariscal

Blue House GUESTHOUSE $
(Map p76; ☎02-222-3480; www.bluehousequito.com; Pinto E8-24 near Almagro; dm/s/d/tr from $9/20/25/36; @📶) This friendly guesthouse has 11 pleasant rooms (dorm rooms with six to eight beds, as well as singles, doubles and triples with private and shared bathrooms) with wood floors in a converted house. It has a front patio for occasional barbecues, a comfy lounge with fireplace, a games room and a kitchen for guest use.

El Cafecito HOSTEL $
(Map p76; ☎02-223-4862; www.cafecito.net; Cordero 1124; dm/s/d $9.50/14/23; ⏰cafe 4-10pm Mon, 8am-10pm Tue-Sat, 8am-8:30pm Sun; 📶) Inside a yellow colonial house, this is a popular budget choice, mostly for its mellow vibe and charming cafe serving breakfasts and sandwiches. The coffee served here is produced in Mindo and roasted on-site; other specialty coffees are also available to sample. The wood-floored dorm rooms are fine, if well-worn; private rooms are on the small side.

Vibes HOSTEL $
(Map p76; ☎02-255-5154; www.vibesquito.com; Pinto near Av 6 de Diciembre; dm $9; 📶) This fun, messy hostel with old furniture in a converted colonial house is good for those looking to party in the Mariscal with other travelers. Sunday mornings, it has the look and feel of a frat house recovering from a blowout the night before. The owner is friendly and laid-back, and there's a tour office, bar and pool table.

Work is underway to add a new swimming pool and sauna.

AIRPORT ACCOMMODATIONS

Following the opening of the sleek new **Wyndham Quito Airport** (☎02-395-8000; www.wyndhamquito.com; Terminal Aeropuerto Internacional Mariscal Sucre; r from $120; 📶) there's talk of several other international chain hotels setting up properties at the airport. Alternatively, a cozy and lovely place located only 10km away is the family-run **Posada Mirolindo** (☎02-215-0363; www.posadamirolindo.com; Oyambarillo; s/d incl breakfast $61/98; 📶). Worth considering for those with early flights to the Galápagos or the Amazon.

★**Hostal de la Rábida** GUESTHOUSE $$
(Map p64; ☎02-222-2169; www.hostalrabida.com; La Rábida 227 near Santa María; s/d incl breakfast $61/85; @📶) Doting service, inviting common areas and elegant rooms make a fine combination in this charming guesthouse. Rooms are bright with crisp white sheets and wood floors, and artwork (botanical prints and the like) adorns the walls. Several have terraces. The fireside lounge and bar is a welcome retreat, particularly on chilly afternoons.

Casa Joaquín HOTEL $$
(Map p76; ☎02-222-4791; www.hotelcasajoaquin.com; Pinto E4-376 near Mera; d/ste incl breakfast from $80/110; 📶) Elegant rooms with polished parquet floors, a cozy bar and reading room and a rooftop terrace with plants make Casa Joaquín an excellent mid-range option in the bustling Mariscal neighborhood. The place is kept spotless and staff are helpful and friendly.

Fuente de Piedra 1 GUESTHOUSE $$
(Map p64; ☎02-252-5314; www.ecuahotel.com; Wilson E9-80 near Tamayo; s/d incl breakfast $55/65; @📶) In an attractive colonial house, the Fuente de Piedra has whitewashed rooms with wood or terracotta-tile floors and sizable windows (great views from some). The open patio doubles as a restaurant. The reception is shared with next-door hotel Anahi (p78).

Another location, **Fuente de Piedra II** (Map p76; ☎02-290-1332; Mera N23-21 near Baquedano; s/d incl breakfast $55/65; @📶) is equally recommended.

Mariscal Sucre

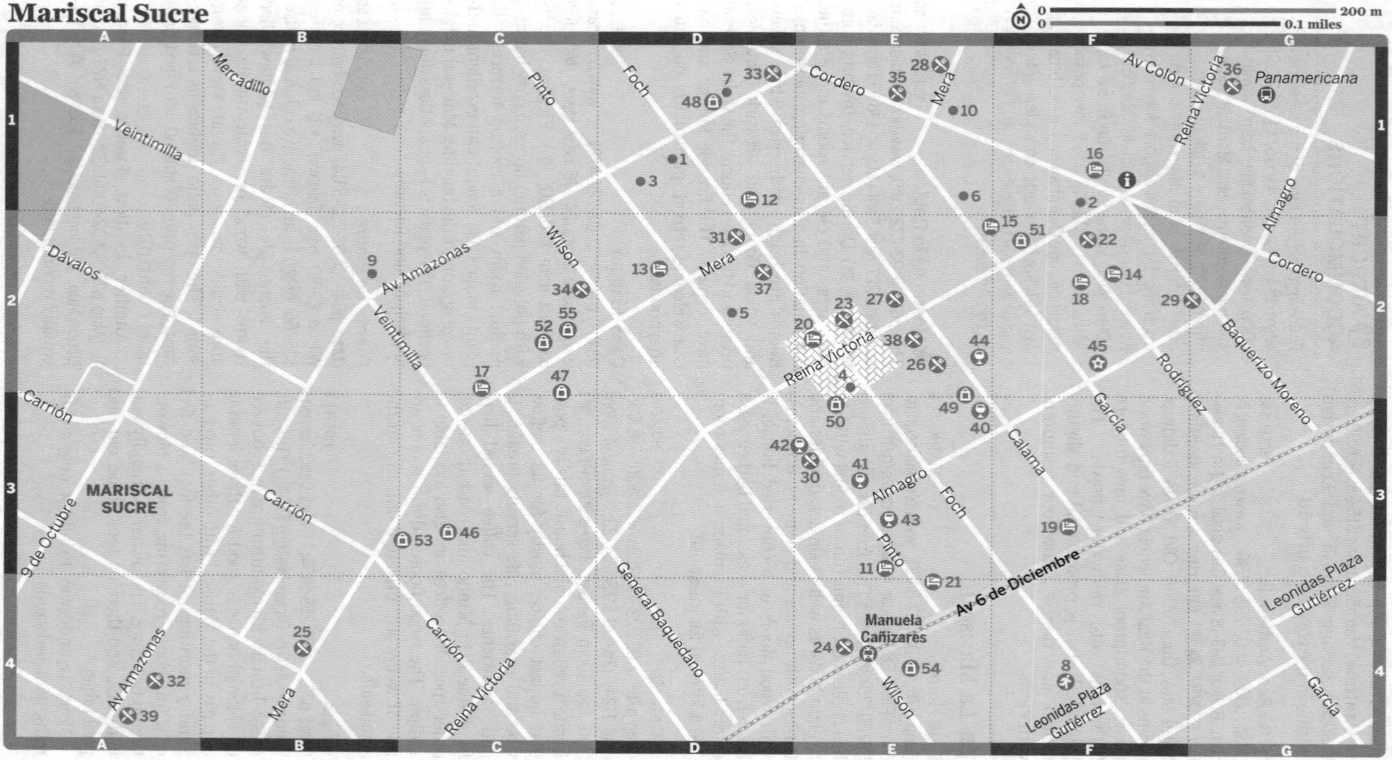
0
200 m
0
0.1 miles
N
A
B
C
D
E
F
G
1
2
3
4
Mercadillo
Veintimilla
Dávalos
Carrión
9 de Octubre
MARISCAL SUCRE
Av Amazonas
Mera
Reina Victoria
Pinto
Wilson
Foch
Cordero
Av Colón
Almagro
Baquerizo Moreno
Rodríguez
García
Calama
General Baquedano
Av 6 de Diciembre
Leonidas Plaza Gutiérrez
Manuela Cañizares
Panamericana
1
2
3
4
5
6
7
8
9
10
11
12
13
14
15
16
17
18
19
20
21
22
23
24
25
26
27
28
29
30
31
32
33
34
35
36
37
38
39
40
41
42
43
44
45
46
47
48
49
50
51
52
53
54
55

Mariscal Sucre

Activities, Courses & Tours

1 Academia Salsa & Merengue D1
Colourful Ecuador .... (see 6)
2 Condor Trekk F1
3 Eos Ecuador D1
4 Gulliver E2
5 High Summits D2
6 Ritmo Salvaje E1
7 Ritmo Tropical D1
8 Simon Bolivar F4
9 Tierra de Fuego B2
10 Zenith Travel E1

Sleeping

11 Blue House E3
12 Casa Foch D1
13 Casa Joaquín D2
14 Cayman Hotel F2
15 El Arupo Bed & Breakfast E2
16 El Cafecito F1
17 Fuente de Piedra II C2
18 Hostal El Arupo F2
19 La Casa Sol F3
20 Nü House E2
21 Vibes E4

Eating

22 Achiote F2
23 Azuca Beach E2
24 Baalbek E4
25 Cacao & Cacao B4
26 Canoa Manabita E2
27 Casa Quebecua E2
28 Chandani Tandoori E1
29 Cosa Nostra G2
30 El Maple E3
31 El Mariachi Taco Factory D2
32 Ethnic Coffee A4
33 Frutería Monserrate D1
34 Kallari C2
35 La Canoa E1
36 La Union G1
37 Magic Bean D2
38 Mama Clorinda E2
39 Suvlaki A4

Drinking & Nightlife

40 Bungalow 6 .... E3
41 Cherusker E3
42 Dirty Sanchez E3
43 Finn McCool's E3
Q .... (see 20)
44 Selfie Club Disco E2

Entertainment

45 Cafe Democrático F2

Shopping

46 Ag C3
47 Casa Mariscal C2
48 Confederate Bookstore D1
49 English Bookstore E2
50 Explorer E3
51 Galería Ecuador F2
52 Galería Latina C2
53 La Bodega C3
54 Librería del Fondo Carlos Fuentes E4
55 Libri Mundi C2

Hostal El Arupo GUESTHOUSE **$$**
(Map p76; ☎ 02-255-7543; www.hostalelarupo.com; Rodríguez E7-22 near Reina Victoria; s/d/tw incl breakfast $30/45/48; @ 📶) A cozy and homey refuge from nearby Plaza Foch's madness, El Arupo is a spotless and warmly decorated converted house with a small, lovely front patio. The rooms have dark wood floors and firm beds. It also offers an immaculate communal kitchen where breakfast is served, and a small lounge.

Its sister hotel, **El Arupo Bed & Breakfast** (Map p76; ☎ 02-252-3528; https://hostalquito.com/; García E5-45 near Reina Victoria; s/d $25/45, without bathroom $20/30; P 📶), has smaller wood-floored rooms and is on a noisier block.

La Casa Sol GUESTHOUSE **$$**
(Map p76; ☎ 02-223-0798; www.lacasasol.com; Calama 127 near Av 6 de Diciembre; s/d/tr incl breakfast $40/65/85; @ 📶) This friendly midrange guesthouse has a warm, inviting lobby with a colonial color scheme and cheerfully painted rooms that face an interior courtyard. There are nice touches throughout, as well as artwork and photos lining the corridors and in the rooms.

Hotel Vieja Cuba GUESTHOUSE **$$**
(Map p64; ☎ 02-290-6729; www.hotelviejacuba.com; La Niña N26-202 near Almagro; s/d incl breakfast $50/75; 📶) In a former colonial home, Vieja Cuba is an attractively designed guesthouse with a Cuban theme, inviting rooms (wood floors are polished to a sheen) and a colorful flair. There's also a small garden.

Casa Foch GUESTHOUSE **$$**
(Map p76; ☎ 02-222-1305; www.hotelcasafoch.com; Foch E4-301 near Mera; s/d/tr incl breakfast from $50/60/82; 📶) In a restored mansion near the heart of the Mariscal, Casa Foch has attractive rooms with high ceilings, polished wood floors, heavy wooden wardrobes and small cast-iron fireplaces. Some rooms have balconies. It has a small outdoor area packed with plants, and a pleasant lounge/

breakfast room. Noise can be a problem on weekends.

Cayman Hotel GUESTHOUSE $$

(Map p76; ☎02-256-7616; www.facebook.com/hotelcayman; Rodriguez E7-29 near Reina Victoria; s/d/tr incl breakfast $46/63/78; @ wifi) This converted home on a relatively quiet Mariscal street has bright and cheery wood-floored rooms, shuttered windows and fluffy white duvets; some are rather cramped. It also has a pleasant indoor lounge and a grassy outdoor space.

Casa Helbling GUESTHOUSE $$

(Map p64; ☎02-222-6013; www.casahelbling.de; Veintimilla E8-152 near Av 6 de Diciembre; s/d $33/45, without bathroom $22/33; @ wifi) In a homey, colonial-style house in the Mariscal, Casa Helbling is clean, relaxed and friendly; and it has a guest kitchen, laundry facilities and relaxing common areas.

Anahi BOUTIQUE HOTEL $$$

(Map p64; ☎02-250-1421; www.anahihotelquito.com; Tamayo N23-95 near Wilson; s/d incl breakfast $115/130; @ wifi) The stylish Anahi brings high-end design to the Mariscal, with sun-drenched, artwork-filled suites (some with balconies) and high-end fittings. Stone walls in corridors (and in some rooms) resemble an Inca temple. There's a Jacuzzi and a top-floor veranda with superb views.

Nü House HOTEL $$$

(Map p76; ☎02-255-7845; www.nuhousehotels.com; Foch E6-12 near Reina Victoria; d/ste $130/210; ❄ wifi) If you want to stay in the heart of the action, Nü House offers a touch of modernism with local touches in a wood-and-glass building rising seven floors over Plaza Foch. Despite the madness below, solid double glazing keeps the noise out of its spacious rooms, which offer clean lines, large windows and splashes of color.

La Floresta & Around

★BoutiQuito HOSTEL $

(Map p64; www.facebook.com/boutiquito; Guerrero 100 near Larrea, Guápulo; dm/d from $10/20; @ wifi) In a fabulous 1970s house with parquet floors and a stylish *Mad Men* vibe, BoutiQuito has four- and eight-bed dorms and private rooms with shared and private bathrooms. There's a great living room with a welcoming fireplace and views over Guápulo, and a kitchen for guests. Breakfast costs $3.

La Casona de Mario GUESTHOUSE $

(Map p64; ☎02-254-4036; www.casonademario.com; Andalucía N24-115 near Galicia; r per person without bathroom $12; wifi) In a lovely old house in La Floresta, La Casona de Mario is outstanding value, with homey rooms, shared bathrooms, a flower-filled garden, TV lounge and guest kitchen.

Hotel Finlandia HOTEL $$

(☎02-224-4287; www.hotelfinlandia.com.ec; Finlandia 35-129 near Suecia; s/d incl breakfast from $80/85; P ❄ @ wifi) A high-rise hotel with boutique-style rooms in Benalcázar, an upscale residential and business district. Several excellent restaurants and cafes are within easy walking distance and Parque La Carolina is only a block away.

Aleida's Hostal GUESTHOUSE $$

(Map p64; ☎02-223-4570; www.aleidashostal.com; Andalucía N24-359 near Salazar; s/d $35/50, without bathroom $25/40; @ wifi) This friendly, family-run guesthouse in La Floresta has comfortably furnished rooms with wood floors. The best have fine views; others are dark with internal windows.

Casa Aliso GUESTHOUSE $$$

(Map p64; ☎02-252-8062; http://casaaliso.com; Salazar E12-137 near Toledo; s/d incl breakfast $140/170; wifi) This charming 10-room guesthouse receives high marks for its friendly service, cozy sitting rooms (where you can sit fireside and enjoy a glass of wine or a cup of tea) and comfortable, classically appointed rooms (some with garden views). It's on a peaceful street, in a converted 1930s home.

Stubel Suites & Café HOTEL $$$

(Map p64; ☎02-601-3499; www.stubel-suites.com; Pasaje Stubel 1, near León Larrea; d/ste from $93/136; @ wifi) Perched high above Guápulo, this top-end place has attractive, modern rooms with luxury fabrics, huge windows and decent amenities (sauna, fitness center, massages). Pricier rooms offer great views, and the well-equipped suites have terraces as well as a kitchen and dining area. The restaurant also offers sweeping views.

Hotel Quito HOTEL $$$

(Map p64; ☎02-396-4900; www.hotelquito.com; González Suárez N27-142; s/d $130/140; @ wifi pool) A Quito landmark, this huge, 215-room hotel with a 1970s vibe sits high on the hill above Guápulo. Some of the rooms (all have balconies) and the 7th-floor bar and restaurant (p85) have memorable views.

Nonguests can use the hotel's outdoor pool, sauna and steam room (included in the room price) for $22.

Eating

Ecuador's culinary capital is a great place to explore the classic dishes from the Andes and beyond. The city's rich and varied restaurant scene also offers a fine selection of international fare. All budgets and tastes are catered for, and you'll find everything from modern sushi restaurants to Italian trattorias. Many restaurants close on Sunday.

The Old Town is where you'll find Quito's most traditional eateries, some of which have been perfecting family recipes for generations. *Seco de chivo* (braised goat stew) is an Ecuadorian classic typically served with yellow rice and *patacones* (plantain fritters). Potatoes, of course, originated in the Andes and are put to imaginative use in dishes like *llapingachos* (fried potato-and-cheese pancakes), often served under grilled steak or fried eggs. A few places also serve *cuy asado* (roasted guinea pig), an indigenous specialty dating back to Inca times.

Head to the new town's Mariscal for the broadest choices and densest concentration of ethnic and international eateries. For more high-end dining and the city's best restaurants, look to La Floresta, La Pradera and neighboring areas. Off the tourist radar but still worth exploring is Benalcázar, an upscale neighborhood of high-rise condominiums, offices, cool cafes and restaurants. It's bounded by Parque La Carolina on the east and Avenida 6 de Diciembre on the west. Take the Ecovia to either Eloy Afaro or Benalcázar.

Old Town

★Cafetería Modelo ECUADORIAN $
(Map p56; www.facebook.com/cafeteriamodelocentrohistorico; Sucre 391 near García Moreno; mains $4-6.25; 8am-7:30pm Mon-Sat, to 6pm Sun) Opened in 1950, Modelo is one of the city's oldest cafes and a great spot to try traditional snacks such as *empanadas de verde* (empanadas made with plantain dough), *quimbolitos* (sweet, cake-like corn dumplings) and tamales. It's also a popular spot for ice cream.

Nearby **Cafetería Modelo II** (Map p56; Sucre OE4-48, near Venezuela; mains $4-6.25; 9am-6:30pm Mon-Thu, to 7:30pm Fri & Sat, 9am-5pm Sun) offers similar old-world trappings plus live music on Friday afternoons from 5pm to 7pm.

San Agustín ECUADORIAN $
(Map p56; 02-228-5082; http://heladeriasanagustin.net; Guayaquil N5-59 near Mejia; mains $5.50-9.50; 10:30am-4pm Tue-Sun;) Kitschy religious icons and old-fashioned radios decorate this old-school classic serving Ecuadorian fare to bustling workday crowds. Opt for first-rate *seco de chivo* (goat stew), *corvina* (sea bass) or *arroz marinero* (seafood rice), followed by old-fashioned *helados de paila* (ice cream handmade in big copper bowls).

Bohemia Cafe & Pizza PIZZA $
(Map p56; www.facebook.com/bohemia.pizzeria; La Ronda Oe3-108 near Venezuela; mains $5-8; noon-midnight Mon-Thu, to 2am Fri & Sat) Feel like a local at this welcoming pizzeria, where the wonderfully energetic owner will greet you like family on repeat visits. The menu includes excellent pizza and layered nachos cooked with homemade corn chips. Wash it down with a giant *michelada*, a mix of beer, lime and salt, accompanied by various salsas.

Café San Blas PIZZA $
(Map p56; 02-228-6762; Antepara near Los Ríos; mains $3.50-6; 6-10pm Mon-Sat;) It could be because this tiny, bustling neighborhood joint was once part of the owner's house that it has such a homely, welcoming atmosphere. The food is equally comforting: well-seasoned pizzas, pastas, sandwiches and salads. Be prepared to wait for a space at the counter or a table.

Cevicheria Puerto Azul SEAFOOD $
(Map p56; 02-228-8798; Mejia Oe445 near García Moreno; mains $6.50-10; 9am-4pm Mon-Sat) *Cevicherias* are few and far between in this part of town, and Puerto Azul's maritime-themed dining room makes for a pleasant place to enjoy a good *cazuela*, a ceviche, an *encebollado* (soup with fish, yuca and onion) and other seafood dishes.

Mercado Central MARKET $
(Map p56; Av Pichincha near Esmeraldas; meals $1.50-4; 7am-5pm Mon-Sat, to 3pm Sun) For stall after stall of some of Quito's most traditional (and cheapest) foods, head straight to the Mercado Central, between Esmeraldas and Manabí, where you'll find everything from *locro de papas* (potato soup served with avocado and cheese) and seafood, to

yaguarlocro (potato and blood-sausage soup) and *fritada* (fried chunks of pork, served with hominy).

Govindas Gopal VEGETARIAN $
(Map p56; Esmeraldas 853; mains $3; ⏲noon-3pm Mon-Sat; 🅥) Proudly serving 100% vegetarian cuisine, the Krishna devotees here whip up tasty, fresh lunch plates from a changing menu, plus yogurt and granola, juices and sweets.

Dulceria Colonial CAFE $
(Map p56; cnr Espejo & Venezuela, Plaza Grande; sandwiches $3; ⏲7am-7pm Mon-Fri, to 11pm Sat, to 9pm Sun; 📶) In business for 27 years, this postage-stamp-sized place is an ideal spot for people-watching on always-busy Plaza Grande. Grab an espresso, a slice of homemade cake or a scoop of ice cream and settle in to observe the parade of humanity that passes by.

La Exquita ECUADORIAN $
(Map p56; Caldas near Av Colombia, San Blas; mains $4-6, set lunch $2.85; ⏲8:30am-3pm) Office workers crowd this two-floor cafeteria for cheap and filling *almuerzos* (set lunches). Convenient for those staying at one of the nearby accommodations.

El Kukurucho del Maní SWEETS $
(Map p56; Rocafuerte Oe5-02 near García Moreno; snacks $0.50-4.50; ⏲8am-7pm Mon-Sat, 9am-6pm Sun) This delightful snack stand cooks up kilos of nuts, corn kernels and *coquitos* (coconut sweets) in a giant copper kettle.

Ari Comida Sana VEGETARIAN $
(Map p56; ☎02-258-4255; Sucre Oe4-48, Centro Comercial Galerías Sucre; mains $2.75-5; ⏲8am-5pm Mon-Sat; 🅥) Tucked away on the 2nd floor of a commercial center, Ari is a colorful, if boxy, space serving vegetarian versions of Ecuadorian classics, such as ceviche, as well as juices and fruit salad.

★**Café Dios No Muere** CAJUN $$
(Map p56; cnr Junín & Flores; mains $5.50-16.50; ⏲9am-10pm Mon-Sat) The Louisiana native who owns this eccentrically designed restaurant attached to a 17th-century monastery takes pride in the quality of the ingredients cooked up in a kitchen that's squeezed into a corner on the ground floor. Space fills up fast, as there are only a handful of tables on two tiny floors, plus a few alleyway tables.

Cajun specials like Po Boy sandwiches and 'Bourbon Street' burgers change daily, and there are various cuts of beef, locally sourced tuna steaks and yuca fries. Local

PANORAMAS OVER QUITO

High up in the Andes and ringed by mountains, Quito does not lack for memorable views. Here are a few of our favorite spots to take in the sweeping panoramas while having a drink or a bite:

Vista Hermosa (p81) The aptly named 'beautiful view' is a top spot to take in the scenery without even having to leave the Old Town.

Casa Gangotena (p74) This historic hotel's terrace provides front-row seats to Plaza San Francisco.

Café Mosaico (p81) Nosh on Greek fare while taking in the sunset.

El Ventanal (p81) This Old Town restaurant is one of the best spots to see the city's lights come on while enjoying meticulously presented haute Ecuadorian cuisine. Best to take a taxi to the hard-to-find entrance.

Pim's (p81) Peacefully set inside Parque Itchimbia.

Hotel Real Audiencia (p75) The top-floor hotel restaurant has sweeping views over Plaza Santo Domingo and beyond.

El Crater (p97) Outside Quito, this restaurant and guesthouse overlooking a verdant caldera has the most magical view of all – well worth the long trip out.

Ananké (p86) In bohemian Guápulo, a splendid setting for a night out.

Tandana (p84) Vegan cafe perfectly positioned for taking in those sweet views over Guápulo.

Techo del Mundo (p85) Hotel Quito's 'Roof of the World' restaurant and bar provides sparkling nighttime city and valley vistas.

microbrews and Ecuadorian organic coffee are also on the menu.

★ Café Mosaico CAFE $$

(Map p56; ☎02-254-2871; https://cafemosaicoecuador.com; Samaniego N8-95 near Antepara; mains $10-17; ⏰4-11pm Mon-Wed, 1-11pm Thu-Sat, 1-10:30pm Sun) Serving up a mix of Ecuadorian and Greek fare near Parque Itchimbia, vine-covered Mosaico is famed for its magnificent views. The open-sided terrace is great for a sundowner. There's a selection of vegan options available and live music on Fridays and Saturdays from 8:30pm.

Pizza SA PIZZA $$

(Map p56; www.pizzasa.com; Espejo Oe2-46; pizzas $10.50-16; ⏰11am-9:30pm Mon-Thu, to 10pm Fri & Sat, 11am-8pm Sun) On a pedestrian lane dotted with restaurants facing the Teatro Bolívar, this casual spot with sidewalk seating bakes up satisfying medium-crust pizzas as well as sandwiches, salads and calzones.

Tianguez ECUADORIAN $$

(Map p56; ☎02-954-4326; Plaza San Francisco; mains $6.50-14.50; ⏰9am-6:30pm; 📶) Tucked into the stone arches beneath the Monastery of San Francisco, this excellent cafe prepares tasty Ecuadorian appetizers (tamales, soups, quinoa salads) as well as heartier mains. Tables on the plaza are perfect for people-watching.

Café del Fraile ECUADORIAN $$

(Map p56; ☎02-251-0113; http://cafedelfraile.com; Pasaje Arzobispal, 2nd fl; mains $10-17.50; ⏰10am-11pm Mon-Sat, to 9pm Sun; 📶) The selection of sandwiches, grilled dishes, ceviches and burgers here are pricey, but you're paying a premium for the comfortable indoor balcony setting and rustic charm (cast-iron lanterns, wood-beam ceilings).

Las Cuevas de Luís Candela SPANISH $$

(Map p56; Benalcázar 713 near Chile; mains $6.50-13; ⏰11am-9pm Mon-Sat) Built in the vaulted cellar of an old-time building, this atmospheric and windowless Spanish/Ecuadorian restaurant has been around since 1963. Bullfighting greats Manolo and Manolete both ate here.

Theatrum ECUADORIAN $$$

(Map p56; ☎02-257-1011; www.theatrum.com.ec; Manabí N8-131, Teatro National Sucre, 2nd fl; mains $14-22; ⏰12:30-3:30pm & 6:30-11pm Mon-Fri, 6:30-11pm Sat & Sun) On the 2nd floor of the historic Teatro Sucre, creative dishes from across Ecuador are served in a theatrically set dining room with heavy curtains and red and black velvets. For pure decadence, try the tasting menu ($42).

There's a classy bar area for an aperitif.

Vista Hermosa INTERNATIONAL $$$

(Map p56; ☎02-295-1401; http://vistahermosa.ec; Mejía 453, 5th fl; mains $13-29; ⏰1pm-midnight Mon-Sat, noon-8pm Sun) A much-loved spot in El Centro, Vista Hermosa (Beautiful View) delivers the goods with a magnificent 360-degree panorama over the Old Town from its open rooftop terrace. Live music on Friday and Saturday from 10pm adds to the magic. Arrive early to beat the crowds.

Octava de Corpus INTERNATIONAL $$$

(Map p56; ☎02-295-2989; www.octavadecorpus.com; Junín E2-167; mains $20-30; ⏰12:30-10pm Mon-Sat) For a completely different dining experience, head to this little-known restaurant inside a colonial home on lovely Junín. Artwork covers every surface of the place, and Jaime, the friendly owner, is also an avid wine collector who can recommend one of more than 300 vintages on hand. The menu features classic meat and seafood (all grilled or steamed). Reservations essential.

El Ventanal ECUADORIAN $$$

(☎02-257-2232; www.elventanal.ec; Carchi near Nicaragua; mains $22-36; ⏰4pm-midnight Tue-Fri, noon-3pm & 6pm-midnight Sat) This restaurant in the San Juan neighborhood, on the lower slopes of Volcán Pichincha, is one of the best spots to see the city's lights come on. The meticulously presented Ecuadorian dishes can be hit and miss, but the setting makes up for it. Best to take a taxi to the hard-to-find entrance.

Pim's ECUADORIAN $$$

(Map p56; ☎02-322-8410; www.grupopims.com; Iquique, Parque Itchimbía; mains $15.50-28.50; ⏰noon-3pm & 6-11pm Mon-Fri, noon-11pm Sat, noon-6pm Sun) Inside the Parque Itchimbia, this popular, slightly upscale chain has fantastic views over the city. Enjoy tasty traditional Ecuadorian fare, plus sandwiches and pastas, and cocktails in the elegant dining room or on the outside patio.

La Mariscal

Kallari CAFE $

(Map p76; www.facebook.com/kallari.com.ec; Wilson E4-266 & Mera; mains $2.50-3; ⏰8am-7:30pm Mon-Fri; 📶) Owned by the Kichwa community of Napo, this co-op serves up satisfying breakfasts and lunches in a bright and airy cafe, which also stocks the community's famous chocolate bars.

Canoa Manabita SEAFOOD $

(Map p76; www.facebook.com/LaCanoaManabita; Calama E7-36 near Reina Victoria; mains $7-10; ⏲10am-8pm Tue-Sun) This casual and unassuming place with picnic-table seating is popular with locals for its tasty ceviche, *cazuelas* (seafood stews), *encebollado* (soup with fish, yuca and onion) and other seafood dishes.

El Maple VEGETARIAN $

(Map p76; 02-290-0000; Pinto E7-68 near Almagro; mains $4-9; ⏲11am-9:30pm Mon & Tue, 8am-11:30pm Wed-Sat, 8am-5:30pm Sun;) This well-loved restaurant serves good vegetarian food with global influences (Asian noodle dishes, creamy pastas, burgers, sandwiches and salads). There's a cheery dining room with a maple tree mural on the wall and shelves of books, and outdoor tables in a pretty courtyard.

Suvlaki GREEK $

(Map p76; Av Amazonas N21-108; mains $5-8; ⏲8:30am-7:30pm Mon-Sat) The go-to spot for skewers of tasty grilled meat (the eponymous souvlaki), this casual spot has a growing following for its speedy service, cheery interior (complete with photos of Greek icons) and outdoor seating.

Chandani Tandoori INDIAN $

(Map p76; Mera 1333 near Colón; mains $4-8; ⏲noon-9:30pm Mon-Sat, to 4pm Sun;) Bouncy Bollywood music and sizzling platters of tikka masala make up the soundtrack to this good, inexpensive and unadorned Indian restaurant. Choose from two-dozen preparations of meat and vegetable dishes.

Cacao & Cacao CAFE $

(Map p76; www.facebook.com/CacaoYCacao; Mera N21-241 near Roca; snacks $3; ⏲8am-8pm Mon-Fri, 10am-7pm Sat;) Only five tables, indoors and on a little outdoor patio, make up this shop selling good coffee, pastries and chocolate made from organically grown local cacao. There's another location nearby at Veintimilla and Reina Victoria.

La Union BAKERY $

(Map p76; cnr Reina Victoria & Colón; sandwiches $2-3.50; ⏲6am-10pm) Bustling La Union always packs a crowd, with its glass displays of croissants, berry tarts and ice cream, plus filling sandwiches.

Mercado Santa Clara MARKET $

(Map p64; cnr Dávalos & Versalles; ⏲8am-5pm Mon-Sat, to 1pm Sun) This is the main market in the new town. Besides an outstanding produce selection, it has cheap food stalls.

Frutería Monserrate ECUADORIAN $

(Map p76; 02-222-2149; www.fruteriamonserrate.com; Av Amazonas near Cordero; mains $4-12; ⏲7am-7:30pm Mon-Fri, 8am-6pm Sat, 8am-3pm Sun) Filling breakfasts, sandwiches, empanadas, ceviche and scrumptious fruit salads are among the offerings at this popular and casual eatery.

There's another **Frutería Monserrate** (Map p64; cnr Saá & Sodiro) just north of Parque La Alameda.

Casa Quebecua CANADIAN $

(Map p76; www.facebook.com/casaquebecuaquito; Calama N24-15 near Reina Victoria; mains $4-8; ⏲9am-11pm Mon-Thu, 9am-midnight Fri & Sat) This Quebecois-owned place serves up the cholesterol-laden signature dishes of the owner's homeland and evokes the wintry feel of a north country log cabin. Fill up on poutine (fries, cheese curds and gravy), cooked up with a variety of extras like chicken and steak. Burgers and hot dogs make it a popular spot for those on a Mariscal pub crawl.

Supermaxi SUPERMARKET $

(Map p64; cnr La Niña & Pinzón; ⏲9:30am-8:30pm Mon-Sat, to 2pm Sun) Well-stocked supermarket near the Mariscal.

Cosa Nostra ITALIAN $$

(Map p76; 02-252-7145; www.pizzeriacosanostra.com.ec; cnr Baquerizo Moreno & Almagro; mains $10-18; ⏲12:30-3:30pm & 6-11pm Mon-Wed, 12:30-4pm & 6-11pm Thu-Sat, 6pm-midnight Sun;) Italian-owned Cosa Nostra has a pleasant front patio, cozy dining room and nearly three-dozen varieties of pizza piled with generous toppings and fired up in a brick oven – we consider it the best in town. It has good gnocchi and other pastas, and tiramisu for dessert.

El Mariachi Taco Factory MEXICAN $$

(Map p76; http://elmariachitacofactory.com/; Foch E4-318, 2nd fl, near Mera; mains $6-11; ⏲noon-11pm) Colorfully woven tablecloths, Mexican mariachi posters and adobe-esque walls conjure a faint impression of Old Mexico in this Mariscal eatery. Sizzling plates of fajitas go nicely with frozen margaritas.

Baalbek MIDDLE EASTERN $$

(Map p76; ☎02-255-2766; http://restaurantbaalbek.com/wp/; Av 6 de Diciembre N23-103 near Wilson; mains $7-17; ⏰noon-5pm Sun-Tue, to 10:30pm Wed-Sat) Authentic Lebanese fare served up quickly in a comfortable and contemporary dining room with a Middle Eastern soundtrack and aesthetic. Most of the menu items can be ordered as a half or full plate, which makes family-style sharing the way to go.

Spanes COLOMBIAN $$

(Map p64; Av Amazonas N20-51; mains $5.50-14.50; ⏰8am-8pm Mon-Sat, to 5pm Sun; 📶) Fast food Colombian-style, including *arepas* and *ajiaco*, a Bogotá specialty of three types of potatoes with chicken and corn. Also serves cheap and filling *almuerzos* (set lunches).

Ethnic Coffee ECUADORIAN $$

(Map p76; Av Amazonas near Robles; mains $6-18; ⏰10:30am-8pm Mon-Fri; 📶) A colorfully decorated spot serving good breakfast, snacks (tamales, empanadas, *quimbolitos*) as well as heartier mains (grilled fish with shrimp). It has outdoor seating among ferns and potted plants.

Crepes & Waffles INTERNATIONAL $$

(Map p64; ☎02-250-0658; http://crepesywaffles.com.ec; La Rábida N26-249 near Orellana; mains $7-14; ⏰noon-10pm Mon-Sat, 9:30am-9pm Sun; 📶👪) Mouthwatering and stomach-enlarging sundaes, as well as more than two-dozen varieties of sweet and savory crepes, waffles, salads and more conventional vegetarian, meat and seafood dishes are on the menu at this South American chain with several other locations in Quito. It has an upscale feel with very warm and welcoming service.

Magic Bean INTERNATIONAL $$

(Map p76; ☎02-256-6181; www.magicbeanquito.com; Foch E5-08 near Mera; mains $8-15; ⏰8am-10pm; 📶) Magic Bean packs a crowd with its ample American-style breakfasts and lunches, plus frothy juices, coffees and desserts, best enjoyed on the covered front terrace.

Azuca Beach SOUTH AMERICAN $$

(Map p76; www.facebook.com/AzucaBeach; Foch near Reina Victoria; mains $7.50-15; ⏰noon-midnight Mon-Thu, to 2am Fri & Sat, to 9pm Sun; 📶) Everyone from students to professionals heads to this buzzing place overlooking Plaza Foch. Dishes from coastal regions throughout South America, including ceviches, are among the hits. Tropical cocktails (try the fruit-flavored mojitos and caipirinhas), a bamboo-trimmed bar and potted palms add to the lounge-like space, which becomes a popular drinking spot at night. Live music Wednesday and Saturday from 9pm.

Mama Clorinda ECUADORIAN $$$

(Map p76; http://mamaclorinda.webs.com/ecuadorianfood.htm; Reina Victoria N24-150 near Calama; mains $8-22; ⏰11am-11pm) This bustling, multifloor restaurant just off Plaza Foch serves tasty national specialties. Try the *llapingachos* (fried pancakes of mashed potatoes with cheese) with steak or, for the adventurous, *cuy* (guinea pig).

La Canoa ECUADORIAN $$$

(Map p76; Cordero E4-375 near Mera; mains $11-26; ⏰24hr, closed 11pm-6am Sun & Mon) This respectable restaurant from Guayaquil is a good place to try Ecuadorian classics: there's *fritada con mote y chicharrones* (slow-cooked pork with white corn), *caldo de morcilla* (blood-sausage soup), *bandera* (a mixed seafood plate) and other treats.

Achiote ECUADORIAN $$$

(Map p76; ☎02-250-1743; http://achiote.com.ec; Rodriguez 282 near Reina Victoria; mains $12.50-25; ⏰noon-9:45pm) Ecuadorian dishes with an upscale twist in a warmly lit contemporary setting. Empanadas, ceviches, rich seafood stews and *llapingachos* (fried pancakes of mashed potatoes with cheese) are all first-rate. Live music Friday to Monday nights.

La Floresta

★**Parque de las Tripas** STREET FOOD $

(Parque Navarro Food Stalls; Map p64; cnr Ladrón de Guevara & Iberia, Floresta; mains $2-4; ⏰4-11pm) To sample some of Quito's most authentic and traditional cooking, head to this attractive park in La Floresta where every evening food stalls are set up selling freshly prepared *tripa mishqui* (grilled cow intestines), *seco de pollo* (chicken stew), empanadas and *morocho* (a kind of spiced corn porridge). Stall holders are happy to let you taste before you buy.

Botánica CAFE $

(Map p64; www.botanicaquito.com; Guipúzcoa E14-104 near Coruña; sandwiches $5-6; ⏰12:30-10pm Tue-Fri, 2-10pm Sat; 📶) Linger over a coffee in the plant-filled covered deck at Botánica. The sandwiches, juices and cakes here are sublime.

Mercado La Floresta MARKET $

(Map p64; Galavis 237 near Isabel La Católica; 6am-5pm Thu & Fri) A small but delightful fruit and veg market (including organic stalls) in the peaceful La Floresta neighborhood.

★ Jürgen Cafe DUTCH $$

(Map p64; 02-323-0088; www.jurgencafe.com; cnr Coruña & Valladolid, La Floresta; mains $6.50-13.50; 7am-8pm Mon-Sat, to 2:30pm Sun) Owned and operated by Jürgen Spelier, a fourth-generation baker from Holland, this casually sophisticated restaurant with clean lines and blond-wood decor does especially good breakfasts and brunches; traditional Dutch pancakes and chicken and waffles are among the highlights.

Z(inc) INTERNATIONAL $$

(Map p64; 02-256-2846; www.zincquito.com; Rivet N30 near Whymper; mains $13-22; noon-midnight Tue-Thu, noon-2am Fri, 7pm-2am Sat, 10:30am-3:30pm Sun) Equal parts restaurant and bar, Z(inc) features a multi-level industrial-chic interior of untreated timber, dark metals, exposed brick and a well-dressed clientele. Sip a lychee-infused cocktail on the front patio before heading inside for brick-oven flatbread pizza, burgers, tempura prawns and other dishes ideal for sharing.

La Cleta CAFE $$

(Map p64; 02-223-3505; www.facebook.com/lacleta.bicicleta; Lugo N24-250 near Guipuzcoa; pizzas $6-9; 11am-11pm Mon-Thu, to midnight Fri, 5-11pm Sat;) Bicycle lovers shouldn't miss this small, cleverly designed cafe-restaurant, where nearly everything (chairs, bar stools, tables, hanging lamps) is fabricated from bicycle parts and there's a whiff of rubber in the air. The wheel-shaped menu includes pizzas, sandwiches, coffee, wine and other drinks.

La Briciola ITALIAN $$

(Map p64; 02-254-5157; http://labriciola.com.ec; cnr Isabel La Católica & Salazar; mains $13-18; 12:30-11pm Mon-Sat, noon-10pm Sun) This longtime favorite has an outstanding and varied menu. The portions are large, and the wine is fairly priced. Reservations are recommended.

Zao ASIAN $$

(Map p64; 02-252-3496; www.zaoquito.com; Rivet N30-145 near Whymper; mains $10-16.50; 12:30-4pm & 7-11pm Mon-Sat, noon-4pm Sun) Adorned with carved wooden screens and statues resembling samurai, Zao is a buzzing spot serving up quality Asian fusion dishes such as sushi, rice noodles, spring rolls and Thai-style curries.

★ UKRO Cocina Local ECUADORIAN $$$

(Map p64; 02-256-3180; www.urko.rest; Isabel La Católica N24-862 near Zaldumbide; small dishes $10-15, tasting menu per person $65; 1-4pm & 7-11pm Tue-Sat, tasting menu 7-11pm Thu-Sat;) Traditional Ecuadorian cuisine is given a contemporary twist at this sophisticated new restaurant. Dishes from across the country are prepared with fresh, ethically sourced local ingredients, including herbs and veg from the restaurant's own rooftop garden. Order two small dishes per person in the casual downstairs 'barra', or book a spot upstairs to sample the tasting menu.

Wash it down with a cocktail made with in-house *licor de caña*, a sugarcane-based liquor infused with local herbs.

Noe Sushi Bar JAPANESE $$$

(Map p64; 02-322-7378; www.noesushibar.com; Isabel La Católica N24-827 near Coruña; mains $18-30; 12:30-11:30pm Mon-Thu, to midnight Fri & Sat, to 10pm Sun) Part of a chain, this stylish, minimalist restaurant offers tender, fresh sushi and sashimi, teppanyaki, Kobe beef and a range of other Japanese delicacies.

Segundo Muelle PERUVIAN $$$

(Map p64; www.segundomuelle.com; Isabel La Católica N24-883; mains $13-36; noon-4pm & 7-11pm Mon-Sat, noon-4pm Sun) Yet another sign that the Peruvians are taking over (at least when it comes to cooking), this innovative modern-dining restaurant is a good place to sample mouthwatering ceviches, nicely spiced risottos and flavorful sharing plates.

La Pradera, La Carolina & Guápulo

Tandana VEGAN $

(Map p64; 02-323-8234; Larrea N27-492 near Pasaje Stübel; mains $5-9; 12:45-7pm Wed & Thu, to 10pm Fri & Sat, to 4pm Sun) At the Mirador de Guápulo (p61), this cafe's wooden benches are perfectly positioned to take in the views. Everything sold here is vegan and fair trade, and many of the ingredients used in dishes such as the bean burgers, pizzas, falafel, curries and homemade cakes come from the vegetable garden outside.

★Zazu FUSION **$$$**
(Map p64; ☎02-254-3559; www.zazuquito.com; Aguilera 331; mains $16-43, 5-/7-course tasting menu $50/70; ⊙11:30am-3pm & 6:30-11pm Mon-Fri, 6:30-11pm Sat) One of Quito's best restaurants, Zazu serves beautifully prepared seafood dishes, grilled meats and ceviches in a stylish setting of light brick, ambient electronica and an inviting, backlit bar. The menu showcases the best of Ecuadorian cuisine with dishes such as Andean grains and veg, confit guinea pig empanada and seafood tamal.

San Telmo STEAK **$$$**
(☎02-225-6946; www.facebook.com/santelmouio; Portugal 440 near Casanova; mains $20-40; ⊙noon-11pm) One of Quito's top steakhouses, San Telmo is an elegant, multilevel, mostly gents' affair with a sizzling grill firing up a wide range of cuts. It has a good wine selection and options for non-meat-eaters (pastas, seafood).

Techo del Mundo ECUADORIAN **$$$**
(Map p64; ☎02-396-4901; www.techodelmundo.com; Av González Suárez N27-142, 7th fl; mains $13.50-19.50, buffet lunch per person $28; ⊙6am-midnight) The restaurant at the Hotel Quito (p78) offers buffet breakfasts and lunches as well as a menu of classic Ecuadorian fare, all served in a formal dining room with white table cloths and stunning views of Cumbayá.

Drinking & Nightlife

Most of the *farra* (nightlife) in Quito is concentrated in and around the Mariscal. A weekend night wandering La Ronda, a cobblestone lane lined with bars and restaurants in the Old Town, shouldn't be missed. For more relaxed, low-key hangouts, head to one of the sophisticated spots in La Floresta, Guápulo or Benalcázar. A spate of microbreweries have opened recently in the city.

Mariscal bars, for better or worse, are generally raucous. Plaza Foch is the neighborhood's epicenter, where the line between 'bar' and 'dance club' is blurry. Bars with dancing often charge admission, which usually includes a drink. Monday to Wednesday nights tend to draw an older crowd, while university-aged Ecuadorians swarm into the area on Friday and Saturday nights.

Hitting the dance floor of one of Quito's *salsatecas* (nightclubs where dancing to salsa music is the main attraction) is a must. If you don't know how to salsa, try a few classes first.

Carry ID when going out at night in case you're carded.

La Oficina CRAFT BEER
(Map p56; www.facebook.com/laoficinaquito; Antepara E4-55 near Los Ríos, San Blas; ⊙6-11pm Mon-Sat) This chilled-out joint has rustic upcycled furniture, dim lighting, creative wall murals and its own San Blas craft beers on tap (the IPA gets rave reviews). There's a theater space at the back for live music, film screenings, salsa nights and stand-up comedy; see its Facebook page for upcoming events. Happy hour 6pm to 8pm.

Bandido Brewing MICROBREWERY
(Map p56; http://bandidobrewing.com; Olmedo E1-136 near Cevallos, San Blas; ⊙4-11pm Mon-Fri, 2-11pm Sat) These guys from Oregon produce their own creative brews, such as La Gran Calabaza Imperial Pumpkin Ale, made with cinnamon, cloves and pumpkin spice, and La Gua.Pa, an American Pale Ale flavored with guayusa, a tea leaf native to the Ecuadorian Amazon. The bar has a vaguely Gothic feel, with stone walls, wooden benches and even a small chapel.

The menu includes freshly baked pizzas and bar snacks, and there's live music on Tuesdays from 7pm.

GAY & LESBIAN QUITO

Quito has a small but active gay scene, with most of the bars and clubs located in the Mariscal. A gay pride parade takes place in June; check the **Orgullo LGBTI Ecuador** Facebook page (www.facebook.com/orgulloEcuador/) for details of the parade and other events.

Bring your passport for entry to clubs.

Tercer Milenio (El Hueco; Map p64; www.facebook.com/discotecatercermilenio; Veintimilla near Av 12 de Octubre; ⊙11pm Fri & Sat) Quito's biggest gay party attracts a mixed crowd of locals and foreigners. DJs spin the tunes and keep the dance floor packed late into the night.

Kika (www.facebook.com/Lademencegayclub; Japón E569 near Av Amazonas; ⊙9pm-4am Thu-Sat) At the northern end of Parque La Carolina, Kika is a haven for the hip. The disco gets going after midnight with pumping Latin pop tunes.

Dirty Sanchez LOUNGE

(Map p76; www.dirtysanchezbar.com; Pinto E7-38 near Reina Victoria; 5pm-12:30am Mon, 3pm-12:30am Tue-Thu, 3pm-2:30am Fri & Sat) The cheekily named Dirty Sanchez is a small art-filled lounge with a bohemian vibe. Decent cocktails (and coffee), better music and a laid-back crowd make this place a standout.

Ananké BAR

(Map p64; www.anankeguapulo.com; Camino de Orellana 781, Guápulo; 6pm-1am Mon-Sat) Well worth the trip out here, Ananké is a stylish and warmly lit bar/pizzeria with small colorfully decorated rooms spread out among an old two-story house. It has a small terrace (complete with fireplace) and several good nooks for hiding away with a beer and a few friends. When the fog clears, the views over Guápulo are superb.

Altar Cervecería CRAFT BEER

(Map p56; www.facebook.com/altarcerveza; cnr Olmedo & León; 5pm-midnight Tue-Sat;) In a hipster haven of polished concrete and blond wood, this new bar has several beers from its own brewery as well as a selection of other local craft beer on tap. The food – burgers, chicken wings, beer-battered fries ($5.50 to $8) – is excellent and there's regular live music, open mic nights and a weekly language exchange.

Santa Rosa Cerveza Artesanal CRAFT BEER

(Map p64; www.facebook.com/santarosabeer; Andalucía N24-234 near Cordero; 4-11pm Tue-Sat) Quito's craft beer scene has exploded in recent years, and family-run brewery Santa Rosa produces some of the city's best. This sleek bar with exposed brick walls has eight of its own brews on tap, including white ale, ginger blonde, dark IPA, mango passion and honey strong. It does good burgers and sharing plates, too.

Traviesas Artesanos del Cafe COFFEE

(Map p64; http://cafetraviesa.com; Humboldt N27-77 near San Ignacio; 10am-9pm Mon-Fri, 1pm-9pm Sat;) Discerning coffee drinkers and aspiring baristas should make their way to this friendly, upscale cafe. Choose your method – pour over, filter, chemex, French press or aeropress – and chow down on a sandwich, salad or cheesecake while you wait.

Cafe Democrático CAFE

(Dávila & Venezuela; mains $6-10; 10am-1am Tue-Sun;) At the Centro de Arte Contemporáneo (p61), red-walled Cafe Democrático is an artsy hangout serving craft beer, cocktails, coffee and a menu of sandwiches and burgers. There's live music from 9pm on Thursday, Friday (salsa) and Sunday.

There's a second Cafe Democrático in La Mariscal.

Bungalow 6 CLUB

(Map p76; www.bungalow6ecuador.com; cnr Calama & Almagro; 8pm-3am Wed-Sat) A popular nightspot among foreigners and locals alike, Bungalow 6 often features long lines on weekends and Wednesday ladies' night (gals drink for free to 10pm). It plays a good mix of beats, with a small but lively dance floor and a warren of colorfully decorated rooms (with table football, pool table and small outdoor terrace) upstairs.

Cherusker BAR

(Map p76; www.facebook.com/CheruskerCerveceria Alemana; Pinto E7-85 near Almagro; 4pm-midnight Mon, 3pm-midnight Tue & Wed, noon-2am Thu-Sat) In a red two-story colonial house, Cherusker has earned a loyal following for its tasty artisanal microbrews, warm bohemian ambience and buzzing front patio. Occasional live bands play on weekends.

Turtle's Head MICROBREWERY

(Map p64; www.facebook.com/TurtlesHeadQuito; La Niña E4-451 near Mera; 4pm-midnight Mon-Thu, to 2am Fri & Sat) Scottish-owned pub serving decent craft beer and pub grub. There's also table football, pool table and occasional bands.

Jugos de la Sucre JUICE BAR

(Map p56; Moreno N2-54 near Sucre; 8am-6pm) For a freshly squeezed serving of vitamins, this juice place is hard to beat. Try *tomate de arbol* (tamarillo), *maracuya* (passion fruit) or *guanábana* (soursop).

La Bodeguita de Cuba BAR

(Map p64; 02-254-2476; Reina Victoria 1721 near La Pinta; noon-10pm Sun-Tue, to midnight Wed-Thu, to 2am Fri & Sat) With its warmly lit interior, graffiti-covered walls and outdoor seating, this is a great place for cocktails, Cuban food and fun. Live bands perform here on Wednesday and Thursday nights (check out attached Varadero for salsa weekend nights).

Finn McCool's IRISH PUB

(Map p76; www.facebook.com/FinnMcCools Quito; Almagro E24-64 near Pinto; 11am-1am Mon-Wed, to 3am Thu & Fri, 9am-3am Sat, 10am-

11pm Sun) Proudly flying the green, white and gold, this Irish-owned bar attracts a mix of locals and foreigners who come for games of pool, table football, pub grub and theme nights (pub quiz on Tuesdays, live bands or open-mic nights, game nights whenever there's soccer on). Not much elbow room on weekend nights.

Q BAR
(Map p76; www.facebook.com/Q.restaurant.bar.lounge; Foch E6-11 near Reina Victoria, Plaza Foch; 6:30am-midnight Mon-Wed, 6:30am-3am Thu-Sat, 6:30am-10pm Sun;) Fashion types gather for midweek cocktails at this hip bar and restaurant, where the ceiling is decorated to resemble Amazonian vegetation ('Q' stands for *quinde*, Spanish for hummingbird). There's live music most nights and a DJ plays lounge-style beats on Saturdays.

Selfie Club Disco CLUB
(Map p76; www.facebook.com/selfieclubdisco; Calama E7-35 near Reina Victoria; $5-10; 9pm-3am Tue-Sat) It's mostly locals bumping and grinding at this open, somewhat industrial space, with video art playing on a large screen above the dance floor. DJs spin a little of everything on weekends.

☆ Entertainment

Quito's theaters stage a variety of dramas, dance performances and concerts, so check ahead to see what's on. Look out too for performances by local musicians playing everything from salsa and merengue to rock, jazz and blues. Several bars and restaurants in the Old Town and the Mariscal have regular live music nights.

Live Music

★El Pobre Diablo LIVE MUSIC
(Map p64; 02-223-5194; www.elpobrediablo.com; Isabel La Católica E12-06 near Galavis; 12:30-3pm Mon, 12:30-3pm & 6:30pm-midnight Tue & Wed, to 1:30am Thu & Fri, 7pm-1:30am Sat) El Pobre Diablo is one of Quito's best places to hear live music. It's a friendly, laid-back place with a well-curated selection of talent (jazz, blues, world music, experimental sounds) performing most nights. It's also a great place to dine, with delectable fusion fare, a solid cocktail menu, candlelit tables and a great vibe.

La Juliana LIVE MUSIC
(Map p64; www.lajuliana.com.ec; Av 12 de Octubre N24-722 near Coruña; admission incl drink $25; 9pm-2am Thu, to 3am Fri & Sat) In an old converted house, La Juliana is a colorfully decorated space with a good mix of bands (rock, salsa, merengue) lighting up the dance floor most weekend nights.

Cafe Democrático LIVE MUSIC
(Map p76; 02-603-4775; García E7-81 near Almagro; 6pm-3am Tue-Sat) Alternative live music (think salsa and Latin jam sessions, jazz-ska nights and flamenco guitar improvisations) and DJs keep the dance floor packed at this bar and club in La Mariscal. Popular with locals.

There's a second branch at the Centro de Arte Contemporáneo.

Casa de la Música LIVE MUSIC
(02-226-1965; www.casadelamusica.ec; Valderrama N32-307 near Mariana de Jesús; box office 9am-1:30pm & 2:30-5pm Mon-Fri) Top-flight orchestras, including Quito's own philharmonic, and musicians from around the world perform at this contemporary hall with great acoustics.

Varadero LIVE MUSIC
(Map p64; cnr Reina Victoria & La Pinta; 8pm-2am Fri & Sat) This space, attached to La Bodeguita de Cuba, comes alive on weekend nights when it's transformed into a lively *salsateca*. If you're lucky you'll catch a performance by the owner, a talented Cuban woman.

Café Libro LIVE MUSIC
(Map p64; 02-250-3214; www.cafelibro.com; Leonidas Plaza Gutiérrez N23-56 near Wilson; $5-10; 12:30-2:30pm Mon, 12:30-2:30pm & 5pm-midnight Tue-Thu, 12:30-2:30pm & 6pm-2am Fri, 6pm-2am Sat) Live music, poetry readings, contemporary dance, tango, jazz and other performances draw an arts-loving crowd to this long-running venue. There are regular tango classes ($10) and *milongas* (tango dance sessions) on Wednesday and Saturday nights.

Pull up a table for a game of chess or cards anytime.

Cinemas

Most Quito cinemas show popular English-language films with Spanish subtitles.

★Ocho y Medio CINEMA
(Map p64; www.ochoymedio.net; Valladolid N24-353 near Vizcaya) This Floresta film house shows art films (often in English) and has occasional dance, theater and live music. There's a great cafe attached.

1

JAMES PENDLETON/SHUTTERSTOCK ©

2

4

JESS KRAFT/SHUTTERSTOCK ©

FOTOS593/SHUTTERSTOCK ©

1. Iglesia de la Compañía de Jesús (p56)
Construction of Quito's most ornate church began in 1605 and took 160 years to complete.

2. Plaza Grande (p55)
The heart of Quito's Old Town, Plaza Grande bustles with activity.

3. Mitad del Mundo (p95)
A 30m-high stone trapezoidal monument topped by a brass globe stands at the center of the Mitad del Mundo.

4. Quito at sunset
A capital city high in the Andes, Quito is dramatically situated, squeezed between mountain peaks, the greenery of which is concealed by the afternoon mist.

Multicines CINEMA
(www.multicines.com.ec; Av Amazonas N36-152 near Naciones Unidas) Multiscreen cinema at the Centro Comercial Iñaquito showing the latest Hollywood movies.

Cinemark CINEMA
(www.cinemark.com.ec; cnr Naciones Unidas & Av América) The most recent Hollywood blockbusters are shown here (usually subtitled rather than dubbed).

Theater & Dance

Teatro Sucre THEATER
(Map p56; ☎02-295-1661; www.teatrosucre.com; Manabí N8-131) Built in 1878, this stately, beautifully restored building in the lively Plaza del Teatro hosts Quito's best theater, dance and music productions. Performances range from jazz and classical music to ballet, modern dance and opera.

Teatro Bolívar THEATER
(Map p56; ☎02-228-5278; www.teatrobolivar.org; Pasaje Espejo Oe243 near Guayaquil) One of the city's most illustrious and important theaters, the Teatro Bolívar stages dance performances, concerts and plays. The wonderful art deco building, completed in 1933, has been in various stages of restoration since it was badly damaged by a fire in 1999.

Ballet Folklórico Nacional Jacchigua DANCE
(Map p64; ☎02-295-2025; www.jacchiguaesecuador.com; cnr Avs Patria & 12 de Octubre; $35; ⏲7:30pm Wed) This folkloric ballet is as touristy as it is spectacular. It is presented at the Teatro Demetrio Agilera in the Casa de la Cultura Ecuatoriana and is quite a show. You can reserve tickets online.

Humanizarte DANCE
(Map p56; ☎02-257-3486; fundacion_humanizarte@hotmail.com; Casa 707, La Ronda) This excellent theater and dance group, currently in La Ronda on weekend nights, presents Andean dance performances. You can also inquire about taking an Andean folk-dancing class.

Teatro Patio de Comedías PERFORMING ARTS
(Map p64; ☎02-256-1902; www.patiodecomedias.org; Calle 18 de Septiembre E4-26 near Amazonas; ⏲box office 6:30-8:30pm Wed-Sat, 5-6:30pm Sun) Presents plays and performances Thursday through Sunday nights, usually at 8pm. It's near the Mariscal between Calle 9 de Octubre and Av Amazonas.

Sports

Estadio Olimpico Atahualpa STADIUM
(cnr 6 de Diciembre & Naciones Unidas) The city's main soccer stadium, opened in 1951, seats 37,750. Ecuador's national team, Deportivo Quito and El Nacional play here. Nearby is the shopping mall Quicentro. Take an Ecovia bus to the Estadio stop.

Shopping

There are some excellent crafts stores in the Mariscal. If buying from street stalls, you should bargain; in the fancier stores, prices are normally fixed. Note that souvenirs are a little cheaper outside Quito, if you have the time and inclination to search them out.

Centros comerciales (shopping malls) are similar to their North American counterparts, and sell international brands.

★**Librería del Fondo Carlos Fuentes** BOOKS
(Map p76; ☎02-254-9817; www.fce.com.ec; Av 6 de Diciembre N24-04 near Wilson; ⏲10am-8pm Mon-Fri, to 7pm Sat, to 2pm Sun) One of Ecuador's best bookshops is located in the former mansion of Galo Plaza Lasso, Ecuadorian President from 1948 to 1952. An excellent selection of titles are displayed beneath the original wood-paneled ceiling and chandeliers, and even the fireplaces have been retained. Up a sweeping staircase there's a gallery space, and there's also a peaceful garden cafe.

Readings and other literary events are often held here; see the website for details.

★**Casa Mariscal** ARTS & CRAFTS
(Map p76; Mera N23-54 near Baquedano; ⏲10am-7pm Mon-Sat) An artists' collective selling beautiful handmade jewelry, prints, bags, textiles and other handicrafts.

★**Tianguez** ARTS & CRAFTS
(Map p56; www.tianguez.org; Plaza San Francisco) Next to Tianguez cafe (p81), this fair trade shop sells a wide selection of quality handmade crafts from across Ecuador. Items are arranged by region, with information on the techniques used to produce them.

Galería Latina ARTS & CRAFTS
(Map p76; www.galerialatina-quito.com; Mera N23-69; ⏲10am-7pm Mon-Sat, 11am-6pm Sun) One of the finest handicraft and clothing shops in the city, Galería Latina has a huge selection of beautifully made pieces: tagua carvings, colorful Andean weavings, textiles, jewelry,

sweaters and handmade items from across Latin America. Prices are high, but so is the craftsmanship.

ARIU JEWELRY
(Map p56; ☎02-228-4157; www.ariustudio.com; Bolívar Oe6-23 near Benalcázar, Plaza San Francisco; ⊙10am-6pm Mon-Fri, to 3pm Sat & Sun) Byron Ushiña, a jewelry designer who learned the craft from his father and grandfather, sells unique, beautifully made pieces, incorporating pre-Columbian designs, semiprecious stones and rare materials native to Ecuador.

Galería Ecuador ARTS & CRAFTS
(Map p76; www.galeriaecuador.com; Reina Victoria N24-263 near García; ⊙9am-9pm Mon-Sat, 10am-8pm Sun) This sparkling two-story complex off Plaza Foch offers top-quality Ecuadorian-made products, ranging from handicrafts, jewelry, coffee-table books and clothing to chocolates, wine and liqueurs.

Folklore Olga Fisch ARTS & CRAFTS
(Map p64; http://olgafisch.com/; Colón E10-53 near Caamano; ⊙9am-7pm Mon-Fri, to 6pm Sat) The store of legendary designer Olga Fisch (who died in 1991) is a good place to go for high-quality crafts, bags and accessories. Fisch was a Hungarian artist who immigrated to Ecuador in 1939 and worked with indigenous artists, melding traditional crafts with fine art.

Mercado Artesanal La Mariscal ARTS & CRAFTS
(Map p64; Washington btwn Mera & Reina Victoria; ⊙8am-7pm Mon-Sat, to 6pm Sun) Half a city block filled by more than 200 crafts stalls, with good prices and mixed quality. It's great for souvenirs.

Arte Rayuela ARTS & CRAFTS
(Map p64; Camino de Orellana 27- 410, Guápulo; ⊙10am-6pm Mon-Fri) This bohemian store is a great place to go on the hunt for handmade crafts, ceramics, paper-mache pieces, wooden items, jewelry and toys, most of them produced by local artists in a shared on-site workshop.

Ag JEWELRY
(Map p76; ☎02-255-0276; Mera 614 near Veintimilla) Ag's selection of rare, handmade silver jewelry from throughout South America is outstanding. You'll also find antiques.

Homero Ortega P & Hijos HATS
(Map p56; www.homeroortega.com; Benalcázar N2-52 near Sucre; ⊙9:30am-1:30pm & 2:30-6:30pm Mon-Fri, 10am-1pm Sat) One of the country's biggest sellers of Ecuadorian straw hats (aka panama hats). The store offers a small but versatile selection of its famous Cuenca brand.

La Bodega ARTS & CRAFTS
(Map p76; Mera N22-24 near Carrión; ⊙10am-1:30pm & 2:30-7pm Mon-Fri, 9:30am-1:30pm & 4-6pm Sat) In business for 30-odd years, La Bodega stocks a wide and wonderful range of high-quality crafts, both old and new.

Galería Beltrán ART
(Map p64; https://galeriabeltran.jimdo.com; Reina Victoria N21-30; ⊙10am-6pm Mon-Sat) This art gallery, which opened more than 30 years ago, sells paintings and sculptures by well-known Ecuadorian artists.

Libri Mundi BOOKS
(Map p76; Mera N23-83 near Wilson; ⊙9:30am-6pm Mon-Fri, to 2pm Sat) One of Quito's best bookstores, with a good selection of titles in English, German, French and Spanish.

Confederate Bookstore BOOKS
(Map p76; www.confederatebooks.com; Amazonas N 24-155 near Foch, 2nd fl; ⊙10:30am-6:30pm Mon-Sat) Excellent bookstore with a large selection of secondhand books in English and several other languages.

El Jardín MALL
(Map p64; http://malleljardin.com.ec/; Av Amazonas N6-114 near Av República; ⊙10am-8:30pm Mon-Sat, to 7:30pm Sun) A sparkling mall with a good supermarket and international chain stores, near Parque La Carolina.

Centro Comercial Iñaquito MALL
(CCI; www.cci.com.ec; Av Amazonas N36-152 near Naciones Unidas; ⊙10am-8:30pm Mon-Sat, to 8pm Sun) Shopping mall and entertainment complex located on the north end of Parque La Carolina.

Explorer SPORTS & OUTDOORS
(Map p76; cnr Foch & Reina Victoria) This store sells pricey, name-brand outdoor apparel and gear right on Plaza Foch.

English Bookstore BOOKS
(Map p76; Calama 217 near Almagro; ⊙10am-6:30pm Mon-Sat) Good selection of used books in English.

Quicentro Shopping MALL
(www.quicentro.com; Av Naciones Unidas near Av 6 de Diciembre; ⊙9:30am-9pm Mon-Sat, 10am-8pm Sun) Popular mall on Naciones Unidas.

Information

DANGERS & ANNOYANCES

Quito has its share of robberies and petty crime, but the dangers can be minimized by taking a few precautions.

- The Mariscal remains a target for muggers and pickpockets, though Plaza Foch and the surrounding streets now have a visible police presence. Take a taxi after dark when traveling more than a few blocks.
- Because most of the shops and restaurants in the Old Town close in the evening, it can feel sketchy wandering some of its outlying dimly lit blocks alone. Pickpocketing, the old-fashioned mustard scam and snatch-and-run robberies do happen here, so keep your wits about you.

Mariscal Police Station (Tourist Police; ☎02-254-3983; Reina Victoria N 21-208 near Roca; ⏱24hr)

Old Town Police Station (☎02-254-3983; Chile btwn Moreno & Venezuela, Plaza Grande; ⏱10am-6pm)

Pickpockets are a problem on the trolley bus system – keep an eye out while riding, and avoid taking it during rush hour and after dark. Always keep your bag close (on your lap); the slicing open of bags (even while between your legs/under your seat, or on your back) is common practice.

Use ATMs in the daytime, choose locations with other people about (shopping malls, banks, etc) and stay alert upon exiting.

If you get robbed, file a police report *(denuncio)* at a police station or tourism security service office; the latter has stations in the airport and Quitumbe bus terminal. Or call ☎02-254-3983 for assistance.

EMERGENCY

Ambulance	☎131
Emergency	☎911
Fire	☎102
Police	☎101
Tourist Info	☎148

INTERNET ACCESS

The Mariscal area has several internet cafes, many with inexpensive international calling rates. There are fewer options in the Old Town. Most charge between $1 and $1.50 per hour. Wi-fi is available throughout the city in cafes, restaurants, bars, hotels and even public parks.

MEDICAL SERVICES

Take out overseas health insurance before you travel to cover medical expenses. Many doctors and hospitals will expect payment in cash.

Hospital Metropolitano (☎02-399-8000; www.hospitalmetropolitano.org; Mariana de Jesús near Arteta)

Hospital Voz Andes (☎02-226-2142; www.hospitalvozandes.org; Villalengua Oe2-37 near Av 10 de Agosto)

Dr John Rosenberg (☎09-9973-9734, 02-252-1104; rosenberg.john@gmail.com; Foch 476 near Almagro)

MONEY

There are a few *casas de cambio* (currency-exchange bureaus) in the new town, along Avenida Amazonas between Avenida Patria and Orellana, and there are dozens of banks throughout town.

Banco de Guayaquil (Av Amazonas near Veintimilla)

Banco de Guayaquil (Av Colón near Reina Victoria)

Banco del Pacífico (cnr Guayaquil & Chile)

Banco del Pacífico (cnr Av 12 de Octubre & Cordero)

Banco del Pichincha (Guayaquil near Manabí)

Western Union (Av de la República 450 near Almagro)

Western Union (Av Colón 1333 near Foch)

TOURIST INFORMATION

Quito Tourism (Corporación Metropolitana de Turismo; Map p56; ☎02-257-2445; www.quito-turismo.gob.ec; Venezuela near Espejo; ⏱9am-6pm Mon-Sat, 9:30-4:30pm Sun; 📶)

Tourist Information (Parque Gabriela Mistral; Map p76; cnr Reina Victoria & Cordero; ⏱9am-5pm Mon-Sat)

Getting There & Away

AIR

Quito's **Aeropuerto Internacional Mariscal Sucre** (☎02-395-4200; www.aeropuertoquito.aero) is 37km east of the city in a broad valley near Tababela. It's a modern facility with the longest runway in Latin America and the second-highest control tower (after Cancun); however, the terminal is significantly smaller than Guayaquil's. There is a **tourist information booth** (☎02-281-8363; aeropuerto@auito-turismo.gob.ec) in the arrivals hall.

BUS

Quito has two main bus terminals (and a smaller third terminal), and they are all a long way from the center (allow at least an hour by public transport, 30 minutes or more by taxi).

Terminals

Terminal Terrestre Quitumbe (☎02-398-8200; cnr Cóndor Ñan & Sucre) Located 10km southwest of the Old Town. It handles the

Central and Southern Andes, the coast, and the Oriente (ie Baños, Cuenca, Guayaquil, Coca and – aside from Otavalo and Mindo – most destinations of interest to travelers). It can be reached by Trole bus south to the last stop. A taxi costs somewhere between $12 and $15. There is a **tourist information office** (☎ 02-382-4815; quitumbre@quito-turismo.gob.ec) located here.

Terminal Terrestre Carcelén (☎ 02-290-7005; Eloy Alfaro) Located in the north, this terminal services Otavalo, Ibarra, Mindo, Santo Domingo, Tulcán and other northern destinations. To get here, take the Trole bus north to Carcelén at the end of the line. A taxi costs about $10 to $15.

Terminal Terrestre La Ofelia (cnr Vásquez de Cepeda & de los Arupos) Located in the north, La Ofelia services destinations to the northwest of Quito such as Nanegalito and Mindo, as well as Cayambe. To get here take the Metrobus north to the end of the line. A taxi costs approximately $10.

Companies

Major bus companies include the following:

Cooperativa Flor de Valle/Cayambe (☎ 02-236-0094; Terminal Terrestre La Ofelia)

Flota Imbabura (☎ 02-382-4810; http://flota-imbabura.com; Terminal Terrestre de Quitumbe)

Panamericana (Map p76; ☎ 02-255-7134; www.panamericana.ec; Terminal Terrestre Quitumbe)

Transportes Ecuador (☎ 02-382-4851; www.transportesecuador.com.ec; Terminal Terreste Quitumbe)

Transportes Occidentales (☎ 02-303-4291; http://transportesoccidentales.com.ec/; Terminal Terreste Quitumbe)

Transportes Baños (Cooperativa de Transportes y Turismo Baños; ☎ 02-382-4843; www.cooperativabanos.com.ec; Terminal Quitumbe)

CAR & MOTORCYCLE

Renting a car to get around Quito is a bad idea – traffic can be a nightmare, and taxis and buses are much cheaper and more convenient than renting a car. However, if you're leaving the city to explore nearby regions, a rental car will give you flexibility and freedom to more easily get off the beaten path. Most rental agencies have offices in town; however, rates for the international companies are generally cheaper if picked up from the airport.

If you want to hire a motorbike, contact **Freedom Bike** (p72).

Car rental companies:

Avis (☎ 02-281-8160; www.avis.com; Airport)

Budget (☎ 02-281-8000, 02-281-8040; www.budget-ec.com; Airport)

 **QUITO'S NEW METRO**

The first line of Quito's new underground rail transport system, the **Metro de Quito** (www.metrodequito.gob.ec), is due for completion in 2019. The metro will connect Quitumbe in the south with El Labrador in the north in just 34 minutes, with 15 stops along the way including Plaza San Francisco, La Almeda, El Ejido and La Carolina.

Hertz (☎ 02-281-8410; www.hertzecuador.com.ec; Airport)

Localiza (☎ 02-600-2975; www.localiza.com/ecuador; Airport)

Thrifty (☎ 02-281-8330, 02-281-8321; www.thrifty.com.ec; Airport)

TRAIN

After massive investment, the country's **train network** (☎ 1-800-873-367; www.trenecuador.com; cnr Guayllabamba & Sincholagua, Estación de Ferrocarril Chimbacalle) is once again ferrying passengers on slow-motion journeys through breathtaking high-altitude scenery. There are currently two routes: the **Tren de los Volcanes** (p131), which makes the round trip to El Boliche in Cotopaxi National Park, and the luxurious **Tren Crucero** (p71), a four-day, four-night luxury train tour from Quito to Guayaquil.

Trains depart from Quito's beautifully renovated Estación de Ferrocarril Chimbacalle 2km south of the Old Town. Book tickets online or at the booking desk at **Quito Tourism**.

Getting Around

TO/FROM THE AIRPORT

Taxi prices into the city are fixed and cost $26 to the Mariscal or Old Town. After exiting customs there's a small kiosk with the rates conveniently posted. Depending on the time of day and traffic, the trip can take between 35 minutes and an hour.

Every half-hour, the **Aeroservicios** (☎ 02-604-3500; www.aeroservicios.com.ec; cnr Av Amazonas s/n & Av La Prensa; one-way $8; ⌚ 3:30am-11:30pm Mon-Fri, 4am-10:30pm Sat & Sun) shuttle bus makes the 30-minute trip between the airport and Parque Bicentenario (the old airport) at the northern end of Avenida Amazonas. From here, taxis are cheaper into the Mariscal or Old Town, respectively only 9km or 15km away.

The least expensive and least convenient alternative is to take a public bus ($2) to or from the **Río Coca bus terminal** (Río Coca near Las Hiedras) north of the Mariscal.

BICYCLE

You can hire bicycles from **Cicleadas El Rey** (☎98-401-4852; www.facebook.com/CicleadasElRey; cnr Cordero & Reina Victoria, El Cafecito; ⏰10am-6:30pm Mon-Fri, 9am-2pm Sun). Quito also has Sunday *ciclopaseos* when key streets are closed to car traffic (p69).

The city's bike share program, **BiciQuito** (p67), is free but you'll need to register at the Agencia Metropolitana de Tránsito on Avendia Amazonas with a completed application form (downloaded from the website) and a color photocopy of your passport photo ID page and Ecuador entry stamp. Once you've registered you can pick up a bike from any of the rental stations.

CAR

With one-way streets and heavy traffic, driving in Quito can be hectic. Don't leave a vehicle on the street overnight. There are private garages throughout town where you can park overnight for around $12.

PUBLIC TRANSPORT

Local buses ($0.25) operate from 6am to 9pm and are convenient since, despite designated stops, you can usually get on and off at any street corner. No route numbers, but the primary and final stops are posted in the front window. Keep a close watch on your bags and pockets. The green buses serve outlying districts and suburbs.

Quito has three electric, wheelchair-accessible bus routes ($0.25): the Trole, the Ecovía and the Metrobus. Each runs north–south along one of Quito's three main thoroughfares, and each has designated stations and car-free lanes, making them speedy and efficient.

Trole Runs through the middle of the city, along Maldonado and Avenida 10 de Agosto. It links Carcelén bus terminal in the north with the Quitumbe bus terminal, southwest of Old Town. In the Old Town, southbound trolleys take the west route along Guayaquil, while northbound trolleys take Flores and Montúfar.

BUSES FROM QUITO

DESTINATION	COST ($)	DURATION (HR)	FREQUENCY
Ambato	3.30	2½	every 10min
Atacames	9	7	6 daily
Baños	4.25	3	every 30min
Cayambe	1.80	1½	every 10min
Coca	10	10	24 daily
Cotacachi	2.25	2½	4 daily
Cuenca	10-12	10-12	every 50min
Esmeraldas	7.25	6	every 25min
Guayaquil	8	8	hourly
Huaquillas	9	11	15 daily
Ibarra	3	2½	every 15min
Lago Agrio	8	7-8	every 40min
Latacunga	1.50	2	every 10min
Loja	14-17	14-15	24 daily
Machala	10	10	22 daily
Manta	10	8-9	hourly
Mindo	3	3	5 departures Mon-Fri, 9 Sat & Sun
Otavalo	2.50	2	hourly
Portoviejo	9	9	hourly
Puerto López	12	10	3 daily
Puyo	6	5½	24 daily
Riobamba	4	4	every 20min
San Lorenzo	7	6½	daily 9pm
Santo Domingo	3	3	every 15min
Tena	6	5	every 1½hr
Tulcán	5	5	every 30min

Ecovía Runs along the eastern side, along Avenida 6 de Diciembre, between Río Coca (from where you can connect to a bus to the airport) in the north and Quitumbe bus terminal in the south.

Metrobus This route runs along Avenida América between La Ofelia bus terminal in the north to Quitumbe bus terminal in the south.

TAXI

Most cabs are yellow. They're plentiful, although at rush hour and on Sundays and rainy days you might have to wait for an empty cab. Taxi companies include **Urgentaxi** (☎02-222-2111) and **City Taxi** (☎02-263-3333).

Cabs are legally required to use their *taxímetros* (meters) by day; however, some drivers may quote a price of anywhere between $2 and $5 for a trip in town, which is usually more than if the meter was on. If you insist on drivers using a meter, they'll often relent. Otherwise, consider flagging down another cab. At night, most taxi drivers turn off their meters, and $2 is the minimum going rate. The minimum fare by day is $1.50. Short journeys will start at that and climb to about $4 for a longer trip.

Several downloadable app services similar to Uber or Lyft – where drivers respond within a few minutes to a request – are now operating in Quito. The most developed is **Easy Taxi** (☎95-883-9483, 99-734-1994; www.easytaxi.ec).

AROUND QUITO

Quito makes a great base for exploring the striking geography and biodiversity of the region, with a number of excellent day trips (including several routes by train) available from the capital. Otavalo, Cotopaxi, Mindo and the hot springs of Papallacta can also be visited on long day trips from the city.

La Mitad del Mundo

In 1736 Charles Marie de La Condamine made the measurements proving that the equatorial line ran through here (well, nearby actually). His expedition's measurements gave rise to the metric system and proved that the world is not perfectly round, but that it bulges at the equator. Appealing perhaps to our childish belief that there is an actual line painted around the world and that an equatorial visit should be checked off a bucket list like skydiving or a boat trip to Antarctica, the area has developed into a kitschy, circus-like environment. There are food and handicraft stalls, bustling weekend crowds and an assortment of sights and attractions, few of which relate to the equator.

Located 7km south of Cayambe, **El Reloj Solar Quitsato** is another equator monument, its massive sundial with a 10m cylinder marking the spot.

Overshadowing the Mitad del Mundo monument is the new headquarters for the **Union of South American Nations** (UNASUR), called 'Nestor Kirchner' in honor of the late Argentine president and fronted by a statue of him. A startling modernist building, with gravity-defying cubist structures resembling a misshapen spaceship, it was designed by Diego Guayasamín and opened for business in December, 2014.

Sights

Mitad del Mundo LANDMARK

(Middle of the World City; www.mitaddelmundo.com; Av Galarza km13.5; adult/child $7.50/3.75; ⏲9am-6pm) At the center of the Mitad del Mundo stands the centerpiece of the park: a 30m-high, stone trapezoidal **monument** topped by a brass globe containing a viewing platform and a museum, which provides a good introduction to the indigenous groups of Ecuador through dioramas, clothing displays and photographs. On the lower floors are new interactive exhibits examining the science behind the myths of the Equator.

Other attractions within the park (included in the entrance fee) include a new **Viviendas Ancestrales** (Ancestral Homes) exhibition, with re-creations of traditional dwellings from the Amazon, Andes and the coast; the **Museo de Cacao** (Cocoa Museum) examining the history of Ecuadorian chocolate production; a 1:200 scale model of colonial Quito; a small **planetarium**, and even a one-room **Museo de la Cerveza Artesanal** (Craft Beer Museum), with displays on the brewing process and beer for sale for $5 a pint.

Museo Solar Inti Ñan MUSEUM

(http://museointinan.com.ec/en/; adult/child $4/2; ⏲9:30am-5pm) A few hundred meters north of the entrance to the main Mitad del Mundo complex, this amusing museum has meandering outdoor exhibits of astronomical geography and explanations of the importance of Ecuador's geographical location. One of the highlights is the 'solar chronometer,' a unique instrument made in 1865 that shows precise astronomical and conventional time, as well as the month, day and season – all by using the rays of the sun.

The real reason to come, of course, is for the water and energy demonstrations, but you'll have to decide for yourself if it's just a smoke-and-mirrors funhouse. It too is supposedly (but not actually) the site of the true equator.

Volcán Pululahua

The 3383-hectare Reserva Geobotánica Pululahua lies about 4km northwest of La Mitad del Mundo. The most interesting part of the reserve is the volcanic crater of the extinct Pululahua. This was apparently formed in ancient times, when the cone of the volcano collapsed, leaving a huge crater some 400m deep and 5km across. The crater's flat and fertile bottom is used for agriculture.

The crater is open to the west side, through which moisture-laden winds from the Pacific Ocean blow dramatically; it is sometimes difficult to see the crater because of the swirling clouds and mist. The moist winds, combined with the crater's steep walls, create a variety of microclimates, and the vegetation on the fertile volcanic slopes is both rampant and diverse. There are many flowers and a variety of bird species.

Sights

Reserva Geobotánica Pululahua NATURE RESERVE
(cnr Kingman & Galarza; 8am-5pm) FREE The crater of extinct Volcán Pululahua can be entered on foot via a steep trail from the **Mirador de Ventanillas** viewpoint just inside the Reserva Geobotánica; you'll need to sign in at the ranger's office at the entrance before starting the walk. From the viewpoint a 1.7km trail leads to the crater and back; allow 90 minutes.

Templo del Sol MUSEUM
(Mirador Volcán Pululahua; $3; 9am-5pm Tue-Sun) Near the Mirador de Ventanillas, you'll pass the castle-like Templo del Sol, a re-creation of an Incan temple, complete with pre-Columbian relics and stone carvings. The guided tour (in Spanish) is a bit gimmicky, led by a heavily decorated 'Incan prince' who touches on presumed ancient beliefs and rituals. The tour ends with a painting demonstration by Ecuadorian art-

MYSTERIES FROM MIDDLE EARTH

The idea of standing with one foot in each hemisphere is an intriguing one, and the closer you get to the equator, the more you hear about the equator's mysterious energy. But what is fact and what is fiction?

There's no point in starting softly, so let's debunk the biggest myth first. La Mitad del Mundo is not on the equator – but it's close. Global Positioning System (GPS) devices show that it's only about 240m off the mark. And no one who sees the photos of you straddling the equator has to know this, right?

Another tough one to swallow is the myth of the flushing toilet. One of the highlights of the Museo Solar Inti Ñan (p95) is the demonstration of water draining counterclockwise north of the equator and clockwise 3m away, south of the equator. Researchers claim it's a crock. The Coriolis Force – which causes weather systems to veer right in the northern hemisphere and left in the southern hemisphere – has no effect on small bodies of water like those in a sink or a toilet. Draining water spins the way it does due to plumbing, eddies in the water, the shape of the basin and other factors.

How about some truth: you do weigh less on the equator. This is due to greater centrifugal force on the equator than at the poles. But the difference between here and at the poles is only about 0.3%, not the 1.5% to 2% the scales at the monument imply.

It is true that the spring and autumn equinoxes are the only days when the sun shines directly overhead at the equator. In fact, that's what defines an equinox. But that doesn't mean the days and nights are equal in length, as many would have you believe – this happens just before the spring equinox and just after the autumn equinox, and the day depends on where you are on the planet.

More fascinating than any of the myths perpetuated by Inti Ñan and the Mitad del Mundo, however, is the fact that the true equator (0.00 degrees, according to GPS readings) resides on a sacred indigenous site constructed more than 1000 years ago. The name of the site is Catequilla, and it sits on a hilltop on the opposite side of the highway from the Mitad del Mundo.

OFF THE BEATEN TRACK

REFUGIO DE VIDA SILVESTRE PASOCHOA

This verdant, mostly intact forested reserve spread over the flanks of extinct Pasochoa is only 30km from Quito, but it feels much further away. At 2900m to 4200m, **Refugio de Vida Silvestre Pasochoa** (8am-5pm) FREE has a wide range of highland trees and shrubs including the Podocarpaceae, the Ecuadorian Andes' only native conifer, plus orchids, ferns and lichens and more than 100 species of birds. Hikers might want to head out here for its feeling of remoteness; there are several trails, from easy short ones to all-day hikes and an eight-hour one that leads out of the reserve and to the summit of Pasochoa.

Buses from Quito's Plaza La Marín (1½ hours) head to the town of Amaguaña, from where the reserve entrance is another 7km south; you can hire a *camioneta* (pickup) to take you the rest of the way. Alternatively, and more conveniently, tour companies in Quito can organize a trip.

ist Cristóbal Ortega Maila, who paints rapidly and adroitly using only his hands (no brushes). There are fine rooftop views.

Sleeping & Eating

Pululahua Hostal HOSTEL $$

(09-9946-6636; www.pululahuahostal.com; s/d from $30/40, without bathroom $20/30) This ecologically friendly guesthouse is located inside the crater. Pululahua Hostal offers a handful of simple, comfortable rooms in a pristine setting. The owners cook tasty meals ($12), using ingredients from their organic farm whenever possible. Guests can use the Jacuzzi ($3.50) and bikes and go horseback riding (from $10 per hour).

El Crater HOTEL $$$

(02-239-8132; www.elcrater.com; Mirador del Pululahua; r incl breakfast from $120;) Near the Ventanillas viewpoint, peacefully set El Crater has 12 spacious, attractively designed rooms with king-size beds and picture windows overlooking the volcanic crater on one side and Quito on the other. The restaurant serves good Ecuadorian dishes against equally impressive vistas.

Getting There & Away

The easiest way to reach the lookout is by an inexpensive organized tour from La Mitad del Mundo. A taxi from Mitad del Mundo is around $5. There is no public bus service.

Northern Highlands

Includes ➡

Best Places to Eat

- ➡ Hostería La Mirage (p112)
- ➡ Sumac (p106)
- ➡ Bizcochos San Pedro (p100)
- ➡ Cafe Fussion (p106)
- ➡ Yumbo's Chocolate (p126)

Best Places to Stay

- ➡ Hostal Doña Esther (p105)
- ➡ La Luna (p110)
- ➡ Hostería Cananvalle (p115)
- ➡ Hacienda Cusin (p108)
- ➡ Casa Divina (p126)

Why Go?

Follow the snaking Panamericana through the awesome Andes to the vibrant market town of Otavalo and the surrounding indigenous villages. As the spine of the Andes bends north from Quito, volcanic peaks punctuate valleys blanketed by flower farms and sugarcane fields. This is Ecuador's beating heart and a cradle of Andean culture: artisans produce their wares using methods unaltered for generations, and visitors find some of the country's best deals here, on everything from leather goods to traditional carpets.

High-altitude landscapes surrender to steamy lowlands in the west, a rich transitional zone where coffee plantations flourish in the spectacular Intag Valley. Further south, Mindo is a base for bird-watching, hiking and outdoor adventures. Remote jungle lodges are scattered around the region for those looking to retreat deeper into nature. Wherever you go, off-the-beaten-path adventures, sustainable community tourism initiatives and volunteering opportunities are close by.

When to Go

Otavalo

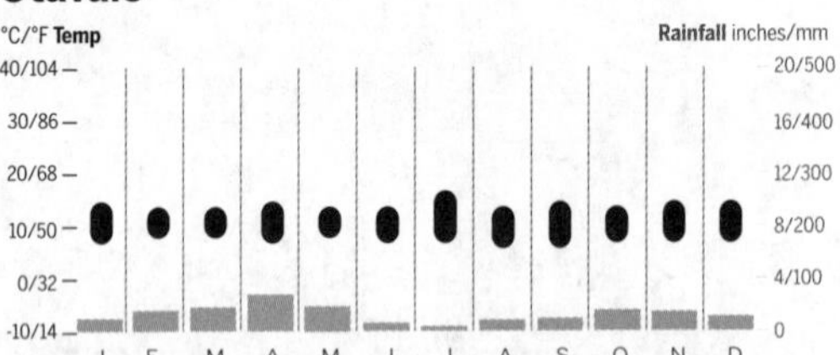

Jun Don't miss Otavalo on June 24, when locals celebrate Inti Raymi, a colorful pagan festival.

Early Sep Try to make it to Otavalo's Fiesta del Yamor, an indigenous harvest festival.

Late Sep Expect music, dancing and lots of food at Ibarra's popular annual fiesta.

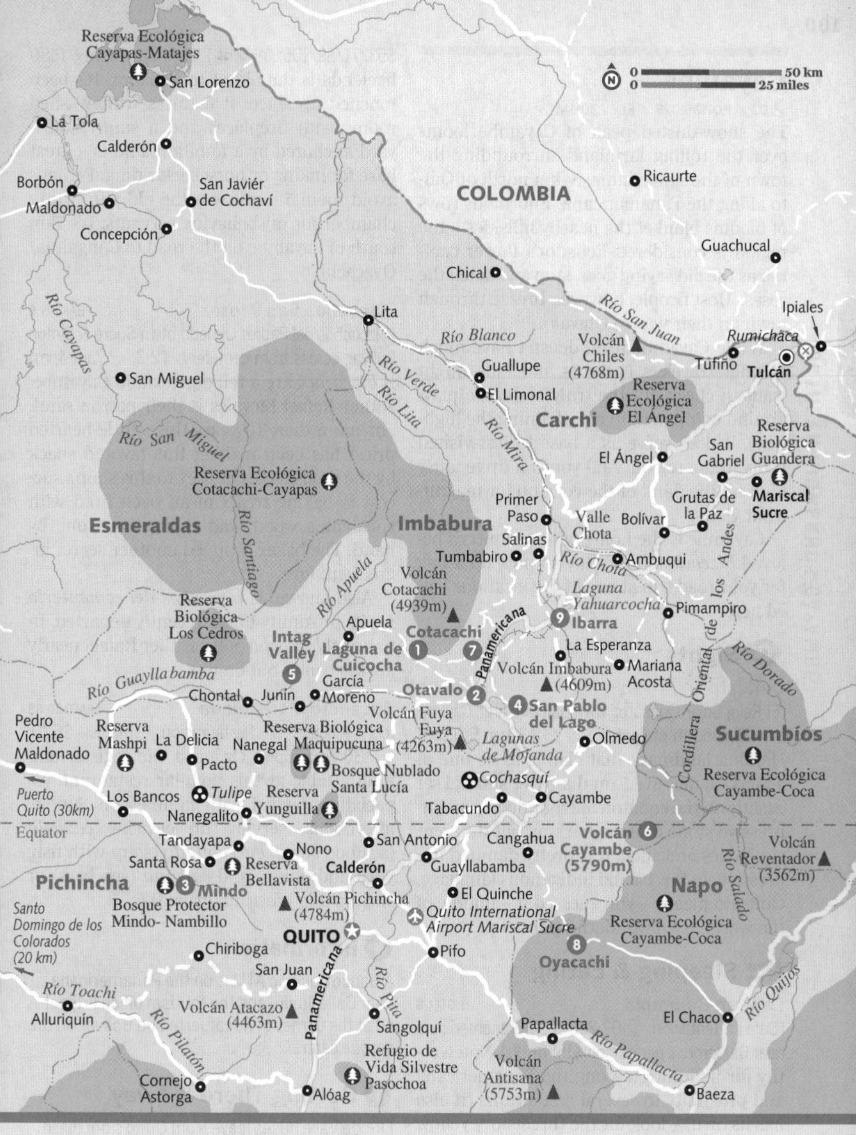

Northern Highlands Highlights

❶ **Laguna de Cuicocha** (p112) Losing yourself on a walking tour in the majestic hillsides above Cotacachi.

❷ **Otavalo Market** (p104) Filling up your luggage with handmade crafts and clothes.

❸ **Mindo** (p124) Ticking off birds wandering through the cloud forests west of Quito.

❹ **Hacienda Cusín** (p108) Horseback riding near a historic, perhaps haunted, manse near San Pablo del Lago.

❺ **Intag Valley** (p117) Seeing the most amazing bird – the cock-of-the-rock.

❻ **Volcán Cayambe** (p101) Summiting the glacier-covered surface of this sleeping giant.

❼ **Cotacachi** (p111) Buying leather goods in the shops of this charming *pueblo*.

❽ **Oyacachi** (p101) Trekking from the highlands to the edges of the Amazon.

❾ **Festival de Los Lagos** (p114) Dancing at one of the biggest parades in Northern Ecuador.

Cayambe

☎02 / POP 39,028 / ELEV 3011M

The snow-dusted peak of Cayambe looms over the rolling farmland surrounding the town of the same name, 64km north of Quito along the Panamericana. Enormous rows of blooms blanket the nearby hillsides – the region is considered Ecuador's flower capital: as the old saying goes, stop and smell the roses. Most people, however, breeze through town on their way to Otavalo.

While Cayambe itself doesn't have much to offer travelers (parents and kids might want to check out the truly elaborate playground equipment in a park lining the highway), it does serve as a base to less-visited spots in the region. And you can drive fairly high up the flank of the volcano for magnificent views.

Cayambe is the home of the country's beloved *bizcochos* (biscuits), so pick up a bag for your road trip at one of the locations listed here.

Sights

Quitsato LANDMARK

(El Reloj Solar Quitsato; www.quitsato.org; Cayambe, 47km north of Quito; $2; ⌚8:30am-5:30pm) Here's a landmark that claims to be one of a kind – a massive 52m-diameter sundial set exactly on the equator. Surrounded by an impressive stone mosaic marking out different equinoxes and such, it is pretty damned impressive. In the Tsa'fiki indigenous language, Quitsato means – you guessed it – middle of the world. It's a wonderful photo op.

Sleeping & Eating

La Gran Columbia HOTEL $

(Cafe La Tentacion; ☎02-236-1238; Panamericana near Calderon; r per person $15; P 📶) Noteworthy for its location along the Panamericana and proximity to several restaurants (it also has its own) – look for the three-story yellow building with red trim. Most rooms, which have comfortable beds and flickering cable TV, also have an awkwardly designed hallway alcove with a desk. Downshifting buses provide early-morning wake-up calls. New ownership was changing the name in the fall of 2017, so you may see both names in some of the signage.

Hacienda Guachalá HACIENDA $$

(☎02-361-0908; www.guachala.com; Cangahua, Panamericana Km 45; s/d/tr/q incl breakfast $53/71/89/105; P 📶 🏊) This sprawling 1580 hacienda is the oldest in Ecuador. It's been touched up since: it features whitewashed rooms with fireplaces and a sunny courtyard anchored by a fountain, and is a great base for hiking or horseback riding. Perhaps avoid room 5 – this was the old jail/torture chamber for misbehaving servants. It's 7km south of Cayambe on the road to Cangahua/Oyacachi.

Bizcochos San Pedro BAKERY $

(Bizcochos del Padre; Olmedo btwn Sucre & Simon Bolívar, across from cemetery; $2-3; ⌚7am-4pm) If *bizcochos* are a religion around Cayambe, Father Rafael Morales is their patron saint. For more than 40 years this gentle-hearted priest has been making this favored snack by the thousands. One key to this shop's success is baking treats in an oven fired with eucalyptus wood, and rolling each one by hand. The baker dropped another secret ingredient: love.

Also known as *bizcochos del cementerio* for its proximity to the recently departed. In national *bizcocho* polls, Father Rafael nearly always comes out on top.

Bucanero Marisqueria SEAFOOD $$

(cnr Alianza & Restauracion; mains $6-10; ⌚7:30am-5:30pm) Order at the register and grab a table at this popular restaurant, especially crowded with families on Sunday afternoons, serving up ceviche, *cazuela* (seafood stew), *encebollado* (soup with fish, yuca and onion) and *corvina* (sea bass) or shrimp *a la plancha* (grilled).

Information

A Banco Pacifico ATM is on the Panamericana near Calle Junín, and the tourism office is located at the corner of Rocafuerte and Bolívar on the *parque central.*

Getting There & Away

Flor de Valle buses leave from Quito's northern Ofelia terminal ($0.75, 50 minutes, every 20 minutes). Alternatively, you can hop on any Ibarra- or Otavalo-bound bus from the Carcelén terminal in Quito. To continue north, you won't have a long wait – buses pass by every 10 minutes or so.

Buses to Cangahua leave every half-hour or so from the corner of Calles Sucre and Restauración. These will stop at the Hacienda Guachalá.

Buses to Otavalo (red and white) leave two blocks south of Hilda Ruiz' bakery from the plaza near the Panamericana ($0.90, one hour).

Reserva Ecológica Cayambe-Coca

Occupying 4031 sq km, **Reserva Ecológica Cayambe-Coca** (www.ambiente.gob.ec/parque-nacional-cayambe-coca) spreads across four provinces, including the Oriente, and includes alpine tundra and rainforest. Volcán Reventador (3562m) and Cayambe (5790m) sit within its bounds. On a clear day, the (alternative) road north from Cayambe to Ibarra, which passes through the village of Olmedo, provides excellent views. Volcán Cayambe is Ecuador's third-highest peak and, at 4600m on the south side, the highest point in the world through which the equator passes.

The entrance to the park is 32km from Cayambe. A convenient entrance point is the village of Oyacachi.

To climb this extinct volcano, get in touch with a tour agency in Quito that specializes in mountaineering. There is a mountain refuge ($20 per person), but you need a 4WD to reach it. The seven-hour climb is more difficult than the more frequently ascended Cotopaxi. Two-day and one-night guided climbs cost around $240 and include transportation, equipment (plus some rudimentary glacier training), meals and a night in the refuge.

You can also hike parts of the reserve from the Termas Papallacta, which is located near the entrance to the park and owns 200 hectares of land there. Termas Papallacta (☎02-256-8989) offers four different guided tours ($6 to $15 per person), the most ambitious of which is seven to eight hours and reaches 4100-plus meters above sea level with views of the Antisana, Cayambe, Choza Longos and Antisanilla mountains and Sumaco volcano. You can use the hot springs as a guest for $22.

Most Tena-bound buses from Quito's Terminal Terreste Cumandá will stop in Papallacta ($2.50, 2 hours).

Oyacachi

☎06 / POP 620

Heading south from Cayambe, you'll encounter the little village of Oyacachi (3200m), surrounded by mountain peaks and known for its indulgent community-run **hot springs** (admission $2.50), which bring in the crowds on weekends.

The two- to three-day **hike** from Oyacachi to El Chaco, which follows a centuries-old route, makes its way across the heart of the Cayambe-Coca Reserve and takes you from the eastern slopes of the Andes to the Oriente. After following the newly paved road for around 10km, it later becomes challenging to follow and turns into true wilderness trekking, and involves several river crossings. Another hike begins at the Las Puntas checkpoint (park entrance) and takes you past high-altitude lakes south to the thermal springs of Papallacta. Guides ($30 per day) are highly recommended and can be found at the community tourism office in Oyacachi's hot springs, or contact a travel agency in Otavalo or Quito.

Getting There & Away

A *camioneta* (pickup truck) from Cayambe is $45 (you can organize this trip from the **Hacienda Guachalá**). There is also a daily 3:30pm bus service from Cayambe ($1.50, 2 hours). The bus in Cayambe leaves from Calle Junin, near Banco de Pacifico.

Otavalo

☎06 / POP 39,354 / ELEV 2550M

Otavalo's market is legendary, but it shouldn't be the only reason you come to this charming Andean mini-city. The buzzing little burg, whose sidewalks are embossed in red, yellow and blue, the colors of the national flag, is a perfect jumping-off point for regional hikes (Cotacachi, Peguche) or train trips (Ibarra, Salinas), and has enough interesting restaurants and cafes to sate your taste buds for a few days. Two days a week the cemetery springs to life as residents honor their dead with vibrant flowers and hearty meals. There's a new brewpub in town and a few fun weekend bars too. And, oh yes, that market (p104).

Sights

Daily Market MARKET

(Panamericana & Colón; 7am-1pm) Next to the Animal Market, this large, covered complex just west of the Panamericana houses the vendors who previously plied their trade in a messy overflow on the city's streets (around Montalvo and Jaramillo). Everything from exotic highland fruits and baggies of ground spices to mops and weaving tools is sold here, and on Saturdays it explodes with even more raw foods. It also features a **food court** where you can chow down with locals.

Otavalo

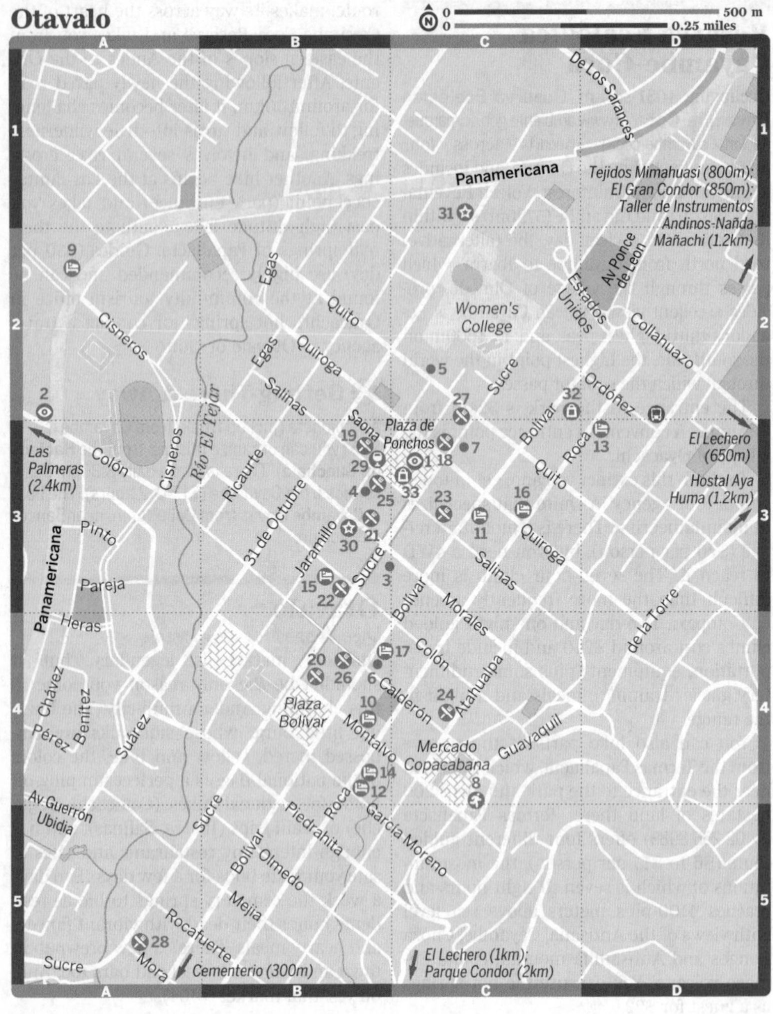

Parque Cóndor BIRD SANCTUARY

(06-304-9399; Via Parque Condor; $4.50; 9:30am-5pm Wed-Sun;) Get an up-close view of Andean condors, as well as, owls, eagles, falcons and hawks, at this Dutch-owned foundation, which rehabilitates these and other birds of prey. Don't miss the free flight demonstrations at 11:30am and 3:30pm. The primary language spoken here is Spanish. The center is perched on the steep hillside of Pucara Alto, approximately 5km from town. You can hit El Lechero and this sanctuary on the same walk uphill.

El Lechero LANDMARK

While this tree outside Otavalo is famous for its magical healing powers, it's more reliable as a great picnic spot, romantic or otherwise, and for great views of town. It's a steep 4km walk or a $4 taxi ride; ask the driver to wait if you don't want to walk back.

Cementerio CEMETERY

(Sucre cnr de las Almas, near Panamericana) Each Monday and Thursday morning, groups of *Otavaleños* summit the Calle de las Almas (Street of Souls) to this hillside cemetery, sharing meals, songs, tears and prayers with relatives who've gone on to the next dimen-

Otavalo

Sights
1 Crafts Market ... C3
2 Daily Market ... A2

Activities, Courses & Tours
3 Ecomontes Tour ... B3
4 Instituto Superíor de Español ... B3
5 Leyton's Tours ... C2
6 Mundo Andino ... B4
7 Runa Tupari Native Travel ... C3
8 Tren Ecuador ... C4

Sleeping
9 Cabañas El Rocío ... A2
10 Hostal Doña Esther ... B4
11 Hostal El Andariego ... C3
12 Hostal Riviera-Sucre ... B4
13 Hostal Samana ... D3
14 Hostal Santa Fé 1 ... B4
15 Hostal Santa Fé 2 ... B3
16 Hostal Valle del Amanecer ... C3
17 Indio Inn ... B4

Eating
Árbol de Montalvo ... (see 10)
18 Cafe Fussion ... C3
19 Cosecha Coffee Shop ... B3
20 Daily Grind ... B4
21 Gran Chifa ... B3
22 Oraibi ... B3
23 Oro Mar ... C3
Quino ... (see 14)
24 Santa Marita ... C4
25 Shanandoah Pie Shop ... B3
26 SISA ... B4
27 Sumac ... C2
28 Yolanda's Chicha de Yamor ... A5

Drinking & Nightlife
29 Cava Caran ... B3

Entertainment
30 Amauta ... B3
31 Peña La Jampa ... C1

Shopping
32 La Casa de Bandolin ... C2
33 Market ... C3

sion. Vendors do a brisk business in flowers, fried fish and pork, and various other types of food and drink. The cemetery is quite basic – mainly plain white crosses or small graves with names painted or scratched on.

Courses

Mundo Andino LANGUAGE
(06-2921-864; www.mandinospanishschool.com; Bolívar No 816 near Calderon, 3rd fl; individual/group lessons per hr $7.75/5.75) This excellent language school offers classes Monday through Friday, homestays with local families and long-term volunteer opportunities where your Spanish will get a workout.

Instituto Superíor de Español LANGUAGE
(06-292-2868, 099-499-1790; www.superiorspanishschool.com; Modesto Jaramillo No 6-69 btwn Morales & Salinas; courses per week from $129) Based in Quito, but with a popular Otavalo outpost, this place receives high marks from readers. It can also arrange homestays. The school is half a block from the Plaza de Ponchos.

Tours

★Runa Tupari Native Travel CULTURAL, OUTDOOR ADVENTURES
(06-292-2320, 099-787-8570; www.runatupari.com; Sucre No 14-15 btwn Quito & Quiroga; closed Sun) Deservedly renowned and respected, Runa Tupari have partnered with indigenous, mestizo and Afro-Ecuadorian rural communities to offer sightseeing, hiking, horseback-riding and biking trips. Rural homestays are $35 per night, while various volunteering options cost $15 per day and include room and board (there's a 15-day minimum).

Offbeat options include a bumpy 2000m mountain-bike descent into the Intag's tropical cloud forest ($85 per person) and a round-trip 10-hour hike up 'Mama' Volcán Cotacachi (4939m; $70 per person). Runa Tupari can customize day- to week-long trips to meet every need and taste.

Not only does Runa Tupari have professional, reliable and enthusiastic guides, but they also offer everyday transportation services so that you can explore the region at your own pace.

Ecomontes Tour ADVENTURE
(06-292-6244; www.otavaloguide.com; cnr Sucre & Morales; closed Sun) This Quito-based agency's Otavalo office offers day and overnight hiking trips, biking ($10), climbing, horseback riding (day trip to El Lechero $45, overnight in El Ángel $125), canyoning and rafting on the Chota, Intag or Mira rivers ($45 to $60). Homestays ($35 including meals) with indigenous families are also

DON'T MISS

OTAVALO CRAFTS MARKET

The **crafts market** (Plaza de Ponchos;) is the reason everyone comes to town. For centuries, Otavalo has hosted one of the most important markets in the Andes, a weekly fiesta that celebrates the gods of commerce. Vendors hawk a dizzying array of traditional crafts as well as an ever-increasing number of slyly disguised imports. Saturday is the big day, but the market runs all week.

The market has become a must-see tourist destination. It certainly feels light years away from the tiny town backpackers visited in the early 1990s. But don't let its popularity dissuade you. *Otavaleños* and *indígena* (indigenous) people from the surrounding villages still wear traditional clothing – women in embroidered white blouses, long wool skirts, *fachalinas* (headcloths), woven belts, canvas sandals and strands of beads; and men in felt hats, blue ponchos and calf-length pants, hair braided in one long strand. And while certainly many struggle to profit from their crafts, Otavaleños are the most commercially successful *indígena* people in Ecuador.

Plaza de Ponchos, the nucleus of the crafts market, is filled every day with vendors selling woolen goods, such as rugs, tapestries, blankets, ponchos, sweaters, scarves, gloves and hats – as well as embroidered blouses, hammocks, carvings, beads, paintings, woven mats and jewelry made from tagua nut (also known as vegetable ivory). But it metastasizes on Saturday, official market day, swelling into adjacent roads and around half of the town center.

Bargaining is expected, especially with multiple purchases. Don't be shy about asking for a deal, but don't be ruthless either. Food stalls set up at the northern end offer vats of chicken or tripe soup boiling on portable stove tops; crispy whole fried fish; scraps of flop-eared suckling pigs served with *mote* (hominy); and scoops of *chicha* (a fermented corn or yuca drink) from plastic buckets.

Between June and August, arrive on Fridays to shop before tour groups choke the passageways.

The markets are not free of pickpockets. While shopping, leave valuables at the hotel and keep your money in a safe spot.

available. A two-day hiking trip to the Intag valley is $120.

Tren Ecuador RAIL
(06-292-8172; www.trenecuador.com; Montalvo & Guayaquil; adult/child $53/37; Wed-Fri 8am-5pm, Sat & Sun from 7am) Now featuring a day-long cultural tour from Otavalo to Salinas, departures are from Thursday to Sunday at 8am. It is recommended to organize trips a few days or a week in advance. The new station rivals Ibarra's brand-spanking new station. At the time of research landslides prevented direct service from Otavalo and trains were departing from nearby San Roque – this was anticipated to be solved by 2018.

Leyton's Tours TOURS
(06-292-2388; www.leytonstoursotavalo.com; Quito & Jaramillo) Leyton's is a full-service tour company offering hiking, horseback riding, rappelling and visits to indigenous communities in the area. It helps that Leyton is a super-friendly guy.

Festivals & Events

Some small surrounding villages still celebrate pre-Columbian rituals that can last up to two weeks.

Fiesta del Yamor CULTURAL
Otavalo's best-known celebration occurs during the first two weeks of September in honor of the fall harvest. An elected queen oversees processions, live music and dancing, and firework displays. Revelers consume copious amounts of *chicha de yamor* – seven varieties of corn are slowly simmered together to produce this unusual nonalcoholic drink (longer-fermented versions are alcoholic).

St John the Baptist Day RELIGIOUS
(Inti Raymi) June 24 is known locally as La Fiesta de San Juan, or by its pagan name, Inti Raymi. It is said that local *indígenas* live and die to celebrate this event, saving money year-round for costumes, food and drink. The festivities continue through June 29, the

Day of St Peter & St Paul. There's a boating regatta on Laguna de San Pablo, as well as celebrations in nearby Ilumán.

Sleeping

Always reserve in advance for the weekend rush, even in budget hotels. The many highly recommended options outside town, often located down rural lanes amid lovely pastoral settings, provide a much different experience and are great places to hole up midweek for quiet and relaxation.

★Hostal Riviera-Sucre GUESTHOUSE **$**
(☎06-292-0241; www.rivierasucre.com; cnr García Moreno No 380 & Roca; s/d/tr/q $25/40/60/75; @ 🛜) The bargain prices have risen some, but we still love Freddy's charming wood-floored, high-ceilinged rooms that surround a delightful inner courtyard with a regal-looking centerpiece fountain, a lovely arupa tree and hammock swings. Prepare a meal or a coffee in the communal kitchen then enjoy it in the flowering garden. Weekend reservations are a necessity.

Hostal El Andariego HOSTAL **$**
(☎62-924-510, 099-594-1029; Bolívar, btwn Salinas & Quiroga; r with/without bathroom $13/11; 🛜) Could you feel more secure than in a *hostal* above the Red Cross office? This new entry to Otavalo is clean, compact and above all, friendly. Smooth cedar floors can be a bit slippery, but guests love the comfy beds and warm showers. The new kitchen and common area make this one a winner, but book early – there are only a couple of rooms.

Hostal Samana HOSTAL **$**
(☎06-292-1458; www.facebook.com/otavalohotels; Roca No 12-08 near Quito; s/d $15/20, $8 per additional person; 🛜) They seem to have put a new layer of spit and polish (and perhaps tiles) on this convenient *hostal*, just a block from the bus terminal. Fifteen rooms feature clean, black-and-white tiled bathrooms, and some have newer flat-screen televisions. This is a nice option and seems more kept-up than some of the older selections in town.

Hostal Santa Fé 2 HOTEL **$**
(☎06-292-0161; www.hotelsantafeotavalo.com; Colón No 507 & Sucre; r per person $15, with breakfast $18; 🛜) Lovers of wooden interiors will find this Southwestern-style place very much to their liking, even if the polished, faux-wood decor shines like plastic flowers. The original, older **Hostel Santa Fé 1** (☎06-292-3640; Roca No 7-34 & García Moreno; r per person $15, with breakfast $18; P 🛜) has smaller rooms, with the bathrooms an especially tight squeeze for the wider-girthed among us.

Cabañas El Rocío GUESTHOUSE **$**
(☎06-2903-776; rocioe@hotmail.com; Barrio San Juan, Los Sigzes & Panamericana; r per person $10; P 🛜) Don't be put off by the faded sign and the Panamericana location: this charming place belies its uninviting exterior and has a range of vaguely alpine rooms and cabins just a short walk from the center of Otavalo. There's a peaceful, well-kept courtyard garden and historic televisions in each of the 15 rooms.

Hostal Valle del Amanecer GUESTHOUSE **$**
(☎06-292-0990; www.hostalvalledelamanecer.com; cnr Roca & Quiroga; r per person incl breakfast with/without bathroom $17/14; 🛜) Very small rooms – couples seeking privacy might want to avoid – surround a welcoming, pebbled courtyard filled with hammocks. There's an on-site restaurant. Bicycle rentals cost $10 per day. While the rooms feel claustrophobic, the courtyard has some lovely coffee plants and avocado trees, and you might spend more time here than in your room. The restaurant is open all day.

★Hostal Doña Esther GUESTHOUSE **$$**
(☎06-292-0739; www.otavalohotel.com; Montalvo No 4-44; s/d/tr $34/49/61; @ 🛜) This small, Dutch-owned colonial-style hotel is cozy, with attractive rooms surrounding a courtyard ornamented with ceramics and ferns. The service is personable; there's a popular book exchange and a recommended restaurant. Just a half-block walk to Plaza Bolívar.

Indio Inn HOTEL **$$**
(Hotel Indio Inn; ☎06-292-2922; www.hotelelindioinn.com; Bolívar No 904 near Calderon; s/d/tr/q $42/64/96/115; P ❄) This former textile workshop is so huge it has two courtyards, as well as a restaurant (La Tulpa) overlooking teeming Calle Bolívar. Neat rooms have flat-screen TVs and clean white-tile bathrooms, while common areas have billiards and foosball tables. You can relax in the Turkish steam room for $15 or boil your troubles away in the hot tub.

Eating

Otavalo has some very good restaurants and some nice dining at lodges outside town; many accept nonguests with reservations.

Keep an eye out for some of the street food, including the snack called *churo:* tiny Andean lake snails that are packed in little baggies with salt, lime and onions, and are sucked out from their shells while on the go.

★Cosecha Coffee Shop CAFE $
(www.lacosechaec.com; Jaramillo near Salinas, Plaza de Ponchos; sandwiches $4-8; ⏰8am-9pm; 📶) Owned by a young American expat, this contemporary cafe with Santa Fe-like adobe walls and minimalistic design wouldn't look out of place in a cool outer-borough NYC neighborhood (it even serves bagels!). Sandwiches on homemade focaccia bread are made with local ingredients, and the cappuccinos are the best in town.

Oraibi VEGETARIAN $
(cnr Sucre & Colón; mains $5-11; ⏰10am-8pm Sun-Fri, 7am-8:30pm Sat; 🖉) Right in the heart of town you'll find this charming vegetarian oasis in the courtyard of an old hacienda. The menu consists of pizza, sandwiches, salads and tortillas, while the decor is rustic-chic. Outside there's a spacious garden complete with white tablecloths, plenty of shade and cool fossilized seashell ashtrays.

Yolanda's Chicha de Yamor ECUADORIAN $
(Auntentica Yamor de Yolanda Cabrera; Sucre & Mora; mains $2.50-4; ⏰10:30am-7pm daily Sep, Sat & Sun only Oct-Aug) Yolanda Cabrera has become famous for delicious local fare such as *tortillas de maíz* (corn tortillas), *empanaditas* (Spanish pies) and the local favorite of *fritada* (fried chunks of pork, served with *mote*). Of course, the real attraction is her *chicha de yamor* (a fermented corn drink), which is stirred out back in bubbling cauldrons over smoky fires. Look for the yellow sidewalk sign.

Daily Grind CAFE $
(cnr Montalvo & Sucre, Plaza Bolívar; food $3-4, drinks $2-5; ⏰8:30am-9pm) Belly up to this corner coffee-bar and watch the action unfold on Plaza Bolívar. Inject your central nervous system with an espresso or downshift with a Baileys, mojito, caipirinha or piña colada. In addition to bagels, you can even order up a peanut-butter-and-jelly sandwich (because they go with everything).

Shanandoah Pie Shop BAKERY $
(Plaza de Ponchos; pie slices $2; ⏰10am-9pm; 🖉) Like the pies, the shopowner Aide can be a bit crusty. Although Shanandoah isn't a salubrious-looking shop, the homemade fruit-flavored pies are the best in Otavalo (39 years in business tells the tale), and there is ice cream on offer for those with hearty appetites.

Oro Mar SEAFOOD $
(Salinas near Sucre, ½ block off Plaza de Ponchos; mains $5-11; ⏰7am-6pm) Feeling landlocked? The blue color scheme, maritime-themed wall paintings and more importantly the huge portions (you can order half-size) of *cazuelas, encebollados,* fried fish and mixed rice dishes will all have you in something of a coastal mood. For thrifty but hungry travelers, economical combos ($3 to $5) are on the menu.

Gran Chifa CHINESE $
(Morales btwn Jaramillo & Sucre; mains $3.50-7; ⏰noon-10pm) Gran-sized portions of good Ecuadorian versions of Chinese fare, plus a small 'fusion' section of street food like *salchipapas* (sausage and fries) are served up in a sparsely decorated, excessively lighted second-floor dining room. Try and grab the window-side table for people-watching.

Santa Marita SUPERMARKET $
(Atahualpa near Calderón) The best modern supermarket in town.

★Cafe Fussion INTERNATIONAL $$
(Sucre near Quiroga; mains $8-14; ⏰10am-10pm; 🖉) Chef Javier, who studied the culinary arts in Peru, painted this place in Caribbean pastels, and the same artful imagination goes into his recipes: smoked ribs with ginger, beef a la pimienta cooked in a reduction of white wine and balsamic vinaigrette, and an array of pasta and vegetarian platters. Hungry for breakfast? How about rainforest crepes in passionfruit sauce?

★Sumac INTERNATIONAL $$
(☎099-423-7153; Quito No 817 near Sucre; 4-course meal $12; ⏰Tue-Sat noon-10pm) 🍃 Ecuadorian chef Jorge David Quilumbaqui, trained in French cuisine in Quito, presents artfully plated meat and fish dishes, as well as delicious desserts, using locally sourced ingredients. He's recently moved from Cotacachi to Otavalo and revised the menu, so expect some even tastier treats.

SISA INTERNATIONAL $$
(☎06-292-5624; Calderón No 4-9 near Sucre; mains $5-12; ⏰9am-10pm; 📶) An attractive three-story complex: the ground floor has

local handicrafts, the second floor sandwiches and the top floor standard international fare, plus up-to-date live folk and jazz in the window-stage on Fridays and Saturdays. Rockers of a certain age will dig the publicity shots of musicians from Yanni to Ray Charles, and from Andean icons to Dire 'Streets.'

Árbol de Montalvo PIZZA $$

(Montalvo No 4-44; mains $9-12; ⏰6-9pm Mon-Thu, noon-10pm Fri-Sun; ✍) Wander back of the Hostal Doña Esther (p105) for Otavalo's only wood-fired oven pizza. Tasty, certainly, and the best in town no doubt, though crusts are cracker-thin and big eaters might need two to do the job. Also on the menu are organic salads, seasonal vegetables and hearty Ecuadorian-inspired soups. Bonuses include a warm canela-honey aperitif and homemade *aji* salsa.

Quino SEAFOOD $$

(Roca near Montalvo; mains $5-9; ⏰noon-9:30pm Mon-Sat) This popular eatery next to Hostal Santa Fé 1 (p105) offers up excellent seafood dishes within its dimly lit walls, but not if you're in a rush: all main courses are cooked from scratch, so expect to wait around half an hour.

Drinking & Nightlife

Cava Caran MICROBREWERY

(☎099-189-7959; www.caran.ec; Plaza de Ponchos, Jaramillo near Salinas; ⏰5pm-2am Wed-Fri, from 10am Wed & Sat) This newly opened funky little brewpub, whose magic formula relies on Ibarra's deep underground springs, is a breath of fresh air on the Otavalo scene. White adobe walls, intricate murals and minimalist wood furniture make this a cool hangout for locals and tourists alike, and every couple of weeks there's a 'rave Andino' to get your spirits flowing.

Some typical bar food is there for picking, and every Saturday the pub hosts a small market of organic producers.

Entertainment

Peña La Jampa LIVE MUSIC

(cnr Av 31 de Octubre & Panamericana; ⏰7pm-3am Fri & Sat) A long-running favorite with locals. Head to this club for a mix of salsa, merengue, *rock en español* and *folklórica* (folk music); usually doesn't get started until after 11pm.

Amauta LIVE MUSIC

(Morales No 5-11 & Jaramillo; ⏰8pm-4am Fri & Sat) Live Andean music, generally after 10pm, is performed at this basement space in the center of town.

Shopping

La Casa de Bandolin MUSICAL INSTRUMENTS

(Instrumentos Ayala; ☎06-292-6951; Bolívar btwn Ordóñez & Quito; ⏰9am-5pm) Santiago Ayala has been making professional-grade instruments for his fellow musicians for a long while, and it's worth a stroll down from the re-sellers on Sucre to see a real artisan in action. His business card even shows you how to tune a guitar, charango or mandolin!

Getting There & Away

Otavalo is well connected to Quito as well as being a major transport hub for smaller towns and villages in the northern highlands. The busy **bus terminal**, basically a parking lot, is on Atahualpa and Ordóñez, conveniently located only a few blocks from the Plaza de Ponchos.

To get to Tulcán and the Colombian border, travel to Ibarra and change buses there.

Old local buses, with fares of roughly $1 per hour of travel, go south to San Pablo del Lago (20 minutes) and Araque (30 minutes). Cooperativa Imbaburapac has buses to Ilumán (30 minutes), Agato (one hour) and San Pablo del Lago (15 minutes). Transportes Otavalo has 7:30am, 10:30am and 2pm departures for Intag (bus sign will read 'Santa Rosa de Pucara'). Buses for destinations except Quito leave roughly every 15 to 20 minutes.

Taxis are cheap, plentiful and easy to flag down. Any in-town trip is $1.50. The following

BUSES FROM OTAVALO

DESTINATION	COST ($)	DURATION
Apuela	2.50	2½hr
Cayambe	0.90	45min
Cotacachi	0.35	15min
Ibarra	0.55	30min
Quito	2	2hr

are a few sample fares: Apuela ($50), Ambuqui ($25), Cayambe ($12), Ibarra ($10), Quinchuqui ($4), Tulcán ($50); haciendas around Laguna de San Pablo ($6). To the Mariscal Sucre airport outside Quito, it's $55 to $60, and $70 to anywhere in downtown Quito.

Around Otavalo

06

Green-checkered farmland creeps up the steep flanks of the mountains surrounding Otavalo, a rewarding combination for visitors seeking heart-pounding exercise and long views. Hikers shouldn't miss the spectacular Lagunas de Mojanda, southwest of Otavalo.

Hidden haciendas, once-grandiose epicenters of colonial society, now invite travelers to enjoy their sprawling grounds. Then there's Ecuador's largest lake, **Laguna de San Pablo**, a more domesticated setting with paddleboats and groomed shoreline hotels. We've heard rave reviews about horseback riding and horse therapy at German-owned **4 Volcanoes** (www.4volcanoes.com; San Pablo del Lago).

Northeast of Otavalo, the villages of **Peguche**, **Agato** and **Ilumán** are known for their weaving workshops; Ilumán is also notable for its 120-member shaman association. Only 6km further, Atuntaqui is worth visiting solely for the **El Museo Fábrica Textil Imbabura** (06-253-0240; Abdon Calderon cnr Junin, La Parroquia de Andrade Marín; adult/child $3/1.50; 9am-5pm Wed-Fri, 10am-6pm Sat & Sun). A convenient way to explore these villages is with a tour operator in Otavalo, as tour prices are not much more than a long taxi rental. Most are also easily reachable by public bus.

Sights

Tahuantinsuyo Weaving Workshop ARTS CENTER

(099-9574-567, 06-2690-195; www.miguelandrango.weebly.com; Main Rd, Agato) Jose Rafael Maldonado, Miguel Andrango's son-in-law, now runs the day-to-day operations of this internationally famous weaving family business, in its fourth generation of creating fabrics entirely by hand (except for that one spindle made of old bicycle parts). You can see the entire workshop for the cost of a donation, but you may also stick around and learn the process for $25 per day. Here in Agato, it's old-school all the way. It's best to call in advance before visiting.

You can walk uphill 2km from the Peguche waterfall; just follow the cobblestone road. At the top of the hill, where the main road comes through, turn left and look for the workshop sign. Cooperativa Imbaburapac buses (red and blue in color) go through Peguche en route to Agato from Otavalo. You can sit it for longer multiday workshops if it suits your fancy. The Andrango family also sells their product at the Hacienda Cusín.

Sleeping

★ **Hacienda Cusín** HACIENDA $$$

(06-291-8316; www.haciendacusin.com; s/d/tr/q $128/152/195/195, ste $195-427, set lunch/dinner $27-30;) This fairy-tale 17th-century hacienda is on the southern outskirts of San Pablo del Lago, 10km from Otavalo. Tall cedar trees shade the garden paths linking the cozy cottages and gracefully aging buildings. Impressive carved wooden doors, European oil paintings and South American textiles and antiques create museum-like interiors. You may feel, though, like you're in a creepy old horror film.

Guests can play squash, ride horses or bikes, lounge in the reading library (every room also comes equipped with its own collection of books), then cozy up to the bar, where a roaring fire cuts the highland chill. The formal, proper dining room (check out the oil canvas depicting a severed head) serves delicious meals made with organic fruits and vegetables grown in the impressive on-site garden. Packages offer everything from overnight horseback-riding expeditions and Spanish-language lessons to weaving courses. Wi-fi can be frustratingly spotty (as in most non-urban areas, let's be honest).

Hacienda Pinsaquí HACIENDA $$$

(06-294-6116; www.haciendapinsaqui.com; Panamericana Norte Km 5; s/d/tr/q incl breakfast $112/144/155/175, set meal $27; P) Hacienda Pinsaquí offers a taste of old-world Ecuador, housed as it is in a former colonial textile hacienda. Wooden-beamed ceilings, grand grounds and refined decor, including antique French washbasins and gaunt portraits, channel the past. Some of the 28 rooms and suites have colonial-era bathtubs and fireplaces, keeping with seventh-generation owner Patricio Saa's theme of pristine preservation.

Constructed in 1790, parts of the property survived the disastrous earthquake of 1857, and the whole place oozes history: Simón

Around Otavalo

Bolívar used to stay here on his route north to Bogotá. The peace treaty ensuring Ecuador's nationhood was signed here. Check out the chapel or the cozy bar, an ideal place to sip *canelazo* (sugarcane alcohol – aguardiente with hot cider and cinnamon). Or get outdoors and go horseback riding astride a mount from the renowned stables.

Las Palmeras CABIN $$$
(☎06-266-8067; www.laspalmerasinn.com; San Jose de Quichinche; r/ste from $97/116; 📶) Offers 16 colorful cottages set in rural hills, with cozy rooms furnished in colonial style (older rooms have a neat antechamber and porches). Rent a bike, go horseback riding, take Spanish lessons or just enjoy the scenery. It also features billiards and ping-pong tables. Meals at the restaurant are excellent.

Cabañas del Lago CABIN $$$
(☎06-291-8108; www.cabanasdellago.com.ec; Araque, San Pablo del Lago; cabañas $155-200; 📶) Cabañas del Lago caters to families (mainly Ecuadorian), with 26 vaguely Polynesian cabins of various sizes and lots of activities. It has mini-golf, a playground with rocking horses, jet skis and all manner of water sports on the east side of the lake (water sports only on the weekend, though). The on-site restaurant fuels the fun.

Getting There & Away

San Miguel has a regular bus service to and from Otavalo. But some of the lodges are a bit off the beaten track and require a taxi if you don't have your own vehicle. Taxis are cheap, but these places are especially recommended if you have your own transport.

Lagunas de Mojanda

A crumbling cobbled road leads high into the *páramo* to three turquoise lakes set like gemstones into the hills. Located 17km south of Otavalo, the area acquired protected status in 2002 and has since become a popular spot for Sunday family outings. If you've come to camp, set up on the south side of the biggest lake, **Laguna Grande**, or in the basic stone refuge (bring a sleeping bag and food). Otavalo tour companies can arrange kayaking trips here. But hiking around the sparkling waters is what seems to draw most here.

Activities

Hiking the steep path up the jagged peak of Fuya Fuya, an extinct volcano (4263m), takes 1½ to two hours and begins close to the taxi drop-off. A shorter, similar climb goes up **Cerro Tourichupa** (3950m).

Another highly recommend option, one that avoids steep ascents and descents, is the circuit that starts out along one side of Laguna Grande and then turns down to Laguna Chiquita and around Cerro Negro (4260m) to a look-out point (4000m), then around to the refuge (with Laguna Negra in view) and then back to the road along Laguna Grande.

Just past Casa Mojanda on the road up to Lagunas de Mojanda is the well-signposted trailhead for **Cascada de Taxopamba**. It's about a half-hour walk to these pretty falls and lagoon in a beautifully pristine setting.

Sleeping

★La Luna GUESTHOUSE $$

(☎099-315-6082, 099-829-4913; www.lalunaecuador.info; camping $8, dm $14, s with/without bathroom $30/22, d with/without bathroom $47/38; P ᯤ) Located 4.5km south of Otavalo on the long uphill to Lagunas de Mojanda, La Luna has million-dollar views for budget-minded travelers. Guests dine in the cozy main house, where the fireplace is the nexus of evening activity. Showers are hot and two of the doubles have a private bathroom and fireplace. Lunchboxes can be arranged for hikes.

Rose Cottage CABIN $$

(Hosteria Rose Cottage; ☎099-772-8115; www.rosecottageecuador.com; dm $14, r from $40, s/d without bathroom $16/35; P ᯤ) If you're looking to combine budget accommodation with spectacular scenery, Rose Cottage is a great choice. Three kilometers from Cotacachi up a steep driveway, a wide range of accommodations allow you to enjoy the Andean scenery while still being close to Otavalo. Library, mirador, and even a 'zip line' made from an old tire feature alongside an antiquated playground.

★Casa Mojanda CABIN $$$

(☎06-304-9253, 098-033-5108; www.casamojanda.com; Via Lagunas de Mojanda; s/d/tr/q incl breakfast $122/159/183/195, fireplace +$10; P ᯤ) On the road to Lagunas de Mojanda is this lovely inn with gorgeous views of steep Andean farmland. Cheerful adobe cottages are equipped with electric heaters and hot-water bathrooms; some have fireplaces. Slip into the outdoor hot tub after a day of hiking or horseback riding. One lovely cabin is a dedicated library/den, and one is perfect for families.

Meals are made from fresh organic garden ingredients, and the owners (Ecuadorian, but former longtime Brooklyn, NY, residents) are knowledgeable and friendly.

Getting There & Away

Taxis between Otavalo and lodges in the Lagunas de Mojanda area cost about $12 each way and will wait 60 to 90 minutes; after that an hourly rate kicks in. Otavalo tour companies offer guided hikes that include transportation. To reach any accommodation, it's a $5 taxi from Otavalo.

The La Luna guesthouse has excellent, detailed hiking maps of the area.

Peguche

In this small and sleepy village known for its weaving, traditional and modern methods of weaving coexist – look out for clotheslines draped with handmade, dyed wool drying in the breeze and listen for the whirring sound of electric looms.

Sights

Cascadas de Peguche WATERFALL

(By donation) Most visitors head out this way to see Cascadas de Peguche, a series of falls sacred to locals – visitors should stay away during Inti Raymi, June's festival of the sun, when men conduct ritual cleansing baths. It's a developed site and the cobblestone street marking the entrance has stalls selling handicrafts, drinks and snacks. You can see some nice birds along the trails, too.

Sign in at the registration desk (free, but donations are requested) and follow the short path to the hot springs, a small bridge below the main falls or two viewpoints on either side of the river.

Sleeping

Hostal Aya Huma HOSTEL $

(☎06-269-0333; www.ayahuma.com; Calle Los Corazos & Calle Ñan Chasquis; s/d/tr/q $23/37/48/60, camping per person $4; P) Abutting the railroad tracks four long blocks from the Panamericana, Aya Huma's office looks like a small-town railway station. Rooms are basic but clean, and the cafe serves hearty breakfasts and good vegetarian food. Best to make reservations; otherwise it might be locked up with no one home. This third-generation family business has nice perks like a wood-fired sauna.

The hostal is 2.5km north of Otavalo, along the railroad tracks.

La Casa Sol HOTEL $$

(☎06-269-0500; www.lacasasol.com; Cascada de Peguche; s/d/ste incl breakfast $59/69/99) Up a steep driveway next to the turnoff for the entrance to the waterfall, this pastel-colored tranquil oasis features terracotta walls and Spanish-tile roofs. Rooms are homey and simply furnished. Most rooms have fireplaces, some have kitchens and balconies with sweet views, so shop around for the best one. A nice option just steps from the falls.

Shopping

Two of the handicraft shops are right on the main plaza, and the guitar man is just down the road.

El Gran Condor ARTS & CRAFTS

(www.artesaniaelgrancondor.com; Main Plaza, Calle Peguche; ⏲8am-7pm Mon-Sat, 11am-6pm Sun) On the central plaza of Peguche, El Gran Condor is the place for textile fanatics who didn't find what they wanted in Otavalo. The shop sells high-quality textiles made locally, including sweaters, scarves and wall hangings. Call ahead to arrange for demonstrations of dyeing and weaving techniques.

Taller de Instrumentos Andinos-Nañda Mañachi MUSIC, HANDICRAFTS

Across from the basketball courts, Jose Luis Pichamba crafts traditional musical instruments, including panpipes, drums, and *charangos,* the 10-stringed mandolin-like instruments traditionally made from armadillo shells (but now made from woods like cedar). Jose's four decades as a professional musician, making instruments for his colleagues, means you'll get a quality item. If you ask politely and you'll get a one-song demo, too!

Follow the road north from the main square about three blocks to reach Jose's workshop.

Tejidos Mimahuasi ARTS & CRAFTS

A demonstration loom sits in the front room, but the real magic lies in the six rooms full of different weavings, spread across two levels. Just across the street from El Gran Condor (p111), and not always well attended.

Getting There & Away

Cooperativa Imbaburapac buses (red and blue in color) go through Peguche en route to Agato from Otavalo. Look for the buses with 'Cascadas' on the front-window signboard.

Cotacachi

☎06 / POP 17,100 / ELEV 2418M

Cotacachi is best known for its leather and its main street, Calle 10 de Agusto, which is lined with shops stocked with good-value leather jackets, luggage, wallets, gloves and shoes. But its appeal, known to an increasing number of North American retirees (you'll notice the white people with white hair and white hats) who have snatched up real estate and built communities of condo-like structures, is its easygoing tranquility, even sleepiness. The feeling is infectious. Relatively prosperous, architecturally uncluttered and with Laguna de Cuicocha and Volcán Cotacachi close by, it would surely draw more travelers if there were more accommodation options.

Sights

Museo de las Culturas MUSEUM

(Garcia Moreno No 13-41; ⏲9am-5pm Mon-Fri, 2-5pm Sat, 10am-1pm Sun) FREE Located in the neoclassical former municipal palace, several small galleries present the ethnohistory of the region, from 8500 BC through colonial and republican periods. It's worth visiting for the indigenous religious festival costumes and photos. Next door to the Land of the Sun hotel.

Sleeping

Land of the Sun HISTORIC HOTEL $$

(☎06-291-6009; cnr Garcia Moreno & Sucre; s/d incl breakfast per person $54/66, mains $4-10; P@🛜) This attractive colonial hotel in the heart of town has an idyllic courtyard around which appealing, wood-floored rooms are arranged; the best have balconies with views of the old convent. Additional amenities include a sauna and an excellent courtyard restaurant (open 6:30am to 8pm).

Note that there are two 'Moreno' streets in Cotacachi; this one is Garcia Moreno.

★ Hostería La Mirage HOTEL **$$$**
(☎06-291-5237; www.mirage.com.ec; 10 de Agosto Prolongacion; r/ste incl breakfast & dinner $295/350; P) One of Ecuador's finest hotels lies beyond an unpaved entry road, past iron gates, white cupolas and columned entrances where peacocks stroll the green. This place is hard to beat if you're looking for serious pampering in a beautiful Andean setting. The decor is Louis XIV-exquisite, with original paintings, canopy beds, flower bouquets and luxurious linens.

If you can pull yourself away from your room, head to the indoor swimming pool and decadent spa. Tennis, bird-watching and mountain biking are offered. The stylish restaurant guarantees a memorable experience in international fusion.

To arrive, turn left on 10 de Agosto on the Prolongacion (confusing, we know).

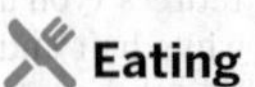

Eating

Mercado Jatuk Cem 'Cotachi' MARKET **$**
(10 de Agosto near Salinas; mains $2-4.50; 6am-4pm) The stalls at this outdoor covered food court serve everything from *marisquerías* to *parrillas* (seafood to BBQ steak). The food is as good as the tourist-oriented white-tablecloth places in town and costs a third of the price. Located next to the bus terminal and the fruit, vegetable and flower market; some places stay open until 7pm.

Cafe Rio Intag CAFE **$**
(Imbabura No 863, Parque San Francisco; sandwiches $2; Sun-Thu 8am-10pm;) Organically grown Intag Valley coffee, cakes and small sandwiches are served at this cool university-like hangout spot with comfy couches and a nifty downstairs nook. Check the noticeboard outside for cultural activities happening in the area.

The Pastry Shop BAKERY **$**
(Plaza San Francisco; $2-3; Mon-Sat 9am-7pm) Next to Rio Intag on the plaza, Robin Lea delights her expat clientele with piping-hot cinnamon rolls and scrumptious carrot cake, among other oven-made treats.

Information

Sunday is market day (not nearly the same scale as Otavalo) and nearly all shops will offer discounts if you pay in cash. There are several ATMs including a Banco Guayaquil on Parque San Francisco at the corner of Rocafuerte.

Getting There & Away

Cotacachi is west of the Panamericana and 15km north of Otavalo. From Otavalo, 6 de Julio and Transportes Cotacachi buses leave every 20 minutes or so ($0.35, 20 minutes) for Cotacachi's bus terminal at the far end of town. You can flag down this bus along the Panamericana if you're coming from Peguche. A taxi between the two towns is $6.

There are three daily buses from here to the Intag Valley (Santa Rosa/Apuela).

Reserva Ecológica Cotacachi-Cayapas

This **reserve** FREE protects a huge swath of the western Andes. The range of altitudes, from Volcán Cotacachi to the lowland rainforests, means tremendous biodiversity. Travel from the highland to lowland areas is nearly impossible due to vegetation density, so most visit the lowlands from San Miguel on Río Cayapas or the highlands from Cotacachi: just before arriving at Laguna de Cuicocha, a rangers' booth serves as the entrance to the reserve (the road to Intag passes by here).

Less than hour's drive east are the popular **Chachimbiro hot springs**, a Disney-like complex with a variety of pools to suit all tastes and some spectacular views. A round-trip taxi from Cotacachi with a stay of several hours is $50 (figure on $10 per hour). Further west of here in the high *páramo* is **Laguna de Piñán**, which has mesmerizing vistas and hiking trails – contact Runa Tupari (p103) in Otavalo for organized trips.

Sights

Laguna de Cuicocha LAKE
Head 18km west from Cotacachi and you'll come upon this eerily still, dark lagoon cradled in a collapsed volcanic crater at 3100m. Some 3km wide and 200m deep, the lagoon features two mounded islands that shot up in later eruptions. The islands look like the backs of two guinea pigs, hence the name: '*cuicocha*' means 'guinea pig lake' in Kichwa. A short path leads up from the parking area near the entrance to several viewpoints.

It's definitely worth doing the around-the-lake **hike**. Referred to as **Sendero Las Orquideas** – it begins just past the final viewpoint – it follows the ridgeline high above the lake shore. Hummingbirds feed on bright flowers, and the occasional condor circles over the glassy expanse. The 14km circuit can take anywhere from 3½ to five hours depending on your fitness level. If the clouds clear, you'll see Volcán Cotacachi.

Boats for hire make short trips around the islands. The Hosteria offers a 25-minute trip for $3.50.

Sleeping & Eating

Hostería Cuicocha GUESTHOUSE $$
(☎06-301-7218, 06-301-7219; www.cuicocha.org; r per person incl breakfast & dinner $55, mains $4-9) Remodeled and refurbished in 2015–16, there are beautiful lagoon and mountain views from three of the six rooms in this brick complex, which also houses a restaurant open to the general public and a rarely staffed information desk. It can feel rather desolate at night if alone (especially with – gasp – no wi-fi). Room rate includes boat tour.

Getting There & Away

In Cotacachi, *camionetas* can be hired to take you to Laguna de Cuicocha (one-way $15, round-trip $25, including a half-hour wait). Or you can hop on a Transportes Cotacachi bus to Quiroga, only 10 minutes midway between Otavalo and Cotachi, and grab a taxi from the plaza there for a few dollars less.

Ibarra

☎06 / POP 139,721 / ELEV 2225M

More than any other northern population, the largest city north of Quito feels *urban*, and moves to the everyday rhythms of its mix of Afro-Ecuadorians (each October 8 the city hosts a large Afrodescendientes festival), *indígenas* and mestizos. Known as *la ciudad blanca* (the white city), most of the buildings have been turned into ordinary shops and there's a bustling commercial atmosphere. Several beautiful plazas with towering palms and baroque churches lend it a distinctively sophisticated feel.

Volcán Imbabura looms impressively nearby and Laguna de Yahuarcocha (in Kichwa it means 'Lake of Blood' for the nearly 30,000 Caranqui warriors killed by the forces of Incan emperor Huayna Capac) is only 3km northeast. Today, it's joggers, cyclists and paddleboaters who occupy the lakeshore. Throw in a couple of small, interesting museums, a worthwhile train journey, good cafes and proximity to Otavalo and other *indígena* villages, and you might wonder why the tourism infrastructure is fairly lacking.

Sights & Activities

Centro Cultural Ibarra MUSEUM
(cnr Sucre & Oviedo; ⏰9:30am-6:30pm Tue-Fri, 10am-4pm Sat & Sun) FREE A small, impressive collection of 14th- to 19th-century religious paintings and archaeological galleries featuring prehistoric ceramics and gold artifacts from Pimampiro. Text in Spanish and English.

Museo Arqueológico y Etnográfico Atahualpa MUSEUM
(García Moreno & Sucre, Teatro Sucre, 2nd fl; ⏰8am-12:30pm & 2-5:30pm Mon-Fri, 9:30am-5pm Sat) FREE Several small galleries with fascinating pre-Columbian artifacts unearthed in the area. The majority of objects – including ceramic ceremonial pieces and sculptures and armaments, as well as intentionally deformed skulls – are from the Caranqui, who were ascendant before the Inca.

Just one block west from Parque Pedro Moncayo.

Parque La Merced PLAZA
(Peñaherrera) Also known as Peñaherrera, the city's main plaza was built at the beginning of the 19th century. The main feature of the **Iglesia de la Merced** (Sánchez y Cienfuentes, Parque La Merced) is a gold-leaf-covered altar for the Virgen de la Merced, patron saint of the armed forces. The church holds a special mass in remembrance of the victims and survivors of the devastating 1868 earthquake.

Parque Pedro Moncayo PLAZA
This gorgeous palm-filled plaza is dominated by the baroque-influenced **cathedral** (García Moreno, Parque Moncayo). The altars are covered in gold leaf, and Troya's paintings of the 12 apostles adorn the pillars. The park itself is named after locally born Pedro Moncayo (1807–88), a journalist and diplomat.

Iglesia de Santo Domingo CHURCH
At the north end of Bolívar you'll find the quaint **Parque Santo Domingo**. The Dominican church behind this small park houses *La Virgen del Rosario*, a painting by famous artist Diego de Robles, on its altar.

Galería Luís Potosí GALLERY
(☎06-293-2056; Parque Central; ⏰8am-6pm) FREE San Antonio, a small village near the

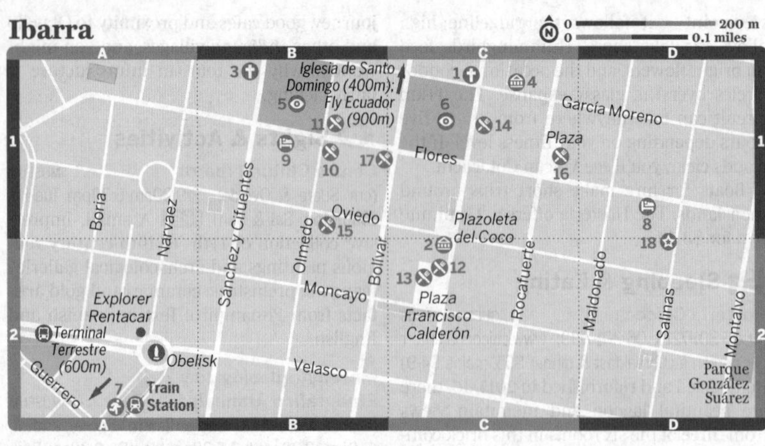

Ibarra

Sights

1 Catedral de Ibarra ... C1
2 Centro Cultural Ibarra ... C2
3 Iglesia de la Merced ... B1
4 Museo Arqueológico y Etnográfico Atahualpa ... C1
5 Parque La Merced ... B1
6 Parque Pedro Moncayo ... C1

Activities, Courses & Tours

7 Tren Ecuador ... A2

Sleeping

8 Backpackers Hostel ... D1
9 Hotel Barcelona ... B1

Eating

10 Ana de Nuñez ... B1
11 Comedores ... B1
12 Donde el Argentino ... C2
13 El Coyote ... C2
14 El Quinde Café ... C1
15 Heladería Rosalía Suárez ... B1
16 La Casa de Frida Bistro-Cafe ... C1
17 Olor a Cafe ... B1

Entertainment

18 Café Arte ... D2

larger city of Ibarra, specializes in woodcarvings. The most renowned gallery here is Galería Luís Potosí. Potosí has achieved fame throughout Ecuador and abroad. Ask to see the workspace he shares with other woodworkers when you visit the gallery.

Fly Ecuador ADVENTURE SPORTS
(☎06-295-3297; www.flyecuador.com.ec; Rafael Troya No 5121 near cnr Jose Vinueza, Parque Avión; per person $67) For breathtaking bird's-eye panoramas of the surrounding countryside, try tandem paragliding from one of the nearby hills. Experienced instructors also offer multiday training courses for those interested in soloing.

Festivals & Events

Fiesta de Los Lagos FIESTA
During the last week of September, Ibarra celebrates this 'festival of the lakes' with a massive parade, folkloric dances, the coronation of Miss Ibarra, and (perhaps) a bit of drinking. The 'Pregón,' or opening parade, occupies much of the city. Dates of the festival vary by year.

Sleeping

While you'll find a couple of decent budget options in town, the nicer accommodations are near the Panamericana west of Ibarra. They're often booked in advance, particularly on weekends and during the last two weeks of September during Ibarra's lively annual fiesta.

Backpackers Hostel HOSTEL $
(☎099-657-3989; Flores btwn Salinas & Maldonado; s/d/tr/q $10/15/24/30) Something new in Ibarra! We like this low-cost option with a small shared kitchen, reliable wi-fi, nicely tiled rooms, modern bunks and flat-screen televisions. The house is 150-plus years old but Nady's attention to her guests is 21st

century. A beautiful courtyard is next to the small shared kitchen. Best low-cost option in town.

Hotel Barcelona HOTEL $

(☎06-260-0871; suarezmagdalena@yahoo.es; Flores No 8-51 near Sánchez y Cifuentes; r per person with/without bathroom $10/8;) Ignore the inauspicious-looking lobby of this whitewashed three-story hotel overlooking Parque La Merced. You'll likely be pleasantly surprised by the large, wood-floored rooms with high ceilings; park-facing rooms get lots of light, plus early-morning noise. Expect some quirks like the bathroom light switch in the shower. There's a nice interior courtyard for sipping a coffee and such.

★ **Hostería Cananvalle** CABIN $$

(☎098-260-9132; www.hosteria-cananvalle.com; s/d incl breakfast $50/60-70, family cabin $130;) Literally on the other side of the tracks, 5km from downtown, this family-owned working farm sits on a bucolic property with canyon and mountain views. There's a main house covered in creeping vines and several stand-alone cabins with Spanish tile roofs and adobe walls. Some of the food served is grown here; they make their own delicious bread and coffee.

Hostería Chorlaví HISTORIC HOTEL $$$

(☎06-293-2222; www.haciendachorlavi.com; Panamericana Sur 4.5; s/d/tr/villa incl breakfast $105/130/180/260;) Weekenders flock to this classic converted hacienda to enjoy the solar-heated swimming pool and mini-golf. It's a charming place, with rooms stuffed full of antiques, yet remains pleasantly understated. It's less peaceful on Saturdays when live music draws Otavalo tour groups and shoppers. The hotel is signed off to the right 4.5km south of Ibarra on the Panamericana.

Eating

There are a surprising number of nice cafes in the center, and an interesting selection on Plaza Francisco Calderón, on Calle Sucre. You can find a few 24-hour *chifas* (Chinese restaurants) south of Flores between Olmedo and Sucre.

Ibarra also seems to be home to the most handmade ice-cream shops (the famous *helado de paila*) in all of Ecuador.

Heladería Rosalía Suárez ICE CREAM $

(Los Legitimos; Oviedo No 7-82; cone/cup $0.95/1.75; 7am-6pm) In 1897, Rosalía Suárez discovered the best ice-cream had no cream at all. Her shop has been a sensation ever since. Now run by her grandson, it serves *helados de paila,* sorbets made from pure tropical fruit juices *(guanábana, naranjilla, maracuyá)* and egg whites, stirred with a wooden spoon in a copper bowl *(paila),* cooled on a bed of straw.

A dueling ice-cream shop with the very same name run by another Suárez descendant is directly across the street. This one is called 'Los Legitimos' for a reason – more distant cousins have opened two other 'Bermejita' shops down the block, discreetly using the family name, too.

Comedores ECUADORIAN $

(Olmedo & Parque La Merced) A half-dozen or so *comedores* and stalls selling the same collection of specialty sweets are sandwiched into little slots in the brick fort on the east side of Parque La Merced. Most prominently displayed is *arrope de mora* (thick blackberry syrup) and *nogadas* (caramel nougat).

Ana de Nuñez SWEETS $

(cnr Flores & Olmedo; 7:30am-9:30pm) A small shop stuffed to the gills with signature Ibarra treats such as *nogadas* (sweetened treats made from walnuts, sugar, milk and egg whites) and *arrope de mora* (blackberry syrup mixed with water or spirits). It's been in business since 1954 (Victor is the third-generation manager) and is so popular it has two other locations in town.

El Coyote MEXICAN $

(Plaza Francisco Calderón; mains $5-8; noon-10pm Mon-Thu, to midnight Fri & Sat;) Heat lamps, as well as tequila, warm things up when dining after dark at this spot with only outdoor plaza seating. The tasty, standard Mexican meals, such as burritos, tacos, enchiladas and fajitas, are enhanced by walls of cartoon drawings of classic rock and pop stars. Go upstairs for a drink at the sister site, **Freaky Monkey**.

El Quinde Café CAFE $

(Sucre btwn Flores & Garcia Moreno, Parque Pedro Moncayo; mains $2-2.50; 11am-9pm Mon-Fri;) Run by a husband-and-wife team, this charming little spot on Parque Pedro Moncayo serves locally grown coffee, and cakes and pastries. The small second-floor perch is a good place to settle in with a book or laptop. New-agey without being pretentious, it also features the prettiest bathroom in all of Ecuador.

La Casa de Frida Bistro-Cafe CAFE $$
(☎098-883-0353; Rocafuerte near Flores, Plaza San Agustin; ⊙5-10pm Mon-Sat) Sandwiches, nachos, coffee and mixed drinks for the most discerning paletes are all served in this comfy cafe based on the theme of 'all things Frida.' Kahlo movie posters, children's books, and walls painted with the Mexican artist's more memorable quotes make for an inspired and relaxed atmosphere for Ibarra's intelligentsia (and *you*, of course).

Donde el Argentino ARGENTINE $$
(☎099-945-9004; Plaza Francisco Calderón; mains $5-18; ⊙noon-9pm Tue-Sat, until 4pm Sun) Transport yourself south in this matchbox-sized cafe packed with ambience. Go for the excellent steaks and fries. Outdoor tables on the square expand the space on sunny days.

Olor a Cafe CAFE $$
(cnr Flores & Bolívar; mains $9-15; ⊙8am-8pm Mon-Sat, until noon Sun; 📶) Downtown Ibarra's literary hangout is housed in a stately colonial-era building, and its operators claim it is the top spot to pop *the* question (a running tally is posted). One wall is lined with highbrow literary fiction for sale. Burgers, Thai chicken with soy pasta, and filet mignon, as well as sandwiches, coffee drinks and pastries are on the menu.

Entertainment

Café Arte LIVE MUSIC, FILM
(Salinas No 5-43; ⊙5pm-midnight Thu, until 2am Fri & Sat) Surprisingly, one of the better live-music venues in Ecuador is here in Ibarra. It hosts bands from as far away as Cuba and Spain. The music ranges from jazz and flamenco to rock. Shows start Fridays and Saturdays around 10pm. Films, dance lessons and art shows are also on the program.

Getting There & Away

Ibarra's modern bus terminal is **Terminal Terrestre** (Av Teodoro Gomez near Espejo). A taxi to/from downtown is $1. Buses to Quito leave roughly every 10 minutes.

Buses to the village of La Esperanza ($0.25, 25 minutes) leave from the north side of Parque German Grijalva in the center of town.

If you want to explore the area on your own, Ibarra's **Explorer Rentacar** (☎06-295-1668; www.rentacarecuador.net; Mariano Acosta No 10-06, across from train station) is the only option; rates start at $38 per day.

La Esperanza

☎06 / ELEV 2992M

This picturesque village just above Ibarra is set against the sloping flanks of **Volcán Imbabura** (4609m). The village is a respite for the road-weary as well as the best spot to climb Imbabura. To climb the peak, start early in the morning and follow the escalating ridge 2000m to the summit, 8km southwest. The last stretch is a scramble over loose rock. You can do it on your own, but if you're not experienced, hire a local guide or go with a tour company out of Otavalo ($60). Allow for six to 10 hours round-trip. Those of middling ambition can try the easier three-hour climb to **Loma Cubilche** (3886m), a hill south of La Esperanza with lovely views.

Sleeping

Casa Aida GUESTHOUSE $
(☎06-266-0221; www.casaaida.com; Gallo Plaza; camping/dm/r per person $6/8/10; 📶) Rest up for your adventure at the affable Casa Aida. Brightly painted rooms are simple but clean and comfortable. Aida, 42 years in the biz,

BUSES FROM IBARRA

DESTINATION	COST ($)	DURATION (HR)	FREQUENCY
Ambato	6.25	5	hourly
Cuenca	16	12	daily 8pm
El Ángel	1.60	1½	6 daily 6am-5:30pm
Guayaquil	14	10	more than 8 daily
Otavalo	0.55	20min	every 10min
Quito	3	2½	every 10min
San Lorenzo	4	4	every 3hr
Santo Domingo	6.50	6	every 3hr
Tulcán	3	2½	hourly until 5pm

DON'T MISS

RIDING THE RAILS

This newly restored route, known as 'Tren de la Libertad,' links Ibarra with the much lower village of Salinas, which feels like a ghost town – tumbleweeds wouldn't be out of place. Only 30km, the round-trip excursion takes six hours because the train chugs along slowly and in Salinas you're given time to visit the mildly interesting salt museum and an Afro-Ecuadorian dance troupe performs for passengers. A handful of private security officers on motorcycles follow along the entire way to ensure the train doesn't hit any cars, trucks or slow-moving livestock – it feels like you're part of a presidential motorcade. **Tren Ecuador** (1-800-873-637, Ibarra station 06-295-0390; www.trenecuador.com; round-trip $30;) operates out of the renovated station in Ibarra. Departures are at 10:30am Thursday through Sunday.

The line between Otavalo and Ibarra began running in 2017 (8am Friday to Sunday), with an immediate snag: winter flooding and landslides moved the operation from Otavalo to nearby San Roque, temporarily.

is a great source of local information and will make you feel at home with her famous hearty pancakes and a fab German goulash. She can help arrange a guide for an Imbabura summit.

Tradiciones San Clemente HOMESTAY **$$**
(06-266-0045; www.sanclementetours.com; San Clemente; r per person with full board $45) This community tourism initiative can arrange homestays in the nearby village of San Clemente. To reach here, when you see the sign for Bella Vista at the end of the paved road from Ibarra, bear right. As you approach the town proper, follow the sign for Pukyupampa about 400m. To make things simpler, a taxi from Ibarra is $5.

Getting There & Away

You can walk here from Ibarra, take one of the frequent buses ($0.25, 25 minutes) or get a taxi for about $5. The buses do not leave from the main terminal: they leave from the north side of Parque German Grijalva in the center of Ibarra. The paved road which now continues on through to Peguche makes things a lot easier on your chassis, human or vehicular.

Intag Valley

Hang on for the dramatic descent into Intag, where trees are weighted with tropical fruit and kids ride horses bridled with a scrap of rope. The lush valley is famous not only for its coffee, but also for its activism.

Run in part by the Union of Peasant and Indigenous Organizations of Cotacachi, Intag communities have begun reintroducing native crops and medicinal plants that have been grown in the Andes for hundreds, if not thousands, of years. The aim is to increase agricultural biodiversity and maintain culinary traditions. You can see and taste the results by booking a stay in a rural, family-run lodge through Otavalo's Runa Tupari (p103).

Worth highlighting is the paving and improving of a road that cuts through the valley via Chontal and Nanegalito. It will make for a scenic alternative route for the journey between Otavalo and Mindo (without having to go through Quito).

Activities

Siempre Verde VOLUNTEERING
(ext 1460 in the US 404-262-3032; www.siempreverde.org; N 0 22' 18) Get off the road just before Santa Rosa for the two-hour walk into Siempre Verde. This is a small community-run research station supporting tropical-conservation education with excellent hiking and bird-watching. Students and researchers are welcome with prior arrangement. $10 entry fee for hiking if you're not staying here.

Sleeping

★**El Refugio de Intag** GUESTHOUSE **$$**
(099-717-5208; www.elrefugiocloudforest.com; Santa Rosa; s/d incl breakfast $45/90;) A river runs through this idyllically situated 75-acre property with several comfortably rustic houses. It's a blood-pressure-lowering refuge from the world for birders or those seeking tranquility. Spanish-speaking guides are available for long walks in the surrounding area. Home-cooked meals ($12) come straight from the farm, and the family of caretakers will charm your socks off. Only 1km from Santa Rosa.

Intag Cloud Forest Cabins HOSTAL $$
(☎099-717-5208; www.intagcabins.com; Santa Rosa; r per person incl all meals $65, cabin for 2 no meals incl $45; P 📶) A more modern choice right next to the Cloud Forest Reserve, these new cabins have flush toilet, ceramic-lined showers and back porches with killer valley views. Owner Sandra Statz, co-founder of the reserve, will walk you around the reserve (she knows where the cock-of-the-rocks live). This is a couple of kilometers down the road from El Refugio (p117) guesthouse.

You can rent a cabin for $45 for two ($10 each additional person) with use of the kitchen. If you want three meals during your stay, it's $65 per person.

Los Cedros LODGE $$
(☎06-301-6550, in Quito 02-361-2546; www.reservaloscedros.org; Reserva Biológica Los Cedros, San Miguel de Chontal, Imbabura; all-inclusive per person $65) This lodge is situated in a fantastic, remote reserve of 64 sq km, whose primary forest is contiguous with the Reserva Ecológica Cotacachi-Cayapas. Facilities include a scientific-research station, dining and cooking facilities, accommodations in dorms or private rooms, hot water and electricity. Always contact the reserve in advance of your visit.

Getting There & Away

Buses from Otavalo ($2.50, 1½ hours) run to Apuela via Santa Rosa six times daily, and from Cotacachi, three times. There are also nine buses daily that return to Otavalo, where you can connect for Quito and other destinations.

To go further into the valley, there are local buses connecting Santa Rosa and Apuela with Junin and La Esperanza.

Apuela

☎06

The tiny town of Apuela hugs the Río Intag, which has carved a vast slit through the mountains as it roars toward the Pacific. On Sundays locals flood the center to play soccer and browse the market for provisions and jeans. It's the center of the coffee-growers' association, and you can taste Ecuador's best coffee all around town.

Activities

Nangulví Thermal Springs SPRINGS
(☎06-3015-892; admission child/adult $1.50/3, cabins per person $25, incl all meals $35; ⏲7am-9pm) This complex of tiled pools is a nice way to relax in the shadow of the volcanoes and remains a gorgeous place to unwind, especially at sunset as the valley grows dark around you. Word to the wise: it fills up early at weekends. There's a cluster of cabins and a restaurant set nicely along the rushing waters with $3 set meals to maximize on-site soaking. Admire the koi pond, with inhabitants longing to make a break for the Rio Intag.

Sleeping

Pachecho Farmhouse HOSTAL $
(☎06-301-5655; www.pachecofarmhouse.com; Main Rd, btwn Apuela & Santa Rosa; cabins per person $15-19; P 📶) Ex-Buenos Aires and New York resident Jimena Larreguí has changed the former Tierra Sol into a fashionable option along the banks of the Intag. Comfy beds with views of distant sugarcane fields are a short walk from the clean common kitchen. Uphill is a garden-in-process where some of your breakfast may originate. Tours of neighboring Soledad coffee plantation available, too. Cash only.

Finca San Antonio CABIN $
(☎06-301-7543; www.cloudforestadventure.com; r per person $8) Go past the hilltop village of Cuellaje to reach this farmhouse with basic cabins or dorm rooms; homestays with local families can also be arranged. There's a kitchen if you want to prepare your own food. Guests can pay extra for guided hikes, a visit to a nearby cheesemaker and trout fishing.

Shopping

Asociación Río Intag COFFEE, HANDICRAFTS
(Café Río Intag; ☎06-256-6029; www.aacri.com) Just downhill from the plaza, visit Café Río Intag, a cooperative coffee factory whose beans are produced by a group of local farmers and artists organized as Asociación Río Intag. It also sell handicrafts made by local women. If you give Franklin Vaca, the director, a few days' notice, he can arrange a coffee tour and tasting ($15-20 per person).

Getting There & Away

Buses from Otavalo ($2.50, 1½ hours) run to Apuela via Santa Rosa six times daily, and from Cotacachi, three times. The new road doesn't mean it's a 'straight' shot by any means – prepare yourself for some stomach-churning curves. There are also nine buses daily that return to Otavalo, where you can connect for Quito and other destinations.

Junín

05 / POP 26,942 (CANTON)

Continue further into remote Andean hills on the road to the politically active town of Junín, still under threat to new mining concessions. Take in the views near the farming village of García Moreno, where a narrow ridge fringed with banana trees drops to hills rolling toward the horizon.

Activities

Cueva de los Tayos BIRD-WATCHING

(06-305-1112; Chontal; 8am-5pm) Contact Ramero Flores for a unique look at the ghostly nocturnal oilbirds (tayo) which live in a cave here, 1km before the Chontal cemetery. The birds fly by night using echo-location, just like bats. He also has the famous cock-of-the-rock on his property, just before the turnoff for Mindo, about 46km from El Refugio de Intag (p117) in Santa Rosa.

Sleeping

Junín Cloud Forest Reserve LODGE $

(987-654-3210, 08-149-1654; www.junincloudforest.com; r per person incl meals $35) The highly recommended reserve operates a three-story bamboo lodge popular with bird-watchers. Relax in a hammock on the terrace, peruse the orchid collection, then hike to waterfalls with Spanish-speaking guides. Bunkrooms are plain but snug, and vegetarian meals come with robust cups of Intag coffee.

This is another DECOIN initiative, intended to preserve the local way of life and environment; your stay here helps.

Contact the center in advance to visit or volunteer ($25 per person or $15 for a homestay; the work varies from teaching English to working on the farm). In the rainy season bus services are limited on the muddy roads; arrange for transportation or a guide with the reserve.

Getting There & Away

You can take the bus from Otavalo to Garcia Moreno three times daily ($3, 3½ hours, 8am, 10am, 2pm) and then take a truck to Junin ($2) or walk the 20 minutes to town.

Northern Carchi

06

The smooth Panamericana snakes north from Ibarra, offering plenty of pavement to spandex-clad cyclists, who pound up this punishing route on weekends. Entering the **Río Chota Valley** at 1565m, the road drops sharply. Round, dry hills covered with cacti surround a lush green valley floor fed by the chocolatey river. Within an hour's drive of Ibarra, this always-warm valley is within arm's reach for day trips.

One place worth checking out is **Grutas de la Paz**, where you'll find a famous grotto converted to a chapel as well as **thermal springs** (open Thursday to Sunday) and waterfalls within easy reach by foot. Other notable sights include the waterfalls at **Las Cascadas de Paluz**, 3km north of San Gabriel.

An example of the unique Afro-Andean culture is *bomba* music, a blend of driving African drums and plaintive highland notes.

Sleeping

★ **Parque Bambú** B&B $

(Bosque de Paz; 06-264-8692; www.bospas.org; Km 108.5 Via Ibarra-San Lorenzo, El Limonal, prior to Jijon y Caamano on Hwy 10; dm/r per person incl breakfast $15/20, volunteers per day/month $20/260) Parque Bambú, rechristened from Bosque de Paz to dissociate it from any funereal implications, is run by a friendly Ecuadorian/Belgian couple. Comfortable lodge accommodations are in a lush setting, a 15-minute walk from the bus stop. The food is wonderful (mains $4 to $7), and guided hikes are offered. On the outskirts of El Limonal, about 1½ hours from Ibarra.

What this place is really all about is connecting to nature through the restorative power of planting. Owner Piet Sab promotes reforestation and organic pest control in this highly deforested area, and a visit is recommend for anyone interested in ecological restoration and permaculture.

Getting There & Away

Your central bus terminal is in Ibarra, which services both El Ángel and Tulcán on a regular basis. There is also regular service between El Ángel and Tulcán, and from Tulcán into Colombia. The main roads in the region are well paved, if you have your own wheels.

Reserva Biológica Guandera

This 1000-hectare, tropical, wet, montane forest reserve was founded in 1994 by Fundación Jatun Sacha. The reserve lies between 3100m and 3600m on a transitional ridge (forest to *páramo*), 11km east of San

Gabriel. Projects include reforestation and finding alternatives to chemical-intensive potato production. Andean spectacled bears (rarely glimpsed), high-altitude parrots and toucans are among the attractions.

From San Gabriel you can take public transport ($1.50) to Mariscal Sucre. From there you can take a *camioneta* to the reserve for $6. You can also take a *camioneta* directly from San Gabriel to the reserve for $15 to $20.

From the village of San Gabriel it is 1½ hours on foot to the reserve, but the **office** (02-243-2240 in Quito; www.jatunsacha.org; Teresa de Cepeda No 34-260 near Republica, 2nd fl, Urbanización Rumipamba, Quito) can arrange a ride with prior notice. You can be dropped in San Gabriel on any bus between Tulcán and El Ángel.

El Ángel

06 / POP 6300 / ELEV 3000M

Tufts of ocher grasses ripple along the hillsides surrounding the stark, still Andean village of El Ángel. The village is the entry point to Páramos El Ángel, a misty, remote wilderness favored by foxes and condors. It's part of the 160-sq-km **Reserva Ecológica El Ángel** (06-297-7597; http://areasprotegidas.ambiente.gob.ec/es/node/909; La Libertad; $2), which is home to *frailejones* – rare, otherworldly plants with fuzzy leaves and thick trunks. The two Lagunas El Voladero are popular and accessible destinations. You can arrange *páramo* visits with tour companies in Otavalo or Ibarra. The village springs to life with a Monday market.

Sleeping

Hostal Paises Andinos HOSTAL $
(09-8613-0892; Rio Frio & 2nd Transerverso; r per person $10; P wi-fi) A sweet family with a sweet dog, and warm blankets. And there's wi-fi! Not much more you can ask for, at this price.

Polylepsis Lodge CABAÑAS $$$
(06-2631-819; El Ángel Reserve, Sector El Colorado; d with 3 meals from $130; P wi-fi) Some very basic cabins and some with hot tubs, depending on your taste and budget. All with electric blankets, fortunately – it gets very cold up here. Guided hikes and horseback riding through the *paramo* put you in the center of the action. There are also occasional lectures on the wildlife around you.

Getting There & Away

Transportes Espejo, on the main plaza, goes to Quito ($4.55, four hours) via Ibarra ($1.60, 1½ hours) every hour. There's also a twice-daily bus to Tulcán ($2, 1½ hours). Buses to Tulcán also pass through San Gabriel.

At the plaza across from the main church (cool condor statue alert) you'll find more frequent buses going north to Tulcán. Private 4WD vehicles can also be rented on the plaza for excursions into the reserve (round-trip with waiting time $30).

Tulcán

06 / POP 53,558 / ELEV 3000M

The busy highland city of Tulcán is the last Ecuadorian stop for visitors headed overland to Colombia. For a border town, especially when compared to Huaquillas on the Peruvian border, Tulcán – with its narrow pedestrian-filled streets, everyday commercial vibe and topiary gardens – feels like Paris. Let's not get carried away, though: other than the uber-cool cemetery, there's no real reason to visit this provincial capital other than to cross the border. Running parallel to one another for several kilometers, Calles Bolívar and Sucre have the majority of hotels, restaurants and shops.

Sights

★ **Cementerio de Tulcán** CEMETERY, GARDENS
(Cotoapaxi & Av del Cemeterio; 7am-7:30pm) FREE Who would have thought the coolest thing you may see in Ecuador would be a cemetery? A maze of cypress trees – sculpted into bulbous, pre-Columbian totems, mythological figures, animals and geometric shapes – lines graves and mausoleums ornamented with candles and plastic flowers. Bushes and hedges take shape as they're trimmed by the son of the original topiary master and another artist. You'll be gobsmacked. A map of the different topiary figures is available in the tourism office, on-site.

Sleeping

Most travelers coming from Colombia continue directly on to Ibarra or Otavalo. If you can't make it those extra couple of hours, though, Tulcán does have a couple of decent places to overnight.

Hotel Lumar HOTEL $
(06-298-7137; hotel_lumar@hotmail.com; Sucre near Pichincha; r per person $18.45; P wi-fi) A com-

OFF THE BEATEN TRACK

WEST OF TULCÁN

Aguas Hediondas Literally 'stinking waters,' these hot, high-sulfur thermal springs 16km from Tulcán and 6km beyond the town of Tufiño certainly live up to their name. Many of the pools are on the Colombian side of the border; you can cross the border on a day pass, but those who want to stay overnight must enter via the Tulcán border crossing. Get there before 4pm, when the springs take on extra stench; go on weekdays to avoid crowds.

Volcán Chiles Beyond Aguas Hediondas (p121) on the main road, this impressive peak (4768m) offers a challenging six-hour summit on the border with Colombia. The peak offers spectacular views; locals say that on a clear day you can see the ocean. Take a bus or taxi to Tufiño and hire a guide in the town's main square. Ask locally about the safety of travel in this remote border region due to ongoing instability in Colombia.

fortable budget choice with freshly painted hallways, clean carpeted rooms, flat-screen TVs and aging furniture. The restaurant downstairs is clean and acceptable.

Grand Hotel Comfort HOTEL **$$**
(☎06-298-8832; http://atates.wixsite.com/hotelcomfort; cnr Colón & Chimborazo; s/d incl breakfast $40/60; P❄🛜) A modern high-rise with brightly painted rooms, plasma televisions, charming animal images stenciled on the walls and large picture windows towering over low-slung buildings several blocks southeast of Parque Ayora. A restaurant, beauty salon and clothing boutique are attached to the hotel.

Eating

The street food in Tulcán unsurprisingly has a Colombian flavor. By the border, there are plenty of snack stalls and fast-food carts. There's even a nice cafe in the center, air-cooled and wi-fi-enabled.

Cafe Tulcán CAFE **$**
(Sucre btwn Junin & Ayacucho; sandwiches $2; ⏲7:30am-7pm Mon-Fri; ❄🛜) A popular and modern spot serving sandwiches, coffee and cake since 1945. Treat yourself to an ice-cream ($2 to $3) too. Jose, the third-generation owner, is kind as can be.

Mercado Plaza Central MARKET **$**
(Boyaca btwn Bolívar & Sucre; mains $3; ⏲7am-5pm) This block-long, well-ordered covered market is an excellent place for a meal. Order from one of the *comedores* and get a fruit juice from a vendor in their respective sections, before grabbing a table or space in the small stadium-seating area.

ℹ Information

Exchanging money (between US dollars and Colombian pesos) is slightly better in Tulcán than at the border. If the currency-exchange centers are closed, try the street money-changers – look for the guys with briefcases. A Banco Guayaquil and Banco Pichincha with ATMs are located on the southern side of Plaza de Independencia.

Colombian Consulate (☎06-225-2458, 06-298-0559; http://tulcan.consulado.gov.co; Olmedo cnr 10 de Agosto, Edificio La Catedral Mezzanine; ⏲8am-1pm & 2:30-3:30pm Mon-Fri)

Tourist Office (iTur; ☎06-298-5760; Cotopaxi & Av del Cemeterio; ⏲8am-6pm Mon-Fri) Friendly Spanish-speaking staff at this small office located at the cemetery entrance.

ℹ Getting There & Away

BORDER CROSSINGS

All formalities are taken care of at the Rumichaca crossing (6am to 10pm daily), 6km from Tulcán. Even day-trippers to Ipiales will need their passport stamped.

Minibuses to the border ($0.85, shared) leave as soon as they are full from the corner of Venezuela and Bolívar on Tulcán's Parque Ayora. Taxis ($3.50) leave from the same location.

On the Colombian side, entrance formalities are straightforward. Check with the Colombian consulate to make sure your nationality doesn't require a visa. Visas are good for 30 to 90 days.

From the border, it's easy to catch a taxi ($1) to Ipiales, the first town in Colombia, 2km away, where there are plenty of hotels and onward bus connections.

BUS

Buses traveling to Ibarra ($3, 2½ hours), El Ángel ($2, 1½ hours) and Quito ($6, five hours) depart from the bus terminal around 2km southwest of downtown on the road to Ibarra. Note that there can be a customs/immigration check between Tulcán and Ibarra, which in our research time delayed the bus by 30 minutes.

The Quito bus does not go to the Ibarra terminal, but stops on the outskirts of town. If you want to go to Otavalo, you can ask the driver to let you off on the Panamericana there for $1 extra.

Getting Around

Taxis from the bus terminal to downtown cost $1.25 or cross the street and catch a city bus ($0.25) running along Bolívar.

WESTERN ANDEAN SLOPES

The old road to Santo Domingo wends past dramatic drop-offs while descending through lush, misty cloud forests. Within just a few hours of Quito, visitors can experience a welcome climate shock in the cool, humid hills. The area is known for its bird-watching, but the landscape inspires mountain biking, horseback riding and hiking as well.

The area includes parts of the remaining swath of the Choco-Andean forest, a corridor that extends to parts of Colombia, southern Panama and the Ecuadorian coast. Its flora and fauna, still relatively unmapped, are threatened by logging, slash-and-burn agriculture and water pollution, the same scourges that have decimated wildlife habitats elsewhere. The reserves themselves, at around 500m to 1400m, are technically in tropical cloud forests and receive a whopping 6000m (236in) of rain annually with an average daily humidity of 85% to 95% (no malaria or dengue, but you should have insect repellent on hand).

Mindo

☎02 / POP 4000 / ELEV 1250M

If there's anything Mindo's about, it's the birds. Did you notice the Andean cock-of-the-rock statue at the town entrance? Or the giant painted hummingbird in the central plaza? Birders come from around the globe to revel in the species density present in and around this very special valley.

With its lovely setting surrounded on all sides by forested mountains, this pint-sized *pueblo* has become a deservedly popular destination for backpackers. Conveniently located just off the main highway between Quito and Esmeraldas, a curvy road descends to a rather ramshackle yet immensely likable town center. It's become a site of sensual sensations, from aromatic coffees to chocolates that dazzle the taste buds and tickle your nose (several tours of each process are available). Hikers and weekenders from Quito and beyond flock here, and locals have created an impressive range of activities (rafting, tubing, ziplining) for enjoying the surrounding cloud forest.

Sights

Tarabita CABLE CAR

(road to Cascada de Nambillo; $5; 8:30am-4pm Tue-Sun) This unique small-motor-powered (2002 Nissan!) cable car takes you soaring across a lush river basin over thick cloud forest to the Bosque Protector Mindo-Nambillo, where you can hike to a number of waterfalls. Not for the acrophobic, the wire basket on steel cables glides 152m above the ground. Your ticket includes a map with routes on it; while the Cascada Nambillo is the closest (15 minutes' walk), it's the series of five waterfalls (one hour's walk) that's really worth it.

It's a $6 taxi or a sturdy uphill walk 7km from town. If you only want to go across and back for the photo op, it's $2.

Cascada Nambillo WATERFALL

(☎093-940-8459; Via al Mariposario, near Mindo Garden Lodge; $5; 8:30am-4pm) Popular with local families on weekends, this series of cascades is the easiest to access in the area. However, it still entails either a trip on the *tarabita* (cable car) or a fairly steep path 2km or so past it. A few spots are roped off for swimming (in the dry season) and there's a rudimentary slide that ends several feet above the water, making for a fun and splashy entry, as does a 12-meter jump for the daring.

A taxi from town runs at $6 to $8.

Mariposario de Mindo BUTTERFLY FARM

(☎099-9202-124; www.mariposasdemindo.com; Via al Mariposario; $7.50; 9am-4pm; P) Mindo's best butterfly garden is like walking through a paint factory with the fans set to slow – a stunning kaleidoscope. Visit in the warmest part of the day, around 11am, when butterflies are most active. If it's raining, the butterflies are dormant and you can use your ticket another day. Kids will love scaling the observation towers, and feeding the giant koi.

The road uphill from town splits for the waterfalls (right, Via a las Cascadas) or the mariposario (left, Via al Mariposario). It also has a restaurant and some above-average **lodging** (☎099-920-2124; r per person $43).

Armonía Orchid Garden GARDENS
(www.birdingmindo.com; Sixto Duran cnr Lluvia de Oro; $3; ⏰7am-5pm) Check out the blooms at this impressive collection of more than 200 orchids – many viewable with a handy microscope. Naturally, the garden is also full of hummingbirds. You can also rent rooms here at **Cabañas Armonía** (☎099-943-5098, 02-217-0131; Lluvia de Oro & Sixto Duran Ballen; s incl breakfast with/without bathroom $25/13, d incl breakfast with/without bathroom $36/26; P 📶).

Activities

Mindo Biking MOUNTAIN BIKING
(☎093-933-5717; www.mindobiking.com; Vicente Aguirre near Quito; $4/hour $8 night tour) Here's a sport that's just catching on in this activity-laden town, and Mindo's hills and valleys will test your lungs and legs. But the views are worth it. Next to Reposteria.

Mindo Canopy Adventure ADVENTURE SPORTS
(☎09-453-0624; www.mindocanopy.com; Via las Cascadas Km 2.5; 2½hr circuit per person $20) Halfway up the road to the *tarabita*, this long-running Costa Rican-owned operation has 10 different cables ranging from 20m to 400m in length, enabling you to fly above the trees – an activity that gets faster in the rain.

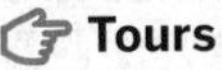

Tours

Chocó Arte FOOD
(Tour de Chocolate; ☎099-488-1922; Los Colibries; $6; ⏰4pm daily) Among Mindo's growing number of culinary tours, Jackie may be the most enthusiastic guide. Her chocolate tour is labeled as the "history, process and enjoyment" of chocolate, and readers commented on how much they were involved in the process, which ends with sampling homemade fondue. You may even be invited back to help whip up the next batch!

La Isla ECOTOUR
(☎02-217-0181, 099-327-2190; www.laislamindo.com; Avs Quito & 9 de Octubre) Offering horseback riding, biking, canopy, canyoning, tubing and bird-watching excursions. English is spoken. Ask for Fernanda 'Ferchis' Patiño, also a respected bird guide.

WORLD RECORD BIRDS: YOU CAN COUNT ON MINDO

Since 1900, twitchers have been using the weeks around the year-end holidays to count avian species – really, really count them. The Audubon Society's annual Christmas Count, set up originally in contrast to 'side hunts' which would document how many species rich, rifle-bearing gentry could kill off, has grown into a social, environmental and political event of global significance, allowing for 'citizen-scientists' to document the total number of bird species present in a 5-mile radius within 24 hours. The counts take place around the world from December 14 to January 5, in all kinds of weather.

Not surprisingly, since entering the fray in 1995, Mindo has topped the charts six times, each time counting more than 400 bird species. The Mindo-Tandayapa circle, or ECNM in Audubon nomenclature, 'won' for four years running from 2008 to 2011, and neighboring circle Yanayaca (ECYY) has since surpassed them a couple of times in a friendly rivalry in which many participate in both counts (not everyone counts on the same weekend, and there are now seven circles in Ecuador alone). Nicole Büttner is the official compiler for the Tandayapa circle, which begins in the dark, pre-dawn hours, sometimes with 'h.o' (heard only) species, and a few owls.

Likely factors in Ecuador's success are the number of species in the country (fourth in the world behind Brazil, Peru and Colombia) and the gung-ho spirit of its hundred-plus participants, who range widely in age and experience, but are unparalleled in enthusiasm – each year they gather the night before the count to get stoked up and receive their free T-shirt.

If you're coming to Ecuador for the year-end holidays, the count is open to anyone. Hey, when was the last time you could say you held a world record?

LOCAL KNOWLEDGE

BIRD-WATCHING IN MINDO

With more than 500 species of birds recorded, the area around Mindo has become a major destination for bird-watching. Mindo has 'won' the Audubon Society's annual Christmas Count six times, counting the most species in a 24-hour period at year's end. If you don't know your rufous-headed chachalaca from your rufous-fronted wood-quail and your interest is casual, you can access trails on your own from Casa Amarilla (Yellow House), located a couple of blocks from the parque central. In addition to a wide variety of birds, locals claim to have spotted pumas, spectacled bears and monkeys here.

Keep in mind that this is an activity for early risers, generally taking place from 6am to 10am. The majority of the top flight bird-watching doesn't happen in Mindo itself but in privately owned reserves (most have admission costs) scattered throughout the area, anywhere from a hike to a two-hour drive away. In addition to the cloud forest reserves and lodges (p128), which undoubtedly are excellent, there are many day-trip destinations:

Rio Silanche Sanctuary Located between Pedro Vicente Maldonado and Puerto Quito at an elevation of around 400m, Silanche is more akin to a tropical rainforest and is known for its very high concentration of birdlife.

Milpe Bird Sanctuary This 250-acre reserve in the upper foothills 15km west of Mindo is close to Los Bancos.

Paz de las Aves Private reserve of subtropical forest an hour from Mindo, off the highway towards Quito.

Yanacocha (Reserva Yanacocha; 02-250-5129; www.fjocotoco.org; Nono; $15; 7am-3:30pm) One of the Jocotoco Foundation's 10 reserves, at 3400m this cloud forest borders the *páramo*. It's around a $60 round-trip taxi ride from town.

Pululahua and Calacalí Temperate forest with arid scrub 50 minutes from Mindo.

23 de Junio Farming community south of Los Bancos renowned for the long-wattled umbrella bird.

Reserva El Bravo Within walking distance at the end of the San Lorenzo Road.

Coyote la Pena Taxi ride and admission $20 each.

Las Tangaras Run by volunteers, a steep, downhill hike off the road to the *tarabita*.

San Lorenzo Along the road to the *tarabita*, the most basic trip for beginners.

Yellow House (Hacienda San Vicente) This private reserve is close to town and features five marked trails. 300 orchid species, 360 bird species and 39 hummingbird species seen here, all for $6.

Las Cotingas Bird Reserve (San Tadeo; 098-0899-882; www.lascotingasbirdreserve.com; San Tadeo, Km 77; $5) A private home at the top of the hill just outside of Mindo, and for $5 it's hummingbird (and tanager) heaven. You might catch the colorful toucan barbet here, too, and the coffee and tea are free.

Jardín El Descanso (Los Colibries; $4; 6:30am-5:30pm) Sit on this family's back porch and be transported by the whir of a thousand wings at this hummingbird airport.

Bird-Watching Guides

Locally there are many competent, professional guides. Most charge a minimum of around $50 to $75, and depending on the number in the group and the particular reserve, that could go up to $100 or more per day.

Irman Arias (099-170-8720; www.mindobirdguide.com)

Marcelo Arias (098-065-9522; marceloguideofbirds@yahoo.com)

Danny Jumbo (099-328-0769; www.mindobirding.com)

Nolberto Jumbo (088-563-8011)

Julia Patiño (098-6162-816; https://mindobirdwatching.wordpress.com)

Sandra Patiño (096-799-6256; https://mindotour.wordpress.com)

Sleeping

There's no shortage of accommodation options; new places pop up all the time, of varying quality and budget ranges. Away from the town center it does get quieter. Don't be shy about asking locals for directions since street signs are virtually nonexistent.

In Town

Rubby's Place GUESTHOUSE $
(099-193-1853; rubbyhostal@yahoo.com; Av Quito; r per person incl breakfast $15; P wi-fi) If you follow Av Quito, the main road through town, to the end past the golf club, you'll find this two-story wood building with six clean and comfy rooms. All have balconies with nice views, and water, coffee and tea are free. Owner Norma blasts out five meg of free wi-fi, and she's a sweetheart, to boot.

Caskaffesu GUESTHOUSE $
(02-217-0100, 099-386-7154; www.caskaffesu.net; Sixto Duran Ballen near Av Quito; r per person incl breakfast $25; wi-fi) Run by a kind Ecuadorian, Caskaffesu is a lovely low-key refuge just off the main road in the center of town. The two stories of brightly painted adobe rooms have a vaguely Mediterranean/colonial feel and surround a small, leafy courtyard. The complex features one room which is fully compatible for people with a disability, with access ramp and shower.

Casa de Cecilia HOSTEL $
(099-334-5393, 02-217-0243; www.lacasadececilia.com; Av 9 de Octubre; r per person $10-15; P wi-fi) The bucolic outdoor patio – even if it is concrete – and riverside location add an out-of-the-way feel and a place to relax for those staying in the maze of single beds. Several good-value private rooms ($15) with more space are in the two-story buildings next door. There's an outdoor fireplace on the hammock deck and an open-air kitchen on the river.

Casa de Piedra GUESTHOUSE $$
(02-217-0436; www.casadepiedramindo.com; r per person incl breakfast $15-25, bungalows $90; P wi-fi pool) Just on the other side of the River Mindo north of the parque central is this pretty property with an always flowering garden, playful dogs and a swimming pool. Henry has really upgraded in recent years, adding stylish bungalows and family cabins ($30 per person) with handmade bedding and fixtures, which feature king-sized beds with new mattresses. Lemon trees abound.

Dragonfly Inn GUESTHOUSE $$
(02-217-0319, 098-238-1830; www.mindo.biz; Av Quito near Rio Canchupi; s/d/tr incl breakfast $29/49/69; P wi-fi) One of the best-looking buildings in Mindo, the Dragonfly stands by the bridge at the town entrance. It's spotless and the all-wood rooms have comfy beds; some have private balconies with hammocks. It's professionally run with friendly service, and the attached restaurant (p127) is one of the best in Mindo. There's ambient noise on the street-facing rooms, so choose a back room if possible.

Sisakuna Lodge CABIN $$
(02-217-0343; www.sisakunalodge.com; Garzón Thomas btwn Quito & Aguirre; s/d/tr/q incl breakfast $60/72/100/123; P wi-fi) A handful of well-built cabins surround a pavilion-style bar and restaurant at this place ('Flowers' in Kichwa) a short uphill walk from town toward the *tarabita*. It's a small, landscaped property, and privacy-seekers may want the concrete adobe buildings, which seem to be more soundproof. Amada, a former Queens, NY, resident has returned home and keeps an eye on things.

Hosteria Arasari CABIN $$
(02-207-1880; www.hosteriaarasari.com; Yaguira; r per person incl breakfast $35, camping per person $5; P wi-fi pool) Over a small footbridge, up a dirt drive is this long, narrow property lined with small stone and wood-paneled cabins. The camping area, which has bathroom facilities, is just across the way on a small, well-mowed volleyball court, which happens to be next to the parking lot. There's a Turkish bath, pool and hot tub.

Mindo Coffee Lodge & Spa CABAÑAS $$$
(098-265-0335; www.lodgemindoecuador.com; next to Hotel Arasari; s/d incl breakfast $85/105; P wi-fi pool) Modern cabañas with flat-screen TVs and stone porches overlook a temperate swimming pool in this new addition to the Mindo accommodation scene. Families can spread out over two rooms ($160), and two of the cabins even have hot tubs – a bit of luxury. Not sure that the coffee tour is worth a separate admission, but it's included with your room.

Outside Town

La Roulotte CABIN $$
(098-976-4484; www.hosterialaroulottemindo.com; off Via Mariposario; r incl breakfast $75; P wi-fi) On the road before the Mariposario

de Mindo (p122) butterfly farm, 2km outside of town, La Roulette's five charming horse-coach-shaped cedar-and-pine rooms, economically styled after gypsy caravans, come with bunk beds, a fireplace (some), a bathroom and lots of color. Those craving space can enjoy the grounds of the hotel, which includes amazing bird activity and a stress-reducing bamboo labyrinth.

Affable owner Ignacio is a member of the local bird guides' association and a font of information on Mindo-based activities.

★El Monte Sustainable Lodge LODGE **$$$**
(☎02-217-0102, 099-308-4675; www.ecuadorcloudforest.com; cabin per person incl meals & activities $130; P 📶 🏊) 🌿 Run by a warm-hearted and knowledgeable American/Ecuadorian couple, El Monte is a lush retreat with three lovely, private riverside cabins. The aesthetic is contemporary, with lots of wood and natural tones. Three cabins sleep up to four people and have bathtubs. Located 4km south of Mindo along a winding dirt road, it's reached by the *tarabita* over the Río Mindo.

The communal lodge has rustic furniture, fire pits, a library and some solar-powered electricity. The food is delicious and mostly vegetarian using ingredients from the organic garden. Guests can wander the on-site trails or swim in the river-fed pool. Reserve ahead so that the owners can arrange transport from Mindo.

★Casa Divina CABIN **$$$**
(☎099-172-5874; www.mindocasadivina.com; s/d incl breakfast & dinner $140; P 📶) 🌿 Highly recommended for seclusion and tranquility with a splash of luxury is this small complex of two-story wooden cabins 2km from town. Porches with hammocks provide roosts for bird-watching, and on-site trails expand the observation territory. The owners are leaders in the local sustainable tourism effort, but don't skimp on comfort, as the delicious breakfasts (banana pancakes, yuca bread) prove.

To reach this divine spot, when coming from town take the road toward the waterfall (right), when it splits off from the road to the mariposario.

Séptimo Paraíso LODGE **$$$**
(☎099-368-4421, in Quito 02-317-1475; www.septimoparaiso.com; r/ste incl breakfast $114/154, mains $6-12; P 📶 🏊) 🌿 On the steep hillside descent from the main road and 2km from Mindo proper is this ecologically minded, hidden-away, country-style collection of wooden buildings. Rooms are rustic (maybe a bit musty) and understated, with wood-paneled walls, splashes of color and some wonderful antiques. The lodge also has an excellent restaurant, The Cloud, a hot tub and heated pool.

Mindo Garden Lodge LODGE **$$$**
(☎099-722-3260; www.mindogarden.com.ec; s/d/tr/q incl breakfast $85/107/137/153; P 📶) This Ecuadorian-Chilean place feels small and personal. Pathways wind through wooded gardens to a main lodge and cozy cabins – some have excellent river views. The restaurant here is recommended. The lodge is 4km uphill from Mindo past the Mariposario de Mindo (p122) butterfly farm. Modern bathrooms and flat-screen tellies give comforting contrast to the rustic surroundings, which include a river overlook.

Las Terrazas de Dana BOUTIQUE HOTEL **$$$**
(☎098-409-9146; www.lasterrazasdedana.com; d $99-109; P 📶) This family from the Canary Islands has created a small, luxury space for romantic getaways high in the hills above Mindo. Incredible valley vistas greet you at breakfast on your private terrace, and modernities like DirectTV make this a more comfortable option for the less rustic of us. Honeymoon suites with special massage offers (coffee massage? chocolate massage?) for loved-up weekenders.

Right next to Casa Divina, about 2km uphill from town.

Eating

A fair smattering of cafes dot the town center, while vegetarian options vary from all-quinoa-based fare to pizzas and *plátanos*. Chocolate is a new trend, with several shops specializing in snacks, sauces and even beers flavored with the magic cacao concoction.

Nearly all of the out-of-town lodges are open to nonguests for meals. Several places offer free refills of water bottles as environmental consciousness grows.

★Yumbo's Chocolate CAFE **$**
(☎099-063-6345, 098-000-4417; www.yumboschocolate.com; ⏲8am-10pm) Owner Claudio Ponce works with an all-female cooperative of cacao growers near Timbiré, *Mujeres Para El Futuro* (Women for the Future), bringing the heat from the Pacific Coast straight to

your Mindo mug, with the best-tasting *chocolate caliente* in town. There's also a short Spanish-English in-store chocolate tour, a small store, and even a chocolate stout from Quito's Pileus Brewery.

★Mishqui Quinde Heladería CAFE $

(Vicente Aguirre cnr Gallo de la Peña, 'Gourmet Avenue'; ice-cream $2; ⏲11:30am-7pm Wed-Mon) Oswaldo has moved from the old van to a more permanent site, but it's still all quinoa, all the time: in burgers ($4 to $5), pudding, homemade sorbet and shakes where you can mix it with other flavors like blackberry, chocolate and passion fruit. The five-juice Cuicocha Lake drink is a surefire hit, but the chocolate liqueur shouldn't be missed.

Arepera VENEZUELAN $

(Venezuelan Soul Food; Av Quito, across from Happy Moment disco; arepas $1.50; ⏲noon-10pm) Budget eaters rejoice! These exiles from Venezuela dish out delicious and ample *arepas*, the stuffed-corn-cake treat which fits any meal, really. Filled with veggies (rice, beans, cabbage), chicken or beef, there's a handful of toppings. You might even get an impromptu jam session going on next to to the baby's crib. There are nice hummingbird and Venezuelan-themed decorations, too. Recommended.

Beehive CAFE $

(Dragonfly Inn; ☎02-2170-296; www.thebeehivemindo.com; sandwiches $8; ⏲8am-8pm Mon-Thu & Sun, to 10pm Fri & Sat; 📶) Run by Ingo and Genny, the Beehive is located on the bottom floor of the Dragonfly Inn (p125), a cool hangout with a Scandinavian design perched over a river. The smorgasbord plate of falafel, hummus, cheese, meatballs, sausages, salad and refrigerator leftovers is the house specialty, but brownies, cakes and coffee drinks are equally good. Romantic dinner here is also recommended.

By Ingo's own admission, his homebrew lagers and ales (both $5) are hit or miss.

Restaurante Pizzeria El Tigrillo PIZZA, ECUADORIAN $$

(Av Quito; pizza $11-15; ⏲10am-midnight) This simple, open-air place across from the Mindo Volunteer Hostel is our favorite pizzeria in town. The pizzas are cooked in a brick oven and offer eight fairly sized slices per pie. Inexpensive breakfasts, *almuerzos* and Ecuadorian mains like tilapia, trout and side of plantains are also on Doña Raquel's menu.

El Quetzal ECUADORIAN $$

(www.elquetzaldemindo.com; Av 9 de Octubre; mains $7-12; ⏲8am-9pm; 📶) This laid-back coffee shop and restaurant, easily the largest in town (for better or worse), has excellent coffee plus locally grown beans and chocolate for sale (with a handy tasting table), a selection of breakfasts and sandwiches, and some Ecuadorian main courses. The American owner's pride is her famous brownie – compare, if you like, to that of **La Reposteria** (Vicente Aguirre; mains $4-6; ⏲7am-8pm; 📶).

Information

The San Miguel de los Bancos ATM accepts most cards on the Mastercard and Maestro networks but not Visa. The Banco Pichincha ATM on the plaza does accept Visa and most other foreign cards.

Getting There & Away

There are several daily buses to Quito ($3.10, 2½ hours, 6:30am, 11am, 1:45pm, 3pm, 5pm Monday to Friday), run by Cooperativa Flor de Valle, which leave from the terminal a few blocks uphill on Av Quito from the main plaza – you can hop out at Nanegalito ($1.50) to grab a *camioneta* to other area destinations. On weekends there are nearly hourly departures from 11am to 5pm.

Cooperativa Kennedy buses leave from the plaza to Santo Domingo ($6, three hours), from where there are connections to Puerto Lopez. Different Kennedy buses travel via Los Bancos (6:30am, 7am; from here there are frequent connections to Esmeraldas) and Pedro Vicente Maldonado to Puerto Quito.

Not to worry if you miss one of these departures. Head out to the 'Y' junction at the top of the hill (taxi $5 or hitch in a truck for $0.50) and hop on one of the frequent buses traveling between Quito and the coast.

Taxis, regulated with fixed prices, line up on the main plaza, right near the giant hummingbird. To Quito it's $60, to the airport $80, and to skip Quito altogether and head north-east to Otavalo it's $150.

Getting Around

A taxi cooperative runs from the plaza. Taxis around town cost $1.50 within the town center. All the *taxistas* go by handles like 'Gorilla' or 'Gato.' (Our favorite was 'La Tortuga', who certainly doesn't drive like a tortoise.) Drivers with private cars provide transport around town and to Quito (one-way, $60).

Cloud Forest Reserves & Lodges

☎02

Although the name 'Mindo' is magic to the nature lover's ear, many of the more specialized and high-end lodges are located a bit outside the town itself, up and down the slopes of the cloud forest between Mindo and the capital. Some of the private reserves allow day visitors for a fee ($10 to $25, guides are additional) and can arrange private transportation from Quito or Mindo. In addition to those reviewed, there are several other community ecotourism initiatives in the area.

Sleeping

Reserva Yunguilla LODGE $

(☎099-954-1537; www.yunguilla.org.ec; camping $5, r per person with full board $35) A little more than 80 families from the village of Yunguilla have developed this community-run ecotourism project to protect nearly 2600 hectares of cloud forest. Accommodations can sleep up to nine in three rooms, there's a space for camping, and you can also arrange for a homestay in the community (book this ahead of time with manager Alex Coyahuasi).

Bellavista Lodge LODGE $$

(☎02-223-2123, 099-416-5868; www.bellavistacloudforest.com; Tandayapa; dm $35, s/d incl meals $130/260) It's worth spending a night or two at this 700-hectare reserve, if only for the jaw-dropping panoramic views from its wooden geodesic dome lodge. There's a library/restaurant/bar on the ground floor, over which are five small rooms topped by a two-story dormitory area with a shared bathroom, restaurant and balcony. If you prefer privacy, larger private cabins are nearby.

About a kilometer away is a research station with a kitchen for self-catering and a 12-bed dormitory for travelers on a budget.

This reserve is on the western Andean slopes at about 2000m above sea level. About 25% of it is primary forest, and the rest has been selectively or completely logged but is regenerating. It was one of the very first ecotourism projects in the area, and various conservation projects are always underway. There are 8km of well-marked trails, and the area is highly recommended by bird-watchers (320 species of birds have been recorded). Guests pay $8 to use the trails, guides cost $18/day, and a taxi from Mindo costs $50; from Quito, $70.

The first recorded *olinguito,* a racoon-like mammal new to science, was recorded here in 2013. It was the first new mammal 'discovered' in 35 years.

Bosque Nublado Santa Lucía LODGE $$

(☎02-215-7242; www.santaluciaecuador.com; Santa Lucia, Nanegal; r per person without bathroom incl meals $50, cabins per person incl meals $90) This beautifully crafted lodge rests on a peak with commanding 360-degree views of lush hills and valleys. Lodge rooms are simple but comfortable with shared bathrooms, composting toilets and solar-powered electricity. Comparatively luxurious cabañas with impressive views over the cloud forest sleep two to three people and have private bathrooms. Excellent meals include salad, potato pancakes and hearty soups.

A foray into Bosque Nublado Santa Lucía is a trip for the adventurous. The reserve is owned and run by a cooperative of 12 families who, looking for a more sustainable future, stopped farming *naranjilla* (tart tropical fruit) with pesticides to work with tourism and preservation. Considered one of the country's best examples of community tourism, Santa Lucía has won numerous awards for sustainability and reducing poverty. Volunteers are welcome.

A minimum stay of three days is recommended, with entry into the reserve and guide service for the first and last day included in the price. Certified guides from the local families speak basic English and know the scientific names for plants and birds. The parking area for the start of the steep one- to two-hour hike up to the lodge is around 1km past Maquipucuna (mules carry the luggage). It's an additional $20 if you'd rather ride the mule up instead.

Maquipucuna Lodge LODGE $$$

(www.maqui.org; Maquipucuna Reserve, Nanegal; r per person incl meals with/without bathroom $155/$112, camping $12) This charmingly rustic lodge is situated on the 60-sq-km Reserva Biológica Maquipucuna, north of Mindo. Guests enjoy great deck views from the hammocks and tasty, healthy meals at the restaurant, which serves its own shade-grown coffee. In addition to a variety of lodge rooms, there's a family cabin with two bathrooms and a private deck.

The reserve, which includes a research station, covers a variety of premontane and montane cloud forests in the headwaters of Río Alambi at elevations ranging from 1200m to 2800m. It has 370 species of birds, including 30 species of hummingbirds; 240 species of butterflies; and 45 species of mammals, including the spectacled bear, which can regularly be seen here during the fruiting season of a small avocado-like fruit called *aguacatillo*.

The nonprofit Fundación Maquipucuna, which administers the reserve, began purchasing parcels piecemeal in the late 1980s. Run by Rodrigo Ontaneda and Rebecca Justicia, a passionate and committed couple, it's a driving force and leader in conservation in the region. A major focus has been to work with area communities, farmers especially, to develop sustainable livelihoods while conserving the environment.

Day guests pay a $10 entry fee and can hire a guide for $25, though it's well worth taking the time to spend at least one night here. Trails range from an easy 1km walk to a demanding 5.5km hike, while specialized guided tours of the coffee-growing process or wild orchids are also available. The Fundación can arrange a private vehicle from Quito for $80. If you're driving, you'll need a 4WD for the 7km from the main road. You can take a public bus here from Quito to Nanegal ($2, 2 hours).

Mashpi LUXURY LODGE **$$$**

(☎02-400-4100, sales 02-400-8088; www.mashpilodge.com; Mashpi; all-inclusive 2 nights per person $1340; ❄📶) 🍃 The luxurious lodge at Mashpi perches on a hilltop overlooking the 1000-plus hectares of its privately protected reserve (in cooperation with the nearby Mashpi community), which features a number of microclimates and four watersheds. The lodge looks like an uber-modernist Hamptons home, yet the scene outside – exposed from the massive ceiling-high windows – resembles a still from *Jurassic Park*.

Tandayapa Bird Lodge LODGE **$$$**

(☎02-244-7520, 099-923-1314, toll-free in the US 800-348-5941; www.tandayapa.com; Tandayapa, Km 52 Via Calacalí-La Independencia (Route 28); s/d incl meals $165/267) This place is a serious bird-watcher's paradise, with such highlights as the Andean cock-of-the-rock, scaled fruiteater and golden-headed and crested quetzals. With just 12 bedrooms (two of which are pleasantly isolated), the feel is intimate and laid-back. The lodge offers multilingual guides, comfortable accommodation with a great viewing balcony, a canopy platform and an enormous number of trails.

ℹ Getting There & Away

Taxis from either Mindo or Quito to this area run to anywhere from $50 to $80. Alternatively, it's easy to grab a bus to Nanegalito, a town 56km along the Quito-Mindo road, which serves as something of a hub; *camionetas* from here to the reserves cost from $20 to $35. The town of Nanegal is another access point. Non-4WD vehicles can make it to most lodges.

Central Highlands

Includes ➡

Best Places to Hike

- Laguna Quilotoa (p143)
- Laguna Limpiopungo (p136)
- Parque Nacional Sangay (p159)
- Volcán Chimborazo (p162)

Best Places to Stay

- Tambopaxi (p137)
- Inti Sisa (p169)
- Hacienda Los Mortiños (p137)
- Llullu Llama (p146)
- Luna Runtún (p156)

Why Go?

The rooftop of Ecuador offers up more adventure per square meter than most places on earth. This vast region cut from fire and ice inspires the imagination and offers a remarkable journey deep into the myth and beauty of the Andes. There are heavenly volcanoes, glacier-capped peaks, high-arching grassy plains, surprisingly quaint colonial cities, bucolic haciendas and precipitous green valleys that take you from highlands down past waterfalls and indigenous villages to the heavy-aired environs of the Amazon Basin.

Most trips to the area will include a couple of days in the region's exceptional national parks and reserves, including Los Ilinizas, Cotopaxi, Llanganates, Chimborazo and Sangay. The Quilotoa Loop brings hiking travelers through traditional indigenous communities to an impossibly deep crater lake. And there are rail adventures and crafts markets, plus plenty of tropical experiences in the verdant valley leading down to the ever-popular town of Baños.

When to Go

Riobamba

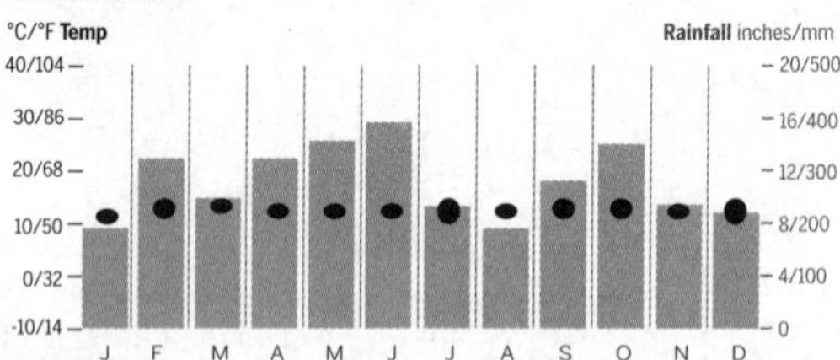

Jun–Sep The dry season is the top time for climbs, bikes and treks.

Sep or Nov Hit up the Mamá Negra festival in Latacunga.

Dec–Jan A dry spell gives way to adventure – plus everything is green!

National Parks & Reserves

For such a small region, the central highlands has quite a collection of protected areas. All but Parque Nacional Llanganates (p151), which is truly a tough wilderness to crack open, have activities for everyone, from leisurely day-trippers to hardcore hikers and climbers. Parque Nacional Cotopaxi (p135) is one of the country's most visited national parks, and is a quick trip from Quito or Latacunga. The Reserva Ecológica Los Ilinizas (p134) encompasses the two Ilinizas peaks, and stretches all the way to Laguna Quilotoa. Volcán Chimborazo is the centerpiece of the Reserva de Producción de Fauna Chimborazo (p162), where roving harems of vicuña (a relative of the llama) scamper across the *páramo* (Andean grasslands). Parque Nacional Sangay (p159) is the region's largest park, with terrain as varied as jungle and glaciated peaks.

Getting There & Around

Latacunga has an airport, but it had no passenger service at the time of research. Buses, of course, go just about everywhere. The most important transportation hubs are Latacunga, Ambato, Baños, Riobamba and Guaranda. For travel to remote areas, you'll often need to switch in those cities.

Getting around by rental car, tour operator or a taxi (rented for the day) is an easy and safe way to get to more remote areas.

Machachi & Aloasí

02 / POP 25,700

Machachi and Aloasí, about 35km south of Quito on opposite sides of the Panamericana, serve as gateways to nearby mountains and wilderness. Aloasí is the more attractive of the two *pueblos*, and serves as a stop on train tours from Quito to El Boliche in Parque Nacional Cotopaxi. Both places are alternate staging points for excursions to Parque Nacional Cotopaxi and the Ilinizas reserve.

The quiet hamlet of Aloasí, on the west side of the highway, sits at the base of the long-extinct volcano El Corazón (4788m), or 'The Heart,' whose name comes from the shape formed by two canyons on its west side.

The busy town of Machachi is on the east side of the highway. The pretty main square has piped-in organ music, and an important **Sunday market** spills all over the town. A boisterous festival celebrating *chagras* (Andean cowboys) rides into town every July 23.

Tours

Tren de los Volcanes RAIL

(1-800-873-637; www.trenecuador.com; adult/child $53/37; 8am-5:30pm Fri-Sun) Departing from Quito's Estación de Ferrocarril Chimbacalle, this pretty tourist train takes passengers on a day trip to El Boliche station near Cotopaxi National Park for a guided walk in the woods, and stops at Machachi station (which is actually in Aloasí) for a traditional dance performance and lunch on a farm, before returning to Quito. Touristy but fun.

Sleeping & Eating

Hostería Granja La Estación HACIENDA $$

(099-277-1578, 02-230-9246; www.hosteriagranjalaestacion.com; Aloasí; s/d incl breakfast $50/70;) This rambling 19th-century hacienda across from the train station in Aloasí is your best bet in the area. It has exposed wood beams in the quaintly furnished rooms, friendly service and plenty of open areas in which to sit and enjoy the views.

In the back courtyard, several spacious rooms with wood-burning stoves have been built to match the house. The restaurant, festooned with farm-related antiques, serves lunch and dinner for $15.

El Café de la Vaca ECUADORIAN $$

(02-231-5012; Panamericana Km 23; mains $7-20; 8am-5:30pm) On weekend afternoons, you will almost certainly have to wait to dine alongside carloads of Quito day-trippers at this restaurant painted like a black-and-white cowhide. Visitors flock to 'The Cow Cafe' for its straight-off-the-farm cheese served with every order. The Ecuadorian dishes and huge variety of breakfast combos (served all day) go down well with a freshly blended fruit juice.

Getting There & Away

Buses departing from Quito's bus terminal for Latacunga can drop you in Machachi ($1.50, one hour) along the Panamericana. To get back to Quito or Latacunga, wave down a bus on the Panamericana.

While the train service is designed for round-trips, you could opt for one-way travel on the **Tren de los Volcanes**, though you would be charged the full ticket price.

Central Highlands Highlights

1. **Quilotoa Loop** (p142) Hiking between remote villages to a stunning crater lake.
2. **Ruta de las Cascadas** (p157) Getting splashed by waterfalls as you plunge from the Andes to the jungle.
3. **Guamote** (p169) Exploring the packed streets full of vendors and shoppers bartering over livestock and potatoes at the village's authentic Thursday market.
4. **Nariz del Diablo** (p170) Riding the rails down an unparalleled switchback descent of a sheer rock face.
5. **Parque Nacional Cotopaxi** (p135) Climbing one of the world's highest active volcanoes, or hiking

or horseback riding around it.

6 **Volcán Chimborazo** (p162) Touching the clouds on an exhilarating bike ride down the volcano slopes, passing families of cute vicuñas as you go.

7 **Salinas** (p161) Taking the high road to this thriving village with excellent local cheeses.

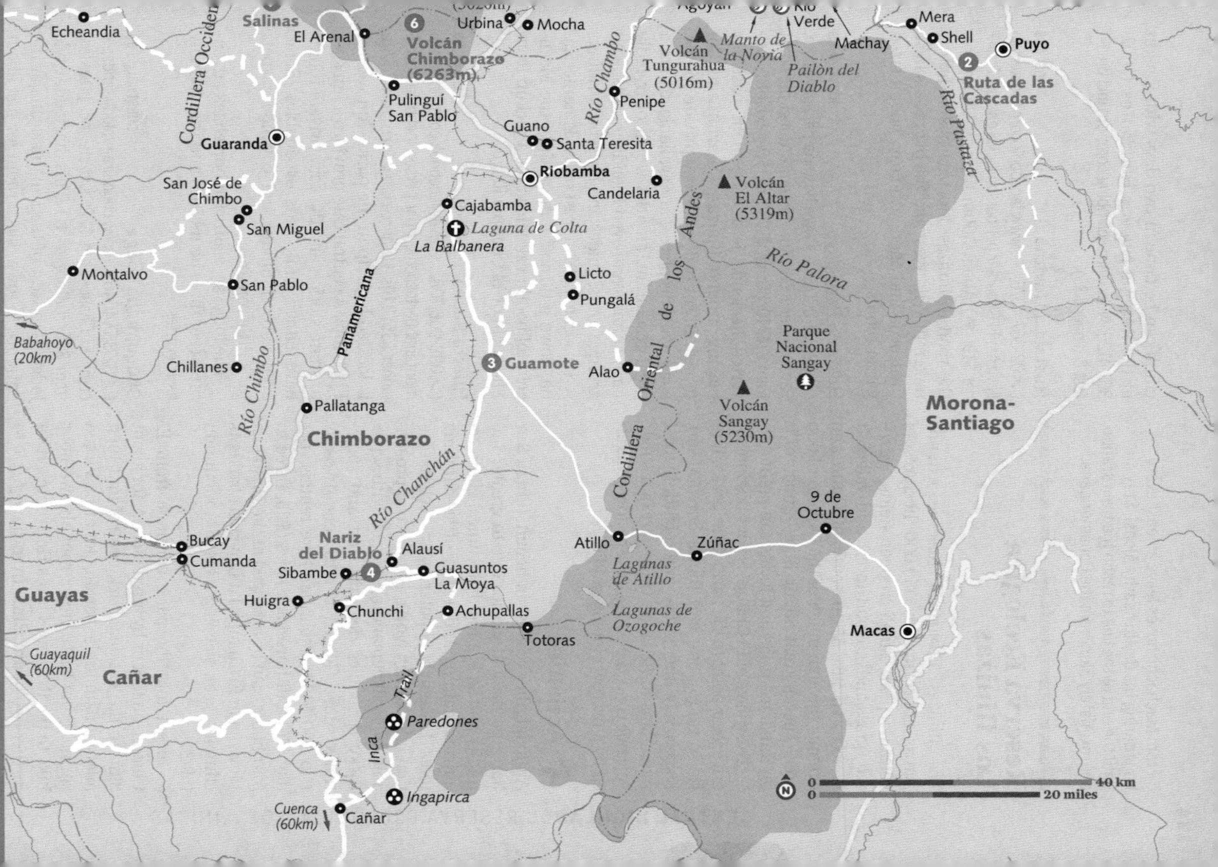

From Machachi, buses leave at least every hour during the day to nearby Aloasí. Stay on until the end of the line to reach the train station, approximately 3km from the Panamericana.

Reserva Ecológica Los Ilinizas

02

Los Ilinizas Ecological Reserve extends across approximately 150,000 hectares of volcanic peak, small-cropper fields, *páramo* (grasslands), cloud forest and valley. It is accessed just 55km south of Quito and extends through much of the Quilotoa Loop area. There's great hiking here – much of it on unnamed trails that locals can point out.

The village of **El Chaupi** is your best northern access point to the park's twin peaks, Iliniza Norte (5126m) and Iliniza Sur (5248m), respectively the sixth- and eighth-highest mountains in Ecuador. Once part of a single volcanic cone, the two spires are now separated by a narrow, sloping saddle.

Activities

Although they're close in height, **Iliniza Sur** has a permanent glacier due to greater humidity and so is a highly technical climb requiring training and a slew of ice-climbing tools. Extremely popular as an acclimatization hike, **Iliniza Norte** is a more approachable, but still demanding, ascent, with scree, rocky scrambles near the top and sometimes snow. Guided climbs (one-/two-day trip $90/$180), mountain-bike rentals (per day $15) and horseback rides ($35, three to four hours) can be arranged at the Hostal La Llovizna in El Chaupi. La Llovizna also rents climbing gear, sleeping bags and mountain bikes.

To get into the park, continue from El Chaupi, on foot or by hired pickup, for about 3km to the national park control and then another 6km to the parking lot at La Virgen shrine. From there, it is a roughly two-hour hike to the Refugio Nuevos Horizontes. It's a further two hours' climb from the *refugio* to the peak of Iliniza Norte; be sure to go with a qualified guide.

Sleeping

A range of sleeping options are available in and around the village of El Chaupi, about 9km from Los Ilinizas car park.

It's possible to climb Iliniza Norte in one day, beginning at 6am; alternatively the climb can be done in two days with a night at the **Refugio Nuevos Horizontes** (02-367-4125; www.ilinizasclimbing.com; dm incl breakfast & dinner $35).

Hostal La Llovizna HOSTEL **$**
(02-367-4076; www.facebook.com/hosterialallovizna; El Chaupi; r per person incl breakfast & dinner $19;) About 500m from El Chaupi on the road to Ilinizas, Llovizna has a slightly unkempt Wild West air. The big rooms have firm beds and there are cozy, hobbit-sized garret rooms.

Hostería PapaGayo HOSTERÍA **$$**
(02-231-0002; www.hosteria-papagayo.com; Panamericana Sur Km 26; dm/s/d incl breakfast from $14/40/50; @) This 150-year-old converted hacienda is a convenient base for playing around Ilinizas, Corazón and Cotopaxi. Dorm beds and cozy private rooms, some with fireplaces, are available, as are a great restaurant, an ark's worth of friendly farm animals and even friendlier hosts, who arrange tours, guides and horseback riding.

It's located 500m west of the Panamericana, down a turnoff 1km south of the Machachi tollbooth; call ahead for a pickup from Machachi or El Chaupi village.

Huerta Sacha LODGE **$$**
(098-906-7082; www.facebook.com/refugiodemontanahuertasacha; r per person incl breakfast & dinner $35) This 40-acre dairy farm and lodge is located high up in the park, 4km west of El Chaupi. A central cafe provides a fun spot to share stories, and the cozy private rooms have either bunk beds or doubles. Some even have chimneys and cowhide carpets for a little romance.

The lodge specializes in horseback adventures (per three hours $30) and is as friendly as it comes.

Chuquiragua Lodge GUESTHOUSE **$$**
(02-367-4046; www.chuquiragualodgeandspa.com; El Chaupi; dm $22, s/d/ste incl breakfast from $35/70/160; @) This hacienda-style lodge, 1km west of the Panamericana at the entrance to town, has a room for just about everybody. There are dorm rooms with fluffy bed covers and thick mattresses; premium rooms with nice views, chimneys and hardwood accents; and the slightly overstuffed (and overpriced) superior rooms. You'll love the spa area with a big hot tub and steam room.

There's also a camping area (per person $12.50).

Getting There & Away

Blue-and-white buses signed 'El Chaupi' ($0.35, 40 minutes) leave Machachi about hourly until dark from Amazonas at 11 de Noviembre, returning from the El Chaupi town square on the same schedule.

If you are driving from Machachi, a sign indicates the El Chaupi turnoff from the Panamericana about 6km south of Machachi. The road continues another 7km to El Chaupi. From El Chaupi, the road turns to dirt and continues another 9km to the Ilinizas parking area, identified by a small shrine to the Virgin.

You can hire a pickup in Machachi ($25, ask around the plaza) to take you directly to the parking area. Trucks from El Chaupi cost around $13.

Parque Nacional Cotopaxi

03

Although you can see **Volcán Cotopaxi** from several provinces, its majestic bulk and symmetrical cone take on entirely new dimensions within the bounds of its namesake **national park** (8am-5pm, last entry 3pm). Covered in a draping glaciated skirt that gives way to sloping gold and green *páramo,* the flanks of Cotopaxi are home to wild horses, llamas, fox, deer, Andean condor and the exceedingly rare spectacled bear.

Get here early for the best views. Hiking and mountain biking to pre-Columbian ruins around the area's lakes and along the park roads can be done with guides or on your own. And an ascent to the top of the peak is a singular experience any fit adventurer should try.

The 32,000-hectare park is easily reached on a day-trip from Latacunga or Quito.

Sights & Activities

Centro Visitantes VISITOR CENTER

(8-4pm) FREE Inside the park, 9km from Control Caspi, this small interpretation center has a few display boards explaining the natural history of the area. Take a minute to have a tea in the cafe (mains $3 to $3.50) or peruse the crafts shop. There's a small botanic garden and an 800m trail through the *páramo* (grassland).

Pucará del Salitre ARCHAEOLOGICAL SITE

On the road to the Río Pita, this Inca fort was built around the end of the 15th century. There are several stone walls and a semi-restored circular building.

A two-hour horseback riding excursion from Tambopaxi (p137) goes past the ruins.

THE SNOWS OF COTOPAXI

The snows of Cotopaxi may someday be no more; Cotopaxi's glaciers shrunk by 40% between 1976 and 2010. Tropical glaciers throughout the Andes are melting at an alarming rate, and many will soon disappear altogether. Many scientists point to rising temperatures in the Pacific Ocean, which have brought rain, instead of snow, to the region's glaciers. The annual snowmelt from glaciers is vital to farmers, hydro-electric projects and urban dwellers, and faster glacial melting could have serious economic impacts on the country.

★**Volcán Cotopaxi** CLIMBING

Summit attempts can be arranged in Quito and Latacunga. Although the climb is not technical – save for a few basic crevasse crossings and heart-pounding shimmies up fallen seracs – it is physically demanding, freezing and, for some people, truly vertigo-inducing.

The ascent starts around midnight from **Refugio José Rivas** (dm incl breakfast & dinner $45). Even experienced, fit and acclimatized climbers can only reach the summit at dawn about one of every two tries (no guarantees, baby!). The reward for those who make it to the top (on a clear day) are awesome views of other mountains and a peek at the crater's smoking fumaroles.

Even people with no mountaineering experience can make it safely to the top. Be sure you have a competent guide, good gear (rip-free ropes and harnesses, ice axe and crampons, warm double boots and jackets – no cotton, as it doesn't stay warm when it's wet like synthetics and wool – sunglasses, water, food, headlamp and emergency gear).

Your guide should teach you to self-arrest and use your ice axe, travel roped-in on glaciers, and put on your crampons the afternoon before the climb. It's important to meet with your guide before you head up. Ask them how many times they've climbed the mountain, what you need to climb the mountain, and if they are certified with the Ecuadorian Mountain Guides Association (ASEGUIM). If your harness is ripped, demand it be replaced; if you're not comfortable with your guide, ask the tour operator for someone else.

Parque Nacional Cotopaxi Area

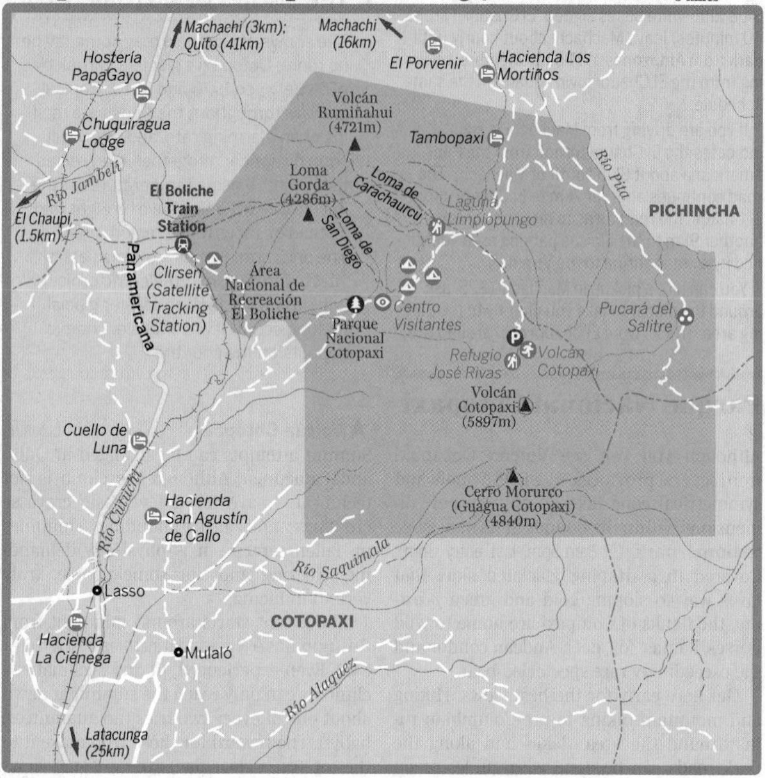

Laguna Limpiopungo HIKING

This shallow, reedy lake at the base of Volcán Rumiñahui is home to local and migrating waterfowl. An easy 2.6km trail circumnavigates the lake, but keep a safe distance from the bulls that like to sip at the shore. There are several viewing platforms around the lake.

North of the lake a trail takes you to the top of the 4721m Volcán Rumiñahui, a long day hike.

Refugio José Rivas HIKING

For a fun lung-buster, climb up the final 200m of the dirt trail from the Refugio José Rivas parking lot to the refuge itself (it will take you at least an hour at this altitude). Don't go onto the glacier (200m up from the refuge) without a guide, as there are crevasses.

Mountain Biking

Cruising around the park's circuit of relatively flat dirt roads is popular, as is a descent down from the *refugio* parking lot to the Control Caspi. Tour operators in Latacunga and Quito (such as Biking Dutchman; p67) can arrange trips.

Bird-watching

Bird-watching in the park is excellent. Keep your eyes peeled for the giant, soaring Andean condor and the Ecuadorian hillstar, one of the world's highest-altitude hummingbirds. Andean lapwing, Baird's sandpiper, Andean coot, caracara, Andean teal, Andean gull and solitary sandpiper are common visitors to Laguna Limpiopungo.

Sleeping & Eating

The luxurious lodges located in and around Cotopaxi National Park are some of the best in the country, and well worth the extra bucks you pay for volcano views. There are campsites in the park at the turnoff for Laguna Limpiopungo, at Tambopaxi and near the train station in the Área Nacional de Recreación El Boliche. Day-trippers can easily stay in Aloasí, El Chaupi or Latacunga.

Most lodges have good restaurants serving breakfast, lunch and dinner. Within the park itself, Tambopaxi serves food all day in their cozy dining room with spectacular views of Cotopaxi, and there's a small cafe at the park's visitor center (p135). The nearest towns for picking up supplies are Machachi to the north of the park and Lasso near the southern entrance.

★Hacienda Los Mortiños LODGE $$
(☎02-334-2520; www.losmortinos.com; dm/s/d/ste incl breakfast $28/74/103/$151; Wi-Fi) A wonderful place to stay not far from Control Norte on the north side of the park, this modern adobe dwelling has beautiful bathrooms, pitched ceilings, comfortable private rooms, dorms that sleep between six and 16 people, and jaw-dropping views of the neighboring volcanoes.

It definitely has a homey feel, and the friendly Fernandez family can offer information on excursions to the park. Call ahead to custom-build your stay. Meals are cooked in the beautiful open kitchen.

Secret Garden Cotopaxi GUESTHOUSE $$
(☎099-357-2714; www.secretgardencotopaxi.com; near Santa Ana del Pedregal; incl full board dm $38, d without/with bathroom $88/98) This lovely rustic property on the way to the northern entrance of Parque Nacional Cotopaxi has superb views (when the clouds clear) and loads of activities: hiking, horseback riding, mountain biking or simply relaxing in a hammock, sitting fireside or soaking in the Jacuzzi. Transfers from Quito are available through the sister hostel (p73).

Included in the room rates are three home-cooked meals a day, made with produce from the vegetable garden when possible; other ecologically conscious practices include compost toilets. Rooms range from dorms with bunks and woodburning stoves to cute hobbit rooms built into the hillside and cabins with private bathrooms. Camping is also available (per tent $23).

Cuello de Luna GUESTHOUSE $$
(☎999-727-535; www.cuellodeluna.com; El Chasqui, Panamericana Km 320; s/d incl breakfast $53/66, superior r $88; Wi-Fi) The 'Neck of the Moon' is a fun midrange option, located 1.5km down a turnoff across from the south entrance of Parque Nacional Cotopaxi. A gang of friendly Saint Bernards patrol the gardens, and the rooms have exposed wood beams and inviting fireplaces. The spacious superior rooms have down comforters.

There's as a sociable bar area and breakfast comes with homemade bread and yogurt produced with milk from the owner's cows.

El Porvenir HACIENDA $$
(☎02-204-1520; www.tierradelvolcan.com; camping per person $12, s/d/ste incl breakfast 44/55/172; ⏲restaurant 7:30-9:30am, 1-3pm & 7-9pm; Wi-Fi) Just 4km from the north entrance to the park, El Porvenir mixes the rustic comfort of an authentic hacienda experience with a strong ecological slant. Up in the roof space, small singles and doubles are separated by bamboo panels and share bathrooms; there are also cozy private rooms and suites. The restaurant is open to nonguests (mains $8 to $14.50).

The setting, high in the *páramo* (grassland) with nothing but views of Cotopaxi for company, is spectacular. There are tons of outdoor activities, such as horseback-riding, a high ropes course and mountain biking, as well as a new spa area with a Jacuzzi, massage rooms and a temazcal sweat lodge. Call ahead for transport.

★Tambopaxi GUESTHOUSE $$$
(☎02-600-0365; www.tambopaxi.com; camping per person $13, dm $24, s/d incl breakfast $91/115; Wi-Fi) Located within the national park boundaries, with Cotopaxi looming close by, Tambopaxi is a certified sustainable-tourism project that hires local workers. It's perfectly positioned for hikes, though you could spend all day gazing at the volcano, llamas and wild horses through the windows of the stove-heated main lodge. The restaurant here is open all day; a set lunch costs $17.50.

Dorm rooms have fluffy down comforters, and a luxurious separate structure has private rooms with woodburning stoves; all have outrageous views of Cotopaxi (be sure to set your alarm for sunrise). Activities include highly recommended horseback excursions ($20 for two hours) and guided hikes. The lodge is located about 25km along the main road from the park's south entrance (and 4km from the north entrance).

Chilcabamba GUESTHOUSE $$$
(☎02-240-8741; www.chilcabamba.com; s/d/ste/cabin incl breakfast $81/100/125/174; Wi-Fi) The volcano views more than make up for the

bumpy drive out to this charming, well-run mountain lodge near the northern entrance to Cotopaxi National Park. Pretty, pink-walled buildings with traditional straw-covered roofs are equally appealing on the inside, with wooden beams and wood-burning stoves. The restaurant serves up surprisingly sophisticated fare, including a 10-course tasting menu.

Hacienda La Ciénega HACIENDA **$$$**
(☎03-271-9093; www.haciendalacienega.com; Panamericana Km 326, near Lasso; s/d/ste incl breakfast $86/122/243;) This 400-year-old hacienda has hosted some illustrious guests, including the French Geodesic Mission, Alexander von Humboldt and Ecuadorian Presidents. A hotel since 1982, it still has hacienda charm: a long, eucalyptus-lined drive, meter-thick walls and an old chapel.

Hacienda San Agustín de Callo HACIENDA **$$$**
(☎03-271-9160; www.incahacienda.com; near Lasso; s/d/ste incl breakfast $230/400/455;) The distinctive, mortarless Incan stonework that forms many of the walls makes this hotel unique and mysterious. Surrounded by luscious gardens in a peaceful, bucolic setting, the 11 meticulously rustic rooms all come with fireplaces, plush spreads and hand-painted walls.

Information

Among the hazards here are the serious threat of altitude sickness and bulls. These problems can be avoided, the first by acclimatizing in Quito for a couple of days, drinking lots of water and donning sun protection, the second by keeping your distance.

VOLCANIC ERUPTIONS

After a period of inactivity lasting more than 80 years, in 2015 Cotopaxi once again began to smoke. By August it was emitting a dense cloud of ash, and fearing a major eruption of lava or a lahar (an avalanche of melted snow, rocks and mud), thousands of local residents fled their homes. But while the volcano continued to spit out plumes of ash and rumble periodically, no big eruption came. Life for locals slowly began to return to normal and in October 2017 the summit was finally reopened to climbers.

Getting There & Away

BUS

Buses to and from Quito, Machachi and Latacunga can be flagged down or drop you off at the Control Caspi turnoff on the Panamericana. From here you can hire a pickup truck to take you to the Refugio José Rivas (one-way/return $30/50). Be sure to be specific if you want to go all the way to the Refugio José Rivas.

CAR

All of the haciendas provide transportation from Quito, often at an additional cost.

On weekends, local tourists visit the park, and there is a good chance of getting a lift from the turnoff to the main entrance and on to Laguna Limpiopungo. Midweek, the park is almost deserted, and you'll probably end up walking if you don't arrange transportation.

There are two entrances to the park:

Control Caspi This is the main southern entrance. It's reached via a turnoff about 22km south of Machachi (or roughly 30km north of Latacunga). From the turnoff, it's 6km northwest over paved roads to Control Caspi and another 9km to the visitor center. Any Quito–Latacunga bus will drop you at the turnoff.

Control Norte (El Pedregal entrance) It's possible to reach the park through this northern entrance via Machachi, but you'll need to hire a pickup or rent a car. The 21km route is well signed and easy to follow.

Latacunga

☎03 / POP 51,717 / ELEV 2800M

Many travelers end up passing through Latacunga to access either the Quilotoa Loop or Parque Nacional Cotopaxi. But for those who stick around, Latacunga also offers a quiet and congenial historic center that has partially survived several Cotopaxi eruptions. You'd never know that such a charming city lies behind the loud and polluted section that greets visitors on the Panamericana.

Volcán Cotopaxi, which dominates the town on a clear day, erupted violently in 1742 and 1768, destroying much of the city both times. The indomitable survivors rebuilt, only to have an immense eruption in 1877 wreak havoc a third time. In 2015 Latacunga was once again coated in ash from Cotopaxi; luckily, no lava flows damaged the town.

To celebrate their rich indigenous and Catholic history, the people of Latacunga put on one of the most famous and magnificent parties in all of Ecuador, the Mamá Negra festival.

LATACUNGA'S MAMÁ NEGRA

One of the biggest celebrations in the highlands, the Mamá Negra (Black Mother) **parade** (late Sep & early Nov) is a combination of Catholic, pre-Columbian and civic rituals that fill the streets of Latacunga with hundreds of costumed and dancing revelers.

Traditionally staged on September 23 and 24, and again on November 8, Mamá Negra now occurs on the closest weekends to those dates. The November occasion also includes a bullfight, but locals say the September revelries are more authentic.

At the head of it all is a statue of the Virgen de las Mercedes, Latacunga's protectress from volcanic eruptions. Believing that the relic has saved the city from Volcán Cotopaxi's wrath many times, people from Latacunga have great faith in her image. (Apparently they overlook the three times that the city *has* been destroyed by Cotopaxi.)

The Mamá Negra, represented by a local man dressed up as a black woman, is said to have been added to the festivities later on. Politically incorrect as it might seem, Mamá Negra is an event loved by all. No one – especially foreign tourists! – can escape the *huacos* (shamans), who execute a ritual *limpieza* (cleansing) by blowing smoke and *aguardiente* (sugarcane alcohol) on spectators. Most impressive are the *ashangueros*, the men who carry *ashangas:* whole roast pigs, flayed open and flanked by dozens of *cuy* (guinea pigs), chickens, bottles of liquor and cigarettes.

Players representing *yumbos* (indigenous people from the Oriente), *loeros* (African slaves), *camisonas* (colonial-era Spanish women) and many more all have a role in this grand street theater.

Sights

Parque Vicente León PARK

Most action tends to center on this main plaza. At the southeast corner stands the republican-era **town hall**, topped by a pair of stone condors. On the south side stands the colonial-style **cathedral**. A 17th-century arcaded building houses the provincial government offices on the west side.

Mirador de la Virgen del Calvario VIEWPOINT

(Av Oriente) On a clear day, this lookout east of town offers views of several distant volcanic peaks. Follow Maldonado up the stairs, go left on Oriente and follow it up to the statue of the Virgin.

Mercado Cerrado MARKET

(cnr Valencia & Vela; 7am-9pm) Latacunga's large markets are quite utilitarian, but that's what makes them interesting. The food stalls on the second floor of the Mercado Cerrado (indoor market) are a great place to to sample local specialties such as *chugchucaras* (a fried pork dish; $1.25 to $2). Stalls spill out into the plazas around the intersection of Echeverría and Amazonas.

Casa de la Cultura MUSEUM

(Vela 3-49; 9am-1pm & 2-6pm Tue-Fri, 8am-4pm Sat) FREE This cultural center is built on the site of a former Jesuit watermill known as **Molinos de Monserrat** and houses a small ethnography and art museum. The stone steps above the river are a nice retreat from Latacunga's busy sidewalks. Check out its schedule for free dance and theater events.

Casa de los Marqueses de Miraflores MUSEUM

(Orellana & Echeverría; 8am-noon & 2-5pm Mon-Fri) FREE Take a break in this archaeological and religious museum housed in a colonial-era mansion. It has good background on the Mamá Negra festivals. The museum was closed for remodeling when we visited.

Tours

Many tour operators have sprung up in recent years. Day trips to Cotopaxi and Quilotoa cost around $40 per person, with price varying depending on group size. Add a bike descent from Cotopaxi for $15. Two-day climbing trips to Los Ilinizas, Cayambe and Volcán Cotopaxi (when open) cost about $250 per person. Hostal Tiana (p140) is a good spot to form groups for your trip.

Volcán Route Expeditions ADVENTURE

(03-281-2452; https://volcanroute.jimdo.com; Guayaquil, near Quevedo; 8am-8pm) Recommended climbing operator offering expeditions to Los Ilinizas, Cayambe, Cotopaxi and Chimborazo.

Tovar Expeditions ADVENTURE

(03-281-1333; www.tovarexpeditions.com; Vivero 1-31, Hostal Tiana) This friendly, long-standing

Latacunga

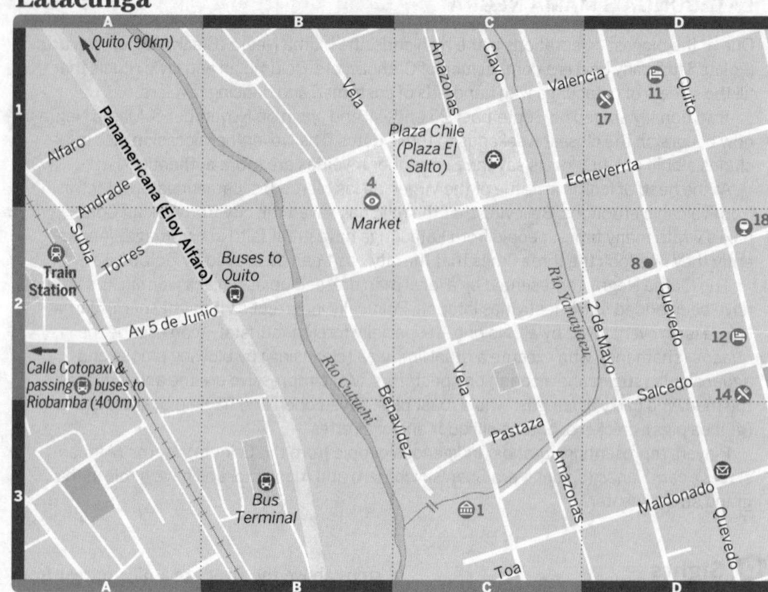

operator based at Hostal Tiana organizes tours to Quilotoa, Cotopaxi, Cayambe and Los Ilinizas.

Sleeping

Hostal Tiana HOSTEL $
(03-281-0147; www.hostaltiana.com; Vivero 1-31; dm/s/d incl breakfast $11/25/32, s/d without bathroom $16/25; @) This good-vibes place has everything a top-notch hostel should: common areas to swap tales, a kitchen, free internet, book exchange, clean rooms and bathrooms, luggage storage, good information and a free breakfast. The old colonial atmosphere lends an air of cool, but the old pipes may leave you wanting come hot-shower time.

Hotel Rodelu HOTEL $
(03-280-0956; www.rodelu.com.ec; Quito 16-31; s/d $18/34;) Popular with the tour groups but still down-home enough to attend to independent travelers, the Rodelu has highly fragranced Andean-style business digs with blaring orange comforters, granite-clad bathrooms and flat-screen TVs.

Its **restaurant** (Quito 16-31; mains $10-14, set lunch $3.70; 7am-9:30pm Mon-Sat) serves tasty pizzas and good-value set lunches.

Hotel Cotopaxi HOTEL $
(03-280-1310; hotelcotopaxi@yahoo.ec; Salcedo 5-61; s/d/tr $15/25/30;) Cotopaxi offers simple but spacious and comfortable rooms with TVs. Some rooms have large windows and pretty views of the central plaza. They can be a bit noisy; ask for a room in the back if you're a light sleeper.

Hotel Makroz BUSINESS HOTEL $$
(03-280-7274; Valencia 8-56; s/d/tr incl breakfast $35/60/75; P) The modern and clean Hotel Makroz is oriented toward business travelers, and you may be put off by the lack of common areas. The spacious rooms have cable TVs, fridges, blow-dryers and nice, big bathrooms.

Eating & Drinking

The classic dish of Latacunga, the *chugchucara* (say that 10 times fast!), is a tasty, heart-attack-inducing plate of *fritada* (fried chunks of pork, served with *mote,* or hominy), *chicharrón* (fried bits of pork skin), potatoes, fried banana, *tostado* (toasted corn), popcorn and cheese empanadas. Many cheap *leñadores* (woodburning ovens) roast chicken along Amazonas between Salcedo and Guayaquil.

Pollos Jimmy's LATIN AMERICAN $
(Quevedo 8-85, near Valencia; mains $4-5; ⏲10:30am-10pm Mon-Sat, to 8pm Sun) Pop in for delicious rotisserie chicken served with rice, potatoes and chicken soup. The place stays busy for a reason.

Guadalajara Grill MEXICAN $
(Quijano y Ordoñez 5-110, near Vivero; mains $5-10; ⏲noon-2:30pm & 6:30-10pm Mon-Fri, 6-10pm Sat; 📶) The only Mexican joint in town, this small, well-conceived spot has a wide variety of Mexican standards like quesadillas, nachos and fajitas. We love the silver dragonflies climbing the wall, and it's a welcome break from double-fried pork.

Chugchucaras La Mamá Negra ECUADORIAN $
(Quijano y Ordoñez 1-67; chugchucaras $9.50; ⏲10am-6pm Tue-Sun) There are several *chugchucara* restaurants on Quijano y Ordoñez, a few blocks south of downtown. They're all family-friendly, but La Mamá Negra is one of the best.

Pizzería Buona D'Juan PIZZA $
(Orellana 1408; pizza $5-7; ⏲1pm-10pm) This warm and inviting pizzeria serves up savory pizza pies, pasta dishes and fresh salads. The split-level dining room features crooked pictures of the leaning tower of Pisa on red walls.

Latacunga

Sights

1 Casa de la Cultura ... C3
2 Casa de los Marqueses de Miraflores ... E1
3 Cathedral ... E3
4 Mercado Cerrado ... B1
5 Mirador de la Virgen del Calvario ... F2
6 Parque Vicente León ... E3
7 Town Hall ... E3

Activities, Courses & Tours

Tovar Expeditions ... (see 9)
8 Volcán Route Expeditions ... D2

Sleeping

9 Hostal Tiana ... E2
10 Hotel Cotopaxi ... E2
11 Hotel Makroz ... D1
12 Hotel Rodelu ... D2

Eating

13 El Alabado ... E3
14 El Gringo y La Gorda ... D2
15 Guadalajara Grill ... E2
16 Pizzería Buona D'Juan ... E3
17 Pollos Jimmy's ... D1
Restaurant Rodelu ... (see 12)

Drinking & Nightlife

18 El Abuelo ... D2

★ **El Alabado** ARGENTINE $$
(www.facebook.com/chefgustavozarate; Maldonado 41-25, near Quijano y Ordoñez; mains $4.50-12; ⏲6-10pm Tue-Fri, noon-10pm Sat; 📶) Contemporary furnishings have transformed a historic building dating from 1668 into a chic restaurant. Along with good-quality beef steaks and dishes such as pork in a spicy passion fruit sauce, the Argentinian chef has infused the menu with the food of his homeland, including *choripan* (Argentine sausage sandwich) and *mate* tea. There's a decent wine list, too.

El Gringo y La Gorda CAFE $$
(☎03-223-3043; www.facebook.com/cafeelgringoylagorda; Salcedo, near Quito; mains $5-15; ⏲10am-10pm Tue-Sat; 🌿) Overlooking a courtyard fountain in a pretty colonial building, this cafe serves hearty breakfasts, huge sandwiches, salads and a good selection of vegetarian meals. Come night time the place takes on a romantic ambience with cocktails, candlelight and warming woodburning stoves.

El Abuelo BAR

(Guayaquil near Quito; 3-11pm Mon-Thu, to midnight Fri & Sat;) This hole-in-the-wall pub has just five cozy tables but plenty of character. There's a well-stocked bar with a lengthy cocktail list and local *cerveza artesanal* (craft beer) on tap.

Information

Banco Guayaquil (Maldonado 7-20)
Banco Pichincha (Quito, near Salcedo)
Hospital (Hermanas Páez, near 2 de Mayo)
Post Office (Quevedo, near Maldonado)

Getting There & Away

BUS

From Quito, buses will drop you at the **bus terminal** (Panamericana) if Latacunga is their final destination. If the bus is continuing to Ambato or Riobamba, it'll drop you on the corner of **Avenida 5 de Junio and Cotopaxi**, about five blocks west of the Panamericana and 10 minutes' walk to downtown.

Buses to Quito ($2.15, 1½ hours) and Ambato ($1.15, 1 hour) leave from the bus terminal and from the corner of Avenida 5 de Junio and Cotopaxi. For Riobamba, the easiest thing to do is catch a passing southbound Cuenca bus from the corner.

TAXI

You can hire taxis and pickup trucks in **Plaza Chile** (also called Plaza El Salto) for visits to Parque Nacional Cotopaxi (park interior $30, Control Caspi entrance $20).

The Quilotoa Loop

☎03

The Quilotoa Loop is a bumpy, ring-shaped road that travels from the Panamericana far into the backcountry of Cotopaxi province. Along the way you'll encounter colorful indigenous markets, a crystal-blue lake that the local people believe has no bottom, a community of painters who are preserving the legends of the Andes, and ancient trails that meander in the shadow of snowcapped volcanoes. The isolation of the loop brings you into contact with Kichwa-speaking indigenous people and their centuries-old way of life.

Several villages offer lodgings, and most travelers go from one place to the next by bus, hired truck or their own two feet. Consider timing your trip to coincide with one of the many market days. Zumbahua has a Saturday market, and Guantualo has a Monday market. Saquisilí's Thursday market is not to be missed.

Getting There & Away

No buses go all the way around the loop. From Latacunga, they only travel as far as Chugchilán, either taking the southern road through Zumbahua and Quilotoa or the northern road via Saquisilí and Sigchos. Tigua is served by regular buses passing between Latacunga and Quevedo. If you're more adventurous, catch a *lechero* (milk truck). If speed is your need, hire a taxi in Latacunga; rates start around $60.

Tigua

ELEV 3500M

From Latacunga, a paved road climbs through a golden patchwork of Andean countryside. On clear days, the views may include Cotopaxi, Rumiñahui and Los Ilinizas. Around Km 49 on the Latacunga–Zumbahua road, there's a signed turnoff to Tigua (a community of farmers and painters, but not a village proper), which is known for bright paintings of Andean life.

Sights & Activities

Galería Arte de Tigua GALLERY

(Latacunga–Zumbahua Rd, Km 53; 7am-6:30pm) The outstanding Galería Arte de Tigua and three other art galleries sell paintings and wooden masks at lower prices than those in Quito. If the gallery is closed poke around and ask for someone to open it (they will, happily).

Cañon del Toachi HIKING

From La Posada de Tigua, there's a six-hour hike up the Cañon del Toachi to Quilotoa. It takes you through a spectacular canyon, past traditional farms and up to the crater lake. A guide will cost you $35.

Sleeping

Posada de Tigua HACIENDA **$$**

(☎03-305-6103, 099-161-2391; posadadetigua@yahoo.com; Vía Latacunga–La Maná, Km 46; dm/r per person incl breakfast & dinner $30/40) La Posada de Tigua is part of a working dairy ranch. The farmhouse dates to the 1890s and is now a rustic and delightfully cozy guesthouse. The rooms, with meter-thick walls, have modern bathrooms and cowhide rugs, and meals include cheese and yogurt made on the farm as well as homegrown potatoes and carrots.

Quilotoa Loop

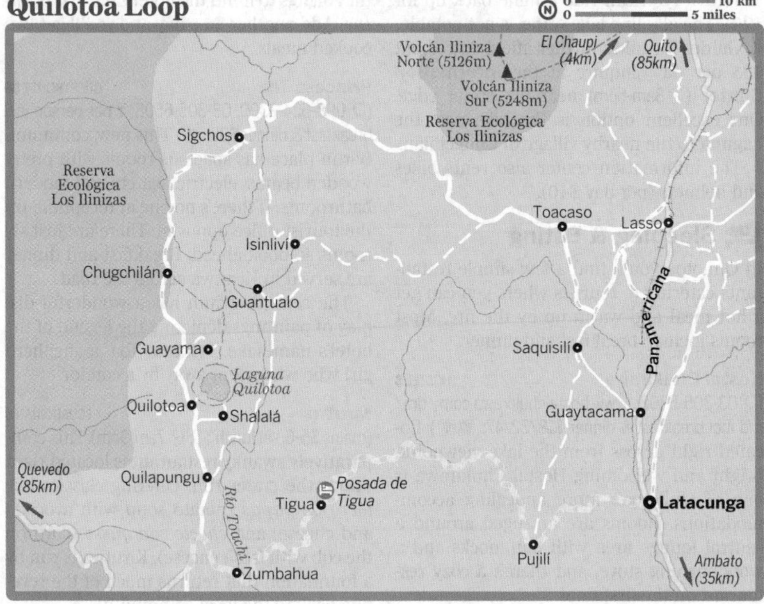

Getting There & Away

Buses to and from Latacunga pass by about once every hour ($2, one hour).

Zumbahua

ELEV 3800M

Some 15km southwest of Tigua, the small town of Zumbahua is surrounded by high bluffs and agricultural fields that soon give way to *páramo* (grasslands). It's worth stopping by its authentic Saturday market.

Sights

Saturday Market MARKET

Zumbahua has a wonderfully authentic Saturday market at which indigenous vendors from the mountains sell their wares. Check out the men on the south side of the market, who use old Singer sewing machines to tailor clothes, and the cuddly *cuy* (guinea pig) trade, which is fun to watch.

Sleeping & Eating

The Saturday Market is a great place to sample authentic Andean food, such as grilled corn and *cuy* (guinea pig). There are a few local eateries around the main plaza, none of them geared towards tourists.

There are several small and very basic hotels around the main plaza and side streets. They always fill up on Fridays, when it could be hard to get a room.

Getting There & Away

Buses to Latacunga depart hourly ($2, 1½ hours).

Quilotoa

ELEV 3914M

About 14km north of Zumbahua, the famous volcanic-crater lake of **Laguna Quilotoa** ($2) is a gasp-inducing sight. A lookout on the precipitous crater rim offers stunning views of the mirror-green lake 400m below and the snowcapped peaks of Cotopaxi and Iliniza Sur in the distance. When you ask the locals how deep it is, they inevitably say it has no bottom, which seems entirely plausible given its awesomeness (the geologists say 250m).

Activities

Fit walkers can hike the crater rim trail in about six hours; another path leads down to the water on a zigzagging trail. At the bottom, you can head out in a canoe or kayak (per 30 minutes $3). The hike down takes about half an hour and more than twice that to return (you can ride a mule back up for $20). The alkaline lake water is not potable.

Guides for hikes further afield cost about $35 per day; inquire at the **Information Center** (8am-5pm) near the crater edge. One excellent option is the hike past the Laguna to the nearby village of Chugchilán.

The information center also rents bikes and helmets (per day $40).

Sleeping & Eating

In Quilotoa you'll find a few simple restaurants catering to tourists where you can get a hot meal and warm up by the fire. Most rooms include breakfast and dinner.

Hostal Chukirawa HOSTEL $

(03-305-5808; www.hostalchukirawa.com; dm/s/d incl breakfast & dinner $18/32/47;) Located right across from the lake viewpoint, bright and welcoming Hostal Chukirawa is one of Quilotoa's more appealing accommodations. Rooms are arranged around a central lounge area with hammocks and a woodburning stove, and there's a cozy restaurant on the first floor.

Hostería Alpaca Quilotoa HOSTEL $

(099-212-5962; www.alpacaquilotoa.com; r per person $20;) Located on the edge of town, about 200m toward the lake from the entrance to Quilotoa, the Hostería Alpaca has quiet rooms with woodburning stoves and a rather abandoned-feeling restaurant area that brings to mind the hotel from *The Shining*. Add another $5 a day and you'll get two cooked meals.

Princesa Toa GUESTHOUSE $$

(098-524-2309, 03-305-6508; r per person incl breakfast & dinner $35;) This new, community-run place has spacious rooms with pretty wooden beams, electric heaters and modern bathrooms. If there's no one at reception, try the tourist office opposite. There are just six rooms so book ahead. Breakfast and dinner are served in Kirutwa across the road.

The central atrium has a wonderful display of paintings depicting the legend of the hotel's namesake, Princess Toa, a shepherd girl who was swept away by a condor.

Kirutwa ECUADORIAN $

(mains $5-6, set lunch $5; 7am-9pm) This comparatively swanky restaurant is located right up on the crater rim. Offering classics like *locro de papas* (potato soup with avocado and cheese) and *choclo con queso* (corn on the cob with fresh cheese), Kirutwa is run by a foundation that returns much of the revenue back to the local community.

Getting There & Away

Buses to Latacunga leave every two hours from 9am to 4pm ($2.50, two hours).

A shared pickup to Zumbahua costs around $5 per person; from there buses leave for Latacunga every hour.

HIKING THE LOOP

For many travelers, the Quilotoa Loop is one of the highlights of their trip to Ecuador. The hiking is fantastic, and although guides are inexpensive and a good way to support the local economy, many *hostales* (small, reasonably priced hotels) and inns also have maps for solo wanderers. Llullu Llama (p146) in Isinlivi is a particularly good source of information.

The loop is shorthand for the circular route clockwise by road from the Panamericana past Tigua, Zumbahua, Quilotoa, Chugchilán, Sigchos and Saquisilí; it's also possible to start at Saquisilí and travel the route in an counterclockwise direction. Isinliví lies off the main road, between Chugchilán and Sigchos.

Hikers usually chose to walk a two- to four-day section of the loop. Sigchos is a good place to start a three-day hike, with overnight stops in Isinliví and Chugchilán, finishing the walk in Quilotoa. Bear in mind that doing the walk in this way means slightly more uphill climbs (good for acclimatization but harder on the legs). Another option is to hike from Tigua to Quilotoa and on to Chugchilán.

Transportation is infrequent, so it takes some planning if your time is limited. It's wise to travel the loop with rain gear, water and plenty of snacks for long waits and hikes, but try to leave your heavy luggage behind and hike with a day pack (Hostal Tiana; p140) in Latacunga has a luggage storage room).

Many travelers have reported problems with dogs along the way. If they charge you, don't run away. Stand your ground, grab a rock and pretend to throw it.

Shalalá

ELEV 3900M

On the eastern edge of the Laguna Quilotoa crater, this small community-run sustainable tourism enterprise has a charming lodge and great views. It makes for an excellent waypoint on the crater-rim trail hike. You'll find a lovely botanic garden here with bouquets of *chuchitos* (bounteous purple flowers) and *pumpo* (reed-looking grass), crafts shopping and a short five-minute trail that takes you up to the crater's edge and an awesome glass-fronted mirador viewing platform.

Sleeping & Eating

The lodge restaurant opens for breakfast, lunch and dinner and makes a good stopping point on the crater rim trail. At weekends and in good weather there are stalls selling barbecued corn and other tempting snacks.

Shalalá LODGE **$$**
(☎093-944-4583, 03-280-0215; www.quilotoashalala.com; Shalalá; r per person incl breakfast $40, camping per person $5, meals $5-7) The nicest spot on the lake, 7km north of Quilotoa road, this community-run ecolodge has just four cabins, beautifully appointed with travertine tiles and hardwood headboards. The vaulted ceilings and exposed wood beams add rustic touches to the new buildings. You'll also love the quiet and seclusion of this wooded setting.

Getting There & Away

To get here, take the bus to Zumbahua and hire a pickup truck from there ($7 to $10), or walk along the crater rim trail from Quilotoa.

Chugchilán

ELEV 3200M

From Quilotoa the road winds down through 22km of breathtaking scenery to Chugchilán, a tiny Andean village that has been greatly enriched by ecotourism but maintains its age-old ways. From here you can hike to nearby villages, visit a cooperatively run cheese factory (6.5km west of town) or ride horses into the nearby cloud forest.

Sleeping

There are three excellent places to stay on the northern edge of town that arrange well-priced horseback riding trips, provide local hiking information, and can help set up private transport in and out of the Quilotoa Loop.

Hostal Cloud Forest HOSTEL **$**
(☎03-270-8181; www.cloudforesthostal.com; dm/s/d incl breakfast & dinner $15/20/30; @📶) The cheapest and simplest of Chugchilán's accommodations, this hostal has wood-accented rooms and clean bathrooms. The Ecuadorian owners serve tasty meals, and guests can chill out in the fireplace-heated common area. Located on the main road.

★**Black Sheep Inn** LODGE **$$**
(☎03-270-8077; www.blacksheepinn.com; incl full board dm $35, s/d $100/190, without bathroom $70/120; 📶) This wonderfully rustic property sits above the valley, 100m north of Chugchilán, and offers spectacular views. Rooms have a cozy cabin feel with stove heaters, tiled floors and exposed wood, and bathrooms are semi-open-air. Ecological practices here include composting toilets, rainwater collection, waste recycling and a wood-fired sauna. Three vegetarian meals a day are included in the rates.

El Descanso de Mama Hilda GUESTHOUSE **$$**
(☎03-270-8005; s/d incl breakfast & dinner $44/70, without bathroom $15/30, meals $7; 📶) This rambling guesthouse in the town center has brick-walled rooms with lofts

TIGUA PAINTINGS

One of Ecuador's homegrown art forms (and a worthy collector's item) is a style of painting called Tigua that originated near the shores of Laguna Quilotoa. The name comes from the small community of Tigua, where indigenous people had decorated drumskins for many generations. During the 1970s, Julio Toaquiza, a young indigenous man from the area, got the idea to turn those skins into canvases and paint colorful scenes from Kichwa legends. The artist, who spent his days growing potatoes and tending llamas, depicted these legends against the beautiful Andean scenery where he lived.

Toaquiza's art has brought fame to Tigua, and today more than 300 painters are at work in the highlands, with about 20 studios in Tigua itself.

and spotless bathrooms. You could spend an entire afternoon lounging in a hammock on your private porch. The real draw is the friendly family that runs it, and helps you arrange excursions, cooks your meals and shares stories about life in rural Ecuador.

Getting There & Away

Buses to Latacunga leave at 3:30am (via Sigchos), 5am (via Zumbahua) and 6am (via Zumbahua) Monday to Friday, at 3am (via Zumbahua) Saturday and 9am, 10am and 11am (all via Zumbahua) on Sunday ($2.50, 3 hours).

Pickups can be hired to Quilotoa ($20), Zumbahua ($25), Isinliví ($30), Sigchos ($20) and Latacunga ($50).

Sigchos

ELEV 2800M

From Chugchilán, it's a journey of 23km through cloud forest to the growing town of Sigchos. You'll likely stop here to catch a bus or while hiking from Chugchilán or Isinliví; otherwise it's not much of a destination, though a stop at the Hosteria San José is worth your time.

Sleeping

There are fewer guesthouses in the town of Sigchos than in other smaller villages along the Quilotoa Loop.

Hostería San José HACIENDA $$
(098-947-6772; www.sanjosedesigchos.com; s/d/tr incl breakfast $70/87/105, meals $12.50; restaurant noon-2:30pm & 7-8:30pm;) Located 2.5km south of Sigchos on the road to Chugchilán, this converted hacienda and working dairy farm has gorgeous gardens, whitewashed walls, a remarkably quaint chapel and comfortable rooms with thick mattresses and a few rustic touches. The enclosed pool, sauna and steam room are open for nonguests ($10), and it is a well worth the stop for dusty trekkers.

There's a games room with table football, a pool table and a karaoke machine, and you can hire horses ($10), quad bikes ($20) or book a massage ($40).

Getting There & Away

Buses to Latacunga ($2.35, two hours) depart at 4am, 5:30am, 11am & 2:30pm Monday to Saturday and noon, 2:30pm & 4pm on Sunday.

Buses to Chugchilán ($1, one hour) depart at about 1:30pm & 3pm daily.

A bus to Isinliví ($1, one hour) departs at about 2:15pm daily except Thursday, when it leaves at 1:15pm.

Pickup trucks make frequent trips to Latacunga (per person $5).

Isinliví

ELEV 2900M

The beautiful and blissfully peaceful village of Isinliví makes a good hike from either Sigchos (11km) or Chugchilán (12.5km). The views of mist-cloaked mountains are spectacular, there are plenty of trails for day hikes and the lower elevation makes nights here less chilly than other spots on the Quilotoa Loop. Locals can direct you to nearby *pucarás* (pre-Incan hill fortresses).

Activities

Guantualo Loop HIKING
A popular day hike is to the Monday-morning market at nearby Guantualo. The 10km round-trip takes three to four hours; Llullu Llama can provide detailed directions and maps for this and other hikes.

Sleeping & Eating

Isinliví's tranquil setting, walking trails and top accommodations make it worth considering spending more than one night here.

Although there are a few tiny stores in the village, it's best to bring your own supplies. Llullu Llama sells good packed lunches ($6.50) that are perfect for bringing on hikes.

★ **Llullu Llama** GUESTHOUSE $
(099-367-8165, 099-292-8559; www.llullullama.com; dm/r/cottage per person incl breakfast & dinner from $19/23/39) Two blocks west of the plaza, Llullu Llama is an enchanting old farmhouse with thick adobe walls, colorful rooms and a woodburning stove. The biggest attractions here are the good-time vibes, friendly hosts and spectacular surroundings. Cottages with exposed wood, fireplaces, large beds and giant showers are well worth the extra cash. Rooms in the main house share bathrooms.

A solar-powered hot tub, steam room and sauna are in a small spa below ($7.50).

Hostal Taita Cristobal GUESTHOUSE $
(099-137-6542, 098-169-351; www.hostaltaitacristobal.wordpress.com; camping $5, r per person incl breakfast & dinner $15;) This budget option one block east of the church has great

views from its spotless rooms, which spread over two floors and all look out to the valley below. There's a garden with a grassy area for tents, and campers can use the shared kitchen and cozy dining room.

Getting There & Away

A Vivero bus leaves Latacunga's bus terminal for Isinliví ($3, three hours) at 1pm all days except Saturday, when it leaves at 11am. Thursday buses leave from Saquisilí at 11am. Buses to Latacunga leave Isinliví at 3:30am.

Saquisilí

POP 5234 / ELEV 2940M

Other than the Thursday morning market, which is worth a look, this small village offers limited attractions and fewer walking trails than other spots along the Quilotoa Loop. Most hikers prefer to continue on to Sigchos and begin walking from there.

Sights

Thursday Morning Market MARKET

(5am-11am Thu) The Thursday morning market in Saquisilí is one of the best in the central highlands. It's a mostly authentic and fascinating place to observe the array of material goods that are part of everyday life in the area.

The market is made up of eight plazas, which are like a bustling outdoor department store with mostly indigenous shoppers; there's a department for *cuy* (guinea pig), *angarillas* (donkey saddles), *sastrería* (tailoring services), *ollas* (pots) and hundreds, perhaps thousands, of other items.

Getting There & Away

Most travelers stay in Latacunga and jump on buses that start running at dawn ($0.40, 20 minutes).

On Thursday buses to Sigchos ($1.75; 1½ hr) leave from the market at 11am and noon.

Ambato

03 / POP 154,370 / ELEV 2577M

While busy Ambato makes it onto few travelers' must-see lists, the town is not without its charms. The central plaza gives an authentic picture of big-city life in the Andes, and it's a town of growing cultural sophistication, housing the best museums in the Central Highlands. Above town, there are fabulous views of the puffing Volcán Tungurahua (5016m), and Ambato's parks and quintas (historic country homes) offer some respite from the bustle of downtown. The **Monday market** fills Ambato's central streets and plazas, and is a major hub in the flower trade.

The city is proud of its cultural heritage and nicknames itself 'Land of the Three Juans' after the writers Juan Montalvo and Juan León Mera, and lawyer/journalist Juan Benigno Malo. All three Juans are immortalized in Ambato's parks, museums and buildings.

In 1947 an earthquake destroyed Ambato, the capital of Tungurahua province, and a modern city was rebuilt.

Sights

★Museo Provincial Casa del Portal MUSEUM

(cnr Castillo & Sucre; 9am-1pm & 2-6pm Mon-Fri, 10am-4pm Sat & Sun) FREE This majestic home was built in 1900 and now houses Ambato's best museum. There are tons of interesting historic photos on the 1st floor. Head up to the 2nd floor and you will find six galleries featuring both original artwork from local painters like Oswaldo Viteri and reproductions of Ecuadorian masterworks.

The amphitheater out back has free performances on Sundays at 11am.

Casa y Mausoleo de Montalvo MUSEUM

(03-242-4938; www.casademontalvo.gob.ec; Montalvo, near Bolívar; adult/child $1/0.50; 9am-noon & 2-6pm Mon-Fri, 9am-4pm Sat) On the northwest side of Parque Juan Montalvo is this museum in Montalvo's pied-à-terre; the grand mausoleum in which the writer is interred is on the same site. Montalvo was politically liberal and his writings were critical of President García Moreno and Ecuadorian politics at the time. He died in France in 1889, where he was living in exile; his remains were returned to Ambato in 1932. The museum contains books, letters and personal objects belonging to Montalvo.

Museo de Ciencias Naturales MUSEUM

(03-282-7395; Sucre, near Lalama; 8:30am-12:30pm & 2:30-6:30pm Mon-Fri) FREE Although a bit dusty, this natural history museum in the Colegio Bolívar houses Ecuador's most thorough collection of stuffed birds, mammals and reptiles. Exhibits include an extensive collection of pre-Columbian bowls, axes and gourds.

Ambato

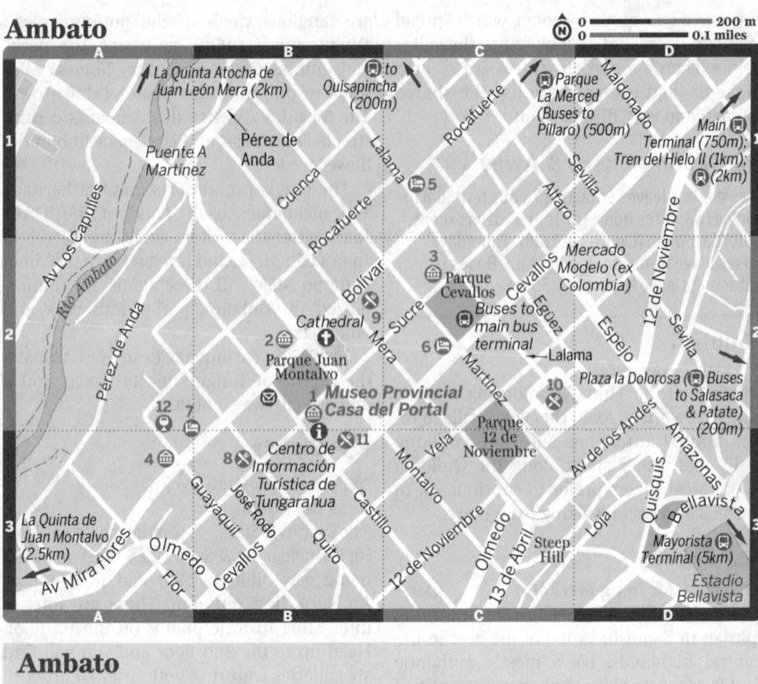

Ambato

Top Sights
1 Museo Provincial Casa del Portal B2

Sights
2 Casa y Mausoleo de Montalvo B2
3 Museo de Ciencias Naturales C2
4 Museo Pictórico Edmundo Martínez.... A3

Sleeping
5 Gran Hotel Napoleón C1
6 Hotel Boutique Mary Carmen C2
7 Hotel Roka Plaza A2

Eating
8 Delicias del Paso B3
9 Los Morochos de la Gata B2
10 Mercado Central C2
11 Pizzería Fornace B3
Restaurant Roka Plaza .... (see 7)

Drinking & Nightlife
12 Los Vinitos A2

Museo Pictórico Edmundo Martínez MUSEUM
(Guayaquil, near Bolívar; ⌚9am-5:30pm Tue-Sat) FREE Housed in a stone-faced mansion, this small museum has occasional live music and rotating exhibits from local artists.

★ **Quinta de Juan León Mera** GARDENS
(☎03-282-0419; Av Rodrigo Panchano; $1; ⌚9am-4:30pm Wed-Sun) Several famous *ambateños* (people from Ambato) had quintas that survived the earthquake. They were once considered countryside homes, but today they are right on the edge of this growing city. Admission to the Quinta de Juan León Mera – set on the banks of the Río Ambato in the suburb of Atocha, about 2km northeast of downtown – includes entry to the Casa Museo Martínez-Holguín and La Liria botanic garden on the same site. To get here, take bus 22 for Atocha from Parque Cevallos; a taxi costs about $2.

Mera's house, built in 1874, has period furnishings and wax figures portraying the life and times of the author and politician, who is best known for writing the lyrics to the Ecuadorian national anthem. It sits in the **Jardín Botánico La Liria**, a lush garden with more than 200 plant species. **Casa Museo Martínez-Holguín** is in the same complex. It's another period quinta formerly owned by relatives of Mera's, an illustrious family of geologists, painters, mountain-climbers, journalists and politicians. Free tours of both museums are offered in Spanish.

Quinta de Juan Montalvo MUSEUM
(03-246-0643; Av Los Guaytambos, Sector Ficoa Las Palmas; adult/child $1/free; 9am-4pm Wed-Sun) This 200-year-old house was the countryside retreat of writer Juan Montalvo, the 'Cervantes of America.' There's a tiny but well-put-together museum dedicated to the author – his house was really small – and the pretty terraced gardens are worth a peek.

The quinta is roughly 3km southwest of Parque Cevallos, on the other side of the river. Taxis from downtown cost about $2.

There is a larger museum (p147) in Montalvo's former townhouse.

Tours

Tren del Hielo II TOURS
(1-800-873-637; www.trenecuador.com; cnr Colombia & Chile; adult/child $22/12; Fri & Sat) This nine-hour train tour (the train looks more like a school bus) takes you through the surrounding countryside to the villages of Cevallos for a visit to a local shoe factory, and Urbina for views of Volcán Chimborazo and crafts shopping. It departs from 100m north of the main bus terminal.

Festivals & Events

Fiesta de Frutas y Flores FESTIVAL
(Fruit & Flower Festival; www.fiestasdeambato.com; late Feb) This annual festival has magnificent displays of, you guessed it, fruit and flowers. There are also bullfights, parades and the Reina de Ambato (Queen of Ambato) pageant. It's held in the last two weeks of February.

Sleeping

Problems have been reported in the budget lodgings around Parque 12 de Noviembre. It's worth paying a bit more for a hotel the other side of Avenida Cevallos.

★**Hotel Roka Plaza** BOUTIQUE HOTEL $$
(03-242-3845; www.hotelrokaplaza.com; Bolívar, btwn Quito & Guayaquil; s/d incl breakfast $45/70;) Housed in an old *casona* (large colonial-era house), this tasty boutique hotel has the nicest rooms in the city center. There are only seven of them, so call ahead. Modern touches blend seamlessly with antiques, and you'll find interesting art throughout.

Gran Hotel Napoleón HOTEL $$
(03-282-4235; granhotelambatoecu@hotmail.es; Rocafuerte 10-45, near Lalama; s/d incl breakfast $25/45;) A recent makeover has freshened up the Gran, where the newly decorated rooms have shiny laminate floors, wallpapered feature walls and flat-screen TVs. The staff are helpful and pleasant, making this your best budget bet.

Hotel Boutique Mary Carmen BOUTIQUE HOTEL $$$
(03-242-0908; www.hotelboutiquemc.com; cnr Cevallos & Martínez; s/d/ste incl breakfast $55/90/200;) A study in contemporary eccentricity, this retrofitted boutique has themed floors that feature ultra-kitsch halograph pictures, odd sculptures and plenty of jungle-print furniture. Choose between zebra, rhino, tiger and old-time-Ambato themed floors. It also has a small dip pool, spa and hot tub on site.

Eating & Drinking

Los Morochos de la Gata ECUADORIAN $
(www.facebook.com/losmorochosdelagata2; cnr Bolívar & Mera; morocho $0.90, snacks $0.75; 7:30am-12:30pm & 3-6:30pm Mon-Fri, 8am-1pm & 4-7pm Sat) A great place to sample an Ambato specialty, a kind of porridge-like milky drink made with the morocho grain, which is ground with spices, soaked in water then boiled with milk and sugar. Try it with *humitas* (ground corn with onions and eggs, cooked in the husk) or *quimbolitos* (a kind of sweet, steamed pudding).

Mercado Central MARKET $
(12 de Noviembre; mains $2; 8am-5pm) The 2nd floor of Ambato's indoor market has particularly good *llapingachos* (fried pancakes of mashed potatoes with cheese), served with eggs, avocado slices and sausage (vegetarians can get it without the meat) for $2. Nearby stalls sells super-fresh juices made with bottled water ($1).

Delicias del Paso CAFE $
(cnr Sucre & Quito; baked goods $1-3, set lunch $3.80; 8am-8:30pm Mon-Sat) This cafeteria has all its tasty quiches, sandwiches and cakes on display out front, and you can order them to go right from the street. Take a seat inside for a sandwich or *almuerzo* (set lunch).

Restaurant Roka Plaza INTERNATIONAL $$
(Bolívar, btwn Quito & Guayaquil; mains $10-20; noon-10pm) In the Roka Plaza's central courtyard, this wonderful restaurant serves grilled meats, fresh juices, international dishes and good sushi. The presentation is better than you'll find anywhere else in

the central highlands, and the ambience is exquisite.

Pizzería Fornace PIZZA $$
(☎03-282-3244; Cevallos 17-28; mains $6-17; ⏲noon-10pm Sun-Thu, to 11pm Fri & Sat) Cooked in a wood-fired brick oven, this is probably the best pizza in town – though some find it to be a bit doughy. Locals enjoy the cuts of meat here as well, and you'll love the candle-lit ambience and the $4 wine carafes.

Los Vinitos PUB
(cnr Rocafuerte & Guayaquil; ⏲noon-11pm Mon-Thu, to midnight Fri & Sat) This cozy two-story bar is perfect for quietly conspiring in a corner. It's one of our faves.

Information

Many robberies are reported on overnight buses here, and it's best to take a cab at night downtown. Take extra care in the areas around Parque 12 de Noviembre at night.

Banco Guayaquil (cnr Mera & Sucre)
Banco Pichincha (Lalama, near Sucre)
Post Office (cnr Castillo & Bolívar; ⏲8am-5pm Mon-Fri, to noon Sat)
Centro de Información Turística de Tungarahua (Tungarahua Tourist Information Center; cnr Castillo & Sucre; ⏲8am-4pm Mon-Fri) For information on trips to seldom-visited spots in the Tungarahua countryside, swing by this friendly information center.

Getting There & Away

Buses to most destinations (but not Baños) depart from Ambato's **main bus terminal** (Av de las Américas), 2km northeast of downtown.

Buses to Salasaca ($0.25, 25 minutes) and Patate ($0.70, one hour) leave every 20 minutes or so from Plaza la Dolorosa in the Ferroviaria neighborhood, a $1 cab ride from downtown.

Buses leave hourly for Baños ($1, one hour) from the **Baños Terminal**, about 5km south of the main bus terminal, near the roundabout at Bolivariana and Julio Jaramillo.

Getting Around

The most important local bus service for travelers is the route between Ambato's main bus terminal and downtown. From the terminal, climb the exit ramp to Avenida de las Américas, which crosses the train tracks on a bridge. On this bridge is a bus stop, where a westbound (to your right) bus, usually signed 'Centro,' will take you to Parque Cevallos for $0.30.

Number 15 buses marked 'Terminal' leave from the Martínez side of **Parque Cevallos**.

Around Ambato

Salasaca

You'll know when you've reached the rather ugly town of Salasaca, about 14km south of Ambato, because of the abundance of men walking around in long, black ponchos over crisp white shirts and trousers. Along with a broad-brimmed white hat, men wear the distinctive black Salasaca poncho. Women wear colorful shawls and long wool skirts with a woven belt called a *chumbi*.

On the Sunday after Easter, a magnificent street dance takes place on the road (slowing traffic considerably), and on June 15 the Salasacans dress up in animal costumes for **Santo Vintio**. Both **Corpus Christi** (on a moveable date in June) and the **Feast of St Anthony** (end of November) are colorfully celebrated.

Sights

Crafts Market MARKET
(⏲8am-6pm) Next to the church on the Ambato–Baños road, behind a statue of a local man donning a black poncho, this market has some great local artisan goods, including Salasaca's famous wool ponchos and hand-woven rugs and tapestries. The busiest day is Sunday, but at least a few stalls open daily.

Museo del Pueblo Salasaca MUSEUM
(☎099-433-1458, 03-274-8974; www.museosalasaka.wordpress.com; Vía Ambato-Baños; suggested donation $5; ⏲9am-6pm) If you're interested in indigenous culture, a look around this museum is well worth your time. However the exhibits, spread over five floors, require some explanation; recommended guided tours are offered in Spanish. The museum is opposite the artisan market on the Ambato to Baños road.

Sleeping

Hostal Runa Huasi LODGE $
(☎099-984-0125; www.hostalrunahuasi.com; r per person incl breakfast $17) This rustic, friendly place in a peaceful setting is run by the indigenous Pilla family. There are wonderful views from the gardens; on a clear day it's possible to see Cotopaxi, Chimborazo, Tungurahua and El Altar among other volcanoes. The simple rooms share bathrooms, and there's a cozy dining room with a few

OFF THE BEATEN TRACK

EXPLORE MORE AROUND AMBATO

Day trips or longer excursions from Ambato can take you to a handful of exciting indigenous villages and a seldom-visited national park. Taxis to these villages cost about $10 per 10km. Get more tips on trips at the Centro de Información Turística de Tungarahua.

Mocha This small village, 24km south of Ambato, has a set of lava tubes.

Parque Nacional Llanganates FREE They say there's lost Inca treasure buried somewhere in the remote and inaccessible wilderness of the 2197-sq-km Parque Nacional Llanganates. The park encompasses broad swaths of *páramo*, cloud forest, tropical forest and 4000m peaks, and is home to tapir, puma, jaguar, capybara and more. You can hire a guide for about $30 a day in the small village of Píllaro, 20km northeast of Ambato. December to February is the best time to visit.

Píllaro The entry point for visits to Parque Nacional Llanganates is known for its festivities, including bullfighting on August 10, and the Diablada festival, featuring parades and locally made devil masks, which runs from January 1 to 6.

Pelileo Looking for a sweet pair of Ecu-Jeans? This is the nation's denim capital. It's an easy stop 19km from Ambato on the road to Baños. Denim shops line the main road.

Quisapincha Just 10km outside of Ambato, this quaint little village is a great spot to pick up leather goods. The views from up here are amazing.

Tisaleo This small village, 17km south of Ambato, is known for guitar manufacturing. Local artisans are happy to share their work.

books and information on the surrounding area.

Getting There & Away

Buses run regularly to Ambato ($0.50, 30 minutes) and Baños ($0.75, 45 minutes).

Patate

Along the banks of the Río Patate, and with great views of Volcán Tungurahua, Patate has become a popular spot for volcano-watchers during recent eruptions. There's a fun hike up the remarkably steep stairway known as **La Escalinata**, just east of town off Soria, while strolling through the lush main square and taking in the air is a favorite pastime for locals and visitors alike.

Sleeping & Eating

The village is known for its *chicha de uva* (a fermented grape beverage) and *arepas* (where squash is added to traditional corn pancakes), lovingly prepared in wood ovens around town. If *arepas* aren't being sold on the plaza, head over to Gonzalez Suarez.

La Casta HOTEL $

(03-570-130; www.lacastapatate.com; s/d incl breakfast from $18/35; wi-fi) Your best bet for sleeping near the town, Casta Restaurant and Hotel is a cozy mountain retreat with an excellent family restaurant and cabin-style rooms with great views. The hotel is just 500m east of town up a steep hill.

Hacienda Manteles HACIENDA $$$

(03-306-3257; www.haciendamanteles.com; r/ste incl breakfast $199/255; @) Hacienda Manteles, about 12km down the Ruta Ecológica, is a beautiful, upscale, rustically styled resort engaged in certified ecotourism practices. Among other things, it supports local communities in creating micro-businesses, has an organic garden and protects 200 hectares of forest, which you can explore.

Getting There & Away

Buses run regularly from Ambato to Patate ($0.75; 40 minutes).

Baños

03 / POP 14,700 / ELEV 1800M

Baños is a mixed bag. The setting is amazing. From town you can see waterfalls, hike through lush forests, rest your bones in steaming thermal springs, hike down impossibly steep gorges, bike or boat all the way to the Amazon Basin, and marvel at the occasional eruption of nearby Volcán Tungurahua. But the town itself is somewhat overwhelmed with garish tour operators, cut-price spas and budget accommodations,

Baños

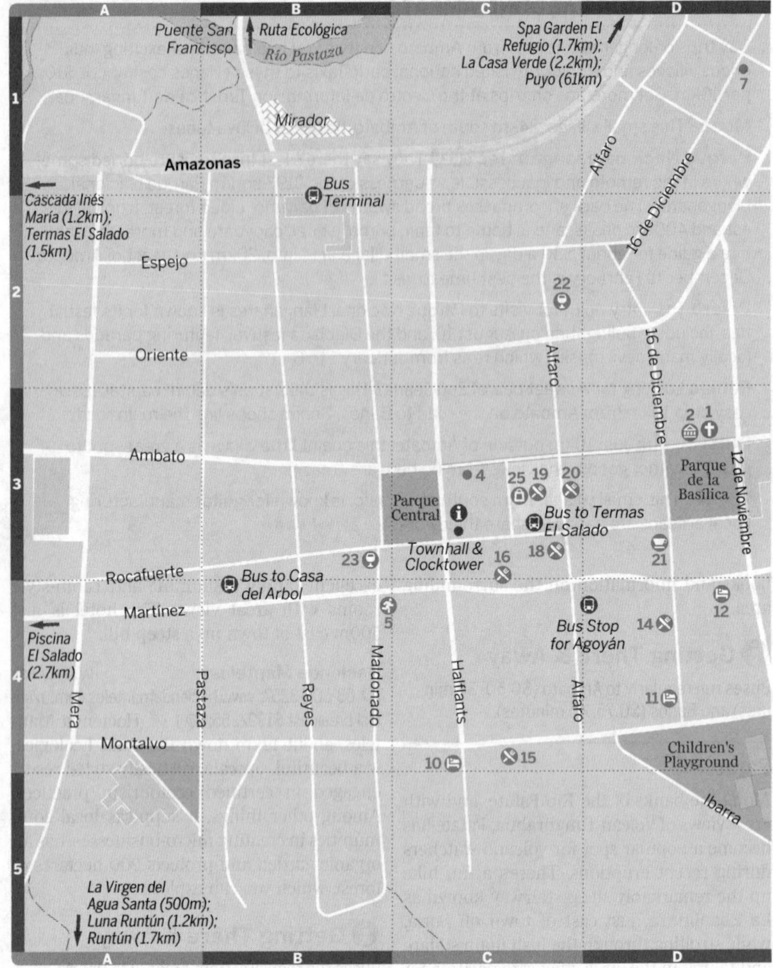

and much of the architecture is rather drab. This said, this is the central highlands' premiere destination for mountain biking, hiking, rafting and partying, and while many folks will have their reservations about the town's look and feel, almost everybody leaves with a big smile on their face and great stories from their adventures.

Sights

Baños is tiny and the mountains towering over town make it easy to find your way around. Almost everything in town is within walking distance from the bus terminal. Note that few buildings in Baños have street numbers.

Basílica de Nuestra Señora de Agua Santa CHURCH

(Ambato, near 12 de Noviembre; ⏲7am-8pm) This Basilica is dedicated to the Virgin of the Holy Water, who is credited with several local miracles. Inside there are several artworks by Father Enrique Mideros depicting the miracles.

Museo Fray Enrique Mideros MUSEUM

(Ambato, near 16 de Diciembre; adult/child $1.50/0.75; ⏲8am-12:30pm & 2-5:30pm Mon-Fri,

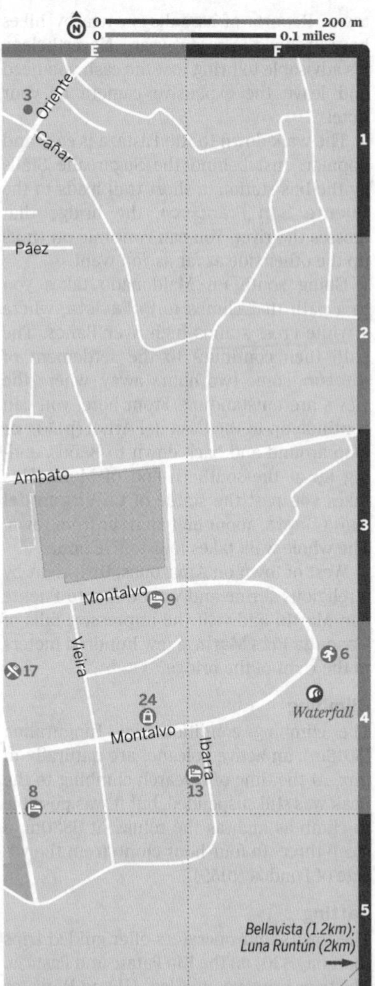

Baños

Sights

1 Basílica de Nuestra Señora de Agua Santa ... D3
2 Museo Fray Enrique Mideros ... D3

Activities, Courses & Tours

3 Baños Spanish Center ... E1
4 Geotours ... C3
5 José & Two Dogs ... B4
6 Las Piscinas de La Virgen ... F4
7 Raíces Spanish School ... D1

Sleeping

8 Casa Arte Huillacuna ... E4
9 Hostal Chimenea ... E3
10 La Floresta ... C4
11 La Petite Auberge ... D4
12 Plantas y Blanco ... D4
13 Posada del Arte ... F4

Eating

14 Café Good ... D4
15 Cafe Mariane ... C4
16 Casa Hood ... C3
17 La Tasca de Baños ... E4
18 Mega Bodega ... C3
19 Mercado Central ... C3
20 Ponche Suizo ... C3

Drinking & Nightlife

21 La Tostaduria ... D3
22 Leprechaun ... C2
23 Stray Dog ... B3

Shopping

24 Maki Awashka ... E4
25 Pasaje Artesanal ... C3

8am-5:30pm Sat & Sun) Adjoining the church, this museum in the priest's former living quarters contains several oil paintings by Father Enrique Mideros as well as his collection of more than 500 pre-Columbian sculptures and utensils. Additional rooms house religious sculptures and assorted taxidermy (pumas, bears, snakes and birds).

Casa del Arbol VIEWPOINT
($1; 7am-6:30pm) Perched on a hilltop behind Baños, just beyond the village of Runtún, this grassy viewpoint is a photographer's dream. As well as a pretty tree house, there are several swings where you can whoosh over the precipice, making for fabulous shots. On a clear day you can see Volcán Tungurahua. Buses leave at 5.45am, 11am, 1pm, 2.15pm and 4pm from the corner of **Pastaza and Rocafuerte** ($1, 1 hour).

It takes about three hours to hike here from Baños (ask for a map at the tourist office; p157).

Activities

Baths

Most baths are fed by thermal springs burbling from the base of Volcán Tungurahua.

★Las Piscinas de La Virgen THERMAL BATHS
(Montalvo; adult/child $2/1, after 6pm $3/1.50; 5am-5pm & 6-9:30pm) These are the only hot pools in the town proper. Built as a community project in 1928, they are named for the Virgin Mary, who is said to have come

here to dip her own feet. Some baths are cold, others warm and one reaches an intense 42°C (118°F). The rooftop pools have lovely views of a nearby waterfall.

Check out the *ojo del agua,* where the water, heated by the volcano, gushes from the earth at a scorching 50°C (122°F).

At the time of research a $6.2 million construction project was underway to expand the complex to create one of the largest thermal baths in South America. A total of more than 10 separate pools will include a large swimming pool with slides and a wave machine.

Termas El Salado THERMAL BATHS

(Salado; adult/child $3/1.50; ⏲5am-8pm) These wonderful hot springs are located in a verdant canyon, some 2.5km from town. There are hot, medium and cool pools surrounded by tree-covered hills, with the soothing sounds of a fast-flowing river close by. You'll need a swimming cap. Buses to here ($0.25, 10 minutes) depart from the stop on Rocafuerte (p157).

Massages & Spa Treatments

Baños has an endless supply of spas with such treatments as the *baños de cajón* (steam baths in a box), massage, medicinal mud baths and, yes, even intestinal drainage. The high-end hotels all have spas open to nonguests.

Spa Garden El Refugio SPA

(☎03-274-0482; www.spaecuador.info; Camino Real; treatments from $8) This day spa in a pretty spot by the river offers steam baths, mud baths, massages, facials and a number of indoor heated pools.

Mountain Biking

Several companies rent mountain bikes starting at about $7 per day ($15 gets you disk brakes and suspension), but check that the bike, helmet and lock are adequately maintained or even ask to take a quick test ride before agreeing to rent. The most popular ride is the dramatic descent past a series of waterfalls on the road to Puyo, a jungle town 61km to the east. Various other mountain-biking options are available and the outfitters will be happy to tell you about them.

Hiking

The tourist office (p157) provides a useful map showing some of the trails around town. Reports of assaults on nearby hikes have dropped in recent years. Nevertheless, it's advisable to bring just the cash you need and leave the expensive camera at your hotel.

The walk down to Río Pastaza is easy and popular. Just behind the Sugarcane Stalls by the bus station, a short trail leads to the **Puente San Francisco**, the bridge that crosses the river. You can continue on trails up the other side as far as you want.

Going south on Maldonado takes you to a path that climbs to **Bellavista**, where a white cross stands high over Baños. The path then continues to the settlement of **Runtún**, some two hours away, where the views are outstanding. From here, you can continue up to the Casa del Arbol (p153), or loop around and back down to Baños, ending up at the southern end of Mera. This takes you past the statue of **La Virgen del Agua Santa**, about half an hour from town. The whole walk takes four to five hours.

West of town on Amazonas, turn right by a religious shrine and walk down to Puente San Martín and visit the impressive falls of **Cascada Inés María**, a few hundred meters to the right of the bridge.

Climbing

The climbing conditions on Tungurahua (5016m), an active volcano, are naturally in flux. At the time of research climbing to the peak was still suspended, but it was possible to climb as high as the refuge at 3830m, a steep three- to four-hour climb from the village of Pondoa (p159).

Rafting

The town's tour operators offer guided trips (half-day $30) on the Río Patate and Pastaza. The trips bring you to Class III and IV water (Class IV is enough to really get your heart pumping). It's also possible to take kayak classes ($80).

Horseback Riding

Horse rentals cost around $10 per hour or $35 per day. Many half- or full-day trips start with a long jeep ride out of town, and the actual riding time is short – inquire carefully to be sure you get what you want.

José & Two Dogs HORSEBACK RIDING

(☎098-420-6966; paulo_climb@hotmail.com; cnr Maldonado & Martínez) Offers horseback riding excursions to nearby springs as well as canyoning, ziplining and salsa classes.

Courses

One-on-one or small-group Spanish classes start from around $10 per hour.

Raíces Spanish School LANGUAGE
(03-274-1921; www.spanishlessons.org; cnr 16 de Diciembre & Pablo Suarez) A good Spanish school with classes held in a brick building on the edge of town.

Baños Spanish Center LANGUAGE
(098-704-5072; www.spanishcenter.banios.com; Oriente 8-20, near Cañar) This well-established school is locally recommended.

Tours

Many Baños tour operators lead trips to the jungle, but they vary somewhat in quality and experience.

Three- to seven-day jungle tours cost about $70 to $85 per person per day, depending on the destination (usually with a three- or four-person minimum). Always full of travelers, Baños is a good place to organize a group if you are not already with one.

Geotours TOURS
(03-274-1344; www.geotoursbanios.com; cnr Ambato & Halflants) For jungle treks, trips to the neighboring national parks, rafting, volcano climbs, canyoneering, bike rentals and more.

Festivals & Events

Baños became the seat of its canton on December 16, 1944, and an annual fiesta is celebrated around this date. There are the usual processions, fireworks, music and a great deal of street dancing and drinking. These festivities rev up again in October as the various barrios of Baños take turns paying homage to the local icon, Nuestra Señora de Agua Santa.

Sleeping

Hostal Chimenea HOSTEL $
(03-274-2725; www.hostalchimenea.com; Martínez, near Vieira; dm/s/d from $9/12/24;) From the rather dark reception area, you wouldn't know that this hostel is the best budget offering in town. The bright and clean rooms and dorms come with rainbow-colored blankets, and the upstairs terrace has great views of the waterfall.

A small dip pool, hot tub ($3) and sauna out back add to the mix. Dorm rooms all have attached bathrooms and sleep four to six people.

Plantas y Blanco HOSTEL $
(03-274-0044; www.plantasyblanco.com; Martínez, near 12 de Noviembre; dm $8-10, r $22-28;) A bit disco in the common areas, the clean and eternally popular 'Plants and White' (you figure it out) scores big points for its rooftop terrace, outstanding breakfasts ($4.50), on-site steam bath and overall value. There's a TV room with Netflix and a games room with a pool table and table tennis. Some rooms share bathrooms.

La Petite Auberge HOTEL $
(03-274-0936; www.lepetit.banios.com; 16 de Diciembre, near Montalvo; s $18-22, d $30-40;) This French-owned hacienda-style hotel has big rooms with *chimeneas* (fireplaces) and lofts as well as smaller, simpler rooms. A large games room makes it popular with families, and there's a shared kitchen. Other than the slightly out-of-date bathrooms, this is a great option for the private-room budget set.

Casa Arte Huillacuna HOSTEL $
(03-274-2909; www.huillacuna.com; 12 de Noviembre, near Montalvo; s/d/tr $25/40/60;) This art lover's paradise houses one of the town's best galleries ($2) and has a large open-air common room with art, antiques, a cozy fireplace and a piano which guests are welcome to play. The rooms are simple but clean, and the friendly owners make you feel at home. There's a shared kitchen for preparing meals.

★**Posada del Arte** BOUTIQUE HOTEL $$
(03-274-0083; www.posadadelarte.com; Ibarra, near Montalvo; s/d/tr incl breakfast $38/72/103;) This exquisite little guesthouse has colorful, comfortable rooms, wood floors, gigantic breakfasts and art all around. Several rooms have waterfall views, some also have fireplaces. There's also an excellent restaurant here which, like the hotel, is a welcoming and cozy place. It serves international dishes, wonderful breakfasts (including Tungurahua pancakes – they don't explode!) and small plates for snacking.

La Floresta HOTEL $$
(03-274-1824; www.laflorestahotel.com; cnr Montalvo & Halflants; s/d/tr incl breakfast $48/72/94;) This comfortable inn situated around a pretty interior garden with plenty of hangout areas offers a quiet retreat. The staff here are friendly, and the spacious, tile-floor rooms have big windows, modern bathrooms and comfortable beds – though we wish they were a little brighter.

La Casa Verde GUESTHOUSE **$$**
(☎03-274-2671; www.lacasaverde.com.ec; Camino Real; incl breakfast s $31, d $54-66) Surrounded by lush mountains and with green walls inside and out, La Casa Verde lives up to its name. The best rooms at the back of the house have wrap-around balconies with hammocks that look straight out at the river and hills, as does the large dining room downstairs. Rooms at the front of the house are smaller and less appealing.

There's a kitchen for preparing food, otherwise it's a 20-minute uphill walk (or five-minute taxi ride) into town. Efforts are made towards environmentally friendly practices.

★**Luna Runtún** RESORT **$$$**
(☎03-274-0882; www.lunaruntun.com; Vía Runtún Km 6; d incl breakfast & dinner $242; @🛜🏊) Perched at the top of a cliff (2260m), gazing down over Baños and up to the Tungurahua summit, Luna Runtún is a luxurious hotel in a fabulous location. Just laying eyes on the infinity pool (open to nonguests for $20) will relax you. There's a wonderful spa complete with local volcanic stones; a herb and vegetable garden supplies the restaurant.

Hostería Chamanapamba LODGE **$$$**
(☎03-277-6241; www.chamanapamba.com; Caserio Chamana; s/d incl breakfast $70/95; 🛜) Tarzan meets Jane at this idyllic lodge perched high in a canyon 1km south of the village of Ulba. It's just 10 minutes to Baños, but you are a world away in this idyllic canyon with its little waterfall and tumbling tropical plants.

Eating

A popular spot on the traveler trail, Baños is full of international eateries catering to backpackers and holidaymakers; quality varies. The town is famous for its *melcocha,* a chewy taffy that's softened and blended by swinging it onto wooden pegs, usually mounted in the doorways of shops. Pieces of chewable *caña de azúcar* (sugarcane) and *jugo de caña* (sugarcane juice) are sold at the **sugarcane stalls** across from the bus terminal.

Casa Hood INTERNATIONAL **$**
(☎03-274-2668; Martínez, near Halflants; mains $4.50-7.50; ⊙noon-10pm; 🛜🌿) Named for owner Ray Hood, a long-standing gringo-in-residence, this excellent cafe has cheap *almuerzos* (set lunches) and a menu of Asian and South American dishes. The Casa is a welcoming place to eat, exchange books, meet with friends or just chill *solito* (alone).

Mercado Central MARKET **$**
(cnr Alfaro & Rocafuerte; meals $2.50-5.50; ⊙7am-6pm) A good place for fresh fruit shakes, ceviche and other local dishes like *llapingachos* (potato pancakes stuffed with cheese), and to pick up fruit and veggies.

Café Good INTERNATIONAL **$**
(16 de Diciembre; mains $5.50-8; ⊙8am-9:30pm; 🌿) The Good serves up better-than-good breakfasts and veggie dishes with wholesome brown rice as well as some chicken and fish.

Ponche Suizo CAFE **$**
(Alfaro, btwn Ambato & Rocafuerte; snacks $1.50-4; ⊙9am-10pm Mon-Fri, to 11pm Sat & Sun) This little spot serves breakfasts, cakes and coffee, but everyone comes for the 'Ponche Suizo,' a trade secret treat that's a cross between a shake and a mousse.

Mega Bodega SUPERMARKET **$**
(Alfaro, near Rocafuerte; ⊙7am-9pm) Stock up at this centrally located supermarket.

★**La Tasca de Baños** SPANISH **$$**
(12 de Noviembre, near Montalvo; tapas $3.50-6; ⊙6:30pm-10:30pm Wed-Fri, 12:30pm-4:30pm & 6:30-10:30pm Sat & Sun) It may be difficult to get a table at this tiny tapas restaurant. The selection of small dishes is excellent, ranging from perennial favorites like *tortilla española* to Andalusian meatballs and shellfish. Order up five to share.

Cafe Mariane FRENCH **$$**
(☎03-274-1947; Montalvo; mains $10-15; ⊙11am-11pm) Cafe Mariane's French-Mediterranean cuisine is a real standout in Baños. The cheese-and-meat fondues are a lot – even for two people – and the pasta and meat dishes are quite elegant.

Drinking & Nightlife

La Tostaduria COFFEE
(cnr 16 de Diciembre & Rocafuerte; ⊙8am-noon & 4-9pm Sun-Mon & Wed-Thu, to 10pm Fri & Sat) Java junkies can get a fix at this hole-in-the-wall coffee joint. The beans from Loja, Pichincha and Imbabura are roasted inside the shop.

Leprechaun CLUB
(Alfaro, btwn Oriente & Espejo; ⊙8pm-2am Mon-Thu, to 3am Fri & Sat) One of the hottest spots in town, this large complex has a bonfire in the back patio, dancing in the middle and a roaring salsa dance party at the *salsateca* Wednesday through Saturday ($5).

Stray Dog BREWPUB

(www.facebook.com/straydoginbanos; cnr Rocafuerte & Maldonado; ⏲4pm-midnight Mon-Thu, to 2am Fri & Sat) This brewpub features artisanal offerings like light Llamas' Breath Belgian and bold Stray Dog Stout.

Shopping

★**Maki Awashka** ARTS & CRAFTS

(Montalvo, near Santa Clara; ⏲8am-7pm) The family from Salasaca who own this shop weave many of the gorgeous wool rug and tapestries in their workshop upstairs. There's a good selection of artisan crafts for sale here, including tablecloths, scarves and blankets.

Pasaje Artesanal ARTS & CRAFTS

(Pasaje Artesanal, btwn Ambato & Rocafuerte; ⏲8am-8pm) At this outdoor crafts market, you'll find endless quantities of locally made baubles and a regional craft called tagua-carving – white, golfball-size nuts that resemble ivory and are dyed and transformed into figurines and jewelry.

Information

Eruptions of Tungurahua force locals to evacuate about every five years. In recent years the volcano has been quite active. This said, it's a well-monitored situation and shouldn't be a major concern. Ask your hotel staff about evacuation procedures in the event of an eruption.

Reports of robberies on the trails outside Baños have dropped. Hiring a guide is a good way to contribute to the local economy and reduce your risk.

Police Station (☎03-274-0251)

Banco del Pacifico (cnr Halflants & Rocafuerte)

Banco Pichincha (cnr Ambato & Halflants)

Hospital (☎03-274-0301; Montalvo) Near Pastaza; pharmacies are along Ambato.

Tourist Office (☎03-274-0483; Halflants near Rocafuerte; ⏲8am-noon & 2-5pm) Lots of info, free maps and emergency evacuation information.

Getting There & Away

The Baños **bus terminal** (Amazonas) is within easy walking distance of most hotels. Transportes Baños offers frequent buses direct to Quito ($4.45, 3½ hours). There are buses every 30 minutes to Salasaca ($0.50, 30 minutes) and Ambato ($1.10; one hour); take a Quito-bound bus for Latacunga ($2, 1½ hours). There are daily buses to Guayaquil ($9, seven hours).

The Baños–Riobamba road via Penipe (damaged during Volcán Tungurahua eruptions) has now reopened; there are great views of the volcano along the way. There are six buses a day to Riobamba ($2, 1½hours); change in Riobamba for buses to Cuenca.

To the Oriente, buses depart regularly for Puyo ($2, two hours), Tena ($4, five hours), Coca ($10, 10 hours) and Macas ($7.50, four hours).

Getting Around

Westbound local buses leave from Rocafuerte, behind the Mercado Central. Marked 'El Salado,' they go to the Piscinas El Salado ($0.25, 10 minutes). **Eastbound local buses** go as far as the Pailón del Diablo ($.50); they leave from Alfaro at Martínez.

Round-trip taxi tours for Pailón del Diablo ($20) leave from the bus terminal.

Ruta de las Cascadas

Nicknamed 'La Ruta de las Cascadas' (Highway of the Waterfalls), the road from Baños to Puyo is one of the region's most dramatic routes. It hugs the Río Pastaza canyon as it drops steadily from Baños, at 1800m, to Puyo, at 950m and passes more than a dozen waterfalls on the way. The bus ride is great, but zipping down on a mountain bike is even better. The first third of the route is mostly downhill, but there are some definite climbs, so ready those legs (it's about 61km if you do the whole thing). Mountain bikes can be rented in Baños.

Getting There & Away

From Puyo (or any point on the way), you can take any passing bus back to Baños, putting your bike in the storage compartment under the bus (the driver's assistant will help you load it). The fare is between $1 and $2, depending where you get on.

Río Verde

One of the highlights of the Ruta de las Cascadas is the village of Río Verde and the spectacular Pailón del Diablo waterfalls. It's worth spending at least a couple of hours here to properly explore the waterfalls, which can be viewed from above and below along two separate trails.

Sights

★**Pailón del Diablo** WATERFALL

(Devil's Cauldron Waterfalls; $2; ⏲9am-6pm) The Devil's Cauldron is a must-stop. There are two terrific trails from Río Verde that take you here. The first is accessed from below

CYCLING THE RUTA DE LAS CASCADAS

Most people go only as far as the spectacular Pailón del Diablo (p157) waterfalls, about 18km from Baños, but if you're up for a much bigger ride, making it to Río Negro allows you to see the change in ecology as you head into the lower elevations. There are plenty of hidden waterfalls and family-run swimming holes along the route; leave an entire day to really explore the area.

Along the way, the road shoots through tunnels that seem to swallow you up like a black hole. Some are quite long, and cyclists or all-terrain-vehicle riders should take the signed, dirt-trail detours that skirt around them. Watch your speed on curves and approaches to the tunnels and ride on the right side of the road. From Puyo (or any point on the way), you can simply take a bus back to Baños, putting your bike in the storage compartment under the bus (the driver's assistant will help you load it).

Make sure that you rent a helmet and a bike lock (and use both!). Insects on the trails can be unrelenting, so bring repellent and don't forget your raincoat.

Baños to Rio Verde

Before the first tunnel, you'll pass the Agoyán hydroelectric project. About 45 minutes' riding time from Baños you'll pass the spectacular **Manto de La Novia Waterfalls**. For a closer look at the falls, take the **Canopy Agoyán** (Km 10; zipline $10-20, cable car $1.50) zipline tour (superman or standard style), which takes you flying near the edge of the waterfall. Return via zipline on a separate cable or take the cable car back.

From the Manto de La Novia, it's a good 30- to 45-minute ride to the village of Río Verde (between the fourth and fifth tunnels), the access point to the thundering Pailón del Diablo (p157), which is a must-see.

Rio Verde to Puyo

Just beyond Río Verde, the road starts to climb. After about a half-hour's riding, you come to **Machay**, a nice place to stop for a picnic lunch and a dip in the river. A 2.5km trail leads into the cloud forest and past eight **waterfalls**, which range from wee tumblers to the beautiful **Manantial del Dorado**, 2.5km in. Several outfits now charge you to access the trails here.

After Machay, you have two good climbs, then it's downhill nearly all the way to Río Negro, 15km from Río Verde. As the road drops, the vegetation rapidly becomes more tropical; the walls of the Río Pastaza canyon are covered with bromeliads, giant tree ferns and orchids. Before you hit Río Negro, you'll pass through the village of **San Francisco**, which has a dirt plaza, a few simple eateries and places to buy water or beer.

After San Francisco, it's only another 10 to 15 minutes to **Río Negro**, a funky little town built up along the main road. There are restaurants (some of which are surprisingly slick) and plenty of places to buy refreshments.

After **Río Negro**, you start really feeling tropical. After 17km you pass **Mera**, which might have a police checkpoint (have your passport ready), and is slowly developing as a tourism spot. At the end of the descent, 61km from Baños, you arrive at the humid jungle town of **Puyo**.

the soccer field, the second is accessed by crossing a bridge east of the village. Signs lead the way. The hikes down to the falls take around an hour round-trip, but you are rewarded with awesome suspension bridges, wicked in-cut trails that cut behind the waterfall and plenty of wildlife viewing.

Sleeping & Eating

There are several low-key eateries close to the waterfalls, and in and around both entrances to the falls you'll find stalls selling fresh tropical fruit, barbecued corn and *maduro con queso* (grilled banana with cheese). Miramelindo has a reliable restaurant with a good range of vegetarian options.

Camping Paraíso CABIN $

(☎03-249-3049; www.facebook.com/paraisocampingecua/; Baños–Puyo Rd Km 53; camping/dm/d $5/7/25) Just east of Río Verde, you'll find the idyllic Camping Paraíso. It offers simple lodgings and camping amid lush and beautiful jungle. There are areas for campfires and a kitchen for preparing meals.

Miramelindo HOTEL $$
(☎03-249-3212; www.miramelindo.com.ec; Baños–Puyo Rd Km 18; r per person incl breakfast from $35; mains $6-14; ⏲restaurant noon-8pm;) This enchanting place has a great spa with a sauna, Jacuzzi and *baños de cajón* (steam boxes). The wonderfully rustic rooms are accented in wood and earthy colors; some have fireplaces. There are jungly common areas and hammocks slung all around. The orchid collection is outrageous.

Getting There & Away

Buses between Baños and Puyo pass regularly along the main road ($1, 45 minutes).

Parque Nacional Sangay

This 2710-sq-km **national park** contains three of Ecuador's most magnificent volcanoes – the mightily active **Sangay**, the remittently active **Tungurahua** and the extinct **El Altar**. Because the park ranges from glaciated mountaintops to tropical rainforests, it offers flora, fauna and terrain of immense diversity.

From the *páramo* (high-altitude grasslands) in the park's western heights, which climb to over 5000m around each of the three volcanoes, the terrain plunges down the eastern slopes of the Andes to elevations barely above 1000m. In between is terrain so steep, rugged and wet (over 4m of rain is recorded annually in some areas) that it remains a wilderness in the truest sense. The whole park is home to some 500 bird species and 3000 plant species, and the thickly vegetated slopes east of the mountains are the haunts of very rarely seen mammals, such as spectacled bears, mountain tapirs, pumas, ocelots and porcupines.

The best times to go are December to March. The wettest months are April and May, and the foggiest are July and August.

Volcán Tungurahua

With a (pre-eruption) elevation of 5016m, Tungurahua (from the Kichwa for 'Throat of Fire') is Ecuador's 10th-highest peak. It *was* a beautiful, cone-shaped volcano with a glacier plopped on top of its lush, green slopes, but since 1999 many eruptions have melted the snow and changed the shape of the cone and crater. Lava and lahar flows from the August 2006 eruption covered about 2km of the Ambato–Baños road (now repaired). Significant recent explosions have triggered occasional evacuations.

At the time of writing the summit of Tungurahua was still officially closed, although some locals were making the climb. When we visited it was possible to hike as far as the (still closed) **Refugio Nicolas Martínez** at 3800m, a three- to four-hour climb along a trail from Pondoa (2470m). The **Pondoa community tourism office** (☎099-839-1072; ⏲8am-5pm) can provide maps, guides for hikes to the refuge (per person including lunch $35) and hire horses (per three hours $25); there are also chalet-style rooms available for overnight stays.

At the time of research a bid for Unesco Geopark status for the area around Volcán Tungurahua – covering Baños, Pelileo, Patate and Píllano – looked set for approval.

Sleeping

Pondoa Community Tourism Center CABIN $
(☎099-839-1072; Pondoa; r per person incl breakfast & dinner $25;) Three cute brick chalets house comfortable rooms with private bathrooms and great views of the surrounding mountains at this community-run complex.

Getting There & Away

Volcán Tungurahua is accessed from **Pondoa**, 3km northeast of Baños. A taxi from Baños to Pondoa costs $10 to $15.

Volcán El Altar

At 5319m, this long-extinct volcano is the fifth-highest mountain in Ecuador and one of its most picturesque and fascinating peaks. Before the collapse of the western side of the crater in prehistoric times, the 'Altar' may have been one of the highest mountains in the world. The crater walls, which surround a jade-colored lake called Laguna Amarilla, actually form nine distinct peaks, most of which have religious-themed names like Obispo (Bishop; 5315m) and Monja Chica (Little Nun; 5080m). In 2000, part of a glacier fell into the lake, creating a massive wave of water that charged down the west slope and over the Collanes plain (3900m), leaving huge boulders strewn across the landscape.

Access to El Altar is from the Hacienda Releche (3070m), near Cadelaria, a 30-minute bus trip from Riobamba. From the Hacienda, it's a five- to six-hour walk to the refugio on the Collanes plain; the route can be extremely muddy and you'll need rubber boots. Up on the plain, you will encounter many bulls (keep your distance), and their poop is spread all over the place (watch your step). Flooding occurs, but rarely. After a night at the *refugio*, it's a two- to three-hour climb to the crater to see the Laguna Amarilla (4200m); it's also possible to camp overnight at the crater. Julio Verne Travel (p165) in Riobamba can arrange guided trips.

Sleeping

Hacienda Releche HACIENDA $
(03-301-4067; www.haciendareleche.com; near Candelaria; dm/s/d $15/20/40, breakfast $6, lunch & dinner $8) The ranch-style Releche, supported by thick wood beams and slung with cowhide rugs, has dorms and private rooms. Meals and packed lunches are available; use of the kitchen costs $10 per group. The owners also hire horses ($45) and can arrange guides ($50) for hikes to El Altar.

The Cedeño family also own the thatch-roofed **refugio** (03-301-4067; per person $10) on the Collanes plain.

Getting There & Away

El Altar is accessed from the **Hacienda Releche** (p160). To get there from Riobamba, take a bus bound for Candelaria from the bus stops at the **Mercado Oriental** (cnr Espejo & Luz Elisa Borja) and ask the driver to drop you at the Hacienda Releche. Buses leave Riobamba at 6:35am, 10:15am, 12:15pm, 1:15pm and 5pm and make the return journey at about 6am, 7:45am, 2:15pm, 3:15pm and 5:15pm ($1.25; 1¼ hours).

Lagunas de Atillo & Ozogoche

With the opening of the Guamote–Macas road, the spectacular *páramo* lakes region of Lagunas de Atillo became easily accessible, and the area is slowly being developed for horseback riding, hiking, trout fishing and even mountain biking. Still, Atillo gets very few visitors, and it's an amazing place to see remote landscape and rural life.

About 79km from Riobamba, the road passes through **Atillo**, which is really a loose grouping of scattered homes. This area is surrounded by the spectacular Atillo lakes. It's possible to hike here from **Ozogoche** – a seven-hour walk for fit hikers – but the route follows an unmarked trail so you will need to go with a local guide; inquire at Julio Verne Travel (p165) in Riobamba about hiring a guide or contact **Anibal Tenemasa** (03-026-688, 099-121-3205; agigsangay2008@yahoo.es).

From Atillo the road descends through the national park, past waterfalls and virgin forest, before ending in Macas in the southern Oriente. Pro Bici (p165) and Julio Verne Travel in Riobamba offer one- and two-day biking trips along the Guamote–Macas road, passing through the lakes area. It's a spectacular route.

Sleeping

Los Saskines HUT
(Vía Guamote-Macos Km 75; hut per person $5, mains $6) This roadside restaurant near the Lagunas de Atillo sells local cheeses and tasty fresh trout. You can stay overnight here in a basic *choza* hut with bunks. There is no heating or hot water and the toilet is in a separate hut.

Getting There & Away

Buses leave Riobamba from **Puruha and Primera Constituyente** (p168) for Atillo three times a day ($2, two hours). Buses to Macas, which depart about once an hour from the Riobamba's **main bus terminal** (p168), also pass Atillo.

Volcán Sangay

Constantly spewing out rocks, smoke and ash, 5230m Sangay is one of the world's most active volcanoes and a highly dangerous ascent. For those who do try, some guides actually recommend carrying a metal shield as protection from rocks blown out of the crater (now *that'll* lighten your load). Hiking up to the base or perhaps just to **La Playa** (the Beach) is possible, especially from December to February, when the area is driest.

Excursions to the volcano are possible from **Sangay Lodge** (03-302-6688; www.guargualla-sangay.com; Guargualllá Chico; per person per night incl meals, guided treks & transport $90), or contact local guide Anibal Tenemasa.

Getting There & Away

Volcán Sangay can be accessed from **Sangay Lodge** (p160). Tours include transport from Riobamba. There are no buses.

Guaranda

☎03 / POP 30,987 / ELEV 2650M

Half the fun of Guaranda is getting there. The 99km 'highway' from Ambato reaches altitudes over 4000m and passes within 5km of the glacier on Volcán Chimborazo (6263m). From here, the mountain almost looks easy to climb. The capital of Bolívar province, Guaranda is small and uneventful. It sits amid seven steep hills that have prompted the moniker 'the Rome of the Andes' – but it certainly didn't get this nickname for its cultural offerings. The Wednesday and Saturday markets in the **Plaza 15 de Mayo** are worth checking out, as are the **Carnaval** celebrations in February, with water fights, dances, parades and a little liquor with local herbs called 'Pájaro Azul' (Blue Bird).

Sleeping & Eating

Hostal Bolívar HOTEL $

(☎03-298-0547; hbguaranda@gmail.com; Sucre 7-04, near Rocafuerte; s/d $20/35; P ⓦ) A good option for discerning travelers, the rooms here are welcoming and clean – though slightly dated save for the flat-screens -- and there's a pleasant courtyard. Breakfast costs $2.80. It's two blocks south of Parque Simón Bolívar.

Los 7 Santos CAFE $

(☎03-298-0612; www.facebook.com/los7santosgda; Convención de 1884, near 10 de Agosto; sandwiches $1.50-3.25; ⏱10am-10pm Mon-Thu, to 1am Fri & Sat) Half a block downhill from Parque Simón Bolívar, Los 7 Santos offers all that you would expect from an artsy cafe in a much larger city. There's breakfast in the morning ($3.50) and small sandwiches and *bocaditos* (snacks) all day.

La Bohemia ECUADORIAN $

(cnr Convención de 1884 & 10 de Agosto; mains $6-8; ⏱2-10pm Mon-Sat) Close to Parque Bolívar, La Bohemia serves *almuerzos* (set lunches; $4), sandwiches and bigger mains in a laid-back but attentive atmosphere. Chase your meal down with one of the giant *batidos* (fruit shakes).

Shopping

Salinerito FOOD

(☎03-298-2205; Av Gral Enriquez 12, near Cándido Rada; ⏱9am-6pm Mon-Fri, to 2pm Sat) Stock up here on the province's famous cheeses ($6 to $7 for a whole wheel), chocolate and other treats.

Information

Banco Pichincha (Azuay, near 7 de Mayo)

Hospital Alfredo Noboa Montenegro (☎03-298-0110; Cisneros, near Selva Alegre)

Clínica Bolívar (☎03-298-3310) One of several clinics and pharmacies near Plaza Roja, south of the hospital.

Post Office (Azuay 309, near Pichincha)

Getting There & Away

Guaranda's bus terminal is a solid 20-minute walk or a $1 cab ride from downtown.

Bus services depart hourly for Ambato ($2.10, two hours) and Quito ($5, five hours). Almost as frequently, there are buses for Guayaquil ($4.50, four hours). There are numerous daily buses to Riobamba ($2.50, two hours) that take in outrageous views; this route passes the Chimborazo park entrance and access road to the mountain refuges, and the views of Volcán Chimborazo are amazing.

Shared taxis for Salinas ($1, 45 minutes) depart frequently from the Plaza Roja, waiting to fill up before they go.

Salinas

☎03 / POP 10,000 / ELEV 3550M

The remote village of Salinas, about 35km north of Guaranda, sits at the base of a dramatic and precipitous bluff surrounded by high *páramo*. Famous as a model of rural development, Salinas is a terrific place to see what successful community-based tourism is all about. A trail above town takes you to the top of the bluff.

Tours

Ask at the tourist office (p162) about horseback riding (3½ hours from $20 per person, plus $30 per group for the guide) and guided walks to nearby caves ($10).

Factory Tours TOURS

(El Salinerito, near Guayamas; tour per person $15; ⏱8am-5pm Mon-Sat) Ask about tours of nearby factories at the Oficina de Turismo Comunitario (p162) in the main plaza. Local guides will take you to cooperative-run factories that manufacture cheese, chocolate, textiles, footballs and herbal remedies, and also to see nearby salt flats. Tours last about two hours.

Sleeping & Eating

There are a few simple but comfortable places to stay in Salinas. Sometimes they fill up

SUSTAINABLE DEVELOPMENT IN SALINAS: FROM CHOZAS TO CHEESES

When an Italian Salesian missionary named Antonio Polo rode into town one July day in 1971, Salinas was still a town of *chozas* (thatch-roofed huts). For generations, *salineritos* (people of Salinas) had lived in dire poverty, unable to demand a fair price for their production of milk, vegetables and wool; half of all Salinas children died before the age of five.

Polo saw a better future for local families making and selling dairy-based products. He helped the *campesinos* (peasants) set up a credit cooperative, buy equipment and bring in technical expertise. Emphasizing high standards of freshness and sanitation, the cooperative eventually opened more than 20 *queserías* (cheese factories) around Salinas and branched out into other provinces. It has also created new cooperatives that produce chocolate, dried mushrooms, wool clothing, salamis, candies and buttons, and it has even started a community tourism project. Check in at the **tourism office** to learn more.

with tour groups, so do book ahead. It gets cold here at night; bring warm clothes.

Hostal La Minga HOSTAL **$**
(☎03-221-0255, 098-626-7586; http://lamingahostal.com; Guayamas, near Salinerito; r per person incl breakfast $15;) This cheery place offers the best accommodation in the village. The bright rooms have fleece sheets and firm beds, and are arranged around a central, plant-filled atrium.

El Refugio HOSTAL **$**
(☎099-240-1454, 03-221-0197; hrefugiotour@gmail.com; r per person incl breakfast $15;) A a simple traveler's lodge three blocks west of the main plaza, with a roaring fireplace in the lobby. Ask for a room with a view.

Pizzeria Casa Nostra PIZZA **$$**
(Guayamas, near Los Tomabelas; mains $6-10; 4-10pm Mon-Fri, 11am-9pm Sat & Sun) Facing the main plaza, Casa Nostra serves freshly baked pizzas loaded with Salinas' famous cheese, as well as a few pasta dishes and other mains. There's beer and wine, too.

Shopping

Tienda El Salinerito ARTS & CRAFTS
(Guyamas, near Salinerito; 9am-6pm) Tienda El Salinerito is Salinas local outlet for all the products made by the communities, including fuzzy wool sweaters, chocolate, cheese and jams.

Information

The **Oficina de Turismo Comunitario** (☎099-563-2095, 03-221-0234; www.salinasmatiavi.com; El Salinerito, near Guayamas; 8am-5pm) is in the main plaza. They can give you the password for free wi-fi in the plaza.

There are no ATMs in the village.

Getting There & Away

Collective taxis to Guaranda leave frequently from Calle Los Tomabelas, one block downhill from the main square ($1, 45 minutes).

Volcán Chimborazo

Called 'Taita' (Father) by indigenous people in the area, Volcán Chimborazo (6263m) is the country's tallest mountain, a hulking giant topped by a massive glacier. Because of Earth's equatorial bulge, Chimborazo is both the furthest point from the center of the earth and the closest terrestrial point to the stars.

Along with its smaller, craggier companion Volcán Carihuairazo (5020m) to the northeast, and the Río Mocha valley that connects them, Chimborazo is a remote, even desolate, place populated by only a few indigenous communities.

Chimborazo and Carihuairazo lie within the **Reserva de Producción de Fauna Chimborazo** (☎03-202-7358; Vía Riobamba-Guaranda Km 45; 8am-4pm) FREE. It is called a 'fauna-production reserve' because it is home to thousands of vicuña (a relative of the llama). Once extinct in Ecuador, they were donated by Chile and Bolivia in the 1980s. Now prospering, it's easy to spot their elegant silhouettes in the mist on the bus ride between Guaranda and Riobamba.

Activities

Climbing Chimborazo or Carihuairazo is an adventure only for well-acclimatized, experienced mountaineers with snow- and ice-climbing gear (contact guides in Riobamba or Quito). From Riobamba, you can organize a day trip that takes you to Chimborazo's Refugio Whymper at 5000m, or just beyond, to Laguna Cóndor Cocha at 5100m.

Care should be taken to properly acclimatize if you plan to do physical activities around Chimborazo and Carihuairazo. If your accommodations are at altitude in the vicinity of Chimborazo and Carihuairazo, then they will probably be good sites to acclimatize, although you should also consult a qualified guide if you are planning hard hiking or climbs on either peak. You can arrange mountain-bike descents from the high-altitude refuges with tour operators in Riobamba.

The small indigenous community of **Pulinguí San Pablo** (3900m) on the Riobamba–Guaranda road is well worth an afternoon visit, and climbers and hikers can stay overnight in the simple community lodge. The Puruhá people have lived on Chimborazo's flanks for centuries and are now working to bring tourism to the region. Locals provide basic guiding services and can take you on fascinating interpretation trails in the area.

Hiking

A good acclimatization hike begins at Chimborazo Lodge and heads up to the **Templo Machay** (4700m), where ancient peoples made offerings to the mountain gods.

Refugio Whymper HIKING

FREE A popular short, high-altitude hike is from the parking lot at Refugio Carrel (4850m) to Refugio Whymper (5050), a distance of about 1km. From here, you can follow signs up about another 300m along the trail to the **Laguna Cóndor Cocha** (really more of a puddle) at 5100m. Take it slowly and drink plenty of water.

Register at the park entrance on the way in and ask about weather conditions. Unless you're prepared to walk the 8km from the park entrance to Refugio Carrel you'll need to arrange your own transport; a taxi from Riobamba costs about $40.

Climbing

Most climbers do multiple acclimatization ascents and spend the night at increasingly higher elevations before tackling Chimborazo, which is a notoriously laborious climb that also requires technical know-how. Most parties these days follow the **Normal Route**, which takes eight to 10 hours to the summit and two to four to return. The **Whymper Route** was unsafe at the time of research.

There are no refuges on Carihuairazo, so guides usually set up a base camp on the south side of the mountain. The climb is relatively straightforward for experienced climbers, but ice-climbing gear is needed.

Mountain Biking

Cycling down Volcán Chimborazo along a new designated bike path from Refugio Carrel to the park entrance is an exhilarating way to experience the mountain. Several agencies in Riobamba, including Pro Bici (p165) and Julio Verne (p165), offer recommended biking excursions (per person from $45), which can include a hike from the first to the second *refugios*. After the initial steep downhill the route gets even more beautiful as you cycle through the *páramo* past families of vicuña.

Sleeping & Eating

Within the park, there is a small cafe selling hot drinks and snacks at the park entrance. At weekends and busy times the *refugios* also sell hot drinks and snacks, but don't rely on them being open (unless, of course, you are staying overnight with a guide). It's best to bring your own supplies, including plenty of water.

It's bone-chilling from the late afternoon on, so bring appropriate clothing and sleeping bags. Temperatures can drop well below freezing at night. July to September, as well as December, are the driest (but coldest) times in this region.

Refugio Whymper CABIN $

(☎03-296-5820, 03-295-1389; refugioschimborazo@gmail.com; per person incl breakfast & dinner $30) The higher of the two *refugios* on Chimborazo, Refugio Whymper is – at 5050m – Ecuador's highest lodging; don't expect a good night's sleep at this altitude. It's named after Edward Whymper, the British climber who in 1880 made the first ascent of Chimborazo, with the Swiss Carrel brothers as guides. Your guide will make reservations.

Refugio Carrel CABIN $

(☎03-295-1389, 03-296-5820; refugioschimborazo@gmail.com; per person incl breakfast & dinner $30) The lower of the two refuges is at 4850m. You'll need a sleeping bag. Your guide will make reservations.

Casa Cóndor HOSTEL $

(☎099-032-5984; Pulinguí San Pablo; per person incl breakfast & dinner $25) This simple backpacker lodge is in the small indigenous community of Pulinguí San Pablo. Families still live in the round *chozas* typical of the area, but Casa Cóndor is a stone building with a basic dorm and private rooms, hot showers and a communal kitchen.

It's run by the local community and you may find the building locked. Ask around in the village to find someone to open up.

Chimborazo Lodge LODGE **$$$**
(☎099-973-3646, 03-236-4258; Riobamba–Guaranda Rd, Km 36; s/d/ste incl breakfast $80/110/130) The only high-end option for miles, this remote lodge sits right below Chimborazo in a pretty, grass-filled valley. The main lodge has a cozy dining room, massive fireplace and picture windows that look up to the peak. The wood cabins feature hardwood accents of cedar and mahogany, small beds and old-time pictures. Best of all, they have heaters.

At 4000m, you will feel the effects of the altitude.

Getting There & Away

Several buses go from Riobamba's main terminal to Guaranda daily via a paved road. About 45 minutes from Riobamba ($1.50), the bus passes Pulinguí San Pablo, and about 7km further it passes the signed turnoff (4370m) for the Chimborazo *refugios* at the **park's entrance** (p162). From the turnoff, it is 8km by road to the parking lot at **Refugio Carrel** (p163) and 1km further (on foot) to **Refugio Whymper** (p163). If you're walking up this road, allow several hours to reach the *refugios*.

Most hotels in Riobamba can arrange a taxi service to Refugio Carrel via this route. It's about $60 to hire a taxi to drop you off and pick you up on a later day. One-way trips cost around $40.

Riobamba

☎03 / POP 156,000 / ELEV 2750M

Riobamba has a strong indigenous presence, which grows to wonderfully colorful proportions during the Saturday market, but the city's layout, large arcaded plazas and architecture are imposing reminders of Spanish colonization.

History

The Puhurá tribe were the first people to live in the vicinity, followed by the Inca for a brief period. In 1534, the Spanish founded the city of Riobamba on the site of Cajabamba, 17km south on the Panamericana, but in 1797 a huge landslide destroyed the city and the people moved it to its present-day site. Spain's grip on Ecuador was officially broken in Riobamba with the signing of Ecuador's first constitution in 1830.

Sights

The handsome, tree-filled **Parque Maldonado** (Primera Constituyente, btwn Espejo & 5 de Junio) is flanked by Riobamba's cathedral on the northeastern side. A few blocks southeast, **Parque La Libertad** (Primera Constituyente, btwn Alvarado & Benalcazar) is anchored, near Alvarado, by its neoclassical **basilica** (Veloz near Velasco), famous for being the only round church in Ecuador. It's often closed, but try Sundays and evenings after 6pm. Just north of downtown, the **Parque 21 de Abril** (cnr Orozco & Ángel León) has an observation platform with views of the surrounding mountains.

★**Museo de Arte Religioso** MUSEUM
(☎03-296-5212; Argentinos, near Larrea; adult/child $3/1; ⏲9am-12:30pm & 3-6pm Tue-Sat) Inside the beautifully restored 18th-century convent, Riobamba's top museum houses one of the country's finest collections of 17th- and 18th-century religious art. More than 200 pieces in 15 different rooms include the painting *La Flagelación de Jesús*; painted by an indigenous artist in the 17th century, it depicts men dressed in Spanish clothes flogging Jesus, a discreet comment on the mistreatment of the local population by the colonial occupiers.

Feria Artesanal MARKET
(Saturday Market; Plaza de la Concepción; ⏲6am-5pm Sat) The Saturday market transforms Riobamba into a hive of commercial activity, when thousands of people from surrounding villages come to barter, buy and sell, spreading out their wares along in and around Plaza de la Concepción, also known as Plaza Roja. Look out for colorful *chumbi,* traditional handwoven belts.

Cathedral CATHEDRAL
The ornate, baroque facade of Riobamba's cathedral was reconstructed from fragments after the 1797 earthquake that destroyed the town. Made from white limestone, the relief depicts both indigenous and Spanish images. The cathedral is often closed, but the building exterior (its most interesting aspect) can be viewed any time.

Museo de la Ciudad MUSEUM
(Parque Maldonado; ⊙8am-6pm Mon-Fri, 9am-6pm Sat, 10am-4pm Sun) FREE Built in the 1900s by the Costales-Dávalos family, this beautifully restored historic building has a few old-time pictures of the city, rotating art exhibits and historic artifacts. It lacks good information, but is an interesting afternoon break nonetheless. Check out the ornate ceilings.

Tours

Thanks to Riobamba's proximity to Chimborazo, the country's highest peak, the city is home to some of the country's best climbing operators and mountain guides. Two-day summit trips start from around $260 per person and include guides, gear, transportation and meals.

One-day mountain-biking trips start at $45 per person. Descents from the refuge on Chimborazo – an exhilarating way to take in the views – are very popular.

Pro Bici CYCLING
(03-294-7479, 03-294-1880; www.probici.com; 2nd fl, Primera Constituyente 23-51, near Larrea; ⊙office 8:30am-8pm Mon-Sat) Located on the 2nd floor through the fabric store, this is one of the country's best mountain-bike operators, with many years of experience and excellent trip reports from clients. It offers mountain-bike rentals (per day $15 to $25), excellent maps, good safety practices and fascinating day tours ($45 to $70) to Chimborazo, Atillo and Colta.

Julio Verne Travel ADVENTURE
(03-296-3436; www.julioverne-travel.com; Brasil 22-40, near León Borja; ⊙office 8:30am-1pm & 3-6pm Mon-Fri) Recommended Ecuadorian-Dutch full-service operator offering affordable, two-day summit trips to Chimborazo and other peaks, as well as multiday treks. The company also offers downhill mountain biking on Chimborazo.

Andean Adventures ADVENTURE
(03-295-1389; www.andeannadventures.com) This respected operation specializes in Chimborazo climbs, but also arranges mountain bikes, treks and other custom adventures. Book through their website or over the phone.

Tren del Hielo I RAIL
(1-800-873-637; www.trenecuador.com; 10 de Agosto, near Carabobo; adult/child $27/21; ⊙8am-2:30pm Sat & Sun) Departing from Riobamba's gorgeously restored railway station at 8am Thursday to Friday, this round-trip train tour takes you along the eastern flank of Chimborazo to the village of Urbina, where you can learn about glacial ice harvesting.

Festivals & Events

Riobamba's annual fiesta celebrates the Independence Battle of Tapi of April 21, 1822. On and around April 21, there is a large agricultural fair with the usual highland events: street parades, dancing and plenty of traditional food and drink.

Sleeping

★**Hostal Oasis** GUESTHOUSE $
(03-296-1210; www.oasishostelriobamba.com; Veloz 15-32, near Almagro; s/d $18/30; P@) When it comes to friendliness, value and down-home cutesiness, this guesthouse is hard to beat. Rooms and apartments are grouped around a garden patrolled by friendly cats, and there's a shared kitchen. We only wish it were a little closer to the downtown action.

Hotel Tren Dorado HOTEL $
(03-296-4890; www.hoteltrendorado.com; Carabobo 22-35; s/d/tr $20/34/45;) Not surprisingly, the 'Golden Train' is close to the train station. Get past the dark reception to reach the spotless, comfortable rooms and airy terraces. The spacious, good-value triples and quadruples are perfect for families. A self-serve breakfast will cost you $4 extra.

Hotel Montecarlo HOTEL $$
(03-296-0577; www.hotelmontecarlo-riobamba.com; 10 de Agosto 25-41; s/d incl breakfast $25/40; @) The Montecarlo occupies an attractively restored, turn-of-the-20th-century house. The use of blue (blue couches, blue carpet, blue trim and blue-plaid bedspreads) can be a bit overbearing, but it's a lovely place nonetheless. Ask for a back room to spare you street noise.

Hotel Zeus BUSINESS HOTEL $$
(03-296-8036; www.hotelzeus.com.ec; Av León Borja 41-29, near Duchicela; s/d incl breakfast $43/61, executive s/d $53/80; P) Between the bus terminal and downtown, Hotel Zeus is a seven-story hotel with a range of room styles and amenities as well as gym access. The pricier rooms are excellent (some have five-star views of Chimborazo).

Riobamba

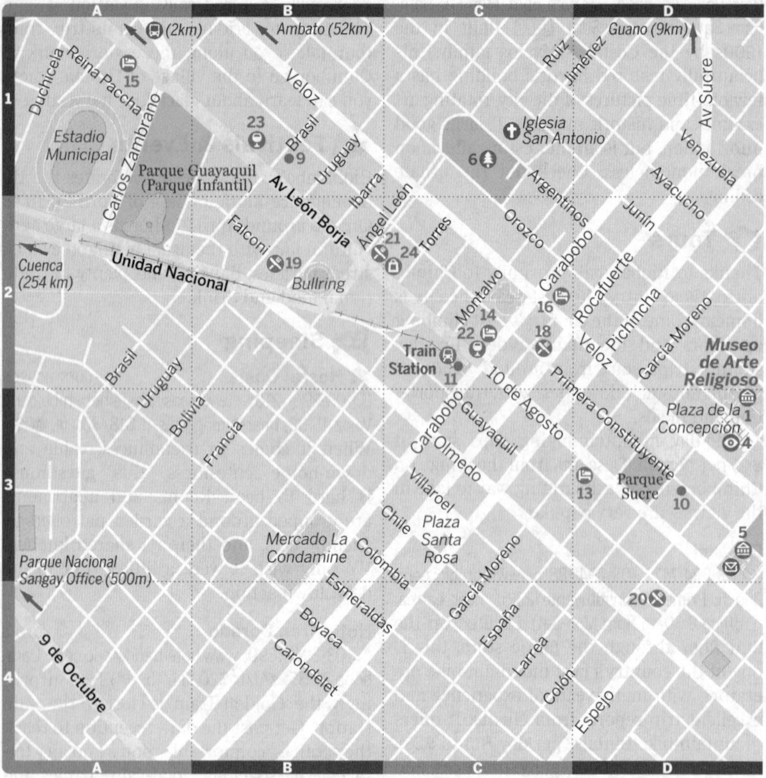

Mansión Santa Isabella BOUTIQUE HOTEL **$$$**
(☎03-296-2947; www.mansionsantaisabella.com; Veloz 2848, near Carabobo; s/d/ste incl breakfast $66/102/150; 📶) A gorgeously appointed courtyard with a fountain and plants is the centerpiece of this boutique hotel in a historic mansion. The vaulted-ceiling rooms in the original house have beautifully restored hard-wood beams and pleasant muted color schemes, but some are rather cramped. Luxurious suites in the new annex are more spacious but lack the character of the older rooms.

Book a massage or use the sauna, steam room and Jacuzzi baths in the hotel's new spa (per person $15).

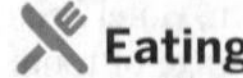

Eating

Mercado La Merced MARKET **$**
(Mercado Mariano Borja; Guayaquil, btwn Espejo & Colón; mains $3; ⏲7am-5:30pm Mon-Sat, to 5pm Sun) The women hawking *hornado* (whole roast pig) put on a pretty hard sell, yelling out for your attention and offering samples. If you can stand the pressure and you're up for dining with flayed Wilburs on every side, then the market is fun and interesting. Wash it down with a *batido* (fruit shake; $1) made with ice from Volcán Chimborazo.

La Parrillada de Fausto ARGENTINE **$**
(Uruguay 20-38, near Unidad Nacional; mains $11-16; ⏲5-10pm Mon-Sat) This fun, Argentine-style grill serves great barbecued steaks, trout and chicken in a ranch-style setting. Don't miss the cave-like bar in the back.

★**El Delirio** ECUADORIAN **$$**
(☎03-296-6441; Primera Constituyente 28-16, near Rocafuerte; mains $8-12; ⏲noon-10pm Tue-Sun) Named for a poem by the great liberator, Simón Bolívar, this former hacienda (now in the city center) serves *comida típica* in a candlelit dining room. The open fire, wooden booths, antiques and artwork-covered

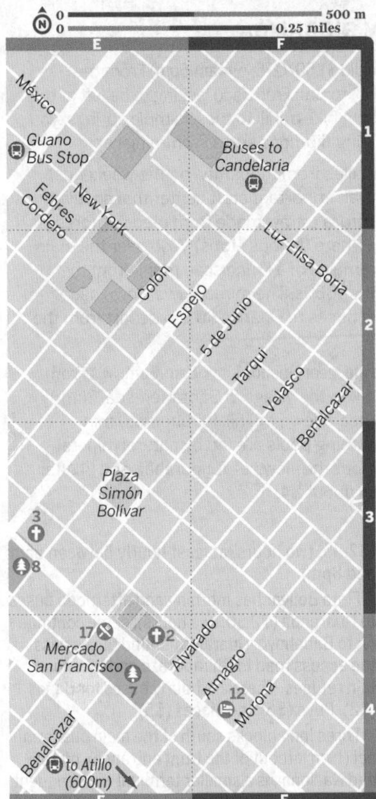

Riobamba

walls make for an inviting atmosphere. Service is slow but the *almuerzos* (set lunches; $10) are excellent and the patio is simply amazing.

Cayfruts ECUADORIAN $$
(☎03-294-1018; Veloz 18-27, near Velasco; mains $8-10; ⏰8am-9pm Mon-Sat; 📶) This friendly restaurant is a good bet for good breakfasts, lunchtime sandwiches and burgers and evening meals. It's open all day, making it a great place to drop in for an afternoon coffee with *humita* (a local snack made with corn flour), or a glass of beer or wine.

Pizzería D'Baggios PIZZA $$
(cnr Av León Borja & Ángel León; pizzas $6.50-12.50; ⏰noon-10pm Mon-Fri, noon-midnight Sat, 3-10pm Sun) Dozens of different kinds of medium-thick-crust pizzas are prepared before your eyes in Baggios' wood oven. The oven keeps the whole place nice and toasty.

Drinking & Nightlife

Beer Garden CRAFT BEER
(☎03-294-0586; www.facebook.com/beergardenpub; León Borja 29-50, near Carabobo; mains $4-9; ⏰5:30-10:30pm Tue-Thu, to 12:30am Fri & Sat) Defying expectations based on its name, Beer Garden is, in fact, an indoor bar, serving a range of local *cerveza artesanales* (craft beers), sandwiches and bar snacks. Murals cover the walls, snaking around cabinets filled with old trumpets, and the upcycled furniture includes a seat made from the trunk of a car. There is live music most weekends.

Gas Plaza BAR
(León Borja near Brazil; ⏰hours vary) This buzzy new complex contains US-style sports bars and fast-food joints fashioned out of shipping containers.

WORTH A TRIP

OFF-THE-HOOK SHORT TRIPS FROM RIOBAMBA

Aguas Termales de Guayllabamba (adult/child $1.50/0.75; 4am-5pm) From the Chambo Terminal take a quick bus ($1, one hour) to San Francisco, asking to be left at the *aguas termales*. From the turnoff, it's an hour-long hike uphill to these simple springs; you might catch a lift with a passing pickup truck. Bring flip-flops and a swimming cap.

Guano Besides serving as a playground for families from Riobamba on the weekends, the village of Guano, 8km north of Riobamba, is an important craft center that specializes in carpets and items made of leather and *totora* (straw made from reeds). Stores selling them are right around the main square (where the bus stops). Also near the main square is a **museum** holding the mummified remains of a Franciscan monk from the 16th century, and ruins of a convent dating to the 1660s. The mirador over town has excellent views (on a clear day) of El Altar. Local buses to Guano ($0.35) depart from the stop at Pichincha and New York in Riobamba.

Parque Acuático Los Elenes (Via Santa Teresita, near Guano; $1; 8am-6pm;) From the main plaza in Guano, continue by bus or walk to the village of Santa Teresita, 2km away. At the end of the bus ride, turn right and head down the hill for about 20 minutes to Parque Acuático Los Elenes, where swimming pools are fed by natural mineral springs. The water is quite cool (22°C, or 72°F), but the views of Tungurahua and El Altar are marvelous. A taxi here from Riobamba costs about $4.

Shopping

The Saturday market (p164) in Plaza de la Concepción is an excellent place to shop for handicrafts. As you're walking around, keep your eyes peeled for locally made *shigras* (small string bags), tagua nut carvings, and *totora* baskets and mats woven by the indigenous Colta from the reeds lining the shores of nearby Laguna de Colta.

Tagua Workshop ARTS & CRAFTS
(Av León Borja 33-24, near León; 9am-1pm & 3-7pm Mon-Sat) Byron Landeta's workshop has Riobamba's best selection of tagua items, carved from the nut of a palm tree. Tagua carving has been in Landetta's family for more than 100 years.

Information

Banco Guayaquil (Primera Constituyente)

Banco Pichincha (cnr García Moreno & Primera Constituyente)

Police Station (03-296-9300; Av León Borja)

Post Office (cnr Espejo & 10 de Agosto)

Su Lavandería (Veloz 14-53, near Morona; per kilo $1) Same-day laundry.

Getting There & Away

Main Bus Terminal (Av León Borja, near Av de la Prensa) About 2km northwest of downtown, this modern terminal has hourly buses for Quito ($4.60, four hours) and intermediate points, as well as buses to Guayaquil ($5.65, 4½ hours), Cuenca ($6, six hours) and Alausí ($2.35, two hours, at least hourly between 5am and 8pm).

Flota Bolívar has morning and afternoon buses to Guaranda ($2.50, two hours); some continue on to Babahoyo. Guaranda-bound buses pass the access road to Chimborazo and the mountain refuges. There are hourly buses for Baños ($2), Puyo ($6) and Macas ($5).

Three long blocks south of the main bus terminal (turn left out of the front entrance), off Unidad Nacional, is a smaller terminal with frequent local buses for Cajabamba, Laguna de Colta and the chapel of La Balbanera. Buses for Guamote leave from Canomigo Ramos near the bypass.

Buses to Atillo in Parque Nacional Sangay leave from the Chambo terminal on Puruhá and Primera Constituyente.

To visit the villages of Guano and Santa Teresita, take the **local bus** ($0.25) from the stop at Pichincha and New York.

Getting Around

North of the main bus terminal, behind the Church of Santa Faz (the one with a blue dome), is a local stop for buses going downtown. These run along Avenida León Borja, which turns into 10 de Agosto near the train station. Going the other way, take any bus marked 'Terminal' on Primera Constituyente. The fare is $0.25.

You can taxi nearly anywhere in town for $1.25.

Laguna de Colta

About 17km south of Riobamba, the Panamericana speeds through the village of **Cajabamba**, the original site of Riobamba until an earthquake-induced landslide buried the city in 1797, killing thousands.

Further south and just off the Panamericana, you'll pass the unmistakable colonial-era chapel of **La Balbanera** in the small village of Colta. On the other side of the highway, the waters of **Laguna de Colta** appear choked with a golden reed called *totora*. For anyone who has ever visited Lake Titicaca in Bolivia, this setting and the small *totora* rafts used to sail around Laguna Colta will look familiar. Ethnobiologists believe that *totora* seeds may have been brought here in prehistoric times, but whatever the case, the reeds form an important crop for the indigenous people of Colta, who use them to make their famous baskets and *esteras* (mats). Women dye the fringes of their hair a startling golden color.

Sights

La Balbanera CHURCH
(Colta; 8am-5pm) Although much of it crumbled in the 1797 earthquake, parts of the facade of this beautiful low-slung church date from 1534, making it one of the oldest churches in Ecuador.

On a clear day Chimborazo peeks out behind the church. Across the plaza is a small **museum** with interesting local artifacts such as a drinking vessel fashioned from a bull scrotum.

Laguna de Colta LAKE
(adult/child $0.60/0.30; 8am-4pm) A trail with broad views of Chimborazo leads around Laguna de Colta, passing through traditional villages and grazing livestock. There's a children's play area on the lake shore and you can rent bikes (per 30 minutes $2) or take a boat trip around the lake (adult/child $1.50/1).

Getting There & Away

You can easily visit any or all of these sites on a day excursion from Riobamba by local buses or hired taxi. Buses from Riobamba heading south on the Panamericana will drop you at any of them. They're close enough to each other that you could walk between them, too.

Guamote

03 / ELEV 3050M

A charming maze of brightly painted adobe buildings, Guamote is a proud indigenous community in little (immediate) danger of losing its identity. The village is famous for its unspoiled Thursday market, one of the largest in rural Ecuador. Although a bit sleepy (there's no ATM in town), it's a place where Kichwa-speaking old-timers gather in the main square to share tales and pass their Sunday afternoons.

Sights

Thursday Market MARKET
(8am-6pm Thu) One of the most authentic markets in the central highlands is held on Thursdays in Guamote, with separate sections for vendors of horses and donkeys; pigs, cow and sheep; guinea pigs and chickens; cereal, fruits, vegetables and rice; traditional clothing; and an area solely dedicated to potatoes.

Sleeping

★ **Inti Sisa** HOSTEL $$
(03-291-6529; www.intisisa.com; Vargas Torres, near García Moreno; dm/s/d incl breakfast $25/50/65; @) Part of a community tourism project, Inti Sisa (the Kichwa words for sunflower) is a welcoming spot that's tastefully decorated and filled with local artwork and crafts. There are dorm rooms with thick mattresses and bright private rooms with exposed wood and minimalist styling. Lunch ($8) and dinner ($10) are served in the colorful dining room.

Inti Sisa runs an early childhood education program in town and offers awesome community tours ($40), horseback trips ($45), Spanish classes ($10 per hour) and cooking classes ($12.50). Ask about volunteer opportunities.

Getting There & Away

Guamote is on the Riobamba–Cuenca bus route, which has several services per day. Unless your bus is actually going to Guamote, you will be dropped off on the Panamericana and have to walk (or take a pickup truck) about 1km up the hill to the main plaza.

Alausí

03 / POP 8111 / ELEV 3340M

Set almost dizzyingly on the edge of the Río Chanchán gorge and presided over by a giant statue of St Peter, Alausí is the jumping-on point for the famous Nariz del Diablo (p170) train run. Alausí is wonderfully picturesque, especially near the railway station and on the cobblestone streets, where old adobe buildings with wooden balconies take you back in time. The town is really just a whistle-stop

DON'T MISS

THE DEVIL'S NOSE

Train buffs will be excited to learn about the illustrious rail system known as the Ferrocarril Transandino (Trans-Andean Railway), built around the turn of the 20th century, that connected Quito and Guayaquil. A technological marvel, it cut the journey time between the cities from two and a half weeks to just two days and was an economic lifeline between the coast and highlands.

Highway construction, along with constant avalanche damage from heavy rains, spelled the demise of Ecuadorian rail transport. However, in the last few years many lines are being restored and targeted specifically at tourists with round-trip service, narration, stops at small museums and more.

The best-known and most exciting of these is the section from Alausí to Sibambe down (and up) the **Nariz del Diablo** (Devil's Nose; ☎1-800-873-637; www.trenecuador.com; Alausí train station; adult/child $32/21; ⏲8am-10:30am & 11am-1:30pm Tue-Sun), a 765m sheer cliff of solid rock. In 1902 track engineers devised a clever way up this monster by carving a zigzag route into the side of the mountain (many lives were lost in the process). The train tugs a bit north, switches track, tugs a bit south and again switches track, slowly making its way up and down the Devil's Nose.

Somewhere along the Nariz, the old choo choo occasionally derails. Not to worry, though! The conductors ask everyone to get off and by using advanced technology – big rocks and sticks – they steer the iron horse back on track. The entire ride should takes about 2½ hours, with an hour stopover in Sibambe, where you are greeted by a local dance troupe and have the chance to buy some artisan goods. A guide accompanies every tour group. Adrenaline-seekers will be sad to hear that you can no longer ride on the train's roof.

these days, but it's a pretty place for a day trip nonetheless.

Alausí lies about 97km south of Riobamba and has a busy **Sunday market**. The train station is at the north end of Avenida 5 de Junio.

Sleeping & Eating

Hotel Europa HOTEL $

(☎03-293-0200; www.hoteleuropa.com.ec; Av 5 de Junio 175, near Orozco; s/d $25/40, without bathroom $15/18; 📶) With old wooden balconies and corridors, the Europa is your best budget option in the town proper. The rooms don't quite live up to the promise, but they have cable TV. It's right across from the bus station. Breakfast costs $3.

Hostería La Quinta HOTEL $$$

(☎03-293-0247; www.hosteria-la-quinta.com; Eloy Alfaro 121; s/d/ste incl breakfast $55/92/150; 📶) Just 300 meters uphill from the train station, this 120-year-old family home has beautiful wooden beams and even better views. Much of the furniture is original and rooms are decorated with family photographs and antiques. Rooms vary in size but all are charming; the best is the family suite with its own private terrace.

Punta Bucana Café MEXICAN $

(Plazaleta Guayaquil; mains $2.50-8; ⏲8am-9pm Tue-Sun) This small eatery on the north end of Avenida 5 de Junio serves up fresh Central American and Mexican food (with an Ecuadorian twist). The service is a bit slow, but the food is worth it.

Getting There & Away

The **bus station** is on Avenida 5 de Junio. Buses for Riobamba ($2,35, two hours) depart hourly; about half of them continue on to Quito, otherwise Quito-bound travelers can change buses in Riobamba. Buses for Cuenca ($6.25, four hours) depart ten times a day. For Guamote ($1.25; 1 hour) take any Riobamba-bound bus.

Many buses between Riobamba and Cuenca enter town – if not, it's a 1.5km walk (all downhill) into town from the Panamericana.

Old buses (or pickup trucks acting as buses) leave from Avenida 5 de Junio for nearby destinations. Some of the bus rides can be quite spectacular, especially the one to Achupallas, the departure point for the Inca Trail hike, about 23km by road to the southeast.

Cuenca & the Southern Highlands

Includes ➡

Best Places to Eat

- ➡ Moliendo Café (p182)
- ➡ Guajibamba (p182)
- ➡ ShamuiCo Espai Gastronòmíc (p191)
- ➡ Zarza Brewing Company (p196)
- ➡ Shanta's Bar (p203)

Best Places to Stay

- ➡ Mansión Alcázar (p181)
- ➡ Hostal Achik Wasi (p191)
- ➡ Grand Victoria Boutique Hotel (p195)
- ➡ Copalinga (p199)
- ➡ Madre Tierra Resort and Spa (p202)

Why Go?

The southern spine of the Ecuadorian Andes ushers intrepid travelers down lush valleys that hide pastel-hued colonial towns and remote villages where indigenous culture thrives. And – with the exception of the famous regional capital Cuenca – the highways and byways are far less traipsed.

Veering from chilly elfin woodland to humid lowland forest, the region is home to hundreds of bird species, thousands of plants and scores of mammals. The sheer diversity of these habitats means a trip to at least one of the region's large national parks should definitely be on the agenda.

Most journeys begin in Cuenca, a classic traveler hub with one of South American's best-preserved colonial centers. From there, you can romp through seldom-visited ancient settlements and untrammeled wild areas towards the vibrant city of Loja and balmy new-age Vilcabamba. From here, forays start up into stark ocher hills, along to verdant lower slopes coated by the plantations rearing Ecuador's best coffee and down into sticky semi-tropical forest.

When to Go

Cuenca

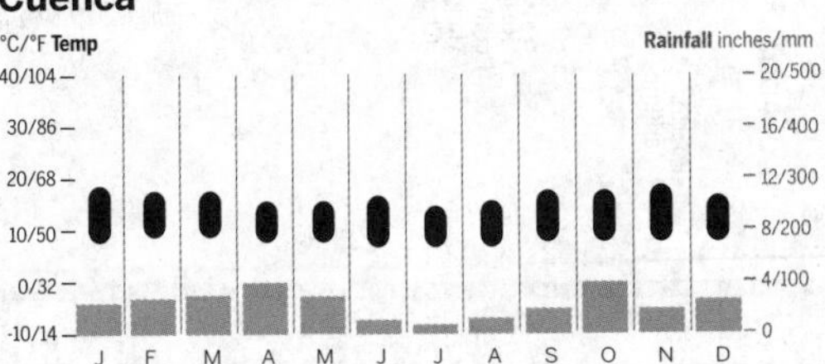

Year-round South of Cuenca, especially around Loja and Vilcabamba, it's spring all year.

Oct–May The rainy season is colder, wetter and greener; morning sun and showers later.

May & Aug Festivals celebrating the Virgen del Cisne bring devotees from around Ecuador.

Cuenca & the Southern Highlands Highlights

1 **Cuenca** (p174) Wandering the cobblestone streets of this colonial town, a Unesco World Heritage Site.

2 **Parque Nacional Cajas** (p186) Hiking in the eerie, lake-bejeweled moors of this windswept highland park.

3 **Ingapirca** (p188) Pondering the engineering mysteries of Ecuador's most important Inca ruins.

4 **DIY Adventures** (p190) Losing the gringo trail amid the region's seldom-visited indigenous communities: unique markets, stunning churches and wildernesses.

5 Gualaceo, Chordeleg & Sígsig (p188) Spending the day shopping for handicrafts at the traditional Sunday markets in the villages near Cuenca.

6 Saraguro (p190) Diving into indigenous culture in this proud and resilient town.

7 Parque Nacional Podocarpus (p197) Keeping your eyes peeled for orchids, birds and rare mammals in the diverse habitats of this national park.

8 Vilcabamba (p200) Perfect the art of relaxation with massages, horseback riding and strolls in the clean country air.

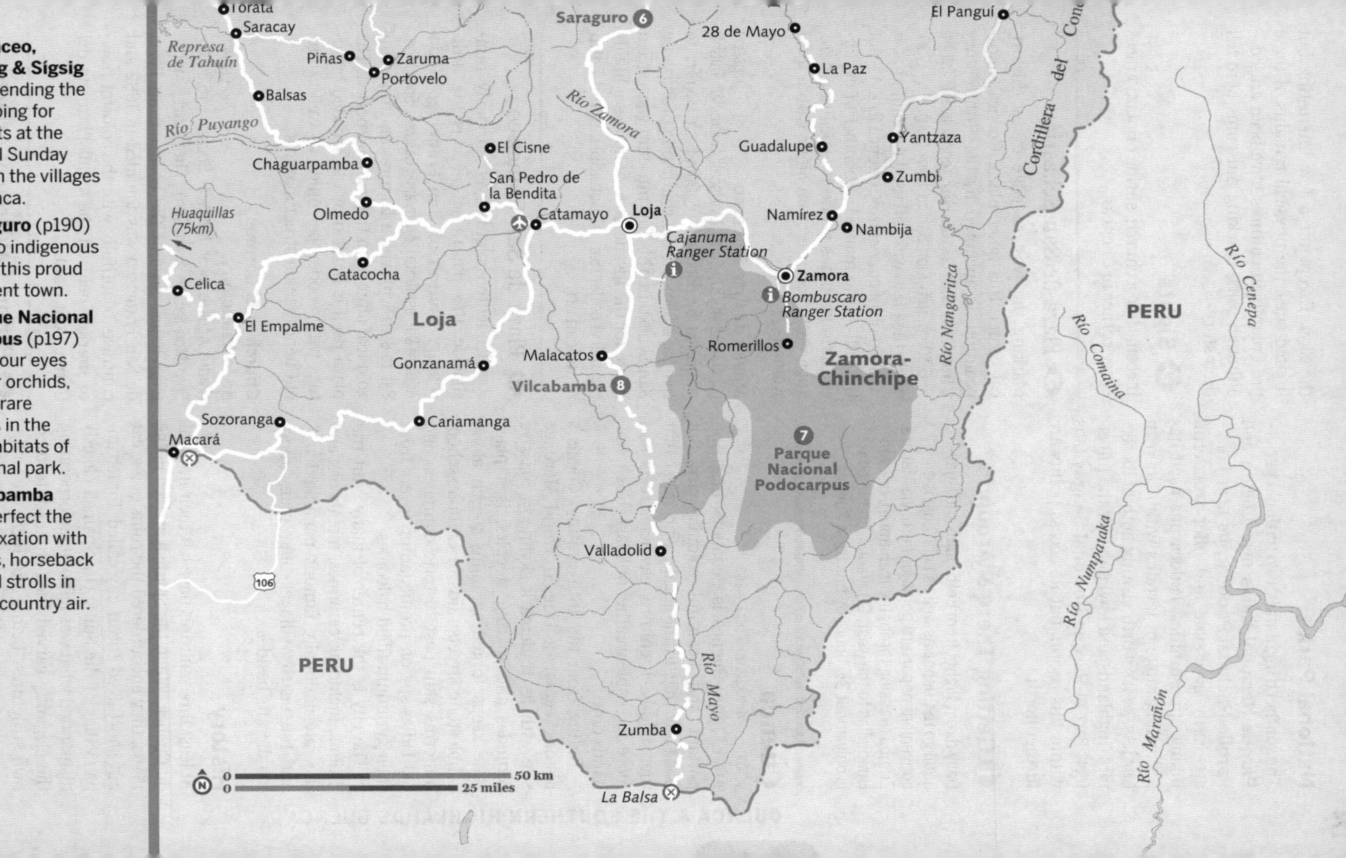

National Parks

The southern highlands' two national parks – **Parque Nacional Cajas** near Cuenca and **Parque Nacional Podocarpus** near Loja – are easily accessible and offer wonderful hiking opportunities. Podocarpus itself has a startling range of terrains within its own borders, so it's worth visiting both of its sectors (highlands and lowlands) for the full effect. Part of **Parque Nacional Sangay** falls within this region, but its access points are further north.

Getting There & Around

Daily direct flights from both Quito and Guayaquil go to Cuenca as well as Loja. Loja is a convenient departure point for Peru, via Macará, Zumba (passing through Vilcabamba), or even Huaquillas to the west. Guayaquil, on the coast, is only about 3½ hours by bus from Cuenca.

Cuenca

07 / POP 332,000 / ELEV 2530M

After Quito, Cuenca is Ecuador's most important and beautiful colonial city. But don't say that to the locals, who insist that their laid-back culture, cleaner streets and more agreeable weather outclass the capital, hands down.

Dating from the 16th century, Cuenca's historic center, a Unesco World Heritage Site with its trademark skyline of massive rotundas and soaring steeples, is a place time keeps forgetting: nuns march along cobblestone streets, kids in Catholic-school uniforms skip past historic churches, and old ladies spy on promenading lovers from their geranium-filled balconies.

The city is the center of many craft traditions, including ceramics, metalwork and the internationally famous panama hat – and the nearby villages offer many more handicrafts besides.

History

At least three cultures have left their imprint on Cuenca. When the Spanish arrived in the 1540s, they encountered the ruins of a great but short-lived Incan city called Tomebamba (Valley of the Sun). The Spanish eagerly dismantled what was left of it, incorporating the elegantly carved Inca stones into their own structures. Before the Inca, the indigenous Cañari people had lived in the area for perhaps 3000 years. They too had a city here, called Quanpondelig (Plain as Big as the Sky). Except for a few interesting but limited sites, the physical remains of these pre-Columbian cultures have been erased – although some cracking museums here tell their story.

Sights

It seems like a church, shrine or plaza graces every corner in Cuenca.

Plaza de San Sebastián

Marking the western edge of the historical center, this quiet plaza, Cuenca's most beautiful, is anchored by the 19th-century **Church of San Sebastián** (cnr Bolívar & Talbot; 6:30am-5pm Mon-Sat, to 8pm Sun). In 1739, when the plaza was still used for bullfights, it was a mob of *cuencanos* (Cuenca folks) – not the bull – who mauled a member of explorer La Condamine's geodesic expedition here, apparently because of an affair with a local woman.

Museo de Arte Moderno MUSEUM
(07-413-4900; cnr Mariscal Sucre & Talbot; admission by donation; 9am-5pm Mon-Fri, to 1pm Sat & Sun) On the south side of Plaza de San Sebastián, this fun museum was once a home for the insane. It now houses a highly regarded collection of Ecuadorian and Latin American art.

Plaza de San Francisco

Resplendently colonial yet curiously ramshackle, this plaza's set-piece is the 19th-century **Church of San Francisco** (Padre Aguirre & Presidente Córdova; 6:30am-5pm Mon-Sat, to 8pm Sun) which features an important gold-leaf altar from the colonial period. The plaza itself is flanked by old arcaded buildings with wooden balconies, as well as one of Cuenca's main street markets.

Church of El Carmen de la Asunción CHURCH
(Padre Aguirre, near Mariscal Sucre; 6:30am-5pm Mon-Sat, to 8pm Sun) The stark, white church just around the corner from Plaza de San Francisco was founded in 1682 and contrasts beautifully with the colorful **flower market** held on the small Plazoleta del Carmen out front.

Parque Calderón & Around

The city's largest plaza is abutted by two stunning cathedrals. The park's name comes from independence hero Abdón Calderón, whose monument graces the center – accessed through prettily hedged walkways.

★Catedral de la Inmaculada Concepción CHURCH
(Parque Calderón; 6:30am-5pm Mon-Sat, to 8pm Sun) Also known as the 'new cathedral,' construction began on this vast cathedral only in 1885. Its giant domes of sky-blue Czech tile are visible from all over Cuenca, and if it looks like the bell towers are bit short, that's because they are – a design error made the intended height of the belfries impossible for the building to support.

★El Sagrario CHURCH
(Parque Calderón; adult/child $2/1; 9am-5pm Mon-Fri, 8am-4pm Sat & Sun) Standing across the park from the new cathedral, the whitewashed El Sagrario is also known as the 'old cathedral.' Construction began in 1557, the year Cuenca was founded, and in 1739 La Condamine's expedition used its towers as a triangulation point to measure the shape of the earth. It's been deconsecrated and serves as a religious museum and recital hall.

Wander out back to the courtyard for a look at some fascinating historical photographs of colonial Cuenca life.

Museo de la Ciudad MUSEUM
(cnr Gran Colombia & Benigno Malo; 8am-1pm & 3-6pm Mon-Fri, 10am-2pm Sat, 10am-1pm Sun) FREE Housed in the former Escuela Central la Inmaculada, this beautifully preserved colonial building has been revamped with sleek, contemporary lines to house art exhibitions in its salons.

Museo del Monasterio de las Conceptas MUSEUM
(07-283-0625; Miguel 6-33; adult/student $3.50/2.50; 9am-6:30pm Mon-Fri, 10am-5pm Sat) This religious museum in the Convent of the Immaculate Conception, founded in 1599, offers a glimpse into the centuries-old customs of the cloistered nuns who live here. You can't see the nuns (they're cloistered, after all) but you can see their primitive bread-making equipment and dioramas of their stark cells, as well as some religious art.

Parque San Blas

On the east end of the historical center and occupying what was once known as the 'low neighborhood,' this slightly decrepit park has one of the city's largest churches, the **Church of San Blas** (Vega; 6:30am-5pm Mon-Sat, to 8pm Sun), at its eastern end. It's the only Cuenca church built in the form of a Latin cross.

Río Tomebamba & Calle Larga

Majestic colonial buildings line the grassy shores of the Río Tomebamba, which effectively separates Cuenca's historic sector from the new neighborhoods to the south. The building facades actually open onto the street of Calle Larga, which runs parallel to and above the Tomebamba, while their back sides 'hang' over the river. This arrangement gives rise to the local name for the fashionable neighborhood, El Barranco (cliff). Steep stone stairways – the most used of which is the wide flight of steps known as **La Escalinata** – lead down to Paseo 3 de Noviembre, an attractive walkway and cycleway which follows the river's northern bank as far west as El Vado.

★Museo del Banco Central 'Pumapungo' MUSEUM
(07-283-1521; www.pumapungo.org; Larga, btwn Arriaga & Huayna Capac; 8am-5pm Tue-Fri,

UNRAVELING CUENCA FASHION

Most travelers will be struck by the vibrant and ornate traditional dress of indigenous women in and around Cuenca. While most men in the region have lost the custom of wearing a poncho, many women still wear their traditional garb with pride. The women's skirts, called *polleras*, fall just below the knee and have a distinctive embroidered hem that can identify which community a woman comes from. Although fine *polleras* can cost hundreds of dollars, no part of an indigenous woman's wardrobe is prized more than her *paño*, a beautiful fringed shawl made with a complicated pre-Columbian weaving technique known as *ikat*. Top that off with a straw hat, clunky metal earrings called *zarcillas*, and a pair of long braids, and you have a look that has withstood every fashion trend the past 100 years have had to offer, including jelly bracelets, acid-washed jeans and bell-bottoms... timeless!

Cuenca

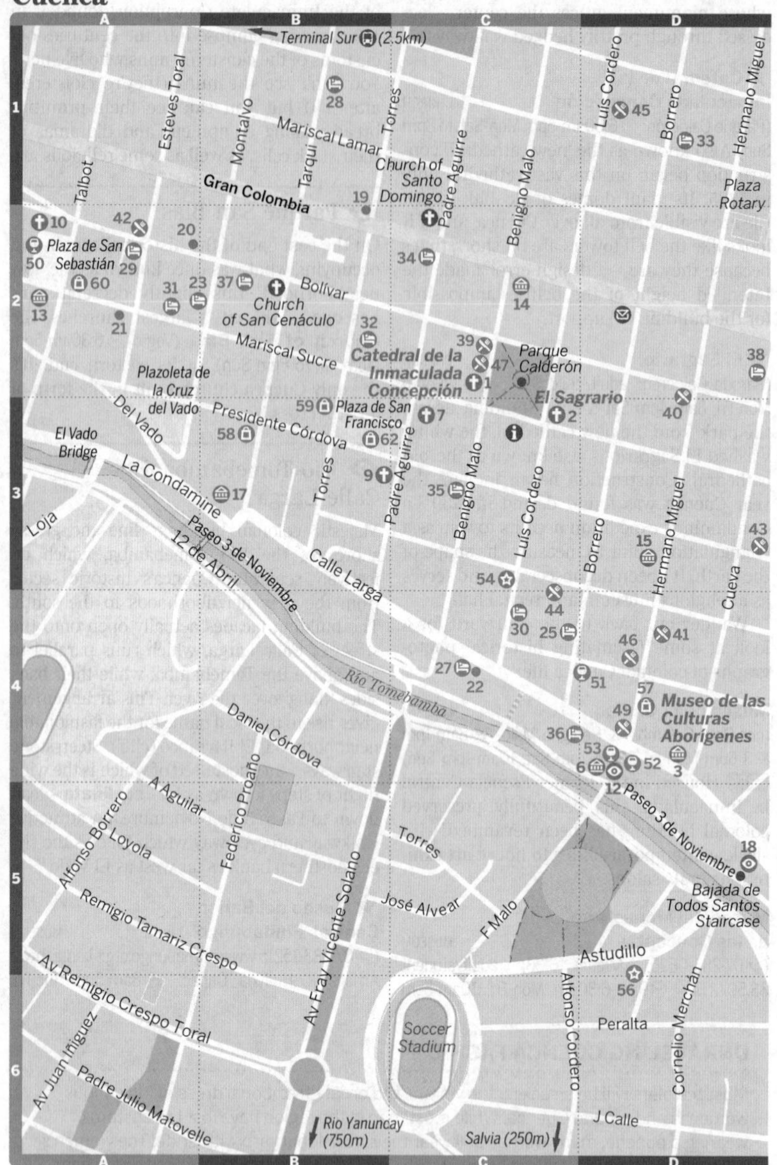

10am-4pm Sat & Sun) FREE One of Ecuador's most significant museums, Pumapungo houses great modern art downstairs, but the highlight is on the second floor. Here begins a comprehensive voyage through Ecuador's diverse indigenous cultures, with colorfully animated dioramas and reconstructions of typical houses of Afro-Ecuadorians from Esmeraldas province, the cowboy-like *montubios* (coastal farmers) of the western lowlands, several rainforest groups and all major highland groups.

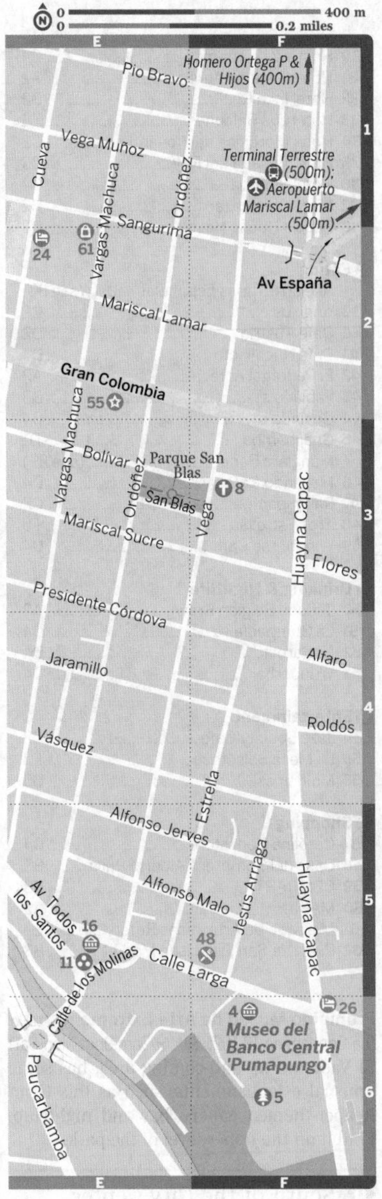

The finale features rare and eerie *tzantzas* (shrunken heads) from the Shuar culture of the southern Oriente. Included in your visit is the **Archaeological Park** (⏲8am-5:30pm Tue-Sat) FREE out back, where you can walk through the extensive ruins of buildings believed to be part the old Incan city of Tomebamba. Thanks to the Spanish conquistadors who carted off most of the stone to build Cuenca, there's not much left – but the park is good for a gander and a stroll, with perhaps a stop at the snack bar at the bottom.

★ Museo de las Culturas Aborígenes — MUSEUM

(☎07-284-1540; www.museodelasculturasaborigenes.com; Larga 5-24; adult/student $4/2; ⏲9am-6pm Mon-Fri, to 2pm Sat) This indigenous culture museum has more than 5000 archaeological pieces representing more than 20 pre-Columbian Ecuadorian cultures going back some 15,000 years. But what makes this such a gem of a museum is the informative self-guided tour – touching upon such unexpected items as combs and obsidian mirrors, and rather sophisticated cooking equipment, as well as explaining the striking designs.

It's one of those rare museums which makes artifacts enthralling to look at. A peaceful courtyard cafe sells wickedly strong coffee.

Inca Ruins — RUINS

A patch of Inca ruins lies near the river, between the east end of Larga and Av Todos los Santos. Most of the stonework was destroyed to build colonial buildings, but there are some fine niches and walls.

Museo Manuel Agustín Landivar — MUSEUM

(cnr Larga 2-23 & Vega; ⏲9am-1pm & 3-6pm Mon-Fri) FREE At the east end of Calle Larga, this museum has archaeological exhibits and tours of the **Ruinas de Todos Santos**, which reveal Cañari, Inca and Spanish ruins, layered one over the other. If you don't want a guide, you can also look at them from below on Avenida de Todos Santos.

Puente Roto — BRIDGE

(Broken Bridge; Av de Todos Santos & Machuca) Most of this bridge, above a pretty stretch of Paseo 3 de Noviembre, was washed away during a flood, but its stone arches make a nice venue for an open-air **art fair** (10am-5pm Sat) and cultural events that take place every Saturday.

Centro Interamericano de Artes Populares — MUSEUM

(Cidap; ☎07-284-0919; www.cidap.org.ec; cnr 3 de Noviembre & La Escalinata; ⏲9am-5pm Mon-Fri, to 4pm Sat) FREE Just down the stairs on the

Cuenca

Top Sights
1 Catedral de la Inmaculada Concepción C2
2 El Sagrario C3
3 Museo de las Culturas Aborígenes D4
4 Museo del Banco Central 'Pumapungo' F6

Sights
5 Archaeological Park F6
6 Centro Interamericano de Artes Populares D4
7 Church of El Carmen de la Asunción C3
8 Church of San Blas F3
9 Church of San Francisco B3
10 Church of San Sebastián A2
11 Inca Ruins E5
12 La Escalinata Staircase D4
13 Museo de Arte Moderno A2
14 Museo de la Ciudad C2
15 Museo del Monasterio de las Conceptas D3
16 Museo Manuel Agustín Landivar E5
17 Prohibido Museo de Arte Extremo B3
18 Puente Roto D5

Activities, Courses & Tours
19 Centers for Interamerican Studies B2
Expediciones Apullacta .... (see 19)
Kushi Waira .... (see 57)
Sampere .... (see 6)
20 Sí Centro de Español e Inglés A2
21 Simón Bolívar Spanish School A2
22 Terra Diversa Travel Center C4

Sleeping
23 Casa Montalvo A2
24 El Cafecito E2
25 Go Hostel C4
26 Hostal Alternative F6
27 Hostal Casa de Barranco C4
28 Hostal Macondo B1
29 Hostal Posada del Angel A2
30 Hostal Yakumama C4
31 Hotel Casa de Aguila A2
32 Hotel Inca Real B2
33 Hotel Los Balcones D1
34 Hotel Morenica del Rosario C2
35 Hotel Posada del Rey C3
36 Hotel Victoria C4
37 Mansión Alcázar B2
38 Pepe's House Hostal D2

Eating
Akelarre Tapas Españolas .... (see 32)
39 Angelus C2
40 Café Austria D2
41 Café Ñucallacta D4
42 El Pedregal Azteca A2
43 Fabiano's D3
44 Govinda's C4
45 Guajibamba D1
Mangiare Bene .... (see 29)
46 Moliendo Café D4
47 Raymipampa C2
48 Tres Estrellas F5
49 Windhorse Cafe D4

Drinking & Nightlife
50 Jodoco Belgian Brew A2
51 La Compañía D4
52 La Parola D4
53 Wunderbar D4

Entertainment
54 Jazz Society Café C3
55 La Mesa Salsoteca E2
56 Multicines D5

Shopping
57 Carolina Bookstore D4
58 Casa del Sombrero Alberto Pulla B3
59 CEMUART B3
60 MAKI A2
61 Mercado de Artesanias Rotary E2
62 Plaza de San Francisco Market B3

riverbank, the Inter-American Traditional Art Center exhibits indigenous costumes, handicrafts and artwork from around Latin America and has a classy, well-priced crafts store.

El Vado

Clustered around the Plazoleta de la Cruz del Vado and Calle La Condamine are galleries, cafes, restaurants and *talleres* (artisanal studios) specializing in everything from traditional embroidery to copperware to saddles.

Prohibido Museo de Arte Extremo GALLERY
(La Condamine 12-102; $1; 9am-9pm Mon-Sat) El Vado, an up-and-coming area, has some unusual establishments, such as this Grim Reaper-themed gallery, bar and nightclub. Find it on the upper level of the park.

South of the City Center

The more modern part of the city south of the Río Tomebamba might lack architectural beauty but it's increasingly the cool place to go out – and has a couple of attractive green spaces worth leaving Cuenca's colonial heart for.

Río Yanuncay PARK

About 1km south of the Old Town's La Escalinita staircase, this peacefully wending river has tree-clad bankside green space perfect for a picnic. Upriver, at the confluence with the city's third waterway, Río Tarqui, is a diverting **botanical garden**. A taxi here costs $1.50.

Mirador de Turi VIEWPOINT

For a lovely view of Cuenca, take a taxi ($5) 4km south of town along Avenida Solano to the stark white Church of Turi. The views of Cuenca's famous, romantic skyline are especially pretty at sunset and on November and December evenings, when the city fires up the Christmas lights.

An alternative way to get here is via double-decker city tour bus ($8), departing every half-hour or so from the north side of Parque Calderón.

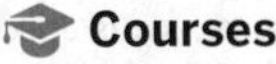

Courses

Most language schools charge around $10 per hour for one-to-one classes.

Centers for Interamerican Studies LANGUAGE

(CEDEI; ☎07-283-9003; www.cedei.org; cnr Gran Colombia 11-02 & General Torres, 2nd fl) A nonprofit language school offering drop-in and/or long-term courses in Spanish, Kichwa and Portuguese.

Sampere LANGUAGE

(☎07-282-3960; www.sampere.com; Hermano Miguel 3-43) A highly recommended and busy Spanish-owned school.

Sí Centro de Español e Inglés LANGUAGE

(☎099-918-8264, 098-277-4464; www.sicentrospanishschool.com; Bolívar 13-28, btwn Toral & Juan Montalvo; lessons per hour $8.50; ⏲9am-1pm & 2-6pm Mon-Fri, 9am-1pm Sat) One of Cuenca's reliable Spanish schools, offering small-group and one-on-one instruction.

Simón Bolívar Spanish School LANGUAGE

(☎07-283-2052, 07-284-4555; www.bolivar2.com; Sucre 14-21, btwn Toral & Talbot; registration fee $35, lessons s/d/group per hour $8/6/5.50) Offers homestays, excursions, plus free salsa and cooking lessons ($3) when you sign up to a course.

Tours

Local operators arrange no-hassle day trips to Ingapirca, Parque Nacional Cajas, nearby villages and markets, and other local attractions. Most operators charge $40 to $50 per person and will pick you up at your hotel.

Expediciones Apullacta ADVENTURE

(☎07-283-7815; www.apullacta.com; Gran Colombia 11-02, 2nd fl; ⏲8:30am-1pm & 2:30-6:30pm Mon-Fri, 9am-noon Sat) A big operation that organizes day tours to Ingapirca ($50), Parque Nacional Cajas ($50) and the Gualaceo area ($55), among other sites. They also run a three-day/two-night Inca Trail trek package ($280), as well as canyoning day trips ($80) with internationally certified bilingual guides and excellent equipment.

Kushi Waira ECOTOUR

(☎099-747-6337, 07-244-0411; www.kushiwaira.com; per person $40) This is one of the Cuenca region's best-run community tourism projects, running on demand to the nearby community of Tarqui. One-of-a-kind daylong programs include visiting a *cuy* (guinea pig) breeding center, demonstrations of typical Inca rituals, picnics with the locals and the like. Trips leave from the Carolina Bookstore (p185; inquire here when the next trip is leaving).

Terra Diversa Travel Center TOURS

(☎07-282-3782, 099-920-4832; www.terradiversa.com; Calle Larga near Cordero) Specializes in biking and horse-riding day trips – as well as overnight horse-riding trips that include staying at haciendas or camping along the Inca Trail north of Ingapirca. They also have Parque Nacional Cajas and Amazon tours, and three-hour Cuenca city tours ($25).

Festivals & Events

Carnaval FESTIVAL

As in other parts of Ecuador, February's Carnaval is celebrated with boisterous water and talcum powder fights in which *no one* is spared.

Semana Santa RELIGIOUS

Holy week in Cuenca is more hectic than most – a week of processions gets perhaps most intense on the Thursday, with devotees doing the rounds of the seven key city churches. Special food, including the cheesy *empanadas del viento* and Cuenca's specific take on Ecuador's complex Easter soup, *fanesca,* helps fuel hungry bellies.

12 de Abril CIVIC

April 12, the anniversary of Cuenca's founding in 1557, often comes on the heels of Easter celebrations. It's a time when school

SANTA SOPA

During Semana Santa, the 'Holy Week' before Easter, signs go up all over Cuenca advertising *fanesca*, a codfish soup that accommodates the prohibition on red meat during the holiday. The base is made of pumpkin, and a dozen kinds of beans and grains representing the 12 apostles of Jesus are thrown in. Garnishes include hard-boiled eggs, fried plantains, and mini-empanadas (the latter symbolize the unbelievers: not involved in the soup's preparation but gladly accepted into the tradition). It's so rich and delicious you won't be hungry until the following Easter. In Cuenca, it's often complemented by a dessert of cinnamon-doused rice pudding.

kids take loyalty pledges to the city, and the Reina de Cuenca (Queen of Cuenca) is selected. *Cuencanos* display their abundant civic pride with elaborate fireworks-laced floats from different neighborhoods.

Corpus Christi RELIGIOUS
This Catholic celebration is usually held on the ninth Thursday after Easter and often coincides with the indigenous celebration Inti Raymi on the June solstice. Carried out with the same fervor as other big Cuenca holidays, it spills into a weekend of processions and fireworks displays. Parque Calderón is transformed into an outdoor candy festival, with vendors selling traditional sweets.

Independence Day CIVIC
Cuenca's Independence Day is November 3, which combines with November 1 and 2 (All Saints' Day and All Souls' Day) to form an important vacation period for the city and the whole country.

Pase del Niño RELIGIOUS
In keeping with Cuenca's strong Catholic identity, the Christmas Eve procession occupies participants with preparations throughout the whole year and culminates in one of Ecuador's most spectacular religious displays.

Sleeping

Cuenca has a vast selection of hotels, many of which are located in old restored houses and mansions. They come in all price categories, but still run a tad higher than elsewhere. During vacation periods they fill up fast and go up in price.

★Pepe's House Hostal HOSTEL $
(☎097-872-5370; Mariano Cueva 9-69; incl breakfast dm $11, s/d from 20/35; 📶) Super-chill and aesthetically appealing in a colorful but minimalist style, Pepe's House is Cuenca's hostel for travelers who've graduated from party mode. Dorms with cushy beds are partitioned with half-walls for some privacy, while private rooms feel like guest bedrooms at a friend's place. Ample common space invites lounging, while the in-house cafe offers wholesome, tasty eats.

Additional perks include free laundry for stays of longer than three days (otherwise, it's a reasonable $5), and free walking tours of the city. Weekend rates are slightly higher.

Hostal Yakumama HOSTEL $
(☎07-283-4353; www.hostalyakumama.com; Cordero, btwn Jaramillo & Vásquez; dm/s/d incl breakfast from $8/17/22, d with private bathroom $31; 📶) As hostels go, the spacious Yakumama is one of Cuenca's best. From the light, roomy 10-bed dorm down through the nicely hand-painted private rooms to the cool common areas (a courtyard full of murals and plants) the owners clearly know what a great hostel needs. There's a great community bulletin board with current activities and events around town.

Staff can be hot and cold, and the place could be a little cleaner, but it remains a go-to spot to meet other travelers and hang in the lounge. Nonguests can also enjoy cocktails in the lounge, which opens to the public from 5pm to midnight.

Hostal Alternative HOSTEL $
(☎07-408-4101; www.alternativehostal.com; cnr Huayna Capac & Cacique Duma; dm/s/d incl breakfast $9/13/22; 📶) Although it's a bit removed from the action, this sparkly hostel (with clean rooms, shared kitchen, TV room and excellent rooftop terrace) has a lot going for it. The modern octagon-shaped building offers small- and medium-size dorm rooms with good mattresses and plenty of space.

Go Hostel HOSTEL $
(☎099-510-1746, 098-837-5810; Borrero 5-47; dm/d incl breakfast from $7/24; 📶) In a pretty, creaky little colonial building, this brand-new hostel is a bargain in central Cuenca. There's zero noise privacy but the feel is convivial and there's a daily happy hour with two-for-$5 drinks.

El Cafecito HOSTEL $

(☎07-411-4765; www.elcafecitohostel.wixsite.com/elcafecito; Cueva 11-28, near Lamar; dm/d $10/30; 📶) Not much has changed at long-term backpacker fave El Cafecito. This is both good (why change a good thing – this probably remains ground zero for meeting other travelers) and bad (rooms look a tad battered, and other hostels in town have overtaken the place in quality). The courtyard cafe-bar is still charming and atmospheric – but rooms nearby stay noisy until the wee hours.

Hotel Morenica del Rosario HOTEL $$

(☎07-282-8669; www.morenicadelrosario.com; cnr Gran Colombia 10-65, btwn Torres & Aguirre; s/d incl breakfast $63/81) Steep stairs at the rather singular Morenica del Rosario wind up around a series of sizable, well-furnished, occasionally dingy rooms, evoking images of some aging aristocrat's once-grand quarters, to a nice roof terrace. Common areas exude a certain Gothic sumptuousness, and it's a very quiet place. All rooms include safes and mini-fridges.

Hostal Macondo HOTEL $$

(☎07-282-1700; http://hostalmacondo.com; Tarqui 11-64; s/d incl breakfast $34/47; 📶) The colonial-style Hostal Macondo has spotless palatial rooms in the front, older section, and small but cozy rooms situated around a big, sunny garden out back, making this one of the best lower-end deals in town. Longer-staying guests will enjoy access to the well-equipped and spotless kitchen, and everyone likes the continental breakfasts with bottomless cups of coffee.

Hotel Inca Real HOTEL $$

(☎07-282-5571; www.hotelincareal.com.ec; Torres, btwn Sucre & Bolívar; s/d from $70/91; P 📶) The Inca Real is the bottom of top-end, rather than top of midrange: its aspirations are clearly grand, and the gorgeous tiled courtyard, abutted by the equally nice tapas restaurant next door, prepares you for stunning rooms. Yet these are only a smidge above average; they tick all the expected boxes with their facilities. One suite is available.

Hotel Posada del Rey HOTEL $$

(☎07-284-3845; www.posadadelreyhotel.com; cnr Benigno Malo & Córdova; s/d/ste incl breakfast from $23/60/99; P 📶) In a restored colonial-style house, 10 rooms with hand-painted murals surround a central courtyard full of wood and iron. It's not quite fit for a king, as the name implies, but all the relatively comfy rooms have balconies, cable TV and an odd disinfectant odor. They could be a *little* more cheerful when showing you the room: doesn't a king deserve that?

Hostal Posada del Angel B&B $$

(☎07-284-0695; www.hostalposadadelangel.com; Bolívar 14-11; s/d/tr incl breakfast $54/81/98; P @ 📶) This yellow-and-blue B&B in a – you guessed it! – colonial-era house has comfortable rooms with cable TV and big beds. Those off the interior balconies have high ceilings, and several others reached by a narrow wooden staircase are tucked away in the quiet reaches (our favorites). Breakfasts in the sunlit lobby are watched over by the eponymous angel.

Casa Montalvo HOSTAL $$

(☎07-284-4997; www.casamontalvo.com; Montalvo 8-33, near Sucre; r/ste incl breakfast from $50/120; 📶) With a colonial aesthetic and modern accoutrements, this midrange spot makes a comfortable base for exploring Cuenca. Rooms surround an attractive courtyard; some rooms tend toward a blander style than the public spaces might lead one to expect.

Hostal Casa de Barranco GUESTHOUSE $$

(☎07-283-9763; www.casadelbarranco.com; Larga 8-41, btwn Benigno Malo & Cordero; s/d/tr incl breakfast from $29/44/58; 📶) Hanging over the high cliffs of El Barranco, this colonial abode has comfortable rooms, four of which have river-facing terraces. The cafeteria, all bare stone walls, haughty furniture and more river views from its terrace, makes a good breakfast spot. Its great location puts it on the map.

★Mansión Alcázar HISTORIC HOTEL $$$

(☎07-282-3918, 07-282-3889; http://mansionalcazar.com; Bolívar 12-55; s/d incl breakfast $145/252; P @ 📶) With unrivaled service and rooms decorated with unique themes, the Alcázar is the best high-end offering in Cuenca. A water fountain spills over with fresh flowers in the interior courtyard, and the sumptuous garden, library and international restaurant all convey the management's tireless attention to detail. Five newer rooms surround a garden at the back. There are several suites, too.

Hotel Victoria HACIENDA $$$

(☎07-283-1120, 07-282-7401; www.hotelvictoriaecuador.com; Calle Larga 6-93; s/d incl breakfast $90/115; P @ 📶) One of several grand

17th-century houses on the *barranco* over Río Tomebamba, the Victoria's 23 impeccable hacienda-style rooms have exposed wooden beams, comfy beds and modern bathrooms. Two suites have giant terraces over the river and many rooms have views, making this a lovely high-end choice. The attentive service and excellent restaurant round out the experience.

Hotel Casa de Aguila HOSTAL **$$$**
(07-283-6498; www.hotelcasadelaguila.com; Sucre 13-56, near Montalvo; s/d incl breakfast from $54/78; P) In this pretty, colonial-style *hostal*, 16 comfortable, wood-floored rooms with modern bathrooms surround a peaceful inner courtyard complete with gurgling fountain. Some rooms have outward-facing balconies with cathedral views. The lovely staff complement the pleasing environs.

Hotel Los Balcones HISTORIC HOTEL **$$$**
(07-284-2103; www.hotellosbalconescuenca.com; Borrero 12-08; s/d/tr $75/110/128; P) We still like this converted colonial-era home with a remarkable chandelier in the central courtyard. Small but well-appointed rooms have hand-painted walls and the rooftop terrace has views fit for a queen. Set the Jacuzzi showers on pulse to feel the wonder of a thousand hands massaging you at once. Amenities include hair dryers, safes, fridges and chocolates.

Eating

★Moliendo Café COLOMBIAN **$**
(07-282-8710; Vásquez 6-24; mains $3-7; 9am-9pm;) This is one of the best little eateries you'll find in Ecuador – and that's why Moliendo Café is always rammed. The hearty *arepas* (maize pancakes) herald from Ecuador's northern neighbors but are a specialty here, topped with anything from beans and cheese to slow-cooked pork. The delicious and filling *almuerzos* (set lunches; $2.50) and *meriendas* (set dinners; $3.50) are also a smashing deal.

Café Ñucallacta CAFE **$**
(http://cafenucallacta.com; Hermano Miguel 5-62, btwn Honorato Vasquez & Juan Jaramillo; light meals $2-5; 8am-6pm Mon-Sat, 9am-1pm Sun;) The best cafe in Cuenca. Artisan Ecuadorian coffee is roasted and the resulting brews are the main reason to stop by – along with gleaning an insight into Ecuador's coffee industry from the knowledgable owner. Note that they also do nice breakfasts and cakes and the tables fill up fast in the mornings.

Windhorse Cafe CAFE **$**
(07-284-9334; Larga 6-16; light meals $2-5; 8am-3pm Thu-Sun) The pies (peanut butter flavor, mmm!) are outstanding, the home-baked cakes are addictive, the salads are enticing and so the Tardis-like Windhorse baits you into lingering awhile. The lingering sometimes morphs into a day-long thing: there's a book exchange, after all – and yoga and meditation classes.

Tres Estrellas ECUADORIAN **$**
(07-282-6968, 07-282-2340; Calle Larga 1-174; mains $4-5; 11:30am-3pm & 5:30pm-1am Tue-Sat) Long in the business, Tres Estrellas roasts up gourmet *cuy* (guinea pig; $17, serves two). If you're not up for that squeaky delicacy, there's outstanding grilled beef, chicken and pork on the menu too.

El Pedregal Azteca MEXICAN **$**
(07-282-3652; Estevez de Toral 8-60; mains $5-9; noon-3pm & 6:30-11pm Tue-Sat, noon-3pm Sun;) El Pedregal serves delicious Mexican food, including lots of vegetarian options, in an atmosphere that's all ponchos, sombreros and *olé!* The portions can be a bit small, however, so fill up on the free homemade chips.

Govinda's INTERNATIONAL **$**
(Jaramillo 7-27; set lunches $2.50, mains $4; noon-3pm Mon, noon-3pm & 6-10pm Tue-Sat;) Pizzas, lentil burgers and a little good karma to wash it down.

Good Affinity TAIWANESE **$**
(07-283-2469; cnr Gran Colombia 1-89 & Capulies; mains $2-4; 9:30am-3:30pm Mon-Sat;) This oddly named Taiwanese cafeteria is the king of soy, gluten and all things vegetarian. *Almuerzos* (set lunches; $2) include a filling soup, entrée and dessert. Outdoor seating is available.

Angelus ICE CREAM **$**
(cnr Benigno Malo & Bolívar; scoops $1.50-4; 8am-10:30pm Mon-Wed, 8am-11:30pm Thu-Sat, 8am-10pm Sun) Cuenca's coolest *heladeria* (ice-cream shop) will freeze you in shock at some of the weirder offerings from its tubs, but we can vouch for the oreo cookie flavor. It's bang on the main plaza – indulging was never easier.

Guajibamba ECUADORIAN **$$**
(07-282-0558, 07-283-1016; guajibambarestaurante@gmail.com; Luís Cordero 12-32; mains $7-12;

IT'S NOT A PANAMA, IT'S A MONTECRISTI

For well over a century, Ecuador has endured the world mistakenly crediting another country with its most famous export – the panama hat. To any Ecuadorian worth his or her salt, the panama hat is a *sombrero de paja toquilla* (toquilla-straw hat), and to the connoisseur it's a Montecristi, named after the most famous hat-making town of all. It's certainly not a paaa...

The origin of this misnomer – surely one of the world's greatest – dates to the 1800s, when Spanish entrepreneurs, quick to recognize the unrivaled quality of *sombreros de paja toquilla,* began exporting them via Panama. During the 19th century, workers on the Panama Canal used these light and extremely durable hats to protect themselves from the tropical sun, helping to solidify the association with Panama.

Paja toquilla hats are made from the fibrous fronds of the *toquilla* palm (*Carludovica palmata*), which grows in the arid inland regions of the central Ecuadorian coast, particularly around Montecristi and Jipijapa. A few Asian and several Latin American countries have tried to grow the palm to compete with the Ecuadorian hat trade, but none could duplicate the quality of the fronds grown here.

The work that goes into these hats is astonishing. First the palms are harvested for their shoots, which are ready just before they open into leaves. Bundles of shoots are then transported by donkey and truck to coastal villages where the fibers are prepared.

The preparation process begins with beating the shoots on the ground and then splitting them by hand to remove the long, thin, flat, cream-colored leaves. The leaves are tied into bundles and boiled in huge vats of water for about 20 minutes before being hung to dry for three days. Some are soaked in sulfur for bleaching. As the split leaves dry, they shrink and roll up into the round strands that are used for weaving.

Some of the finished straw stays on the coast, but most is purchased by buyers from Cuenca and surrounding areas, where it is woven into hats. Indeed, you'll see more panama hats in and around Cuenca than you'll see anywhere else in Ecuador.

The weaving process itself is arduous, and the best weavers work only in the evening and early in the morning, before the heat causes their fingers to sweat. Some work only by moonlight. Weaves vary from a loose crochet (characteristic of the hats you see sold everywhere) to a tighter 'Brisa' weave, which is used for most quality panama hats.

Hats are then graded by the density of their weaves, which generally fall into four categories: standard, superior, *fino* (fine) and *superfino* (superfine). Most hats you see are standard or superior. If you hold a real *superfino* up to the light, you shouldn't see a single hole. The best of them will hold water, and some are so finely woven and so pliable that they can supposedly be rolled up and pulled through a man's ring!

After the hats are woven, they still need to be trimmed, bleached (if they're to be white), blocked and banded. Then they're ready to sell. Although standard-grade hats start at around $15 in Ecuador, a *superfino* can cost anywhere between $100 and $500. While it may seem expensive, the same hat will easily fetch three times that amount on shelves in North America and Europe. And considering the work that goes into a *superfino,* it rightly should.

noon-3pm & 6-10pm Mon-Sat) This restaurant has a small menu of traditional plates such as *seco de chivo* and gourmet *fritada* (fried chunks of pork, served with hominy, avocado and other garnishes). It's one of the best places to try *cuy* (guinea pig; $21.50) if you're game; call an hour before you go for prep time. It's liveliest in the evenings.

Raymipampa ECUADORIAN **$$**
(Benigno Malo 8-59; mains $5-11; 8:30am-11pm Mon-Fri, 9:30am-10pm Sat & Sun;) This Cuenca institution is overwhelmingly popular with locals and travelers and stays open late. The menu hangs somewhere between Ecuadorian comfort food and diner fare. Get a pew on the upstairs deck for a view of what Ecuadorian meals are all about.

Café Austria EUROPEAN **$$**
(07-284-0899; cnr Hermano Miguel & Bolívar; mains $6-12; 8am-10:30pm;) Does exactly what it says on the label. Austrian-esque comfort food such as goulash, strudel and

Sachertorte taste particularly divine after days/weeks on the road, and the corner location is an attractive spot to check emails over coffee or play some chess with local enthusiasts.

Fabiano's PIZZA $$
(cnr Presidente Córdova & Cueva; pizzas $6-17;) Amiable, family-friendly Fabiano's is a tried and tested gringo hangout but garners a following among Ecuadorians too. Pizzas are generous and tasty. Try the stodge-fest which is lasagne pizza – should it prove too much, these guys'll willingly wrap it up for you for take home.

Mangiare Bene ITALIAN $$
(07-282-6233; cnr Estevez de Toral & Bolívar; mains $6-9; noon-3pm & 5-10pm Mon-Sat, noon-3pm Sun) The Italian place worth knowing about in Cuenca is this sophisticated spot below Hostal Posada del Angel, although it's more about artfully made pastas than pizza. Good wine list.

Akelarre Tapas Españolas SPANISH $$
(Torres 8-40; plates $3-10; 11am-10pm Mon-Fri, 3-5pm Sat;) Akelarre serves petite plates of Spanish classics such as *papas bravas* (spicy fried spuds) and Galician squid, not to mention a delicious paella, in a cozy and classy interior.

Drinking & Nightlife

Cuenca has a lot of nightlife on offer: pick from intimate taverns with live music to Hollywood-style clubs catering to the hook-up scene. Discos are open Thursday through Saturday nights from 10pm, but things don't really get moving until around midnight. Bars are generally open nightly, often as early as 5pm.

A good bet for a wild night out is Presidente Córdova around Hermano Miguel and along Calle Larga from Benigno Malo right down to Av Todos los Santos: bar-clubs with dance floors, dressed-up 20-somethings and myriad themes.

Many of the town's museums offer theater and cultural performances, and the galleries in the El Vado neighborhood are also worth checking out. Movies cost about $4 per person and are listed in Cuenca's newspaper *El Mercurio*.

Jodoco Belgian Brew CRAFT BEER
(097-909-3186; www.jodocobelgianbrew.com; Sucre, next to Church of San Sebastián; 4pm-midnight Tue, from 11am Wed-Sat;) Blessedly authentic Belgian beer, brewed in Cuenca and served alongside lovely bistro fare, is poured at this plaza-side spot with patio seating. A jazz soundtrack and clean, moody interior set the scene for a relaxed sip of craft beer bliss.

La Compañía BREWERY
(099-887-4099; cnr Borrero & Vásquez; 4pm-11:30pm Mon-Thu, to 2am Fri & Sat) Cuenca's first microbrewery is still the best (but only by a beer mat's breadth) – it caters to a young rocker crowd and offers up decent hand-crafted stouts, Irish reds and golden brews. And if you're not into beer, they do great cocktails as well.

La Parola LIVE MUSIC
(cnr Larga & Hermano Miguel; 4:30pm-2am Tue-Sat) Food and cocktails complement a great variety of live music at this hangout high on the cliffs of Barranco. It's right above the La Escalinata staircase.

Wunderbar BAR
(07-283-1274; Escalinata 3-43; noon-midnight Mon-Thu, to 2am Fri, 3pm-2am Sat) This Austrian-owned place is *wunder*ful if you want a classic bar with big wooden tables to sit around with friends. Food is served, and there's a happy 'hour' from 11am to 6pm. They have an American pool table and big-screen sports.

☆ Entertainment

★**Jazz Society Café** JAZZ
(in English 093-934-2714, in Spanish 099-588-8796; jazzsocietyofecuador@gmail.com; 5-101 Cordero, near Jaramillo; 6:30-10pm Wed-Sat) The performance venue of the Jazz Society of Ecuador provides soothing aural therapy with Ecuadorian musicians as well as international artists. The Jazz Society also cultivates young local talent, and though there's rarely a cover charge, a humble donation of $5 is suggested – a bargain for the caliber of performances hosted here.

La Mesa Salsoteca DANCE
(07-421-3276; Gran Colombia 03-35; 9pm-2am Wed, to 3am Fri) *The* place to show off or refine your salsa moves, but don't expect to get going until late.

Multicines CINEMA
(www.multicines.com.ec; Astudillo, Milenium Plaza) Get your stadium seats, buckets of popcorn and blockbuster Hollywood flicks in English (with Spanish subtitles).

Shopping

Cuenca is the center of the *paja toquilla* (toquilla straw, or 'panama') hat trade. *Cuencano* nested baskets, gold- and silver-filigreed jewelry from the nearby village of Chordeleg, and ceramics of varying quality are typical finds. Cuenca's markets are some of the best places to pick up these products.

Casa del Sombrero Alberto Pulla HATS
(☎099-519-1987; Tarqui 6-91; ⏰8am-1pm & 2-6pm Mon-Fri, 8am-1pm Sat) The hats of Cuenca's most famous hatter have graced the noggins of Presidents, celebrities and hundreds of local indigenous women. Alberto Pulla himself died in 2010; his legacy has not.

Plaza de San Francisco Market MARKET
(cnr Padre Aguirre & Presidente Córdova; ⏰8am-5pm) The Plaza de San Francisco Market has an interesting combination of basketry, ceramics, ironwork, wooden utensils, plastic trinkets, gaudy religious paraphernalia and guinea pig roasters (great gift for Mom, but tough to get home). It also has a large contingent of *otavaleños* (people from Otavalo) selling sweaters and weavings on its north side.

Homero Ortega P & Hijos HATS
(☎07-280-9000; www.homeroortega.com; Gil Ramirez Davalos 03-86; ⏰8am-12:30pm & 2:30-6pm Mon-Thu, 8am-12:30pm Fri & Sat) More akin to a hat emporium, this is Ecuador's best-known hat seller. The company exports around the world and has a huge selection of high-quality straw hats. They now have a fascinating museum charting the history and manufacture of hats, where you can see each part of the complex production process. Located a block north of the bus station.

CEMUART MARKET
(Centro Municipal Artesanal; ☎07-284-5854; Torres 7-33; ⏰9am-6:30pm Mon-Fri, to 5pm Sat, to 1pm Sun) On the west side of the Plaza de San Francisco is this artisan market, which houses more than 100 craft stalls selling handmade musical instruments, embroidered clothing, baskets, jewelry and more.

Mercado de Artesanias Rotary MARKET
(Sangurima, btwn Cueva & Machuca; ⏰8am-7pm) Basketry, ceramics, wooden utensils, plastic trinkets, religious paraphernalia and decorative souvenirs can be purchased at this low-pressure, pleasant outdoor market.

Eduardo Vega CERAMICS
(☎07-281-7177; www.ceramicavega.com; Vía a Turi 201; ⏰8am-5:30pm Mon-Fri, 9:30am-1:30pm Sat & Sun) Just below the Mirador de Turi – and 4km south of the center – is the home, workshop and studio of Eduardo Vega, Ecuador's most important ceramic artist. His colorful terracotta and enamel murals grace walls all over Cuenca and the rest of Ecuador. Sculpture, vases and plates are for sale.

MAKI ARTS & CRAFTS
(☎07-282-0529; maki@fairtrade.ec; Sucre 14-96, near Talbot; ⏰10am-7pm Mon-Fri, to 5pm Sat & Sun) Featuring high-quality textiles, baskets, clothing, jewelry and ceramics, this fair-trade shop is a wonderful showcase from which to scoop up souvenirs you can feel good about.

Carolina Bookstore BOOKS
(Hermano Miguel 4-46; ⏰9am-6pm Mon-Fri, from 10am Sat) Carolina has the best selection of English-language books around, plus maps and a wealth of local info. They offer Spanish lessons, too.

Information

DANGERS & ANNOYANCES

Cuenca is pretty safe for a bigger city. This said, at night it's best to walk on well-lit streets. The area around Plaza San Francisco can get slightly sketchy after dark.

Police Station (☎07-284-0476; Plaza de San Francisco; ⏰8am-8pm)

LAUNDRY

La Química (cnr Borrero & Presidente Córdova; per kg $1; ⏰8am-6:30pm Mon-Fri, 9am-1pm Sat)

Lavandería Nieves (Calle Larga 11-55; per kg $1)

MEDICAL SERVICES

Clínica Hospital Monte Sinaí (☎07-288-5595; www.hospitalmontesinai.org; cnr Av Solano & Miguel Cordero) An excellent clinic with some English-speaking staff.

POST

Post Office (cnr Borrero & Gran Colombia)

TOURIST INFORMATION

Tourist Office (iTur; ☎07-282-1035; Mariscal Sucre, near Luís Cordero; ⏰8am-8pm Mon-Fri, 9am-4pm Sat, 8:30am-1:30pm Sun) Friendly and helpful; English spoken.

Airport Terminal Information Office (☎07-286-2203)

Bus Terminal Information Office (☎07-282-4811)

USEFUL WEBSITES

www.cuenca.com.ec Cuenca's tourism website.

www.cuencanos.com Loads of Cuenca information, mostly in Spanish.

www.gringotree.com Aimed at resident expats but good English info on a variety of topics.

Getting There & Away

AIR

Cuenca's **Aeropuerto Mariscal Lamar** (07-286-2095, 07-286-7120; www.aeropuertocuenca.ec; Av España) is 2km from the heart of town and just 500m from the Terminal Terrestre bus station. **TAME** (07-286-2193, 07-286-6400; www.tame.com.ec; Aeropuerto Mariscal Lamar; 7am-8pm Mon-Fri, 8am-noon Sat, 6-8pm Sun) has daily flights to Quito ($99 to $131) and Guayaquil ($73 to $150).

BUS

Cuenca's main bus station is **Terminal Terrestre** (Av España), about 1.5km from downtown, across the street from the airport. It has daily buses to Ingapirca and Gualaceo, Chordeleg and Sigsig.

Two routes go to Guayaquil: the shorter via Parque Nacional Cajas and Molleturo ($8, four hours), and the longer via La Troncal and Cañar ($8, five hours).

Services are frequent on all routes.

CAR

The national chain **Localiza** (1-800-562-254, 07-280-3193/8) rents economy cars and 4WDs at the airport.

Getting Around

Regular buses head downtown ($0.25) from in front of Terminal Terrestre. From downtown to the terminal, take any bus marked 'Terminal' from stops on Padre Aguirre near the flower market. Taxis cost about $2 between downtown and the airport or the bus terminal – or it's a 20-minute walk.

Local buses for Turi ($0.25), 4km south of the center, go along Avenida Solano – or a taxi is $5.

Around Cuenca

07

Cuenca is an easy base for day trips to indigenous villages in the surrounding area. Many are invested in community-based tourism, so you can support local people by hiring local guides and buying traditional crafts. Gualaceo, Chordeleg and Sigsig can all be done together in one day, while Principal, Cajas and the ruins at Ingapirca are separate day trips of their own.

Parque Nacional Cajas

Parque Nacional Cajas (Cajas National Park; 07-237-0126; 8am-4:30pm) FREE is only 30km west of Cuenca and encompasses 2854 sq km of golden-green, moor-like *páramo* (mountainous Andean grasslands) dotted with hundreds of chilly lakes that shine like jewels against a rough, otherworldly countryside.

BUSES FROM CUENCA'S TERMINAL TERRESTRE

DESTINATION	COST ($)	DURATION (HR)
Alausí	6	4–5
Ambato	9	7
Azogues	0.75	¾
Gualaquiza (via Sigsig)	10	7
Guayaquil	8	4–5
Huaquillas	7	5
Latacunga	10	8½
Loja	7.50	4
Macas (via Guarumales)	10.95	7
Machala	5.50	4–5
Piura (Peru)	15	10 (via Machala) to 14 (via Macará)
Quito	12	9
Riobamba	7	5–6
Saraguro	5	3
Sigsig	1.50	1½
Zamora	10.50	6

Parque Nacional Cajas

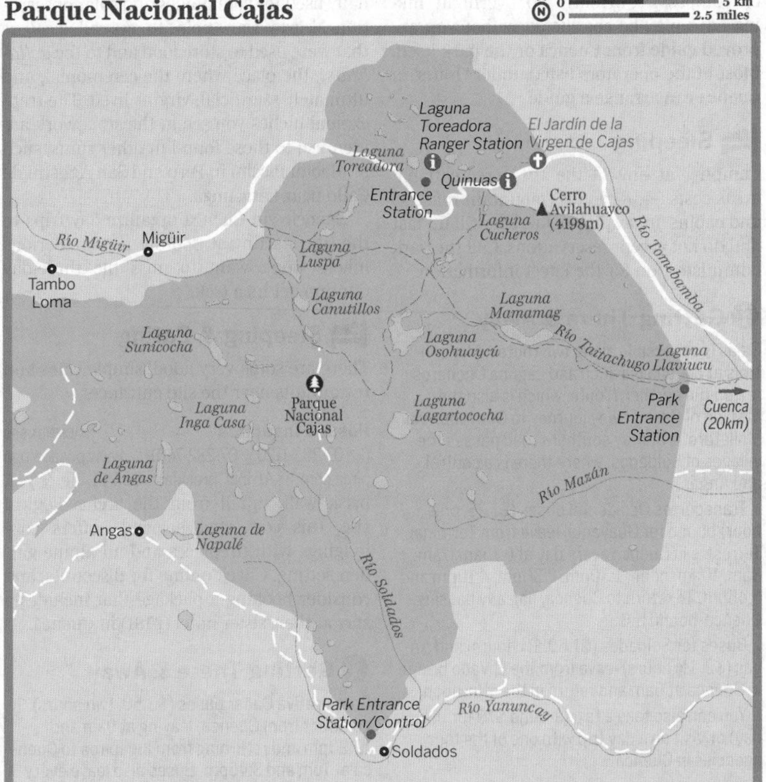

This extremely wet and foggy area feeds rivers that flow into Cuenca and is considered a major conservation area for birds, mammals and flora: in fact, this is the most biologically diverse portion of *páramo* in the entire Andes range.

Especially important are small forests of Polylepis trees that are found in sheltered hollows and natural depressions. Polylepis trees have adapted to grow at higher elevations than almost any other tree in the world, making this one of the highest forests on earth. And wandering into one of these dense dwarf forests is like entering a Brothers Grimm fairy tale.

Sights

The park is named Cajas, according to some folks, because the park's lakes look (rather dubiously) like *cajas* (boxes). More likely, the name comes from *caxas*, the Kichwa word for cold. And cold it is ... so cold that getting lost, which is easy to do, is a rather dangerous proposition. Night temperatures can drop below freezing, especially in the dry season. Driest months are August to January, but it can rain anytime. Altitudes within the park vary between 3000m and 4300m.

Three main recreational areas, all at scenic lakes, lie along the Cuenca–Molleturo road: **Laguna Llaviucu**, which is closest to Cuenca and has a **control**; **Laguna Cucheros**; and **Laguna Toreadora**, which has an information center. A second **control** appears at Quinuas, 3km west of Cucheros. The controls provide free topographical trail maps, which are also available at the tourist information office in Cuenca.

Outside the designated areas around Laguna Llaviucu, Cucheros and Toreadora, groups of eight or more are required to be accompanied by a guide, and all hikers outside these areas must register with the ranger stations (they must also carry a GPS or compass). Currently no overnight hiking trips may be conducted without an approved guide from Cuenca or the park itself. Most of the operators listed under 'Tours' in Cuenca can arrange a guide.

Sleeping

Camping at any of the three recreational areas costs $4. *Refugios* (mountain refuges) and cabins are available, but they fill up fast and do not accept reservations. Call the park administration for the latest information.

Getting There & Away

Cajas is accessible along two routes. The controls at Laguna Llaviucu and Laguna Cucheros are on the northern route, which is also the first leg of the highway journey to Guayaquil via Molleturo. A bumpy southern road passes the villages of Soldados, where there is a control, and Angas.

Transportes Occidental buses ($1.25, one hour) bound for Guayaquil leave from Terminal Terrestre in Cuenca every day at 6:15am, 7am, 8am, 10am, noon, 1:30pm, 2:30pm, 4:10pm and 5:45pm. To return to Cuenca, flag any passing Cuenca-bound bus.

Buses for Soldados ($1.50, 1¼ hours) and Angas ($2, 1¾ hours) leave from the El Vado bridge in Cuenca at 6am and return in the afternoon.

You can also take a taxi (around $70 for the day) or visit on a day trip with one of the tour agencies in Cuenca.

Ingapirca

07 / ELEV 3150M

Ecuador's most preserved archaeological site, **Ingapirca** (07-221-7107; www.complejo ingapirca.gob.ec; entry incl guided tour $2; 8am-6pm), with its semi-intact temple, grazing llamas and open fields, is definitely worth a stopover if you are headed this way. The ruins were originally used by the Cañari people as an observatory. The strategic site was later taken over and developed by the Inca during the 15th century as a military stronghold.

Unfortunately, the Spanish carted away much of Ingapirca's stone to build nearby cities. What's left of the site is still important to the indigenous Cañari, and they now control the administration of the ruins and the **museum** (admission included with Ingapirca) displaying Inca and Cañari artifacts.

The centerpiece of the site is the Temple of the Sun, a large structure that was originally used for ceremonies and solar observation. Nearby, signs point to pits called *colcas* that were used to store food and to the *acllahuasi,* the place where the ceremonial, and ultimately sacrificial, virgins lived. The trapezoidal niches you see in the stonework are identical to those found in other ruins, such as Machu Picchu in Peru and San Agustín de Callo near Latacunga.

Agencies in Cuenca organize day trips to the site, starting at $50 per person. Serious hikers won't want to miss the three-day Camino del Inca trek.

Sleeping & Eating

There are some very good, simple cafes and restaurants near the site entrance.

Posada Ingapirca HACIENDA **$$$**
(07-283-1120, 07-282-7401; www.posadainga pirca.com; s/d incl breakfast $67/91; P) A brisk walk uphill from the archaeological site, this converted hacienda offers cozy lodgings with fireplaces and an alpine garden setting. Check online for discounts, and consider booking a package that includes a stay at their sister hotel (p181) in Cuenca.

Getting There & Away

Cooperativa Cañar buses ($3.50, two hours) go direct from Cuenca, leaving at 9am and 12:20pm and returning from Ingapirca to Cuenca at 1pm and 3:45pm. Buses also leave every half-hour from Cuenca for El Tambo, located 8km below Ingapirca. From El Tambo, buses leave about every half-hour to Ingapirca, or take a taxi ($5).

Gualaceo, Chordeleg & Sigsig

If you start early, you could easily visit the Sunday markets at all three of these towns and be back in Cuenca for happy hour. Between them all you'll find many traditional handicrafts: woven baskets, fine gold and silver filigreed jewelry, woodwork, pottery, guitars and *ikat* textiles – made using a pre-Columbian technique of weaving tie-dyed threads.

GUALACEO

07 / POP 13,981 / ELEV 2591M

Along the banks of a small, swift-moving river lies the craft-shopper's paradise of Gualaceo. *Ikat* weavings and *paños* (indigo-dyed cotton shawls with intricate macramé fringe) are especially sought-after here.

Sights

La Casa de la Makana HANDICRAFTS
(099-569-9163; Sector San Pedro de los Olivos) FREE Visit La Casa de la Makana to see how *makanas* shawls are made, and how the different dyes are mixed. These are sought-after items: one *makana* can take days or even weeks to produce. Quality *makanas* are on sale for about $40.

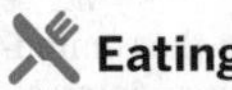

Eating

Mercado 25 de Junio ECUADORIAN $
(cnr Cuenca & Vicente Peña Reyes) For lunch in Gualaceo, try the Mercado 25 de Junio, two blocks north and then three east of the main plaza.

Information

On Gualaceo's main plaza, the **Tourist Information Office** (iTur; 07-225-5131, 098-437-0632; 7-68 Gran Colombia; 8am-5pm Mon-Fri) can provide good info on nearby hiking and adventure opportunities.

CHORDELEG

07 / POP 4209

About 10km south of Gualaceo, hilly Chordeleg has been an important jewelry-making center since before the arrival of the Inca. Its characteristic style is fine filigree. Fakery is common, however, so know how to discern high-quality gold before laying out the big bucks.

Chordeleg also produces wood carvings, pottery, textiles and plenty of panama hats.

Sights

Museum MUSEUM
(8am-5pm Tue-Sun) FREE On the central plaza, this small museum details the history and techniques of wood carvings, pottery, textiles and panama hats, and sells some locally made work.

Sleeping

Hostal Colonial Chordeleg GUESTHOUSE $
(07-222-3486; www.hostalcolonialchordeleg.com; cnr Guayaquil & 24 de Mayo; r per person incl breakfast $25; P) This colonial abode near Chordeleg's main plaza is a comfortable base. The owner can also arrange overnight horseback trips into the waterfall-laden countryside (per person $55).

SIGSIG

07 / POP 3330

About 26km south of Gualaceo lies Sigsig (2684m), a charming vestige of a colonial-era indigenous town, best known for its panama hats.

CAMINO DEL INCA

Though it sees only a fraction of the traffic of the Inca Trail to Machu Picchu, the three-day trek to Ingapirca is popular. For approximately 40km, it follows the original Ingañan Incan royal road that linked Cuzco with Tomebamba (at present-day Cuenca) and Quito. In its heyday, this transportation and communication network rivaled that of the Roman Empire.

The starting point for the hike is **Achupallas**, 23km southeast of Alausí. From there, the Trail climbs, passing rivers and lakes and eventually the ruins of an Incan town. The next day takes you past the ruins of an Incan bridge and a large structure at **Paredones**, where some walls are still standing. At times you'll be able to easily make out the Ingañan itself. On the third day the hike lets out at the magnificent ruins at Ingapirca.

You'll need a GPS and three 1:50,000 topographical maps (*Alausí, Juncal* and *Cañar)*, available at the Instituto Geográfico Militar (IGM) in Quito. Also be prepared for extremely persistent begging from children; most travelers refuse to hand anything out in order to discourage begging.

To get to Achupallas, take one of the daily midday buses from Alausí or, more reliably, hire a taxi-pickup for about $10 to $15 one-way. Alternatively, south-bound Panamericana buses from Alausí can drop you at **La Moya** (also known as **Guasuntos**), where you can wait for passing trucks headed to Achupallas, 12km up a slim mountain road. You can hire guides in Achupallas for $30 to $40 per day, or **Julio Verne Tour Operator** (p165) in Riobamba runs trips for about $320 per person. If you want to go on your own, check out a hiking guide, such as *Ecuador: Climbing and Hiking Guide* by Rob Rachowiecki and Mark Thurber.

Getting There & Away

From Cuenca's Terminal Terrestre bus terminal, buses leave every half-hour to Gualaceo ($0.90, one hour), Chordeleg ($1, one hour) and Sigsig ($1.50, 1½ hours). Buses run from town to town for $0.50 and can be flagged down from the main street. For Sigsig, you might need to change in Gualaceo.

Saraguro

07 / POP 9045 / ELEV 2520M

Surrounded by emerald hills that have been sown with hearty tubers and grains for thousands of years, Saraguro, 165km south of Cuenca, is the center of indigenous Saraguro culture. This prosperous and proud indigenous group originally lived near Lake Titicaca in Peru but ended up here in the 1470s as a result of the Inca Empire's system of resettlement, or *mitimaes*.

Saraguro's excellent community tourism projects are applauded across Ecuador – there are few better places in South America to go off grid and authentically experience indigenous highland culture.

Sights & Activities

The villages around Saraguro, most within a half-hour walk or 10-minute bus ride ($0.20), are full of outdoor and cultural activities. Buses to any of these places leave from the main square in front of the cathedral: information is available at Operadora de Turismo Comunitario Saraurku.

Las Lagunas VILLAGE

Tupus and textiles are made in the community of Las Lagunas, making this an interesting cultural excursion. Catch a bus ($0.20, 10 minutes) from the main road, or get walking directions at Saraurku.

Tuncarta VILLAGE

The community of Tuncarta is known for producing fine Saraguro hats. Catch a bus ($0.20, 10 minutes) from the main road, or get walking directions at Saraurku.

Baños del Inka WATERFALL

($2.50) Just north of town on the Panamericana, this nature area has impressive waterfalls and large rock formations.

WORTH A TRIP

DIY ADVENTURES OUTSIDE OF CUENCA

There are plenty of DIY adventures to be had from Cuenca in the nearby towns of Baños, Girón, Jima and Paute. Here are some hints to get you started.

Paute Good mountain biking and hiking are to be found at this seldom-visited town 41km northeast of Cuenca off the road to Gualaceo. It's an easy day trip from Cuenca, but staying the night will help out the community more.

Azogues The bustling capital of Cañar province, 33km north of Cuenca, has a distinctive church and a Saturday market where woven panama hats are sold – and sent to Cuenca for the finishing touches.

Biblián The huge church of Santuario de la Virgen del Rocio (Sanctuary of the Virgen of the Dew) is carved dramatically into a sheer cliff above this little town, 6km north of Azogues, and is the site of a huge pilgrimage on September 8 (and another on Good Friday). Cuenca to Cañar buses pass by.

Cañar 32km north of Azogues, this dusty town is interesting to visit on Sundays for the lively market. The Cañari people – wearing their colorful woolens – gather; the men wear their distinctive *chumbis* (woven belts decorated with indigenous/Catholic motifs). These can be bought on the market and in the town prison, where inmates sell them (you'll be allowed in to make purchases).

Baños Just outside Cuenca, this small village has thermal springs and a neat little church.

Girón Some 43km southwest of Cuenca on the road to Machala, Girón offers hiking to a 60m waterfall. After busing it here from Cuenca, hire a truck for $5 to take you to the waterfall. Hire a guide from the first waterfall to take you to two hidden falls nearby.

Jima This peaceful agrarian village two hours south of Cuenca serves up easy access to a neighboring cloud forest in a community-run reserve. There's a *hostal* and information center in town where you can arrange a guide. Get here by bus from Cuenca.

DRESS LIKE A SARAGURO

During the last century, Saraguros have relocated (this time, of their own accord) to significantly lower altitudes to the southwest and often alongside Shuar communities in the Ecuadorian Amazon. In both the chilly mountains and humid lowlands, the Saraguro dress in traditional woolens. Women wear broad-brimmed black or white hats, long pleated skirts, ornate pins called *tupus* and elaborate beaded collars known as *chakiras*. Men wear fedora-like black hats, black ponchos and knee-length black shorts, and they may also don small white aprons and woven, double-pouch shoulder bags called *alforjas*.

Each part of this attire is an important craft tradition, maintained in nearby communities, which are fun to visit – for their stunning scenery, as well as for cultural reasons.

Sunday Market MARKET
(7am-2pm Sun) The Sunday market draws Saraguros – dressed finely for the occasion – from the surrounding countryside. None of the several ATMs in town accept cards issued by Visa, so arrive with the cash you need.

Bosque Protegido Washapamba HIKING
($2.50) The Washapamba Forest Reserve, just south of town, is great for hiking.

Tours

Operadora de Turismo Comunitario Saraurku CULTURAL
(07-220-0331, 098-694-1852; www.turismosaraguro.com; cnr 18 de Noviembre & Loja; 8:30am-6pm Mon-Fri) One block west of the main plaza, this community-based tour operator also serves as a tourist information center. They can arrange day trips to nearby sites, horseback-riding and mountain-biking trips, and visits to the Saraguro communities in the Amazon for $50 to $120 per person per day. English-speaking guides are available with advance notice.

Sleeping & Eating

★ **Hostal Achik Wasi** HOTEL $$
(07-220-0058; Intiñan, Barrio La Luz; r per person incl breakfast $23; P) A 10-minute walk up and out of town (taxi $1), this large adobe-and-wood *hostal* is by far the best place to stay. It has comfortable, clean rooms with thick wool blankets and beamed ceilings. The great views and charming service are also big pluses. It's part of a well-run tourism project that benefits the community.

Tupay ECUADORIAN $
(096-971-4663; 10 de Marzo & Vivar; dishes $1-16; 8am-10pm Sun-Fri) Serving up typical Ecuadorian fare from tamales to full *almuerzos* (set lunches), community-based restaurant Tupay utilize as many organic ingredients as they possibly can, in the process educating local farmers on sustainable techniques and benefits. They compost, buy most ingredients locally and brew a mean cuppa (with Loja beans).

Mamá Cuchara ECUADORIAN $
(Parque Central; mains $3; 8am-5pm Sun-Fri, to 3pm Sat) 'Mother Spoon,' as the name aptly means, serves up hearty, tasty meals right on the main plaza. Money goes to the indigenous women's association that runs it.

★ **ShamuiCo Espai Gastronòmic** FUSION $$
(07-220-0590; shamuicorestaurant@gmail.com; cnr Loja & 10 de Marzo; small dishes $2-6; 11am-10pm Wed-Sat, to 9pm Sun) A surprising find in Saraguro, this unpretentiously sophisticated spot is run by a local chef who trained in some of Europe's best restaurants. Bold cuisine falls somewhere along the lines of highland Ecuadorian tapas.

Getting There & Away

Any Loja-bound bus from Cuenca will drop you a block from Saraguro's main plaza ($5, three hours, hourly). Buses to Loja ($2.10, 1½ hours) leave hourly-ish during the day. The bus office is a block from the main plaza, at Azuay and El Oro.

Loja

07 / POP 181,000 / ELEV 2100M

Once upon a time, Loja was the thriving base from which Spanish conquistadors sallied forth to explore the jungle just over the mountains. Loja's main lure will always be its proximity to one of Ecuador's most diverse protected areas, the vast Parque Nacional Podocarpus, spanning chilly highland *páramo* (grassland) and sweltering jungle within its wild confines (and, indeed, the

Loja

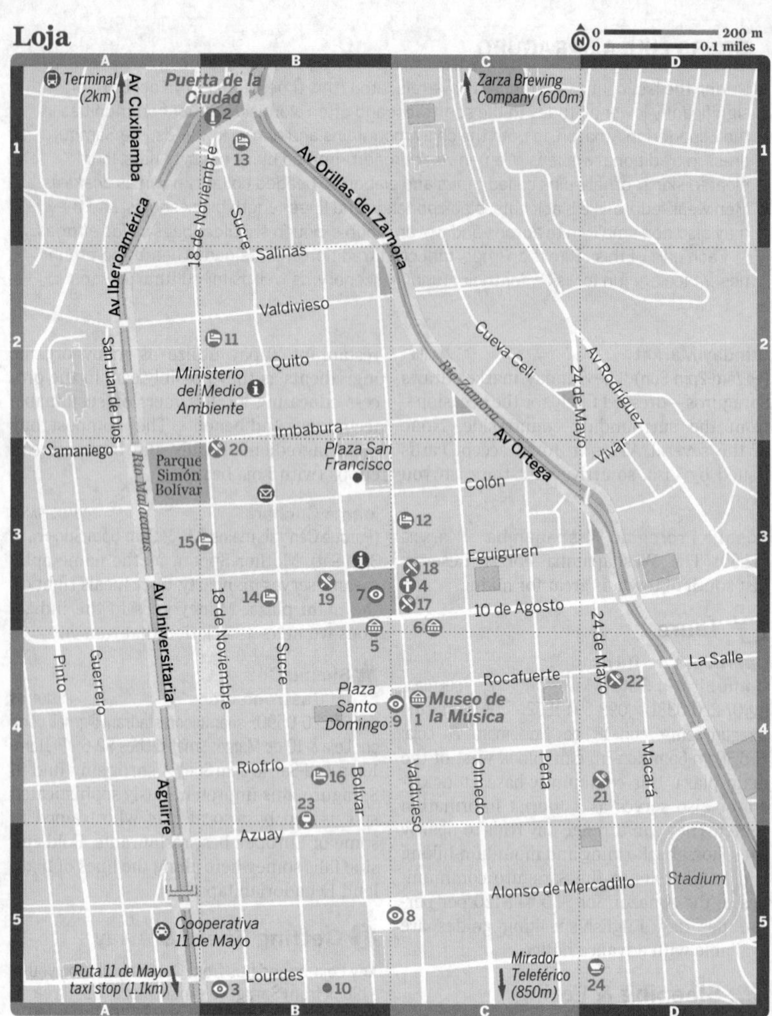

chilled traveler hangout of Vilcabamba just south of town).

But Loja boasts plenty of bait itself. Its cuisine, its musical traditions and its university are known across Ecuador and beyond. Its streets, although traffic-clogged and a tad tame after Cuenca, offer inroads into the local culture its more famous rival to the north cannot. Lying dramatically along the bottom of the Valle de Cuxibamba, Loja's surrounding slopes are fringed with the country's main coffee plantations, and several miradors (viewpoints) offer unforgettable city views.

Sights

From the ornate Puerta de la Ciudad at the northern entrance to the historical center, an inviting series of parks and plazas pepper the ensuing blocks, offering plenty of diversion along the way.

City Center

★Puerta de la Ciudad MONUMENT

(Door to the City; ⌚8am-8pm Mon-Fri, 9am-8pm Sat, 9am-7pm Sun) FREE With perhaps more pomp and circumstance than you'll encounter anywhere else in Loja, the City

Loja

Gate greets you into downtown from the northern corner. It's a giant castle with an arched doorway spanning Sucre, a street forging south (from the confluence of Ríos Zamora and Malacatus) towards the central plazas.

Inside, the helpful staff, second-floor archaeological museum, cafe and several lookouts orchestrate an ideal intro to the city.

★Museo de la Música MUSEUM
(Valdivieso 09-42; ⏲8am-2pm & 3-7pm Mon-Fri) FREE This fun museum located in an old school explores the lives of famous musicians who hailed from Loja (most peaking in success during the golden 1890–1940 period). Many old instruments and scores of music are on display, and a shop here (often closed) sells music.

Parque Central PLAZA
Loja's main square is always busy with shoeshine boys, newspaper vendors and local devotees stepping into the **cathedral** for their daily devotions to the Virgen del Cisne.

Museo de la Cultura Lojana MUSEUM
(10 de Agosto 13-30; ⏲8am-1pm & 2-5pm Mon-Fri, 10am-4pm Sat & Sun) FREE On the south side of Loja's Parque Central square, a characterful republican-era building houses this museum and its exhibits, which include good local art, archaeology and ethnography. Most interesting are the old photographs of Loja and the room devoted to the Saraguro culture.

Museo del Monasterio de Madres Concepcionistas MUSEUM
(10 de Agosto; $1; ⏲8am-noon & 2-6pm Mon-Fri) A half-block east of Parque Central, this monastery has three public rooms housing religious treasures from the 16th to 18th centuries.

Plaza Santo Domingo PLAZA
(cnr Valdivieso & Rocafuerte) Make a beeline a block south of Parque Central for this plaza, mainly notable for the **Church of Santo Domingo**, adorned with religious paintings.

Plaza de la Independencia PLAZA
(Plaza of Independence; cnr Alonso de Mercadillo & Valdivieso) The plaza is hemmed in by the **Church of San Sebastián** and colonial-era buildings with pillared overhangs and shuttered wooden balconies. A brightly tiled fountain depicts Ecuadorian wildlife.

Calle Lourdes STREET
This narrow lane is the oldest colonial street in Loja. There are some nice art galleries here (if only the street were pedestrianized, they would be much more tempting to linger in).

Outside the City Center

Mirador Teléferico VIEWPOINT
Loja's best viewpoint is at the top of the cable car from Parque Pucará, 1km south of Plaza de la Independencia up Olmedo. Walk or get a taxi ($1) to the cable car base. Tourist robberies have happened on the trail which goes up from the park, so taking the

cable car, and not taking valuables, is highly recommended.

Parque Universitario PUEAR PARK
(Parque Universitario de Educación Ambiental y Recreación; 302-7795; https://puear-unl.jimdo.com/; $1; 9am-4pm) Almost 5km south of the center, the 90-hectare reserve has excellent trails. You'll need to cab it here ($1.25).

Parque Recreacional Jipiro PARK
(Santiago de las Montañas, near Salvador Bustamante) North of town, this kid-friendly park offers a giant chessboard, a skate park, a Chinese pagoda, a pint-size Kremlin, small animal enclosures and a paddleboat pond. Green buses ($0.25) go there from the southeast corner of Eguiguren and Peña.

Tours

Exploraves BIRD-WATCHING
(098-515-2239, 07-258-2434; www.exploraves.com; Lourdes 14-80; tours per day from $80) Offers bird-watching tours in Podocarpus, as well as tours to Mindo and other areas.

Festivals & Events

El Día de La Virgen del Cisne RELIGIOUS
(20 Aug) Huge processions mark this Catholic festival.

Independence of Loja CIVIC
(18 Nov) The celebrations may go on for a week.

Sleeping

Hotel Londres HOSTEL $
(07-256-1936; Sucre 07-51; r without bathroom per person $6;) With creaky wooden floors and saggy beds, Hotel Londres is as basic as they come, but it's a tried-and-true travelers' favorite, with spotless shared bathrooms and friendly young owners. Get a room with French doors that open above the street.

Hotel Metropolitano HOTEL $
(07-257-0007; 18 de Noviembre 06-31; r per person $15;) The Metropolitano is a decent budget option: comfortable rooms with hardwood floors, decent beds and cable TV. It's dark, though, so try to score a window.

Zamorano Real Hotel BUSINESS HOTEL $$
(07-257-0921; http://zamoranorealhotel.com; Riofrío, btwn Sucre & Bolívar; s/d/ste $46/75/86; P) A small step down in class from the Grand Victoria but a step up from everything else, the Zamorano is the business choice – smart and slick and delivering exactly what you'd expect such a place to do. There is a good, if slightly soulless, restaurant. Suites have Jacuzzis.

Floy's International Hotel HOTEL $$
(07-257-3821; www.hotelfloysinternacional.com; cnr 18 de Noviembre & Valdivieso; s/d $30/40 incl breakfast; P) The welcome may be the only aspect of Floy's likely to get international respect but this personable hotel does offer incredibly good value for big, clean rooms – some of which have nice murals – and a pleasant cafeteria.

Hostal Aguilera Internacional HOTEL $$
(07-257-2892; hostal_aguilera@hotmail.com; Sucre 01-08 y Ortega; s/d/tr incl breakfast $25/40/50; P) International is a slight overstatement. But this is family-owned, it is right next to Puerta de la Ciudad and it has nice, well-lit rooms.

Hosteria Quinta Montaña CABIN $$
(07-257-8895; Barrio Colinas del Norte; s/d $25/45; P) City address; countrified experience – 2km north of the bus termi-

BOUNTIFUL BEANS

Compared to its neighbors, Colombia and Peru, Ecuador's coffee production is small-scale, but where many believe it wins out over both is in its fine aroma. The Loja/Vilcabamba area is the powerhouse of the plantations producing these highly revered beans.

It's the location that does it. The milder climates that circulate as the hills drop away into the humid lowlands create ideal coffee-growing conditions similar to those in Sumatra and Ethiopia. Coffee grown here produces a soft, smooth brew with just a note of acidity – vastly differing altitudes (800–2000m) ensure plenty of variety.

The best cantons for coffee growing hereabouts are Gonzanamá and Quilanga. Look out also for Zamora-Chinchipe province's Río Mayo label: a chocolatey, creamy flavor permeates through, with maybe an inkling of citrus.

Caffeine fiends can begin their journey at Loja's Equanativa (p196) or sign up for a coffee plantation trip at Vilcabamba's La Tasca Tours (p202).

SOUTHERN DELIGHTS

For many Ecuadorians living overseas, nothing beckons them home more than the smell of corn- and plantain-based *delicias* (delights, or treats). They're common throughout the highlands, but everyone knows that they're better the closer you get to Loja. Many people wash them down with coffee or dress them with *ají* (hot sauce). Here's a primer:

Humita A corn dumpling steamed in a corn husk. The *sal* (salty) versions come with cheese; the *dulce* (sweet) versions are often flavored with anise.

Quimbolito A light, sweet, corn-based cake steamed in *achira* leaves, usually topped with a raisin.

Tamales de Loja Close to a *humita,* but usually stuffed with shredded chicken.

Empanada A pocket of dough stuffed with sweet or savory fillings and fried to a golden, light crispiness. The *masa* (dough) in *empanadas de verde* is made with young plantain; *empanadas de maíz* are made of corn.

Tortilla de choclo A grilled pancake made with rough corn flour.

Maduro con queso A grilled, sweet plantain with cheese.

Bolón de verde A molded ball of young mashed plantain, fried with sausage.

nal, serene Hosteria Quinta Montaña's well-kept cabins skitter down a steep hillside. Grounds include a nice restaurant, a great pool and even a sauna. Swinging on a hammock might be commonplace in the jungle but in Loja, doing so with such a lush view is the preserve of guests staying here.

Grand Victoria Boutique Hotel HISTORIC HOTEL $$$
(☎07-258-3500; www.grandvictoriabh.com; cnr Valdivieso & Eguiguren; s/d incl breakfast $116/140; P ❄ @ ☜ ≋) Bringing the 'boutique hotel experience' to Loja, the Grand Victoria remembers all the little details, like bathrobes and rose petals, 800-thread-count cotton sheets and aromatherapy in the pool area. The rooms are supremely comfortable but lack the charm of the common areas. The service, including in the three international restaurants, is far above par.

Eating

While Loja's specialty dishes have long been talked of fondly, quality sit-down cafes/restaurants seemed light years away until recently – now, there are lots.

Loja's biggest specialty, *cuy* (guinea pig), is commonly served on Sundays. Other local delights include *cecina* (salty fried pork served with yuca) and some of the country's best *humitas.*

West of Bolívar, succulent grilled-chicken joints line Alonso de Mercadillo, where you can pick up a quarter-chicken with soup and fries for about $2.

Biscuit & Co CAFE $
(☎07-256-5656; cnr 24 de Mayo & Rocafuerte; snacks $2-6; ⏲10am-9pm Mon, from 9am Tue-Fri, from 4pm Sat) It's hard to say when we like dropping by this cute French-Ecuadorian place most: probably early evening, as a prequel to a night out. From organic teas to quiches and sweet treats, you'll find something to tickle your taste buds.

El Tamal Lojano ECUADORIAN $
(☎07-258-2977; www.tamallojano.com; 18 de Noviembre 05-12; dishes $1-4, set lunches $2; ⏲8am-8:30pm Mon-Fri, 8:30am-noon & 3:30-8pm Sat & Sun) The *almuerzos* (set lunches) are good, but the real reason to come to El Tamal Lojano is for the delicious *quimbolitos, humitas, empanadas de verde* and *tamales lojanos* – all the Loja region's foodie classics. Order at the counter. There's also a new branch on 24 de Mayo.

Lecka Bistro Alemán GERMAN $
(☎07-256-3878; leckabistroaleman@yahoo.es; 24 de Mayo 10-51; meals from $5; ⏲5pm-10:30pm Mon-Thu, to 11:30pm Fri) Good, authentic German offerings (particularly the cakes and the beer!) in an intimate setting.

El Jugo Natural JUICE BAR $
(☎07-257-5256; eljugonaturalloja@gmail.com; Eguiguren 14-20; light meals $1-4; ⏲7am-8pm) Pure, all-natural juices, yogurt shakes and fruit salads make up the menu at this small cafe: Loja's definitive breakfast stop and *numero uno* meeting-up spot for old-timers. It's been in the juice business over 30 years.

★ **Riscomar** SEAFOOD **$$**
(☎07-258-5154; www.riscomarloja.com; cnr Rocafuerte & 24 de Mayo; mains $10; ⌚9am-4pm & 7-10pm Mon-Sat, 9am-4pm Sun) Serving some of Loja's best seafood, Riscomar prepares delicious, Ecuadorian-style ceviche in a civilized dining room. The *chivo en cerveza* (goat in beer) is a surprise addition to the menu.

Dumas Trattoria & Restaurante PIZZA **$$**
(☎07-256-1494; Eguiguren & Valdivieso; mains $5-13; ⌚noon-9pm Mon-Fri, to 4pm Sat) Wood-fired pizzas, decent wines, homemade pasta and a cozy atmosphere give Dumas an edge over other pizza joints. House specialties include Argentine-style steak tenderloin with chimichurri, and chicken milanesa, with salads and other vegetarian options also on offer.

Dejà Vu INTERNATIONAL **$$**
(☎07-258-2347; Valdivieso 07-50, 3rd fl, Centro Comercial Colibrí; mains $7-19; ⌚noon-10:30pm Mon-Sat) Service: indifferent. Meat and fish dishes: good. Views from the balcony over Parque Central: the best. Book at weekends if you want the best seats. It's accessed via stairs within the shopping center below.

Drinking & Nightlife

Many cafes have unadvertised, low-key live music during the evenings.

★ **Zarza Brewing Company** MICROBREWERY
(☎07-257-1413; www.zarzabrewing.com; cnr Puerto Bolívar & Esmeraldas; dishes $4-9; ⌚4pm-midnight Mon-Wed, to 2am Thu-Sat) In the El Valle neighborhood, this brewpub is as popular with locals as with Loja expats. The owner is Texan and clearly knows a thing or two about microbrewing and Mexican food. They do unusual-for-Ecuador brews such as lambics and Belgian wits, and make what are possibly Ecuador's hottest barbecued ribs. A taxi here costs about $1.40.

★ **Equanativa** CAFE
(☎07-256-1830; Lourdes, btwn Peña & 24 de Mayo; ⌚10am-1pm & 3:30-7:30pm Mon-Fri, 3:30-7:30pm Sat) The region's best caffeinated brews are served in this out-of-the-way little cafe, which also sells coffee by the bag. The owners are true experts on Loja coffee, and it's a real treat to see the rich beans grown in the *fincas* (farms) hereabouts finally get showcased and served with aplomb.

El Viejo Minero PUB
(☎07-258-5878; elviejominerobar@gmail.com; Sucre 10-76; ⌚5pm-midnight Mon-Thu, to 2am Fri & Sat) This rustic old watering hole is the perfect place for a relaxed beer and snacks in a friendly pub-like environment. Catch live music here on weekends.

ℹ Information

EMERGENCY

Police Station (☎07-257-5606; Valdivieso btwn Imbabura & Quito) Just north of the city center.

LAUNDRY

VIP Lavandería (Alonso de Mercadillo btwn Olmedo & Peña; per kilo $0.85; ⌚8am-1pm & 2-6pm Mon-Fri, 3-6pm Sat)

MEDICAL SERVICES

Clinica San Augustin (☎07-257-7339; www.hospitalclinicasanagustin.com; cnr 18 de Noviembre & Azuay; ⌚24hr) Recommended hospital for foreigners.

MONEY

Banco de Guayaquil (Eguiguren, near Valdivieso) Bank with ATM.

Banco de Pichincha (cnr Bernado Valdivieso & 10 de Agosto) Functioning ATMs.

POST

Post Office (cnr Colón & Sucre)

TOURIST INFORMATION

Tourist Office (iTur; ☎07-258-1251/07-257-0485; cnr Bolívar & Eguiguren; ⌚8am-6pm) Helpful, with some maps available.

Ministerio del Medio Ambiente (☎ext 109 07-257-7125; Sucre 4-35, 3rd fl; ⌚8am-5pm Mon-Fri) Responsible for administering Parque Nacional Podocarpus; provides information and simple maps.

USEFUL WEBSITES

www.loja.gob.ec Municipal website.

www.lojanos.com Loja's 'virtual community.'

ℹ Getting There & Away

AIR

Loja is served by La Toma airport in Catamayo, 30km to the west. Buses bound for Macará head there ($1.30). **TAME** (☎07-257-0248; www.tame.com.ec; Av Ortega, near 24 de Mayo; ⌚8:30am-1pm & 2:30-6pm Mon-Fri, 9am-12:15pm Sat) flies to/from Quito (from $86, Monday to Saturday) and Guayaquil (from $69, Monday to Friday).

BUS & TAXI

Almost all buses leave from the **bus terminal** (Terminal Terrestre Reina del Cisne; Av 8 de Diciembre), about 2km north of downtown. There is an iTur office here to help you.

Vilcabambaturis has fast minibuses to Vilcabamba ($1.30, 1¼ hours, every 30 minutes from 5:45am to 8:45pm). A faster way is via *taxi colectivo* (shared taxi; $2, 45 minutes), from Avenida Universitaria, about 10 blocks south of Mercadillo in Loja; ask a local taxi driver to take you to the Ruta 11 de Mayo **taxi stop** (cnr Aguirre & Mercadillo).

Huaquillas, the main border crossing to Peru, can be reached by a bus leaving at 5pm ($10, seven hours), so you can avoid backtracking to Machala. Loja is also a departure point for buses to southern border crossings into Peru via Macará and Zumba (now connected via a direct route from Loja to Jaén, Peru).

You can go directly to Piura (Peru) from Loja without stopping in Macará. The service ($13, nine hours) is offered with **Loja International** (☎ 07-257-0505, 07-257-9014). The bus stops at the border, waits for passengers to take care of exit/entry formalities, then continues to Piura. It's advisable to buy your tickets at least a day before you travel.

There are frequent bus services to most destinations.

Getting Around

Most taxi rides in town will cost about $1.25. For the airport, ask your hotel to call a *colectivo* (shared taxi), which charges $5 per person for the 40-minute trip, or catch a bus to Catamayo ($1.30, 45 minutes) from the bus terminal.

Parque Nacional Podocarpus

Podocarpus National Park (refugios $3) FREE fills in much of the triangle between Loja, Zamora and Vilcabamba as well as a huge swath to the southeast. Because altitude ranges so greatly within the park borders – from around 900m in the lowland sector to over 3600m in the highland sector – Podocarpus has some of the world's greatest plant and animal diversity. Perhaps 40% of its estimated 3000 plant species occur nowhere else in the world, and close to 600 bird species have been recorded. Rare mammals include foxes, deer, puma, mountain tapirs and bears.

Sights

Podocarpus' varied landscape is mesmerizing: high, windy *páramo* (grassland) that looks vaguely like a coral-rich sea floor; jewel-like lakes that sit in glacial depressions; fairy-tale woodland buffeted by harsh weather; and lush, towering forests seething with the hum of insects and birdlife.

The park is named for the giant Podocarpus, Ecuador's only native conifer, but don't bank on seeing one, or any larger animals, for that matter. Loggers stole most of the Podocarpus years ago, and the mammals have been hunted down to small populations driven deep into the forest. On top of these threats, which continue despite the park's protected status, both legal and illegal mining and agriculture encroach on habitat throughout the park.

Birds, however, are found in abundance. In the highland sector, they include such exotic-sounding species as the lacrimose mountain tanager, streaked tuftedcheek, superciliaried hemispingus and pearled treerunner; the lowland sector is home to coppery-chested jacamar, white-breasted

DAILY BUSES FROM LOJA

DESTINATION	COST ($)	DURATION (HR)
Ambato	18	11
Catamayo	1.30	¾
Cuenca	7.50	5
Gualaquiza	7.50	6
Guayaquil	12	8–9
Macará	7.40	6
Machala	7	5
Piura (Peru)	13	9
Quito	17	14–15
Riobamba	11	9–10
Zamora	3	2
Zumba	10	6

LA VIRGEN DEL CISNE

Throughout Ecuador, but especially in Loja province, you'll see figurines, shrines, pendants and all manner of trinkets dedicated to the Virgen del Cisne (Virgin of the Swan). According to legend, the Virgin Mary protected a medieval knight who appeared before his lover in a boat shaped like a swan. The knight's chivalric acts and the Virgin's kindly auspices inspired Franciscan monks so much that they erected statues of the 'Virgen del Cisne' throughout Europe. The Franciscans later hauled one of these statues to Ecuador, where she has been credited with miracles aplenty, mostly involving sickness and storms.

The Virgin you see today, installed by adoring *campesinos* (peasants) in 1594 in a little town also called El Cisne (70km west of Loja), wears gilded robes and a towering crown. This Virgin, the 'original,' lives in the town's Santuario, a Gothic-style cathedral, most of the year. Virgens del Cisne in other parts of Ecuador wear vestments inspired by local indigenous costumes, or even the Ecuadorian flag (especially when the national soccer team is playing a big game).

A huge festival is held in the Virgin's honor in El Cisne on August 15, after which thousands of pilgrims from Ecuador and northern Peru carry the statue on their shoulders to Loja, with many of the pilgrims walking the entire way. The Virgin finally arrives in Loja on August 20, where she is ceremoniously installed in the cathedral. On November 1, the process is repeated in reverse, and the Virgin rests in El Cisne until the following August. There is another major (if smaller) festival in El Cisne on May 30.

For most of the year, tours and buses make day trips to the village from Loja and Catamayo to see El Santuario and the statue. But on procession days, forget it! You walk like everybody else – the road is so full of pilgrims that vehicles can't get through. In recent years, cyclists have taken to riding this gorgeous route through the mountains alongside the pilgrims. No matter how you go, this display of devotion always amazes.

parakeet and paradise tanager. Rainfall in both sectors is heavy and frequent, so be prepared. October through December is the driest period.

Highlands Sector

Access to the highland sector of the park is through Cajanuma control, about 10km south of Loja. From here, a dirt road leads 8.5km uphill to the park office and adjacent **refugio** (cabin per person $3), which has seven basic cabañas with mattresses and a camping area.

From the *refugio,* several self-guided trails wend through the cloud forest. More strenuous and wide-ranging is the 5km **Los Miradores loop trail**, a four-hour hike up through the cloud forest and into the *páramo* (grasslands) – expect strong winds. Another trail that branches off the Miradores leads 14.5km to the highland lakes of **Lagunas del Compadre** and requires a minimum of three days' round-trip for most hikers. There's no water between the trailhead and the lakes.

The Ministerio del Medio Ambiente (p196) in Loja can provide detailed information, and the control (where you'll sign in) has simple maps.

Getting There & Away

Buses heading toward Vilcabamba cost $0.50. A taxi from Loja to the Cajanuma control is $5 – up to the park office/*refugio* it's $10-15. It's important to realize the difference: from the Cajanuma control on the Loja–Vilcabamba road it's an 8.5km walk to the start point for the main trails; from the park office/*refugio* it's 8.5 meters!

There is no transport offered between Cajanuma control and the park office/*refugio*. Set out from Loja early and you can hike for several hours before walking the 8.5km back to the Loja–Vilcabamba road (enjoyable if you're coming down). There are rarely cars on the park road, so don't expect to be able to hitchhike.

Lowlands Sector

The main access to the lowland sector is the Bombuscaro control, 6km south of Zamora by a dirt road that follows the Río Bombuscaro. From the parking area at the end of the road it's a half-hour walk on a wide, uphill trail to the control point.

There are several short, maintained (but sometimes muddy) trails that meander into the forest, the most popular of which leads you to the **Cascada Poderosa** and **Chismosa Waterfalls**. The 6km **Los Higuerones** trail takes you into some primary forest, as does the five-hour **El Campesino** trail. The very fit can scramble uphill about an hour on the **El Mirador** trail, while another trail leads to a deep (but very swift) swimming hole called the *área fotográfica* on the Río Bombuscaro.

Another infrequently used entrance is at the tiny village of **Romerillos**, about 25km south of Zamora by a different road.

The climate is hot and humid but beautiful, and the rainiest months are May through July. May and June are the best months for orchids.

Getting There & Away

The easiest way to get to the Bombuscaro entrance is by taxi from Zamora ($4); find them behind the bus terminal. Taxis from Loja will cost $10 to $12 one-way. You can have the driver from Zamora return to pick you up at the end of the day (additional $4), or you can walk back in about 1½ hours on the flat road. Zamora also has buses to the Romerillos entrance ($1.50, two hours, 6am and 2pm).

Zamora

07 / POP 13,400 / ELEV 970M

The hot and humid capital of the Zamora-Chinchipe province is part Oriente and part Sierra. Perched between these regions in the Andean foothills, it attracts settlers from the high-altitude communities of Saraguro and the Amazon Basin Shuar. The town bills itself as the 'City of Birds and Waterfalls.' Tourism here is all about nearby Parque Nacional Podocarpus.

Decades of colonization by miners and growth into a provincial hub have created a town of mostly unremarkable, concrete structures. Zamora has, however, experienced a bit of a revival, with renovations to bridges, a spruced-up bus station and a beautiful new *malecón* (waterfront) along the Río Zamora. And if you need to know what time it is, just look up: the big hill above the bus station has a massive clock. The minute hand is 11 meters and 34 centimeters long. This may very well be the largest timepiece in Ecuador and, according to some, the biggest in the world.

Sights

Take some time out... and get a gander at the big clock across the street from the bus station and market. It's particularly – ah – surreal at nighttime. The plaza with its parrot cresting the central fountain and overwhelmingly salmon-pink building facades is worth a look-see. Yet Zamora's principal attraction is nearby Parque Nacional Podocarpus. On the way out here, there's also a good **swimming hole**, before you get to the Copalinga lodge. In town, few central streets are signed.

Refugio Ecológico Tzanka WILDLIFE RESERVE
(099-675-7730, 07-260-5692; refugioecologicotzanka@yahoo.es; Mosquera, at Tamayo; adult/child $2/1; 11am-5pm Mon & Wed-Fri, 9am-5pm Tue & Sat & Sun) Head a block southwest of the main plaza and hang a right on the dead-end lane to find this wildlife rescue center. Housing colorful parrots, coatis (big, acrobatic rodents), monkeys, sloths and a boa constrictor, the refuge also has short-term volunteer opportunities.

Sleeping

Hotel Betania HOTEL $
(07-260-7030; Francisco de Orellana; s/d $17/30; P) Two blocks west of the bus station, the Betania is a comfortable, modern hotel with generously sized rooms and firm beds. It's one of the cleanest budget hotels in all of Ecuador, and we love the nudes in the showers (ooh la la!).

Hotel Chonta Dorada HOTEL $
(07-260-6384; Jaramillo Alvarado near Amazonas; s/d $13/22; P) A friendly and decent if unatmospheric choice for bedding down, three blocks west of the bus station.

Hotel Samuria HOTEL $
(07-260-7801; hotelsamuria@hotmail.com; cnr 24 de Mayo & Diego de Vaca; s/d incl breakfast $25/38; P) Located half a block north of the main plaza, Zamora's most upscale hotel (it's all relative) has firm beds, blow-dryers, flat-screens and relatively quiet and modern rooms. The air-con helps on hot nights; the restaurant bolsters the scant eating options around.

★ **Copalinga** LODGE $$
(099-347-7013; www.copalinga.com; Vía al Podocarpus Km 3; cabins incl breakfast with/without bathroom s $44/32, d $111/53) Bird-watchers, ahem, *flock* to this Belgian-owned private reserve for sure-thing sightings of exotic avian species. Even non-birders will love the orchid collection, hummingbird feeders, trails and secluded ambience. Take your pick of rustic or luxury cabins, and let the rushing river lull you to sleep. Hydropower runs

WORTH A TRIP

CABAÑAS YANKUAM

East of Zamora, the Río Nangaritza flows past the vast Cordillera del Cóndor, a region of unparalleled biodiversity that is also home to indigenous Shuar communities. Traveling by boat along a blackwater tributary (it's actually a brown hue, caused by naturally occurring tannins), you'll see odd rock formations, waterfalls, rare birds and cliffs covered in orchids. **Cabañas Yankuam** (☎099-947-0740; www.lindoecuadortours.com; r per person incl breakfast $30, lunch or dinner $10, multiday tour & accommodation packages per person $113-196), outside the river's port of Las Orquídeas, can immerse you in this lost world, which is truly the end of the line for most travelers. They offer some fascinating two- to three-day tours to surrounding sights, including canyons and caves frequented by oilbirds.

the whole place, and meals are generous and tasty.

Book at least three days in advance. It is 3km southeast of town and a 30-minute hike from the entrance of Parque Nacional Podacarpus.

Eating

Tio Bolo ECUADORIAN $
(☎07-260-7005; Mercadillo, near Diego de Vaca & Aldean; meals $5; ⏲5:30pm-late Tue-Sat) Overlooking the *malecón* (waterfront) and river, enjoy sublimely grilled meat with all the usual accompaniments on an intimate, smokey, open-sided terrace.

La Choza ECUADORIAN $
(☎07-260-7246; Sevilla de Oro; mains $3-9; ⏲7am-7pm Mon-Fri, 8am-4pm Sat) Serving fried fish, *churrasco* (fried steak with eggs and rice) and fried frogs' legs (which are delicacies, so command high prices), La Choza is a health foodie's nightmare, but it's good, and the fish is local and fresh. To get here, head toward the clock from the main plaza.

Information

Banco del Austro On the Plaza, with a functioning ATM.
Hospital (cnr Sevilla de Oro & Orellana)
Ministerio del Ambiente (☎07-260-6606, 07-260-5318; Sevilla de Oro near Orellana; ⏲8:30am-4:30pm Mon-Fri) Information on Parque Nacional Podocarpus.
Post Office (24 de Mayo near Sevilla de Oro)

Getting There & Away

The **bus terminal** (cnr Av Heroés de Paquisha & Amazonas) is across the street from the big clock.

Buses leave almost hourly to Loja ($3, two hours) between 3am and 11pm. There are five daily buses heading north to Gualaquiza ($3.50, four hours). For Cuenca (seven hours), Guayaquil (about 11 hours) or Quito (about 16 hours), head first to Loja and catch one of the frequent buses departing from there.

Buses to Las Orquídeas (for Cabañas Yanquam; $4) leave from Zamora daily at 4am, 6:30am, 11:15am and 12:30pm. In Las Orquídeas, you change to a pickup for the rest of the journey.

Vilcabamba

☎07 / POP 5000 / ELEV 1700M

Oh, Vilcabamba: where mountains soar alluringly above town, where the balmy air is synonymous with longevity (it shot to fame for its high number of centenarians after *Reader's Digest* did stories on them in 1955), where those who encounter it simply get waylaid – sometimes for months, sometimes years…

The area's beautiful scenery, mild weather and laid-back vibe attract waves of visitors: backpackers as well as North American and European retirees. The hills are dotted with big new houses, and the town plaza with expat-owned businesses. Gringo-ization has created tension about the cost of land and living, but the flip side is that jobs in tourism and construction are more plentiful than ever, and Vilcabamba is the rare Ecuadorian *pueblo* where young people have little ambition to leave for the big city.

Activities

Vilcabamba offers perfect weather for hiking and horseback riding, as well as access to remote sections of Parque Nacional Podocarpus, but it's also an excellent place to chill. Legions of specialists are ready to facilitate your relaxation with inexpensive massages, pedicures and meditation sessions.

Most naturalists and horse guides charge about $15 for two hours, $25 for four and $35 for the whole day.

Most hotels have hiking trail maps; some even have their own trail systems. Many area

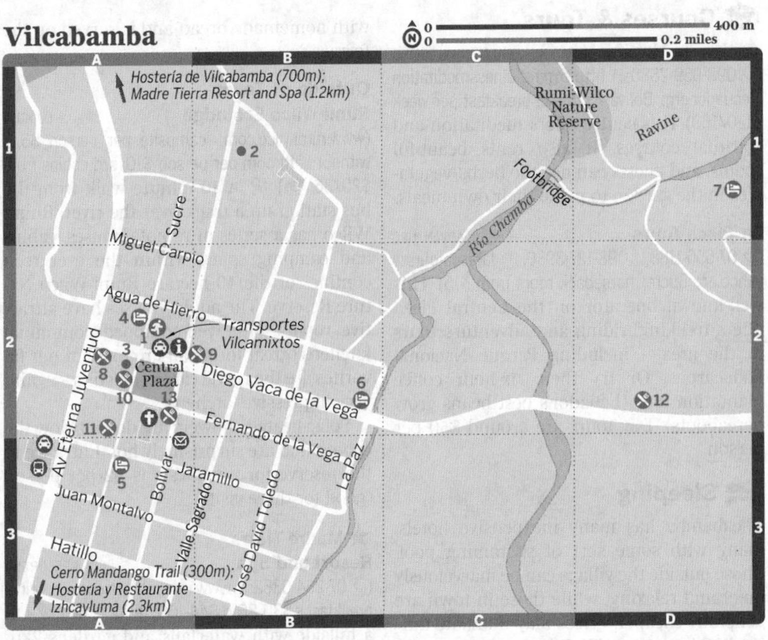

Vilcabamba

Activities, Courses & Tours
1 Caballos Gavilán A2
2 Centro de Meditación B1
El Chino .... (see 1)
3 La Tasca Tours A2

Sleeping
4 Hostal Jardín Escondido A2
5 Hosteria Las Margaritas A3
6 Rendez-Vous Hostal Guesthouse B2
7 Rumi-Wilco Ecolodge D1

Eating
8 La Baguette A2
9 La Terraza B2
10 Layseca's A2
Midas Touch .... (see 10)
11 Restaurante Katherine A2
12 Shanta's Bar D2
13 UFO A2

Drinking & Nightlife
Juice Factory .... (see 10)

hikes are on private land, and you may need to pay a nominal fee ($1 to $2) to use the trail. The **Cerro Mandango** trail ascends the distinctive peak west of town and takes four hours out and back. Ask locally about hiking independently, as it was considered safe at the time of research, but there were some tourist robberies on the ascent some years ago. Heading into Parque Nacional Podocarpus from the Río Yambala west of town, there's a long five- to eight-hour hike to a waterfall known as **Cascada el Palto**. For an afternoon spin, consider the quick hike out to **Agua de Hierro**, a small natural spring – signs will take you there. The 40-hectare **Rumi-Wilco Ecolodge** ($2) has many excellently signed trails ranging from one to three hours in length.

Caballos Gavilán HORSE RIDING
(☎07-264-0415, 098-133-2806; gavilanhorse@yahoo.com; Sucre 10-30; from $25) Highly recommended, Gavin is a New Zealander who has lived here for years. He guides two-hour to three-day horseback-riding trips with overnight stays in his refuge near the park.

El Chino CYCLING
(☎098-187-6347; cnr Sucre & Agua de Hierro; bikes/motorbikes per day $10/50; ⏰8am-6pm) Rents bikes and motorbikes; for a little extra, they'll offer tours on both sets of wheels too. Check the shop next door: wondrous sculptures made out of bicycle parts!

Courses & Tours

Centro de Meditación HEALTH & WELLBEING
(☎098-959-2880; http://mindfulnessmeditationinecuador.org; Bolívar; s/d incl breakfast per week $120/160) This centre offers meditation and spiritual courses. It also rents beautiful rooms, and guests can use the herbs/vegetables in the garden to make their own meals.

La Tasca Tours ADVENTURE
(☎07-556-1188, 098-127-3930; latascatours@yahoo.ec; Sucre; horseback tours from $15) This well-known operator on the Central Plaza offers trekking, riding and adventure tours in the area – including Parque Nacional Podacarpus. Or try their six-hour coffee plantation tour (Ecuador's best beans grow hereabouts). Day tours are around $50 per person.

Sleeping

Vilcabamba has many inexpensive hotels, many with some sort of swimming pool. Those outside the village can be marvelously quiet and relaxing, while those in town are generally cheaper. Prices may fluctuate during high season and holidays.

Central

★Hosteria Las Margaritas HOSTERIA $
(cnr Jaramillo & Sucre; s/d incl breakfast $15/30; P) Las Margaritas' high white walls conceal clean rooms in a tidy German-style home, with a fantastic breakfast room overlooking the pool, all wrapped in a lush garden. It's not the backpacker hangout that other addresses in the center are, but it's better value than the lot of them.

Hostal Jardín Escondido HOSTEL $
(☎07-264-0281; www.jardin.ec; cnr Sucre & Agua de Hierro; dm/s/d incl breakfast $15/25/30;) Built around a tranquil interior garden filled with songbirds, this is a good budget bet. All rooms have high ceilings and big bathrooms, and breakfast comes with homemade bread and good coffee. A great spot to meet other travelers.

Rendez-Vous Hostal Guesthouse HOTEL $
(☎099-219-1180; www.rendezvousecuador.com; Diego Vaca de la Vega; s/d/tr $28/38/54, without bathroom s/d $19/28; @) Call it adobe chic. Each of the meticulous rooms at French-owned Rendez-Vous Hostal has its own little terrace that looks out onto a calm, feng-shui interior garden enclosed by high red walls. Breakfast (included in prices) comes with homemade bread and is served on the terraces.

Outside of Town

Rumi-Wilco Ecolodge LODGE $
(www.rumiwilco.com; campsite per person $5, r without bathroom per person $10, s/d cabins from $20/36;) A 10-minute walk from the bus station up a track over the river, Rumi-Wilco has a series of remote houses, cabins and camping space within the evergreen confines of the 40-hectare Rumi-Wilco Nature Reserve. The adobe houses have attractive rooms with well-equipped communal kitchens (great for small groups) but our favorites are the rustic cabins on stilts – again: very impressive kitchens!

Solar-heated showers are down below the cabins, and are surprisingly hot. Entrance to the reserve for nonguests is $2 per person (good for three visits).

★Madre Tierra Resort and Spa SPA & RESORT $$
(☎07-264-0362; www.madretierra.com.ec; incl breakfast s $30-86, d $44-100; P @) On a hillside with waterfalls and gardens 2km north of town, Madre Tierra has a strong New Age vibe, replete with candles and healing ions. Rooms are meticulously and individually decorated; standard rooms have hammocks with views, while deluxe rooms include private balconies, inset rock floors, and bathrooms like fairy-tale grottos. The excellent spa is open to the public.

Hostería y Restaurante Izhcayluma RESORT $$
(☎07-302-5162; www.izhcayluma.com; dm $11, s/d from $32/43, without bathroom from $23/29, cabins s/d $44/55; P) Located 2km south of town, German-owned Izhcayluma is excellent value, a refined hilltop retreat. The outdoor dining area serves German-Ecuadorian cuisine and has sweeping panoramic views. A 'holistic wellness room' offers massages and other treatments, and there is a bar and swimming pool. The cabins and rooms are quiet and spacious.

The newest cabins, clocking the best views of Cerro Mandango and the new trail system through the grounds, are stunning and tastefully decorated with Valdivia culture artifacts. This place is always packed, so book your room at least a week in advance. A direct shuttle service ($15) runs from Cuenca's La Cigale hostel. Breakfast is not included in rates, but 7:30am yoga is.

Eating & Drinking

La Baguette BAKERY $

(☎098-957-7107, 099-046-8701; cnr Eterna Juventud & Vaca de la Vega; snacks from $2; ⊙7am-5pm Wed-Sat, to 2pm Sun) Divine French goodies – pain au chocolat, quiche, and even gluten-free bread on Wednesdays – to take out.

Restaurante Katherine ECUADORIAN $

(☎07-264-0055; cnr Sucre & Jaramillo; meals $3) Enjoy great *comida típica* at local prices at Katherine (pronounced 'kat-REEN'), just off the plaza. It's family-run, inexpensive, unpretentious and delicious – what's not to love?

Midas Touch BREAKFAST $

(Sucre 11-35; breakfasts & lunches $3-5; ⊙7:30am-5pm Mon & Wed-Thu, to late Fri-Sun; ✎) While it's open all day, this popular hangout is mostly about the great breakfasts – the banana and cinnamon hotcakes and the 'pumpkin eggs' are particularly addictive. Using organic and local ingredients, they also offer good vegetarian options.

Layseca's BAKERY $

(cnr Sucre & Vaca de la Vega; snacks $0.50-1.50; ⊙10:30am-8pm Tue-Sun) Owned by a Belgian-Ecuadorian couple, this little café has delicious homemade chocolate, cookies, cakes and bread, and the town's best coffee and espresso. The bags of granola make great hiking snacks.

★**Shanta's Bar** PIZZA $$

(Diego Vaca de la Vega; mains $6-10; ⊙1-9pm Tue-Sun) We love Shanta's – and have done for years. It serves pizza and big plates of frogs' legs in an innovative rustic setting with saddle seats at the bar and a bartender with a handlebar mustache. Ask about the *licor de serpiente* (snake liquor).

UFO MIDDLE EASTERN $$

(United Falafel Organization; ☎07-264-0148; www.unitedfalafel.org; Fernando de la Vega 09-18; ⊙11am-8pm Wed-Sun, to 8:30pm Fri & Sat; ✎) Besides the clever name and enviable location next to the church, the Turkish-run UFO gets jammed for its inexpensive and tasty breakfasts, Middle Eastern favorites, gluten-free desserts, fantastic coffee and a variety of vegetarian and vegan options.

Hostería y Restaurante Izhcayluma ECUADORIAN $$

(☎07-264-0095; www.izhcayluma.com; mains $5-9; ⊙7-10am & noon-9pm Tue-Sun, 7am-10am & 5-9pm Mon; ✎) Bavarian specialties and classic Ecuadorian dishes are the fare here. Using local ingredients where possible, Izhcayluma also offers excellent vegetarian substitutions for the meat dishes and some vegan selections. It's 2km down the main road south of town, and worth the trip up the hill for a meal with a lovely view.

La Terraza INTERNATIONAL $$

(cnr Diego Vaca de la Vega & Bolívar; mains $5-12; ⊙9am-9:30pm) Do your best to snag a table outside for a beer and some Central Plaza people-watching, as the location might be the best reason to come here. This busy spot serves pastas, grilled meats and Mexican-style favorites like fajitas.

Juice Factory JUICE BAR

(Sucre; ⊙8:30am-4pm Tue-Sat, to 2pm Sun) Tasty juices and good healthy, light lunches too, right on the west side of the central plaza. Some of the profits go back to helping the community.

Information

There were a few muggings on the trail up Cerro Mandango around 2012, but safety is not currently an issue. Ask about the current situation at the iTur and leave valuables in your hotel as a precaution.

Police Station (☎07-264-0896; Agua de Hierro near Bolívar)

Hospital (☎07-267-3188, 07-264-0188; Av Eterna Juventud, near Miguel Carpio)

Internet (Bolivar on Plaza; per hr $1.15; ⊙9am-9pm)

Lavandería (Bolívar on plaza; per kilo $1; ⊙8am-9pm)

Post Office (Bolívar btwn Fernando de la Vega & Jaramillo)

Tourist Office (iTur; ☎07-264-0090; cnr Bolívar & Diego Vaca de la Vega; ⊙8am-1pm & 3-6pm) Helpful with good info and maps of area hikes.

Getting There & Away

Transportes Vilcamixtos (☎07-264-0044) is a taxi-truck cooperative on the main plaza (you can't miss the green-and-white trucks). Most charge $1.50 to $4 for nearby destinations.

Buses, minivans and taxis leave from the tiny **bus terminal** (Eterna Juventud & Jaramillo). **Taxis colectivos** ($2, 45 minutes) depart frequently to Loja after four people cram in; Vilcabambaturis minibuses ($1.30, one hour) leave on the hour.

Buses from Loja stop in Vilcabamba on their way south to Zumba ($9, around five hours) and

WORTH A TRIP

TAPICHALACA RESERVE

The small **Tapichalaca Reserve** (☎ in Quito 02-250-5212; www.fjocotoco.org/tapichalaca; $15, with guided walk to feeding station $30), 75km south of Vilcabamba, protects one of Ecuador's most rare and endangered birds, the jocotoco antpitta (Grallaria ridgelyi), which has fewer than 20 known breeding pairs. Some of the birds have been habituated to eating grubs put out by the caretaker, however, so a sighting is likely. The rest of the reserve is an oasis of cloud forest in a region of heavy deforestation, and the hummingbird feeders are abuzz all day. To get there in time for the antpittas' breakfast, catch the 5am bus from Loja or spend the night at the reserve's beautiful **lodge** (☎ 02-227-2013; http://jocotoursecuador.com/destination/casa-simpson-tapichalaca-reserve; Tapichalaca Reserve; s/d incl meals from $125/170;).

the Peruvian border, from where there is onward transportation to Chachapoyas, Peru.

Zumba & the Peruvian Border

☎ 07

Vilcabamba is the end of the road for most. However, a slowly improving road heading south to Zumba and Peru may tempt more travelers to use this route south to the world-class ruins at Chachapoyas.

Zumba was an important military outpost during the wars with Peru between the 1940s and 1990s. The wars are over, but there's still an Ecuadorian military post here, and soldiers roam all over town. The main activity here is the adventurous journey on into Peru. From Loja or Vilcabamba, it's an all-day trip to the Peruvian town of San Ignacio – the best place to spend the night.

Getting There & Away

Transportes Nambija runs a direct overnight service from Loja through Zumba to Jaén, Peru (from where you can pick up *colectivos*/buses to Chachapoyas).

Transportes Nambija ($10, six to seven hours) and Cooperativa Cariamanga buses, among others, leave Loja for Zumba; all stop in Vilcabamba one hour after leaving Loja.

From Zumba, *rancheras* (open-sided trucks) leave at 8am, 10:30am and 5:30pm for the border at La Balsa ($3, 1½ to 2½ hours), where you get your exit stamp (or entry stamp, if coming from Peru). The condition of the road between Zumba and La Balsa varies greatly, depending on recent weather. On the other side of the 'international bridge' in Peru there are taxi *colectivos* (*combis*) to San Ignacio (9 soles/$3, 1½ hours), where you can spend the night. Money-changing can be done at La Balsa or San Ignacio.

From San Ignacio, there are regular minibuses to Jaén ($3.50, three hours) beginning at 4am. Once you're in Jaén, take a mototaxi (motorcycle taxi) to the *colectivo* stop and then get a *colectivo* to Bagua Grande (one hour). From Bagua Grande you then get a bus to Chachapoyas (three hours), the first town of any real size.

Catacocha

☎ 07 / POP 6617 / ELEV 1886M

Declared a National Cultural Heritage Site in 1994, Catacocha is proud of its places of worship, sun-baked adobe houses and wooden balconies, but has yet to capitalize on its tourism potential. Strolling its streets is the best way to appreciate the timeless cycle of highland life.

Sights

Templo de Lourdes CHURCH

FREE The Templo de Lourdes is worth a peek inside for its replicas of famous European religious paintings. You won't mistake this church for the Louvre, but the canvases by a local monk give the surroundings an earnestly faithful if slightly kitschy feel.

Peña de Shiriculapo VIEWPOINT

(sunrise-sunset) FREE The infamous Peña de Shiriculapo is a shrine-cum-mirador (lookout) known for its vertigo-inducing views of the Casanga Valley. Access it through the small hospital a five-minute walk from Plaza Independencia.

Sunday Market MARKET

(Las Paltas; Plaza Independencia; 7am-noon Sun) The Sunday market is the most important event of the week. At dawn church bells beckon everyone to mass in the Plaza Independencia, and by 7am they are buying and selling homemade cheese, donkey saddles, farm-fresh eggs and mountains of veggies all over town. By dusk, the same plaza is a gathering spot for old-timers and bored teenagers.

Sleeping

Hostal Tambococha HOTEL $
(☎07-268-3551; cnr 25 de Junio & Lauro Gerrero; r per person $10; P) Has clean, well-lit rooms, many of which look over Plaza Independencia. All have cable TV and electrically-heated showers.

Getting There & Away

Buses from Loja ($3, two hours, 10 daily) stop here en route to Macará and Piura (Peru). Quicker *colectivos* (shared taxis) to Loja charge $5.

Macará & the Peruvian Border

☎07 / POP 19,018 / ELEV 470M

The descent from Catacocha toward the Peruvian border offers sweeping views of mountains and deep, dramatic valleys that give way to hilly, dry tropical forest. Adobe ruins bake under the strong sun, and livestock roams untethered along the road.

At the bottom of all this is anti-climactic Macará – a sleepy border town, although fairly innocuous as such places go. Surrounded by terraced rice fields, it's infested with crickets that jump about the streets and hotel rooms. If you're entering Ecuador through here, don't worry, it gets better heading north.

The hallmark tree of the surrounding arid forest is the ceiba (kapok). It stands out majestically – and sadly – with its green-tinted, swollen trunks and gnarly, usually leafless branches on hillsides that have been logged and grazed. In these barren areas, the lonely giants have been spared the chainsaw because they are mostly hollow and of little utilitarian value.

Sights

Jorupe Reserve WILDLIFE RESERVE
(☎in Quito 02-250-5212; www.fjocotoco.org; $15) The Jorupe Reserve is run by Fundación Jocotoco outside of Macará. Primarily a bird-watching reserve, Jorupe is home to the white-tailed jay, blue-crowned motmot and Ecuadorian trogon. Hire a taxi ($3) to take you to the reserve about 5km down the road from Macará toward Sozoronga, but be sure to book ahead of your visit.

It's advisable to arrange a visit beforehand and – to enjoy the reserve at its optimum – stay over in the **lodge** (☎in Quito 02-250-5212; www.jocotoursecuador.com/en/our-lodges/urraca-lodge-jorupe-reserve; s/d incl full board $168/294).

Sleeping & Eating

Hotel Los Arrozales HOTEL $
(☎07-269-4300; cnr 10 de Agosto & Amazonas; s/d incl breakfast $18/34; P ❄ 📶) The Arrozales (rice fields; named after the town's economic mainstay) is Macará's fanciest option: sparkling, big rooms (all air-conditioned), private bathrooms, corridors opening out onto small terraces and a small cafeteria.

Hostal Santigyn HOTEL $
(☎07-269-4539; cnr Calderón & Rengel; r per person incl breakfast from $12; ❄) A joint-smoking Mona Lisa looms over reception, but this clean, smart hotel has small but well-lit rooms of various sizes. Some have air-con; all have cable TV.

Caña y Tapa TAPAS $
(☎07-269-4970; Amazonas 41-15; tapas $3-8; ⏲4-10pm) An atmospheric tapas bar.

D'Marco's ECUADORIAN $
(cnr Roldós & Amazonas; mains $5-6) This nice option serves seafood.

Information

Banco de Loja (cnr Ventimilla & Calderón) has an ATM ($200 limit) but no currency exchange. For Peruvian soles, exchange your money on the border.

Getting There & Away

Transportes Loja Internacional (☎07-269-4058; Vaca & Jaramillo) buses leave four times a day to Loja ($7.40, six hours) and take the Catacocha route.

Unión Cariamanga (☎07-269-4047; cnr Loja & Manuel E Rengel) has seven buses a day to Loja ($7.40, six hours) via Cariamanga.

The crossing into Peru via Macará is much quieter than at Huaquillas and busier than at Zumba. Macará is 3km from the actual border crossing, or *puente internacional* (international bridge). Most people buy tickets direct to Piura (Peru) from Loja, but both companies listed above leave Macará for Piura twice a day ($4, three hours). The bus stops at the border, waits for passengers to take care of exits/entries, then continues to Piura.

The Oriente

Includes ➡

Best Places to Eat

- ➡ EscoBar (p240)
- ➡ El Jardín (p241)
- ➡ Gina's (p211)
- ➡ JungLab (p243)
- ➡ Tienda Ahimsa (p231)

Best Places to Stay

- ➡ Hotel Termas de Papallacta (p210)
- ➡ Napo Wildlife Center (p220)
- ➡ Sacha Lodge (p220)
- ➡ Hamadryade Lodge (p235)
- ➡ Kapawi Ecolodge & Reserve (p245)

Why Go?

The vast tract of land locally known as Amazonía holds more drama than a rip-roaring flood. Rivers churn from the Andes into the dense, sweltering rainforest on course for the Amazon basin. Along the way, ancient indigenous tribes call the riverbanks home and astounding wildlife can be seen among the trees. Those lucky enough to reach the remoter jungle lodges (several hours downriver from the nearest towns) can fish for piranhas on silent blackwater lakes, hear the menacing boom of howler monkeys, spot the shining eyes of caiman at nighttime, see colorful parrots feasting at the famous clay licks (areas where birds gather to feed on nutrient-rich clay), and perhaps catch sight of an elusive tapir or jaguar.

Exploring the Oriente gives you the unforgettable experience of seeing the natural world up close and personal. But this region is not just jungle. Ecuador's best thermal spa, its most spectacular waterfall, its most active volcanoes and its most formidable white-water rapids also await.

When to Go

The Oriente

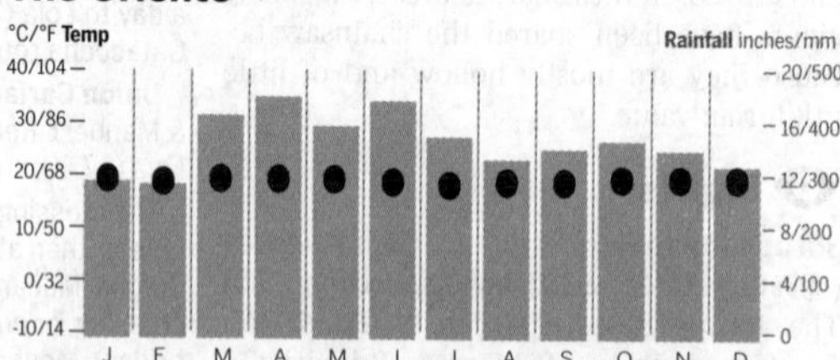

Dec–Mar The driest time of year, when some rivers become impassable due to low water levels.

Apr–Jul The wettest time of year – make sure you've got a good raincoat!

Oct–Nov The best time of year: the rivers are all passable, it's not too wet, and wildlife is easy to spot.

THE NORTHERN ORIENTE

From Quito to Lago Agrio

The road from Quito to Lago Agrio traverses the misty Andean slopes before descending into the lowlands of Amazonía. The journey along this road takes travelers through a beautifully diverse swath of Ecuadorian ecosystems – from high-altitude cloud forest to steamy equatorial rainforest. If you're not flying to Lago Agrio for a trip down the Río Cuyabeno, this journey can be done in one long day by road, or enjoyed in stages with stops for hot-spring soaking, bird-watching and white-water rafting.

Papallacta

POP 920 / ELEV 3300M

Slip into this tiny village's steamy, therapeutic waters to soothe sore muscles or combat the high-altitude chill. At Termas de Papallacta, more than a dozen sparkling pools offer the country's most luxurious thermal baths experience. The main spa complex is 3km above the village of Papallacta and is a good day trip from Quito, 67km (two hours) away. Be prepared for cold nights and intense sun.

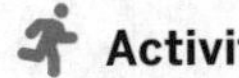

Activities

Spas & Thermal Pools

The Termas de Papallacta is the main event here, but (in order up from the Quito-Baeza road junction in Papallacta village) La Choza de Don Wilson (p210), Hostería Pampallacta Thermales and Hostal Antisana also have thermal pools.

Termas de Papallacta THERMAL BATHS
(☎06-289-5060; www.papallacta.com.ec) The setting of Termas de Papallacta, 3km above the pretty little village of Papallacta, is grand: on a clear day you can see the snowcapped Volcán Antisana (5753m) 15km south, beyond the lush sheep- and cow-dotted hillsides. The hot springs are a poorly kept secret; opt for a weekday visit if possible, or come after dark, when it's particularly magical and far less crowded.

There are two sets of pools: the **Balneario** (adult/child $8.50/4; 6am-10:30pm, last entry 9pm) and the **Spa** (adult/child $22/14.50; 9am-8pm Sun-Thu, to 9pm Fri-Sat). Together they number more than a dozen pools, with temperatures varying from cool to 40°C, all surrounded by plush grass, red-orange blossoms, quaint interconnecting bridges, and beyond, mountains laced by tempestuous clouds. Towels and lockers ($5 deposit) are available for a small fee.

There's little reason to visit the Spa pools, although they are less crowded, smaller and filled with jets. An indoor sauna can loosen you up for a spa treatment (the sauna is free at the Spa). Treatments (ranging from $12 to $69) include hydrothermal massages, reflexology, body wraps with Andean mud, Turkish baths, body lymphatic drainage and body exfoliation. Pool waters are changed in late afternoon daily.

Hiking

Few spa-goers explore this option, but right by the gates of the Balneario is a back entrance to the 400,000-hectare **Reserva Ecológica Cayambe-Coca**. The spa has been acclaimed over the years for its approach to conservation, and owns a 250-hectare protected swath of land at the park entrance known locally as the **Rancho del Cañón**. There is an interpretation center in the spa complex and guided hikes into this terrain of Andean meadows and lonely lakes (making this perhaps the best starting point for exploring the reserve). Ask about the challenging two-day **hike** through to the village of Oyacachi (more thermal springs await).

Sleeping & Eating

Hostería Pampallacta Termales GUESTHOUSE $$
(☎06-289-5014; www.pampallactatermales.com; s/d incl breakfast from $36/75; P) This *hostería* is the best midrange option in Papallacta. Warm (fireplaces) and charming (all rooms have huge stone bathtubs you can fill with thermal spring water). Management is friendly and there are a number of small thermal pools in which to relax – if you don't fancy walking the 1km to Termas de Papallacta that is.

Hostal Antisana GUESTHOUSE $$
(☎06-289-5016; s/d incl breakfast $20/40; P) This 10-room *hostal* sits just meters from the Termas de Papallacta, but is a fraction of what you would pay to stay within the spa confines. It's chilly and a tad dark, but slightly worn rooms are good enough. Bring warm clothes, or take refuge in one of the thermal pools out back.

The Oriente Highlights

1 Papallacta (p207) Soaking in pristine steaming waters, watching the mist move across the mountainsides above.

2 San Rafael Falls (p211) Standing in the thunderous spray of Ecuador's highest waterfall.

3 Parque Nacional Sumaco Napo Galeras (p226) Hiking through three different vegetation zones to gaze out over jungle and cloud forest on the country's most volatile volcanoes.

4 Reserva Producción Faunística Cuyabeno (p215) Watching for an astonishing range of birds and animals in this blackwater paradise.

5 Parque Nacional Yasuní (p223) Sleeping in one of the world's most biodiverse jungles at river lodges, and visiting its parrot clay lick and rainforest canopy towers for wildlife-watching.

6 Laguna Pañacocha (p222) Fishing for piranhas and looking out for gigantic arapaimas and pink river dolphins.

7 Tena (p227) Taming white-water rapids on a rafting adventure on multiple nearby rivers.

8 Puyo (p238) Visiting indigenous communities within the rainforest on a guided jungle tour.

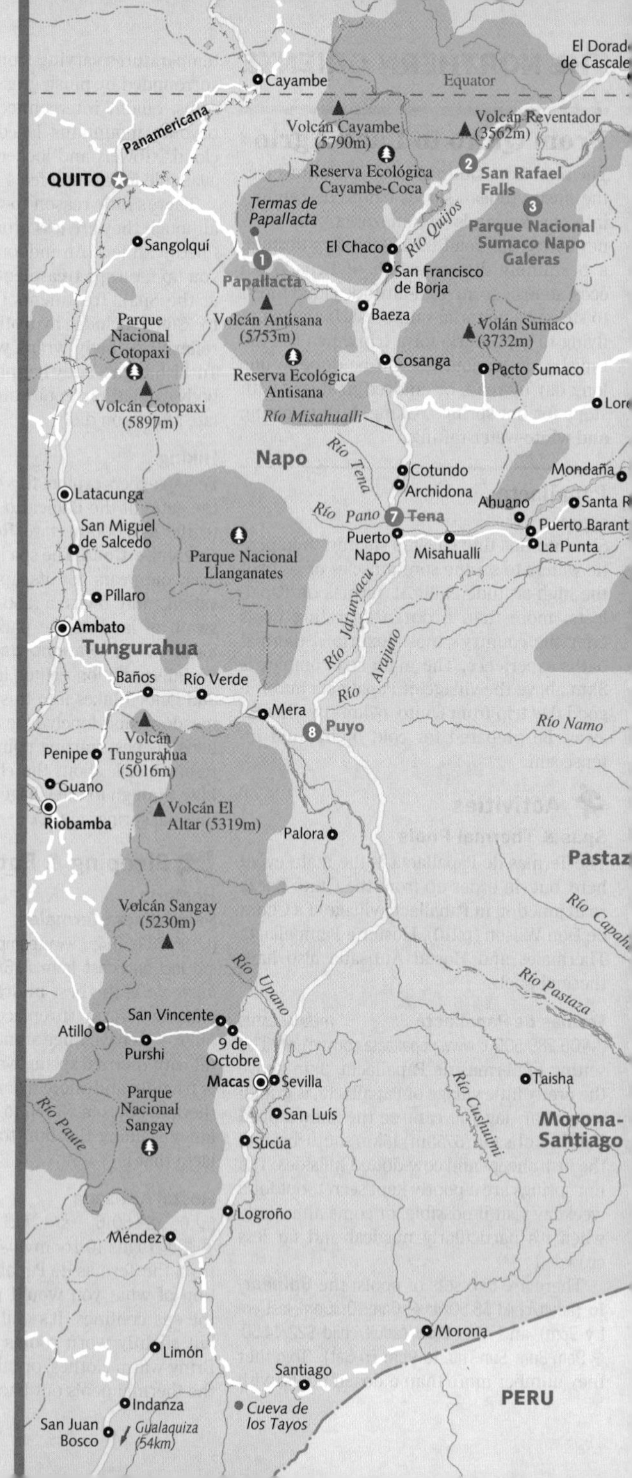

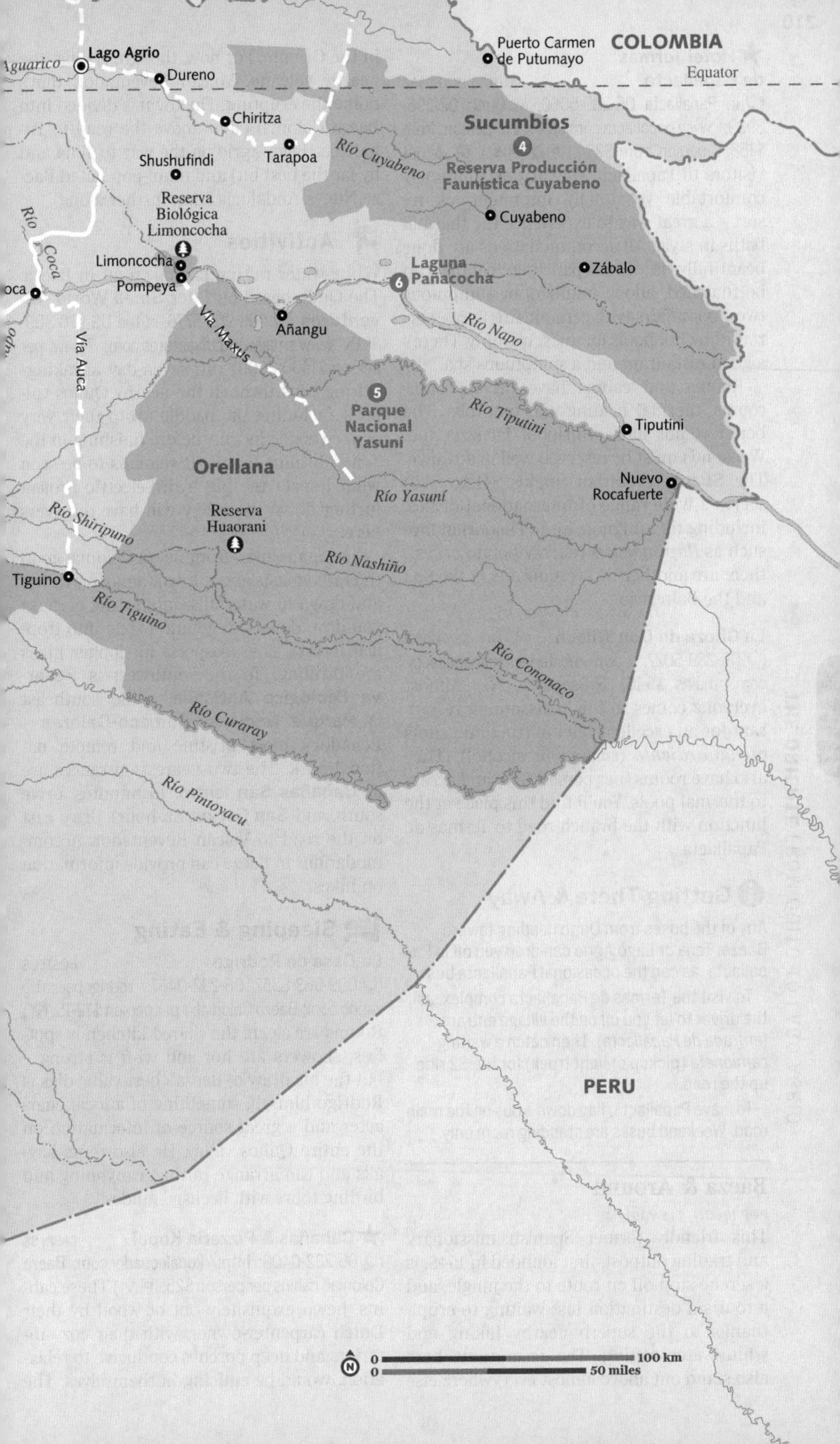

COLOMBIA
Equator
Puerto Carmen de Putumayo
Lago Agrio
Aguarico
Dureno
Chiritza
Tarapoa
Shushufindi
Río Cuyabeno
Sucumbíos
4
Reserva Producción Faunística Cuyabeno
Cuyabeno
Zábalo
Reserva Biológica Limoncocha
Limoncocha
Pompeya
Río Coca
Laguna Pañacocha
6
Río Napo
Añangu
Vía Maxus
Vía Auca
5
Parque Nacional Yasuní
Río Tiputini
Tiputini
Nuevo Rocafuerte
Orellana
Río Yasuní
Reserva Huaorani
Río Shiripuno
Río Nashiño
Tiguino
Río Tiguino
Río Cononaco
Río Curaray
Río Pintoyacu
PERU
0 100 km
0 50 miles

★Hotel Termas de Papallacta LUXURY HOTEL $$$
(☎in Papallacta 06-289-5060, in Quito 02-256-8989; www.papallacta.com.ec; r 1-3 person from $158, 6-person from $234; P @ ☜ ☒) Most visitors to Papallacta stay at this supremely comfortable yet totally unpretentious resort – a great way to experience the thermal baths in style. All accommodations are done beautifully in wood paneling: cabins can be thatched, adobe numbers or sumptuous two-floor affairs with ceramic fireplaces, surrounding hot pools for guest use only. There's a good restaurant and a sumptuous spa.

Rooms and cabins have private bathrooms, thermal heating and bathtubs. The better rooms have whirlpool Jacuzzis, too. Weekends must be reserved well in advance. The **Sucus** restaurant (mains $11 to $20) serves a wide range of international dishes, including filet mignon, and Ecuadorian fare such as *llapingachos* (cheesy potato cakes); there are another two restaurants in the Spa and the Balneario.

La Choza de Don Wilson SEAFOOD $
(☎06-289-5027; www.hosteriachozapapallacta.com; mains $5-10; ⏲8am-9pm; ☜) Almost everyone comes to this unassuming restaurant for an excellent fillet of trout and shots of *aguardiente* (sugarcane alcohol). They also have rooms (per person $20) and access to thermal pools. You'll find this place at the junction with the branch road to Termas de Papallacta.

Getting There & Away

Any of the buses from Quito heading toward Baeza, Tena or Lago Agrio can drop you off in Papallacta, as can the occasional Papallacta bus.

To visit the Termas de Papallacta complex, ask the driver to let you off on the village entrance (*entrada de Papallacta*). Then catch a waiting *camioneta* (pickup or light truck) for the $2 ride up the road.

To leave Papallacta, flag down a bus on the main road. Weekend buses are standing room only.

Baeza & Around

POP 1960 / ELEV 1914M

This friendly former Spanish missionary and trading outpost, first founded in 1548, is a serene stop-off en route to the jungle, and a tourism destination just waiting to erupt, thanks to the superb nearby hiking and white-water rafting. The restaurants here also stand out above almost everywhere else in the Oriente. For now, though, it's just the nearby volcano, Volcán Reventador, that's doing the erupting. The town is divided into Baeza Colonial (1km above the road to Papallacta/Lago Agrio on the way to Tena and by far the best bit) and more-populated Baeza Nueva Andalucia (1km further along).

Activities

White-water rafting has taken off in Baeza. The Quito-based outfitter **Small World Adventures** (☎093-958-5776, in the US 970-309-8913; www.smallworldadventures.com; 7-days per person $1400-2000) run seven-day kayaking/rafting trips through the nearby Quijos valley – including the paddle up to their very own riverside lodge – before finishing in the Tena/Misahuallí area. It remains to be seen what impact the big hydro-electric project further down the valley will have on rivers here.

The main hikes from Baeza Colonial go to the radio masts above town (amazing views) and down to waterfalls (interesting because you drop down a vegetation zone into tropical forest). The prospects for longer hikes are thrilling. To the southwest is **Reserva Ecológica Antisana**, while southeast is **Parque Nacional Sumaco-Galeras** – Ecuador's most pristine and remote national park. The two nearest entrances are at **Cabañas San Isidro**, 15 minutes' drive south, and **San Carlos**, an hour's drive east on the road to Volcán Reventador. Accommodations in Baeza can provide information on hikes.

Sleeping & Eating

La Casa de Rodrigo HOSTEL $
(☎099-963-8357, 06-232-0467; rodrigobaeza1@yahoo.com; Baeza Colonial; r per person $12-15; ☜) Rooms are clean, the shared kitchen is spotless, showers are hot and wi-fi is strong – but the big draw of Baeza's best-value digs is Rodrigo himself, something of a local character and a great source of information on the entire Quijos valley. He also rents kayaks and can arrange rafting, canyoning and birding tours with licensed guides.

★Cabañas & Pizzeria Kopal CABIN $$
(☎06-232-0408; http://kopalecuador.com; Baeza Colonial; cabins per person $25; P ☜) These cabins, hewn exquisitely out of wood by their Dutch carpenter-owner, with their cozy interiors and deep porches conducive to relaxation, would be enticing in themselves. The

DON'T MISS

SAN RAFAEL FALLS

Ecuador's highest waterfall is spectacular 131m **San Rafael Falls** (7am-5pm) FREE and it absolutely deserves a stop on the road between Baeza and Lago Agrio.

While this incredible waterfall is at its powerful best in the winter, a hydroelectric dam and power plant 20km (12 miles) upriver, completed in 2016, reduces the flow by half during the summer months.

The power plant issue polarized the country, which, since the election of former President Rafael Correa in 2007, has actively sought to expand Ecuador's sustainable energy production.

Those who supported the scheme said that the power plant would not affect the strength of the Coca River, which feeds the falls and, as such, this natural wonder was not in danger.

Others disagreed, stating that water flow to the falls had been dropping in recent years, and that the plant would not be able to operate for much of the year due to low water flow from the Coca River.

In the end, the falls are still an impressive sight and worth a visit if you're heading this way. An access road has been built to ease your trip here, sign-posted off the road just below Hostelería Reventador (and just before, if you're coming from Quito). This takes you down to a small visitor center where you'll begin the easy 15- to 20-minute hike down to the viewpoint, which is breathtaking.

handmade, forced-relaxation deck chairs are good enough reason to stay. But there's also one of Ecuador's best **pizzerias** (Baeza Colonial; mains $5-15; 5-7pm).

Quinde Huayco B&B $$

(06-232-0649; Baeza Colonial; r per person incl breakfast $25;) Does it get better than sleeping in one of two secluded rooms, surrounded by lush gardens renowned for the hummingbirds they attract, knowing that next morning brings one of Ecuador's most lovingly prepared breakfasts, complemented by proper espresso, and taken in the atmospheric attached cafe? Not really.

This is one for the ornithologists and the coffee addicts. Cafe opening hours for nonguests are erratic, but breakfast/brunch is a safe bet.

Río Quijos Eco Lodge LODGE $$

(www.rioquijosecolodge.com; r per person incl breakfast from $22; P) Birders, rafters and fans of bucolic Andean retreats will love this ecolodge. About 12km north of Baeza, this riverside spot has trails through the trees and more than 90 acres of reserve land across the river. It's well placed for excursions to San Rafael Falls, river put-ins and caving adventures, and the helpful staff can organize all manner of tours.

Cabañas San Isidro CABIN $$$

(06-289-1880, 099-358-1250; www.cabanasanisidro.com; s/d incl breakfast $87/130; P) Once a cattle ranch, this 3700-acre nature reserve 15km south of Baeza enjoys a spectacular setting at 2000m. It offers first-class bird-watching; co-owner Mitch Lysinger is one of the top birders in South America. Comfortable cabins have decks with forest views. Full board is an extra $46 per person.

Nearby hiking trails weave through wonderful subtropical cloud forest within Reserva Ecológica Antisana.

Advance reservation is required; book online or through the **Quito office** (02-289-1880; cnr Av Siena 318 & Calle A, Edificio MDX, Oficina 310, Sector la Primavera, Cumbaya). To get here, turn off the Baeza–Tena road just north of Cosanga village.

Gina's ECUADORIAN $

(Baeza Colonial; mains $2-8; 7:30am-10:30pm;) Those who love little mountain towns will feel right at home in this wood-plank restaurant plastered with rafting stickers. Hearty fare includes trout prepared a thousand ways – and whichever manner you choose, it is the dish to order here.

Getting There & Away

Flag down one of the many buses going to and from Lago Agrio, Tena and Quito and hope there's room.

Coming from Quito, it's best to take a Tena-bound bus from the main terminal, as these stop in Baeza Colonial and Baeza Nueva Andalucia ($4, 2½ hours).

PREPARING FOR A JUNGLE TRIP

While it's possible to visit the jungle on your own, organized tours and jungle lodges get you into the wilderness quicker and without all the logistical challenges. Moreover, going alone means foregoing encounters with indigenous peoples who prefer to see tourists who are accompanied by guides.

First, figure out how much you can spend, what you want to see and how much time you have. The further you travel from roads, well-plied rivers and development, and the more time you spend in the jungle, the more wildlife you'll see. The same applies for cultural experiences – longer, more remote trips result in more exciting experiences and encounters.

The Differences

Lodges and large hotel-style boats offer daily excursions from a comfortable base. Other tours may include camping or sleeping in communities.

Lower costs may translate to more basic accommodations, Spanish-speaking guides, non-naturalist guides, larger groups, boiled instead of purified water and visits to developed areas with less wildlife. In some cases, operators may cut corners with practices that are not ecologically sound, including hunting for food (the rainforest is over-hunted; a no-hunting policy is a must).

Equally, money doesn't buy a more authentic (ie more wildlife, more indigenous culture) trip. The opposite can indeed be true: lower-cost trips with jungle camping can lend a far better insight into flora, fauna and rainforest tribes.

Different operators emphasize different aspects of the jungle, and can advise you on the probability of seeing specific wildlife. Observation towers enhance the chances of seeing birds and monkeys. However, it is no longer the case that community tourism (the most authentic type of trip, as it signifies that indigenous villages get tangible benefits from it) is exclusively high-end. Check itineraries carefully if this is important to you. Any community tourism is best suited to Spanish speakers with a flexible itinerary.

Some unscrupulous outfitters will offer *ayahuasca* or other psychotropics used ritually in indigenous cultures. These illegal substances should be regarded with extreme caution.

Buses to Lago Agrio ($7, four to five hours) stop only at the junction of the Tena turn-off.

Volcán Reventador

Following the 2002 eruption of this spectacular volcano, hiking to the 3562m-summit became impossible: it's currently Ecuador's most active volcano, belching out smoke and boulders several times hourly. For updates on Reventador's activity, consult Instituto Geofisico (www.igepn.edu.ec).

The volcano is within the eastern boundaries of **Reserva Ecológica Cayambe-Coca**, a rarely visited reserve that rises to over 5500m and a transition zone between Andes and Oriente. There are no signs or entrance stations here and the guard station is 20km away in the town of **El Chaco**, half-way between Baeza and Hostería Reventador (which can advise on hiking possibilities).

Volcano-watchers should not despair, however. You can appreciate Volcán Reventador by signing up on a hardcore adventure tour in the privately owned cloud forest reserve of Reserva Alto Coca.

Activities

Reserva Alto Coca WILDLIFE-WATCHING
(Map p64; ☎in Quito 02-252-8019; www.altococa.com; per person $50-120) The best way to appreciate Volcán Reventador is actually to sign up on a hardcore adventure tour in this privately owned cloud forest reserve, sitting between 1500 and 2000m on the other side of the valley from the volcano. Trips must be booked in advance through their Quito office.

After a tough four-hour hike up from the village of San Carlos, you reach what must be one of Ecuador's remotest accommodation options.

Basic cabins are strung with hammocks and garner great views of Reventador's antics. Hikes then lead off into the adjoining Parque Nacional Sumaco Napo Galleras. Wildlife sightings are great here, as devel-

Wherever you go, it's essential that you have a guide when outside towns and villages. Whatever choices you make, tread lightly and respect local communities.

Tour Bookings

Numerous operators have offices in Quito, allowing for quick comparative shopping. Agencies can get you into the jungle with a few days' notice. Once booked on a tour, you usually have to arrange your own travel to the town where it begins (most often Lago Agrio or Coca). Thoroughly discuss costs, food, equipment, itinerary and group size before reserving.

Booking a tour from Lago Agrio, Coca, Tena, Puyo or Macas often means traveling with guides who have a superior knowledge of the surroundings to Quito-based operators. The Cofán, Huaoranis, Kichwa, Shuar and other groups offer trips guided by their own community members.

Guides

A good guide will show you things you would have missed on your own, whereas an inadequate guide will spoil the trip. Guides should be able to produce a license on request and explain their specialties. Recommended guides are always preferable, and many lodges are known for their quality guiding services. Make the most of guides – ask questions and let them know exactly what you're interested in seeing. Be prepared to tip your guide, and recommend their services to others if they prove to be good.

What to Bring

Jungle towns have only basic equipment, including bottled water, tarps (for rain) and rubber boots in an array of sizes. Nearly all guided tours provide the essential boots and rain gear, but check beforehand. Mosquito nets are usually provided in places that need them. If you're serious about seeing wildlife, bring your own binoculars. Some guides will carry a pair, but will need them to make sightings. Besides general travel supplies, bring a flashlight, sunblock, a sun hat and repellent with DEET. Depending on the time of year and your destination, you may need malaria pills.

opment within the park has mercifully been minimal.

Sleeping

Hostería Reventador HOTEL $$

(☎06-302-0110; http://hosteriaelreventador.com; s/d $38/49; P 📶 🏊) The most obvious option hereabouts is this pleasant roadside place, a friendly and recently renovated lodge by San Rafael Falls. Rooms are modern and include all creature comforts. The nine-hour route up Reventador starts nearby; ask about the chances of tackling it or other hikes in the vicinity. There's also an excellent restaurant here.

Any bus from Quito or Baeza to Lago Agrio will pass right outside the hotel.

Getting There & Away

Buses heading to Lago Agrio from Quito or Baeza will skirt the eastern side of Reserva Ecológica Cayambe-Coca, where the volcano is located. Ask the bus driver to let you off at Hostería Reventador, if you're heading there or to San Rafael Falls.

Lago Agrio

☎06 / POP 57,730

This seedy, gray town pulses with the life of the oil industry, a chaotic market, dusty streets, thick traffic and gritty bars. The first oil workers nicknamed Lago Agrio 'bitter lake,' after Sour Lake, Texas, the former home of Texaco, which pioneered local drilling. The city's official name is Nueva Loja, although no one calls it that. Locals settle for 'Lago.' Certain realities exist here, including a high amount of prostitution and crime related to the nearby Colombian border: take care at all times, especially after dark. Lago is mainly visited as the entry point to the spectacular Reserva de Producción Faunística Cuyabeno (Cuyabeno Reserve), which offers some of Ecuador's best wildlife-spotting opportunities.

Sleeping & Eating

Hotel D'Mario HOTEL **$**
(☎06-283-0172; www.hoteldmario.com; Av Quito 26-2, near Amazonas; r incl breakfast $20-60; ❄📶🏊) Tour groups favor this staple in the center of town, along a strip of midrange hotels on Avenida Quito. Arranged around a courtyard with a pool and outdoor sitting areas, the bright but sometimes cramped rooms are perfectly comfortable. The downstairs restaurant is best known for its pizzas ($6 to $16) and is one of the best options in town.

Araza Hotel HOTEL **$$**
(☎06-283-1287; www.hotel-araza.com; Av Quito 536, near Narvaez; s/d incl breakfast from $48/62; P❄📶🏊) Hands down, the best, friendliest place in town: popular with oil industry travelers. Average-sized rooms are spotless, anonymous and business-style, with desks, TV and private bathrooms. There's also a pleasant tropical courtyard, a restaurant, a bar with big-screen TV, a gym and swimming pool.

Sacha Micuna Wasi ECUADORIAN **$**
(☎06-283-0557; Alfaro, near 20 de Junio; meals $5; ⏲10am-5pm) Look for the grill outside, where the *maitos* (*tilapia* grilled in palm leaves) are prepared by Kichwa pros. Served whole, alongside steamed *maduro* (green plantain) or yuca (cassava) and pickled onions, with a refreshing pitcher of iced *guayusa* (Amazonian herbal tea), this is the urban intro to cuisine a la Amazonía.

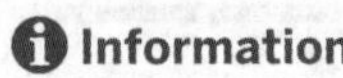

Information

The ongoing conflict in neighboring Colombia has made border towns such as Lago Agrio havens for Colombian guerrillas, anti-rebel paramilitaries and drug smugglers. It is not recommended to cross into Colombia here. In town, bars can be risky and side streets unsafe, so stick to the main drag (especially at night) or take a taxi to restaurants further out. Tourists rarely have problems.

Banco de Guayaquil (cnr Av Quito & 12 de Febrero; ⏲8am-4pm Mon-Fri, 9am-noon Sat)

Banco del Pichincha (cnr Av Quito & 12 de Febrero)

Colombian Consulate (☎06-283-2114; http://nuevaloja.consulado.gov.co; Av Quito, near Colombia, Edificio Moncada, 4th fl; ⏲8am-4pm Mon-Fri)

Getting There & Away

AIR

Flights fill up fast with jungle-lodge guests and oil workers traveling home for the weekend; book early. If you can't get a ticket, go to the airport and get on a waiting list in the hope of cancellations, which are frequent because tour companies book more seats than they can use.

TAME (☎06-283-2365; Orellana near 9 de Octubre) has daily flights between Quito and Lago Agrio.

The airport is about 3km east of Lago Agrio; taxis there (yellow or white pickup trucks) cost about $3.

BORDER CROSSINGS

The Colombian border is less than 20km north of town but it's best to avoid it. The area is notorious for smugglers and guerrilla activity. The most frequently used route from Lago Agrio is to La Punta (about 1½ hours) on Río San Miguel. Taxi-trucks leave Lago Agrio from the corner of Eloy Alfaro and Avenida Colombia and go to La Punta during the day.

BUS

The drive from the jungle into the Andes (and vice versa) is dramatic and beautiful, and worth doing in daylight. The bus terminal, about 2km northwest of Lago Agrio center, has a wide selection of routes and options. In addition, Transportes Putumayo buses go through the jungle towns of Dureno and Tarapoa for travelers wanting access to the Río Aguarico side of the Cuyabeno Reserve – although it's far more rewarding to go with a guided tour. Services run daily and are relatively frequent.

BUSES FROM LAGO AGRIO

DESTINATION	COST ($)	DURATION (HR)
Baeza	7	4–5
Coca	3	2
Guayaquil	20	13
Puyo	13	8–9
Quito	12	8
Tena	10	6

Reserva Producción Faunística Cuyabeno

This beautiful reserve is a unique flooded rainforest covering 6034 sq km around Río Cuyabeno. Seasonally inundated with water, the flooded forest provides a home to diverse aquatic species and birdlife – not to mention pink river dolphins, manatees, caiman and anacondas, several monkey and cat species, tapirs, peccaries and agoutis. Macrolobium and ceiba treetops thrust out from the underwater forest, creating a stunning visual effect. The blackwater rivers, rich in tannins from decomposing foliage, form a maze of waterways that feed the lagoons.

Due to its remoteness, and to protect the communities within it, travelers should only visit the reserve on guided tours – which are significantly cheaper, and often yield richer wildlife sightings, than in Parque Nacional Yasuní.

History

The boundaries of the reserve shift with the political winds, but the area is substantially larger than it was originally. The reserve was created in 1979 to protect rainforest, conserve wildlife and provide a sanctuary in which the indigenous inhabitants – the Siona, Secoya, Cofán, Kichwa and Shuar – could lead customary ways of life.

Its protected status notwithstanding, Cuyabeno was opened to oil exploitation almost immediately after its creation. The oil towns of Tarapoa and Cuyabeno and parts of the trans-Ecuadorian oil pipeline were built within the reserve's boundaries. Roads and colonists followed, and tens of thousands of hectares of the reserve became logged or degraded by oil spills and toxic waste. Many of the contaminants entered Río Cuyabeno itself.

Various groups set to work to try to protect the area (although legally protected, in reality it was open to development). Guard stations were established, Siona and Secoya were trained to work in wildlife management, and an Ecuadorian environmental-law group that challenged the legality of allowing oil exploitation in protected areas was instrumental in getting the government to shift the borders of the reserve further east and south and enlarge the area it covered.

The result is that the new reserve is more remote and better protected. Vocal local indigenous groups – supported by Ecuadorian and international nongovernmental organizations (NGOs), tourists, travel agencies and conservation groups – are now proving to be its best stewards.

Tours

Most people sign up on tours online or in Quito, where there is more choice. Transport from Quito to Lago Agrio is rarely included in packages – and neither are entrance fees (per person around $5) to communities within the reserve.

About 10 lodges currently operate close to each other on the river; a few are close by on a lagoon. No location is significantly privileged; all have similar opportunities for spotting wildlife. Travel is mainly by canoe except between December and February, when low water levels limit river travel. Most visitors come during the wetter months of March to September.

The best rates, especially for solo travelers, are obtained by squeezing into an existing trip. When booking, check to see whether: transportation to and from Lago Agrio is included; the travel day is considered a tour day; water is boiled or purified (purified is preferred); and whether you can expect naturalist/native guides. A naturalist is preferred as they are able to tell you far more about plants scientifically, but native guides give the traditional uses and can show how indigenous people prepare various products. A naturalist will nearly always speak English.

Sleeping

Jamu Lodge JUNGLE LODGE **$$$**
(www.jamulodge.com; 3 nights per person incl full board $334;) Squirrel monkeys cavort above the walkways at highly rated Jamu lodge, where the jungle feels close at hand. Dugout canoe trips, walks through swamps knee-deep in mud to spot the likes of anacondas and pink river dolphins, swims in lagoons and memorable nighttime excursions all contribute to a vivid wilderness experience; the lodge also stands all by itself in the reserve, which makes it seem more remote.

Facilities are clean and as high-end as it gets in the jungle, all powered by solar. Guides have a reputation for their knowledge and enthusiasm.

Cuyabeno Lodge LODGE **$$$**
(02-292-6153 in Quito; www.cuyabenolodge.com.ec; s/d 3 nights incl full board from $480/760)

This highly recommended place is run by Quito-based Neotropic Turis (p72), in close cooperation with the local Siona people. Thatched huts and towers with hot-water bathrooms and solar electricity are spread over its hillside location (which is never inundated). Upgraded tower rooms are more spacious and have private balconies. Bilingual naturalist guides get top reviews from guests.

The food and attention are excellent (request vegetarian, vegan or gluten-free preferences upon booking). Prices include transfers from Lago Agrio. Canoes and kayaks are available to paddle around the lake when the water is high enough.

Tapir Lodge LODGE **$$$**
(☎in Quito 02-380-1567; www.tapirlodge.com; 3 nights incl full board $650) Established in 1999, Tapir Lodge features multitiered tower lodgings that get guests into the trees. Simple but comfortable rooms come fitted out with screens, mosquito nets, hot water and balconies. Solar-powered electricity is provided 24/7. The lodge works in partnership with the local Siona community, and the guides here have a great reputation for being knowledgeable and enthusiastic.

Getting There & Away

Guided tours include transport to, from and on the river. Trips to Cuyabeno generally begin at the Lago Agrio airport.

Coca

☎06 / POP 45,200

The unavoidable starting point for many of Ecuador's most fascinating jungle tours, Coca will be most visitors' unsexy introduction to the Río Napo. In the 1990s the town was transformed by the oil industry from a tiny river settlement with dirt roads into a hot, teeming mass of concrete. The capital of the Orellana province since 1999 (and officially known as Puerto Francisco de Orellana), Coca is the last real civilization before the Río Napo transports you deep into the rainforest to the Parque Nacional Yasuní and beyond into the Amazon basin.

Though decidedly not a destination in itself, Coca isn't altogether charmless – an attractive little park adorns the center, and a pretty *malecón* (waterfront) runs along the riverfront, anchored by the excellent Museo Arqueológico Centro Cultural de Orellana (MACCO) that opened in 2016. A stunning new suspension bridge now spans the Napo, taking traffic bound down Via Auca towards Tiguino (another starting point for rainforest forays).

Sights

★MACCO MUSEUM
(Museo Arqueológico Centro Cultural Orellana; www.macco.ec; cnr 9 de Octubre & Espejo; $5; ⏲8am-5pm Tue-Fri, 9am-5pm Sat-Sun) This excellent archaeological museum of the Orellana region's cultural legacy is a must-visit museum in Coca. Housing exquisitely restored and diverse artifacts from the region – from funereal vases to purely ceremonial axes – the curation and bilingual interpretive explanations are nuanced and beautifully arranged. Various Amazonian cultures are presented in both historical and contemporary contexts, with delicate artwork enhancing the exhibits.

Tours

A jungle tour can offer a very different experience to staying at lodges (which do, of course, have their own tours): more flexibility and more adventurous possibilities. Groups are generally smaller and prices cheaper overall – although there are fewer creature comforts. In addition to the operators in Coca, there are plenty of tour options in Quito.

★Amazon Wildlife Tours WILDLIFE
(www.amazonwildlife.ec; cnr Napo & García Moreno, Hotel El Auca; per person per day from $100) This is the best reason to book a jungle jaunt within Coca: an experienced agency with an array of nature-watching tours, including a specialty jaguar expedition in Yasuní National Park, tours to see Amazon dolphins and general wildlife-watching in the Limoncocha Reserve.

Jorge Carriel JUNGLE TOUR
(☎093-971-2597; loresalavarria84@hotmail.com; cnr Alejandro Labaka & Camilo de Torrano; per person per day $120) Jorge specializes in six- to eight-day adventure trips deep into the jungle (you pay a little more because of corresponding diesel costs) – down to the Nuevo Rocafuerte area near the Peruvian border – on blackwater tributaries where there are higher chances of seeing more exciting wildlife. Accommodation is in basic jungle shelters.

Coca

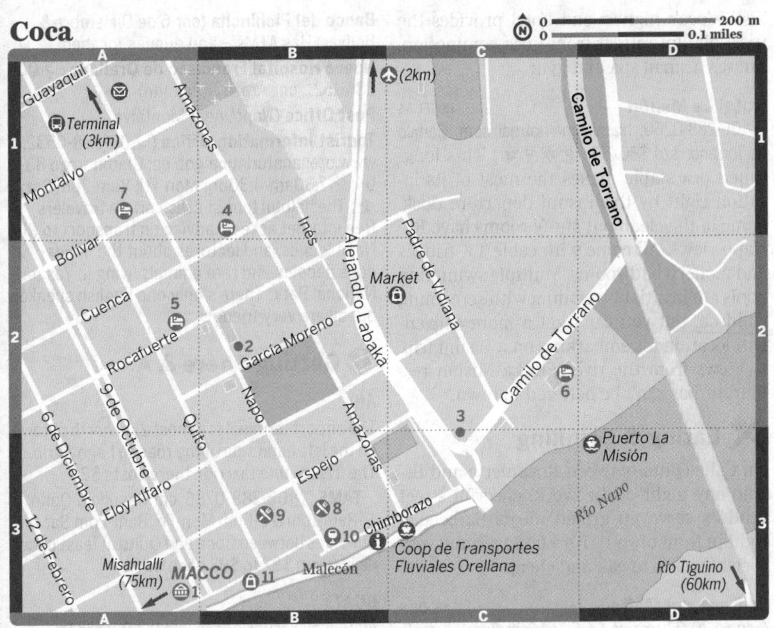

Coca

Top Sights
1 MACCO ... A3

Activities, Courses & Tours
2 Amazon Wildlife Tours ... B2
3 Jorge Carriel ... C3

Sleeping
4 Heliconias Grand Hotel ... B1
5 Hostal Jungle Santa María ... A2
6 Hotel La Misión ... C2
7 Hotel Río Napo ... A1

Eating
8 Cevichería Colorado ... B3
9 La Casa del Maito ... B3

Drinking & Nightlife
10 Bar Pappa Dans ... B3

Shopping
11 Kallary Kawsay ... B3

Otobo's Amazon Safari TOURS
(www.rainforestcamping.com; per person per night $200) Operated by indigenous Huaorani Otobo and his family, this remote site on the Río Cononaco has platform tents and a thatched-roofed lodge. Visitors hike in the Parque Nacional Yasuní with an English-speaking native guide, and visit lagoons and a local village.

Sleeping

Hotel Río Napo HOTEL $
(06-288-0872; www.hotelrionapo.com; Bolívar 76-06; s/d incl breakfast $23/40;) This smart, clean and bright midrange hotel in the center of town has 29 comfortable air-conditioned rooms with cable TV. You can opt out of breakfast for a slightly cheaper rate. Importantly, it's safe and has the friendliest staff in town.

Hostal Jungle Santa María HOTEL $
(06-288-0287; Rocafuerte, btwn Quito & Napo; s/d without bathroom $10/13, s/d with air-con $15/20;) Here you'll find the cheapest acceptable bed in town, in neat, clean rooms with room-temperature water only. Don't hit your head on the low ceiling in the stairwell on the way upstairs.

Heliconias Grand Hotel HOTEL $$
(06-288-2010; www.heliconiasgrandhotel.com.ec; Cuenca, near Amazonas; s/d incl breakfast from $42/66; P) With more than 40 tiled, faux-colonial rooms surrounding a lovely

pool, Coca's highest-end hotel provides the most blissful retreat from Coca commotion. There's a small spa and gym.

Hotel La Misión HOTEL $$
(06-288-0260; hlamision@hotmail.com; Camilo de Torrano; s/d $30/50; P ❄ 📶 ≋) This long-time Coca staple makes the most of its location right by the Yasuní departure dock. Some of the clean but stuffy rooms have Río Napo views. All come with cable TV, fridges and modern bathrooms. Multiple swimming pools are invariably teeming with screaming children, but you can't get a more convenient location for embarking on a Yasuní trip.

Views from the riverside La Misión restaurant/bar can't be bettered in town.

Eating & Drinking

On Calle Quito between Rocafuerte and Espejo any night of the week, cheerful street vendors serve up grilled meats barbecued right in front of you – it's a fantastic and very sociable place to eat, and cheap.

La Casa del Maito SEAFOOD $
(Espejo 70-02; mains $4-6; 6am-8pm) Locals flock in to lunch on delectable fish (mostly *tilapia* and piranha) cooked in palm leaves on the grill outside. The friendly owner, Luis Duarte, also offers guiding services.

Cevichería Colorado SEAFOOD $
(098-967-4646; Napo, near Chimborazo; mains $5-9; 7:30am-4pm) Down towards the river, this popular spot is *the* place for a bowl of frothy ceviche and a cold beer.

Bar Pappa Dans BAR
(06-288-1345; cnr Chimborazo & Napo; 6pm-late Mon-Sat) Coca's first decent-looking bar is a *palapa*-style place with prime river views and good cocktails. There's sometimes a small cover charge for live music and dancing on weekends.

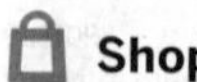

Information

Banco del Austro (06-289-1900; cnr Chimborazo & Quito; 9am-4:30pm Mon-Fri) Has reliable ATMs on the Quito side.

Banco del Pichincha (cnr 6 de Diciembre & Bolívar) Has ATMs – and queues for them.

Nuevo Hospital Francisco de Orellana (06-286-1521; cnr Arazá & Palmito)

Post Office (Napo, near Montalvo)

Tourist Information Office (06-288-0532; www.orellanaturistica.gob.ec; Chimborazo 83-04; 7:30am-4:30pm Mon-Fri, 8am-2pm Sat; 📶) The helpful tourist office offers travelers free internet access, advice on transport to Río Napo lodges, and lectures about the indigenous peoples and rare animals living in Yasuní National Park. There's only one English speaker, but all are very friendly.

Getting There & Away

AIR

The airport terminal is almost 2km north of town on the left-hand side of the road to Lago Agrio. The five-minute taxi ride there costs $2.

TAME (06-288-0786; cnr Castillo & Quito; 8am-1pm & 2-6pm Mon-Fri, 8am-2pm Sat & Sun) flies between Coca and Quito at least once daily (from $82 to $98 each way).

BOAT

Almost all Yasuní lodges use the **Puerto La Misión** dock within Hostería La Misión.

Coop de Transportes Fluviales Orellana (06-288-2582; Chimborazo at docks) offers an upriver passenger service in a covered 60-passenger canoe. Buy your ticket early. It departs Sunday, Wednesday and Thursday at 7am for Nuevo Rocafuerte ($18.75, 8 to 10 hours) on the Peruvian border. It returns to Coca, departing Nuevo Rocafuerte on Wednesday, Saturday and Sunday at 5am (12 to 14 hours).

Although there's usually a stop for lunch, bring food and water for the long trip – and be ready at Coca's main dock 30 minutes before departure. Ask at the dock about faster boats, which big groups can charter for around $70 to the border.

BUS

Coca, among its growing number of boasts, has one of Ecuador's best new bus terminals – 3km north of town. A taxi here costs around $2.50. All main destinations are served.

Rancheras (open-sided buses, or trucks mounted with uncomfortably narrow bench seats – also known as *chivas*) leave from the market on Alejandro Labaka two blocks back from the river, heading for various destinations between Coca and Lago Agrio, and to Río Tiputini to the south. **Cooperativa Camionetas Río Napo** pickup trucks and taxis provide services around/outside town.

Buses run to Tena ($8.75, 4 hours) as well as Oriente destinations further to the south, Lago

Agrio ($3.75, 2 hours) and Quito ($12.50, 10 hours).

Vía Auca

06

This unfortunately named road ('auca' means 'savage' in Kichwa) from Coca crosses the Río Napo and continues south across Río Tiputini and Río Shiripuno, ending near the small community of Tiguino on Río Tiguino. The area used to be Huaorani territory and virgin jungle, but when this oil-exploration road was built in the 1980s, the Huaorani were pushed out. The area is being colonized, and cattle ranches and oil rigs are replacing the jungle in spite of conservationist efforts.

The rivers crossed by the road provide access to remote parts of both the Huaorani reserve and Yasuní, but you should only enter with authorized guides.

Sleeping

Shiripuno Amazon Lodge LODGE **$$$**
(02-227-1094 in Quito; www.shiripunolodge.com; 3 nights incl full board per person $670) Some 75km south of Coca you'll find Shiripuno Lodge, one of the few lodges within Yasuní National Park. It's a simple place with no electricity, deep in the forest and perfect for those seeking a real jungle experience. Volunteer opportunities are also available here at the Shiripuno Research Center, with a minimum commitment of four weeks.

Getting There & Away

Daily *rancheras* go as far as Tiguino. If you're staying at Shiripuno Amazon Lodge, most packages include round-trip transport from Quito.

Lower Río Napo

06

The Río Napo flows east from Coca on a steady course toward the Amazon River in Peru. Just after Coca, the river widens into a powerful waterway that can flood villages and islands. This long, lonesome stretch of the Napo, running along the edge of Parque Nacional Yasuní, houses some of Ecuador's best jungle lodges and boasts some of the country's better wildlife-spotting possibilities. On the way there, you'll spot some of the oil development causing ongoing controversial headlines.

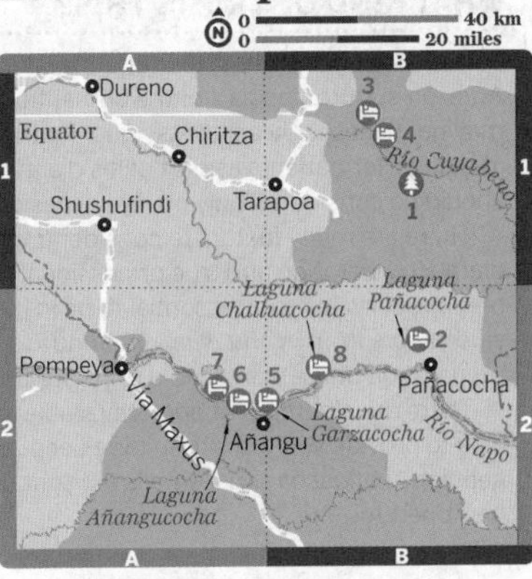

Lower Río Napo & Around

Sights
1 Reserva de Producción Faunística Cuyabeno B1

Sleeping
2 Amazon Dolphin Lodge B2
3 Cuyabeno Lodge B1
4 Jamu Lodge B1
5 La Selva Jungle Lodge B2
6 Napo Cultural Center A2
Napo Wildlife Center .... (see 6)
7 Sacha Lodge A2
8 Sani Lodge B2
Tapir Lodge .... (see 4)

Activities

Anakonda River Cruises CRUISE
(02-336-0887 in Quito, 1-786-220-3251 in the US; www.anakondaamazoncruises.com; s/d cabin 3 nights incl full board $3279/4392) See the Río Napo on three- to seven-night cruises that ply the river as far as Nuevo Rocafuerte. The *Anakonda*, a 40-passenger-capacity luxury vessel built in 2013, offers a nigh-on boutique hotel experience. Excursions and activities are included, while add-ons like glamping cost extra. Impressively spacious cabins have private balconies and Jacuzzis. Meals are spectacularly gourmet.

Along the way, there's the chance for a spot of jungle glamping.

Sleeping

Due to the uniquely challenging environment that is the Amazon rainforest, as well as the need to tread sensitively and ethically in the homeland of the local indigenous

WHAT KIND OF TRIP IS THIS?

Think twice if your jungle tour offers *ayahuasca*, a psychotropic plant used ritually in Amazon cultures, as part of the authentic experience. Only a professional shaman (who may not necessarily be 'dressed up' for the occasion) has the trained ability to carry out 'readings' for patients as part of his diagnostic arts. The intake of this psychotropic plant should be considered only on rare occasions.

There are many factors to consider prior to taking *ayahuasca*, such as the need for dietary preparation and true professional supervision and guidance, and the timing of menstrual cycles – it's essential to be in the hands of a professional shaman. Dangerous side effects from *ayahuasca*, either due to medication you might be taking or negligent preparation of the plant, could ruin your trip.

There are a number of books available on the subject. A good tour operator should be able to provide you with these for a deep-rooted, preliminary understanding of what a genuine *ayahuasca* ritual entails – if your operator can't supply these resources, find a new operator.

people, it is strongly recommended – and a richer experience – to arrange travel to the Lower Río Napo region through a lodge or tour operator. Book directly with lodges online or at their Quito offices.

★Napo Wildlife Center LODGE $$$

(☎800-176-647 in Australia, 02-600-5893 in Quito, 800-0325-771 in the UK, 800-250-1992 in the US; www.napowildlifecenter.com; s/d 3 nights incl full board $2126/2834; @) As the lodge most ensconced within Parque Nacional Yasuní, the sumptuous Napo Wildlife Center (NWC) enjoys a pristine setting with rarely paralleled access to wildlife. This ecotourism project is 100% owned by Añangu's Kichwa community; they make up almost the entire lodge staff.

One of the most enjoyable aspects here is simply arriving: you'll be paddled a couple of hours from the Río Napo, down a thrillingly wild blackwater creek replete with birds and animals.

Eventually you'll arrive at Añangucocha, the lagoon where NWC's 16 red-hued rooms enjoy a prime position on the far side. The rooms are stylishly well appointed, with lake views from most. Four suites are even bigger, with outdoor Jacuzzis on terraces at the back. The fabulous communal areas are spacious and open, with a lovely wooden deck, small library and elevated viewing platform. Meals here are delicious and varied.

Trips are guided by local Añangu villagers trained as Yasuní park rangers and bilingual naturalist guides. Two parrot clay licks on the property are a major attraction for bird-watchers, who also come from surrounding lodges to see parrots, parakeets and macaws. Between late October and early April is the best time to see up to 10 species of parrot – sometimes numbering in the thousands. A short hike from the lodge, a 36m steel tower offers a spectacular canopy panorama and prolific birdlife. The rare zigzag heron has been spotted on the property.

The center has won numerous awards, not only for its connection to the local community, but for ecologically sound practices, including an environmentally sustainable sewage system, composting latrines, solar panels and quality guiding. It's generally held to be the most luxurious and most environmentally sensitive of the lower Río Napo lodges and is highly recommended.

Those on a budget can also stay within Parque Nacional Yasuní at the sister site Napo Cultural Center, run by the same community. The lodge is actually within the Kichwa village alongside the Río Napo, so while the experience is somewhat less wild, it's a wonderful place to learn more about Kichwa culture, and the lodge facilities are excellent.

Sacha Lodge LODGE $$$

(☎02-256-6090 in Quito, 800-706-2215 in the US; www.sachalodge.com; s/d 3 nights incl full board $1575/2100; @) Enjoying a spectacular setting on the inland lake of Pilchecocha (Laguna El Pilche), a short hike and canoe ride from the Río Napo, Sacha Lodge is one of Ecuador's best jungle lodges. Opened in 1992, this Swiss-run place has never rested on its laurels and offers one of the most luxurious rainforest experiences possible.

As well as employing and training indigenous people to work in the tourism industry,

Sacha has been steadily purchasing plots from Ecuadorian smallholders who were using it to farm, and allowing the rainforest to reclaim the land purchased. The lodge sits on 5000 acres of reclaimed land now fully protected for forestation, and is the largest private reserve in Ecuador.

Guests are welcomed to the open-air, lakeside dining terrace, which serves as the main restaurant. The lodge's boardwalks tentacle out to 26 cabins, each with a spacious, modern bathroom, dry box for cameras, 24-hour hot water and electricity, and a hammock deck for shady siestas and wildlife-watching. Older units are built deeper into the jungle – but as a result present better wildlife-watching opportunities. All rooms have safes and are very well screened – mosquito nets aren't used because the threat is small. Food is superb, and there's a pleasant upstairs bar in a central *palapa*, popular in the evenings.

Hikes and canoe trips typically consist of about five tourists, with a bilingual naturalist and local guide. The terrain includes flat and hilly rainforest, various lakes, coiling rivers and swamps. The 5000 acres are visited by six kinds of monkey, toucans, poison dart frogs, peccaries, sloths, anacondas, caiman and black agoutis.

The lodge's showpiece is a massive metal canopy walkway that stretches between three platforms, 60m off the ground. Birdwatchers covet the early morning experience of standing on the creaking giant to watch the fog lift on an array of avian and primate life. A separate 45m-high wooden observation deck atop a huge ceiba tree is another way to get high up.

Getting here is an adventure – a two-hour motorized canoe ride from Coca is followed by a leisurely walk through the forest on an elevated boardwalk. You're then taken on a 15-minute paddle up a blackwater canal and across a lake in a dugout canoe.

Napo Cultural Center JUNGLE LODGE **$$$**
(☎02-254-7758; www.yasuniecolodge.travel; s/d 3 nights incl full board from $868/1460; 📶) 🍃 The lodge formerly known as Yasuní Ecolodge (same excellent community-run lodge) offers four spacious cabañas, each housing four luxurious rooms fitted out with spacious showers and bathrooms, wood construction and vaulted ceilings, terraces with cozy chairs and comfortable, mosquito-netted beds. Its beautifully landscaped grounds sit harmoniously in Añangu village, so guests are somewhat ensconced in the quotidian activities of a well-to-do Kichwa community.

La Selva Jungle Lodge LODGE **$$$**
(☎02-515-4000 in Quito, 800-032-8271 in the UK, 866-87-3109 in the US; www.laselvajunglelodge.com; s/d 3 nights incl full board $1580/2430) The oldest lodge on the lower Napo, Norwegian-Ecuadorian owned La Selva Jungle Lodge stands on the shores of Laguna Garzacocha. Recently refurbished, the new-look accommodations are in light, airy and rather elegant suites, making this absolutely top-end.

Spacious (20 sq meter) rooms now feature beautiful king-size beds, ceiling fans, mosquito nets, extensive closets, luxury bathrooms and either private porches or balconies with lake views. Three family suites also get hot tubs. Raised walkways connect the complex. Meals are delicious and presented in a spacious dining room overlooking the lake.

With more than 500 bird species, La Selva is a major bird-watching spot. A 43m-high canopy platform, 20 minutes' walk from the lodge, affords even better viewing. Monkeys and other mammals are frequently seen, and brilliantly colored butterflies flit about in an enormous butterfly-breeding complex that's open to visitors. Swimming and canoeing are also both possible on the lake.

La Selva is about 2½ hours downriver from Coca in a motorized canoe. It's then reached by a gentle walk through the jungle, followed by a canoe trip across the lagoon.

Yarina Ecolodge LODGE **$$$**
(☎02-250-4037 in Quito; www.yarinalodge.com; s/d 3 nights incl full board $690/920) The Río Manduro meets the Napo an hour downstream from Coca, and a further 10 minutes down this blackwater stream you'll find Yarina Lodge, a hillside camp of 26 bamboo, thatched-roofed cabañas. Yarina is geared toward budget travelers and doesn't feel as remote as those camps further downstream, but it provides excellent services and has enthusiastic and professional English-speaking guides.

Meals, with vegetarian options, are well prepared in a communal lodge that features hammocks. Two- and three-bed cabins come equipped with mosquito nets, modern bathrooms, electricity and 24-hour hot water.

Besides the expected jungle walks and activities, there is a nearby 'rehabilitation area,' where animals rescued from traffickers in

Coca spend time before being released into the wild. Kichwa cookery classes are on offer too. Rates include all meals and tours with Spanish- and English-speaking local guides.

Book online or via the **Quito office** (☎02-250-4037; www.yarinalodge.com; Av Amazonas N24-240 near Av Colón).

Sani Lodge JUNGLE LODGE $$$

(☎02-243-6801 in Quito; www.sanilodge.com; s/d 3 nights incl full board $1270/2116;) Owned by the local Sani community, Sani Lodge is one of the lower-priced options around, but unlike other economy lodges it's located very deep in the rainforest, enjoying one of the most beautiful locations of any jungle lodge in Ecuador.

The lodge came into being as part of a deal between the local community and the Occidental Oil Company. In exchange for allowing Occidental to explore for oil on its land, the Sani community asked them to build a tourist lodge they could run. Occidental did not find oil, but Sani Lodge was nevertheless built. All profits from tourism go back into the Kichwa community in the form of scholarships, a community store that eases the need for local hunting, emergency medical funds etc.

After traveling up a small tributary of the Río Napo, visitors are greeted with a welcome at the lodge's open-air bar, overlooking Challuacocha, Sani's enchanting blackwater oxbow lake. Ten cabins each sleep two to three people and have private hot-water bathrooms, comfortable beds, mosquito screens and a small porch. There are also four family-sized cabins and a camping area in a separate area reachable by canoe. The latter can be a great money-saver – tents are provided and share a staffed kitchen and bathrooms with running water.

Monkeys, sloths and black caiman are regularly spotted, and the lodge's bird list records more than 570 species (the 30m-high tree tower will help you find them). Guides here (native and English-speaking naturalists) are excellent for their knowledge of, and respect for, the jungle. Most enjoy showing visitors the Sani community to reinforce how the lodge has created an important, sustainable economy.

Getting There & Away

Lower Río Napo river lodges include transport to and from Coca in their rates. The lodges' dedicated canoes depart only on days on which guests are booked, so it's recommended to reserve in advance.

TO/FROM PERU

Exit and entry formalities in Ecuador are handled in Nuevo Rocafuerte; in Peru, try your best to settle them in Pantoja, with Iquitos as backup. Private boats from Nuevo Rocafuerte charge $60 per boat to Pantoja. Cargo boats travel from Pantoja to Iquitos (a three- to five-day trip) when they have enough cargo to justify the trip. A hammock and 19L of water, in addition to food, are recommended – food on the boats can be dodgy. The experience can be rough: there may be only one bathroom, crowded conditions and lots of livestock on board. Boats vary in quality, but if you've been waiting a long time for one to arrive, you may not want to be picky.

Laguna Pañacocha

This quiet, hidden blackwater lagoon is a short boat ride off the Río Napo through a wild network of creeks brimming with wildlife. Pañacocha, which means 'Lake of Piranhas' in Kichwa, is frequently visited by local lodge tour groups, who come up here on day trips to fish for piranha and spot some of the pink freshwater dolphins that can often be seen in the lagoon. Nearby oil development has reduced sightings, however.

Ask when you book your tour/lodge whether the lagoon features on the itinerary.

Sleeping

Amazon Dolphin Lodge JUNGLE LODGE $$$

(☎02-250-4037 in Quito; www.amazondolphinlodge.com; per person 3 nights incl breakfast $600) One of several lodges near Laguna Pañacocha, and probably the best. Simple, with 11 cabins.

Getting There & Away

The lagoon can be explored independently, although you'll have to rely on a bit of luck to find a fairly priced boat operator when you need one. Hire a local canoe where the Río Pañayacu meets the Río Napo, which can be reached by a Nuevo Rocafuerte-bound boat from Coca.

Pañacocha is four to five hours downstream from Coca (depending on your motor), or about halfway to Nuevo Rocafuerte.

Nuevo Rocafuerte

A distant dot on the map for many people, Nuevo Rocafuerte is in no danger of losing its mystery. While backpackers may bubble with excitement at the idea of floating the

Napo all the way to Peru and the Amazon River, only the most intrepid travelers rise to the occasion. In this truly off-the-beaten-track adventure, aspiring 'survivors' may have to endure cramped and wet travel, the possibility of seeing their next meal slaughtered, and potential illness.

Nuevo Rocafuerte is on the Peruvian border, eight to 10 hours from Coca along the Río Napo. This is a legal border crossing with Peru, although regular passenger-boat transport is lacking and accommodations are basic.

Arrange a tour in Parque Nacional Yasuní or Cuyabeno reserve while you wait for your onward transportation: more and more tours from Coca use the blackwater rivers around Nuevo Rocafuerte as there's less pollution and more animal sightings than upriver.

Sleeping

Hostal Yurag Wasi HOSTAL $
(☎06-238-2184; yuragwasi@gmail.com; s/d $10/18) Simple, clean, basic rooms.

Hostal Chimborazo HOTEL $
(☎06-238-2109; r per person $10; 📶) Clean and comfortable wood-paneled rooms. Breakfast is available ($3). The hotel can also arrange onward transportation.

Information

For local information, tours or to hire a boat, contact local guide Juan Carlos 'Chuso' Cuenca (06-238-2182); his house is the second one after the marina.

Getting There & Away

Coop de Transportes Fluviales Orellana (p218) passenger canoes to Coca depart at 5am on Wednesday, Saturday & Sunday. The trip ($18.75) takes approximately eight to 12 hours, with a lunch stop in Pañacocha. The canoe is covered but you should still bring rain gear, food and water. Low-water conditions may prolong the trip. Even if you have a ticket, be sure to be at the departure point by 4:30am, as boats leave once they're full.

If you are continuing to Peru, inquire at the **Coop de Transportes Fluviales Orellana** (p218) in Coca, when you buy your ticket downstream, for phone numbers of cargo boats which may be connecting to Pantoja/Iquitos. But nothing guarantees timing; there's a good chance you'll get stuck here, so be prepared. Bring adequate supplies of water-purification tablets, insect repellent and food. Also, consider getting Peruvian currency in Quito before arriving.

To get to Iquitos, Peru (from where boats head down to Brazil and Colombia) it's best to travel downstream across the border to Pantoja. (Canoes can be hired for $60 per boatload.) Pantoja has a hotel, restaurant and disco.

Parque Nacional Yasuní

With a massive 9620 sq km section of wetlands, marshes, swamps, lakes, rivers and tropical rainforest, **Yasuní National Park** ($2, parrot clay lick $20) is Ecuador's largest mainland park. Its staggering biodiversity led Unesco to declare it an international biosphere reserve, and it was established as a national park shortly after, in 1979. Because this pocket of life was untouched by the last ice age, a diverse pool of species has thrived here throughout the centuries, including more than 600 bird species, some previously unknown elsewhere. Resident animals include some hard-to-see jungle wildlife, such as jaguars, harpy eagles, pumas and tapirs.

History

Yasuní stands today as one of the last true wildernesses in Ecuador. Its inaccessibility has preserved it in ways that active protection cannot. Bordered by Río Napo to the north and Río Curaray to the southeast, the park encompasses most of the watersheds of Ríos Yasuní and Nashiño, as well as substantial parts of Río Tiputini. Its diverse habitats consist of 'terra firma' (forested hills), which are never inundated even by the highest floods; *varzea* (lowlands), which are periodically inundated by flooding rivers; and *igapó* (semipermanently inundated lowlands).

A small number of Tagaeri, Taromenani and Oñamenane people live within the park. Park territory has been altered to protect these traditional populations of hunter-gatherers, who vehemently resist contact with the outside world. The nearby Reserva Huaorani contributes as an ecological buffer zone for the national park.

Oil discovery within the park has complicated this conservation success story. In 1991, despite Yasuní's protected status, the Ecuadorian government gave the US-based oil company Conoco the right to begin oil exploration. Since then the concession has changed hands several times. Conoco was soon replaced by the Maxus Oil Consortium,

1

FOTOS593/SHUTTERSTOCK ©

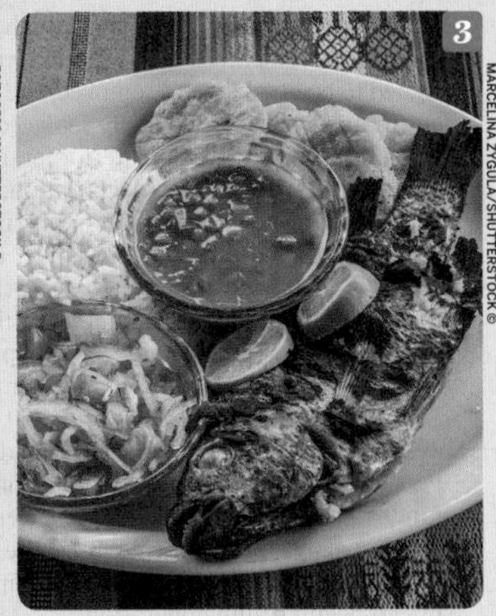

MARCELINA ZYGULA/SHUTTERSTOCK ©

1. San Rafael Falls (p211)
Spectacular San Rafael Falls is Ecuador's highest waterfall.

2. Laguna Pañacocha (p222)
Pañacocha means 'Lake of Piranhas' in Kichwa and visitors come here to fish for piranha and spot pink freshwater dolphins.

3. Tilapia Rio Negro
Tilapia (river fish) features in many Ecuadorian specialties.

4. Puyo (p238)
Art from the Ecuadorian Amazon.

VOLANTHEVIST/GETTY IMAGES ©

whose legacy is the Maxus road, which slices 150km into the park. While the road was designed to be lifted up and removed, the forest cut in its wake is not as easily replaced, and the subsequent link to the interior for outsiders causes its own kind of degradation.

In 2007 the Ecuadorian government launched the Yasuní-ITT Initiative under which it effectively promises to leave the estimated 846 million barrels of oil within the vast ITT (Ishpingo-Tambococha-Tiputini) oilfield underground in exchange for some $3.6 billion of foreign money and debt relief over 13 years. However, in 2013, Ecuadorian President Rafael Correa concluded that the funds raised – while considerable – were not economically sufficient. He closed the Initiative: sadly, oil companies have since moved in and begun drilling operations.

Getting There & Away

River lodges and tour operators include boat transport and sometimes airport transfers in their packages. Coca serves as the usual jumping-off point into the park.

Parque Nacional Sumaco Napo Galeras

A smooth, paved road connects Coca via Loreto to Tena, passing by the southern entrance to this large and stunning slice of little-explored cloud forest. Nowhere else in Ecuador is there such a vast area totally free of development – making its myriad ecosystems, including thick rainforest, cloud forest, hidden caves and cliffs and bare, volcanic uplands – precious indeed.

The centerpiece of the 2052-sq-km park is 3732m **Volcán Sumaco**, which is plagued by wet weather. The volcano is currently dormant, although vulcanologists believe it could become active. It lies about 27km north of the Cocai-Loreto-Tena road.

Activities

The tough hike to the summit is a three- to five-day round-trip. Making the effort will reap dividends: this is one of Ecuador's few trails transecting the three distinct climatic zones of rainforest, cloud forest and *páramo* (exposed mountainous uplands). Overnight stays are in one of the volcano's three new *refugios* (mountain refuges). Trails are muddy year-round, but drier between October and December. On the upper slopes, the rare woolly monkeys can be seen – as well as a host of birdlife throughout.

Guides are required for any summit attempts in this national park, as it is a conservation area rather than a recreational one, and summiting involves bushwhacking along poorly marked trails. Hire guides (per day $35) through the **Centro de Turismo Comunitario** (098-421-8470, 06-301-8324; infosumaco@gmail.com) in the village of Pacto Sumaco, 9km north (uphill) from the Loreto road. The national park has an **office** (06-301-8303, 06-301-8325) at the start of the track up from the main road, and can offer basic accommodation and help arrange guide services.

Sleeping

There's a good range of lodgings in the area, although all are fairly simple. If you're doing a multiday trek, you'll be camping in rainforest, cloud forest and *páramo* as you ascend – be prepared for wet weather.

Casita CABIN **$**
(Pacto Sumaco; per person $30) A simple place with self-catering facilities and an incredible roof terrace where wheeling toucans often provide evening entertainment. Ask at Wildsumaco Lodge or in the village for more information.

Reserva Biológica Río Bigal LODGE **$$**
(098-930-6988, 098-710-5385, 099-812-3023; http://bigalriverbiologicalreserve.org; per person incl full board visitor/volunteer $70/55) Río Bigal welcomes visitors interested in a purely back-to-nature experience (three-night minimum), and those who wish to get their hands dirty in participatory research are also welcome, with a minimum commitment of seven days when opportunities are available. All stays include accommodation, full board, activities, night walks and mule porter for the hike in. Reservations are essential.

Transport via 4WD from Loreto (one hour) is not included. Volunteer opportunities for construction or education work are also available; contact the reserve for specifics.

Wildsumaco Lodge LODGE **$$$**
(06-301-8343, in Quito 02-333-1189; www.wildsumaco.com; s/d full board $177/323) Located 1km south of Pacto Sumaco, the Wildsumaco Lodge makes a good base for climbing Volcán Sumaco. Set on a hilltop with panoramic mountain views, a wooden house with

a deck serves as a gathering spot for guests, most of whom come for the birds, a unique mixture of cloud forest, foothill and Amazonian species. Booking ahead is mandatory.

Concrete rooms are simple but tasteful with wood floors, comfy beds, plenty of hot water and electricity. A web of trails starts at the lodge, providing access to the abundance of birds and wildlife. The price includes basic guide services; specialized bird guides can be requested in advance. The Swedish and American owners are conservation-minded and started the Río Pucuno Foundation (www.riopucunofoundation.org) to preserve forest in the area.

Getting There & Away

Buses from Quito to Coca head east on the Loreto road; the turnoff at Wawa Sumaco leads up to Pacto Sumaco.

Cotundo & Archidona

06

While Tena is by no means a metropolis, its outlying towns of Cotundo and Archidona offer more of a relaxed, small-town Amazonía pace. If you're not in the area for a dose of foreigner-friendly white-water adventure, these little towns make great bases for exploring the other local attractions without the distractions of bigger-city rattle and hum.

Situated 7km south of Cotundo, Archidona, originally a mission founded in 1560, is a village of sleepy pastel facades, with a zebra-striped church poking up out of a manicured plaza. Sundays are market days.

Sights

The road south from Quito to Tena descends near the lonely village of Cotundo into the **Valle de los Petroglifos**, where fascinating petroglyphs are etched into valley rocks. A trail is marked from the main road but to see the best, it's worth enlisting the services of a guide: ask at accommodating Huasquila Lodge. Caving hereabouts is good. The **Gran Canyon**, 4km north of Cotundo, is a half-day canyon hike full of swimming holes and caves along a tributary of the Río Jondachi.

Cuevas de Jumandí CAVE

($3; 9am-5pm) About 4km north of Archidona, you'll find Cuevas de Jumandí. This cave system, the best known in the area, has three main branches that remain partly unexplored. Forgo the sketchy waterslides that dump into a river-water pool, and tread slowly (with a flashlight) to see stalactites, stalagmites and odd formations. Rubber boots and old clothes will serve you well.

For thorough exploration, you'll need a guide from Tena or on-site – ask guide companies in Tena for a customized day trip to the caves.

Sleeping

Huasquila Lodge LODGE $$

(02-237-6158 in Quito; www.huasquila.com; per person incl dinner & breakfast $69, 4 nights incl all meals and activities per person $460) Cresting a hillside 3km above Cotundo, Huasquila Lodge has 20 rustic but well-appointed and cozy cabins. There's a good restaurant, a pool and a mix of tours from secondary jungle hikes to petroglyph-spotting and caving. A taxi from Cotundo's main square is $3.

Hostería Orchids Paradise HOTEL $$

(06-288-9232; www.elparaisodelasorquideas.com.ec; r per person incl full board $60; P) The best local accommodations, this friendly hotel occupies its own sprawling grounds just outside town on the Tena road. There's a spacious thatched-hut restaurant-bar, a huge pool and cabins with screened windows and hot water. The lodge operates a monkey-rescue program – see the results swinging in the trees – and can arrange for day trips and multiday packages.

Getting There & Away

Buses from Tena ($0.25) leave for Cotundo and Archidona throughout the day.

Tena

06 / POP 23,300 / ELEV 598M

Unusually for a jungle transport hub, Tena is a charming place where many travelers find themselves hanging around quite happily for days before or after a trip into the rainforest. While it won't win architectural prizes anytime soon, Tena has a friendly population, a gorgeous setting surrounded by jungle-covered hills and lots of backpacker infrastructure. White-water fanatics from around the globe come to paddle and play on the high concentration of surrounding rivers, and the town is home to lots of experienced and highly recommended kayaking operators.

Tena

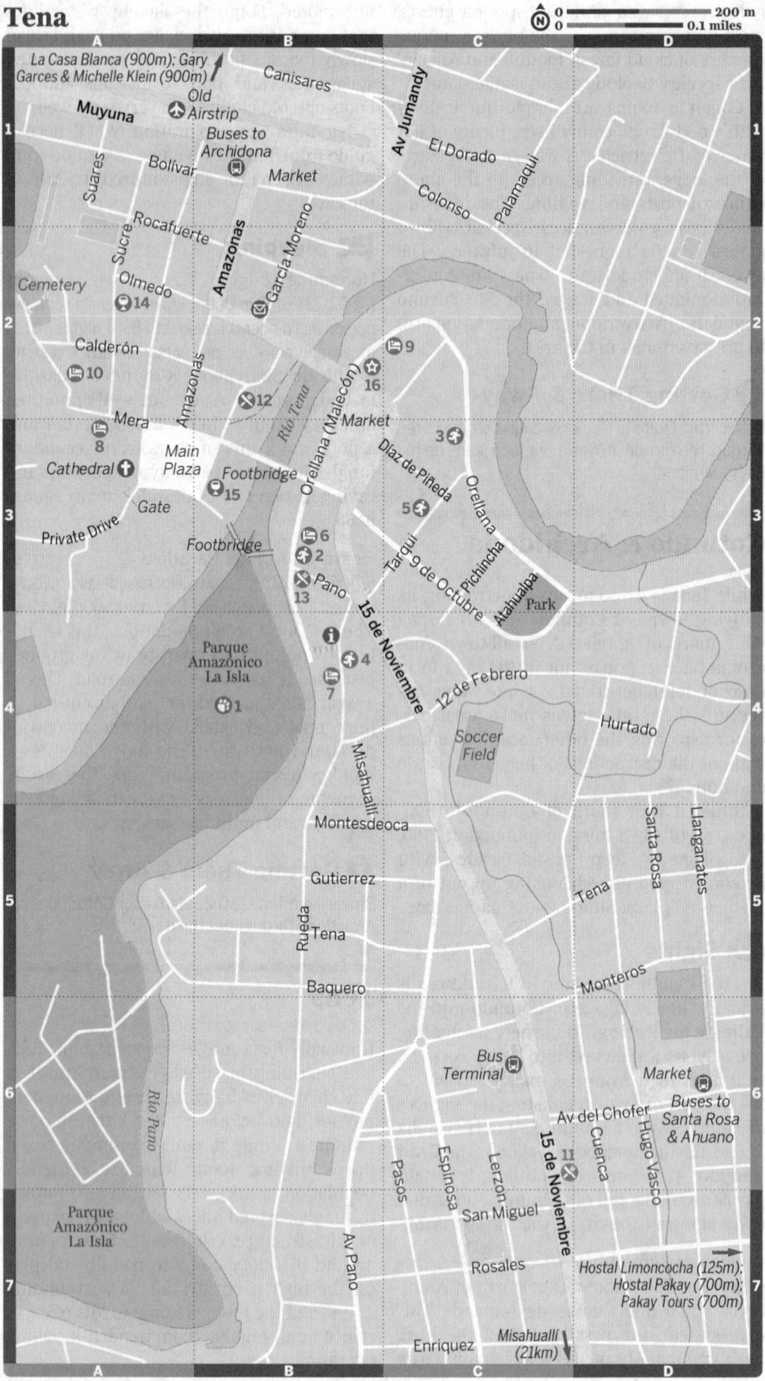

0 — 200 m
0 — 0.1 miles

A B C D
1 2 3 4 5 6 7

La Casa Blanca (900m); Gary Garces & Michelle Klein (900m)
Canisares
Muyuna
Old Airstrip
Buses to Archidona
Av Jumandy
El Dorado
Suares
Bolívar
Market
Colonso
Palamaqui
Rocafuerte
Sucre
Amazonas
García Moreno
Cemetery
Olmedo
14
Calderón
9
16
10
Amazonas
12
Río Tena
Orellana (Malecón)
Market
Mera
8
3
Main Plaza
Cathedral
Footbridge
15
Díaz de Piñeda
Orellana
Gate
5
Private Drive
Footbridge
6
2
Pichincha
Tarqui
9 de Octubre
Pano
13
Atahualpa
Park
15 de Noviembre
Parque Amazónico La Isla
1
4
7
12 de Febrero
Hurtado
Soccer Field
Misahuallí
Montesdeoca
Santa Rosa
Llanganates
Gutierrez
Tena
Rueda
Tena
Monteros
Baquero
Bus Terminal
Market
Buses to Santa Rosa & Ahuano
Av del Chofer
Río Pano
Hugo Vasco
15 de Noviembre
Cuenca
11
Pasos
Espinosa
Lerzon
San Miguel
Parque Amazónico La Isla
Av Pano
Rosales
Hostal Limoncocha (125m); Hostal Pakay (700m); Pakay Tours (700m)
Enriquez
Misahuallí (21km)

Tena

Sights

1 Parque Amazónico La Isla B4

Activities, Courses & Tours

2 AquaXtreme B3
3 Caveman Adventures C3
4 Raft Amazonía B4
5 Ríos Ecuador C3

Sleeping

6 Brisa del Río B3
7 Hostal Los Yutzos B4
8 Hotel Cristian's Palace A3
9 Hotel Pumarosa C2
10 La Casa del Abuelo A2

Eating

11 Asadero de Pollos Sin Rival C6
Café Tortuga (see 6)
12 Pizzería Bella Selva 2 B2
13 Restaurante La Isla B3
Tienda Ahimsa (see 6)

Drinking & Nightlife

14 Guayusa Lounge A2
15 La Araña Bar Coctelería B3

Entertainment

16 Discoteca La Gallera B2

The capital of Napo province, Tena was founded in 1560 and plagued by early indigenous uprisings. Jumandy, chief of the Kichwa, led a fierce but unsuccessful revolt against the Spaniards in 1578. The anniversary of the town's foundation is celebrated on November 15 with live music and community events.

Sights & Activities

On a clear day it's sometimes possible to see Volcán Sumaco looming from the jungle 50km away. To imbibe the Tena vibe, take a turn along the inviting *malecón* (waterfront) which runs east and west along the banks of the Río Tena for a few blocks. Tena's newer (southernmost) footbridge, connecting across to Parque Amazónico, has a futuristic-looking mirador (viewing tower). Cross the river on this one; come back on the old footbridge, just north. Market days are Friday and Saturday.

Parque Amazónico La Isla ZOO

(btwn Ríos Pano & Tena; 8am-5pm) FREE Take the snazzy new footbridge part-way across the river to this 27-hectare island. There's a self-guided trail whisking you past labeled local plants and animal enclosures, including those of tapirs and monkeys. It's worth the clamber up to this urban park's lofty mirador to see Tena's rather stunning surrounding terrain.

White-Water Rafting

Tena is Ecuador's white-water rafting center. However, mining around the town is forcing operators to take groups further away to find unspoiled river. Trips range from gentle scenic floats to exhilarating rapids and first descents in gorgeous landscapes. Serious outfitters will have everything you would expect – decent life jackets, professional guides, first-aid supplies and throw bags. Many use safety kayakers who paddle alongside the boat in case of capsizings. It's worth signing up with one of these outfits. Kayakers can hire guides or arrange for transportation and put-ins in town.

One of the most popular local trips is to the upper Río Napo (called Jatunyacu locally, which means 'big water' in Kichwa), where rafters tackle a fun 25km stretch of Class III+ white water, suitable for all levels. For more excitement, the Río Misahuallí has wild Class IV+ rapids and includes a portage around a waterfall.

★ **River People** RAFTING

(099-544-0234, 06-286-5197; http://riverpeopleecuador.com; Vla a Inchillaqu) Run by the Dent family from England, River People is a top-notch outfitter that consistently gets rave reviews. River People has been pioneering rafting on previously untried rivers throughout the region, including the remote Río Hollín, where groups of experienced rafters camp overnight in pristine rainforest. One popular tour is the challenging two-day expedition to the nearby Río Quijos, site of the 2005 World Rafting Championships.

Guides have a minimum of eight years' experience and speak English. Jungle camping, kayaking instruction and tailor-made trips are possible.

Caveman Adventures RAFTING

(06-288-8394; www.cavemanecuador.com; Orellana 666, near Tarquí; 8am-7pm Mon-Sat) The name is the only bad thing about this adventure outfit. Kayaking novices get some of the best instruction there is at this outfitter with

US-trained guides. They also run memorable multiday trips for kayakers and rafters of all levels, down classic white-water stretches like the Jatunyacu ($60) and the Jondachi and Hollín ($80).

Raft Amazonía RAFTING
(☎06-288-6853; www.raftamazonia.com) Run by a local indigenous family, Raft Amazonía offers rafting and kayaking trips with friendly, experienced, licensed guides (who get excellent reviews from guests). They also run caving and cultural tours from their base in Tena.

Ríos Ecuador RAFTING
(☎099-680-4046, 06-288-6727; www.riosecuador.com; Tarqui) This long-standing outfitter doesn't have quite the reputation it did but offers wide-ranging rafting trips for all tastes. Most popular is the day trip ($65) down a 25km stretch of the Jatunyacu. Another trip suitable for beginners is a one-day excursion to the Ríos Toachi and Blanco, boasting some of Ecuador's longest white-water runs ($87). Many other river trips are also available.

Guides mostly speak English. Be aware that the Tena office is usually closed so booking online is the best bet.

AquaXtreme RAFTING
(☎06-288-8746; www.axtours.com; Orellana, near Pano; ⌚9am-6:30pm Tue-Sat) This operator, based on the Tena riverfront, has full-day trips on the Jatunyacu ($63) and the Misahuallí ($75), plus plenty of other destinations. The company also offers horseback riding, caving, kayaking and biking trips. Guides speak English.

Tours

Juan Garces JUNGLE TOURS
(☎098-461-4199, 06-306-2907; joseluisgarces2002@yahoo.com) Enterprising guide Juan Garces speaks fluent English, French and Kichwa and, more critically, knows the jungle hereabouts like the back of his hand. Kayaking, chocolate-making and jungle hikes are all available, as are multiday adventures downriver towards the Peruvian frontier. Prices start around $50 per person per day – more, naturally, if you stay at his Sacha Sisa Lodge out past Misahuallí.

Pakay Tours JUNGLE TOURS
(☎06-284-7449, 099-033-5295; www.ecuadorpakaytours.com) Based out of Hostal Pakay (p230), English- and German-speaking guide Tony Altamirano specializes in rainforest hikes and cultural immersion experiences with rainforest communities. Want to use a blowgun or taste lemon ants? Look no further. Further-afield tours, such as to Parque Nacional Cuyabeno, are available.

Gary Garces & Michelle Klein JUNGLE TOURS
(☎099-549-8228, 099-549-8118, in the US 480-264-8470) The husband-and-wife duo behind hostel La Casa Blanca, Gary and Michelle, also offer interesting tours. Gary has more than a decade's guiding experience and does several off-beat trips around Tena; one of their most popular is a jungle adventure (from $180) featuring seven activities over two days, sleeping in cabins with hot water, comfortable mosquito-netted beds and great food.

Sleeping

★**Hostal Pakay** HOSTEL $
(☎06-284-7449; above Av Perimetral; incl breakfast dm $13, s/d $26/34/48, without bathroom $22/30/45; P 📶) Surrounded by woodland, a stay at the ecofriendly Hostal Pakay is more like a jungle lodge experience than a town hostel experience. Wooden rooms are clean and tidy, kayakers and backpackers love the chill-out terrace, and the on-site tour agency is increasingly renowned. Much of the breakfast fruit is grown in the lush grounds.

It's a steep 20-minute hike up from the bus station so get a taxi here.

★**La Casa del Abuelo** GUESTHOUSE $
(☎06-288-8926, 06-288-6318; www.tomas-lodge.com; Calle Mera 628; s/d/tr $22/34/50; P ❄ @ 📶) This nicely refurbished colonial-style home, tucked away on a quiet street, easily maintains its place among the city's elite digs. Public areas are full of eclectic arts and crafts; rooms themselves have a cozy, homey feel with high ceilings, adobe walls and wood floors. Free coffee; breakfast costs $3 to $5 extra. Ask the owners about their rural guesthouse on the river, 5km away.

La Casa Blanca HOSTEL $
(☎099-549-8228, 06-231-0456; www.casablancatena.com; cnr Churiyuyo & Ishpingo; dm/s/d $12/19/38; 📶) Situated 1.5km northwest of the center, laid-back, spick-and-span Casa Blanca aims to provide weary backpackers with everything they wanted to find in a hostel elsewhere, but couldn't. The wonderfully equipped kitchen, spacious rooms

hung with Otavalo tapestries, 'honesty system' for chilled beers, special boot-wash area, washer-dryer, in-house tour agency... Gary and Michelle have it nailed.

There are discounts for weekly and monthly stays. La Casa Blanca is in the Aeropuerto Dos neighborhood north of the old airstrip: taxi drivers mostly now know it.

Brisa del Río GUESTHOUSE **$**
(☎06-288-6444, 06-288-6208; Orellana, near Pano; per person with/without bathroom $15/9; ❄📶🏊) Rarely are backpacker places in the jungle so clean and well located. Right on the riverfront, there is also a kitchen and a miniscule plunge pool. Shared bathrooms are very clean, while rooms with private bathrooms also have air-con.

Hostal Limoncocha HOSTEL **$**
(☎06-284-6303; www.hostallimoncocha.com; Paso Urco, btwn Av del Chofer & Rosales; dm $7, s/d $14/26, without bathroom $9/16; P❄@📶) Backpackers frequent this spot on the hill, 300m southeast from the bus station, because they're the cheapest beds worth having in Tena, because of the great views, and because this is a time-tested traveler hangout. Rooms are chipper, with clean private bathrooms. Breakfast ($3) is available, and there's a guest kitchen and on-site tour operator.

Hostal Los Yutzos HOTEL **$$**
(☎06-288-6717; yutzos@outlook.com; Rueda 190; s/d incl breakfast $27/46, with air-con $40/54; P❄📶) The spacious, comfortable rooms and tranquil riverside setting make this Tena's best accommodation option. There's a tiled balcony with wooden loungers, overlooking the gurgling river. The garden is thick with green and hammocks. Be sure to book ahead at the weekend and during holidays.

Hotel Pumarosa HOTEL **$$**
(☎096-759-8667, 06-288-6320; Orellana, near 15 de Noviembre; s/d from $15/30; P❄📶🏊) Inviting rooms at Hotel Pumarosa have high wooden ceilings, large armoires and modern white-tiled bathrooms. There is reliable hot water, cable TV, lush gardens and billiards in the open-air lobby. The disco and roller-rink next door mean loud weekend nights, but, on the plus side, guests enjoy free entry. The most intriguing tour possibility is to visit the cacao plantations that produce Kallari chocolate.

Hotel Cristian's Palace HOTEL **$$**
(☎06-288-6047; hotelcristianpalace@gmail.com; Mera; per person incl breakfast $25; P❄📶🏊) The swishest spot in town is on the large side by local standards. Rooms are spacious with good bathrooms, TV and writing tables in most, and surround a murky pool, a sauna and gym, which are all free for guests to use. Insider tip: ask for a mini-suite, which costs the same as a standard room.

Eating

★Café Tortuga INTERNATIONAL **$**
(Orellana; snacks $1.50-5; ⏲7am-7:30pm Mon-Sat, to 1pm Sun; 📶) Everyone in town seems to drop by this super-popular Swiss-run riverfront joint, whether it's for the wide choice of breakfasts, delicious *batidos* (fruit shakes) or range of salads, sandwiches and cakes. Tortuga is especially popular with backpackers, and is a great place to meet other travelers. There is a good book exchange.

Tienda Ahimsa VEGETARIAN **$**
(☎06-301-9172; almuerzos $4; ⏲11am-9pm Mon-Sat) The lovely owner of this excellent vegetarian eatery prepares most dishes to order, so unless you request the daily *almuerzo* (set lunch), don't be in a hurry. You'll want to savor the mostly vegan, wholly delicious *arepas,* burritos, veggie burgers and desserts. She doesn't have a formal menu, so ask what's being served the day(s) you visit – vegans, note: desserts sometimes incorporate dairy.

Restaurante La Isla PIZZA **$**
(☎06-287-1026; cnr Orellana & Pano; dishes $4-9; ⏲10am-10pm; 📶👪) Right on the *malecón* across from the southern footbridge, this friendly, open-air spot serves up good, topping-laden pizzas, chicken wings, sandwiches and juices.

Asadero de Pollos Sin Rival CHICKEN **$**
(15 de Noviembre, btwn San Miguel & Av del Chofer; quarter/half/whole roasted chicken $3/6/12; ⏲10am-3:30pm) Believe the translation of this place (chicken without rival) if you believe no other sign in Ecuador. It's only open lunchtimes – until that roast chicken is gone.

Pizzería Bella Selva 2 PIZZA **$$**
(mains $3-18; ⏲5-10pm) The pizza here is just about as good as you'll get in the Oriente and as a riverfront melting pot of local families, businessmen and tourists it's the most

buzzing place for dinner. Oh, and their salsa: aiaiai!

Drinking & Entertainment

Dance floors pulse on weekends, so slip into the mix. Discos open from approximately 8pm to 2am Sunday to Wednesday, and to about 3am Thursday to Saturday.

Guayusa Lounge LOUNGE
(☎06-288-8561; Sucre, near Olmedo; cocktails $4; ⏰4-11pm Tue-Sat) Inside or out, the ambiance at this hip spot is invitingly chill. The interior, brightened by huge picture windows, feels spacious and jungle-industrial, while the outdoor patio in enclosed in greenery and the sounds of chirping frogs. Come here for cocktails concocted with Amazonian herbs like *guayusa* and *ishpingo*, and stay for the refreshingly different rice bowls, salads and appetizers.

La Araña Bar Coctelería BAR
(Main Plaza; ⏰5pm-midnight Mon-Thu, to 2am Fri & Sat) The most popular place for drinking and carousing is the raucous 'spider,' across the river at the end of the footbridge. It's busy nightly, and rammed with locals and travelers on the weekend. Expect a hangover.

Discoteca La Gallera DISCO
(Orellana; $2) Found next to Hotel Pumarosa, La Gallera has a fun but grown-up atmosphere, even though there's an attached roller-rink. Hotel guests enter for free.

Information

Banco del Austro (15 de Noviembre) This bank has an ATM.

Banco Pichincha (15 de Noviembre) Almost opposite the fuel station; has the most reliable ATMs.

Hospital (☎06-284-6786, 06-284-6755; 15 de Noviembre, btwn Eloy Alfaro & Ambato) South of town on the road to Puerto Napo.

Police Station (☎06-288-6101; main plaza)

Post Office (cnr Olmedo & Moreno) Northwest of the old footbridge.

Tourism Office (iTur; ☎06-288-8046; Rueda; ⏰7:30am-5pm Mon-Fri) The friendly staff here will do their best to help you with whatever you need. Some staff members speak English.

Getting There & Away

The **bus terminal** (Terminal Terrestre; 15 de Noviembre) is at the southern end of town. **Café Tortuga** (p231) keeps a very useful complete list of current bus times. Services to all destinations are frequent.

Destination	Cost ($)	Duration (hr)
Ambato	6.25	4
Baños	5.25	3
Coca	8.75	4
Puyo	3.15	2½
Quito via Baeza	7.50	5

Getting Around

Local buses to **Archidona** ($0.25, 15 minutes) leave every 30 minutes during the day from the west side of the market, near the **old airstrip**. Other local buses leave from **15 de Noviembre**, near the terminal, to Ahuano ($1.50, one hour), Misahuallí ($0.75, 45 minutes) and Santa Rosa/San Pedro ($3.75, three hours).

There's a large **gas station** along Av 15 de Noviembre on the way from the center to the bus terminal.

Misahuallí

☎06 / POP 5127

Once an important transit point for travelers arriving by river from Coca, Misahuallí (mee-sah-wah-*yee*) sank into obscurity when the Loreto road connecting Coca to Tena was built. Positioned between two major rivers – at the literal end of the road – the town has a lovely sandy beach, a famous cadre of monkeys adept at swiping sunglasses from visitors, and little else.

However, the region's **Aeropuerto Jumandy** actually means that for those flying from Quito, you'll likely hit Misahuallí before you reach Tena. And many prefer this diminutive but spirited village over Tena as a base for exploring the Río Napo and its jungle. Traveller facilities are good, with several key tour operators stationed here.

Be aware that the surrounding area has been colonized for decades, which means wildlife has diminished greatly.

Sights

Sinchi Warmi CULTURAL CENTRE
(☎06-306-3009; www.sinchiwarmiamazonlodge.com; meals $3-10, cabañas from $13) Founded, built and run by a group of Kichwa women, this community center introduces visitors to their culture through activities such as jungle walks, traditional dance performances and chocolate-making demonstrations. Enjoy Kichwa cuisine and consider staying

Around Tena

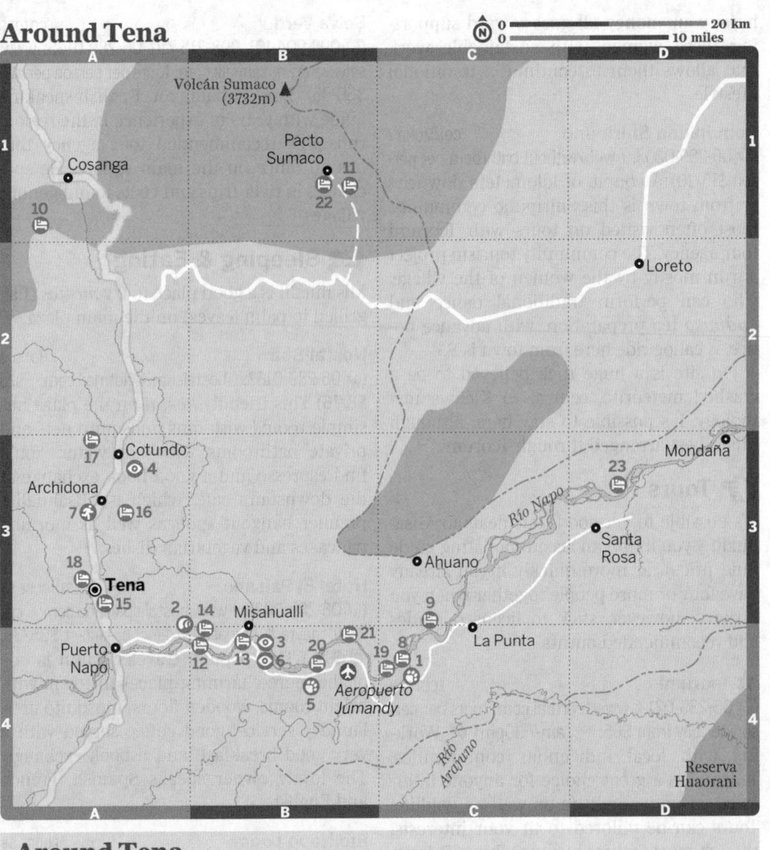

Around Tena

Sights

1 AmaZOOnico C4
2 Cascada Las Latas A3
3 Comunidad Shiripuno B4
4 Cuevas de Jumandí A3
5 Reserva Biológica Jatun Sacha B4
6 Sinchi Warmi B4

Activities, Courses & Tours

Ecoselva Pepe Tapia .... (see 3)
Gary Garces & Michelle Klein .... (see 18)
Pakay Tours .... (see 15)
7 River People A3
Selva Verde .... (see 3)
Teorumi .... (see 3)

Sleeping

8 Anaconda Lodge C4
9 Arajuno Jungle Lodge C3
10 Cabañas San Isidro A1
11 Casita B1
12 Cotococha Lodge B4
13 France-Amazonia B4
14 Hamadryade Lodge B4
15 Hostal Limoncocha A3
Hostal Pakay .... (see 15)
Hostal Shaw .... (see 3)
16 Hostería Orchids Paradise A3
Hotel El Paisano .... (see 3)
17 Huasquila Lodge A3
18 La Casa Blanca A3
19 La Casa del Suizo C4
Liana Lodge .... (see 1)
Misahuallí Amazon Lodge .... (see 3)
20 Reserva Biológica Jatun Sacha Cabins B4
Río Napo Lodge .... (see 3)
21 Sacha Sisa Lodge B4
22 Wildsumaco Lodge B1
23 Yachana Lodge D3

Eating

El Bijao .... (see 3)
El Jardín .... (see 3)

Transport

Compañía Trans Dumbiki .... (see 3)

here; your money all goes toward supporting these women with sustainable work that allows them to continue a traditional lifestyle.

Comunidad Shiripuno COMMUNITY

(☎06-289-0203; r with/without bathroom per person $15/10) A couple of kilometers downriver from town is this Shiripuno community, most often visited on tours with Teorumi tour agency. The community tourism project is run mostly by the women of the village, who can perform traditional dance and *guayusa* tea preparation, with advance notice. A canoe ride here from town is $5.

On site is a huge rock believed to be a crashed meteorite, central to Kichwa mythology. It's possible to stay here, although this is best arranged through Teorumi.

Tours

It's possible to get good tour deals in Misahuallí – you'll find an accommodating guide (and price) far more quickly if you already have four or more people together when you arrive – however, stick to licensed guides and recommended outfits.

★Teorumi ECOTOUR

(☎06-289-0213; www.teorumi.com; tours per person per day from $65; ⌚7am-7:30pm) Working with local indigenous communities, Teorumi is a great choice for anyone interested in native culture as well as wildlife. Tours can be tailored to fit your interests, though most feature bird-watching, fishing, medicinal plant demonstrations and jungle hikes. Other activities include panning for gold and horseback riding. English and French are spoken. The office is on the main square.

Their nearby Shiripuno Lodge is often a base for activities.

Teorumi's owner is one of Ecuador's foremost authorities on snakes and their venom, and has helped create several antidotes.

Ecoselva Pepe Tapia ECOTOUR

(☎099-789-8900, 06-289-0019; http://ecoselvapepetapia.com; tours per day from $45) Pepe Tapia González takes visitors on enjoyable one- to 10-day tours, including nature walks and canoe trips, with overnight stays at his rustic lodge or jungle camps. He speaks fluent English, has a biology background and is knowledgeable about plants, birds and insects. Ecoselva is located on the main square.

Selva Verde ECOTOUR

(☎098-904-101, 998-215-710, 06-289-0165; www.selvaverde-misahualli.com; tours per person per day $60-95) Luís Zapata, an English-speaking guide with years of experience in the region, runs this recommended tour agency that has an office on the main square. He specializes in river trips and visits to indigenous villages.

Sleeping & Eating

Misahuallí is a good place to try *maitos* (fish grilled in palm leaves) on the main plaza.

Hostal Shaw HOTEL $

(☎06-289-0163; hostalshaw@hotmail.com; s/d $8/16) This friendly *hostal* on the plaza has simple rooms with fans, mosquito nets and private bathrooms with hot water. You'll find espresso and a good book exchange at the downstairs cafe, which is Misahuallí's premier hangout spot, as well as morning pancakes and vegetarian dishes.

Hotel El Paisano GUESTHOUSE $$

(☎06-289-0027; www.hostalelpaisano.com; cnr Rivadeneyra & Tandalia; s/d incl breakfast $25/35; P@🛜) This popular traveler haunt is one of the more charming places in town, with bright rooms, wooden floors, mosquito nets, laundry service, good coffee served with a very good breakfast, and a book exchange. The lovely owner speaks Spanish, French and English.

Río Napo Lodge LODGE $$

(☎06-289-0071; www.rionapolodge.com; s/d incl breakfast $30/60; 🛜) Run by a local indigenous family that also grows cacao, this peaceful lodge on the south side of the Río Napo makes for a quiet retreat outside of town. Rooms are in wooden duplex cabins, with hammock-slung terraces and a lovely garden setting.

France-Amazonia GUESTHOUSE $$

(☎06-289-0009; www.france-amazonia.com; Av Principal; r per person incl breakfast $18-24; P🛜🏊) Just outside of town on the lip of the river, shady thatched huts surround a sparkling pool and sandy fire pit. Beds are small but rooms are sizeable and pleasantly rustic. The garden offers plenty of nooks for enjoying the pleasant climate and the sound of the river – which can be accessed via a small trail.

Misahuallí Amazon Lodge HOTEL $$$

(☎06-289-0063, in Quito 02-224-9651; www.misahualliamazonlodge.com; s/d incl breakfast from

$80/120;) A fussy, manicured version of a jungle camp, this hotel has a resort feel and is popular with Ecuadorian families. It has a great position overlooking the river and Misahuallí (from which you have to take the complimentary canoe to get here). Newer hotel-style rooms are sophisticated, while the stilted cabins are rather aged.

El Bijao ECUADORIAN $
(mains $5; lunch & dinner) On the plaza, this is a great place to try the *maito* – an Ecuadorian jungle specialty where *tilapia* (river fish) or chicken are wrapped in a jungle leaf and grilled, then served with rice, yuca and *guayusa* (Amazonian herbal tea). Stop by around lunch for the freshest ones.

El Jardín ECUADORIAN $$
(06-289-0219; www.eljardinmisahualli.com; mains $10-15; noon-4pm & 6-10pm Mon-Sat;) Over the bridge up on the road to La Punta, El Jardín is a beautiful addition to the local dining scene. In a flower-festooned garden, you can dine on the huge platters of pricey but well-prepared meat, *tilapia* (river fish) and seafood.

Information

There is no bank or post office in Misahuallí. Carry your passport on buses, boats and tours in the region, and have a stash of small bills for boat travel.

Getting There & Away

Buses leave from the plaza approximately every hour during daytime; the last bus is at 6pm. The main destination is Tena ($1, one hour). There's a daily 8.30am bus to Quito ($6, five hours) that leaves from the main square.

You can also catch a **Compañía Trans Dumbiki** (06-289-0051) *camioneta* on the plaza for nearby destinations as well as to Tena and beyond.

The need for passenger canoes has dried up thanks to the Tena–Coca (Loreto) road and others along the Río Napo. You can arrange trips with boat drivers on the beach for about $30 per hour, but nearby agencies offer better deals.

Upper Río Napo

06

The Río Napo gains momentum south of Tena and just before Misahuallí. It widens and quickens as it passes nature reserves, small jungle communities, oil rigs and lodges. Unfortunately, road construction has altered wildlife habits for good, and visitors will see fewer animals and birds here now than deeper in the jungle.

West of Misahuallí

When you leave Tena behind and hit the river bridge at Puerto Napo, the mass of churning water below you is the beginning of the Río Napo proper. These early stages of the mighty waterway flow east past surprisingly luxurious lodges, while good roads run along both banks as far as Misahuallí.

The northern shore road, trawled about hourly with buses, passes **Cascada Las Latas**, an impressive waterfall more or less half-way between Puerto Napo and Misahuallí (and 15 minutes' drive from either).

Sleeping

★ **Hamadryade Lodge** BOUTIQUE HOTEL $$$
(098-590-9992, 098-822-5413; www.hamadryade-lodge.com; d incl breakfast & dinner from $198;) Perched on a hillside a few kilometers upriver of Misahuallí and accessed by the road along the northern shore, this stylish, ecofriendly French-owned jungle lodge departs from the standard look with sleek, contemporary decor. Each private bungalow has a balcony with jungle views; there's a fantastic pool and lounging area perched over the rolling landscape; traditional massage is also available.

With just five bungalows, this a great place for travelers to chill out in style. The deluxe bungalow, which sleeps up to six people, is perfect for families. Multiday packages include excursions to Reserva Biológica Jatun Sacha, local indigenous communities and AmaZOOnico (p237).

Cotococha Lodge LODGE $$$
(in Quito 02-244-1721, 02-512-3358; www.cotococha.com; d 3 nights incl full board from $550) This is the first lodge you see on the nascent Río Napo, 17km from Tena along the southern shore. It's a quiet collection of 22 thatched-roofed bungalows, connected by winding river-rock pathways in a lush setting. Oil lanterns create a romantic glow, and cabins have hot water and private river-facing decks (though no electricity).

English-speaking guides lead walks and trips to waterfalls; tubing, rafting and visits to local communities can be arranged. It's a good way to get into the rainforest without having to take a long river trip.

Getting There & Away

Lodges here can arrange private transport, for an additional fee. Tena buses heading to Misahuallí ($0.75, 45 minutes) depart almost hourly throughout the day.

Reserva Biológica Jatun Sacha

The 25-sq-km **Reserva Biológica Jatun Sacha** ($6) biological station and rainforest reserve is located on the south shore of the Río Napo, 23km east of Puerto Napo. It is run by **Fundación Jatun Sacha** (☎02-331-8156, 02-243-2240, 099-490-8265; www.jatunsacha.org; Psje Eugenio de Santillan 34-248, Quito; $6), an Ecuadorian nonprofit organization that was formed to promote rainforest research, conservation and education.

Many new species have been discovered here since the 1990s, including the butterfly *Passiflora jatunsachensis,* and biodiversity is very high for the area, with an estimated 1500 types of plants in a single hectare.

With neighboring areas being rapidly cleared for logging and agriculture, the biodiversity of Jatun Sacha is precious. Besides counting and tracking local species, the foundation develops reforestation initiatives and agro-forestry alternatives with local farming communities and indigenous groups.

Biostation workers and other guests stay in rustic **cabins** (per person incl full board $30) with shared bathrooms just up from the entrance on the Misahuallí–La Punta road. Water is solar-heated and meals are included. The restaurant by the office at the reserve entrance serves healthy Ecuadorian and international meals.

Go bird-watching or meander through the surrounding forest trails, then check out the plant conservation center and botanical garden. You can also borrow a climbing harness and scale the vertigo-inducing 30m observation tower in the middle of the reserve. There are discounts for groups and students.

Getting There & Away

To get to Jatun Sacha from Tena, take an Ahuano or Santa Rosa bus and ask the driver to drop you at the main entrance/research station. A taxi to the entrance from Misahuallí is $5, but for buses, you'll need to first make it 2km up to the junction of the main Tena–Ahuano road (the road along the southern shore of the Río Napo).

La Punta, Ahuano & Around

Splintering off the Tena–Santa Rosa road is the turning to La Punta and Ahuano, along which you'll also find the new Aeropuerto Jumandy, which serves the Misahuallí and Tena area. The river port of La Punta is the usual colorful microcosm of Oriente life and has a couple of basic riverfront restaurants.

From here the main destination is Ahuano, a sleepy village across the river. While it's still in secondary, deforested jungle, being accessible only by river makes Ahuano feel like the start of a remote rainforest adventure, and it is indeed a relatively easy way to get assimilated into jungle culture.

CHICHA, THE BREAKFAST OF CHAMPIONS

Before you could get a Coke and a smile in the Amazon Basin, there was *chicha* – not the boiled highland version, but a highly portable nutritional drink. Stored as a paste wrapped in leaves, *chicha* materializes when you add water.

The recipe is simple – *chicha* is yuca (cassava) or chonta palm masticated by women (and only women). For millennia, *chicha* has been a prime source of nutrition and vitamins for remote communities. It's an important staple in the jungle, where people eat very little and drink up to 6L a day. When fresh, *chicha* tastes mild and yogurt-like, but as time passes, it becomes more alcoholic as bacteria from the saliva turn carbohydrates into simple sugars. The older the *chicha,* the more potent it is. The flavor depends on the individual who made it; each woman's unique bacteria creates a distinctive taste.

Really terrible *chicha* is considered a portent of something bad – but will something bad happen to you, the visitor, if you try it? Contrary to what you might think, problems result not from the saliva (which starts the fermentation process but only constitutes a tiny percentage of the finished product) but from unfiltered river water that may have been mixed with the paste. However, very few people experience trouble after tasting just a sip. A highlight of many visits to local communities in Oriente is being able to see *chicha* being made and tasting it afterwards, too. Enjoy!

Sights

AmaZOOnico

WILDLIFE RESERVE

(www.amazoonico.org; adult/child $4/2.50) You're guaranteed to see all manner of jungle wildlife at AmaZOOnico, a well-known animal rehabilitation center located on the grounds of Selva Viva, a 17-sq-km reserve of primary forest on Río Arajuno, a narrow tributary of the Napo about 3km east of Ahuano. A Swiss-Kichwa couple founded the center in 1993 to care for confiscated or displaced rainforest animals.

While it's great to be able to see toucans, capybaras, monkeys and boas close up, the circumstances betray an ugly reality. These animals have been displaced because illegal traffickers sold them for quick cash or their habitats were destroyed. Some of the stories you'll hear from the excellent tours are heartbreaking – animals abandoned in hotel rooms, rare birds whose owners died, and severely traumatized 'pets' intercepted during trafficking attempts. Some healthy animals are released back into the rainforest, but an unfortunate number of animals arrive too domesticated to be re-released.

Spanish- and English-speaking volunteers, who know the animals intimately, lead all tours. The center is always looking for volunteers (who must pay $250 per month for living expenses), especially veterinarians, for a two-month-minimum stay.

Get in touch via the website to give advance warning if you want to visit; phone reception is unreliable, and there is no phone number to call.

Sleeping

★ Anaconda Lodge

JUNGLE LODGE $$$

(06-301-7723; www.anacondalodgeecuador.com; Isla Anaconda; per person incl full board from $110;) Run by the warmly welcoming Chilean-Colombian couple Francisco and Silvia, Anaconda Lodge is their jungle lodge dream come true. Screened wooden cabins on stilts are set within neat garden environs, with an open-air restaurant serving as social hub. Visiting their neighboring Kichwa community, wildlife-watching in the jungle, rafting and tubing are all on the agenda on this tranquil Napo island.

Healthy, delicious meals – which can accommodate dietary restrictions – night walks and excursions round out the experience. Dog lovers are especially welcome, as three giant German shepherds are a roving part of the family here.

Yachana Lodge

LODGE $$$

(02-252-3777 in Quito; www.yachana.com; s/d 3 nights incl full board from $567/810) Situated on a 2500-acre nature reserve, Yachana Lodge is the newer iteration of a long-running lodge along the Río Napo. A training center educates local residents for sustainable career opportunities; revenues from the lodge help support the training center. It's a win-win, as guests are exposed to the wonders of jungle and river, as well as introduced to indigenous culture.

Sacha Sisa Lodge

JUNGLE LODGE $$$

(098-461-4199, 06-306-2907; www.sachasisaamazon.com; d/t incl breakfast $100/150;) Sacha Sisa Lodge, run by Tena guide Juan Garces, sits on a river cliff – aside from the great views, it is also mercifully fresh and mosquito-free. Guests generally stay overnight as part of Juan's highly recommended tours involving kayak trips and intrepid jungle hikes.

Arajuno Jungle Lodge

JUNGLE LODGE $$$

(098-268-2287; www.arajuno.com; 2 nights incl full board per person $399) If small and out of the way is your thing, check out former Peace Corps volunteer Thomas Larson's Arajuno Jungle Lodge, slung on a bend of the Río Arajuno. A handful of hillside cabins are snug and screened and have solar-powered hot water. The thatched main lodge has a sprawling wooden deck and dining area perched over the river.

Guests can roam the 80 hectares of forest, hike, canoe and visit nearby AmaZOOnico.

The lodge works with local communities to develop new food sources and spread information about health and nutrition. Volunteers are accepted for stays of three to six months. The chef cooks up locally inspired gourmet food, such as smoked *cachama maitos* (fish grilled in palm leaves) and *tortilla de yuca* (cassava bread). Grown-up kids will love the rope swing that launches into the river. Services are in Spanish and English.

Liana Lodge

JUNGLE LODGE $$$

(06-301-7702; www.selvaviva.ec; per person incl full board 2/3/4 nights $194/291/388, single supplement per night $16) Each of Liana Lodge's nine cabins has two double rooms, a hot shower and no electricity. The carefree riverside atmosphere revolves around bonfires, walks through the woods and a round bar overlooking the river. Packages include meals, tours (including lessons on making *chicha* and building a balsa raft) and canoe transport from Puerto Barantilla. Reserve in advance online.

Ask about **Runi Huasi**, an indigenous-run lodge nearby that's managed by the Liana owners. Kichwa, English, Spanish, German and French are spoken here.

To get here, take a Tena bus to Santa Rosa ($2, one hour) and get off at Puerto Barantilla. Walk down the dirt road to the river, where a canoe will be waiting to pick you up.

La Casa del Suizo HOTEL $$$

(☎02-250-9504 in Quito, 800-706-2215 in the US; www.lacasadelsuizo.com; s/d incl full board $181/290; ❄📶🏊) Most visitors come to stay at the Swiss-owned **La Casa del Suizo**, a walled fortress on the Río Napo that offers a pampered glimpse of the jungle. A maze of covered boardwalks links thatched hotel-style rooms that have high ceilings, pale adobe walls, electricity, fans, hot showers, and hammock-hung balconies, most of which boast river views.

Transport to the lodge from La Punta or Ahuano is not included.

Getting There & Away

Bus services from Tena run eight times a day to La Punta or Ahuano ($1.50; one hour), about 28km east of Puerto Napo; you can sometimes catch a *colectivo* back to Tena for the same price as the bus. From La Punta, you can catch a boat to your Río Napo destination – if your stop happens to be Ahuano, the bus will motor onto a barge for the five-minute chug across the river before continuing on to Ahuano and villages beyond.

Puyo

☎03 / POP 36,560

Puyo is an enigma: whereas most towns make efforts to spruce up their centers and leave the outskirts stagnating, this place does the direct opposite. While it retains some vitality as the capital of the Pastaza province, overall this is just a built-up town with little to attract you. Regardless, anyone traveling in southern Oriente is quite likely to pass through. Dense green jungle flourishes close around the town's edges, and – thanks in part to travelers from Baños making the hour-long drive down to do a rainforest reconnoiter – accommodations are good and plentiful, with some of the best jungle tour operators located here.

Sights

Parque Etnobotánico Omaere PARK

(www.fundacionomaere.org; adult/child $3/1.50; ⏲9am-5pm Tue-Sun) Less than 1km north of the city center, this ethnobotanical park offers one- to two-hour guided tours (included in admission fee) of rainforest plants and indigenous dwellings, by mostly indigenous guides. The park is run by Shuar plant expert Teresa Shiki and her biologist husband, Chris Canaday, a font of knowledge about everything from jungle plants to ecological dry toilets.

Teresa helped found and plant the park and prepares natural medicine.

Get here by following Loja north of town for about 300m until you reach a gas station on the left. Turn right and follow the road right to arrive at the park entrance, across a footbridge over the river and past the El Jardín hotel (p240). To return, a beautiful trail (called the *paseo turístico*) continues past Omaere for 1.7km along the river to the Puyo–Tena road, where you can flag down a bus back to town every 20 minutes, or return along the trail.

Volcán El Altar VOLCANO

Early risers may see the jagged white teeth of Volcán El Altar (5319m), the fifth-highest mountain in Ecuador, about 50km southwest. On clear days look southwest to see Volcán Sangay (5230m).

Paseo de los Monos PARK

(☎03-303-0801, 099-474-0070; www.losmonos.org; adult/child $3/1.50; ⏲8am-5pm) At Paseo de los Monos you can see a variety of rescued animals, including six kinds of monkeys, turtles and birds. Some animals are caged, while others run free. For an extra fee, guides lead four-hour walks into the surrounding jungle to see more of the center's animals. Volunteer opportunities are available, with a minimum commitment of one week (per week $130).

Jardín Botánico las Orquídeas GARDENS

(☎03-253-0305; www.jardinbotanicolasorquideas.com; $5; ⏲8am-6pm) Visitors rave about this privately run botanical garden, located 15 minutes south from Puyo on the road to Macas. Enthusiastic owner Omar Taeyu guides visitors through hills of lush foliage and fish ponds to see gorgeous plants and countless rare orchids. Call ahead to let them know you're coming.

Puyo

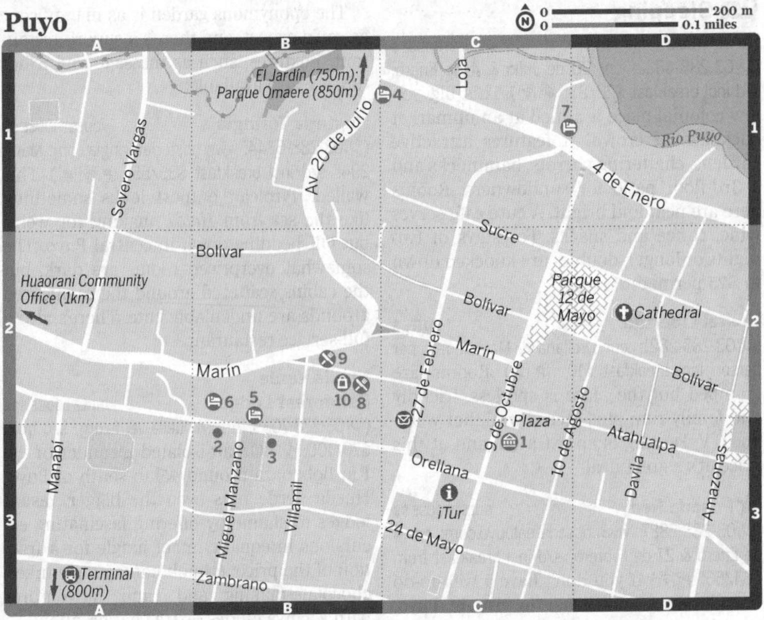

Puyo

Sights

1 Museo Etnoarqueológico C3

Activities, Courses & Tours

2 Papangu Tours B3
3 Shiran Nantu B3

Sleeping

4 Hostal Las Palmas C1
5 Hostal Libertad B2
6 Hostería Turingia B2
7 Posada Real C1

Eating

8 El Fariseo B2
9 EscoBar B2

Shopping

10 Waorani B2

Museo Etnoarqueológico MUSEUM

(☎03-288-5605; cnr Atahualpa & 9 de Octubre; $1; ⊙8am-5pm Tue-Sun) Puyo's tiny Museo Etnoarqueológico has ceramics, artifacts, models of various traditional indigenous homes and an excellent map showing the distribution of native populations.

Tours

Papangu Tours TOURS

(☎099-550-4983, 03-288-7684; info@papangutours.com.ec; Orellana, near Manzano; 3-day tour per person from $45; ⊙Mon-Fri) Papangu Tours is an indigenous-run agency with a focus on community tourism. Trips go to Sarayaku (a Kichwa community) and Cueva de los Tayos (Shuar). Guides are indigenous and speak Spanish and Kichwa, and some of the fees go to participating communities. Highly recommended by readers.

Shiran Nantu ADVENTURE

(☎03-288-5667; www.shirannantu.com; Orellana, near Villamil; per person per day from $50; ⊙8:30am-7:30pm Mon-Sat) Adventurous jungle trips with flexible itineraries. Tours involving longer boat trips are more fun, but entail a higher fee to cover petrol costs. An eight-day odyssey takes you right down the Río Curaray to the Peruvian border.

Festivals & Events

Fiestas de Fundación de Puyo CULTURAL

This week-long celebration of Puyo's founding takes place in early May.

Sleeping

Hostal Las Palmas GUESTHOUSE $
(03-288-4832; cnr 20 de Julio & 4 de Enero; s/d incl breakfast $22/33;) This big yellow colonial place is aimed at an upmarket backpacking crowd. It features attractive gardens, chattering parrots, hammocks and a 3rd-floor patio for sundowners. Rooms here are neat and bright. A cute cafe serves wine, coffee and snacks. For stays of two nights or longer, doubles are knocked down to $25 per night.

Hostal Libertad HOTEL $
(03-283-2821; cnr Orellana & Manzano; r per person incl breakfast $10;) Rooms are cramped but the place is spotless, friendly and family-run; plus there's wi-fi, hot water and TV. Parking is an extra $3, and at this price, it's a great deal.

★**Posada Real** GUESTHOUSE $$
(03-288-5887; www.posadarealpuyo.com; cnr 4 de Enero & 27 de Febrero; s/d incl breakfast from $34/56;) If you don't have a well-to-do Ecuadorian grandmother to visit in Puyo, staying in this immaculately kept locale is the next best thing. Only two blocks down from the main square, Posada Real enjoys a set-back location in quiet grounds. Spacious rooms have cozy reading lamps and antique furniture; most have balconies. Breakfast in the dignified cafeteria is a pleasure.

El Jardín HOTEL $$
(03-289-2253; www.eljardinpuyo.com; Paseo Turístico, Barrio Obrero; s/d incl breakfast from $46/77;) This gorgeous spot is just across the footbridge by the entrance to the Parque Omaere, 1km from the center of town. It feels more like a jungle lodge than a city hotel, with 10 rooms housed in a wooden building on two floors and decorated with local arts and crafts.

The eponymous garden is as magnificent as you'd expect, and there's a superb restaurant. Luxuries, such as massage and a hot tub, are also available.

Hostería Turingia GUESTHOUSE $$
(03-288-6344; www.hosteriaturingia.com; Marín 294; s/d incl breakfast $35/55;) This walled, Tyrolean outpost looks something like the set from *Heidi,* making for weird but OK bedding-down in central Puyo. The somewhat overpriced rooms are dark, but the cabins scattered around the manicured grounds are undeniably cute. There's also a full-service restaurant.

Huella Verde Rainforest Lodge JUNGLE LODGE $$$
(03-278-7035; http://huella-verde.org; s/d from $70/100;) On an isolated meander of the Río Bobonaza around 45km south of Puyo, Huella Verde puts even the bigger Yasuní lodges to shame by offering fascinating excursions in equally intact jungle for a fraction of the price: ethnobotanic jungle hikes, chocolate-making and canoe adventures with Kichwa guides (extra charges apply).

There is also a restaurant (mains $6-15). Two bungalows, each with private bathrooms and hammock-slung terraces, have capacity for just six – making reservations obligatory.

Head to the village of Canelos, off the Puyo–Macas road (a $25 taxi ride from Puyo), from where there's a complimentary canoe.

Eating

EscoBar ECUADORIAN $
(cnr Atahualpa & Marín; mains $4-8; 9am-late) With panache to punch its weight in Quito's coolest neighborhoods, EscoBar makes *palapas* (rustic, palm-thatched dwellings) seem chic. Sample Ecuadorian microbrews,

BUSES FROM PUYO

DESTINATION	COST ($)	DURATION (HR)
Ambato	3.65	3
Baños	2.50	1½
Coca	10.50	5-6
Guayaquil	12	8
Macas	5.60	2½
Quito	7	5½
Tena	3.25	2½

cocktails and a menu of *patacones* (fried bananas), yuca (cassava) or salads served with meat within the 2nd-floor open-sided bar-restaurant. Service is as slow as a motorless canoe heading upriver, but it's still the place to hang.

El Fariseo INTERNATIONAL $

(Atahualpa, btwn Villamil & 27 de Febrero; light mains $2-6; 7:30am-9pm Mon-Sat;) It may not look like much, but this cafe boasts one of the Oriente's few espresso machines – and knows how to use it. They serve up surprisingly delicious fare, including a very tasty *churrasco* (steak served with a fried egg). Burritos, burgers and steaks round out the menu. As do the inviting cakes.

★ **El Jardín** ECUADORIAN $$

(03-288-7770; Paseo Turístico, Barrio Obrero; mains $8-16; noon-4pm & 6-10pm Mon-Sat;) The best food in the Oriente may be at this ambient house by the river inside the charming hotel of the same name, 1km north of town. The award-winning chef-owner Sofia prepares fragrant *pollo ishpingo* (cinnamon chicken – *ishpingo* is a type of cinnamon native to the Oriente); its decadent, delicate flavors awake the palate.

Try the *lomo plancho* (grilled steak) for a tender, perfectly cooked slab among artfully arranged vegetables. Top-notch vegetarian and fresh fish dishes are other plusses.

Shopping

Waorani ARTS & CRAFTS

(Asociacion De Mujeres Waorani De La Amazonia Ecuatoriana; Atahualpa, btwn Villamil & 27 de Febrero; 9am-12:30pm & 2-6:30pm Mon-Fri) Sells artisanal crafts made by Waorani women, including jewelry, spears, hammocks, blowguns and palm string bags. Artisans receive a portion of every sale.

Information

Banco de Guayaquil (Marín, near Av 20 de Julio)

Banco del Austro (Atahualpa, near 27 de Febrero)

Hospital General Puyo (www.hgp.gob.ec; cnr 9 de Octubre & Feicán)

IESS Hospital (03-288-5378; cnr Marín & Curaray)

iTur (03-288-5122 ext 227, 03-288-5937; cnr Orellana & 27 de Febrero; 8:30am-12:30pm & 3-6pm Mon-Fri) At the town hall. Either the booth downstairs or the office upstairs will be open. There's another smaller office at the bus terminal.

Post Office (27 de Febrero)

Getting There & Away

The bus terminal is 1km southwest of town. There are several services daily to each destination.

Getting Around

A taxi ride from downtown to the bus terminal costs $1, as should all rides within the city. Small local buses go to Shell ($0.25) every 30 minutes or so from south of the market along Calle 27 de Febrero.

THE SOUTHERN ORIENTE

The southern Oriente may be the envy of its northern sister: here the jungle is wilder, and more pristine. Rivers snake through vast tracts of rainforest dotted with tiny indigenous settlements and no roads. Inaccessibility remains, for the most part, because of a lack of industry, although mining and oil exploration may change all that in the future. Most visitors come to visit indigenous tribes such as the Shuar, an adventurous pursuit that involves few creature comforts – the tourism industry has yet to bloom.

Macas

07 / POP 19,000

Bienvenidos to a jungle town with few tourist trappings: clamoring markets, *huecos* (basic hole-in-the-wall eateries) and glass-and-concrete houses are the first impressions of Macas. It gets better. A couple of good hotels and restaurants make this the best base for tours into the least-explored corners of the Ecuadorian rainforest – including opportunities to visit the Shuar and Achuar indigenous groups. The longest continuous stretch of white water in the country also lures kayakers. Untrammeled as the nearby nature might be, Macas itself is the brashly modern provincial capital of Morona-Santiago. Tribesmen wear traditional beads over Nike T-shirts, and trucks overloaded with jungle produce honk on traffic-clogged streets that keep thoughts of rivers at bay. It's raucous, and raw – but it's real.

Macas

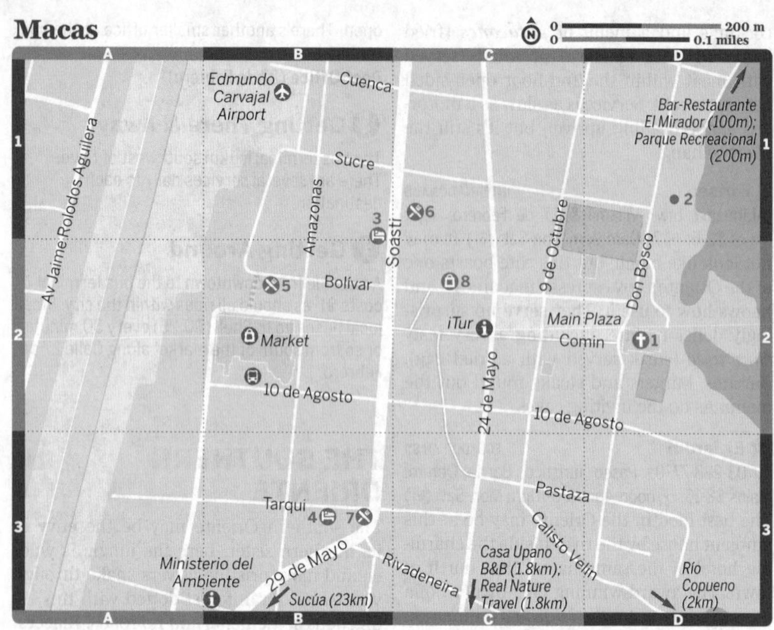

Macas

Sights
1 Our Lady of Macas Cathedral D2

Activities, Courses & Tours
2 Tsuirim Viajes D1

Sleeping
3 Hostal Casa Blanca B1
4 Hotel Sol de Oriente B3

Eating
5 JungLab B2
6 La Maravilla C1
7 Tisho's Pizzeria B3

Shopping
8 Fundación Chankuap C2

Sights

Our Lady of Macas Cathedral CHURCH

The cathedral announces itself with a Technicolor virgin, looming over a plaza resembling an elaborate skate park. Inside, a tranquil, column-free space with stained glass telling episodes from the town's past ushers you up to the tiled altar depicting Macas in front of a bellowing volcano. Miracles are attributed to the painting of the Virgin of Macas (c 1592) on the altar.

Parque Recreacional PARK

(Don Bosco & Pasaje la Randimpa; dawn-dusk)
We all feel the urge for a peaceful, green picnicking spot sometimes – particularly in Macas, where there's a dearth of them. Parque Recreacional delivers – with Río Upano views.

Volcán Sangay VOLCANO

The perfect snow-covered cone of Volcán Sangay (5230m), some 40km to the northwest, can be glimpsed on a clear day. It's Ecuador's seventh-highest mountain and one of the world's most active volcanoes; early missionaries construed it as hell.

Tours

Macas is the place to book trips into the southern Oriente. Services are not as comprehensive as those up north; then again, more unspoilt rainforest and lack of other tourists adds authenticity to adventures. Know that the Shuar do not want unguided visitors in their villages; certain villages refuse visitors entirely. It's therefore essential to travel with a professional guide who can arrange access and is sensitive to the Shuar's stance on tourism. Tena operators have more possibilities for rafting on rivers around Macas.

Tsuirim Viajes TOURS
(☎07-270-1681, 099-737-2538; leosalgado18@gmail.com; cnr Don Bosco & Sucre; tours per person per day from $60) Offering a range of jungle tours, including Shuar community visits, shamanic rituals, canyoning, caving, rafting, tubing and jungle-trekking. Owner Leo Salgado grew up in a Shuar community and knows the area well. His unique offerings include Shuar weddings or vow renewals and multiday caving expeditions with licensed, experienced guides.

Real Nature Travel BIRD-WATCHING
(☎07-270-2525, 07-252-5041; www.realnaturetravel.com; Av la Ciudad; day trip per person $120, 9-day 2-person tour $2000-3600) Birders and nature lovers should look no further: these bird-watching tours cover the Macas area, including Parque Nacional Sangay (good if you've just got a day) but usually run much further afield into the cloud forest and Andean *páramo* (high mountains). The longer you go for, the richer the sightings. Fluent English is spoken.

Festivals & Events

Chonta Festival CULTURAL
During the last week of May, the Chonta Festival is the most important Shuar celebration of the year. Shuar guides can help you garner an invitation to this grand event, where participants dance for four consecutive hours to help ferment the *chicha* (a fermented corn or yuca drink).

Sleeping

Hostal Casa Blanca HOTEL $
(☎07-270-0195; Soasti, btwn Sucre & Bolívar; r incl breakfast $15-35; ❄📶🏊) The older, most pleasant rooms surround the small pool in the garden out back, even though they face the common social area. Cheaper rooms don't have air-con. Casa Blanca remains best option in the city center.

Hotel Sol de Oriente HOTEL $
(☎07-270-2911; Tarqui, btwn Amazonas & Soasti; s/d $15/30) This six-floor place will pass in a pinch. Some rooms are pokey; all have acceptable private bathrooms. English is spoken.

★**Casa Upano B&B** GUESTHOUSE $$
(☎07-270-2674; www.casaupano.com; Av la Ciudad s/n; s/d incl breakfast $50/80; P@📶) Perhaps this is an inkling of what Macas' future could hold: a serene retreat for travelers tucked away from the city mayhem. Four balconied rooms look out on a huge fruit-tree-dotted garden which falls away towards the Río Upano. The English-speaking owners rustle up a scrumptious breakfast with super-local ingredients (ie from their garden or a nearby house).

It's mostly birders stopping by, as the owners also run great birding tours. It's 1km from the junction of Juan de la Cruz and Av la Ciudad.

Eating & Drinking

La Maravilla ECUADORIAN $
(Soasti, near Sucre; mains $3-6; ⏲4pm-midnight Mon-Sat) Easily the most charming place in town, this blue casita is all ambience, from the twinkling porch lights to the stuffed red-leather armchairs. Come to chill with *tablas* (cutting-boards) of meat and cheese and yuca (cassava) fries. There's live Andean music here at weekends, making it the town's best entertainment option, too.

The drink menu gets creative, with herbal aphrodisiacs and *hueso de chuchuguazo* (a root mixed with rum).

JungLab FUSION $$
(☎07-270-2448; cnr Bolivar & Amazonas; mains $5-15; ⏲noon-11pm Mon-Sat) Has fusion food reached Macas? It would seem so with this serendipitous, intimate spot near the bus terminal. Meat dishes are what you would expect in the Ecuadorian jungle – but done creatively. Ask about the famous *cerveza de cacao* (cocoa beer).

Tisho's Pizzeria PIZZA $$
(☎098-622-9400, 07-270-4663; cnr Tarqui & 29 de Mayo; small/large pizza $9/16; ⏲noon-11pm Tue-Thu, 2pm-midnight Fri-Sat, 11am-11pm Sun) The owner of Tisho's spent some years in the States, and here are the results: big thick-crust pizzas and even Philly cheese-steak sandwiches. Pizzas are so big they're pushed over on trolleys.

Bar-Restaurante El Mirador BAR
(☎07-270-0491, 098-515-6283; Pasaje la Randimpa & Parque Recreativo; mains $4.50-12; ⏲4-10:30pm Mon-Sat) Five blocks north of the main square, this is where Macas folks come

to chill with a couple of cold ones (including Ecuadorian microbrews, if you're into that sort of thing ... which we are) on the terrace here alongside Parque Recreacional, overlooking the mirador (viewpoint) over the Río Upano. Edible offerings include steak, pasta and salads.

Shopping

Fundación Chankuap ARTS & CRAFTS
(07-270-1176; www.chankuap.org; Bolívar, btwn Soasti & 24 de Mayo; 8:30am-1pm & 2-8:30pm Mon-Fri, 8:30am-2:30pm Sat & Sun) This foundation aids the Shuar and Achuar by selling crafts, herbal remedies and beauty products. Our personal favorite? The soap made from local cinnamon – but there's also the cinnamon itself, chocolate made from locally grown cacao and coffee beans.

Information

iTur (cnr Comín & 24 de Mayo; 8am-5pm Mon-Fri) Tiny; tries to help.

Ministerio del Ambiente (cnr Juan de la Cruz & 29 de Mayo; 8am-5pm Mon-Fri) Has basic information about Parque Nacional Sangay.

Getting There & Away

AIR

Although **TAME** (07-270-4940; Edmundo Carvajal Airport) had suspended service to Macas at the time of writing, daily flights may once again connect the small **Edmundo Carvajal Airport** (Amazonas btwn Sucre & Cuenca) with Quito.

On the flight to Quito, the left side of the plane offers the best mountain views, including those of Sangay/Cotopaxi on clear days.

BUS

The **bus station** is on Amazonas, right in the center of town.

Sucúa

07 / POP 12,620

The wide, neat streets of spread-out Sucúa mark the transition from Macas bustle to serene jungle. As – truth be told – this is a nicer town than Macas, it's worth a half-day trip out here. Old men slowly pedal bicycles as a vendor grills meats under the town's only stoplight, across from a plaza of ficus trees and chirping cicadas. The Sucúa area is home to many people of the Shuar tribe, who can be seen around town. Market day is Sunday.

Sights

Parque Botánico PARK
(07-274-0211; off Av Oriental; 8am-5pm Tue-Sat) FREE Parque Botánico, 3km southeast of central Sucúa, has a visitor interpretation center, a restaurant, a well-kept *orquideario* (orchid farm) and paths through subtropical forest. Taxis from the center of Sucúa charge $1.50.

Sleeping & Eating

Hostal Romanza HOSTAL $
(07-274-1141; Olson & Carvajal; s/d incl breakfast $15/30;) Just off the park, Hostal Romanza is a clean, safe and perfectly fine place to lay your head in Sucúa.

Tisho's Pizzeria PIZZA $
(07-274-1131; cnr Pástor Bernal & Sangurima; mains $3-7; 11am-11pm) A block off the main plaza, Tisho's Pizzeria offers American dishes inspired by the owner's years in the States, including Philly cheese-steak sandwiches and a 'Texas' pizza.

Getting There & Away

Frequent buses or pickups leave for Macas ($1, 45 minutes) from dawn until dusk at the

BUSES FROM MACAS

DESTINATION	COST ($)	DURATION (HR)
Cuenca	11	7
Gualaquiza	10	6
Guayaquil	12.50	8
Puyo	5	2.5
Quito	12	8
Riobamba	6.50	4
Sucúa	1	¾

corner of the main plaza. Others head south to Gualaquiza ($9, five hours).

Gualaquiza

07 / POP 9230 / ELEV 950M

Spread against a gently sloping hillside surrounded by dense jungle, colonial Gualaquiza is the southern Oriente's most appealing settlement. A church with a fan of turquoise-painted steps crowns the town.

Sights & Activities

Gualaquiza is just awaking from a long hibernation where tourism is concerned. The main activity is gawping at (or bathing in) the waterfalls around town. They get more impressive as you head out. First up is **Cascada Las Culebrillas**, the entrance to which is a 1.5km jaunt (or $2 taxi) along the Macas road. A further 12km along is **Caverna y Cascadas la Dolorosa** (good for bathing) and then there's the spectacular falls at **Reserva Ecológica al Bosque Paraíso**, 20km from Gualaquiza. Macas-bound buses can drop you at the entrance to these.

Ask locally for information on the excellent caving 15km west of town near the village of Nueva Tarquí (flashlights and spare batteries are essential).

Ciclos CYCLING

(07-278-0579; Orellana 4-35, near the market; 8am-6pm) Visit Ciclos, a bike shop run by Angel and Erwin Barros, for advice on outings. An excellent ride swoops through the hills to La Florida (2½ hours). It's best to have your own bike, but they may be willing to rent.

Sleeping & Eating

Posada D'León GUESTHOUSE $

(099-095-6649, 07-278-1983; cnr Gonzalo Pesántez & Domingo Comín; s/d $10/20;) Posada D'León has a clean-cut cream edifice with 10 substantial, nicely kept rooms. It's a few paces down from the main square.

Los Pinchos FAST FOOD $

(Plaza; mains $1-6; noon-midnight) On the main square, atmospheric Los Pinchos is a bar which serves the eponymous *pinchos* (skewered grilled meat and vegetables) street-side for a dollar a pop.

Information

The **tourist booth** (07-278-0109; García Moreno, near Pesantez; 9am-5pm Mon-Fri) has information about nearby Inca sites and attractions.

Getting There & Away

The bus terminal is four blocks downhill from the main square. Multiple daily buses go to Loja ($7.50, 5½ hours) via Zamora ($3.50, four hours). You can also forge through to Cuenca via Sigsig ($10, seven hours). Buses heading north go to Sucúa ($9, five hours) and Macas ($10, six hours).

Kapawi Ecolodge & Reserve

Located in the heart of Achuar wilderness, in one of the most remote parts of the Ecuadorian Amazon, **Kapawi** (310-598-3402 in the US; www.kapawi.com; s/d 3 nights incl full board from $1388/2136) offers a pristine, ecologically and culturally sound experience. Many outfits claim similar practices, but few execute like this. The lodge has received many accolades for its approach and is operated and run exclusively by the Achuar.

The lodge is made up of 18 thatched, screened cabins built on stilts over a lagoon, each with private bathroom and a balcony. Low-impact technology such as solar power, trash management, recycling, sound water treatment and biodegradable soaps are used in daily operations.

Instead of just photographing the Achuar, guests are invited to their homes and offered yuca (cassava) beer, which begins a unique cultural exchange. Small groups are accompanied by an Achuar guide and a bilingual naturalist, who work in tandem to explain the intricacies of the rainforest, both ecologically and culturally.

The lodge is just off Río Pastaza, on an oxbow lake on Río Capahuari, and is reached by canoe from the nearby landing strip. The nearest town is a 10-day walk away. Packages include all meals, guided tours and round-trip transportation from Quito.

North Coast & Lowlands

Includes ➡

Why Go?

Ecuador's north coast doesn't make it onto the itineraries of many international travelers – it's hard to compete in a country that offers so much variety. But for surfers, backwoods explorers and nature lovers, this is a hidden treasure.

Here you'll find quiet beaches, uncrowded waves, little-explored mangrove forests, indigenous jungle settlements and entrancing Afro-Ecuadorian villages. Although noticeably poorer than most of Ecuador's other regions, the north coast makes up for this with its fascinating cultural mix.

Further south, the sun-kissed beach towns of Same, Mompiche and Canoa are the top backpacker draws, with good surf, peaced-out vibes and bacchanalian booze-ups that carry on 'til dawn.

Sadly, the 2016 earthquake, whose epicenter was near Manta, devastated the region, and its effects were still being felt in late 2017 when we visited.

Best Places to Eat

➡ Amalur (p264)
➡ Azuca (p258)
➡ Seaflower Lateneus (p258)
➡ Trovador Cafe (p267)
➡ Hermanacho (p266)

Best Places to Stay

➡ Playa Escondida (p259)
➡ Bam-Bú (p261)
➡ Hotel Bambu (p263)
➡ Casa Ceibo (p265)

When to Go

Manta

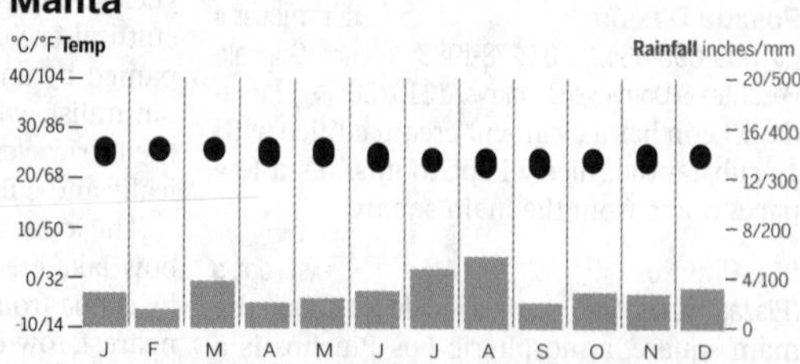

Dec–Mar Surf's up. The rainy season brings downpours and bugs, but there's still heat and sun.

Jul–Aug Beach resorts heave with Ecuadorian tourists and the coast is alive with holiday fun.

Sep–Nov Come and enjoy the coast at its quietest while the weather is still great.

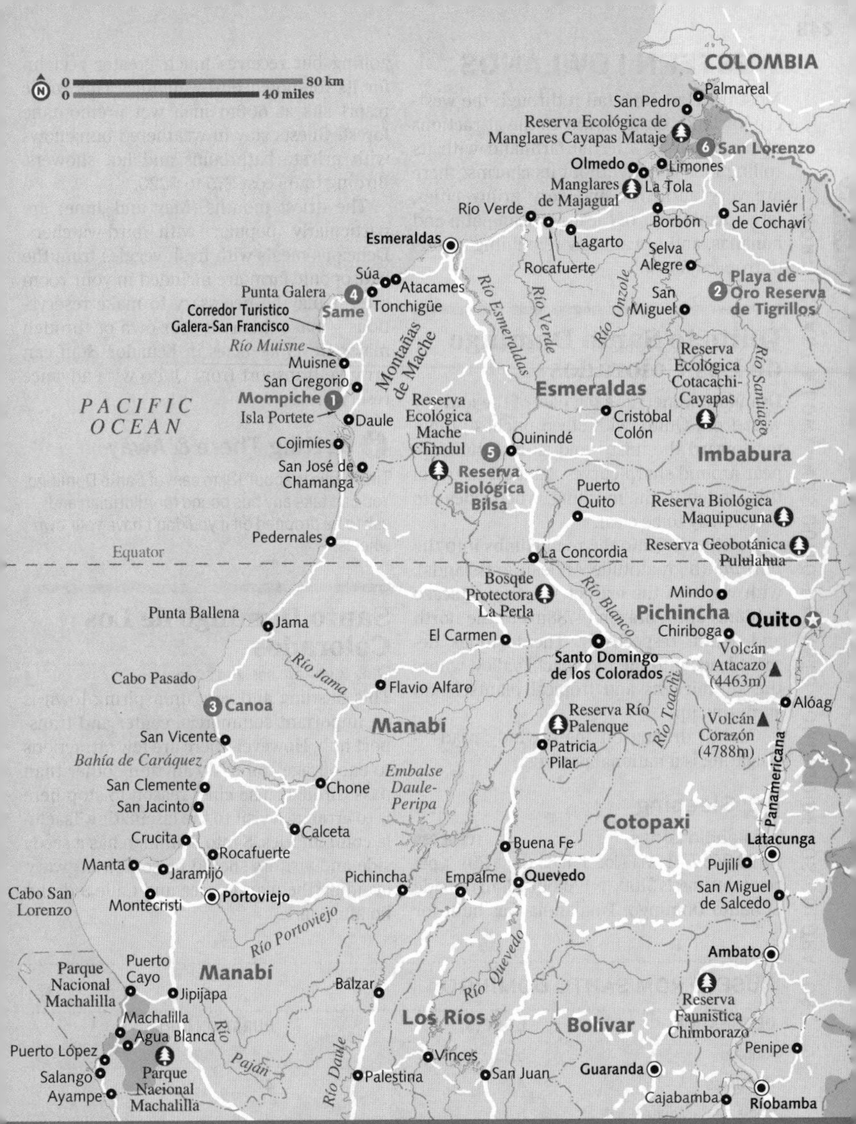

North Coast & Lowlands Highlights

1. **Mompiche** (p260) Walking for miles on the lost, lonely and out-of-this-worldly lovely beaches.

2. **Playa de Oro Reserva de Tigrillos** (p252) Hiking beneath the lush jungle canopy.

3. **Canoa** (p262) Taking in the laid-back beach and surfer scene in the region's top backpacker spot.

4. **Same** (p258) Frolicing in the waves in the idyllic beachside settings.

5. **Reserva Biológica Bilsa** (p259) Marveling at the verdant, wildlife-rich scenery.

6. **San Lorenzo** (p250) Enjoying Afro-Ecuadorian rhythms near Ecuador's steamy northern border.

WESTERN LOWLANDS

Most travelers high-tail it through the western lowlands on their way to the attractions of the coast. This fertile farmland with its rolling hills is not without its charms: there are very authentic and very grimy cities, large plantations of cacao, African palm and bananas, and a scant few remaining stands of tropical forest.

Quito to Santo Domingo de Los Colorados

Dramatic scenery is a big part of the journey west from Quito, with steep pitches plunging toward the misty void as lush hills appear around sharp curves. It's best to travel this stretch in the morning, when skies are more likely to be clear.

Outside of Quito the road climbs into the *páramo* (high-altitude Andean grasslands), with views of the extinct Volcanes Atacazo (4463m) and Corazón (4788m) to the north and south, respectively. The tortuous descent leads into the Río Toachi valley, where the air thickens and tropical plants begin sprouting up.

Careful driving on these windy roads – tailgating is a national pastime.

Sleeping

Tinalandia Lodge LODGE **$$$**
(99-946-7741; Vía Alog, Km 85 (Ruta 20); r per person incl meals $100; P) About 16km outside of Santo Domingo, Tinalandia was built for golfing but receives much greater acclaim for its top-notch bird-watching. This rustic resort sits at 600m in a wet premontane forest. Guests stay in weathered bungalows with private bathrooms and hot showers. Birding tours cost $75 to $220.

The driest months (May and June) are particularly popular with bird-watchers. Delicious meals with fresh veggies from the hydroponic farm are included in your room rate. It may be necessary to make reservations – make them on your own or through major travel agencies in Ecuador. Staff can arrange transport from Quito with advance reservations.

Getting There & Away

Tinalandia is about 18km east of Santo Domingo. You can take any bus bound for Alluriuian and ask to be dropped off if you don't have your own wheels.

Santo Domingo de Los Colorados

02 / POP 270,835 / ELEV 500M

This bustling and very uninspiring town is an important commercial center and transport hub. However, there are few attractions to encourage you to do anything other than pass through. The chief reason to stop here is to arrange a visit to the fascinating Tsáchila communities. Santo Domingo has a seedy side and visitors should be somewhat wary, avoiding the market area and Calle 3 de Julio after dark.

BUSES FROM SANTO DOMINGO

DESTINATION	COST ($)	DURATION (HR)
Ambato	5.25	4
Atacames	4	4
Bahía de Caráquez	5	5
Loja	11	12
Coca	13	16
Esmeraldas	4.75	3½
Guayaquil	7.25	5
Ibarra	9	6.5
Manta	8	6
Mindo	4.50	2
Muisne	7.50	5
Puerto Viejo	6	5
Quito	3.50	3

LOS TSÁCHILAS

The Tsáchilas, dubbed 'the Colorados' by colonists, are well known for their *curanderos* (medicine men) as well as for their beautiful woven crafts in shocks of rainbow colors. The group's signature dress is easy to recognize: they paint their faces with black stripes, and men dye their bowl-shaped haircuts red.

Nowadays it is much more probable to see Westernized Tsáchilas. With curio shops selling their postcard images, gawkers in Santo Domingo calling them 'painted tigers', and bus drivers protesting that the hair dye stains the backs of their seats, it's no wonder that the Tsáchilas have closeted their customs. Nevertheless, there have been some important victories for the Tsáchilas in recent years, most notably the creation of their own province in 2007, granting the group a much more prominent role in the nation's political system.

Kasama, the New Year (coinciding with Easter Saturday), is a time for the Tsáchilas to reaffirm their roots. It unites all of the villagers, who gather to wish one another prosperity in the coming year. Cane sugar *chicha* (a fermented corn or yuca beverage traditionally drunk by many indigenous cultures in Ecuador) is served and the festive atmosphere ignites with music, dance and theater. Despite being the most important Tsáchila celebration, it was shelved for 30 years and only began to be celebrated again in 1998. With the return of this celebration springs the small hope that other important features of the landscape – such as the *guatusa* (agouti, a type of rodent) and the armadillo – will eventually return as well.

Sights & Activities

Tsáchila Communities COMMUNITY

(admission $10-20) The Tsáchila people number about 3000; their eight communities spread across a 10500-sq-km reserve around Santo Domingo. A community tour is available that includes a demonstration of plants used for medicinal purposes, an explanation of customs and traditions, and even dancing. Locals produce lovely hand-woven goods in their signature wild rainbow colors, as well as jewelry.

Contact **José Aguabil** (☎09-770-8703; day tour from $15), leader of the El Poste community, to arrange a visit. You can also visit Chihuilpe, located 17km from Santo Domingo on the road to Quevedo. Contact **Tsapini Calasacón,** (☎098-884-9835) the leader of the community there. To visit **Los Naranjos** (☎098-557-0207; tour with aura cleansing $12.50, overnight stay $25), contact Alejandro Aguibil. Visitors are charged about $10 to $20 depending on the activities in which they partake. Tour agencies in Mindo can help you in contacting these folks.

Sleeping & Eating

Hotel Del Pacífico HOTEL $$

(☎02-275-2806; Av 29 de Mayo 510 btwn Ibarra and Latacunga; s/d $30/40, with air-con $38/$48; P ❄ ≋) There's not really any reason to stay in Santo Domingo, but if you get caught overnight, try this central spot. It has clean and spacious rooms with tile floors and glazed windows; you'll find it in the center of town between the main square and the market.

La Tonga INTERNATIONAL $

(☎02-276-7950; cnr Río Toachi & Galapagos; mains $4-5; ⏱7am-10:30pm) A crisp and formal setting with a varied menu of well-prepared international dishes, vegetarian options and criollo (of Spanish influence) specialties. It's located in the Gran Hotel Santo Domingo. The *tonga* a special coastal dish of chicken and plantains in a peanut sauce, is served on Wednesdays and draws a crowd.

Getting There & Away

Santo Domingo is an important transportation hub, with connections all over Ecuador. The bus terminal, almost 2km north of downtown, has frequent buses to many major towns, as well as internet access, an ATM and luggage storage facilities. Most major destinations have hourly bus departures.

THE NORTH COAST

The north coast is a lush green swath of tropical rainforests and tangled mangroves, with a sprinkling of inviting beaches, dirt-poor backwater villages and laid-back surf

STAYING SAFE IN NORTHERN ECUADOR

Previously, the US State Department had a travel warning for Ecuador's northern border region, including the provinces of Sucumbios, northern Orellana, Carchi and Northern Esmeraldas (from Esmeraldas to San Lorenzo). Kidnappings and crime were a big threat. Although those threats have lessened, you should still stay alert in this region. Top tips to stay safe include the following:

- Cross the border to Colombia from San Lorenzo with caution, if at all.
- Walk in groups – especially at night. Better yet, take a taxi.
- On the coast, do not leave the central tourist district (the strip with all the booming bars) at night.
- Avoid cocaine. Dabbling in drugs is particularly dicey in these parts.
- Take limited amounts of cash and leave your camera and other expensive items locked up in your hotel.
- As a general rule, if you see women and children around, it's safer.

towns. This is home to the country's largest Afro-Ecuadorian population, which gives the area its marimba music and lively festivals as well as outstanding seafood dishes.

Common sense and a taste for adventure are essential tools for travelers heading to this region. Some visitors are turned off by the obvious poverty, higher crime rates and lack of creature comforts. The party-hearty beaches are not for all tastes either, but if you look hard, slivers of solitude peek through.

This region was also hardest-hit by Ecuador's devastating 2016 earthquake, and you'll still see the after-effects in many of these towns. If you're up for it, your tourist dollars can help to support the rebuilding process.

San Lorenzo

06 / POP 20,209

Encircled by verdant jungle, at the edge of a dank, still river, San Lorenzo is a decrepit and dangerous hodgepodge of blaring heat, tropical beats and crumbling storefronts. Hollow marimba notes and salsa is what flavors this mostly Afro-Ecuadorian town. It has a few good music festivals, plus it also makes a great base for visiting the nearby Reserva Ecológica de Manglares Cayapas Mataje.

With road access only completed in the mid-1990s, the area still has the air of a forgotten outpost. It is extremely poor, tourism is barely developed and getting around isn't easy. But if you like the vibe of old port cities, you might enjoy the atmosphere here.

Sights

Reserva Ecológico de Manglares Cayapas-Mataje NATURE RESERVE

(02-398-7600; www.ambiente.gob.ec/reserva-ecologica-manglares-cayapas-mataje) Millions of migratory birds pass through this coastal paradise in June and July, creating a cacophonous and memorable spectacle. The 513 sq km reserve supports five species of mangrove, and includes the tallest mangrove forest in the world – Manglares de Majagual – near the villages of La Tola and Olmedo. Most of the reserve is at sea level and none of it is above 35m. San Lorenzo lies in the middle of the reserve, making it a good base for exploration.

A highlight is the pristine 11km island beach of San Pedro near the Colombian border, but visitors should inquire about safety before venturing into this area. You can reach the reserve by paved road from San Lorenzo or Borbón, but for a more immersive experience, organize a boat tour with a local agency.

Tours

Trips to nearby beaches leave at 7:30am and 2pm ($3). Tour guide **Andrés Carvache** (06-278-0161; andrescarvache@yahoo.es) arranges these and other trips. He can be found in a stilted Ecuador Pacifico office to the right of the pier.

Touring the mangroves isn't really possible via public transportation. To arrange a trip, contact **Cooperativa San Lorenzo del Pailón** (099-795-0944), an authorized service offering private tours in boats for $20 to $30 per hour (it's next to the office of the *capitanía* – the port captain). You can also arrange tours through Andres Carvache for $60 and $80 for a two- to three-hour trip.

Festivals & Events

San Lorenzo Marimba Festival MUSIC
(May) This three-day festival normally held in the last week of May will set your rump-shaker a'shaking.

Fiestas de San Lorenzo MUSIC
(Aug) Held around August 10, this vibrant festival has lots of live salsa music, dance performances and more.

Sleeping & Eating

Pickings are slim, but consider mosquito nets and fans as essentials, especially in the rainy season.

Gran Hotel San Carlos 2 HOTEL $
(06-278-1189; Av 26 de Agosto, near José Garcés, next to a BanEcuador branch; with/without air-con s $12/15, d 25/30; P) The Gran Hotel San Carlos 2 is comfortable with state-of-the-art air-con, cable TV and spotless floors. It's worth the $5 splurge if the original Gran Hotel San Carlos is a little too basic for you.

Gran Hotel San Carlos HOTEL $
(06-278-0284; cnr Imbabura & José Garcés; s/d without bathroom $8/15, s/d incl air-con $13/25; P) The Gran Hotel San Carlos No 1 has clean, bright rooms with large windows. Kitschy, rainbow-hued decor prevails in the common areas. Its brother hotel, the San Carlos 2, however, is a bit nicer for a few bucks more.

Doña Luca ECUADORIAN $
(Eloy Alfaro; mains $2.50-8; 6am-9pm) Probably the best place in town, this laid-back joint serves breakfasts and a wide variety of food, dishes from meat to delicious local seafood. It's in the center of town between the main drag and Parque Central.

El Chocó ECUADORIAN $
(Imbabura, near Tácito Ortiz; mains $2-6; 7am-midnight Mon-Sat) On the main street, this clean and well-liked spot serves all the local seafood favorites including ceviche and *encocado de camarones* (shrimp and coconut stew).

Information

Cyber San Lorenzo (Tacino Ortiz; 8am-8pm) Internet cafe next to Hotel Pampa de Oro with reliable access.

Hospital Divina Providencia (06-278-0188; Av Carchi & Av Principal) Main hospital in town; a Catholic institution with a reputation as one of the region's finest. Located next to San Lorenzo Technical College and near the bus terminal (Terminal Terrestre).

Ministerio del Ambiente (06-278-0184; Parque Kennedy; 9am-7pm Mon-Fri) Offers information on Reserva Ecológica de Manglares Cayapas Mataje.

Police Station (06-278-0672; opposite Parque Central) If you're traveling into or out of Colombia on the coast road (which is not highly recommended), take care of passport formalities here, or with the port captain at the pier.

Getting There & Away

BOAT

Ecuador Pacífico (06-278-0161; andres carvache@yahoo.es; Simon Bolívar, near Imbabura) services depart daily to Limones ($3, 1½ hours) at 7:30am, 10:30am and 1pm, from which you can catch a connecting service to La Tola ($5, 45 minutes). At La Tola, you can connect to Esmeraldas by bus.

To cross the Colombian border, there are daily departures at 7:30am, 2pm and 4pm ($3), which also require bus connections to Tumaco in Colombia. The safety situation has improved in recent years, but it's still worth inquiring locally about the current risks before crossing here.

BUS

La Costeñita departures for Esmeraldas ($5.50, five hours) leave the bus terminal (cnr Av Esmeraldas and Av Armada Nacional) hourly from 5am to 4pm. Trans Esmeraldas buses leave regularly from in front of the church on 10 de Agosto to Quito ($16) via Ibarra ($7) and to Manta ($9).

San Miguel

06 / POP 1092

San Miguel is a modest and friendly Afro-Ecuadorian community of stilted thatched huts set in the forest, with Chachi homes scattered nearby along the shores of the river. The village is the main base from which to visit the lowland sections of the Reserva Ecológica Cotacachi-Cayapas.

The Cotacachi-Cayapas Ranger Station overlooks the village in the San Miguel Lodge.

Sleeping

San Miguel Lodge LODGE $
(06-0303-5008; San Miguel; r per person incl breakfast $10, meals $3-4) This basic six-bed lodge overlooks the village and has a cool

veranda, spectacular views and basic rooms with mosquito nets. The food is basic. Contact Merlin or Leiler Nazareno at the number listed for further information.

Getting There & Away

The driver of the daily passenger canoe from Borbón (a down-on-its-luck lumber port 30km downriver) spends the night about 15 minutes downriver from San Miguel. He won't return to San Miguel unless passengers have made previous arrangements, so book ahead by informing the **San Miguel Lodge** (p251) when you plan to return. The canoe leaves San Miguel at around 4am.

La Costeñita and Transportes del Pacífico run buses to Esmeraldas ($3, four hours) or San Lorenzo ($1.50, one hour) about every hour from 7am to 6pm.

A daily passenger boat leaves at 11am for San Miguel ($8, three hours). Ask for the 'Canoa San Miguel.' This boat can drop you at any location on Río Cayapas or at San Miguel. Various boats run irregularly to other destinations – ask around at the docks.

Playa de Oro

As the Río Santiago leads inland from Borbón, the last community upriver is the remote settlement of Playa de Oro. Populated with the Afro-Ecuadorian descendants of slaves brought here to pan for gold 500 years ago, Playa de Oro's charm lies in its authenticity. Locals do what they and their ancestors have always done, whether that be roaming the forest, riding the river currents, panning for gold, making drums or encouraging their children in traditional dances. When visitors show interest in their way of life, locals are quietly proud.

This is a great entrance point to the surrounding Playa de Oro Reserva de Tigrillos.

Sights

Playa de Oro Reserva de Tigrillos WILDLIFE RESERVE

FREE Half an hour upstream from Playa de Oro, this 100-sq-km reserve is owned and operated by the community of Playa de Oro. It borders the Reserva Ecológica Cotacachi-Cayapas and protects native jungle cats – but you'll need to work hard to sight one.

Visits to the reserve can be organized through the Maquipucuna (p128) NGO, located near Mindo. If you're staying at one of Playa de Oro's lodges, you can also coordinate a visit through your hosts.

Sleeping

Playa de Oro Lodge LODGE $$

(☎99-421-8033; www.maquipucuna.org/playa-de-oro; r per person incl meals $84) Maquipucuna, an NGO which manages a cloud-forest lodge near Mindo, also helps the Playa de Oro community manage this lodge. A group canoe trip to the lodge costs $80, and a guide costs $25 per day. The lodge has three different cabins as well as more rustic camping sites and a research station.

PROTECTING PARADISE

Located hours inland from the coast in a roadless wilderness, Playa de Oro's end-of-the-earth location has helped to keep it a natural paradise, the kind of place where the huffing of margays can still be heard at night outside your window. Amid mounting pressures from the mining industry, locals have turned to tourism in the hope it might help to keep their jungle home intact.

Much of the area around the reserve has changed dramatically in the last 15 years, owing to gold-mining activity. Small villages have disappeared and in their place lie heaps of gravel piled up by machinery sluicing for gold; the river water has become contaminated by cyanide and arsenic used in the mining process. So far the villagers have resisted overtures from gold-mining and lumber companies to receive goods and services (a generator, a new road, jobs to log their own forest) in exchange for their land.

In Playa de Oro every villager over the age of 14 gets to vote on important issues. Some villagers have long argued that ecotourism is the sensible, nondestructive way forward, but their insistence on maintaining control of their own ecotourism, and not allowing it to fall into the hands of large tour agencies who take a big cut, forces them to rely on independent travelers and small groups. Recently, however, they've partnered with Maquipucuna (www.maquipucuna.org), an NGO that manages an ecolodge between Quito and Mindo and pledges to bring tourism to the region in a responsible manner. The question remains whether this trickle of income will be enough to sustain them.

Tigrillos Lodge CABIN $$
(www.maquipucuna.org/playa-de-oro; r per person inc meals $84) Located upriver from Playa del Oro, these rustic, community-managed accommodations include eight rooms, each with a private bathroom. To get here, you'll have to arrange river travel with the Maquipucuna NGO, located near Mindo.

Getting There & Away

The village of Playa de Oro is about five hours upstream from Borbón, but there are no regular boats. You have to take a bus from Borbón to Selva Alegre ($3, two hours). From Selva Alegre, only if you made a reservation, a boat from Playa de Oro will motor you up to the village or the reserve.

It's best to plan your trip through **Maquipucuna Lodge** (p128). Located between Quito and Mindo, Maquipucuna is essentially the community's conduit to the outside/tourist world, and will coordinate with the community as to the best and safest time to traverse the river, as well as other logistics.

Reserva Ecológica Cotacachi-Cayapas

To really get off the beaten track, this reserve, the largest protected area of Ecuador's western Andean habitats, might be just the place. As altitudes increase from about 200m to 4939m, habitats change quickly from tropical forests to premontane and montane cloud forest to *páramo* (high-altitude Andean grasslands). This rapid change produces the so-called 'edge effect' that gives rise to an incredible diversity of flora and fauna.

The lower reaches of the reserve are home to the indigenous Chachi, famous for their basketwork which you might be able to purchase directly from artisans. About 5000 Chachi remain, mostly fishers and subsistence farmers, living in open-sided, thatched river houses on stilts. Over the last few decades, the Chachi have been swept by an epidemic of river blindness that's carried by black flies, which are particularly prevalent in April and May. Vaccination efforts have stymied the disease locally, but to protect yourself, use insect repellent and take malaria medication.

When to Go

River levels are high during the rainy season (December to May), making for swifter travel. At this time mosquitoes, black flies and other insects are at their highest concentrations; definitely cover up at dawn and dusk when they come out in full force.

Even during the rainy months, mornings are often clear. Up to 5000mm of rain has been reported in some of the more inland areas, although San Miguel is somewhat drier. The drier months of September to the start of December are usually less buggy, and you have a better chance of seeing wildlife, although river navigation may be limited.

Sights & Activities

Guided tours of the reserve can be arranged at the **Cotacachi-Cayapas Ranger Station** (06-278-6029; http://areasprotegidas.ambiente.gob.ec; 8am-5pm) in San Miguel. The rangers here can serve as guides, and charge about $10 per day (entrance to the reserve is free). Two guides are needed for trips, with one for each end of the paddle-and-pole-operated dugout canoe. Alternatively, you can visit on a guided tour arranged through one of the lodges (p251) in San Miguel.

These hills are the haunts of rarely seen mammals including giant anteaters, Baird's tapirs, jaguars and, in the upper reaches of the reserve, spectacled bears. However, the chances of seeing these animals are very remote. You're more likely to see monkeys, squirrels, sloths, nine-banded armadillos, bats and a huge variety of bird species.

Getting There & Away

To visit the reserve you can approach from the highlands (at Laguna Cuicocha, near Cotacachi) or San Miguel. Hiking between these regions may well be impossible; the steep and thickly vegetated western Andean slopes are almost impenetrable.

It's about two or three hours by canoe from San Miguel to the park boundary. Another one or two hours brings you to a gorgeous little waterfall in the jungle. A guide (pre-arranged in San Miguel) is essential as the reserve's few trails are poorly marked. The **lodge** in Playa de Oro is also an access point for the reserve.

Esmeraldas

06 / POP 161,868

Esmeraldas is ugly, dangerous and dirty, and there's really no reason to stay here. Most tourists just spend the night (if they have to) and continue southwest to the popular beach destinations of Atacames, Súa and Mompiche. You can, at least, make a number of bus connections here.

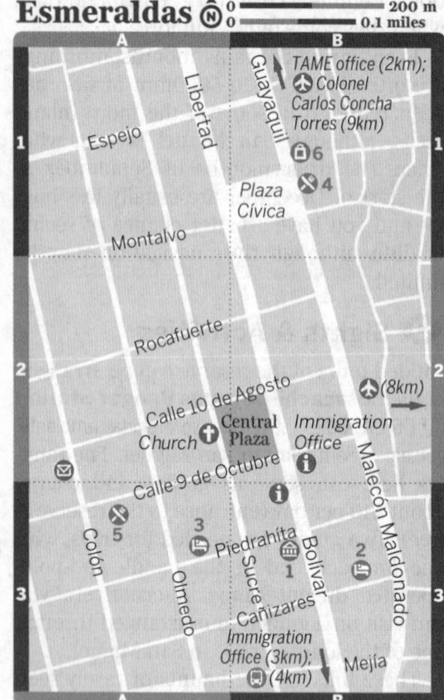

Esmeraldas

Sights
1 Centro Cultural Esmeraldas B3

Sleeping
2 El Trébol B3
3 Hotel Perla Verde A3

Eating
4 AKI Supermercado B1
5 Parrilladas El Toro A3

Shopping
6 Centro Artesenal B1

While you're here, stop to grab a seafood lunch along the *malecón* (waterfront) and check out the cultural center, where you can learn about the Spanish conquistadors' first Ecuadorian landfall, which happened right here.

Sights

Centro Cultural Esmeraldas MUSEUM
(Bolívar 427; 9am-5pm Tue-Fri, 10am-4pm Sat & Sun) FREE This combined museum, library and bookstore contains materials ranging from recent local history to fine ceramics and gold work from the ancient Tolita culture. Some of the exhibit signs and documentary videos are in English, and the staff is very obliging. When we visited the museum was closed for construction on weekends, but staff promised to open again soon.

Tours

Mandagua Tours TOURS
(991-391-649, 98-145-6235; pandafinu@hotmail.com) Javier Valencia runs tours to destinations all over Esmeraldas Province.

Sleeping

Hotels and hostels are plentiful, but the cheapest ones are just about intolerable. During the wet months you'll want a mosquito net in your room.

El Trébol HOTEL $
(06-272-2101; Cañizares 1-18; r per person $16;) A fern-lined hotel offering oversized rooms with cable TV, but no hot water. Like the owner, it shows a combination of age and charm.

Hotel Perla Verde BUSINESS HOTEL $$
(099-501-2909; www.hotelperlaverde.ec; Piedrahíta btwn Olmedo & Sucre; s/d incl breakfast $45/55;) This is the best hotel in town, boasting spacious rooms with lots of creature comforts (as long as you don't mind some truly awful art on the walls and darkish corridors). The staff is friendly and you're in a central location. The downstairs restaurant is also recommended.

Eating

The food in the many cheap sidewalk cafes and *comedores* (cheap restaurants) is often good – try those along Olmedo between Mejía and Piedrahíta. There is also a number of food stands across from the Terminal Terreste bus station.

AKI Supermercado SUPERMARKET $
(cnr Malecón Maldonado & Montalvo, Plaza Civica) This is a good supermarket for stocking up on provisions. In addition to this downtown locale, there's another branch next to the bus terminal (Terminal Terreste).

Parrilladas El Toro STEAK $$
(Calle 9 de Octubre 4-23; mains $7-10; 5pm-midnight) Beyond the uninviting decor you'll find a decent steakhouse specializing in beef and chops. The thatched courtyard seating is preferable to sitting inside.

Shopping

Centro Artesenal ARTS & CRAFTS
(cnr Malecón Maldonado & Plaza Cívica; ⏲8am-5pm Mon-Fri, 9am-5pm Sat & Sun) This is where to come to browse for tapestries, baskets, *tagua* (vegetable ivory) carvings and other Chachi pieces.

Information

Esmeraldas is arguably the most dangerous city in Ecuador. Avoid arriving after dark, do not walk around at night; take a taxi instead.

Immigration Office (☎06-272-4624) At the Policía Civil Nacional, 3km out of town (take a taxi). Have your passport stamped here for entry or exit via the rarely used coastal route to Colombia. You can also inquire at the main police building on the main plaza (Libertador and 9 de Octubre).

Police Station (cnr Bolívar & Cañizares) Two blocks south of the central plaza.

Post Office

Tourist Office (☎06-272-7340; www.turismo.gob.ec; Bolívar; ⏲9am-noon & 2-6pm Mon-Sat) Located between Calle 9 de Octubre and Piedrahíta.

Getting There & Away

AIR

The **TAME office** (☎06-272-6863; www.tame.com.ec; Centro Comercial, Av Maldonado near Manabi; ⏲10am-8pm Mon-Sat, until 7pm Sun) is on the lower floor of the snazzy mall at the Centro Comercial, about five blocks from downtown on Maldonado; it also has an office at the **airport** (☎95-956-0672; Highway 15) itself. TAME has daily flights to Quito (one way $75), and Guayaquil (one way $138, with one stop) and Cali, Colombia (one way/return $196/$240; one-way fare sold only to Colombian nationals).

BUS

The new bus terminal, Terminal Terreste, is 4km from the city center on the road to Atacames. Note that you'll pay more for a comfy coach-cama seat on long-distance rides, but your spine may thank you. A taxi from the terminal to the city center is $2.50.

Getting Around

The **airport** is 8km from town, across the Río Esmeraldas. A taxi charges about $25 to go directly from the airport to Atacames, thus avoiding Esmeraldas completely. A taxi to downtown Esmeraldas from the bus terminal costs $2.50.

A taxi to the beach costs $1.50, or you can take a Selectivo bus signed 'Las Palmas No 1' northbound along Bolívar. Taxis charge a $1.50 minimum, which doubles after 11pm.

Atacames

☎06 / POP 16,855

It's hard to 'get' Atacames. The beach is just OK, the town is dirty, kind of dangerous and crowded as hell, and still *serranos* (highlanders) love it for the partying, the beachfront ceviche stalls and the easy trips to nearby beaches. If you want to get down to all-night reggaeton and cheap drinks, this is certainly a good spot. If not, head further south for better beaches, bigger waves and more relaxation.

Tours

Fishers on the beach can take you on a boat tour around the area, passing by Isla de Pajaros just offshore. Plan on about $20 per person for a 75-minute tour, and $40 per person for a fishing trip.

Sleeping

Atacames is packed with hotels, but it can get awfully crowded on holiday weekends. Reserve in advance if arriving during the high season.

BUSES FROM ESMERALDAS

DESTINATION	COST ($)	DURATION (HR)
Atacames	1	1
Guayaquil	11-12	9
Manta	12	10
Mompiche	3.90	2½
Muisne	2.50	2
Quito	9-11.25	6
San Lorenzo	5.30	5
Santo Domingo	4.75	4

Atacames

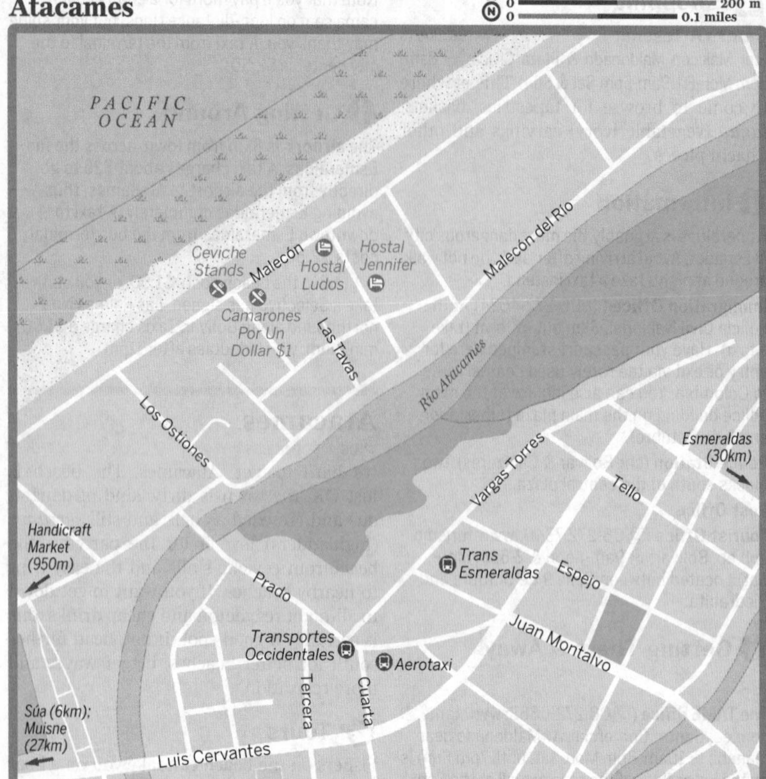

Hostal Ludos HOTEL $
(98-191-5052; Malecon; r per person $10-20;) This new bamboo structure along the *malecón* has a karaoke veranda and clean rooms with nice sea breezes and little 'attic' spaces. Cable TV and a Jacuzzi add to the 'luxe' factor. Staff offer loads of information on tours, including an excursion to an interesting archeological museum in the small northern coastal town of Àfrica. Most rooms are comprised of bunk beds.

Hostal Jennifer HOTEL $
(06-273-1055; near Malecón; s/d with hot water $18/35, without hot water $15/25;) This simple, straightforward place has kind staff and clean, spartan rooms that get a decent amount of light (there are windows in every room). It's a concrete block structure with small swimming pool, only half a block from the action.

Eating

Cocada (a chewy coconut sweet) and *batidos* (fruit shakes) are two local specialties sold everywhere. Seafood shacks dominate the beachfront.

Ceviche Stands SEAFOOD $
(Malecón; ceviche $5-10) There are ceviche stands on the beach and in a couple of central spots along the *malecón*. Pick a stand that looks clean, and dive into fresh-caught *ceviche de concha* (shellfish ceviche) or *ceviche de pescado* (fish ceviche).

Camarones Por Un Dollar $1 SEAFOOD $$
(Malecón; lunch specials $4-6; mains $7-20; 11am-10pm;) Don't be fooled by its name – the only thing on the menu that costs $1 is a serving of rice. Nevertheless, this cozy seafood restaurant packs in the crowds. Its recipe for success? Big family plates that

are piled high with fresh seafood, plus daily lunch specials and soups from just $2.

Shopping

Handicraft Market ARTS & CRAFTS
(Malecón; 9am-8pm) There's a tiny handicraft market daily at the west end of the *malecón*.

Information

The beach has a strong undertow and lifeguards work only midweek to weekends. People drown here every year, so stay within your limits.

The beach is considered unsafe at night, when assaults and rapes have been reported. Stay near the well-lit areas in front of the hotels, and avoid the isolated stretch between Atacames and Súa, as knifepoint robberies have been reported. Needless to say, the beach is not a place to bring your valuables at any time of the day.

Banco del Pichincha (Malecón; 8am-2pm Mon-Fri) Next to Hotel Castel, the bank has an ATM. There is also a Banco de Guayaquil ATM at this location.

Getting There & Away

All buses stop by the *taxis ecológicos* on the main road to/from Esmeraldas; there is no bus terminal, and bus offices are scattered around the town center. Buses for Esmeraldas ($0.80, one hour) normally begin from Súa. Most buses from Esmeraldas to Atacames continue on to Súa (10 minutes), Same (20 minutes) and Tonchigüe (25 minutes) for about $0.50. There are also regular buses to Muisne ($2, 1½ hours). *Ecovias* (motorcycle taxis) charge $2 to Súa and $7 to Same.

Bus companies including **Transportes Occidentales** (06-276-0547; cnr Prado & Cuarta), **Trans Esmeraldas** (cnr Vargas Torres & Juan Montalvo) and **Aerotaxi** (Cuarta) operate a daily service to Quito ($9, seven hours) as well as to Guayaquil ($11 to $12, eight hours). If you're returning to Quito on a Sunday in the high season, be sure to buy your ticket in advance.

Tonsupa

Just 5km north of Atacames, Tonsupa has a high-rise beachfront skyline and a big, hard-packed golden-gray-sand beach with plenty of space to roam. There's less partying here, but that also makes for a better night's rest. Head to the beach to make arrangements for a whale-watching tour for $15 to $20 (depending on group size and your bargaining skills).

Sleeping & Eating

Aside from the massive Makana Resort, there are plenty of more affordable lodgings on the 'other' side of town (hostels and hotels), closer to the Malecón.

Makana Resort RESORT **$$$**
(06-246-5242; www.ghlhoteles.com; Grey St, northern edge of Tonsupa's beach; r incl breakfast $122-159; P) This gleaming beachfront resort and condo complex has 31 massive post-modern inspired rooms. All come with ocean views, private balconies and kitchenettes. With a large infinity pool, Jacuzzi, restaurant and gym to boot, it's the nicest hotel for a hundred miles. It stands apart from the rest of Tonsupa, barricaded by construction and other high-rise buildings.

Wendy Restaurant SEAFOOD **$**
(Malecón; meals $7-12; 8am-9pm) Right on the main drag, Wendy serves up northern beach fare like fish soup, *langostina* (king prawns) and fresh ceviche in a thatched-roof, open-air restaurant. It's opposite Checho's Bar and next to the Fogón Manabita Hotel on the 'land' side of the street. Beach vendors selling sunglasses and other wares may interrupt your meal (not only here, though!).

Getting There & Away

To get here, take Bus Interplaya ($0.30, 10 minutes) from the main road in Atacames. If you're coming from Esmeraldas, it's $1 to Atacames, where you'll transfer.

Súa

02

Groups of scissor-tailed magnificent frigatebirds wheel over the roiling surf in Súa, a more family-oriented, quieter and less popular seaside spot than neighboring Atacames, with more-reasonable weekend hotel prices. That said, the cocktail bars along the beach still screech out music, so it's hardly the place for an idyllic break. Humpback whales can be seen off the coast from June to September. You can walk here on the beach from Atacames, but watch the tide and don't do it at night (take an *ecovia*).

Sleeping & Eating

Hotel Chagra Ramos HOTEL **$**
(06-247-3106; hotelchagraramos@hotmail.com; north side of Malecón; r per person $13; P)

Nestled against the beach, this friendly, wind-battered classic is the most popular guesthouse in town. Rooms are clean if a little weathered, with antiquated bathrooms, softer-than-wonderbread mattresses and pretty darned nice views. There's no hot water, but there's a good-value restaurant. Octogenarian owner Aida is an inspiration.

You'll feel like you're in a medieval fort when you scale the mirador and scan the horizon for pirates.

Kikes SEAFOOD $

(Malecón; mains $7-10, breakfast $3; ⏲7am-9pm) For a bamboo beachfront eatery, try Kikes. It serves up mouthwatering *encocada de camarón* (shrimp and coconut stew, $8).

Getting There & Away

Bus services to and from Esmeraldas run about every 45 minutes. From Súa it takes 10 minutes to get to Atacames ($0.30) and about an hour to get to Esmeraldas ($1). If you want to go further along the coast to Muisne, you have to wait out of town along the main road for a bus that's heading south from Esmeraldas (flag it down anywhere along the road). Getting to and from Atacames is easy in an *ecovia* ($1.50) when the buses aren't running at night.

Same & Tonchigüe

☎06

Same (*sah*-may) is a real mixed bag of a resort town, boasting a wonderful beach and a genial atmosphere, while also being dominated by a vast resort and condo complex called Casablanca. The beach itself, while certainly beautiful, is far from pristine and would benefit from a community-wide effort to keep it clean, such as that seen in Mompiche.

It must be said that the community *has* rallied and organized better private security up and down the little road which leads to the beach. All in all, Same is an unbridled delight compared to Atacames – *mucho mas tranquilo*, you might say. You can rent stand-up paddleboards (per hour $10) on the beach, and there are a surprising number of fine little dining establishments in this hidden nook.

Tonchigüe is a tiny fishing village about 3km west of Same, along the same stretch of beach. Go early in the morning to see the fisherpeople unloading their catch.

Sleeping

Azuca HOTEL $

(☎98-882-95881; azuca2@hotmail.com; Same; r per person $10; 📶) This incredibly cheap place is just a short walk from the beach (at the turn-off where Same's main 'street' leaves the coastal road). It has a decidedly atavistic air and five pretty comfortable and spacious wooden rooms (two with shared bathrooms) with balconies and mosquito nets – though the sheets are slightly dirty. Artist-owner-chef Evelyn, from Cali, Colombia, serves up the catch of the day ($9 to $15).

El Acantilado CABIN $$

(☎06-302-7620; www.elacantilado.net; s/d $45/90, cabana sleeping up to 6 $120, camping $20; P📶🏊) Perched on a cliff above the crashing waves, El Acantilado offers unobstructed sea views from its rooms, which make it great for whale-watching from June to September. Rustic suites are open to the elements, with just bug screens separating the rooms from individual private gardens and views down to the sea and beach below. Camping is available, too.

New management took over in September 2017. Be forewarned that the cabins are often full of student groups.

Isla del Sol HOTEL $$

(☎06-247-0470; www.cabanasisladelsol.com; Tonchigüe; d/q/ste $60/72/112; P❄📶🏊) With new modern suites replete with living areas, beachfront decks, air-con and flatscreen TVs (and a few cheaper worn-down cabins out back with wood floors, beamed ceilings and small verandas), this is a good midrange bet. English is spoken and kayaks are available (per two hours $10).

Eating

La Terraza PIZZA $

(Same; pizzas $8-10; ⏲noon-4pm, 6pm-11pm; P📶) Spanish-owned La Terraza has a great beach setting and turns out good pizzas that keep it packed with locals throughout the week. Pepo, who was one of Same's original expats three decades ago, can also rent you a room up top ($15 per person).

★**Seaflower Lateneus** SEAFOOD $$

(☎06-247-0369; Same; mains $15-25; ⏲9am-11pm) Boasting one of the best chefs along the north coast (born here, trained in Europe), Seaflower serves delicious plates of grilled seafood (try the *spaghetti marin-*

OFF THE BEATEN TRACK

RESERVA BIOLÓGICA BILSA

Rugged adventurers looking to get truly off the beaten path and into nature should head to Reserva Biológica Bilsa, 30km west of Quinindé. Crashing waterfalls and spectacular wildlife adorn this 30-sq-km reserve in the Montañas de Mache. Biodiversity is exceptionally high in these last vestiges of premontane tropical wet forest, with howler monkeys, endangered birds, jaguars and pumas all present. The reserve, administered by **Fundación Jatun Sacha** (02-243-2240; www.jatunsacha.org; La Yecita, Km 80 Esmeraldas Quinindé; r per person incl all meals $30), sits in the 1200-sq-km Mache Chindul Ecological Reserve, which ironically only preserves 2% or 3% of the original forest from the area, the rest being used for logging, oil and other industrial enterprises.

This trip is for the hardy: rainy season access (January to June) requires hiking or mule-riding a mud-splattered 25km trail. From October to December you can make this journey by car or truck. Contact Fundación Jatun Sacha before visiting.

era). It's worth reserving a table on weekends, when it's often packed with a smart crowd of cocktail-sipping weekenders – it also doubles as Same's best bar, with an array of hanging bottle decorations (watch your head!).

Rooms for rent here, too – one's even categorized as a 'suite'!

Toquilla y Mar PERUVIAN $$
(099-384-1496; Same; mains $9-20; 8am-10pm; P) There is a Peruvian sensibility to the fresh seafood served at this relaxed, open-air beachfront spot. It offers fried rice with shellfish, garlic crab and nine varieties of ceviche. When it's time for dessert, don't doubt the house coffee, which comes from the family finca in Loja down south. Like other restaurants in the area, Fabiola will rent you a comfy room.

Getting There & Away

Buses heading northeast to Esmeraldas and south to Muisne pick up and drop off passengers at both Same and Tonchigüe. *Rancheras* (open-sided buses, or trucks mounted with uncomfortably narrow bench seats – also known as *chivas*) head to Tonchigüe from Esmeraldas.

Corredor Turistico Galera-San Francisco

About 3km south of Tonchigüe, there's a turn-off to this rough lost coast, which sports a few cool hotels, forgotten Afro-Ecuadorian villages and plenty of virgin coastline.

Sleeping

★**Playa Escondida** CABIN $
(99-650-6812, 06-302-7496; www.playaescondida.com.ec; Corredor Turistico Km 10; camping per person $8.50, cabin per person $25, beach day use $5;) Look no further for seclusion: the lovely and remote Playa Escondida offers accommodation in rustic cabins surrounding a beautiful beach cove, set amid 1 sq km of protected land. There's a restaurant serving seafood, meat and vegetarian dishes, and tours and other activities are offered. Children under 12 pay half price. It's just one kilometer east of Cumilinche Club.

Cumilinche Club CABIN $$
(06-302-7526; cumilincheclub@hotmail.com; Corredor Turistico Km 11, near Punta Galera; s/d/tr $41/61/80) Set on a secluded cove with just a sliver of beach, this remote lodge has thatched-roof adobe cabañas with large living areas that can sleep the whole family. There's a restaurant on-site and you will love hanging out in a hammock from your private porch. There's no air-con, but good ocean breezes cool things down.

Getting There & Away

It's easiest to travel here in your own car, or by taxi from Atacames ($20). The road eventually turns to dirt as it follows the coast, before finally arriving in Muisne.

From Atacames, Sua, Same or Tonchigue, you can also take a local bus ($1, runs every two to three hours) headed to Punta Galera. Ask the driver to let you off in Playa Escondida. You can also take a bus to Abdon Calderon or Tonchigüe and then a tricycle-taxi or *camioneta* for 10km to Playa Escondida ($5).

Muisne

Muisne is a tumbledown, working-class island surrounded by river and sea, its ramshackle little port bustling with a minor banana-shipping industry. Being relatively remote, Muisne attracts far fewer visitors than the more popular beaches, but it makes an interesting foray off the beaten track. The long and lonely palm-lined beach at its back is its best feature, and the few remaining mangroves in the area are protected and worth a visit.

Muisne was badly affected by the earthquake of 2016, and the main road along the island was still being rebuilt during our visit in late 2017. However, it has an amazing new pedestrian bridge from the mainland, another project of the Correa government, and a splendid little plaza on the mainland side, with soccer-ball adornments at the foot of the bridge.

Note there is no ATM on the island, so plan ahead.

Sights & Activities

Congal Bio-Station NATURE RESERVE
(02-2243-216; www.jatunsacha.org/congal-bio marine-station) Only 2km from Muisne, this 6.5-sq-km marine reserve established by Jatun Sacha in 2000 focuses on mangrove conservation and organic aquaculture. Volunteers are needed, but visitors are also welcome. There are great opportunities for snorkeling and scuba diving, plus comfortable private cabins with seafood on the menu. Room and full board costs $40 per person per day.

Fundecol ECOTOUR
(Foundation for Ecological Defense; 06-248-0519; tours per day $25-50) Community and mangrove tours are organized by this outfit based in the local area. Costs vary depending on the type of tour and the size of your group, with tours including boat trips up Río Muisne to see the remaining mangroves and the impact of commercial shrimping. It's across the street from the hospital on Muisne.

Sleeping & Eating

Most of the island's lodgings didn't survive the quake. If you do find a place, during the rainy months mosquitoes can be bad, so be sure to get a room with a net.

There are a few places to eat and sleep on the mainland before you cross, including **Viejo Willy** (3 de Octubre; $5-6; 7pm-11pm), a local fave which moved after the quake. Walk all the way to the beach for a seafood feed, though. You'll be glad you did.

Las Palmeiras SEAFOOD $
(Beach; mains $7-13; 7am-7pm) This simple beach restaurant serves up shrimp or freshly caught fish with a sea view. It was one of the few businesses to survive the earthquake, and there's a funky bar right across the little road on the beach with a pit fire.

Getting There & Around

Buses from Esmeraldas go as far as the cement launch of El Relleno. From here take a motorized canoe across the mottled-blue Río Muisne to the island ($0.20). With the new pedestrian bridge, however, you can just walk across to the island any time. Cars can also take a ferry until 5pm.

Buses depart from El Relleno about every 30 minutes to Esmeraldas ($2, 2½ hours) passing Same, Súa and Atacames en route. There are five buses daily to Santo Domingo de los Colorados ($6, five hours), where connections to Quito or Guayaquil are made. **Transportes Occidentales** (06-243-4009; cnr Calle Principal & El Relleno) has a nightly bus to/from Quito ($9, 8½ hours). To go further south, take a bus to El Salto and then a bus to Pedernales ($3, three hours), from where you can connect to other towns down the coast.

Muisne's main road leads directly away from the pier, crossing the center to the beach. It's 2km from end to end. *Ecovias* vie for passengers at the pier. It's $1 well spent for the wild ride at top rickshaw speed over potholes and sharp, rolling rubble. The road was being resurfaced during our visit.

Mompiche

05

Famed for its world-class waves and gorgeous 7km-long strip of pristine (if grayish) sand beach, this little fishing village has long been popular with backpackers and surfers for its good waves, and cheap eats and lodgings. Mompiche had barely been touched by the modern world until the creation of a good new road nearly a decade ago, but even now there's not extensive vehicular traffic, and everyone in town still knows everyone else. Besides its fabulous stretch of palm-fringed sands, Mompiche has little else (not even an ATM), and that's its beauty.

Like much of the region, Mompiche's businesses were hit hard by the 2016 earthquake and are still attempting to rebound. Rising sea levels have also brought the high tide all the way to the sea wall, effectively eliminating beach time for a quarter of the day, and cutting off land access to the beach hotels north of here.

Activities

November through February sees the best surf, with waves up to 2m – the rest of the year it's pretty flat. There's a river break north of town and a steep point break (for experts) to the south. Two friendly competitors in town rent surfboards and give lessons for the same price: Jefferson Panezo at **La Peña Escuela de Surf** (9672-74-255; La Fosforera; 8am-5pm) is one of them.

Head to the beach to arrange whale-watching tours as well as trips to Isla Portete, Muisne, nearby mangroves, and a bunch of lost beaches. Boats cost about $25 per person per hour, depending on occupancy. Ask for Ramon at the **Banana Hotel** (099-739-6244), who runs popular jungle tours.

Sleeping

The Mudhouse HOSTAL **$**

(093-911-2203; www.the-mud-house.com; Via a Mompiche; dm/d $9/25-30, family cabin $50-60; P wi-fi) This newish entry on the Mompiche scene is run by a friendly American expat couple and has both private rooms and dorms, the nicest of which have outdoor stone showers. It has capacity for singles, couples and families, and Mendy has a wealth of information on local activities in her handy spiral notebook.

It's across from the police station, before you hit 'downtown' proper.

Bam-Bú HOTEL **$**

(095-978-0941; www.bambu-hotel.com; 100m north of T-Junction, btwn La Fosforera & Gaviotas; r per person incl breakfast $25; P wi-fi) This three-story scatterjam of support beams, arches, walkways and terraces is made almost entirely from bamboo (and withstood the 2016 earthquake well). The rooms (six with ocean views) are big, with modern bathrooms, comfy beds and very simple appointments. There's a friendly restaurant and bar downstairs – probably the most fun you can have in town. Yoga and laundry services are available, too.

A sweet third-floor veranda is open to guests who don't have ocean views.

Iruña CABIN **$$**

(Las Pigualas; teremompiche@yahoo.com; d $40, r from $50) A 45-minute walk down the beach from Mompiche's center takes you to this wonderfully isolated spot. Six spacious wooden cabañas surround a pleasant restaurant and social area right on the beach among the palms, and come with mosquito nets, fridges and fans. Good meals can be provided by arrangement.

The hotel can arrange to pick you up in Mompiche, or organize a boat transfer from Muisne. You can't get here by land at high tide.

Los Balcones de Mompiche HOTEL **$$**

(Via a Mompiche; d $45; P air-con wi-fi) If Mompiche had a five-star hotel, we suppose this would be it. With air-con, wi-fi, cable TV and even a small, clean swimming pool, you might not feel like you're in Miami Beach, but if you want a few creature comforts, here you are. It's set back a bit from the road noise on the main drag, too.

Eating

La Facha INTERNATIONAL **$**

(www.lafachahostel.com; 100m north of T-Junction, across from La Casona; mains $5-8; 8am-10pm) A charming team of young locals (who also run the hostel in the same building, and are all keen surfers) serve up mouthwatering burgers, salads and sandwiches. It's on Calle Fosforeras, parallel to the *malecón*. You can rent a decent room here, too ($13 to $15 for shared bathroom, $20 private).

La Chillangua SEAFOOD **$**

(Via a Mompiche; mains $5-8; 7am-7pm) This basic *comedore* on the main drag, across from Farmacia Rogers, no longer has sweet seaside views, but it remains a dependable choice, with filling breakfasts like *majado de verde* (green plantains, white cheese and peppers, with a fried egg on top).

PLAYA NEGRA: BLACK SANDS & THE SHADOW OF MINING

Generations of Mompicheans remember picking up oysters on the black-sand beach of Playa Negra. But the alluring sand also holds titanium deposits, and since 2012 locals have been waging a war against the bulldozers tearing up the beach. An online petition at change.org garnered more than 5,000 signatures in 2017. You can find out more at #SalvemosPlayaNegra. Minister of Tourism Enrique Ponce de León has called the mining actions 'a crime against the environment and tourism.' Stay tuned.

El Chivo Pizzeria ITALIAN $
(Chivo's Pizzeria; ☎098-300-7557; La Fosforera, 100m north of T-junction; mains $6-9; ⏰6-10pm) Formerly called Suly's, this pizzeria has a nice mix of Italian faves like lasagna, spaghetti, pizza and overstuffed calzones.

Getting There & Away

Buses go to and from Esmeraldas a few times daily ($5, 3½ hours), passing Same and Atacames on the way.

Isla Portete

Just 2km south of Mompiche, this palm-frocked island has a long beach with blond sands and little traffic. There are a few seafood shacks right on the beach, and a large resort hotel just across the estuary. Other than that, you get decent surf (with a long 1m-high right-hander from December through March), and a lost island world all to yourself. Check with local fishers about boat tours to nearby islands and further afield. From the Royal Decameron resort you can walk close to an awesome arched rock that's been carved by the sea.

Sleeping

Cabaña Caña Brava CABAÑAS $$
(☎099-191-8054; s/d $35/50) Since our former island favorite (Donde Tito) didn't withstand the earthquake, Cabaña Caña Brava is a more-than-adequate back-up just across the estuary from Decameron. Some rooms have nice balconies with views; all have mosquito netting. Basic, but reasonable.

Royal Decameron RESORT $$$
(☎06-299-7300; www.decameron.com.ec; accessed from mainland 1km south of Mompiche; d/tr/q all-inclusive $177/191/317; P❄📶🏊) This mega-resort geared towards the Ecuadorian elite is located right across the estuary from Isla Portete on the mainland. It has nearly 200 rooms spreading over a hodgepodge of pools, gyms, tennis courts, bars, buffet restaurants, discos and more. The deluxe rooms have ocean views, Ecuadorian textiles, and plenty of modern amenities.

There's a beach club with kayaks and other water toys just across the way on Portete (which guests access via a free boat service).

Getting There & Away

There is no public transport here. Take a taxi ($5) or walk the 2km from Mompiche, then hop on a river ferry ($0.50) to cross the estuary to the island.

Cojimíes

This lost spit of sand is a bit out of the way, but it's worth the trip if you're looking to escape the crowds of Canoa and Mompiche. There's a pretty riverfront beach with light-brown sand right in town, plus a long gorgeous strip of virgin sand that stretches all the way to Perdernales 38km to the south.

A gaggle of beachfront food stands and boat trips to the remote Isla del Amor (one way per boat $15) are the number one and two attractions in this low-key village. There's a running joke that two people go to the island, and three come back (ie with baby in arms).

Sleeping & Eating

Hotel Santorini HOTEL $
(☎099-377-9957; santorini_hotel@hotmail.com; 200m north of Malecón Turistico; s/d $15/30; P📶) This super-lean cement-block hotel is just close enough to the ocean to catch the breeze. The double-decker rooms don't have ocean views, but you do get bunk beds, a funky common sitting area and easy access to the beach.

Restaurant Aurita SEAFOOD $
(☎05-239-1236; Malecón; mains $6-10; ⏰7am-8pm) Overlooking the fishing boats bobbing on the water, this simple waterside restaurant serves delectable Manabí seafood. It's famous for the huge shrimp native to the area, but also prepares tasty ceviche, *concha* (shellfish) and *encocado de pescado* (fish cooked in a rich, spiced coconut sauce). The vibe is casual: dine at plastic picnic tables and dig your heels into the sand.

Getting There & Away

To get here, grab a *buseta* (intercity bus) from Pedernales, on the corner of Juan Pereira and Velasco Ibarra ($1, 45 minutes).

Canoa

☎05 / POP 6887

A sleepy village with a heart of gold, Canoa has a lovely stretch of beach framed by picturesque cliffs to the north and a disappearing horizon to the south. Despite its growing popularity with sunseekers and surfers, the village remains a low-key place, where kids frolic on the sandy lanes at dusk and fishers head out to sea in the early hours before dawn. In the evenings the beachfront bars and guesthouses come to life as backpackers swap travel tales over rum cocktails.

International surf competitions come in the high season (January to March), when waves reach over 2m and accommodation becomes hard to find.

Note that Canoa's comeback from the 2016 earthquake may take some time.

Sights & Activities

Tides are strong here, so stay close to the beach. At low tide you can reach caves at the north end of the beach, which house hundreds of roosting bats. A popular bike trip takes you on the bike path that runs from here to Bahía de Caráquez in about an hour. Surf Shak (p264) offers kayaking cave tours ($25, three hours), paragliding ($45, 20 minutes) and surfing classes ($25, 1½ hours).

Reserva Ecologico Jama-Coaque NATURE RESERVE
(Comuna Camarones) We're hoping this reserve, 26 km south of Perdanales and 3km off the main highway, opens to tourism soon. Last we heard, Third Millenium Alliance (www.tmalliance.org) was working with the community and government to establish accessible trail-heads and basic services. In this wonderland of biodiversity, more than 40 new frog species have been discovered since 2009, and its grounds are designated an Important Bird Area (IBA) by Birdlife International.

It's currently possible to volunteer here by contacting Third Millenium Alliance.

Río Muchacho Organic Farm OUTDOORS
(☎05-302-0487; www.riomuchacho.com; via Canoa Jama Km 10, Troncal del Pacifico, northeast of Canoa) Get your hands dirty learning about sustainable farming practices at tropical Río Muchacho Organic Farm. Most people come here on a three-day, two-night tour costing $172 per person, with discounts for larger groups; there are also short programs from one to three days, plus courses from one week to month ($300 to $1200). You can also volunteer here for $300 per month.

Guest groups are kept small and reservations are preferred. On the accommodation front, cabins are rustic, with shared showers and composting toilets (dorm/private room $8/$18). The coveted spot is a tree-house bunk. Lying along the river of the same name, the farm is reached by a rough 7km unpaved road branching inland from the road north of Canoa. Transportation is by horseback or a $10 taxi from Canoa.

Surfing

There are only beach breaks here. But unlike other spots on the coast, they keep working year-round – getting really big from January through March. Surfboard rentals (per half-/full day $5/$15) and classes (90-minutes, $25) are available at most guesthouses.

Sleeping

★**Hotel Bambu** HOTEL $
(☎05-258-8017; www.hotelbambuecuador.com; Malecón, north end; dm/s/d $10/30/40, camping $20; P ☎) The nicest hotel in town has a great sand-floored restaurant and bar area, cabins with exposed cane roofs, wood-panel windows and mosquito nets, plus delicious hot-water showers. Only a few have ocean views, but most catch a breeze and stay cool. A new addition is the good-value, fully equipped camping spot with a raised bed. There's ping-pong and billiards, too!

★**Casa Shangri-La** GUESTHOUSE $
(☎099-146-8470; Antonio Aviega, 100m north of town on the main road; camping/r per person $7.50/10; ☎ ☎) This fantastic place is owned by a friendly Dutch guy, Jeroen, who has created a chilled-out surfer spot with a big garden, a plunge pool, very nice rooms and a super-relaxed vibe. There's a bar and a library, with surfboards available for rent. It's a short walk from town, which also means you won't hear the reggaeton from the beachfront bars all night.

Jeroen rebuilt the place following the 2016 earthquake, which is surrounded by starfruit and papaya trees. He also offers a tour of a beautiful cacao plantation in nearby El Águila, a site full of birdlife and howler monkeys.

Hostal Canoamar HOSTAL $
(☎05-258-8081; www.canoamar.com; Malecón; s/d $20/25; P ☎) There are good ocean views (sometimes with accompanying welcome breezes) from this three-story spot with cane-walled rooms including mosquito nets and nice firm beds. Budget travelers will like the shared kitchen. It's next to La Vista Hotel, on the beach.

Posada Olmito GUESTHOUSE $

(☎099-553-3341; www.olmito.org; Malecón; d $26, breakfast $3; P 📶) Right on the beach you'll find this decidedly rustic and rather higgledy-piggledy structure perfect for beach bums. The funky, fan-cooled bamboo rooms have small private bathrooms with hot water, and are clean enough. The vibe is beyond relaxed, complete with hammocks and dozing dogs. The bar and barbecue fire up at night.

Amalur GUESTHOUSE $

(☎098-303-5039; www.amalurcanoa.com; cnr San Andres & Francisco Aveiga; dm $10-12, s/d $20/25; 📶) Overlooking a drab soccer pitch, two blocks from the ocean, this guesthouse is a nice option away from the madding crowd. Rooms have bamboo beds, hardwood floors, bright showers and super sheets. The downstairs restaurant glows orange-pink and oozes light jazz; there's also a ping-pong table and yoga classes.

La Vista Hotel GUESTHOUSE $

(☎099-228-8995; Malecón, next to Coco Loco; s/d/tr/q $25/35/45/55; P 📶) La Vista is an upscale-ish four-story guesthouse. Its spacious, nicely designed rooms have beamed ceilings and glass (rather than screened-in) windows, and it's right on the beach. Like nearly every place in Canoa, rates go up $5 per night on weekends.

Cocoa Inn HOTEL $$

(☎099-228-9372; www.cocoainn.com; Malecón, south end; d/q/ste $30/40/50; P 📶) Neat, clean and with nice colorful bedspreads, this newish Chilean-run hostel survived the 2016 earthquake with only a few raised floor tiles. It's located at the southernmost end of the developed part of the *malecón*, and because of its age (or lack thereof) is a better option at this price range than some nearby hotels.

Eating

Amalur SPANISH $

(www.amalurcanoa.com; cnr Francisco Aviega & San Andres, inside Amalur Hotel; mains $7-12; ⊙8am-10pm; 📶) Owned by a Spanish chef (Amalur means 'Mother Earth' in Basque), this trim, minimalist restaurant is a major step up from your average Ecuadorian small-town restaurant. A chalkboard lists the day's specials – a few recent favorites include fresh calamari *a la plancha*, *pulpo a la Gallega* (boiled octopus with paprika), homegrown, nicely seasoned eggplant in salsa and a marvelously tender sea bass.

Surf Shak INTERNATIONAL $

(Malecón; mains $5-10; ⊙8am-midnight; 📶) The 'Shak' serves up pizzas, burgers, filling breakfasts and plenty of rum cocktails to a fun-seeking foreign crowd. Its California dreamin' surf vibe is spot on.

Information

There are no banks in Canoa (San Vicente has the nearest ATMs).

Getting There & Away

Buses between Bahía de Caráquez ($1, 45 minutes) and Pedernales or Esmeraldas will all stop in Canoa. The office for Coachtur is about three blocks inland from Hotel Bambu and has hourly services to Portoviejo ($4, 2½ hours), Manta ($5, 3 hours) and Guayaquil ($9, 6 hours).

Bahía de Caráquez

☎05 / POP 26,100

Gleaming-white high-rises and red-tile roofs fill this bustling peninsula city. With the Río Chone on one side, flowing into the Pacific on the other, this tidy former port city basks in the sun and enjoys a wonderfully laid-back feel. There's a pretty beach and it's popular with Ecuadorian tourists, though not many foreigners stay here.

In the first half of the 20th century the city was Ecuador's principal port, but eroding sandbanks let the honor drift to Guayaquil and Manta, and Bahía was left to its housekeeping.

The city was devastated by the 2016 earthquake, with many businesses reduced to rubble. Tourism has yet to recover.

Sights & Activities

Head to the beach to organize boat tours to heart-shaped Isla Corazón, and whale-watching tours (per hour $25).

Church of La Merced CHURCH

(Plaza Sucre) Built of materials imported from the US and Europe in 1912, this church has survived two big earthquakes. Alberto Santos, a big-time businessman of the time, left his mark on the city with his donations for this building and the statues along the waterfront.

Museo Bahía de Caráquez MUSEUM

(www.museos.gob.ec/redmuseos/bahia/bahia.html; cnr Malecón Santos & Peña; ⊙8:30am-

4:30pm Tue-Fri, 9am-2:30pm Sat) FREE You'll find a good introduction to the area's indigenous history at this well-curated modern museum. The collection includes hundreds of pieces of pre-Colombian pottery, as well as local crafts for sale.

Mirador La Cruz VIEWPOINT
(Barrio de La Cruz, near Av 3 de Noviembre) High above the peninsula and boasting great views of the city, sea and river, this viewpoint at the south end of town can be reached on foot or by a short taxi ride.

Isla Corazón ISLAND
(☎05-267-4836; www.islacorazon.com; San Vicente or Puerto Portovelo; admission incl 2hr guided tour from $10) Bird-watchers shouldn't miss a visit to Isla Corazon, where you can take guided tours through mangroves in search of frigate birds, herons, egrets and other species. It's 7km east of San Vicente, reachable by bus ($0.50) or taxi ($5). For tours, contact Leonidas Vega or Juan Montalvo at the Santa Rosa church in San Vicente on the phone number listed.

Sleeping

With Bahía's hotel scene still recovering from the 2016 earthquake, you're likely to find more options further down the coast.

Centro Vacacional Life CABIN $
(☎05-269-0496; cnr Octavio Vitteri & Daniel Hidalgo; r per person $20; ❄📶) Just two blocks from the beach, these cabins aren't much to look at from the outside, yet all come with kitchens, two bedrooms, comfy furniture, plasma TVs and sleep up to five people. There's also a grassy playground, a pool table and ping-pong. Since everything else fell down in the earthquake, it's pretty much the only option in the town center.

Casa Ceibo LUXURY HOTEL $$$
(☎05-239-9399, 099-470-3622; www.casaceibo.com; Av Sixto Durán Ballén; d/ste incl breakfast from $110/240; P❄📶🏊) If you're looking for pampering and seclusion, this gated luxury hotel 4km from central Bahía (on the road out of town, just beyond the bus terminal) is the place for you. With plush rooms that have all the creature comforts, minimalist public areas and huge manicured gardens that lead down to the river, this is definitely the smartest place in town.

Kayaking, biking, use of the gym, Jacuzzi and pool are all included, and there's a full-service restaurant here as well.

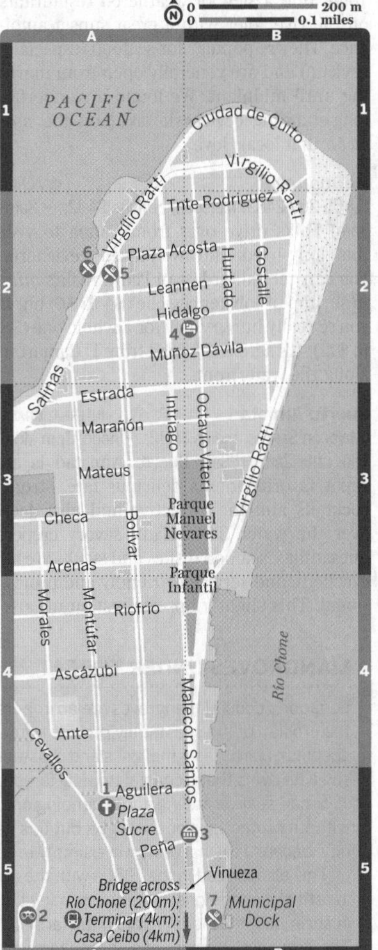

Bahía de Caráquez

Eating

You'll find a slew of weathered restaurants on the river pier with a great sunset ambience. They're popular for seafood (especially ceviche) and are generally open from morning until midnight. We found a wonderful, long-standing cevicheria right on the *malecón* that locals love.

Hermanacho CEVICHE $
(05-269-2483; Malecón; ceviche $4-12; 8am-3pm) Folks drive over from Canoa to visit this long-lived and well-loved cevicheria. You can get half orders of Pedro Avila's *mixto* shrimp or lobster ceviche ($4 to $6) but if you're really hungry, pay for a whole one ($8 to $12). It's across the road from D'Camaron, along the waterfront.

Puerto Amistad INTERNATIONAL $
(Malecón Santos; mains $6-12; noon-11pm Mon-Thu, until 2am Fri-Sat) Puerto Amistad is an expat favorite for its delicious fare, strong cocktails and the attractive and airy deck over the water. The salads, savory crepes, quesadillas, seafood dishes and steaks are all excellent, and service is friendly and professional. This slightly upscale restaurant also functions as Bahía's yacht club and is the place to bump into other visiting yachties.

D'Camaron SEAFOOD $
(www.dcamaron.com.ec; Bolívar btwn Plaza Acosta & Leannen; mains $7-11; 9:30am-6pm Mon-Fri, 8:30am-6pm Sat & Sun) As the name implies, shrimp is the specialty at this casual open-air spot near the water. Order them grilled, with a cocktail, and enjoy the ocean breezes. For a change, try the *arroz marinera*, with loads of different shellfish.

Information

Banco de Guayaquil (cnr Bolívar & Riofrío) Cashes travelers checks and has an ATM.

Getting There & Away

A bridge connects Bahía to San Vicente (and the rest of the north coast) over the Río Chone. This eliminates the need for long drives around the bay or a ferry ride across the river.

The bus terminal is 4km from the center of town on the *malecón* as you head towards Chone. From there you'll find buses that offer regular or *ejecutivo* (1st-class) services – they head to Quito (regular/*ejecutivo* $10/$12, eight hours, four daily) via Santo Domingo (regular/

MANGROVES UNDER THREAT

Ecuador's coastal mangroves are an important habitat. In addition to helping to control the erosion of the coast, they provide homes, protection and nutrients for numerous species of birds, fish, mollusks and crustaceans. Unfortunately, it has been difficult to say who owns these coastal tropical forests, which has left them open to exploitation.

Small-scale crabbing and shrimping operations initially took over areas of mangroves without protections or oversight, but this never posed a serious threat to mangrove ecology, because the harvests were simply too small.

This all changed in the 1980s with the arrival of shrimp farms, which produced shrimp in artificial conditions in numbers many times greater than could be caught by traditional shrimping methods. To build the farms, it was necessary to remove the mangroves. The prospective owner of a shrimp farm purchased the land from the government, cut down the mangroves and began the shrimp-farming process. The net profits of the shrimp farms were very high, and the idea soon caught on and spread rapidly along the coast, resulting in the removal of 80% to 90% of Ecuador's mangroves during the 1980s and early 1990s. (Driving along the coast, it's hard to miss the shrimpers in their long, flat boats.) Although there are now laws controlling this destruction, these are difficult to enforce in the remote coastal areas.

The shrimp farms have had many negative short- and long-term effects. Previously, many families could find a sustainable livelihood in the mangroves, whereas shrimp farms employ only a handful of seasonal workers. Where before there were mangroves protecting a large diversity of species, now there's just commercial shrimp. Coastal erosion and pollution from the wastes of the shrimp farms have become serious problems. A combination of disease and economic decline means that today many farms lie abandoned. Meanwhile, efforts are being made in Muisne, Bahía de Caráquez and a few other coastal towns to start replanting mangroves. You can take mangrove tours around most major tourist centers.

ejecutivo $5/$6), and there are services to Guayaquil ($7.50, six hours, seven daily), Manta ($3, three hours, three daily) and Canoa ($1.25, 45 minutes, half-hourly).

Manta

05 / POP 217,553

The largest city in the province (and the fifth largest in Ecuador), Manta is a bustling and prosperous port town graced with high-rises, and a few urban beaches that draw mostly domestic tourists. As an important center for the fishing and tuna-processing industries, it's the kind of place you smell before you arrive, and its quirkiest sight is a huge statue of a tuna. Indeed, there aren't a lot of reasons to come here – the beaches are far better elsewhere on the coast – but it's an important transportation hub and has a lively nightlife scene. You may pass through if you're visiting the handicraft town of Montecristi.

Sights

Museo Arqueológico del Banco Central MUSEUM
(Malecón btwn Calle 9 & Av 2; admission $1; 8:30am-5pm Mon-Fri) The fully modernized city museum reopened in its new location in 2009, and showcases valuable artifacts from pre-Colombian Manta culture, a selection of Ecuadorian paintings and quirky fishing paraphernalia.

Playa Murciélago BEACH
(Malecón, btwn Calle 30 & Calle 19) This beach is less protected than most beaches in the area and has bigger waves (although they're not very big) along with a powerful undertow. It's a couple of kilometers northwest of downtown (near Hotel Balandra) and is the town's most popular beach, backed by snack bars, restaurants and umbrella-rental spots.

Tarqui Beach BEACH
(Malecón) The east end of this stretch of sand is a hive of activity early in the mornings, as vendors sell row upon row of shark, tuna, swordfish, dorado and other fish (the sizes of which seem to decrease with each passing year). You'll also find the so-called Parque del Marisco here: lots of stalls serving up fresh fish and seafood in a variety of different styles right on the beach, including what locals will swear to you is the best ceviche in the country.

The beach is suitable for swimming.

Sleeping

Manakin GUESTHOUSE $$
(05-262-0413; hostalmanakin@hotmail.com; cnr Calle 17 & Av 21; s/d incl breakfast $55/65;) Near the heart of all the nightlife, Manakin is a converted one-story house with a pleasant laid-back vibe. Narrow, well-ordered and highly perfumed rooms are nicely furnished, and the house offers fine places to unwind – including the front patio. And it's near the mall. Truly, what more could one ask for?

Hotel Balandra HOTEL $$$
(05-262-0545; www.hotelbalandra.com; Av 7 near Calle 20; s/d $103/152, deluxe r $155;) This small but upscale hillside hotel offers pleasantly furnished deluxe rooms and two-bedroom cabins, some with balconies looking out to sea. Outside you'll find sculpted shrubbery, a small gym and sauna, a pool and a playground. Family groups can make for a less-than-relaxing experience on weekends.

Eating

Seafood *comedores* line the east end of the beach on Malecón de Tarqui. Playa Murciélago has cafes front and center for enjoying beach action.

Trovador Café CAFE $
(05-262-9376; Av 3 & Calle 10, Pasaje Hermanos Egas Miranda; mains $2-5; 7:30am-6pm Mon-Sat) On a pleasant pedestrian lane set back just a short distance from the *malecón*, this place offers frothy cappuccinos, sandwiches and inexpensive lunch plates. There's outdoor seating in this old colonial home.

Parrillada Oh Mar GRILL $$
(cnr Av 20 & Flavio Reyes; mains $9-12; noon-11pm Mon-Sat) This amenable glass-walled grill in the center of Manta's nightlife area is a great place for a filling steak and a glass of good Argentinian red wine.

Information

Municipal Tourist Office (05-262-2944; Av 3 N10-34; 8am-12:30pm & 2:30-5pm Mon-Fri) Friendly and helpful.

Police (Av 4 de Noviembre, near Calle 104)

Post Office (Calle 8) Located at the town hall.

Getting There & Away

AIR

Located on the Manta waterfront, past the open-air theater, is the **TAME office** (05-262-2006;

Manta

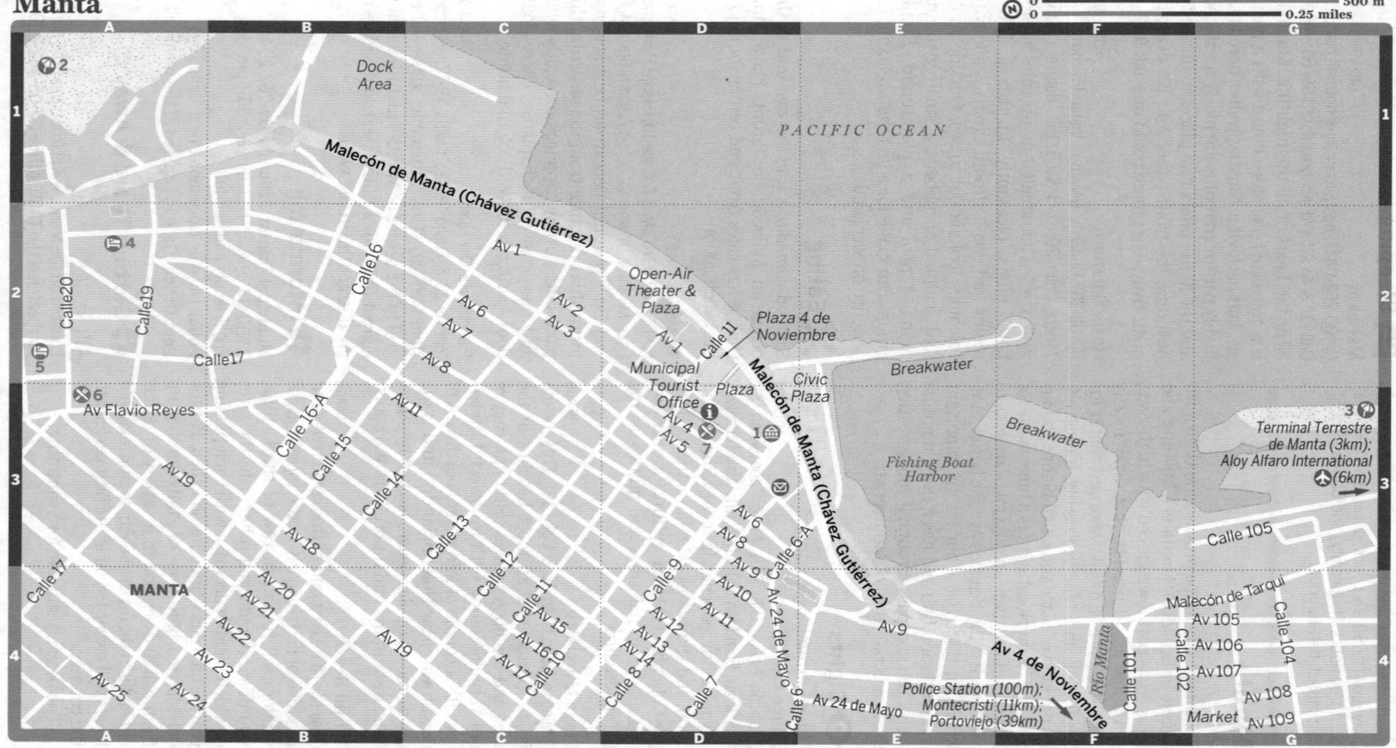
500 m
0.25 miles
PACIFIC OCEAN
Dock Area
Malecón de Manta (Chávez Gutiérrez)
Open-Air Theater & Plaza
Plaza 4 de Noviembre
Municipal Tourist Office
Plaza
Civic Plaza
Breakwater
Breakwater
Fishing Boat Harbor
Terminal Terrestre de Manta (3km); Aloy Alfaro International (6km)
Police Station (100m); Montecristi (11km); Portoviejo (39km)
Av 4 de Noviembre
Malecón de Tarqui
Río Manta
MANTA
Av Flavio Reyes
Av 24 de Mayo
Calle 105
Calle 104
Calle 102
Calle 101
Av 105
Av 106
Av 107
Av 108
Av 109
Market

Manta

Malecón de Manta betw. Av 13 & 14). TAME has one to two flights daily to/from Quito (one way from $86, 30 minutes). You can buy tickets at the airport on the morning of the flight, but the planes are sometimes full on weekends and holidays. Buying tickets a few days in advance seems to offer big discounts if you can plan ahead.

The airport is some 3km east of Tarqui, and a taxi costs about $2 for the 10-minute trip.

BUS

Most buses depart from the new Terminal Terreste near the airport. Buses to nearby Manabí towns and villages, such as Montecristi ($0.50, 15 minutes), also leave from the terminal.

Buses serve Jipijapa ($0.90, one hour), Canoa ($4, 3½ to four hours), Bahía de Caráquez ($2.50, three hours), Guayaquil ($5, four hours), Esmeraldas ($7, six hours) and Ambato ($8, 10 hours).

Ejecutivo buses to Quito ($10, nine hours) and Guayaquil ($7.50, four hours) leave from a smaller nearby terminal on the *malecón* throughout the day.

Montecristi

05 / POP 46,312

Montecristi produces the finest straw hat on the planet, even if it is mistakenly referred to as the 'Panama' hat. Ask for yours as a sombrero *de paja toquilla,* a fine, fibrous straw endemic to this region. Hat stores line the road leading into town and the plaza, but most of their wares are cheap and loosely woven.

The city was founded in around 1628, when manteños fled inland to avoid the frequent plundering by pirates. Today its many unrestored colonial houses give the village a rather tumbledown and ghostly atmosphere. The key draw here is hat shopping, but Montecristi's main plaza has a beautiful church which contains a statue of the Virgin to which miracles have been attributed, as well as a statue of native son Eloy Alfaro, who was twice Ecuador's president. His tomb is in the town hall and there's a new museum in his honor on the hilltop.

Sights

Museo Historico de Montecristi MUSEUM
(Centro Cívico Ciudad Alfaro; www.ciudadalfaro.gob.ec; Prolongacion 10 de Agosto; 9am-4:30pm) FREE Revolutionary and two-time president Eloy Alfaro was born in Montecristi, and here is an amazing tribute to the man: a hilltop museum with a panoramic view of the city below. There' s an old train engine in honor of Alfaro's pioneering efforts with the Guayaquil-Quito line connecting the Andes to the Pacific, and gobs of letters and artifacts honoring the person who brought dignity, citizenship and military rank to the nation's formerly dispossessed: the indigenous, the Afro-Ecuadorians and women.

On a side note, the bathrooms here are really, really nice.

Basilica Santisima Virgen de Montserrat CHURCH
(Calle Sucre, La Madre Parque) Dating back to the early 20th century, this beautiful church contains a statue of the Virgin to which miracles have been attributed. While the Museo Historico de Montecristi further up the hill may house the city's political heritage, this site is its spiritual center.

Shopping

José Chávez Franco CLOTHING
(Rocafuerte 386; 7am-7pm) Here you can snatch up high-quality straw 'Panama' hats for under $100, but check them closely. None are blocked or banded, but they're cheaper than just about anywhere else in the world.

José is quick to point out that he also sells higher-grade sombreros for far more than that, too, so take your time shopping.

Getting There & Away

Montecristi can be reached during the day by frequent buses ($0.50, 30 minutes) from the bus terminal in Manta.

South Coast

Includes ➡

Best Places to Eat

- El Morro Restaurant (p301)
- Manso Mix (p282)
- Pique & Pase (p283)
- Delfín Mágico (p293)
- Pigro (p297)

Best Places to Stay

- Mansion del Rio (p280)
- Hostería Mandála (p289)
- Balsa Surf Camp (p295)
- Chescos (p299)
- Hostería Farallón Dillon (p298)

Why Go?

Wide sandy beaches, lush nature reserves and biologically rich islands are just a few of the attractions of Ecuador's southern coastal region. For wildlife watching, outdoor activities (like surfing, hiking and paragliding) or just relaxing on the beach, this is a great place to be.

The gateway to the region is Guayaquil, a buzzing, tropical city that has gone through a remarkable transformation in recent years. To the west lies the coastal Ruta Spondylus, where you can watch migrating humpback whales or visit colonies of blue-footed boobies off Puerto Lopez, join the surf and party crowd in Montañita, or unwind in the peaceful seaside enclaves of Ayampe and Olón.

South of Guayaquil is mostly banana country, featuring miles and miles of *oro verde* (green gold). Machala celebrates its banana legacy, and is the entry point to the rustic, mangrove-covered island of Jambelí. Meanwhile, Zaruma is a picturesque colonial mountain town.

When to Go

Guayaquil

Jan–May Rainy season is hot, humid and sunny with occasional heavy downpours.

Jun–Dec Dry season is cooler and more overcast. Humpback whales visit June to September.

End Dec–Apr This is high season, when Ecuadorians visit coastal resorts.

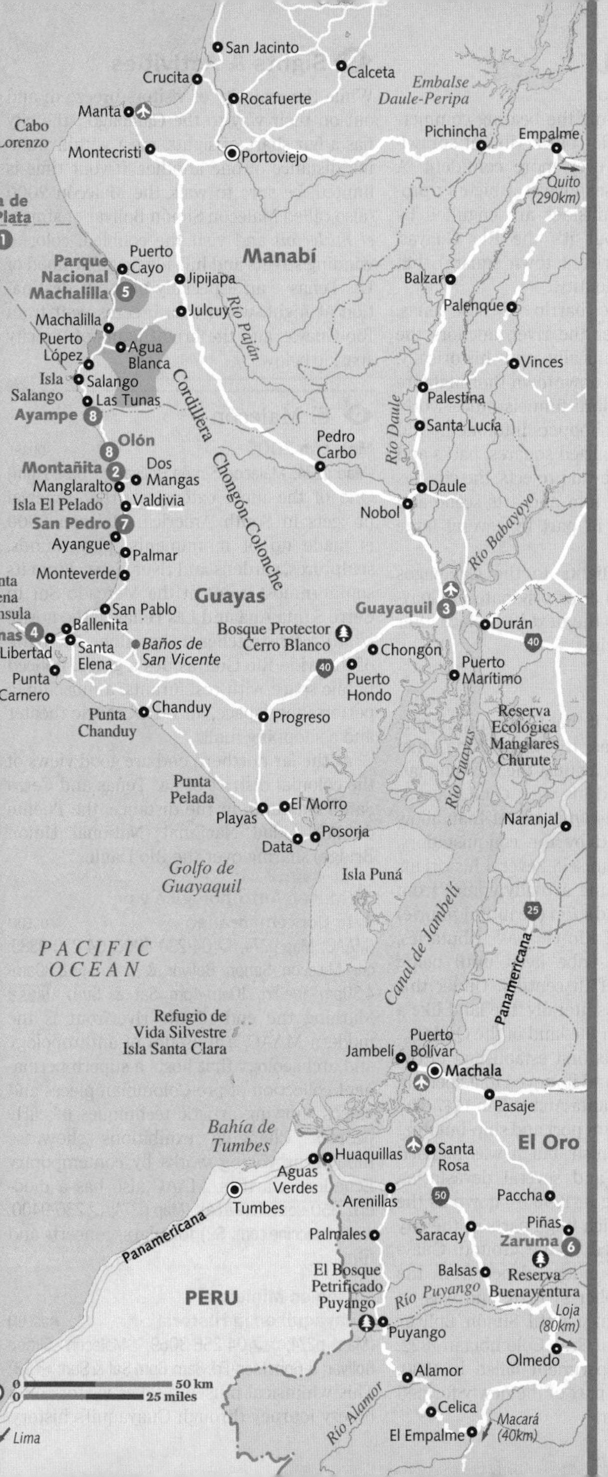

South Coast Highlights

1. **Isla de la Plata** (p292) Getting up close and personal with nesting boobies and other birdlife.
2. **Montañita** (p294) Frolicking in the waves and sipping fruity cocktails to tropical beats at this surfing mecca.
3. **Guayaquil** (p272) Strolling the *malecón*, dining in some of Ecuador's best restaurants and wandering the cobbled lanes of Cerro Santa Ana.
4. **Salinas** (p299) Paddleboarding, jet skiing and banana boating at Ecuador's answer to Miami Beach.
5. **Parque Nacional Machalilla** (p291) Spotting massive humpback whales on their annual migration, breaching only meters away from your boat.
6. **Zaruma** (p304) Wandering around a beautiful former mining town, breathing in the cool air and spectacular mountain views.
7. **San Pedro** (p298) Flying like a bird along the coastline on a paragliding adventure.
8. **Olón and Ayampe** (p293) Slowing down and relaxing in these peaceful seaside villages.

GUAYAQUIL

04 / POP 2.69 MILLION

Guayaquil is not only the beating commercial heart of Ecuador but a vibrant sprawling city, growing ever more confident. A half-dozen high-rises give it a big-city profile, and several hillsides are engulfed by colorful favelas, but it's the Río Guayas' *malecón* (the riverfront town square) that defines the city's identity.

The picturesque barrio of Las Peñas, which perches over the river, anchors the city both geographically and historically, while the principal downtown thoroughfare Avenida 9 de Octubre funnels office workers, residents and shoppers into one hybrid stream. Amid revitalized squares, parks and massive urban-renewal projects, the city has a growing theater, film and arts scene and lively bars, fueled in part by several large universities.

Note that all flights to the Galápagos Islands either stop at or originate in Guayaquil, so the city is the next best place after Quito to set up a trip.

History

Popular legend has it that Guayaquil's name comes from Guayas, the great Puna chief who fought bravely against the Inca and later the Spanish, and his wife, Quill. Guayas is said to have killed Quill rather than allow her to be captured by the conquistadors, before drowning himself. Several historians claim the city's name actually comes from the words *hua* (land), *illa* (beautiful prairie) and Quilca, one of Río Guayas' tributaries, where the Quilca tribe lived until being wiped out in the 17th century. Under this theory, Guayaquil is literally 'the land like a beautiful prairie on the land of the Quilcas.'

A settlement was first established in the area around 1534, and it moved to its permanent home of the Santa Ana Hill in 1547. The city was an important port and ship-building center for the Spanish, but it was plagued by pirate attacks and several devastating fires, including one in 1896 – known as the Great Fire – in which huge parts of the city were simply burned to the ground. Guayaquil achieved its independence from the Spaniards on October 9, 1820, and was an independent province until Simón Bolívar annexed it as part of Gran Colombia in 1822. When Bolívar's experiment failed in 1830, Guayaquil became part of the newly formed republic of Ecuador.

Sights & Activities

While the majority of visitors breeze in and out on their way to the Galápagos, the city has a fair share of sights, most within walking distance of one another. If your time is limited, be sure to walk the Malecón 2000 (also called Malecón Simón Bolívar or simply *el malecón*) and visit the cobbled, colorful winding streets and hillside neighborhood of Las Peñas – an especially pleasant destination at night, when cool breezes waft from Río Guayas and the bright lights of the city sparkle below.

El Malecón

Malecón 2000 SQUARE

(Map p274; Malecón Simón Bolívar; 6am-11pm)

One of the most extensive urban-renewal projects in South America, Malecón 2000 is made up of monuments, playgrounds, sculptures, gardens and river views. From its southernmost point at the Mercado Sur to Cerro Santa Ana and Las Peñas in the north, *el malecón* stretches 2.5km along the bank of the wide Río Guayas. It's a gated, policed public space with restaurants, a museum, a performance space, an IMAX movie theater and a shopping mall.

At the far northern end are good views of the colonial district of Las Peñas and Cerro Santa Ana and, in the distance, the Puente de la Unidad Nacional (National Union Bridge) soaring over the Río Daule.

★ **Museo Antropológico y de Arte Contemporáneo** MUSEUM

(MAAC; Map p274; 04-230-4000, 04-230-9385; cnr Malecón Simón Bolívar & Loja; 8.30am-4.30pm Tue-Fri, 10am-4pm Sat & Sun) FREE

Marking the end of the riverfront is the modern MAAC, a museum of anthropology and archaeology that hosts a superb permanent collection of pre-Colombian pieces and videos showing artistic techniques of early peoples. Changing exhibitions showcase thought-provoking works by contemporary Ecuadorian artists. MAAC also has a modern 350-seat **theater** (Map p274; 230-9400; www.maaccine.com; $2) for plays, concerts and films.

Museo en Miniatura 'Guayaquil en la Historia' MUSEUM

(Map p274; 04-256-3069; Malecón Simón Bolívar; 3-6pm Mon-Fri, 8am-6pm Sat & Sun; $3)

This whimsical museum takes visitors on a breezy journey through Guayaquil's history, with elaborate miniature sets that relate key events over the past 500 years (including pirate attacks, devastating fires, revolutionary fervor and more recent but equally bold revitalization projects). The whole tour takes about 45 minutes, and is available in English.

La Rotonda MONUMENT

(Map p274; Malecón Simón Bolívar) Around halfway along the *malecón* you'll soon come to one of Guayaquil's more impressive monuments, particularly when illuminated at night. Flanked by small fountains, it depicts the historic but enigmatic meeting between Bolívar and San Martín that took place here in 1822.

La Perla SCENIC FLIGHTS

(Map p274; www.laperladeguayaquil.com; Malecón Simón Bolívar; Tues-Fri/Sat & Sun $3.50/5; ⏲10am-10pm Tue-Sun) Ride this giant 187ft-high Ferris wheel, the largest in South America, for views over the city, old town and the rivers beyond.

Las Peñas & Cerro Santa Ana

These two historic neighborhoods are some of Guayaquil's oldest, with parts untouched by the many fires that have ravaged the city over the years. Perched here for more than 400 years, the streets and buildings have been restored into an idealized version of a quaint South American hillside village, with brightly painted homes and cobblestone alleyways. The views from the top are spectacular, especially at night. Small, informal, family-run restaurants and neighborhood bars line the steps and it's completely safe, patrolled by friendly security officers who make sure foot traffic up the steep stairway flows unimpeded.

Numa Pompilio Llona STREET

(Map p274) This historic street, named after the well-known *guayaquileño* poet (1832–1907), begins at the northern end of the *malecón,* to the right of the stairs that head up the hill called Cerro Santa Ana. The narrow, winding street has several unobtrusive plaques set into the walls of some of its houses, indicating the simple residences of past presidents. The colonial wooden architecture has been allowed to age elegantly, albeit with a gloss of paint.

Several artists live in the area, and there are art galleries and craft shops scattered along the lane.

Keep going along the street and it eventually meets back up with the river, with a pleasant paved walkway skirting along its edge.

Cerro Santa Ana AREA

(Map p274) One of Guayaquil's most iconic sights is this hillside enclave, which is dotted with brightly painted homes, cafes, bars and souvenir shops. Follow the winding path up the 444 steps to reach the hilltop **Fortín del Cerro** (Fort of the Hill; Map p274). Cannons, which were once used to protect Guayaquil from pirates, aim over the parapet toward the river and are still fired today during celebrations.

You can climb the **lighthouse** (Map p274; ⏲10am-10pm) FREE for spectacular 360-degree views of the city and its rivers, and stop in a tiny chapel across from it.

Museo de la Musica Popular Guayaquileña Julio Jaramillo MUSEUM

(Map p274; Edificio 3 Bldg, 2nd fl; ⏲10am-5pm Wed-Sat, to 3pm Sun) FREE This small, quaint museum is worth a peek while strolling through this historic area. One part is dedicated to the great singers and songwriters of Ecuador (especially the legendary Julio Jaramillo), with old Victrolas and vintage mandolins among the memorabilia. The other part of the museum is dedicated to beer, ie Pilsener, which once had a brewery nearby.

Don't miss Pilseners on draft (from $4) in the attached cafe. To find the building, head east along Numa Pompilio Llona and into the pedestrianized courtyard.

Iglesia de Santo Domingo CHURCH

(Map p274; near Pedro Carbo & Sgto Buitrón) Behind the open-air Teatro Bogotá is the oldest church in Guayaquil. Founded in 1548 and restored in 1938, it's worth a look.

Downtown

Avenida 9 de Octubre, downtown Guayaquil's main commercial street, is lined with shoe stores, high-end electronics shops, department stores and fast-food restaurants.

Museo Nahim Isaias MUSEUM

(Map p274; ☎04-232-4182; cnr Pichincha & Ballén; ⏲8:30am-5pm Tue-Fri, 10am-4pm Sat) FREE Nahim Isaias, in the Plaza de Administración building, exhibits more than 2,000 pictorial and sculptural works, paintings and artifacts from the 16th to 19th centuries, including colonial and religious objects.

Guayaquil – City Center

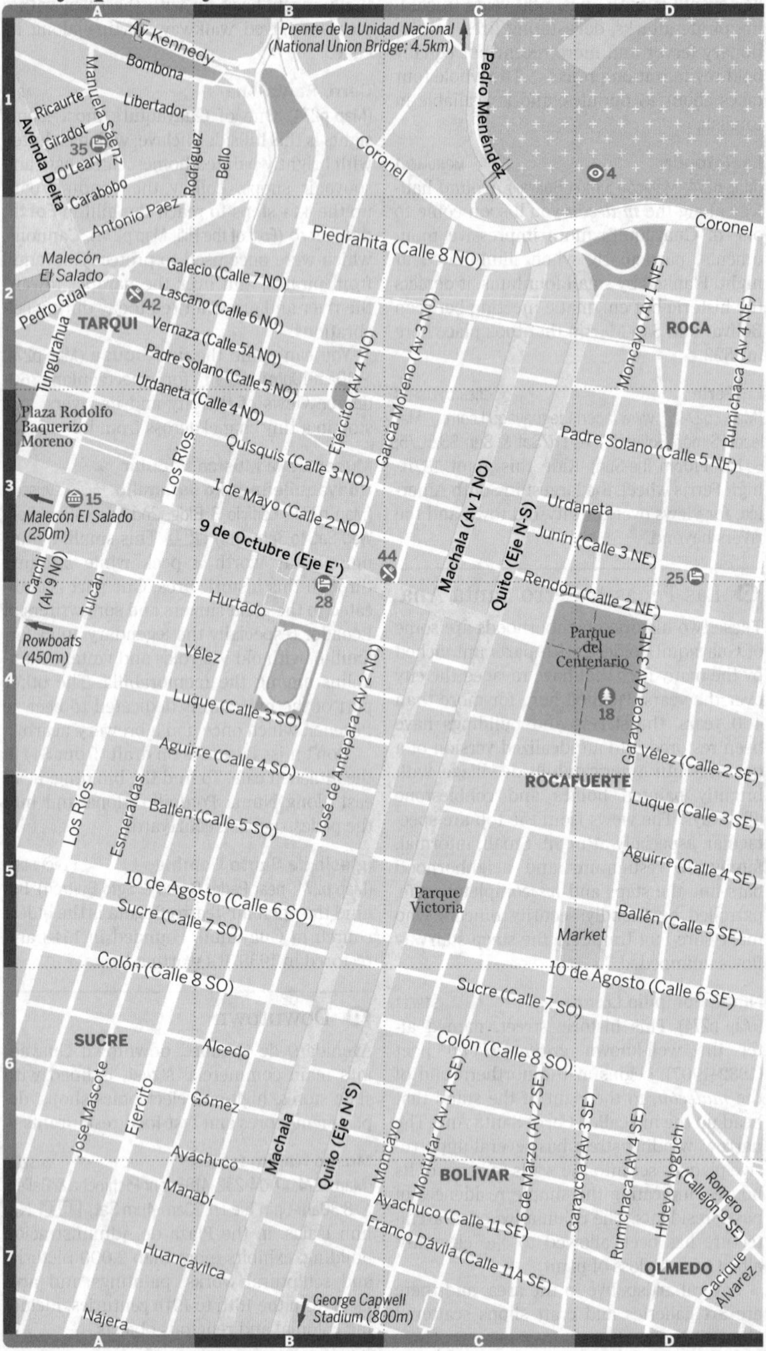

SOUTH COAST GUAYAQUIL

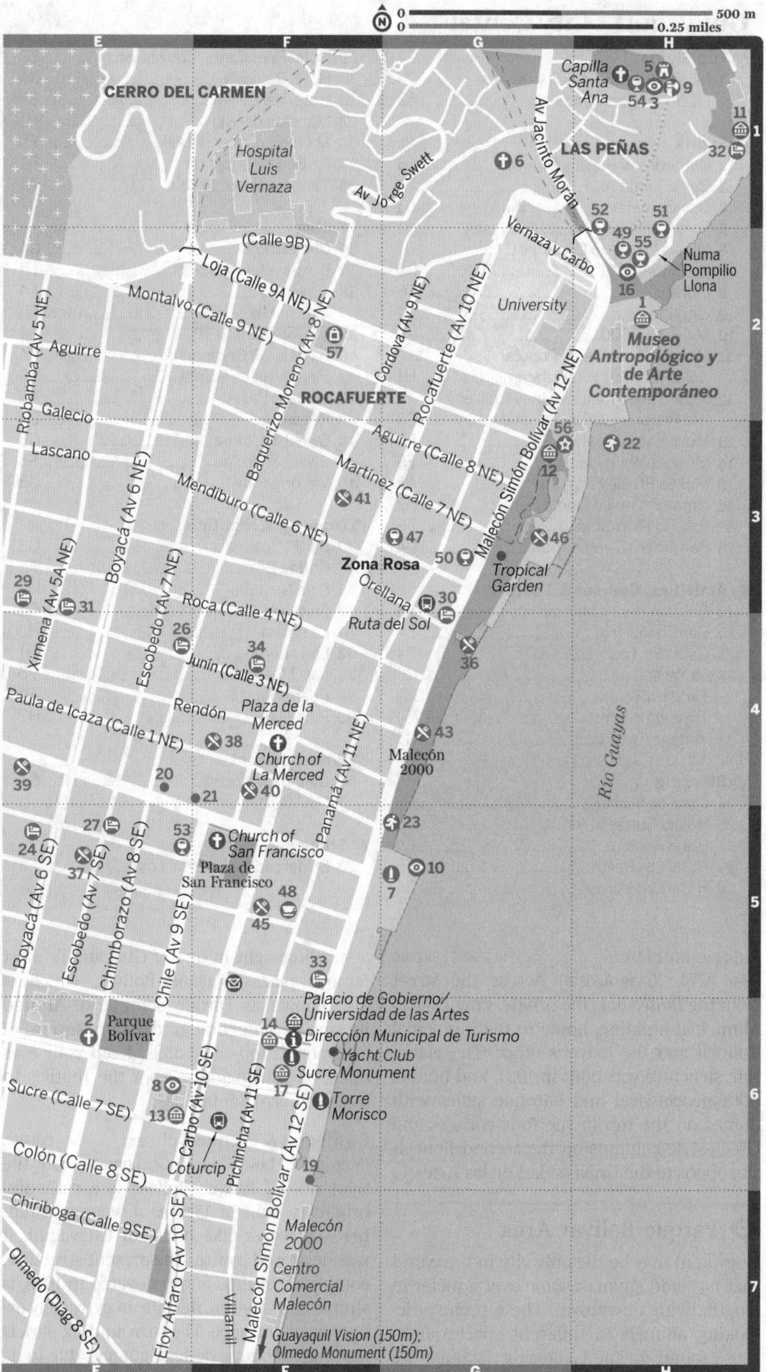
0 500 m
0 0.25 miles
CERRO DEL CARMEN
Hospital Luis Vernaza
Av Jorge Swett
Capilla Santa Ana
LAS PEÑAS
Av Jacinto Morán
Vernaza y Carbo
Numa Pompilio Llona
University
Museo Antropológico y de Arte Contemporáneo
(Calle 9B)
Loja (Calle 9A NE)
Montalvo (Calle 9 NE)
Aguirre
Galecio
Lascano
Riobamba (Av 5 NE)
Baquerizo Moreno (Av 8 NE)
Cordova (Av 9 NE)
Rocafuerte (Av 10 NE)
ROCAFUERTE
Aguirre (Calle 8 NE)
Martínez (Calle 7 NE)
Mendiburo (Calle 6 NE)
Malecón Simón Bolívar (Av 12 NE)
Boyacá (Av 6 NE)
Escobedo (Av 7 NE)
Ximena (Av 5A NE)
Zona Rosa
Tropical Garden
Orellana
Ruta del Sol
Roca (Calle 4 NE)
Junín (Calle 3 NE)
Rendón
Plaza de la Merced
Paula de Icaza (Calle 1 NE)
Church of La Merced
Panamá (Av 11 NE)
Malecón 2000
Río Guayas
Church of San Francisco
Plaza de San Francisco
Boyacá (Av 6 SE)
Escobedo (Av 7 SE)
Chimborazo (Av 8 SE)
Chile (Av 9 SE)
Parque Bolívar
Palacio de Gobierno/ Universidad de las Artes
Dirección Municipal de Turismo
Yacht Club
Sucre Monument
Torre Morisco
Sucre (Calle 7 SE)
Carbo (Av 10 SE)
Pichincha (Av 11 SE)
Coturcip
Colón (Calle 8 SE)
Chiriboga (Calle 9SE)
Olmedo (Diag 8 SE)
Eloy Alfaro (Av 10 SE)
Villamil
Malecón Simón Bolívar (Av 12 SE)
Malecón 2000
Centro Comercial Malecón
Guayaquil Vision (150m); Olmedo Monument (150m)
SOUTH COAST GUAYAQUIL

Guayaquil - City Center

Top Sights
1 Museo Antropológico y de Arte Contemporáneo ... H2

Sights
2 Cathedral & Parque Bolívar ... E6
3 Cerro Santa Ana ... H1
4 City Cemetery ... D1
5 Fortín del Cerro ... H1
6 Iglesia de Santo Domingo ... G1
7 La Rotonda ... G5
8 Library ... E6
9 Lighthouse ... H1
10 Malecón 2000 ... G5
11 Museo de la Musica Popular Guayaquileña Julio Jaramillo ... H1
12 Museo en Miniatura 'Guayaquil en la Historia' ... G3
13 Museo Municipal ... E6
14 Museo Nahim Isaias ... F6
15 Museo Presley Norton ... A3
16 Numa Pompilio Llona ... H2
17 Palacio Municipal ... F6
18 Parque del Centenario ... D4

Activities, Courses & Tours
19 Captain Henry Morgan ... F6
20 Centro Viajero ... E4
21 Galasam Tours ... F4
22 La Perla ... H3
Tangara Tours ... (see 35)
Trips & Dreams ... (see 25)
23 Vintage Train Car ... G5

Sleeping
24 Casa de Romero ... E5
25 Hostal Suites Madrid ... D3
26 Hotel Andaluz ... E4
27 Hotel Las Peñas ... E5
28 Hotel Oro Verde ... B4
29 Hotel Presidente Internacional ... E3
30 Hotel Ramada ... G4
31 Hotel Versailles ... E3
32 Mansion del Rio ... H1
33 Manso Boutique Hotel ... F5
34 Re Bed & Breakfast ... F4
35 Tangara Guest House ... A1

Eating
36 Chop Chops ... G4
37 Dulceria La Palma ... E5
38 Lorenabo ... F4
Manso Mix ... (see 33)
39 Mi Comisariato ... E4
40 Pasteles & Compania ... F4
41 Picanteria La Culata ... F3
42 Pique & Pase ... A2
43 Resaca ... G4
44 Sweet & Coffee ... C3
45 Sweet & Coffee ... F5
46 Victoria Cafe ... G3

Drinking & Nightlife
47 Bar El Colonial ... G3
48 Coffee Box ... F5
49 Diva Nicotina ... H2
50 Frutabar ... G3
51 La Paleta ... H2
52 La Taberna ... H1
53 Las 3 Canastas ... E5
54 Puerto Pirata ... H1
55 Rayuela ... H2

Entertainment
56 Cinema Malecón ... G3
MAAC Theater ... (see 1)

Shopping
57 El Mercado Artesanal Loja ... F2

Palacio Municipal HISTORIC BUILDING
(Map p274; 10 de Agosto) Across the street from the *malecón* is the ornate, gray Palacio Municipal building, home to the Municipal Council and the mayor's office. The elaborate structure was built in 1921, and honors both neoclassical and baroque styles with domes on the top in the four corners and Greek-style columns on the second floor. It sits opposite the Universidad de las Artes.

Parque Bolívar Area

Guayaquil may be the only city in the world that has land iguanas, some over a meter in length, living downtown. These prehistoric-looking animals (a different species from those found on the Galápagos Islands) are a startling sight in one of Guayaquil's most famous plazas, Parque Bolívar, which is also known as Parque Seminario. Around its small ornamental gardens are several of Guayaquil's top-end hotels. Keep your eyes open, as you may also spot the reptiles in lanes of Cerro Santa Ana.

Cathedral & Parque Bolívar CHURCH
(Map p274; btwn Chile & Chimborazo) On the west side of Parque Bolívar is a cathedral originally built in 1547 as a wooden building – however, like much of Guayaquil, it was destroyed by fire. The present structure, completed in 1948 and renovated in 1978, is simple and modern, despite an extremely ornate front entrance. The surrounding park is also called Parque de Las Iguanas, due to its

reptilian residents. Look closely and you can spot iguanas grazing on the rocks here.

Museo Municipal MUSEUM

(Map p274; ☎04-259-4800; http://museodeguayaquil.com; Sucre; ⏰9am-5:30pm Tue-Sat) FREE A block south of Parque Bolívar, you'll find this museum and the municipal **library** (Map p274; 10 de Agosto; ⏰9am-5pm Mon-Fri, 9am-2pm Sat), which is on the opposite side of the building. The archaeology room on the ground floor has mainly Inca and pre-Inca ceramics, and several figurines from the oldest culture in Ecuador, the Valdivia (c 3200 BC). Also on the ground floor is a colonial room with mainly religious paintings and a few period household items. Upstairs there's a jumble of modern art and ethnography rooms.

Downtown North

Malecón El Salado PLAZA

(⏰6am-midnight) Just like it's better known-brother Malecón 2000, Malecón El Salado is another attractive waterfront renewal project that's popular with residents. There are several eateries and cafes in a streamlined modern building along the estuary, plus a micro theater named **Sala La Bota** (tickets $5 to $25) with a funky adjacent coffee shop. **Rowboats** (per 30 min US$4) can also be rented (one to five people per boat).

Local families with children in tow head to Malecón El Salado on weekend nights to see the 'dancing fountains', a choreographed waterworks display at 7pm, 7:30pm and 8pm. The large square just south of the *malecón,* called the Plaza Rodolfo Baquerizo Moreno, is dominated by a large modernist structure. Expositions and events are held here periodically.

Museo Presley Norton MUSEUM

(Map p274; ☎04-229-3423; Av 9 de Octubre; ⏰8:30am-4:30pm Tue-Fri, 10am-4pm Sat & Sun) FREE This museum, featuring an impressive collection of archaeological artifacts, including pottery and figurines made by the original settlers of Ecuador, is housed in a beautifully restored mansion. It occasionally stages concerts and screens films. Exhibit info is in Spanish.

Parque del Centenario PARK

(Map p274; cnr Monocayo, Garaycoa, Velez & Victor Manuel Rendon; ⏰8am-7pm) This plaza, along Avenida 9 de Octubre, is the largest in Guayaquil and marks the midway point between the Río Guayas and the Estero Salado. It is four square city blocks of manicured gardens, benches and monuments, the most important of which is the central **Liberty Column** surrounded by the founding fathers of the country.

City Cemetery CEMETERY

(Map p274; ☎04-229-3849; www.cementeriopatrimonial.org.ec; Pedro Menéndez) Incorporated into the city landscape a short ride from the city center is this landmark cemetery, founded in 1823. It contains hundreds of above-ground tombs (and 700,000 graves in total) stacked atop one another so that it resembles a crowded apartment complex. A walkway leads to several monuments and huge mausoleums, including the impressive grave of President Vicente Rocafuerte.

Outside Guayaquil

Parque Histórico Guayaquil ZOO, MUSEUM

(☎04-283-2958; www.parquehistorico.gob.ec; Av Esmeraldas; ⏰9am-4:30pm Wed-Sun) FREE Colonial history meets the animal kingdom at this large site across the Puente Rafael Mendoza Aviles Bridge, east of Río Daule. The park is divided into three 'zones': the **Endangered Wildlife Zone**, which has 45 species of birds, animals and reptiles in a semi-natural habitat; the **Urban Architecture Zone**, which has a restaurant and showcases the development of early-20th-century architecture in Guayaquil; and the **Traditions Zone**, which focuses on local traditions, with an emphasis on rural customs, crafts and agriculture.

A taxi from the city costs around $5 to $6, or you can take a Durán-bound bus from Terminal Río Daule. It's easier to catch the bus back to the city from in front of the large mall on the main road, about a 200m walk from the park.

Tours

Prices for Galápagos cruises are no lower here than they are in Quito; however, flights to the islands are slightly cheaper. For Guayaquil city tours and beyond, My Trip to Ecuador is highly recommended.

My Trip to Ecuador TOURS

(Map p281; ☎09-8727-3727; http://mytriptoecuador.net; Victor Emilio Estrada 727 near Guayacanes, Luis Antonio Bldg, 2nd fl, office 2; tours per person from $65) Run by enthusiastic guide

Mario, this could be the best tour operator in the country. Mario's enthusiasm for his home nation is addictive. He's charming, knowledgeable and flexible, running everything from quick city tours of his native city Guayaquil to week-long Galápagos and Amazon adventures. English and Portuguese are spoken; customized tours and transfers are available.

The Fisherman's Trail tour (per person $110) takes visitors to a quiet, non-touristy village around an hour from the big city, where they can enjoy the local crab and seafood and then go on a dolphin cruise. The Guayaquil and Cacao Trail tour (per person $95) goes to the old town of Guayaquil and then onto a local cacao farm for lunch, chocolate-making and tasting.

Trips & Dreams TOURS
(Map p274; ☎099-235-1335; www.tripsanddreams.com; Quísquis 305 near Rumichaca) This is an agency that shares space and management with Hostal Suites Madrid. Ask for Christopher Jimenez, the extremely knowledgeable and affable manager. Can arrange all manner of trips, including to the Galápagos and Amazon.

Tangara Tours TOURS
(Map p274; ☎04-228-2828; www.tangara-ecuador.com; Ciudadela Bolivariana, cnr Manuela Sáenz & O'Leary, Block F, Casa 1) Run out of the guesthouse of the same name, built over Cañari and Inca ruins. This outfit is highly recommended for local day tours to Cuenca.

Tren Ecuador RAIL
(☎1800-873-637; www.trenecuador.com; round trip $22; ⏲tours 8am Thu-Sun) An all-day train excursion takes you from Durán to Yaguachi and on to Bucay, 88km east of Guayaquil, through banana, sugar cane and pineapple plantations. Once in Bucay, you'll have about four hours of free time, which you can spend on a range of outdoor activities.

Tour operators meet the train in Bucay and provide you with options for horse riding, mountain biking and visiting waterfalls (you can even rappel down them) – all of which cost extra. The return journey happens by bus, and you'll arrive back in Guayaquil around 5:30pm. It's a bit touristy (a dance troupe puts on a show at Bucay station), but still an enjoyable outing that's popular with Ecuadorian travelers. A taxi to the start of the trip in Durán should cost around $8 from the city center. Tickets are sold from the **vintage train car** (Map p274; Malecón Simón Bolívar; ⏲9am-12.30pm & 1.30-6pm Mon-Fri, 10am-12.30pm & 1.30-4pm Sat & Sun) on the *malecón*.

Captain Henry Morgan BOATING
(Map p274; ☎04-251-7228; Simón Bolívar Pier, near Sucre; adult/child $7/5; ⏲4pm, 6pm & 7:30pm Mon, Wed & Thu, 4pm & 6pm Fri, 12:30pm, 2pm, 4pm, 6pm, 7:30pm & 9pm Sat, 12pm, 2pm, 6pm & 7:30pm Sun) Named after the infamous pirate (who never made it to Guayaquil), this replica sailboat makes hour-long trips along the river. There's booze and dancing, but the tour itself is child friendly.

Guayaquil Vision BUS
(☎09-6882-3935, 04-292-5332; www.facebook.com/GuayaquilVision/; adult/child $8/4; ⏲booking office 9am-8pm Tue-Sun, to 7pm Mon) Runs double-decker hop-on-hop-off bus tours of downtown and surrounding suburbs. There are numerous tours a day starting from Plaza Olmedo on the *malecón*.

SANTAY ISLAND

The mangrove-covered protected reserve of Santay Island has a different feel from the other attractions in Guayaquil. Part of the government's plans to add more green space to the city, Santay is one of the initiatives in the ecotourism project Guayaquil Ecológico, aimed at recovering spaces with environmental and tourism potential. In 2014 a vehicle-free bridge was completed, providing pedestrian access to the island.

The allure: this peaceful 2200-hectare island in the Río Guayas makes a pleasant refuge from the bustle of downtown. It's also a good bird-watching spot, with more than 128 species in residence; if you're lucky, you might also spy caimans in the muddy waters. Wooden walkways on the island lead through a small fishing community of around 200 residents (with simple eating options on the island). A second bridge also connects the island to the canton of Durán.

The 840m-long Santay Island bridge is located a few kilometers south of the *malecón*, opposite El Oro street.

Dreamkapture Travel TOURS
(☎04-227-3335; www.dreamkapture.com; Villa 21, Juan Sixto Bernal) Good deals on Galápagos cruises and other trips. Tours available with French-, Spanish- and English-speaking guides.

Centro Viajero TOURS
(Map p274; ☎099-235-7745; www.centroviajero.com; Baquerizo Moreno 1119 near Av 9 de Octubre, office 805, 8th fl) Organizes Galápagos packages and customized tours to the beaches and Amazon. Spanish, English and French are spoken; ask for the manager, Douglas Chang.

Galasam Tours TOURS
(Map p274; ☎04-230-4488; www.galasam.com.ec; Av 9 de Octubre 424, Grand Pasaje, ground fl, office 9A) Organizes Galápagos cruises and tours; look out for last-minute deals on the website.

Festivals & Events

Carnaval CULTURAL, RELIGIOUS
(Malecón Simón Bolívar; Feb or Mar) Guayaquil's waterfront erupts with color and fiestas on the days immediately preceding Ash Wednesday and Lent. In addition to the festival's traditional throwing of water, Carnaval includes different floats celebrating Ecuador's various customs, with around 1500 dancers and musicians participating.

Simón Bolívar's Birthday & Founding of Guayaquil CULTURAL, HISTORICAL
(24 & 25 Jul) The city goes wild with parades, art shows, beauty pageants, fireworks, and a great deal of drinking and dancing for Simón Bolívar's Birthday (called Día de Simon Bolivar) and Guayaquil Foundation day.

Independence Day & Día de la Raza CULTURAL, HISTORICAL
(Oct) These two events combine to create a long holiday full of cultural events, parades and bigger-than-usual crowds on the *malecón*. Independence Day is October 9 (1820) and Día de la Raza is October 12.

New Year's Eve CULTURAL
(31 Dec) Life-sized puppets (*viejos*), made out of papier-mâché, represent the old year. Some look like famous people and political figures and are displayed on the main streets of the city, then burned at midnight in bonfires. Roads around the city close around midnight, as it's a dangerous drive. Watch out for fireworks and bonfires when walking.

Sleeping

The city has a range of options from plush high-end business-style hotels to boutique guesthouses and hostels. Some visitors choose to stay in the northern suburbs, but that is really no more convenient to the airport or bus terminal than staying downtown, and you'll be forced to take taxis wherever you go. If you do choose to stay there, be sure to base your decision on each accommodation's merits.

Downtown

Street noise can be an annoyance regardless of the category of hotel; bring earplugs if you're a light sleeper.

Hostal Suites Madrid HOTEL $
(Map p274; ☎04-230-7804; www.hostalsuitesmadrid.com; Junín 305 near Rumichaca; r incl fan/air-con from $25/30; P ❄ @ 📶) Geared toward foreign travelers (English, French and Italian are spoken), this place has a Moroccan feel, with a colorful tiled lobby, high ceilings and exotic wall decor. It's a super-clean and secure refuge within 10 minutes' walk of the *malecón*. A pretty rooftop terrace has city views and computers for guests, and there's also a kitchen for self-caterers.

Hotel Andaluz HOSTEL $
(Map p274; ☎04-231-1060, 04-231-1057; www.facebook.com/pg/hotelAndaluzgye; Baquerizo Moreno 840 near Junín; s/d/tw $25/34/40; ❄ @ 📶) The rooms aren't as charming as the facade, but the Andaluz certainly has character. An antique theme runs throughout, including a large Singer sewing machine, vintage clocks, historic photographs and model ships in the lobby. A friendly, good-value option: rooms are bright with touches of Ecuadorian artwork and the upstairs terrace is a fine spot for relaxing.

Casa de Romero B&B $
(Map p274; ☎04-603-6244; www.hostelromero.com; cnr Vélez 501 & Boyacá, 7th fl; s/d $30/40, with shared bathroom $22/36; ❄ @ 📶) For a taste of downtown *guayaquileño* living, try this friendly place with nine good-sized rooms located over two floors in a high-rise apartment building. All rooms come with TVs, and some with balconies. There's also an attractive lounge area and a kitchen (and

laundry) for guests. Continental breakfast is included.

Hotel Versailles HOTEL $

(Map p274; ☎04-308-778; www.hotelversailles.com.ec; cnr Junín & Ximena; s/d from $27/35; ❄@📶) While it inevitably falls short of its namesake, the Versailles is a fair deal only a few blocks from Avenida 9 de Octubre. The large marble-floored rooms are spacious (though some are dark and windowless) and have high-end shower fixtures, minifridges and flat-screen TVs. At the time of research an adjacent restaurant was being built.

★ **Manso Boutique Hotel** HOTEL $$

(Map p274; ☎04-252-6644, in US 786-245-4973; www.manso.ec; cnr Malecón Simón Bolívar & Aguirre; dm $15, s/d/tr incl breakfast from $55/63/82, with shared bathroom $38/$48/60; ❄@📶) The unrivaled *malecón* location aside, Manso is both a hostel and boutique hotel, housed in an atmospheric period property. Rooms vary in comfort and style – the best being bright, with high ceilings, framed artwork, and a splash of color. There's a certain bohemian vibe, with wooden sculptures, photography exhibitions and a balcony hammock in common areas, and an appealing pescatarian restaurant.

Hotel Las Peñas HOTEL $$

(Map p274; ☎04-232-3355; www.hlpgye.ec; Escobedo 1215 near Vélez; s/d/tr incl breakfast $49/61/67; P❄📶) Good-value Las Peñas has extremely spacious rooms with old TVs, minifridges, safes and hot-water showers. It's a short walk from the *malecón* and Avenida 9 de Octubre. Ask for a corner room, with big windows and a decent view. There are three kinds of breakfast, including Americano and Guayaco style.

Hotel Presidente Internacional HOTEL $$

(Map p274; ☎04-230-6779; www.presidenteinternacional.com; Junín near Riobamba; s/d $40/67; ❄@📶) A traditionally outfitted doorman is a surprise in this worn-down part of the city; however, the nine-story Hotel Presidente is real value considering the polished-wood floors, quality bathrooms and low-key artwork – there's even a small gym and Jacuzzi.

Re Bed & Breakfast GUESTHOUSE $$

(Map p274; ☎04-231-0111; www.rebandb.com; Junín 428 near Córdova, 3rd fl, apt D; dm/s/d incl breakfast $17/44/59; ❄📶) Tucked away in an apartment building, this small five-room guesthouse has simple rooms decorated with stencils, pop art and colorful curtains. There's a kitchen for guests, a small living room with lots of natural light and a friendly bohemian vibe that makes everyone feel at home.

★ **Mansion del Rio** HOTEL $$$

(Map p274; ☎04-256-6044; www.mansiondelrio-ec.com; Numa Pompilio Llona 120, Las Peñas; r incl breakfast from $177; ❄@📶) Housed in a lovingly restored home from the 1920s and hidden down a riverside cobblestone street in Las Peñas, the rooms at Mansion del Rio are handsomely designed with well-curated antique furnishings and many original details (chandeliers, vintage wallpaper, brass fixtures). The rooftop terrace offers great views.

Hotel Oro Verde LUXURY HOTEL $$$

(Map p274; ☎04-232-7999; www.oroverdehotels.com; cnr Av 9 de Octubre & García Moreno; r incl breakfast from $160; P❄@📶≈) About four blocks west of Parque del Centenario, the Oro Verde is still the classiest hotel in town – not so much for superior-quality rooms as for its high-end facilities, casino and several excellent restaurants, plus a sauna and gym.

Hotel Ramada HOTEL $$$

(Map p274; ☎04-2565-555; www.ramada.com; Malecón Simón Bolívar & Luzarraga; s/d incl breakfast from $93/105; P❄📶≈) Smart and sleek business-style hotel on the *malecón*, with river view rooms. There's also a swimming pool and gym.

Northern Suburbs

Several standard-issue, business-class hotel chains like Hilton (p282), Sheraton and Howard Johnson are near the Mall del Sol.

★ **NucaPacha** HOSTEL $

(Map p281; ☎04-261-0553; www.nucapacha.com; Bálsamos Sur 308; dm $11.50, s/d $22/35, without bathroom $19/29; @📶≈) On a peaceful street in Urdesa, this appealing guesthouse has a pool and patio, and hammocks rimmed by mango and papaya trees and tropical foliage. Some simple rooms have colorful artworks, all have fans. There's also a clean shared kitchen (with filtered water for drinking) and free walking tours. The staff are friendly and the price is right.

Washing is $6 per load. Guests should be pet-lovers; the hostel has a friendly dog named Nacho.

Guayaquil – Northern Suburbs

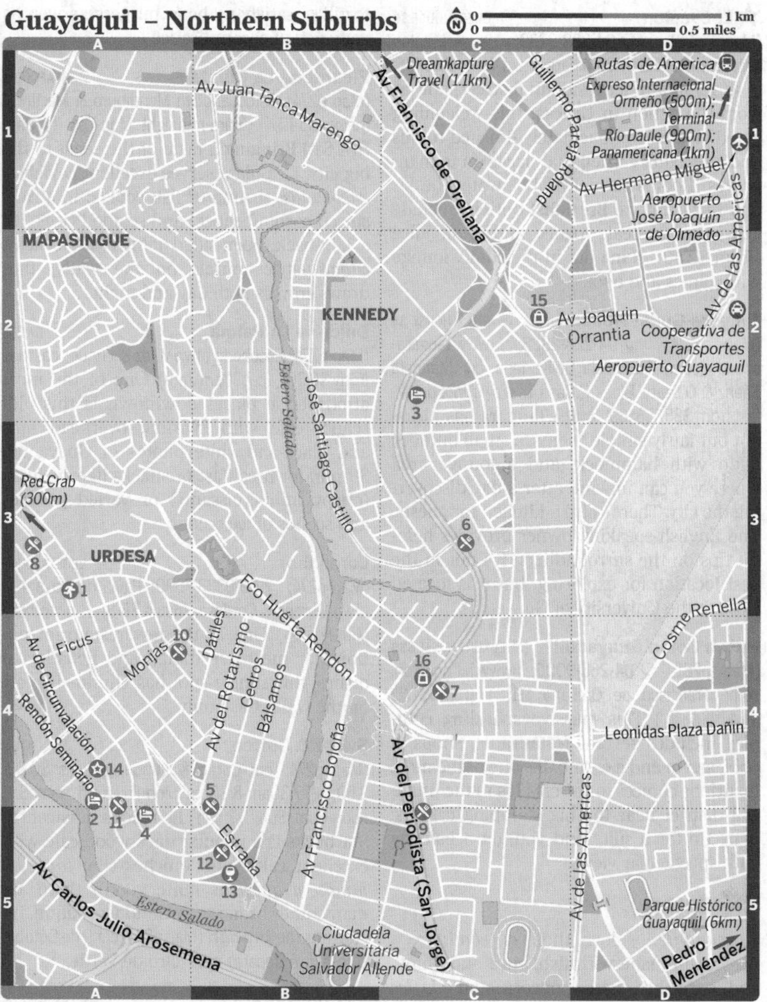

Guayaquil - Northern Suburbs

Activities, Courses & Tours
1 My Trip to Ecuador A3

Sleeping
2 El Escalon A4
3 Hilton Colón Guayaquil C2
4 NucaPacha A5

Eating
5 Café El Español B4
6 Cocolon C3
7 La Alameda de Chabuca C4
8 Lo Nuestro A3
9 Maverick C5
10 Palo Ceviches A4
11 Puerto Moro A4
12 Sushi Isao B5

Drinking & Nightlife
13 Live by Chavela B5

Entertainment
14 Pop Up Teatro Cafe A4

Shopping
15 Mall del Sol C2
16 San Marino C4

★ El Escalon GUESTHOUSE **$$**
(Map p281; 04-328-8239; www.escalonhotel.com; Rendon Seminario; s/d from $60/85;) In a quiet residential street, not far from the action in Urdesa, this welcoming gated villa has immaculately finished rooms and a relaxing garden that backs on to mangroves. Rooms have TVs, hot water, desks, and refrigerators. Breakfast options include eggs, toast, cereal, yogurt, and fresh juice (from $2.50). Hang out in the comfy lounge with games and books.

Tangara Guest House GUESTHOUSE **$$**
(Map p274; 04-228-2828; www.tangara-ecuador.com; Ciudadela Bolivariana, cnr Manuela Sáenz & O'Leary, Block F, Casa 1; s/d/tr incl breakfast from $35/56/69;) Tangara has pleasant but fairly simple rooms, a small outdoor patio with hammock, and a lounge area where you can unwind after a day discovering the city. There's also a kitchen for guests. The English-speaking owner provides helpful tips on the surroundings. It's not in the best location for exploring, but it is located close to the University of Guayaquil.

Hilton Colón Guayaquil LUXURY HOTEL **$$$**
(Map p281; 04-268-9000; www.hiltoncolon.com; Francisco de Orellana 111; r from $172;) This massive sparkling complex includes several restaurants, shops, a pool, a gym and a casino. It's one of the most luxurious choices in the city. It's in the financial district near the big shopping centers. Pony up for a suite and you get a balcony with spectacular views.

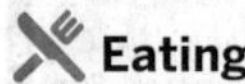

Eating

Guayaquileños love their *encebollado,* a tasty soup made with fish, yuca and onion, and garnished with popcorn and *chifles* (crispy fried banana slices). The best *encebollados* are found in cheap mom-and-pop restaurants, which usually sell out by lunchtime. *Cangrejo* (crab) is another local favorite. Many of the best restaurants are in the northwestern suburb of Urdesa, 4km northwest of downtown.

Downtown

Manso Mix FUSION **$**
(Map p274; 04-252-6644; cnr Malecón Simón Bolívar & Aguirre; mains $7-9; 8am-10pm;) Inside the bohemian Manso Boutique Hotel (p280), this colorful cafe serves up tasty organic and vegetarian fare, including quinoa tortillas, satisfying bean burgers as well as tasty fish in coconut sauce.

Picanteria La Culata SEAFOOD **$**
(Map p274; Córdova, btwn Mendiburo & Martínez; mains $5-10; 6am-midnight Mon-Thu, to 2am Fri & Sat) Bringing a taste of the coast to the big city, La Culata serves excellent ceviches, *encocados* (shrimp or fish cooked in a rich, spiced coconut sauce) and seafood rices. It's a laid-back, open-sided joint (with beachy, *cabaña*-style murals on the walls) that draws crowds both day and night.

Dulceria La Palma CAFE **$**
(Map p274; Escobedo btwn Vélez & Luque; pastries from $0.30; 7:30am-7pm) One of the most atmospheric places downtown is this old-school cafe with swirling overhead fans and black-and-white photos of Guayaquil. Stop in for breakfast or snacks like *cachitos* (crispy mini-croissants) or varied pastries and scoops of ice cream.

Lorenabo VEGETARIAN **$**
(Map p274; 09-9383-7990; Paula de Icaza 427, btwn Moreno & Cordova; mains $5-8; noon-5pm Mon-Fri;) One of the few restaurant options for meat-free Italian and Ecuadorian dishes, this simple spot has Hindu-style art on the walls. Cash only.

Sweet & Coffee CAFE **$**
(Map p274; cnr Carbo & Luque; snacks $0.60-3.50; 7:30am-8:30pm Mon-Fri, from 9am Sat, noon-6pm Sun;) Ecuador's answer to Starbucks is a popular dark-wood cafe with excellent cakes and quiches (the *torta de jamón y queso* is quite good); there are many other branches around Guayaquil, including the **branch** (Map p274; cnr 9 de Octubre & José de Antepara) near Oro de Verde.

Mi Comisariato SUPERMARKET **$**
(Map p274; Av 9 de Octubre, btwn Avilés & Boyacá; 9am-8pm) This cavernous grocery is the most convenient downtown option for self-catering. Looks like a clothing store from outside.

Pasteles & Compania CAFE **$**
(Map p274; 04-256-1022; www.pastelesycompania.com.ec; Cordova 1015; sandwiches from $3.50; 10am-8:30pm Mon-Sat;) Local chain selling sandwiches and cakes in an informal bakery setting. This is a good place to grab an inexpensive packed lunch or low-priced snack – the smoothies are fresh and cheap, too (from $1.30).

Chop Chops ECUADORIAN $

(Map p274; www.chopchops.com.ec; Malecón Simón Bolivar; dishes $3-12; ⌚10am-10pm) This modern Ecuadorian chain on the *malecón* is a good option if you need a quick inexpensive fix while promenading the waterside. It serves typical dishes like *patacones* (plantain fritters) with cheese, as well as various meat, rice and bean dishes, plus heaped salads.

Pique & Pase ECUADORIAN $$

(Map p274; Lascano, btwn Tulcán & Carchi; mains $8-15; ⌚noon-11pm; 📶) The best restaurant for traditional Ecuadorian specialties also has traditionally dressed waiters. Sit at the tables with wooden benches and share several small dishes, like *bolon verde* (fried plantain with mashed cheese), *humitas* (corn dumpling steamed in a corn husk) or *guatita con moro de lentejas* (beef tripe stew with mixed rice and lentils) before a meat or seafood main.

Maverick PIZZA $$

(Map p281; ☎09-9610-0129; www.facebook.com/Maverickpizzaec; Av del Periodista; pizzas $10-23; ⌚5-10pm Tue-Sat, 4-9pm Sun; ❄📶) This unassuming place on main road Av del Periodista (San Jorge) has white walls, black benches and simple chalkboards with funny slogans and cute drawings. It's a self-proclaimed 'unorthodox' joint, creating delicious handmade pizzas made with yuca bases. Order them with veggie, carbonara, beef, chicken, pork or chimichurri toppings. Regular dough pizzas are also available.

Victoria Cafe ECUADORIAN $$

(Map p274; ☎098-594-8506; www.facebook.com/VictoriaCafeGye; Malecón Simón Bolívar; mains $7-17; ⌚11am-11pm) This lovely shaded eating spot sits alongside a small duck pond. Tuck into Ecuadorian eats, ceviches, salads, meat and fish dishes, or stop in for a pasta, sandwich, desert or coffee. It's *malecón* prices, but well located for breaking up your waterfront wanderings.

Resaca INTERNATIONAL $$

(Map p274; ☎09-9942-3390; Malecón Simón Bolívar, near Junín; mains $11-19, cocktails from $9; ⌚noon-midnight Mon-Sat, to 8:30pm Sun) This festive two-story spot on the *malecón* serves filling Ecuadorian classics like ceviche and shrimp soup, plus salads and mixed meat and rice dishes. It also has a lovely rooftop deck, a fine spot to enjoy a house-made margarita, piña colada, frozen daiquiri or Long Island iced tea.

Northern Suburbs

Palo Ceviches CEVICHE $

(Map p281; ☎04-604-8223; Calle 11B NO; ceviches from $7.50; ⌚10am-5pm Tue-Fri, 9am-5pm Sat & Sun) Fresh, tangy ceviches are served up in glass tankards (with a garnish of plantain chips) at this new casual, modern spot in Urdesa. Tuck into shrimp, fish, octopus or seafood ceviche mixed in the special house sauce, at the inside or outside seating. Sides include crunchy calamari, plantain chips and hot salsa.

Café El Español CAFE $

(Map p281; www.elespanolgourmet.com; cnr Estrada & Cedros; crepes from $3.25, sandwiches from $4.99, mains from $7; ⌚8am-8pm; ❄📶) Two-story upscale cafe and Spanish-style delicatessen (ham and cheese is the specialty), serving good sandwiches. Indoor and outdoor seating available.

Sushi Isao JAPANESE $$

(Map p281; ☎04-288-9936; Balsamos 102, near Estrada; mains $9-16; ⌚11am-11pm Tue-Thu & Sun, 10am-midnight Fri & Sat) One of the top Japanese restaurants in town, Sushi Isao is a small, casual spot that's popular with Japanese expats. Ingredients are fresh and dishes are skillfully prepared. The heaping bowls are superb value; choose from salmon, shrimp, tuna, octopus and eel over seaweed, shredded *tamago* (egg) and rice.

Puerto Moro STEAK $$

(Map p281; ☎04-288-4630, 09-8948-8750; www.facebook.com/pg/puertomoroec; Circunvalación Sur 320; mains $9-20; ⌚noon-11pm Mon-Thu, to midnight Fri & Sat, to 10pm Sun) Barbecue, seafood and steak restaurant serving up South American and Ecuadorian flavors with modern decor and punchy cocktails. Meat dishes come accompanied by different sauces, including herb and olive oil, spicy salsa and cheese.

Cocolon ECUADORIAN $$

(Map p281; ☎04-263-4181; Av Francisco de Orellana; mains $8-14; ⌚noon-11pm) Not far from the Hilton Colon Guayaquil and Mall del Sol, Cocolon has a modern, fun interior with bright red chairs and photos decorating the walls. Well-known for its Ecuadorian dishes: *La ultima cena* (grilled loin with rice, beans and all the fixings) is a classic. Adventurous palates should try *guatita* (a tripe and potato stew in a seasoned, peanut-based sauce).

★ **Lo Nuestro** ECUADORIAN $$$
(Map p281; ☎04-462-7233; www.lonuestro.com.ec; Estrada 903; mains $15-40; ⏰noon-11pm) Housed in a century-old mansion complete with wooden shutters and period furniture, Lo Nuestro is one of the most atmospheric places in Guayaquil to feast on ceviche, sea bass with crab, and other seafood dishes. Musicians play on weekend evenings, when reservations are recommended. Leave room for some of the homemade cakes, displayed on a trolley. Good wine selection, too.

Red Crab SEAFOOD $$$
(☎04-238-0512; www.redcrab.com.ec; Estrada 1205, near Laurales; mains $13-22; ⏰10am-10pm Sun-Fri, to 11pm Sat) The iconic crustacean is prepared in more than a dozen different ways at this popular and festive restaurant. The theme is underwater world, with bad lighting and tasty (but overpriced) crab, seafood and fish dishes.

La Alameda de Chabuca PERUVIAN $$$
(Map p281; ☎04-269-0641; Pasaje 9, off Av Francisco de Orellana; mains $12-17; ⏰12:30-4:30pm & 7-10pm Tue-Sun) Across from the San Marino Mall, this elegantly set dining room is a showcase for some of Guayaquil's best Peruvian cooking. The expansive menu features mouthwatering ceviches, rich *parihuela* (seafood in a rich white wine broth) and tender *lomo saltado* (sliced steak, potatoes, onions and tomatoes over rice).

Drinking & Nightlife

The former red-light district (still called the Zona Rosa) behind the *malecón* between Aguirre and Orellana has a dozen or so garish bars and clubs (various cover charges apply on weekends). Las Peñas, the hillside to the north of downtown, is the place to enjoy a sangria or glass of wine, while more chic offerings can be found in the northern suburb of Urdesa and the Samborondón area.

Las 3 Canastas JUICE BAR
(Map p274; cnr Vélez & Chile; drinks from $1.60, fruit bowls from $2.30; ⏰8:30am-6:30pm Mon-Sat) A busy daytime spot with street-side tables, bar stools and a large variety of fruit drinks, fruit bowls, granola, and cream-topped fruity desserts.

Live by Chavela LOUNGE
(Map p281; ☎09-9691-7926; Circunvalación Sur 106 (Av de Circunvalación), near Estrada; ⏰10pm-late Wed-Sun) This stylish Urdesa lounge is the hottest nightspot du jour, drawing a well-dressed dance-loving crowd with deep pockets. Minimum consumption is typically around $25, and there's also an excellent steak restaurant on-site to fuel up before cocktails.

La Paleta BAR
(Map p274; www.facebook.com/lapaleta.enlasrocas; Numa Pompilio Llona 174; ⏰8pm-3am Tue-Sun) La Paleta is a great little lounge to while away an evening, with cave-like nooks, a hipster crowd and good ambient grooves. Serves beers and high-end cocktails, as well as tapas.

Puerto Pirata BAR
(Map p274; ☎09-323-7231; Escalón 384; ⏰5pm-2am) After summiting Cerro Santa Ana, stop in for a breather at this faux pirate ship below the lighthouse. It has drinks and food, and live music on weekends, plus karaoke on Tuesday nights.

Frutabar JUICE BAR
(Map p274; ☎04-230-0743; www.frutabar.com; Malecón Simón Bolívar 504; juices from $1.75, mains $5-7; ⏰11am-midnight Mon-Sat, to 11:30pm Sun) This surfer-themed eating and drinking spot serves up gourmet sandwiches, snacks and tasty tropical fruit juices and cocktails. It's a fun spot for a drink, with a soundtrack of reggae and loungey beats.

Coffee Box CAFE
(Map p274; ☎04-600-2302; www.coffee-box.net; cnr Pichincha & Luque; ⏰7:30am-7pm Mon-Fri, 10:30am-8pm Sat) Close to the *malecón*, this convenient modern cafe offers a proper caffeine fix (one of the few places that actually uses fresh beans), plus cakes and sweet pastries.

Rayuela BAR
(Map p274; ☎09-8339-7261; Numa Pompilio Llona; cocktails from $7; ⏰6pm-3am Tue-Sat) This hip spot has a candlelit, lounge-like vibe that's just the right setting for a few drinks with friends. Well-mixed cocktails are on hand, plus there are low-key bands on certain nights. Minimum consumption is around $15 per person. It's also open for brunch and daytime drinking (with two-for-one drink specials until 8pm)!

La Taberna BAR
(Map p274; Cerro Santa Ana; ⏰7pm-late) Walking up the steps in Las Peñas, take the first lane off to the left to reach this lively, bohemian drinking den. It has salsa beats, a fun crowd, and plenty of love for Guayaquil's Barcelona

PLAZA LAGOS

One of Guayaquil's most charming and upscale settings for a bite or a drink is **Plaza Lagos** (☎04-511-5800; www.plazalagos.com.ec; Km 6.5 Via Puntilla; ⊙8am-11:30pm Mon-Thu, 8am-1am Fri & Sat, 8am-10:30pm Sun), a handsomely designed complex of restaurants, designer boutique shops, wine bars and outdoor cafes set amid palm trees, gurgling fountains, walkways and an artificial lake. With its colonial-inspired architecture and tropical breezes, it feels a bit like Miami meets the Mediterranean.

Around two dozen eating spots are clustered here, serving up everything from South American fusion to Spanish tapas. In addition to higher-end dining rooms, a handful of cafes serve up Italian, gourmet sandwiches, desserts and the like. It's a relaxing spot to dine al fresco, particularly on weekends, when some places host live music. Keep in mind that prices are higher here – but in general so is the quality.

It's located across the Río Daule in the upscale district of Samborondón. From downtown Guayaquil, a taxi costs about $10.

Sporting Club with its hanging jerseys and old football mementos.

Bar El Colonial BAR

(Map p274; ☎096-774-6535; www.facebook.com/ElColonialGYE; Rocafuerte 623; ⊙5pm-midnight Tue-Wed, to 3am Thu-Sat) You can't miss this lime-green pub with life-sized figurines hanging out of the window – it's one of the Zona Rosa's long-surviving hotspots, often with live music on weekend nights.

Diva Nicotina BAR

(Map p274; ☎04-504-8763; www.facebook.com/DivaNicotinaBar; Cerro Santa Ana; ⊙7pm-midnight Mon-Thu, to 2am Fri & Sat) At the foot of the hill, the atmospheric Diva Nicotina draws a festive young crowd who pack the house when there's live music.

☆ Entertainment

Pop Up Teatro Cafe PERFORMING ARTS

(Map p281; ☎09-9123-4500; Av de Circunvalación; tickets from $5; ⊙6:30pm-midnight Tue-Thu, to 2am Fri & Sat) A funky micro-theater and cafe that attracts a hip crowd who come to watch short performances throughout the evening. An audience of around 20 people changes during the night; visitors typically see five performances. Between shows, the cafe serves tapas dishes and great coffee. Note: performances are in Spanish, although non-Spanish speakers might get lucky with a dialogue-free show.

Cinemas

Filmgoers in the northern suburbs have their choice of several multiscreen cinemas in large malls. For an **IMAX** (Map p274; ☎04-256-3078; www.cinemamalecon.com; Malecón Simón Bolívar, near Loja; tickets $5, 3D movies $6) experience head to the *malecón*.

Sports

Guayaquileños bleed yellow and black, the colors of their beloved soccer team, Barceloña Sporting Club. On game days much of the city looks like it's gone into hiding, since those not at the 90,000-seat **Estadio Monumental Isidro Romero Carbo** (Barceloña Sporting Club, Estadio Monumental Banco del Pichincha; ☎04-220-0550; https://barcelonasc.com.ec; Av Barcelona, btwn San Eduardo & Bellavista; tickets $5-20) in the northern suburb of El Paraíso are glued to their TVs at home or in bars. However, the city's other team, Emelec, whose **George Capwell Stadium** (Emelec; ☎04-241-6000; www.emelec.com.ec; Quito, btwn José de San Martín & General Gómez) is in Centenario just south of downtown, has arguably been the better side in recent years. When Barceloña and Emelec meet it's best to avoid wearing either team's colors, especially if attending the game in person (tickets from $5), so as not to provoke the ire of partisan fans. For game schedules check out the team's websites.

Shopping

One of the largest malls in all of South America is **Mall del Sol** (Map p281; ☎04-208-2100; www.malldelsol.com.ec; Av Juan Tanca Marengo; ⊙10am-9pm Mon-Sat, 10am-8pm Sun) near the airport. **San Marino** (Map p281; www.sanmarino.com.ec; Av Francisco Orellana; ⊙10:30am-9pm Mon-Thu & Sun, 10am-10pm Fri & Sat), in the suburb of Kennedy, is a large, equally high-end mall.

El Mercado Artesanal Loja MARKET

(Map p274; Baquerizo Moreno; ⏲9am-7pm Mon-Sat, 10am-4pm Sun) This large artisans market has a huge variety of crafts from all over Ecuador, including Otavalo-style sweaters, plus Panama hats, carved chessboards and mass-produced paintings, wallets, scarves, leather goods, gifts and trinkets. Bargaining is expected.

Information

DANGERS & ANNOYANCES

Guayaquil has its fair share of poverty and urban woes, but nothing to justify paranoia. The main tourist areas of Avenida 9 de Octubre, the Malecón 2000, Las Peñas and the restaurant strip in Urdesa are perfectly safe. It's common to see security guards in flack jackets outside restaurants, and tourist police on the streets, but there's no need to be alarmed, they're always here. The area directly north and south of the Parque del Centenario can feel dodgy at night, but simply use common sense and take the normal precautions you would for visiting any large city.

EMERGENCY

Cruz Roja (Red Cross) ☎131

Police ☎101

MEDIA

El Universo and *El Telégrafo* are Guayaquil's two main local papers, which report cultural goings-on about town.

MEDICAL SERVICES

A number of 24-hour pharmacies can be found on Avenida 9 de Octubre. **Clínica Kennedy** (☎04-228-9666; Av del Periodista) hospital is also open 24 hours.

MONEY

Major banks and stand-alone ATMs are all over downtown, especially around the city's plazas.

POST

Post Office (Map p274; cnr Carbo & Aguirre; ⏲8am-6pm Mon-Fri, to noon Sat) For local and international mail.

TOURIST INFORMATION

Dirección Municipal de Turismo (Map p274; www.turismo.gob.ec; cnr Pichincha & Ballén, Museo Nahim Isaias; ⏲9am-5pm Mon-Fri) This small office for city and regional tourist info is friendly, but usually Spanish-speaking only.

Getting There & Away

AIR

Sleek and modern **Aeropuerto José Joaquín de Olmedo** (GYE; Map p281; ☎04-216-9000; www.tagsa.aero; Av de las Américas) is located on the east side of Avenida de las Américas, about 5km north of downtown. Anyone flying to the Galápagos Islands either leaves from here or stops here on their way from Quito. Free wifi access is available throughout. A tourist information desk can help with accommodation and transport information in the arrivals hall.

Domestic

There are many internal flights to all parts of the country. The most frequent flights are to Quito (one hour) with **Avianca** (☎1-800-003-434; www.avianca.com; Av Francisco de Orellana), **LAN** (☎04-259-8500; www.lan.com; Aeropuerto José Joaquín de Olmedo) or **Tame** (☎04-256-0728; www.tame.com.ec; Av 9 de Octubre 424, Gran Pasaje). One-way tickets start at $78. For the best views, sit on the right side when flying to Quito.

Tame also flies to Cuenca (return from $85, 50 minutes) and Loja (return from $96, 60 minutes)

BUSES FROM GUAYAQUIL

DESTINATION	COMPANY	DURATION (HRS)	FREQUENCY	PRICE
Máncora	Cruz del Sur	8	Once daily at either 9am or 2pm, rotating on various days	$41
Trujillo	Cruz del Sur	18	Once daily at either 9am or 2pm, rotating on various days	$60 to $80
Lima	Cruz del Sur	24	Once daily at either 9am or 2pm, rotating on various days	$90 to $100
Lima	Expreso Internacional Ormeño	26	Daily, times vary	$90
Chiclayo	CIVA	15	Once daily at 9pm	$25 to $32

daily. There are usually flights to Tulcán, Latacunga and Esmeraldas as well. Avianca, Tame and LAN fly daily to Baltra (two hours, return from $278) and San Cristóbal (two hours, return from $256) in the Galápagos.

BUS

The enormous **Terminal Terrestre** (☎04-213-0166; http://ttg.ec; Av Benjamin Rosales), just north of the airport, is as much a sprawling mall (shops, restaurants, internet cafes etc) as it is a transportation hub. There are more than 100 bus companies with small offices lined up along one side of the bottom floor of the building. The kiosks are grouped by region, and most of the destinations and departure times are clearly marked. Buses depart from the 2nd and 3rd floors.

Most bus companies sell tickets in advance, which will guarantee you a seat. Otherwise, just show up at the terminal and you'll usually find a bus to your destination leaving the same day. Departures on Friday nights and holidays can sell out.

The best services to Quito are the direct evening departures with **Panamericana** (☎04-213-0638; www.panamericana.ec; Terminal Terreste; $10; eight hours). For Cuenca, buses leave from **Terminal Terrestre** (p287) and run both via El Cajas ($8.25, four hours) and the more indirect route via La Troncal ($7.25, five hours).

Buses to Peru

The easiest way to get to Peru is with one of the international lines departing from the **Terminal Terrestre**. These services are very convenient because the bus waits for you to take care of border formalities.

Cruz del Sur (www.cruzdelsur.com.pe) has newer buses than those of the domestic lines, with larger, more comfortable seats, better-quality lunches, and sometimes-working wi-fi.

Another recommended operator is **CIVA** (http://civa.com.pe), which travels daily from Guayaquil to Chiclayo, with onward connections to Lima and beyond.

Expreso Internacional Ormeño (www.grupo-ormeno.com.co; Centro de Negocios El Terminal, Bahia Norte, Office 34, Bloque C) has daily departures for Lima. Its office and terminal is on Avenida de las Americas, just north of the main bus terminal.

Minivan

For Salinas, **Ruta del Sol** (Map p274; ☎04-294-2060; www.rutadelsol.com.ec; Panama 501 near Orellana) runs direct shared minivans (around $10, 2½ hours) from behind the Hotel Ramada on the *malecón*. These leave hourly from 6am to 8pm, but it's best to reserve ahead.

For Machala, **Coturcip** (Map p274; ☎04-239-6439; Pichincha and Carbo) has shared minivans leaving hourly from downtown (around $12, 2.5 hours), or airport transfers from the airport in Machala to the airport in Guayaquil (around $60, three hours).

Getting Around

TO/FROM THE AIRPORT

The airport is about 5km north of downtown. A **taxi** (☎04-282-3333; www.fastline.com.ec) in either direction should cost around $5 and take around 20 minutes. The majority of taxis at the airport are yellow and labeled **Cooperativa de Transportes Aeropuerto Guayaqui** (Map p281; ☎04-216-9141)l; these will take you into the city or, for that matter, anywhere else in the country. Rates are posted in the back seats.

By bus, cross the street in front of the airport to take a green line **Metrovia** (☎04-259-7680; http://metrovia-gye.com.ec) downtown ($0.30). The 'Plaza del Centenario' stop on Avenida Machala is the most convenient downtown stop. Heading back out to the airport, catch the Metrovia one block south on Avenida Quito. The journey should take roughly 45 minutes.

TO/FROM THE BUS TERMINAL

The bus terminal is about 2km from the airport. A taxi between the two is approximately $3 or you can hop on a north-bound Metrovia ($0.30), which arrives at Terminal Río Daule, across from the bus terminal.

From the city center, there are two convenient **Metrovia** lines that go to **Terminal Río Daule**, across from the bus terminal. Handy stops include Avenida Quito (near Parque del Centenario) and Rocafuerte, one block north of Avenida 9 de Octubre.

A taxi to/from downtown is around $5.

Bosque Protector Cerro Blanco

Located about 15km west of Guayaquil, this **reserve** (☎09-8622-5077; www.bosquecerroblanco.org; Km 16, Hwy 40, Via a La Costa; $4; ⏲8am-4pm Sat & Sun, weekdays by reservation) is one of the few areas of tropical dry forests left in the country, and counts jaguars, pumas, monkeys, deer and raccoons among its residents. More than 200 bird species also call the 6078-hectare Cerro Blanco home – including the rare great green macaw (the reserve's symbol), which is considered critically endangered. People usually visit on a day trip from Guayaquil.

This private reserve is administered by Fundación Pro-Bosque. There's an organic farm, an education center with exhibits on the local ecology and birdlife (in Spanish), and a wildlife rescue center where endangered species are cared for, including a large aviary for several Guayaquil macaws. Spanish-speaking guides are available for nature-trail hikes (two to four hours, per group $12 to $20).

Activities

Just west of Cerro Blanco are the **Puerto Hondo Mangroves**. Charged with the protection of this threatened environment is **Spa and Recreation Center Puerto Hondo** (09-9140-0186; kayaking per hour $5; 10am-4.30pm Tue-Sun), which helps to arrange pleasant kayak rides through the area.

On the highway in the direction of Santa Elena is a watersports lagoon named **Laguna Park** (09-9734-4003; Km 27, Hwy 40, Via a La Costa; activities one hour/day $5/10, camping per person $16, ste per person $30; 10am-6pm Tue-Sun;), with 17 activities ranging from paddleboarding to fishing. Plus the treetop adventure park **Bosque Aventura** (09-9102-4573; www.bosqueaventuraec.com; Km 33, Hwy 40, Via a la Costa; $15; 9am-6pm Sat & Sun); both are ideal antidotes to Guayaquil's busy city life.

Getting There & Away

To get to Cerro Blanco and Puerto Hondo, take a Cooperativa de Transportes Chongón bus from the corner of Calle 10 de Agosto and García Moreno in downtown Guayaquil, or hop on any Playas- or Salinas-bound bus from **Terminal Terrestre** (p287) in the northern suburbs. Ask to be dropped off at the park entrance; you should see a sign.

RUTA SPONDYLUS

Formerly known as the Ruta del Sol, this coastline has much more to offer than just sun and sand. The area's geography runs the gamut from dry scrub and cactus to lush mountainous cloud forests, beautiful beaches and offshore islands teeming with unique flora and fauna.

Puerto López

05 / POP 16,000

A long, wide beach and the proximity to the wonders of the Parque Nacional Machalilla have turned this quiet fishing village into a traveler's base on Ecuador's coastline. During whale-watching season especially, tourists wander the *malecón* and the dusty streets – home to a surprising number of good accommodation options, cafes and restaurants. In the wee morning hours – before tour groups escape for the day and the handful of sunbathers take up their positions on the sand – fishermen gut their catch on the beach, and the air teems with frigate birds and vultures diving for scraps.

Activities

Travesia Surf & Bikes SURFING, BIKING
(09-9957-0396, 09-8864-6618; www.facebook.com/travesiasurfnbikes; 2hr lesson $30) To learn to surf (or to hone your skills), sign up for lessons with Miguel, the English-speaking owner of Hostal Yemayá. He also hires out surfboards, SUPs and kayaks (per hour $15), and offers daily mountain-bike hire ($20) including a helmet, bike lock and snorkel kit.

Tours

Numerous agencies offer tours to Isla de la Plata or the mainland part of the park. Hiking, horseback riding, mountain biking and fishing trips are also available. Some companies have English-, German- and French-speaking guides.

From June to September, whale-watching tours combined with visits to Isla de la Plata are popular (from $45). During July and August, whale sightings are pretty much guaranteed, while in June and September sightings may be brief, distant or just of single animals. On Isla de la Plata groups are given lunch, a guided hike and a brief opportunity to snorkel. The journey to the island takes well over an hour and can be rough; bring a rain jacket for the wind and spray.

Licensed companies are found along Córdova and Malecón Julio Izurieta. We don't recommend bargain-hunting for cheaper whale-watching trips on the street, because fishing boats on those trips tend to be slower and smaller and lack officially mandated equipment.

Outside of the whale-watching season, similar tours to the island are offered to see birds and sea lions, and you may well see dolphins, too. Most of the operators will also arrange a variety of other local trips, such as visits to local beaches, and camping and/or horseback riding in the Agua Blanca and San Sebastián areas. It is usually cheaper to make your own way to Agua Blanca.

Exploramar Diving DIVING
(☎02-256-3905; www.exploradiving.com; Malecón Julio Izurieta; 2-dive package from $140, snorkeling $40; ⊙8am-6pm) This PADI-certified dive center on the *malecón* runs dive sessions and snorkeling off the coast.

Machalilla Tours ADVENTURE
(☎09-3984-5839; www.machalillatours.org; Malecón Julio Izurieta; tours from $45; ⊙9:30am-5:30pm) Runs standard tours, as well as excursions for horseback riding, kayaking, mountain biking and paragliding, plus trips to Los Frailes Beach and Agua Blanca.

Sleeping

Be sure to reserve ahead during the busy whale-watching season, and during the coastal high season (end of December to April). Off-season the rates listed will drop; ask for discounts if the place has few occupants.

Hostal Yemayá HOSTEL $
(☎09-9957-0369, 09-8864-6118; www.facebook.com/YemayaPuertoLopez; General Córdova; dm $10, r per person $15-20;) The Yemayá offers good value for money a couple of minutes from the beach. The handful of fan-cooled rooms (some have air-con) have hot water, TVs and are simple and clean. There's a pleasant interior courtyard with plants, tables and chairs. Miguel, the friendly English-speaking owner, also runs activity tours, and a tiny adjacent cafe which serves the town's best coffee.

Hostal Maxima GUESTHOUSE $
(☎09-9056-1950; www.hotelmaxima.org; Gonzáles Suárez, near Machalilla; r per person with/without bathroom $10/7;) This good-value hotel has shabby but clean rooms with fans, and a friendly English-speaking owner. The grassy courtyard is strung with hammocks, and faces an open-sided kitchen where you can whip up a meal. You can also pitch a tent here (per person $5).

★**Hostería Mandála** CABIN $$
(☎05-230-0181; www.hosteriamandala.info; d $35-155;) Easily the nicest place to stay in town, Mandála has a beachfront location north of the *malecón* – you can't miss the giant rainbow whale tail beckoning you in. Cabins are scattered throughout a thick and lush flower garden, and the rooms are rustic and sophisticated: wood, bamboo and colorful textiles combine to make charming, cozy hideaways.

Hostería Itapoá HOSTEL $$
(☎05-230-0071, 09-9314-5894; www.hosteriaitapoa.com; Malecón Julio Izurieta, near Calle Abdon Calderon; s $16, d $20-40;) A handful of thatch-roofed cabins are tucked away in a lush courtyard at Itapoá, a friendly, family-run operation opposite the beach. Cabins have a tropical island hideaway feel, with private bathrooms, hot water, mosquito nets and balconies with hammocks. There's a small restaurant and bar, plus a cocoa project onsite, where you can try 100% organic chocolate.

A good breakfast ($3) is served on the raised wooden platform cafe out the front. The owners donate some of their profits to the Itapoá Reserve Rainforest Project, which helps to protect the surrounding habitat. Guests can also rent mountain bikes and surfboards.

Nantu Hostería HOTEL $$
(☎05-230-0040; www.hosterianantu.com; Malecón Julio Izurieta; s/d $40/56;) On the beachfront, Nantu has smart recently refurbished rooms with crisp white walls, wooden features, and bright colored accents in the soft furnishings and subtle floral wall paintings. There's natural tones, rustic chunky wood wall hangings, and thatched roofs at the cabins. All have hammocks on the porches. There's a small pool and Jacuzzi, and the two-story lounge has a bar, restaurant and billiard table.

Punta Piedrero GUESTHOUSE $$
(☎05-230-0013, 09-8337-7774; www.puntapiedreroecolodge.com; Malecón Julio Izurieta; s/d from $30/50, camping from $8;) Punta Piedrero is the last sleeping spot on the beach heading south (past the pier). It's a tranquil place with 14 clean, tile-floored rooms with TVs and hot water, with delightful sea views. You can relax in a hammock on the beach-facing balconies, or at the barbecue and fireplace social areas. There's also a guest kitchen, and camping is available.

Eating & Drinking

Find informal, affordable restaurants selling Ecuadorian and seafood dishes (made with the catches of the day), plus Italian eateries and a number of pleasant cafes selling European pastries.

Restaurant Danica ECUADORIAN $
(mains $4; ⊙8:30am-10pm) Despite the cement floor and plastic tables, this rough and

ready outdoor eatery always draws crowds. The key to its success: delicious chargrilled fish, prawns, chicken or pork chops (served with rice and lentils). Follow the wafting smoke along the waterfront (it's on the side road near the Banco del Pichincha).

Cafe Madame CAFE **$**
(09-8436-7851; Malecón; crepes from $2.50, mains from $6; 10am-6pm;) A beachfront bar and organic cafe with a shaded veranda and wooden tables. Order crepes, ice cream, coffee, fruit smoothies, sandwiches, omelets and salads, or enjoy a sundowner in this pretty location.

Fercho's Cafe CAFE **$**
(Malecón; dishes $3.50-$6; 7:30am-9pm Fri-Wed) Located inside some arches on the *malecón,* this little cafe has only five tables and a ceiling decorated with magazine pages, photos and newspaper clippings. It serves inexpensive, hearty breakfasts (continental, American or ranchero – with sausage or bacon) as well as salads, ceviches, sandwiches, hamburgers and coffee.

Restaurant Carmita SOUTH AMERICAN **$$**
(09-9372-9294; Malecón; mains $6-13; 9am-9pm;) The patio dining is a good people-watching spot at this popular Ecuadorian restaurant on the *malecón*. It serves well-priced fish dishes plus ceviches, mixed rice, and chicken plates. The octopus in garlic sauce has to be tried. Ask about lunch and dinner specials.

Bellitalia ITALIAN **$$**
(09-9617-5183; Juan Montalvo; mains $9-12; 6-10pm Mon-Sat) You won't stumble upon this delightful spot hidden in a backstreet, but you should seek it out for its high-quality Italian cooking in a romantic, garden-like setting. It's one block inland from the beach. Reserve ahead, especially on weekends.

Shopping

Pacha Chocolates CHOCOLATE
(05-230-0323; Av Machalilla; tours $25, chocolate bars $4; 9am-7pm) Out on the main highway, this place is a chocolate-lover's dream, with all manner of cocoa temptations – hot chocolate, chocolate crepes, brownies and mousse, plus household soap, cocoa butter and more. Pacha offers three-hour morning cocoa tours (minimum 4 people) in which to watch (and taste!) the chocolate-making process, learning about the route from bean to bar.

Information

Banco del Pichincha (Malecón Julio Izurieta; 9am-4pm Mon-Fri) has a reliable ATM.

The **tourism office** (off Ruta del Spondylus; hours vary) is on a side street off Ruta del Spondylus, but is often unmanned. Alternatively, ask at guest houses and tour operators for local info.

Getting There & Away

All buses now run out of the new **bus terminal** (Terminal Terrestre; Ruta del Spondylus), located 2.5km north of town. A moto-taxi ride to/from the town center should cost around $1.

TO QUITO

Carlos Aray Ejecutivo has buses to Quito ($14, 10 hours) at 5:05am, 9:15am and 7pm via Jipijapa, Portoviejo, Chone and Santo Domingo. Alternatively, you can catch the bus to Portoviejo or Manta to make connections.

Reina de Camino (05-303-6002;) has the comfiest service to Quito ($14, 10 hours), with one first-class bus at 8pm.

TO THE SOUTH COAST

Cooperativa Manglaralto has buses heading to Santa Elena ($4, 1½ hours) every 20 minutes from 4am to 7pm, stopping in Montañita ($2.50).

Getting Around

The whole town is walkable, but if you're feeling sluggish look for moto-taxis buzzing around (around $1). A round-trip taxi to either Agua Blanca or Los Frailes beach costs from $16, or $26 to visit both.

Parque Nacional Machalilla

05

Ecuador's only coastal national park is a reminder of what much of the Central and South American Pacific coast once looked like. Now almost entirely disappeared, it's one of the most threatened tropical forests in the world. The park, which was created in 1979, preserves a small part of the country's rapidly vanishing coastal habitats, protecting about 50km of beach, some 400 sq km of tropical dry forest and cloud forest, and around 200 sq km of ocean (including offshore islands, of which Isla de la Plata is the most important).

Aside from rare exotic species, the park is also home to an important archaeological site that dates from the Manta period

Parque Nacional Machalilla

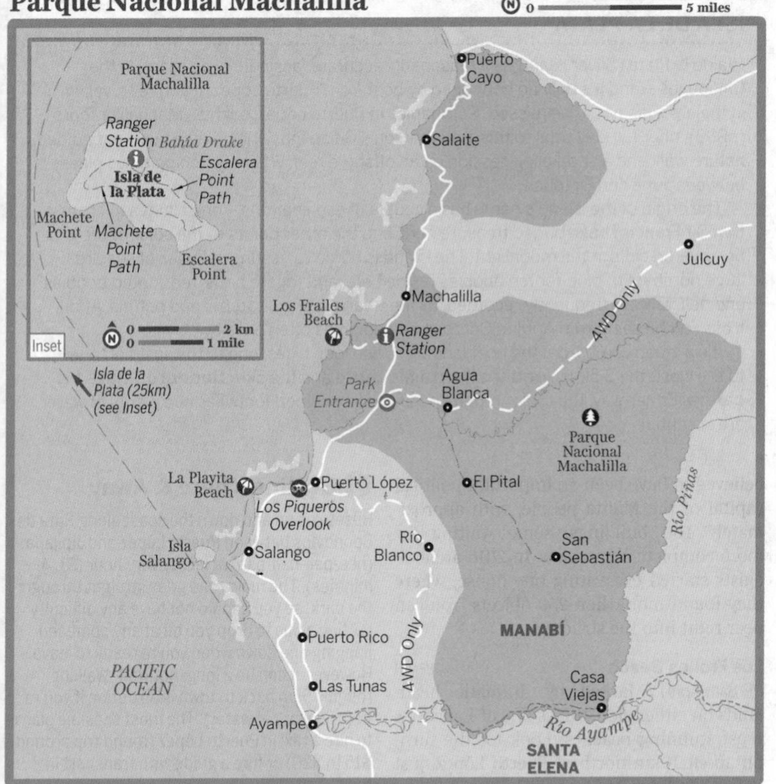

– beginning around AD 500 and lasting until the Spanish conquest. There are also remains of the much older Machalilla and Chorrera cultures, dating from about 800 BC to 500 BC, and of the Salango culture from 3000 BC.

Sights & Activities

Parque Nacional Machalilla NATIONAL PARK
FREE Preserving isolated beaches, coral formations, two offshore islands, tropical dry forest, coastal cloud forest, archaeological sites and 200 sq km of ocean, Ecuador's only coastal national park is a marvelous and unique destination. Within its nature-rich, strange-looking forest are more than 200 species of birds, including coastal parrots and parakeets, and seabirds such as frigates, pelicans and boobies – some of which nest on the offshore islands. Animals include deer, squirrels, howler monkeys, anteaters and a variety of lizards, snakes and iguanas.

Agua Blanca VILLAGE
(09-8161-0095; www.comunidadaguablanca.com; $5; 8am-5pm) A visit to this small indigenous community and its surrounding territory is a opportunity to escape tar-and-concrete modern Ecuador. You'll find the turn-off, where you pay an entry fee (which covers museum admission and a guide), about 5.5km north of Puerto López on the right. From here it's another 6km down a dusty, bumpy road to the village. Once there, you can see pre-Colombian art, soak in a sulfur pool, get a free mud mask, and hike the surrounding forest.

Archaeological Museum MUSEUM
(09-9443-4864; www.comunidadaguablanca.com; 8am-5pm) This museum is well worth a visit. Spanish-speaking guides explain the significance of the artifacts, including well-preserved ancient tools, ceramics and funeral urns. The informative tour continues a short walk away at the Manta site,

DON'T MISS

ISLA DE LA PLATA

Isla de la Plata (Silver Island) is a reasonably accurate facsimile of an island in the Galápagos – and it's only an hour or so by boat from Puerto López. If you're traveling in the area, it's not to be missed. Companies in Puerto Lopez, such as Machalilla Tours (p289), offer full-day trips to this 'poor person's Galápagos', including a two-hour guided nature walk and a snorkeling session on an offshore reef. Whale-watching takes place between June and October.

The origin of the island's name has a couple of explanations – one alludes to claims that Sir Francis Drake buried treasure here, and the other points to the color of the guano-covered cliffs in the moonlight. The island is home to nesting colonies of seabirds: large numbers of blue-footed boobies reside here, and frigate birds, red-footed boobies and pelicans are frequently recorded, as are a variety of gulls, terns and petrels. Albatross can be seen from April to October, and dolphins often pass by.

It's a steep climb from the boat landing to two loop hikes, one to the east and one to the west: the 3.5km **Sendero Punta Machete** and the 5km **Sendero Punta Escalera**. Either way, the trail is rough and exposed, so good footwear and plenty of water are essential.

believed to have been an important political capital of the Manta people, with approximately 400 buildings, some waiting for more complete excavation. In 2016 archeologists started excavating one house, where they found more than 250 objects. You can peer right into the structure.

Los Frailes Beach BEACH
(⏲8am-4pm) Marked by dramatic headlands on either side, this is one of Ecuador's most stunning beaches. Look for the turnoff about 10km north of Puerto López, just before the town of Machalilla. After passing the ranger station, it's another 3km along a dirt road to the beach. Mototaxis (tuk tuks) wait by the entrance and deliver visitors to the beach ($2).

There's also a scenic lookout point to the north of the beach (bring your binoculars during whale-watching season), and a 4km nature trail that runs through the dry forest to two secluded beaches; make it to the furthest beach and you'll likely have the place to yourself – keep your eye out for blue-footed boobies. Swimmers take caution in these waters during big swells, as there can be strong undertows.

San Sebastián & Julcuy HIKING, HORSE RIDING
This excellent four- to five-hour hike or horseback ride is southeast of Agua Blanca. The trail ascends a transition zone to humid remnant cloud forest at San Sebastián, about 600m above sea level. Horses can be hired if you don't want to hike the 20km round trip, and guides ($20) are mandatory.

ℹ Getting There & Away

Buses run up and down the coast along Ruta de Spondylus between Puerto López and Jipijapa (hee-pee-*hah*-pah) at least every hour ($1, 4 minutes). The main road goes straight through the park, so you should not have any difficulty getting a bus to drop you off at any point and flagging one down when you're ready to leave. However, it can be a long, hot wait. Walking roughly 5km back to town is an option if you're fit (bring lots of water). The most sensible plan is to hire a taxi in Puerto López (round trip around $15 to $20) or hire a guide with transport in town.

Boat trips to Isla de la Plata (Silver Island) can be arranged through tour agencies based in Puerto López and at hostels and hotels along the coast.

Salango, Las Tunas & Ayampe

Along the coast you'll find the sleepy towns of Salango, Las Tunas, and Ayampe – where the Río Ayampe empties into the ocean (the strong undertow here makes swimming difficult), and the luxuriant green hills close in on the beach. If you're looking to get away from people, the guesthouses in these parts offer solace, peace and quiet. Only 6km south of Puerto López is the little fishing town of **Salango**. From here you can hire fishing boats to buzz the 2km out to **Isla Salango**, a haven for birdlife – including blue-footed boobies, pelicans and frigate birds – with good snorkeling, too.

Sights & Activities

Salango Archaeological Museum

MUSEUM

(05-257-4304; www.salango.com.ec/museo-arqueologico-salango.php; adult/child $2.50/1.50; 9am-5:30pm) A fascinating collection of more than 245 ceramics pieces is exhibited here. Objects date from between 3000 BC to 1500 AD and account the settlements of the Valdivia, Machalilla, Chorrera Engoroy, Bahia and Guangala peoples. Archeologists are still making discoveries in this very spot, and there's a lab for research on site. The museum has a few cabins (per person $15) on the beach for those wanting to stay and get involved with archeology projects and research (by prior arrangement only).

The Festival de la Balza takes place annually around October 12th, and sees locals sail replicas of traditional bamboo boats along the shore. These boats would have been used for trade and to transport goods as far as Mexico. The museum is on the northern edge of Salango, a block in from the beach.

Abel Munoz

BOAT GUIDE

(09-9399-8515; per person $15-20) Local guide and boat driver Abel Munoz offers 1½-hour boat trips to Isla Salango to visit the untouched beach and spot pelicans, boobies and other wildlife. Abel also has snorkeling equipment you can use (included in the price).

Sleeping & Eating

La Buena Vida

GUESTHOUSE $$

(09-9486-3985; http://surflabuenavida.com; near Ruta del Spondylus, Ayampe; r incl breakfast $40-75;) Operated by an Ecuadorian-American couple, La Buena Vida has seven colorful rooms, all with fans and ocean views. Friendly hosts, good breakfasts, and an inviting open-sided cafe-bar that's perfect for a sundowner have made this a popular spot. Surf lessons are also available ($25).

Finca Punta Ayampe

CABIN $$

(09-9189-0982; www.fincapuntaayampe.com; Ayampe; r $60-70;) Surrounded by rainforest, this idyllic place feels like an end-of-the-road hideout. The high-ceilinged bamboo bedrooms are filled with light, while a big lounge area has chunky wooden tables and spectacular sea views. Surfing, diving, kayaking and bird-watching tours can be arranged, and there's a good restaurant serving fresh ceviches, burritos, fish dishes, pastas, salads and sandwiches.

Cabañas La Tortuga

CABIN $$

(05-257-5178, 05-257-5163; www.latortuga.com.ec; Ayampe; d/tr incl breakfast $70/90;) Cabañas La Tortuga's beachside thatch-roofed cabins are well maintained with fans, mosquito nets and hot water. Guests can make use of a swimming pool, shared kitchen, pool table and barbecue area. Kayaks and bikes are available to rent (per hour $10), and there's a restaurant and bar in high season.

Azuluna Eco-Lodge

LODGE $$$

(05-234-7093, 09-9951-0542; www.azuluna-ecuador.com; off Ruta del Spondylus, Las Tunas; d from $79-149;) Secluded on a hill south of Salango are these thatch-roofed bungalows made from bamboo, wood and palm leaves. Each has a mesmerizing view of the ocean and a balcony with a hammock from which to enjoy it. Thoughtful touches include hand-painted nature murals, windows with colored glass detailing, and bathrooms with tiled floors.

There's also an attractive restaurant (mains $5 to $12) and lounge area. Azuluna has a sustainable ethos, making an effort to recycle and build with natural materials. In addition, 10% of room fees goes to supporting development projects in and around Las Tunas.

Delfin Mágico

SEAFOOD $$

(05-2574-4291, 09-9951-3938; www.delfinmagico.com.ec; Salango; mains $12-25; noon-7pm;) In Salango, it's worth stopping in at the under-the-sea-themed Delfin Mágico, which serves outstanding seafood. Order everything from cherna and grouper to corvina, octopus, shrimp and sea bass, marinated in all manner of delicious sauces and prepared using local and Spanish techniques. Go early to avoid long waits.

Getting There & Away

Buses run up and down the coast along Ruta de Spondylus between Montañita and Puerto López every hour or so; flag them down anywhere along the route. Alternatively, local taxis and mototaxis between towns cost around $3 to $7.

Olón

A few kilometers north of Montañita is the coastal village of Olón, boasting a long beach (with beginner waves) and an inland landscape that marks the beginning of a dramatic departure from the dry scrubland further south. This lush cloud forest is part of the Cordillera Chongón-Colonche, which climbs over a low coastal mountain range. It's one of the few places in the world with a cloud forest and a beach in such close proximity; jaguars, howler monkeys and the endangered great green macaw all reside here.

Sleeping

La Mariposa HOTEL $
(☎04-278-8120; www.lamariposahostal.com; Calle 13 de Diciembre, near Rosa Mística; d $30-35; ❄📶) Two minutes from the beach, the Italian-run La Mariposa has pretty gardens with coconut trees and is a relaxing, welcoming place. Upper floors have ocean views and there's a pleasant courtyard strung with hammocks. Continental breakfast is available (from $3.50).

Samaí Lodge GUESTHOUSE $$$
(☎099-462-1316; www.samailodge.com; d incl breakfast from $114; ❄📶) Overlooking the forest, Samaí Lodge feels like an idyllic oasis. Twelve cabins are scattered throughout the property; many with floor-to-ceiling windows and hammocks from which to enjoy views all the way to the coast – with a chance to spot both whales and monkeys in the same place. There's also a Jacuzzi, yoga classes, a spa, pool and tasty food.

A taxi to/from Olón (7km) costs approximately $7. The lodge is reached via 2km of dirt road – don't get dropped off at the main road, as it's a long (and sometimes muddy) hike up the hill, especially with luggage.

Getting There & Away

Comfortable **CLP buses** (☎04-293-3001, 04-293-3009, 04-294-4322; http://libertadpeninsular.com) leave from just north of Olón on the main road, headed to Guayaquil ($6.25, 2½ to three hours, five to six daily). Buses have TVs (with movies), wifi, air-con, reclining seats and a bathroom. This route also stops in Montañita. Check at the bus station or on the website for current timetable info.

Montañita

☎04 / POP 1,200

The beachfront village of Montañita is a party place with a surfing problem. There's a laid-back atmosphere and steady stream of cosmopolitan backpackers, with as many South Americans as gringos. Cheap digs and a Rasta vibe mean some travelers put down temporary roots, paying their way by hair braiding, jewelry making or staffing the front desk at a guesthouse. Montañita is ideal for the kind of person who, regardless of age, baulks at the typical restaurant dress code: bare feet and no shirt is practically de rigueur here.

Activities

The beach break is rideable most of the year (though it's best from December to May), but beginners should keep in mind that waves can be big, and riptides are common. Real surfers ride the wave at the point, at the northern end of the beach, a right hander that can reach 2m to 3m on good swells. Most hostels and hotels arrange surfboard rentals.

Balsa Surf Camp is a recommended outfit that offers surf lessons, as is **Montañita Surf & Dive** (☎09-8098-5370; diving from $19, surf lesson $25, one-hour surfboard hire $5; ⏲10am-6pm). Diving, bike tours, nature hikes and Spanish courses are also on offer here.

Courses & Tours

Montañita Spanish School LANGUAGE
(☎09-9758-5207; www.montanitaspanishschool.com; near Ruta Del Spondylus; 20hr group/private language classes $170/240, 5-day surf classes $80) Overlooking town, Montañita Spanish School is *the* place to take language classes. They offer Spanish and surf lesson combos. Find it on an unnamed road, east of the main village of Montañita, off Ruta del Spondylus. Ask a local or call the school for directions.

Machalilla Tours ADVENTURE
(☎099-169-4213; ⏲9am-6pm) On the main street near Banco Bolivariano, Machalilla Tours offers a wide range of activities, including walking tours through the rainforest ($35), cycling excursions ($35), horseback riding ($45), paragliding ($40) and parasailing ($35).

Sleeping

Noise is an issue in this party town, and earplugs are recommended for the central hotels and hostels, especially on weekends and during the high season. If you're interested in peace and quiet, check out the places on the main road into town and on the beach. Most hotels have mosquito nets, and sea breeze for ventilation; some places only have cold water, so check before you book.

In Town

Tiki Limbo HOSTEL $

(04-206-0019; www.tikilimbo.com; d incl breakfast from $30;) Tiki Limbo outdoes its competitors in terms of in-town location and decor: the stylish pastel-colored rooms have beds made of bamboo, and zebra-print bedspreads. Each has air-con and a private bathroom with hot water. You can relax in a hammock or lounge chair in the second-floor lounge, or sign up for surf lessons. The downstairs restaurant is rather good too.

Casa Blanca HOSTERÍA $

(09-9918-2501; r per person $10) One of the anchors of the busiest intersection in town, you can't beat this location for this price. Casa Blanca is in the center of the action, with simple, clean (if a little shabby) private bedrooms with crisp white sheets. Some have balconies with hammocks. Consider bringing some earplugs if you're staying at the weekend.

Boutique Hotel Rocio BOUTIQUE HOTEL $$

(04-206-0181; www.rocioboutiquehotel.com; d incl breakfast from $60;) The most charming guesthouse in town could have been plucked straight from a Greek island, with its stone brick walls and crisp white and blue accents. Bedrooms are well finished; some have patterned tiled floors and balconies overlooking the town. There's a rather good restaurant on the first floor serving Mediterranean food – hummus, falafel, Greek salads and kofte.

The hotel is a few blocks back from the beach, parallel to Ruta del Spondylus.

Hotel Hurvínek HOSTERÍA $$

(04-206-0068, 09-8454-5354; www.hurvinek.ec; Calle 10 de Agosto; s/d/t incl breakfast $30/40/55;) The spacious, fan-cooled rooms at this bright and sunny guesthouse are beautifully designed, from the polished-wood floors and rustic wood furniture to the charmingly tiled bathrooms. A buffet breakfast is served in the ground-floor lounge area. To find the Hurvínek, make your first left after turning into town from the highway; it's located halfway down on the right.

Out of Town

Hostal Mamacucha GUESTHOUSE $

(09-9402-9356; dm from $8, r per person from $10;) Adorned with murals and color-saturated walls, this uber friendly hostel is good value, with simple rooms surrounding a small garden courtyard. Bathrooms have hot water, there's a pool table and TV room, mosquito nets, free tea and coffee and guests often make dinner together like a family. Offers great deals on bike tours, surf lessons and nighttime nature walks too.

Find it on the northern side of the river, a couple of blocks back from the beach.

Hostal Esperanto HOSTERÍA $

(099-970-4569; www.esperantohostal.com; dm $15, d from $30;) Just past the domed Dharma Beach Hotel, slightly set back from the beach, this distinctive four-story building has cozy wood-accented rooms with fans, balconies and a rooftop deck with panoramic views. There's also a small lounge and communal kitchen with free coffee. Hotel activities include ukulele lessons (per hour $7) and Spanish lessons (per hour $10).

It's one of the more eco choices in Montañita; the hostel recycles waste and reuses water in its gardens.

★ **Balsa Surf Camp** BUNGALOW $$

(04-206-0075; www.balsasurfcamp.com; s/d from $40/60;) This lovely hideaway of handcrafted two-story thatch-roofed bungalows is set in a lush garden across a sandy pathway to the beach. The vibe is laid-back surfer, and the design aesthetic is Balinese retreat. There's also a hot tub and spa (massages from $30) and a surf school (board-hire per hour from $5, lessons $25).

Find it in the lane parallel to the beach.

★ **Hostal Kundalini** HOSTEL $$

(09-5950-5007; www.hostalkundalini.com.ec; r incl breakfast $42-105;) Sitting on the beach in front of a surf break, Kundalini was once nothing more than a thatch-roofed building set out on a lawn with four rooms. Now it's a smart tropical-themed 22-room hostel/boutique hotel, including a top beachside restaurant and exceptionally finished rooms with bamboo headboards.

The grounds have well-kept lawns, bordered by hedges and palm trees, with hammocks and brightly colored sun loungers for relaxing. Free yoga lessons take place weekly, and guests can hire surfboards (two hours $5).

Montañita Estates BOUTIQUE HOTEL $$

(09-3903-6465, 04-206-0153; www.montanitaestates.com; Ruta del Spondylus; d incl breakfast $50-80, house per person $45; P) Just out of town on the main road you'll find

WORTH A TRIP

DOS MANGAS: DETOUR FROM THE SUN

Most often visited as a side trip from Montañita, the inland village and national park of **Dos Mangas** is a starting point for walks or horseback rides further into the tropical humid forest of the Cordillera Chongón-Colonche.

Tagua (vegetable ivory) carvings and *paja toquilla* (toquilla straw) crafts can be purchased in the village. Visitors can go to remote coastal villages and stay overnight with local families for a nominal fee that includes meals, guides and mules. It's usually an easy day's walk or horseback ride to the village of Manglaralto (around 12km north). Overnight tours can be arranged including bird-watching and visiting remote waterfalls and other natural attractions.

Guides and horses can be hired at the **Centro de Información Sendero Las Cascadas** (☎09-9734-6906; near Ruta Spondylus; park entry per person $2.50; ⌚8:30am-4:30pm), a small kiosk in Dos Mangas. Friendly guides ($20, Spanish-speaking only) will take you on a four- to five-hour hike through the forest to an elevation of 60m, and to the 80m waterfall (may be dry in the warm season). You can also hire horses (per person $10), arrange lunch, and rent boots ($1) – recommended when it's muddy. Book in advance through **Vicente Laines** (☎099-202-0348; tours up to 8 people $20) and Machalilla Tours (p294) or simply show up in the morning and cross your fingers.

Grab a taxi ($5, 30 minutes) for the 7km from Montañita to Dos Mangas.

this tropical hotel with two swimming pools, pretty gardens and nice views. All rooms have TVs, king-sized beds and air-con; luxe rooms include fridges, safes, hot tubs and hammocks. There's also a house (sleeps nine) with its own kitchen and an ocean-facing balcony.

The place has a restaurant, bar, kids park, gym, spa and pool table – and 11 resident cats. Yoga classes ($8) and surfboard hire (per day $20) are available.

Nativa Bambu CABIN $$$
(☎04-206-0097; www.nativabambu.com; Ruta del Spondylus; d/ste incl breakfast $90-110/115-140; ❄📶) These peaceful all-wood cabins with thatched roofs and small front decks have lovely views overlooking Montañita and the ocean beyond. Nativa Bambu is known for its friendly, professional service and high-end fittings (good beds, coffee makers, Direct TV in some cabins). It's also eco-conscious, with solar panels, a recycling program and a garden selling plants you can take home.

Look for the signed entrance off the highway near Calle Principal.

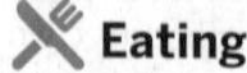

Eating

Almost every street-side space has been converted into an informal restaurant, including street carts selling fruit salads, empanadas, sandwiches, *encebollado* (soup with fish, yuca and onion), ceviches, burgers and bubbling *cazuelas* (seafood stews). Those catering to Ecuadorians are more likely to offer economical *almuerzos* (set lunches; from $2 to $4) and *meriendas* (inexpensive set dinner menus). International meal options are also readily available.

Donde Garci BAKERY $
(cakes $0.60-1.20; ⌚6am-11pm) Home to some tasty Colombian-style cookies, pastries and cakes – try the dulce de leche–filled pastry cones.

It's at the intersection of the highway and Calle Principal.

Restaurant Surf Food ECUADORIAN $
(meal deals from $3.50; ⌚8am-midnight) Always packed with locals, this cafe has zero atmosphere (it's very basic with simple tables and chairs), but is *the* place to get a satisfying and inexpensive Ecuadorian meal. Decent plates include breaded shrimp or fish in coconut sauce, accompanied by rice, lentils and plantain. Meal deals include a soup and a drink. Menus change daily.

Mas Alla EMPANADAS $
(Ruta del Spondylus; empanadas from $1, pizza slices from $1.25; ⌚noon-10pm; 📶) For a quick and cheap snack, head to this hippy-vibe cafe with informal inside and outside seating. It sells coffees, beers, slices of handmade pizza (the veggie one is heaped with with peppers, eggplant and broccoli), and fresh empanadas with cheese, chicken, ham and more.

It's just by the bridge.

Papillon INTERNATIONAL $
(crepes $6.50-13; 8am-11pm;) You'll find Tex-Mex, Ecuadorian, seafood, paella and an excellent variety of sweet and savory crepes at Papillon. It's got a rustic feel with chunky wooden tables and is on the main street lined with cocktail vendors, with the beach at its western end.

★Tiki Limbo INTERNATIONAL $$
(09-9954-0607, 04-206-0019; www.tikilimbo.com; mains $8-15; 8:30am-midnight;) In the epicenter of town, Montañita's best restaurant has an eclectic menu of global dishes (fajitas, falafels, homemade burgers, sesame-crusted shrimp, seafood platters) served in a charming setting of well-kept bamboo furniture with crisp white cushions. To finish your meal, try the milkshakes loaded with Nutella and vanilla ice cream or the bannoffee waffles. There's a good range of breakfasts, too.

Pigro ITALIAN $$
(09-8153-0076; www.facebook.com/restaurantepigro; mains $7-14; 12:30pm-11:30pm;) For an upscale dining experience that won't break the bank, head to Pigro for homemade creamy risottos, tasty seafood pastas, hearty lasagna and other Italian favorites (no pizzas, though), as well as good cocktails and a laid-back setting. Find it on the eastern end of the main street to the beach, the one with all the cocktail vendors.

Drinking & Nightlife

The side street that ends at the beach is lined with carts doling out tropical cocktails, beers and shakes until late most nights. One block over, **Lost Beach Club** (www.lostbeachclub.com; Malecón; entry from $25; 10pm-late) throws big dance parties, with DJs from Ecuador and abroad. Restaurant by day, **Hola Ola** (www.facebook.com/hola.ola.cafe; mains $7-14; 8am-midnight) becomes a key nightspot when the sun goes down, with live music and dancing.

★Montañita Brewing Company BREWERY
(www.montanitabrewingcompany.com; noon-10pm) At the northern end of the beach, overlooking the sand, the one and only micro-brewery on Ecuador's coast serves up Amazonian IPA, chocolate stout, blackberry, jalapeno and passion-fruit blondes, and tropical ciders (mango, lime, ginger) – all fresh out of the keg. They don't export these top-notch brews, so you can only experience them in Montañita.

There's live music most weekends, including everything from jazz bands to classical concerts. The next-door restaurant serves sushi, which you can enjoy with your pint.

Information

Women should be cautious about walking alone along the beach at night as there have been reports of assaults.

Banco Bolivariano, **Banco de Guayaquil** and **Banco Pichincha** (near the taxi stand) all have ATMs in town.

Getting There & Away

CLP (p294) buses are the most comfortable option. They depart from Olón and stop in Montañita on their way south to Guayaquil ($6, 2½ to three hours, six daily). Other buses stop on their way to Santa Elena ($3, two hours), La Libertad ($2.50, 1¾ hours), or north to Puerto López ($2.50, 1¼ hours) every 20 minutes or so. The main **bus station** (04-266-0203; Segundo Rosales, near Ruta Spondylus) and ticket office are on the main road.

The two local taxi companies are **Montañisol S.A** (09-3914-0192, 09-8279-5312, 04-206-0217; montanisol@gmail.com; 24hr) and **Montañisol Compañía De Taxis** (09-6891-1333; www.montanisol.com). Located just in from the highway, they offer services to destinations from Puerto López ($25) to as far away as Guayaquil ($80).

SANTA ELENA PENINSULA TO GUAYAQUIL

East of Santa Elena Peninsula, the landscape seems fit for a cowboy. It becomes increasingly dry and scrubby, and the ceiba trees give way to 5m-high candelabra cacti. But at its westernmost point, Salinas is the glitziest beach town on the south coast, with an immaculate stretch of beach (and lots of watersports) backed by concrete apartment blocks and hotels. There's a significant scenic lookout here marking the westernmost point in Ecuador. While Puerto Lopez to the north has better marketing, whale-watching in this location is arguably better, as the migration happens closer to shore. Salinas is also home to a fascinating whale museum. Inland from Salinas is the transport hub of Santa Elena.

Located a couple of blocks from the main road, on the west side of Santa Elena, is **Los Amantes de Sumpa** (☎04-294-1020; ⏲9am-5pm Tue-Sun) **FREE**, a museum that sits on an ancient cemetery of the indigenous Sumpa people. The main displays feature several 5000- to 8000-year-old skeletons, including two embracing as *amantes* (lovers) in the position they were found.

On the outskirts of Ballenita, just north of Santa Elena, is the clifftop **Hostería Farallón Dillon** (☎04-295-3640; www.farallondillon.com; r from $69;). The brainchild of an ex-captain, the place is filled with boaty memorabilia – from the full-sized mast, complete with crow's nest, and scattered life-preservers, anchors and navigation lights, to an original steel ship door leading into the restaurant's kitchen. All-wood rooms have jaw-dropping sea views, and clever touches include side lamps that look like lighthouses, with lampshades made of nautical maps. This brilliantly bizarre place has to be seen to be believed – at the very least it's worth stopping for a peek around and a spot of lunch or a drink.

Not far from the town of San Pedro, you can go **paragliding** (☎09-8113-1666; Km 41, off Ruta del Spondylus, San Pedro; per person $30; ⏲10am-6pm) from this grassy cliff edge just north of Ayangue. Pilots here offer thrilling, and inexpensive, 15-minute tandem glides along the coastline. Agencies based in Montañita can book trips here, or you can simply show up.

Salinas

☎04 / POP 50,000

At first glance Salinas looks like Miami Beach: a row of tall white condominiums fronts a pale sandy expanse filled with sun worshippers. Although the backstreets look more 'down-and-out' than a playground for wealthy Ecuadorians, Salinas is one of the smarter beach towns and certainly the biggest resort town on the south coast. It also boasts the most westerly point on the Ecuadorian mainland – a scenic spot named La Chocolatera – a must-visit for those passing through.

The resort itself stretches for several kilometers along the beach, and the *malecón* is lined with restaurants and bars. On one side it ends at the large Barcelo Colon Miramar hotel; on the other is the yacht club, town plaza and church, while further west is more sedate, but just as pretty Chipipe Beach – a good option for those wanting to escape the crowds during the high season (from mid-December through April).

Sights

La Chocolatera NATIONAL PARK

(entry via Salinas naval base; ⏲8am-5pm) **FREE** The westernmost point of Ecuador has three main attractions: **La Fae Beach**, with a boarded walkway where you can watch a seal colony; **El Morro** (or little hill), with a lighthouse and incredibly spectacular views over Salinas; and **La Chocolatera** – a point named for the way the tempestuous waves break on the rocks, creating foam and the impression of a big bowl of chocolate.

It's possible to walk or cycle to La Chocolatera from Salinas, but the heat can be exhausting. The best way to go is by taxi ($6 to $9) – ask them to wait while you visit all three sites. La Chocolatera is accessed via the Salinas naval base, so bring ID.

Surfing competitions sometimes take place at La Fae Beach, and speed skaters favor the hills and perfectly paved winding roads around the park.

San Lorenzo Beach BEACH

(Malecón) Salinas' main, and most crowded, beach sits on the *malecón* opposite dozens of restaurants and hotels. It has volleyball courts, a pier (from which you can take a boat ride or whale-watching trip) and plenty of watersports. The water is generally calmer than the other beaches in the area, due to its sheltered crescent shape, making it ideal for swimming.

Chipipe Beach BEACH

To the west of San Lorenzo Beach is Chipipe – equally well maintained, but with a fraction of its neighbor's crowds. If you're looking for a quieter beach experience, or more space to play beach games, this is the option for you.

Whale Museum MUSEUM

(Bar de Ostras, Oystercatcher Bar; ☎04-277-8329, 09-9787-4425; www.museodeballenas.org; Enríque Gallo, btwn Calles 47 & 50; $3; ⏲7am-8pm by appointment only) Run by the passionate Ben Hasse, a pioneer of whale-watching in the area, this small and informative whale museum has several whale skeletons, including one fully assembled 11m humpback frame. Other interesting specimens include dolphin fetuses, sea lion samples and squid jaws. Look out for the 80-year-old beaked whale skull.

Activities

Whale-watching trips are the major draw from June through October. Beginning about 13km offshore from Salinas, the continental shelf drops from 400m to more than 3000m (about 40km offshore), so a short, one-hour sail can take you into really deep water for excellent **sport fishing**. Hope for the likes of swordfish, sailfish, tuna, dorado and black marlin (the best season is September to December).

Watersports are in abundance at Chipipe and San Lorenzo Beach; simply ask on the beach about banana boating, jet skiing or paddle boarding.

Soerma Tours WHALE WATCHING, WATER SPORTS
(09-9617-7537; soermatour@gmail.com; Malecón; tours from $16) Tour operator offering 1½-hour whale-watching trips between June and September, departing from the pier on San Lorenzo Beach. Also offers watersports including banana boat rides ($3), kayak rental ($10), jet ski rides ($20), paragliding ($25) and fishing trips ($60).

Sleeping

Accommodation in Salinas is varied; you'll find the odd funky hostel and five-star resort hotels, as well as lots of dated guesthouses catering to domestic local travelers. Prices often drop by 20% to 30% from May to mid-December and are higher during Easter week, Christmas, New Year and Carnaval.

★ **Chescos** HOSTAL $
(02-770-875, 09-9160-6612; www.chescos.com; Malecón; dm from $10, s/d from $20/24;) This funky new hostel on the *malecón* is where the young people hang out. It has a welcoming atmosphere and a TV lounge with swings as seats, plus games like Jenga and beer pong. Rooms are small but clean, with minimalist decor and bright colorful accents. A bar was being built at the time of research, adjacent to a balcony with beach views.

Coco's Boutique Hostal GUESTHOUSE $
(04-277-0361; www.hostal-cocos.com; Malecón; s/d $25/35;) Boasting a central waterfront location, Coco's is a good option for its attractive but simply decorated rooms (though some of them lack natural light), with artwork throughout, plus private bathrooms and TVs. It's at the western end of the *malecón*.

Hotel Francisco III HOTEL $
(09-9155-2127, 04-277-0881; www.hotelfranciscoecuador.com; cnr Malecón & Calle 27; d from $30;) The nicest of the Salinas Franciscos is well located in the middle of the *malecón*. The sunny outdoor hallways are a nice touch, though unfortunately the rooms themselves could use more natural light.

Big Ralph's Hostal & Restaurant GUESTHOUSE $$
(04-312-7120, 09-9618-8111; www.bigralphhostal.com; cnr Av San Lorenzo & Carlos Espinoza; s $25, d $34-48;) About 10-minutes' walk from the *malecón*, English/Ecuadorian-owned Big Ralph's earns high marks from homesick Europeans. It's decorated with English memorabilia, from Union Jacks to scenes of London. In the restaurant they even serve fish and chips and a proper English breakfast ($8). Simple rooms with adobe-style walls cluster around a relaxing courtyard and have terracotta-tiled floors.

Hotel Marvento I HOTEL $$
(04-277-0975; www.hotelmarvento.com; cnr Guayas & Enríquez Gallo; r per person incl breakfast $35-60;) If sea views aren't a priority, the Marvento, only a block from the *malecón*, is an option. Everything from the polished marbled floors to the rustic wooden furniture is in good condition. The rooftop has a small pool and there's a restaurant on site.

Barcelo Colon Miramar HOTEL $$$
(04-2771610; www.barcelo.com; Malecón, near Calle 38; r per person incl full board from $167;) The largest hotel in town is the most luxurious option. It has the facilities of a resort complex: a pool, gym, sauna, three restaurants (meals and cocktails included), and several bars and lounges. Free activities include beach football, table tennis and volleyball; there are also different entertainment options for adults and kids each week. Still, it's of questionable value.

Eating

Most of the restaurants are located either on the *malecón* or a block or two away. There's a good range of options including barbecue, empanadas, French, Italian and lots of seafood joints. Note: some may be closed or have limited hours during the low season (May to mid-December).

Pedro's Empanadas EMPANADAS $

(Cosme Renella; empanadas from $1.80; ⏲4pm-11pm) Away from the main tourist drag, one block inland from Chipipe Beach, you'll find this inexpensive local empanada shop with plastic chairs, selling fine hand-baked patties made with plantain outer shells. Flavors include shrimp and beef, cheese and chicken, crab and more. Wash them down with fresh juices like papaya, melon, strawberry, blueberry or coconut and lime.

Cevicheria Lojanita SEAFOOD $

(cnr Enriquez Gallo & Aviles; mains $5.50-10; ⏲8:30am-8:30pm) Cevicheria Lojanita is a large, yellow complex with a foodcourt-style setup. Ceviche portions are large and fresh, and come in various flavors. Other dishes include rice with crab, shrimp or seafood, grilled fish fillets, seafood spaghetti or omelets, plus grilled lobster and dozens of other plates inspired by the ocean.

Oui Chef FRENCH $$

(☎09-8007-2240; Enriquez Gallo; mains $6-15; ⏲noon-3:30pm & 6:30pm-10:30pm Thu-Sat, 9am-9:30pm Sun) This new edition is one of the coolest hangout spots in town. A converted VW campervan food truck fronts onto a sleek patio with fairy lights and wooden tables, offering typical French dishes like crepes and beef bourguignon. Finish with a chocolate dessert and proper ground Ecuadorian coffee. All ingredients are sourced from local farms. It's behind the Barcelo Colon hotel.

Luv 'n' Oven ECUADORIAN $$

(☎09-9957-8101; Malecón; mains $6-16, lobster from $26; ⏲11am-9pm; 📶) This welcoming waterfront spot serves good seafood plates, including ceviches, risottos, tasty *encocados* (seafood stew with coconut milk), and octopus rice. Plus, there's pastas, steak, and stuffed chicken with cheese and ham. There's another branch further along the *malecón* with inside seating (and air-con).

Casa Grill GRILL $$

(☎04-277-2509; Malecón; lunch from $6, dinner mains from $9-$12.50; ⏲noon-midnight) With big glass windows and a shiny new porch overlooking the waterfront, Casa Grill is a carnivore's heaven. The best-value option is to order the grill plates to share. Parilla Casa Grill ($32) has two pork chops, two steaks, one chicken fillet, one portion of lamb, one blood, chorizo and longaniza sausage, plus roasted corn on the cob and a salad.

Lui e Lei SEAFOOD $$

(☎09-9957-8101; Malecón; breakfast from $4, dinner $9-16; ⏲8am-10pm) Lui e Lei is a simple eatery that does pancakes and continental breakfast in the morning; by night, it's all about the seafood. Specials include Lui e Lei shells (shells with seafood sauce), *cazuela de mariscos* (seafood stew with smashed plantain, peanuts and spices) and *mariscos gratinado* (mixed seafood in white sauce, baked into a gratin with mozzarella and ham). You'll find it at the western end of the *malecón*.

Drinking & Nightlife

Most of the restaurants on the *malecón* offer cocktails and beers; for a more lively atmosphere try **Aloha Bar** (☎09-8857-2755; www.facebook.com/AlohaBarEcuador; Malecón; ⏲7pm-2am Mon-Sat; 📶).

Information

There's no shortage of ATMs available to you in Salinas. On the malecón, try **Banco Pichincha** or **JEP**.

Tourist Information (San Lorenzo Beach; ⏲9am-5pm) is located at the far western end of the beach, this little hut can provide travelers with maps, information and tips on the local area.

Getting There & Away

CITSE bus 30C goes to/from Salinas ($1, 45 minutes) to **Santa Elena bus station** (Hwy 15, btwn Santa Elena & Ballenita) throughout the day, departing when full. Taxis to/from Santa Elena cost $5.

TO GUAYAQUIL

Turismo Ruta del Sol (☎04-277-0358, 09-9464-0915) runs minivans between Salinas and Guayaquil ($12, 2½ hours) every hour between 6am and 8pm. You can pay a little extra to be dropped directly outside your hotel. Call ahead to arrange pick-up.

Buses to Guayaquil depart from Santa Elena ($4.25, 2½ hours, every 15 minutes from 4am to 7pm).

TO THE NORTH

Buses to Montañita ($1.70, 1½-2 hours, every 20 minutes from 4.45am to 7pm) depart from Santa Elena bus station. Some of the these buses also service other coastal villages to the north. Alternatively, transfer in Montañita for buses traveling further up the coast.

Make sure you tell your driver when you want to get off, as it may not be a scheduled stop.

Playas

04 / POP 35,000

Weekending *guayaquileños* don't come to crumbling and dusty Playas looking for urban sophistication; they come for the long, broad and relatively close expanse of beach and delicious fresh seafood.

Sleeping & Eating

★La Posada del Sueco HOTEL $$

(099-372-2888; Km 2; d $65-75; P 🛜 ❄) Owned by a friendly Swedish-Ecuadorian couple, this lovely remote eco-minded beachfront complex has six attractive rooms surrounding a lush garden of bougainvillea, passionfruit vines and fruit trees. It's about 2km from Playas on the way to Data.

Restaurant Jalisco SEAFOOD $

(cnr Paquisha & Alexander; mains $3-10; 10am-8pm) Jalisco, a local institution with plastic chairs, has been serving cheap *almuerzos*, seafood plates and ceviches for some 40 years. Ask about $2.50 lunch specials.

Getting There & Away

Transportes Villamil (04-276-0942, 04-276-1675; www.cooperativavillamil.com.ec; Mendez Gilbert; 4am-11pm) and **Transportes Posorja** have buses to Guayaquil ($2.85, two hours, every 30 minutes from 4am to 8pm). Villamil buses go direct, while Posorja buses pass through Posorja en route.

SOUTH OF GUAYAQUIL

Though it is usually seen by travelers as a place to pass through on the way south to Peru, this agriculturally important part of the country has nature reserves, cocoa farms you can visit, and a charming mountain town.

Reserva Ecológica Manglares Churute

04

This 500-sq-km **national reserve** (near Hwy E25; 8am-5pm) FREE protects an area of mangroves southeast of Guayaquil. Much of the coast used to be mangrove forest – an important and unique habitat. This is one of Ecuador's few remaining mangrove coastlands; the rest have been destroyed by the shrimp industry. Inland is some tropical dry forest, on hills reaching 700m above sea level.

Studies of the area within the reserve indicate that the changing habitat from coastal mangroves to hilly forest supports a wide biodiversity with a high proportion of endemic species. Dolphins have frequently been reported along the coast, and many other animal and bird species can be seen by wildlife-watchers.

The reserve's **information center** (09-3919-6806; off Hwy E25; 8am-5pm) is on the left side of the main Guayaquil–Machala

WORTH A TRIP

EL MORRO

A 10-minute drive east of Playas brings you to the little-known fishing village of El Morro. Off the international tourist trail, it has a completely different feel from Playas, with attractions including one of the oldest remaining **churches** (Provincal Playas-Puerto del Morro, El Morro; 9am-noon & 3-6pm Tue-Fri, 9am-noon Sat) in the region and a historic 125-year-old **bakery** (El Morro; bread from $0.50; hours vary). It sells incredibly good sweet bread, baked every morning using the traditional technique – in the stone oven, 90 loaves at a time.

But El Morro Port is the real reason to make the journey here – bordering the mangrove-lined Rio de Horno, it is home to dolphins and exotic frigate birds. **Tour agencies** (09-9130-2594, 09-6793-7980; tours from $30; 9am-4:30pm) offer boat tours to see both; when you're done, tuck into the best crab soup of your life by the dock.

The easiest way to get to El Morro from Playas is by taxi ($3, 20 minutes); don't forget to book one for your return trip.

Look for **El Morro Restaurant** (09-8141-0236; El Morro; lunch $3-8; 8am-3:30pm), a truly delicious eatery with no name on the 2nd floor (the 1st floor is a different restaurant) of the orange and white house at El Morro's pier. It's nothing to look at, just a handful of wooden tables and plastic chairs, but it serves the best crab soup you'll ever eat. When it's gone for the day, it's gone.

highway headed towards Machala, 50km southeast of Guayaquil. Stop here to register before visiting the park.

Any bus between Guayaquil and Naranjal or Machala can drop you off at the park's information center. When you're ready to leave, flag down a bus at the sign on the road (drivers know the sign); be prepared to wait.

A return taxi from Guayaquil is around $50 to $60.

Several tour companies in Guayaquil run day trips to the reserve, including My Trip to Ecuador (p277).

Machala

07 / POP 241,791

Surrounded by banana plantations – *oro verde* (green gold), the region's moniker – Machala is the commercial and administrative capital of El Oro province. The dusty city is a transport hub and there's not much to see, but it's a convenient stop south from Guayaquil on the way to the Peruvian border to refuel and recharge, or for those making journeys further into the mountains directly to the east. Puerto Bolívar, only 7km away, is the local international port and seafood center.

Parque Juan Montalvo is the main plaza at Machala's epicenter. The bus stations, most hotels and restaurants are within six blocks of here. The **World Banana Fair** (Feria Mundial del Banano; 07-370-0300; www.facebook.com/feriabananoec), held the third week in September, is when Machala celebrates all things banana.

Sleeping

Hotel Bolívar Internacional HOTEL $

(07-293-0727, 02-293-887; cnr Bolívar & Colón; s/d $20/30; P ❄ wi-fi) Clean, friendly and only a short walk from several bus companies. Some of the tiled rooms have windows overlooking a small park, rooms also have cable TV. There's a restaurant and conference center on site.

Veuxor Executive Hotel HOTEL $$$

(07-293-2423; http://hotelveuxor.com.ec; cnr Bolívar & Juan Montalvo; s $69-92, d $83-104; P ❄ wi-fi) One of the top upscale options downtown, Veuxor is a safe bet near the main plaza, with spacious, nicely designed rooms, some of which have views over the city. There's a gym, restaurant, and decent buffet breakfast. Cheaper on weekends.

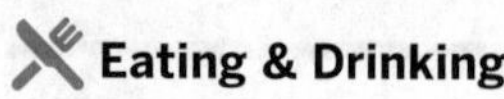

Eating & Drinking

Romero's ECUADORIAN $

(Sucre 1304, near Santa Rosa; set lunch $2.75, dinner mains $4-10; 6:30pm-11pm; wi-fi) Romero's has no sign, so can be tricky to find, but you'll be pleased if you do. The basic eatery serves up tasty grilled meats by night and inexpensive set lunches by day. Dine on the tiny front patio or the nicely set dining room inside.

Nutripan BAKERY $

(www.facebook.com/nutripandelicias; Guayas, btwn Av 25th de Junio & Sucre; sweet rolls $0.50; 7am-8pm Mon-Sat, 8am-6pm Sun) For midday snacks, nothing beats the piping-hot sweet rolls or dulce de leche–smothered pastries served here.

★ **Zona Refrescante** INTERNATIONAL $$

(Guayas, near Pichincha; mains $6-12; 9am-10:30pm) The best dining option in town is this inviting air-conditioned place specializing in grilled meats. The *seco de pollo* (passionfruit chicken) is delightful, served with fresh avocado, rice, plantain and french fries. Other choices include Cuban sandwiches, pork and chicken grills (with salad, salsa fries and plantain), and *churrasco ecuatoriano* (steak in garlic and cumin with fries and salad).

It's also a good spot for an evening drink (with outdoor seating in front).

Sir Cafe CAFE

(07-600-1262, 09-9324-5070; www.facebook.com/sircafemachala; Ayacucho, near Av 25th de Junio; 11am-11pm) With a classic European-style feel (decorated with upholstered dining chairs, chandeliers, a picture of the Leaning Tower of Pisa, a small model of a penny farthing, and chintzy painted teapots), this tiny cafe is one of the few places in town you can get a proper cup of coffee. Hot drinks are served in painted tea cups.

Information

A handful of major banks with ATMs are located around Parque Juan Montalvo, including **Banco Pichincha** (Guayas near Rocafuerte).

Post Office (Correos del Ecuador; cnr Bolivar & Juan Montalvo; 9am-6pm Mon-Fri)

Tourist Information (cnr Av 25 de Junio & Av 9 de Mayo, Carrera Central; 8am-1pm & 2:30-5:30pm Mon-Sat) This office can provide city and area maps, but only Spanish spoken here.

Machala

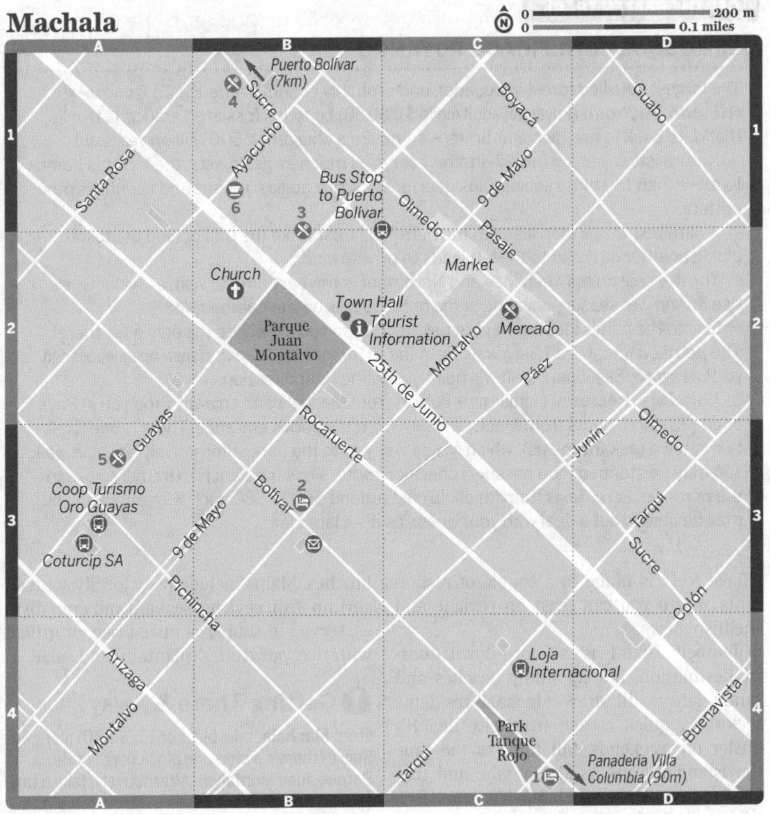

Machala

Sleeping
1 Hotel Bolívar Internacional C4
2 Veuxor Executive Hotel B3

Eating
3 Nutripan B2
4 Romero's B1
5 Zona Refrescante A3

Drinking & Nightlife
6 Sir Cafe B1

Getting There & Away

AIR

Flights to Quito (from $27, 1¼ hours) with **Tame** (07-2932-710; www.tame.com.ec; Montalvo, near Pichincha; 9am-6pm Mon-Fri) depart from Santa Rosa Airport, 40 minutes south of Machala. Jump on any bus heading to Huaquillas (ask the bus driver to stop at the airport), or take a taxi ($30).

BUS

Machala has no central bus terminal, though most bus companies cluster about five blocks southeast of Parque Juan Montalvo.

MINIVAN

A handful of minivan companies line Guayas between Pichincha and Serrano, including **Coturcip SA** (07-296-2963; cnr Guayas & Pichincha) and **Coop Turismo Oro Guayas** (07-293-4382; cnr Guayas & Pichincha). These have hourly departures to Guayaquil ($10 to $12, three hours).

Puerto Bolívar & Jambelí

07

Only 7km from Machala, Puerto Bolivar and the island Jambelí are of interest to seafood connoisseurs and those who want to glimpse the mangrove-lined landscapes along the coast. The area around the pier, while not pretty (it has an industrial fishing

OFF THE BEATEN TRACK

EL BOSQUE PETRIFICADO PUYANGO

The largest petrified forest in Ecuador, and probably in South America, **El Bosque Petrificado Puyango** (Puyango; adult/child $1/$0.50) contains fossilized araucaria trunks that date back to pre-dinosaur times – some are a staggering 500 million years old.

Naturalists will enjoy this 27-sq-km reserve as much as geologists; the forest is home to more than 130 bird species, plus deer, ocelots, armadillos, pumas and countless other critters.

A 4km boardwalk loop leads to the petrified forest (take the trail behind the toilet block; another dirt road to the left leads to private land).

The dry season between May and November is the best time to visit, as water levels rise during wet season, covering some of the fossils on the riverbed.

Due to the park's location, it gets few visitors, so you'll likely be the only ones there. The petrified forest is a 1.3km walk from the **information center** (www.bosquepuyango.ec; Puyango; ⏲8am-5pm); staff will point you in the right direction.

Loja Internacional (Tarqui, near Bolívar) from Machala and Loja will drop you in Puyango ($3, three hours from Machala), 5km from the park's entrance. There is one local taxi in town (ask the locals), which will deliver you to the park. Alternatively, you can walk. You may be stopped for a passport check en route, since the park is extremely close to the border of Peru. Taxis from Machala cost around $60 to $80 each way, although you may be able to cut a deal with your driver, as it's a large fare.

village feel), is home to a couple of restaurants where you can feast on ceviche and shellfish stews.

Jambelí island is a worn-down tourist destination, but its sunny beaches and sandy lanes still draw Machala residents seeking a quick escape from city life. It's busier on weekends, but most of the time the island retains its sleepy vibe and ragged, unkempt charm. Jambelí's canal is a good spot for bird-watching, with plenty of pelicans, egrets and gray herons nesting in the undergrowth. Keep your eyes peeled for male frigates showing their big red pouches.

Sleeping & Eating

Las Tórtolas CABIN $$
(☎09-9929-7926; Jambelí; d $40, f $60; ❄📶) On the beach about a 10-minute walk north of the pier, Las Tórtolas has pleasant wood cabins with brightly colored soft furnishings and natural wood features. They surround a pretty courtyard and garden with coconut trees, hammocks and a barbecue. All of the tidy, clean rooms have fridges and hot water, some have TVs.

Nuevo Eden SEAFOOD $$
(☎07-292-8236; Sucre, near Malecón; mains $11-15; ⏲8:30am-9:30pm; ❄📶) Inside this clean, modern building with big windows and sleek furniture (including pale green chairs, white walls and spotlights), businesspeople schmooze with their guests over seafood lunches. Mains include tasty locally sourced shrimp, fish, ceviche, seabass and crab dishes, served in soups, as mixed rice, or grilled with rice, *patacones* (plantain) and salad.

Getting There & Away

From **Machala**, take bus 1 or 13 ($0.30) along Sucre (there's a stop one block north of the Parque Juan Montalvo). Alternatively, take a taxi ($3, 20 minutes).

To Jambelí, passenger boats (return $4, around 30 minutes) depart on the hour from **Muelle De Cabotaje Pier** (Malecón, near Ave Rocafuerte; ⏲6am-6pm Mon-Fri, to 7.30pm Sat & Sun).

Zaruma

☎07 / POP 23,000 / ELEV 1200M

This charming old gold-mining town (founded in 1549) is a revelation, with its narrow, hilly streets, wooden balustrades decorated with potted plants, a well-kept plaza and quaint **Virgen del Carmen** church rising above it. The journey into Zaruma itself is part of the appeal; winding up and over lush mountains with gushing streams pouring through the foliage, the final climb to the colonial town feels like the end of a pilgrimage. While most mines are closed to the public, you can visit one – **La Mina el Sexmo** (El Sexmo; ⏲8am-noon & 1-4:30pm Tue-Sun, last entry 3.30pm) FREE – and learn about the industry that once made this area flourish.

The nearby secluded Reserva Buenaventura – a cloud-forest reserve – offers nature hikes and some magnificent bird-watching opportunities.

Sights

Reserva Buenaventura NATURE RESERVE
(02-505-129, 09-9997-2958; www.fjocotoco.org/buenaventura2; off Av Angel Salvador Ocha; $15; 8am-3pm) Run by the Fundación Jocotoco, this 27-sq-km cloud-forest reserve is a fantastic spot for bird-watching. There are a number of short trails, simple wooden cabins (per person including full board $130), and a restaurant (day visitors should pre-order meals before their visit) with hummingbirds whirring about. Half-a-dozen hummingbird feeders are set up on the balcony, so you can see them up close. Other species in the area include umbrella birds, toucans and parakeets.

At the time of research there was a coati family living near the lodge. It's located about 9km from Piñas down a dirt road. Ask for comprehensive directions when you book, as it's tricky to find.

Sleeping & Eating

★ **Hostería El Jardín** HOSTERÍA $
(07-297-2706; www.hosteriaeljardinzaruma.com; Av Isidro Ayora, Barrio Limoncito; s/d from $25/40; @) Outside the town center, El Jardín is a peaceful, family-run guesthouse with a pretty courtyard garden and comfortable rooms. It's a short taxi ride ($1.50) to the town center. American, continental or Ecuadorian breakfast is $4.

Zaruma Colonial HOTEL $
(07-297-2742; www.hotelzarumacolonial.com.ec; Sucre, near Sexmo; s/d/tr $15/30/45; P) This friendly four-story hotel has 35 attractive brown-and-beige modern rooms, the best of which have pretty views.

Pizza Pimini PIZZA $
(09-8789-6117, 09-5963-8611; El Sexmo; pizzas from $4; 4:30pm-10:30pm) This simple little cafe with white walls and chunky pine tables serves hand-prepared pizzas. Order a classic margherita, salami and ham, tuna and onion, or a Hawaiian. All are made with fresh tomato sauce and mozzarella. Also on the menu: spaghetti carbonara or bolognese, with banana and nutella crepes to finish. Service can be slow.

200 Millas/Cafe Zarumeno ECUADORIAN $$
(07-297-2600; Alonso de Mercadillo; mains $5-10; 8am-10pm;) A 10-minute walk downhill to the left from Plaza de la Independencia you'll find Zaruma's top restaurant. Part coffee shop and part Ecuadorian eatery, dishes include meat every which way (breaded, fried or barbecued), plus seafood (ceviche, with rice, or grilled) and a selection of salads. Good breakfasts and coffee, too.

Information

There are a number of ATMs in town including **JEP** (Sucre, near Sexmo).

The friendly **tourism office** (07-297-3533; www.visitazaruma.com; 9 de Octubre; 8:30am-5:30pm Mon-Fri, 9am-3pm Sat) is on the edge of Plaza de la Independencia. Spanish only.

Getting There & Away

The two bus companies (Piñas and TAC) are located near the cemetery at the base of town. It's around a 2km walk uphill (or $1.50 taxi) to Plaza de la Independencia. An informal **bus stop** is next to the gas station on the way into town.

In your own vehicle it's about a two-hour drive to/from Zaruma to Machala. Some street parking is free, but most is $1.50 for three hours; purchase passes from restaurants and shops.

Peru via Huaquillas

The only reason to come to Huaquillas is to cross the border from Ecuador into Peru – it's the route taken by most overland travelers between the two countries. Huaquillas is about 80km from Machala on the highway, which passes through banana and palm plantations, as well as the dusty market towns of Santa Rosa and Arenillas.

Huaquillas is a fairly populated place, and like most of the world's border towns it's not spectacular to look a. Those passing through these dusty streets will find a busy market, just off the main plaza, plus a collection of basic hotels and eateries.

Getting There & Away

CROSSING THE BORDER

There are two ways to cross the border, by road (bus/car) and by foot (using a pedestrian bridge), but only the road route has official offices.

The easiest way to cross over to Peru is by road with one of the international lines that depart

MONEY MATTERS

It's best to avoid the informal moneychangers on either side of the border. Problems with fake currency are common and moneychangers will tell patent lies like 'the machines don't work.' Banks in Huaquillas or Aguas Verdes don't normally do exchange transactions, but it's worth trying. Alternatively, there are ATMs on both the Ecuadorian and Peruvian sides.

If you're leaving Peru, it's best to get rid of as much Peruvian currency as possible before arriving at the border. If you're leaving Ecuador, your US currency is easily exchanged in Peru, but it's best to wait to do the bulk of your transactions until you're further south of the border.

from **Guayaquil**'s main bus terminal. **Cruz del Sur** (p287), **CIVA** (p287), **Expreso Internacional Ormeño** (p287) and **Rutas de America** (Map p281; ☎ 04-223-8673; www.rutasenbus.com; La Garzota, Camilo Nevarez Vasquez) have daily departures for Lima. These services are very convenient because the bus goes to the Ecuadorian Immigrations Office and waits for you to take care of border formalities.

Alternatively, the pedestrian border crossing is in the center of **Huaquillas** at Río Zarumilla. An international footbridge goes over a mostly dry riverbed linking Huaquillas to **Aguas Verdes** in Peru. The bridge guards and police won't bother you with formalities. You can walk back and forth as you please, but remember that without an exit stamp from Ecuador and entry stamp into Peru you will have problems leaving Peru at any other official border crossing or airport.

The official **Ecuadorian Immigrations Office** (⏲24hr) and the **Peruvian Immigration Office** are in new complexes, some 4km north of the bridge on the North Panamerica Highway. All entrance and exit formalities (including passport stamps) are carried out here. If you're coming by non-international bus, it's easiest to disembark in Huaquillas and hire a taxi to take you to the immigration office. Taxis ask around $5 there and back.

Across the footbridge you will find *colectivos* (shared minivans; $3) in Aguas Verdes, plus mototaxis ($5) running to Tumbes in Peru, which has plenty of hotels, as well as transportation to take you further south. **Transportes Flores** (http://floreshnos.pe) has four daily departures from the Peruvian side of the border south to Lima ($30, 20 hours) and destinations en route. More comfortable premium bus options might be available for a few extra dollars.

If you're leaving Peru and entering Ecuador, after walking across the international bridge you'll find yourself on the main road, which is crowded with market stalls and stretches out through Huaquillas. Take a taxi ($5; double if you ask them to wait and return to the town) to the Ecuadorian and Peruvian immigration offices. For onward northbound transport you'll have to return to Huaquillas, where the buses and minivans depart.

To make your way further into Ecuador, head to one of the bus companies scattered within a few blocks of one another near the footbridge.

CIFA (www.cifainternacional.com; cnr Santa Rosa & Machala) has buses at least every hour to Machala ($2, two hours), where you can transfer for Cuenca, Loja, Piñas, Zaruma and Guayaquil. They also have six daily departures for Guayaquil ($7, four hours).

Transfrosur (☎ 07-299-5288; http://transfrosur.com; Santa Rosa; ⏲5am-8pm Mon-Sat, from 7am Sun) runs hourly minivans to Guayaquil ($20, four hours), with wi-fi and air-conditioning.

Panamericana (www.panamericana.ec; cnr Teniente Cordovez & 10 de Agosto) has 11 buses daily to Quito ($15, 11 hours) via Ambato or via Santo Domingo. If you're in a rush to get to Colombia, there's a daily 4.10pm trip to Tulcan ($25, 19 hours) near the Colombian border.

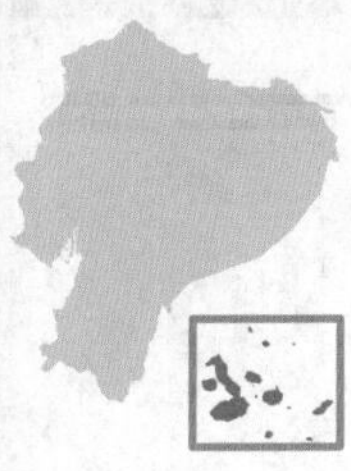

The Galápagos Islands

Includes ➡

Best Places to Eat

- Coco Surf (p331)
- Almar (p317)
- Garrapata (p317)
- Isla Grill (p317)

Best Places to Stay

- Casa Blanca Galapagos (p323)
- Iguana Crossing Boutique Hotel (p330)
- Lodging House Casa del Lago (p315)
- Casa de Nelly (p324)

Why Go?

The Galápagos Islands may just inspire you to think differently about the world. The creatures that call the islands home, many found nowhere else in the world, act as if humans are nothing more than slightly annoying paparazzi.

This is not the Bahamas and these aren't typical tropical paradises; in fact, most of the islands are devoid of vegetation and some look more like the moon than Hawaii. However, more humans live here than is commonly assumed, and there's a surprising level of development in the islands' towns, mostly geared toward the thriving tourism industry.

This isolated group of volcanic islands and its fragile ecosystem has taken on almost mythological status as a showcase of biodiversity. Yet you don't have to be an evolutionary biologist or an ornithologist to appreciate one of the few places left on the planet where the human footprint is kept to a minimum.

When to Go

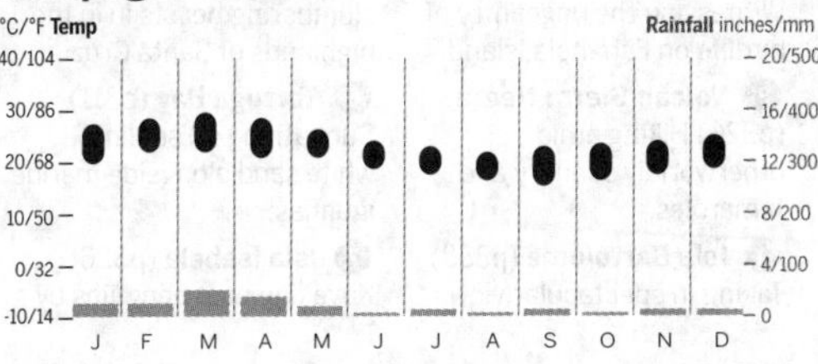

Jan–May Sunny, warm, occasional short downpours. Water is less rough and winds slacken.

Jun–Dec The cool and dry season. Seas tend to be choppier due to the Humboldt current.

Jun–Dec Sea mammals and land birds tend to be at their most active.

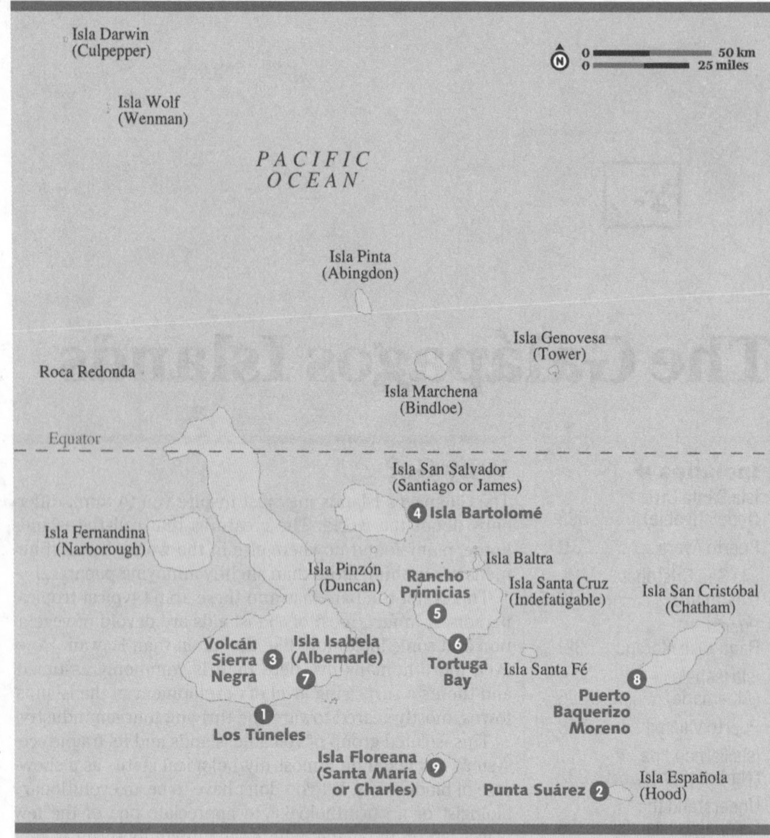

The Galápagos Islands Highlights

1 **Los Túneles** (p327) Locking eyes with sea horses among superb lava formations.

2 **Punta Suárez** (p334) Witnessing the pageantry of birdlife on Española Island.

3 **Volcán Sierra Negra** (p326) Hiking amid otherworldly scenery and fumaroles.

4 **Isla Bartolomé** (p333) Taking in spectacular views and snorkeling with sea turtles around Pinnacle Rock.

5 **Rancho Primicias** (p309) Gawking at the slumbering beasts in in the highlands of Santa Cruz.

6 **Tortuga Bay** (p311) Sunbathing on sublime white sand alongside marine iguanas.

7 **Isla Isabela** (p326) Kayaking past penguins by day and enjoying beachside cocktails by night.

8 **Puerto Baquerizo Moreno** (p321) Surfing, snorkeling, kayaking, biking or diving within minutes of Isla San Cristóbal's port town.

9 **Isla Floreana** (p333) Relaxing after days of adventuring on a pretty, peaceful beach.

ISLA SANTA CRUZ (INDEFATIGABLE)

The island of Santa Cruz has the largest and most developed town in the Galápagos; almost every visitor to the islands spends at least some time here, even if it's simply commuting from the airport on nearby Isla Baltra to a cruise ship in the harbor of Puerto Ayora. However, to anyone who stays for longer, the island of Santa Cruz is more than just a way station or place to feel connected to the modern, man-made world. It's a destination in itself, full of visitor sites, easily accessible beaches and remote highlands in the interior, and a base for adventurous activities far from the tourism trail.

Sights

Several sites of interest in the highlands of Santa Cruz can be reached from the trans-island road and are part of the itineraries of many cruises.

★El Chato Tortoise Reserve — WILDLIFE RESERVE

($5; 8am-5pm) South of Santa Rosa is El Chato Tortoise Reserve, where you can observe giant tortoises in the wild. When these virtually catatonic, prehistoric-looking beasts extend their accordionlike necks to feed, it's an impressive sight. The reserve is also a good place to look for short-eared owls, Darwin's finches, yellow warblers, Galápagos rails and paint-billed crakes (these last two are difficult to see in the long grass). The reserve is part of the national park and a guide is required.

Rancho Primicias — WILDLIFE RESERVE

($3; 8am-5pm) Next to El Chato is this private ranch, owned by the Devine family. There are dozens of giant tortoises, and you can wander around at will. The entrance is beyond Santa Rosa, off the main road – ask locals for directions. Remember to close any gates that you go through. There is a cafe selling cold drinks and hot tea, which is welcome if the highland mist has soaked you.

Lava Tunnels — TUNNEL

($5; 8am-5pm) These impressive underground tunnels southeast of the village of Santa Rosa are more than 1km in length and were formed when the outside skin of a molten-lava flow solidified. When the lava flow ceased, the molten lava inside the flow kept going, emptying out of the solidified skin and thus leaving tunnels. Because they are on private property, the tunnels can be visited without an official guide. The tunnels have electrical lighting (you can also hire flashlights/torches). Tours to the lava tunnels are offered in Puerto Ayora.

El Garrapatero Beach — BEACH

A 30-minute taxi ride from Puerto Ayora through the highlands, plus a 15-minute walk, brings you to this beautiful beach. It has tidal pools that are good for exploring and snorkeling on calm days, and a lagoon with flamingos, white-cheeked ducks and black-necked stilts.

Cerro Crocker — HIKING

A path north from Bellavista leads toward Cerro Crocker (864m) and other hills and extinct volcanoes. This is a good chance to see the vegetation of the scalesia, miconia and fern-sedge zones and to look for birds such as the vermilion flycatcher, the elusive Galápagos rail and the paint-billed crake. It's around 5km from Bellavista to the crescent-shaped hill of **Media Luna**, and 3km further to the base of Cerro Crocker. This is national park, so a guide is required.

Los Gemelos — NATURAL FEATURE

Part of the highlands that can be visited from the road are these twin sinkholes (not volcanic craters), surrounded by scalesia forest. Vermilion flycatchers are often seen here, as are short-eared owls on occasion.

ISLAND BASICS

The islands lie in the Pacific Ocean on the equator, about 90 degrees west of Greenwich. There are 13 major islands (ranging in area from 14 sq km to 4588 sq km), six small islands (1 sq km to 5 sq km) and scores of islets, of which only some are named.

Five of the islands are inhabited. About half the residents live in Puerto Ayora, on Isla Santa Cruz in the middle of the archipelago. Puerto Baquerizo Moreno on Isla San Cristóbal (the easternmost island) is second in importance to Puerto Ayora when it comes to tourism.

The other inhabited islands are Isla Isabela (the largest island, accounting for half the archipelago's land mass), with the small, increasingly popular town of Puerto Villamil; Isla Baltra; and Isla Santa María, with Puerto Velasco Ibarra. The remaining islands are not inhabited but are visited on tours.

Most of the islands have two, or sometimes three, names. The earliest charts gave the islands both Spanish and English names (many of these refer to pirates or English noblemen), and the Ecuadorian government assigned official names in 1892. The official names are used in this guide in most cases.

Isla Santa Cruz

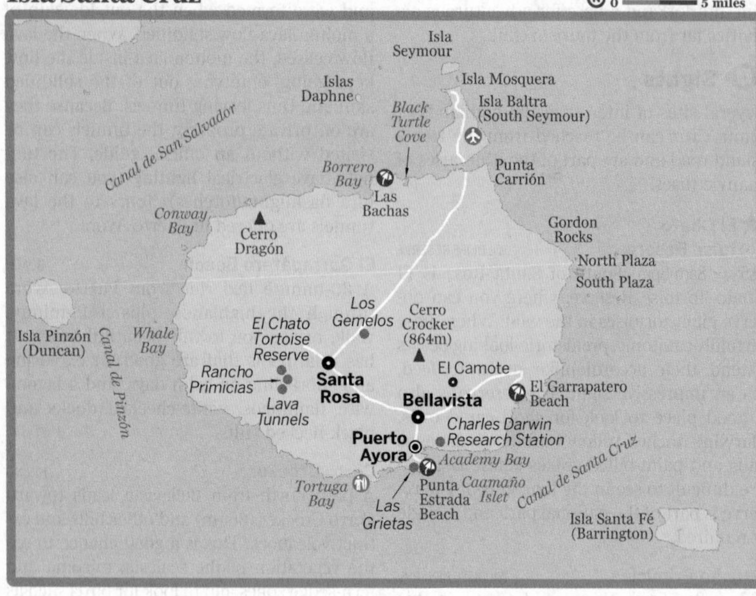

Los Gemelos are about 2km beyond Santa Rosa on the trans-island road. Although the sinkholes lie only 25m and 125m from either side of the road, they are hidden by vegetation, so ask your driver to stop at the short trailhead.

Punta Estrada Beach BEACH

The small beach in front of the Finch Bay Hotel is a good place to while away a few hours. The water here is pristine and sharks have been known to pass through the cove.

Coastal Sites

The remaining Santa Cruz visitor sites are reached by boat and with guides. On the west coast are **Whale Bay** and **Conway Bay**, and on the north coast are **Black Turtle Cove** (Caleta Tortuga Negra) and **Las Bachas**. Conway Bay has a 1.5km trail passing a lagoon with flamingos; north of here is **Cerro Dragón**, with two small lagoons, which may have flamingos. It also has a 1.75km trail that leads through a forest of palo santo (holy wood) trees and opuntia cacti to a small hill with good views. There are some large repatriated land iguanas here.

There is no landing site in Black Turtle Cove, which is normally visited by *panga* (small boats used to ferry passengers from a larger boat to shore). The cove has many little inlets and is surrounded by mangroves, where you can see lava herons and pelicans. The main attraction is in the water: marine turtles are sometimes seen mating, schools of golden mustard rays are often present and white-tipped sharks may be seen basking in the shallows. The nearby Las Bachas beach, although popular for sunbathing and swimming, is often deserted.

Sleeping

While most of Santa Cruz's accommodations options are in Puerto Ayora, there are a handful of highland hotels and lodges that range from bare-bones basic to break-the-bank luxurious.

Royal Palm HOTEL $$$

(☎05-252-7408; www.royalpalmgalapagos.com; r from $300; ❄@📶🏊) If Puerto Ayora is too 'bright lights, big city' for you, try the Royal Palm Hotel, a beautifully designed luxury hotel in the highlands around Santa Rosa.

Casa Natura LODGE $$$

(☎05-450-6016; www.casanaturahotel.com; Via al Camote; r incl 3 meals from $285) A few kilometers from Bellavista, this is a fine, ecofriendly place to enjoy the peacefulness of the highlands. Food served in the garden is grown in the lodge's gardens; tours are available.

Puerto Ayora

☎05 / POP 20,000

This town, the largest in terms of population and size in the Galápagos, is a surprise to most visitors, who don't expect to find anything but plants and animals on the islands. Puerto Ayora looks and feels like a fairly prosperous mainland Ecuadorian coastal town, despite the sea lions and pelicans hanging around the waterfront. Most of the hotels, restaurants and tourist facilities line Avenida Charles Darwin, and the airport is on Isla Baltra, around an hour away to the north. Several blocks inland, travel agencies give way to ordinary, humble dwellings and shops. Some descendants of the handful of Norwegian, Swiss and German families that originally settled here four generations ago maintain an active presence in the tourism industry.

Sights & Activities

★MAPRAE MUSEUM

(Museo de Arte Precolombino de Realidad Aumentada; ☎05-252-5197; www.maprae.com; Av Darwin & Av Binford; $5-10, includes tablet with headphones; ⏲10am-10pm) The first of its kind in the world, this museum uses augmented reality to showcase a permanent exhibition of 55 pre-Columbian artifacts. The ancient cultures of Ecuador's Amazon and coastal regions are brought to life as visitors point their smart phones or tablets at one of the relics, with historical information and three-dimensional images appearing directly on the devices.

Charles Darwin Research Station WILDLIFE RESERVE

(☎05-252-6146; www.darwinfoundation.org; Av Darwin; ⏲8am-12:30pm, 2:30pm-5:30pm) FREE Just northeast of Puerto Ayora is this iconic national-park site, where more than 200 scientists and volunteers are involved with research and conservation efforts, the most well known of which involves a captive breeding program for giant tortoises. Paths leading through arid-zone vegetation take you past tortoise enclosures, where you can get a good look at these Galápagos giants. There's also a **baby-tortoise house** with incubators (when the tortoises weigh about 1.5kg or are about four years old, they're repatriated to their home islands).

Several of the 11 remaining subspecies of tortoise can be seen here. Other attractions include a small enclosure containing several land iguanas, with explanations in Spanish and English concerning efforts to restore their populations on islands where they've been pushed to the brink of extinction. Follow paths through arid-zone vegetation such as saltbush, mangroves and prickly pear, and see a variety of land birds, including Darwin's finches. The research station is supported by contributions to the Galápagos Conservancy (www.galapagos.org).

Tortuga Bay BEACH

In terms of sheer white-sand beauty, this beach is the rival of any in South America. You'll find it at the end of a 2.5km paved trail southwest of Puerto Ayora. In addition to swimming (a spit of land provides protection from the strong and dangerous currents on the exposed side), surfing or just sunbathing, you can see sharks, marine iguanas, pelicans and the occasional flamingo. There's no drinking water or other facilities. It's about a half-hour walk from the start of the path – often used by local runners – where you must sign in between 6am and 6pm.

Centro Comunitaria de Educación Ambiental Miguel Cifuentes Arias MUSEUM

(⏲7:30am-12:30pm & 2-5pm Mon-Fri, 8am-noon Sat) At the foot of the hill before the start of the path to Tortuga Bay is this educational center, where you can learn about conservation efforts and issues in the waters around the archipelago. To get here, you have to take the road out of Puerto Ayora about 500m before reaching the paved path that begins at the top of a hill and runs the rest of the way to Tortuga Bay.

Playa Mansa LAGOON

If you walk the length of Tortuga Bay, you'll reach this picturesque lagoon lined with mangroves. Here you can spot marine iguanas, brown pelicans and blue herons, among other species. On the nearby dunes, sea turtles lay their eggs. The placid, shallow water is a great swimming spot for kids. **Kayaks** (per person per hr $10; ⏲9am-6pm) are available for hire.

Laguna de las Ninfas LAGOON

FREE This peaceful lagoon has a short boardwalk path, where you can stop to take in the mangroves while looking for stingrays, baby sharks, sea turtles and other creatures sometimes spotted here.

Puerto Ayora

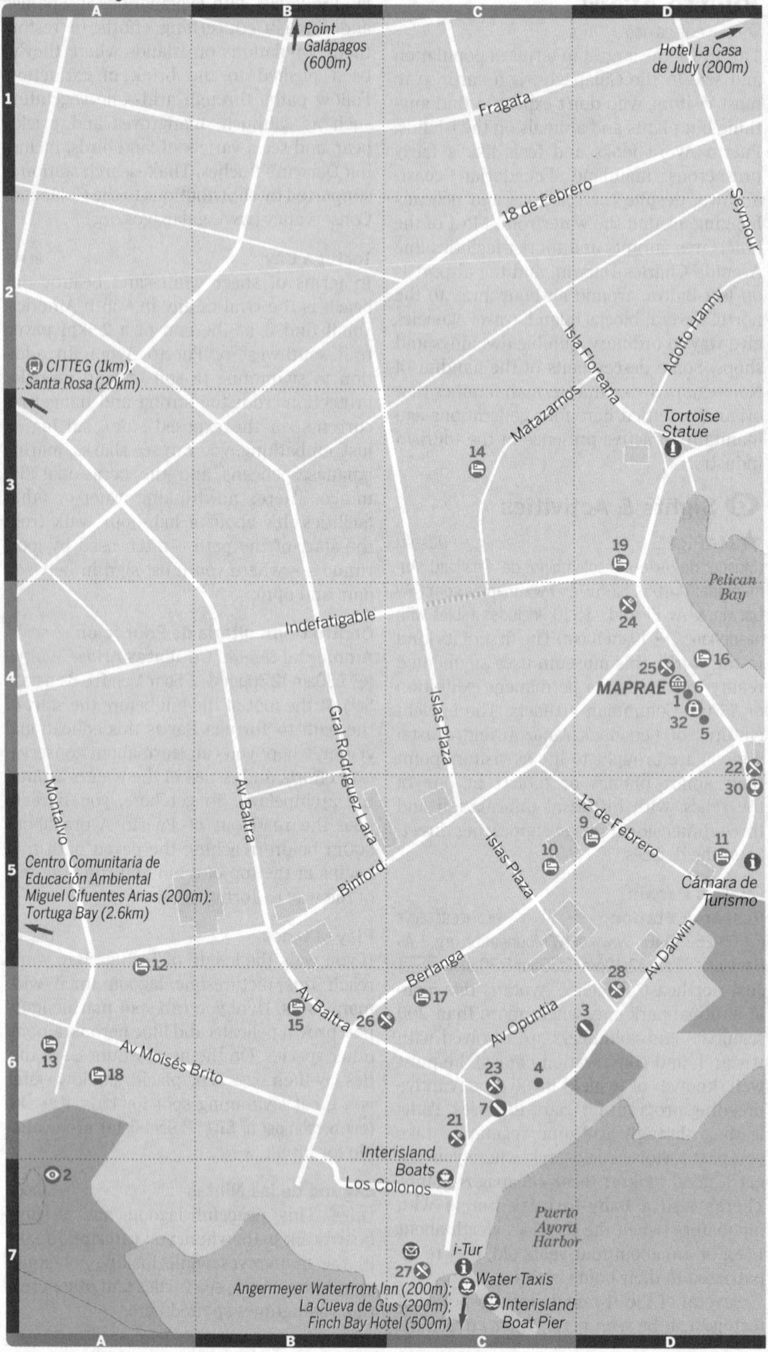

A
B
C
D
1
2
3
4
5
6
7
Point Galápagos (600m)
Hotel La Casa de Judy (200m)
Fragata
18 de Febrero
Seymour
Adolfo Hanny
Isla Floreana
Matazarnos
Tortoise Statue
CITTEG (1km); Santa Rosa (20km)
14
19
Pelican Bay
24
Indefatigable
16
25
MAPRAE
6
1
32
5
Islas Plaza
Gral Rodriguez Lara
Av Baltra
Montalvo
22
30
12 de Febrero
9
10
11
Cámara de Turismo
Islas Plaza
Binford
Centro Comunitaria de Educación Ambiental Miguel Cifuentes Arias (200m); Tortuga Bay (2.6km)
Av Darwin
28
Berlanga
12
17
Av Baltra
15
26
3
Av Opuntia
13
Av Moisés Brito
18
23
4
7
21
Interisland Boats
Los Colonos
2
Puerto Ayora Harbor
i-Tur
27
Water Taxis
Angermeyer Waterfront Inn (200m); La Cueva de Gus (200m); Finch Bay Hotel (500m)
Interisland Boat Pier

Puerto Ayora

Top Sights
1 MAPRAE D4

Sights
2 Laguna de las Ninfas A7

Activities, Courses & Tours
3 Academy Bay Diving D6
4 Albatros Tours C6
5 Aquatours D4
6 Moonrise Travel D4
7 Nauti Diving C6
8 Scuba Iguana F2

Sleeping
9 Galapagos Native D5
10 Hostal Gardner C5
11 Hostal Los Amigos D5
12 Hotel Crossman A5
13 Hotel Fiesta A6
14 Hotel Mainao C3
15 Hotel Sir Francis Drake B6
16 Hotel Sol y Mar D4
17 La Posada del Mar C6
18 Lodging House Casa del Lago A6
19 Peregrina B&B D3
20 Red Mangrove Aventura Lodge F2

Eating
Almar .... (see 20)
Casa del Lago Café Cultural .... (see 18)
21 Descanso del Guia C6
Galápagos Deli .... (see 17)
22 Garrapata D4
23 Hernan Café C6
24 Il Giardino D4
25 Isla Grill D4
26 Lo & Lo B6
27 Proinsular Supermarket C7
28 Rock D6

Drinking & Nightlife
29 Bar Tolomé F2
30 Bongo Bar D5
La Panga .... (see 30)

Shopping
31 Galería Aymara E3
32 Tortoise Gallery D4

Diving

Because live-aboards are costly and space is limited, most divers experience the underwater wonders of the Galápagos on day trips booked from Puerto Ayora. These are suitable for intermediate to advanced divers – currents can be strong and most are drift dives.

Gordon Rocks, Caamaño Islet, La Lobería, Punta Estrada and Punta Carrión

WORTH A TRIP

LAS GRIETAS

For nice swimming and snorkeling, head to **Las Grietas**, a water-filled crevice in the rocks. Talented and fearless locals climb the nearly vertical walls to plunge gracefully (and sometimes clumsily) into the water below. Take a water taxi (per person $0.60 from 6am to 7pm) to the dock for the Angermeyer Point restaurant, then walk past the Finch Bay Hotel, then past an interesting salt mine, and finally up and around a lava-rock-strewn path to the water. Good shoes are recommended for the 700m walk from the dock. Keep an eye on any valuables that you leave on the rocks.

are popular dives sites, as is North Seymour Island, a short boat trip from Isla Baltra. Devil's Crown, Enderby or Champion off the northern tip of Isla Santa María are good for barracudas, rays and sharks. One of the recommended sites for those with a few dives under their belt is Academy Bay off the Puerto Ayora harbor.

The standard rate for two boat dives starts at $180 ($160 if booked 'last minute'); all offer PADI certification courses to newcomers and have English-speaking divemasters.

Scuba Iguana DIVING
(☎05-252-6497; www.scubaiguana.com; Av Darwin; ⊙9am-12pm & 3-6pm Mon-Fri, 3-6pm Sat) Run by two of the most experienced divers in the Galápagos.

Nauti Diving DIVING
(☎05-252-6982; www.nautidiving.com; Avs Baltra & Darwin; ⊙10am-8pm Mon-Sat & 3:30-8pm Sun) Runs hotel-based diving tours as well as day trips. Prices begin at $185 per person for one dive, with equipment, lunch and transfers included.

Academy Bay Diving DIVING
(☎05-252-4164; www.academybaydiving.com; cnr Av Darwin & Islas Plaza; ⊙8am-7:30pm Mon-Sat & 2-7:30pm Sun) Whether you're a novice or an expert, this is your one-stop shop for all things scuba – it offers lessons, day tours and live-aboard excursions.

Surfing

There are several good surf breaks near Puerto Ayora itself, including **La Ratonera** and **Bazán** near the Charles Darwin Research Station beach. If hauling your board a few kilometers is no problem, Tortuga Bay has several good breaks.

An hour or so by boat takes you to **Punta Blanca** and further north to **Cerro Gallina**, **Las Palmas Chica** and **Las Palmas Grande**, considered to be three of the best breaks in the Galápagos. There are also several breaks off the west side of Isla Baltra.

Point Galápagos SURFING
(☎05-822-1926; www.thepointgalapagos.com; 18 de Septiembre & Piqueros) Offers surf camps, yoga retreats, SUP, kayaking and snorkeling, plus multi-adventure day-tour packages around Santa Cruz and beyond.

Biking

A *ciclovia* (bicycle path) runs from Puerto Ayora up to Bellavista and Santa Rosa, but it's a long, tough climb to the highlands. A good DIY adventure is to hire a bike and take a taxi up to either Los Gemelos or El Camote, then bike back. Returning from Los Gemelos, you can stop in El Chato and the lava tunnels. Another option is to taxi instead to El Camote, from which you can continue by bike down to El Garrapatero Beach for a full day's outing. Many shops in town offer rentals by the hour, half-day or full day.

Tours

Daily trips to Islas Santa María, Isabela, Bartolomé and North Seymour, as well as nearby Santa Cruz sites, are offered by almost every travel agency in town. Some include snorkeling as well as visits to land-based sites for wildlife.

Aquatours TOURS
(☎05-252-7303; www.galapagosaquatours.com; Av Darwin) Offers glass-bottom boat tours around the bay, which includes snorkeling and a visit (on foot) to Las Grietas.

Metropolitan Touring TOURS
(☎05-252-6297; www.metropolitan-touring.com; ⊙8am-5pm) Located at the Finch Bay Hotel, this outfit books the M/V *Santa Cruz*, yachts *Isabela II* and *La Pinta* and any land- or water-based tours in the islands.

Moonrise Travel TOURS
(☎05-252-6402; www.galapagosmoonrise.com; Av Darwin) Run by a family of Galápagos experts and guides, who can arrange camping at their private highlands ranch, plus boat- and hotel-based tours and diving trips.

Albatros Tours TOURS
(☎05-252-6948; albatrostours@gpsinter.net; Av Darwin) Santa Cruz day tours, snorkel gear rental and dive trips.

Sleeping

You get much less bang for your buck compared to the mainland. Most of the hotels are within a few blocks of Avenida Darwin, and prices tend to rise during the heaviest tourism seasons (December to January and June to August).

Around the Southern End of Avenida Charles Darwin

Hotel Sir Francis Drake HOTEL $
(☎05-252-6221; www.sirfrancisdrakegalapagos.com; Av Baltra; s/d from $25/30;) Hidden behind a small department store, the Sir Francis Drake is one of the better value places in town. Ask for one of the ground-floor rooms all the way in the back – these have large windows that let in lots of natural light. Common space is limited to an inner patio with no seating and a single balcony. It's located just a short walk from the pier.

La Posada del Mar GUESTHOUSE $$
(☎05-301-4976; posadadelmargalapagos@gmail.com; Tomás de Berlanga near Av Baltra; s/d incl breakfast $70/85) Above the Galapagos Deli, this place has handsome rooms with russet-colored ceramic-tile floors and balconies with views over the greenery beyond town. Breakfast in the first-rate Galapagos Deli (p316) is a bonus.

Hotel Crossman HOTEL $$
(☎05-252-6467; www.crossmanhotel.com.ec; cnr Juan Montalvo & Charles Binford; s/d $25/40;) Draped with bougainvillea, this attractive red-roofed guesthouse has decent if somewhat plain rooms. Though unadorned, they're good-sized with strong wi-fi and cable TV, and some have balconies.

Galapagos Native GUESTHOUSE $$
(☎05-252-4730; www.galapagosnative.com.ec; Tomás de Berlanga near Av 12 de Febrero; s/d from $25/30) This place offers decent value for its clean rooms with white adobe-like walls. Three rooms (the best) are bright and airy with balconies.

Hostal Gardner HOSTAL $$
(☎05-252-6979; Tomás de Berlanga; s/d from $20/35;) The budget-minded Gardner has simple rooms and a covered rooftop patio with lounge chairs and hammocks.

★**Lodging House**
Casa del Lago APARTMENT $$$
(☎05-252-4116; www.casadellagogalapagos.com; cnr Moisés Brito & Juan Montalvo; d/tr incl breakfast from $99/170;) Ideal for laid-back families or small groups. Choose from several suites with fully stocked kitchens and charming private patios or porches: everything is made from recycled materials and decorated with colorful tiles and textiles. A short walk from the harbor and next to Laguna Las Ninfas, it's run by an environmentally conscious owner who also runs the charming attached cafe.

Hotel Fiesta HOTEL $$$
(☎05-252-6440; www.galapagoshotelfiesta.com; Av Moisés Brito near Juan Montalvo; r incl breakfast $125;) Next to the Laguna Las Ninfas, the Fiesta has spotless modern rooms set around an attractive courtyard set with cacti, palms, scalesia trees and an enticing pool. Excellent breakfasts.

Around the Northern End of Avenida Charles Darwin

Hostal Los Amigos HOSTAL $
(☎05-252-6265; hostal.losamigos@gmail.com; Av Darwin; s/d without bathroom $15/30;) Possibly the best-value cheapie in town. The lack of private bathrooms (aside from one room for four) is excused by the absolutely central location and gleaming wood-floored, though admittedly small, rooms. A kitchen and a lounge with TV is available for guests.

Peregrina B&B HOTEL $$
(☎05-252-6323; www.laperegrinagalapagos.com.ec; cnr Av Darwin & Indefatigable; s/d incl breakfast $45/70;) Not exactly a typical B&B, this collection of simple rooms, some larger and more nicely decorated than others, occupies prime real estate. A few hammocks in the small cactus garden contribute to the impression of a relaxing hideaway.

Hotel La Casa de Judy HOTEL $$$
(☎05-252-7343; www.hotellacasadejudy.com; cnr Fragata & Scalesia; s/d $77/95, with sea view $119/150;) Million-dollar rooftop ocean views and sun-splashed top-floor rooms with balconies are the big draw at this hotel, also known as Hotel Galápagos Inn. Some of the smaller standard rooms

(not recommended) open up onto a courtyard pool. It's on a quiet block, almost on the outskirts of town, although still only a short walk from the *malecón* (waterfront).

Hotel Mainao HOTEL **$$$**
(☎05-252-7029; www.hotelmainao.com; Matazarnos; r incl breakfast from $140; ❄@📶) A mix of Greek island and Moroccan casbah, this white stucco complex features a nicely landscaped flowering courtyard. Rooms are clean and spacious, if unexceptional, for the price.

Waterfront

Angermeyer Waterfront Inn HOTEL **$$$**
(☎05-252-6561; www.angermeyer-waterfront-inn.com; r from $240; ❄@📶) Across the harbor (accessible by water taxi) is this sun-splashed complex that has simple rooms and outstanding views from the garden patio, as well as from the rooms with balconies in the newer multi-story annex.

Finch Bay Hotel RESORT **$$$**
(☎05-252-6297; www.finchbayhotel.com; r from $379; ❄@📶🏊) Power down and disconnect at this ecologically minded beachside retreat across the bay from Puerto Ayora. Lava gulls and herons hang out by the pool and every facet of the property evokes a sense of place. The rooms aren't especially large or luxurious, but the grounds, hot tub and restaurant are worth coming for.

Metropolitan Touring (p314), based in the hotel, can arrange any outdoor activity imaginable.

Red Mangrove Aventura Lodge HOTEL **$$$**
(☎05-252-6564; www.redmangrove.com; Av Darwin; r incl breakfast from $350; ❄@📶) Nestled in a shady mangrove cove, this charmingly designed red-adobe inn at the northern end of town feels like a secret hideaway. While the standard rooms are suitably comfy, it's quite a step up to the next level of accommodation in terms of size, luxury and sunniness with its outdoor porches and tiled bathrooms. It has an attractive waterside restaurant, Almar, and all manner of day and overnight trips can be arranged.

Hotel Sol y Mar HOTEL **$$$**
(☎05-252-6281; www.hotelsolymar.com.ec; Av Darwin; r incl breakfast from $250; ❄@📶🏊) Occupying a sought-after waterfront location with pelicans, sea lions and marine iguanas for neighbors, this hotel (for better or worse) resembles a Florida condo complex. The rooms are no-nonsense, efficient and comfortable, each with a small private balcony; however, it is the seaside hot tub, pool, bar and restaurant area that justify consideration.

Eating

More than a half-dozen popular food kiosks sell inexpensive and hearty meals – mainly seafood – along Charles Binford, just east of Avenida Baltra. It's liveliest at night, particularly on weekends, when there's a festive atmosphere among the outdoor tables set out on the street.

Proinsular Supermarket SUPERMARKET **$**
(Av Darwin; ⊙7am-8pm Mon-Sat, 9am-5pm Sun) A short stroll from the pier, this place has food, beer, wine, toiletries, sunblock and other necessities. Don't miss the decent cinnamon rolls and croissants (on the left after you enter). The upstairs cafe offers a good view of the pier.

Galápagos Deli DELI, PIZZERIA **$$**
(Tomás de Berlanga; mains $5-9; ⊙7am-10pm Tue-Sun; 📶) Tired of standard *almuerzos* (set lunches)? Head to this sleek and modern place for brick-oven pizza (small $5) and high-quality deli sandwiches, as well as fish and chips, espresso and delicious gelato. Because it's on a block with few pedestrians, it feels like a secret.

Rock ECUADORIAN, INTERNATIONAL **$$**
(cnr Av Darwin & Islas Plaza; mains $8-23; ⊙11am-11pm Tue-Sun; 📶) This lively restaurant on the main strip serves up seafood and grilled dishes, including peppery seared tuna, pork ribs with pineapple salsa, and linguini with coconut and lobster. For something lighter (and cheaper), the big menu also features pastas, quesadillas and sandwiches.

Lo & Lo ECUADORIAN **$$**
(Berlanga; mains $9-19; ⊙7am-3:30pm Wed-Mon; 📶) A little open-sided place that does ceviche, grilled fish, *seco de chivo* (goat stew) and *balones* (mashed plantain balls).

Casa del Lago Café Cultural CAFE **$$**
(cnr Moisés Brito & Montalvo; mains $7-9; ⊙7am-7pm Tue-Sat; 📶✎) This boho cafe with a few indoor and outdoor patio tables serves excellent breakfasts, sandwiches, empanadas and salads, as well as homemade cakes, fruit drinks and brewed coffee.

Descanso del Guia ECUADORIAN **$$**
(Av Darwin near Los Colonos; mains $7-17; ⏰6am-8pm) Near the passenger pier, this bustling cafeteria is a handy spot for a quick bite.

Hernan Café ECUADORIAN, INTERNATIONAL **$$**
(Av Baltra; mains $8-20; ⏰8am-10pm; 📶) Owing to its location at the busiest intersection in town, lively Hernan Café often packs a crowd, and serves up decent (if unmemorable) pasta, pizza, fish and meat dishes.

Isla Grill BARBECUE, INTERNATIONAL **$$$**
(Av Darwin; mains $13-25; ⏰noon-10pm Tue-Sun) This buzzing grillhouse serves satisfying plates of grilled meat and seafood. Among the top picks: *costillitas* (pork ribs), *mariscada* (char-grilled shrimp, octopus and calamari) and *churrasquito de mimi* (a particularly tender cut of steak). The plump salads are also first-rate.

Il Giardino INTERNATIONAL, ICE CREAM **$$$**
(cnr Av Darwin & Binford; mains $16-32; ⏰8am-10pm; 📶) This open-air Italian trattoria boasts a lovely patio dining area, good meat and seafood dishes, plus decadent desserts. An *heladería* (ice-cream shop) is attached.

Almar JAPANESE **$$$**
(Av Darwin, Red Mangrove Aventura Lodge; mains from $16-24; ⏰8am-10pm; 📶) Located inside Red Mangrove Aventura Lodge, Almar prepares its seafood dishes with ingredients sourced from local suppliers. The big draw is sitting on the back waterside deck where sea lions have free rein.

Garrapata ECUADORIAN **$$$**
(Av Darwin; mains $15-30; ⏰11am-10:30pm Mon-Sat) Good tunes, cool breezes and tasty Ecuadorian and international dishes (seared tuna, grilled seafood platters and fish in coconut sauce) draw a lively crowd most nights. It's pricey but casual, with open sides and a pebble floor.

La Cueva de Gus INTERNATIONAL **$$$**
(☎05-252-6561; mains from $15-30; ⏰5-10pm) This picturesque open-air spot perched over the water serves tasty fish and lobster, pizzas and bistro fare. It's attached to Angermeyer Point Hotel; to get there, take a water taxi from the pier.

Drinking & Nightlife

Bongo Bar BAR
(Av Darwin; ⏰7pm-2am; 📶) What nightlife there is in Puerto Ayora centers mainly on this bar, a trendy 2nd-floor spot replete with flat-screen TVs, music and a lubricated mix of hip locals, guides and tourists. Surprisingly, you'll also find some of the best sushi on the islands here (rolls $10 to $14).

La Panga CLUB
(Av Darwin; ⏰8pm-3am) Downstairs from Bongo Bar, this disco is where to go to grind the night away.

Bar Tolomé BAR
(Av Darwin; ⏰10am-midnight Mon-Sat; 📶) At the northern end of town, this outdoor lounge features festive fairy lights and recessed alcoves with couches. The kitchen serves up tapas and there's sometimes live music on weekends.

Shopping

Every imaginable item has been covered with a Galápagos logo or creature and is on sale in Puerto Ayora.

Tortoise Gallery JEWELRY
(Av Darwin; ⏰9:30am-1:30pm & 3-10pm) You'll find one-of-a-kind gifts at this jeweler, with exquisite handmade works by Ecuadorian artisans. Some pieces incorporate lava forms, others feature pre-Columbian art and themes from native Ecuadorian wildlife.

Galería Aymara GALLERY, JEWELRY
(www.galeria-aymara.com; cnr Av Darwin & Seymour; ⏰8am-noon & 3-7pm Mon-Sun) A high-end artists boutique selling uniquely designed handicrafts, jewelry and ceramics.

Information

INTERNET ACCESS

The majority of midrange and top-end hotels offer wi-fi in public spaces; in rooms, it's less often. Several restaurants and cafes also provide wi-fi. Internet cafes are scattered throughout town and along Avenida Darwin – most charge around $2.50 per hour and some have headsets for Skype users.

MONEY

There are two ATMs near the pier and in front of Proinsular Supermarket.

Banco del Pacífico (Av Darwin near Isla Floreana; ⏰8am-3:30pm Mon-Fri, 9:30am-12:30pm Sat) has an ATM and changes traveler's checks.

POST

Post Office Near the harbor.

TOURIST INFORMATION

Cámara de Turismo (p47) Has hotel information and maps; some staff speak English.

Report any complaints here about boats, tours, guides or crew.

i-Tur (Av Darwin, entrance to water-taxi pier) A small kiosk with flyers, maps and basic hotel and travel-agency info.

Getting There & Away

AIR

Three airlines fly to the Galápagos (p341). Reconfirming your flight departures with **Avianca** (p286), **Lan** (05-269-2850; Av Darwin; 8am-6pm Mon-Sat & 10am-1pm Sun) or **Tame** (05-252-6527; cnr Av Darwin & Av 12 de Febrero; 8am-noon & 2-5pm Mon-Fri, 8am-1pm Sat) offices is recommended. Flights are often full, and you may have difficulty changing your reservation or buying a ticket.

Emetebe (p342) and **Fly Galápagos** (p342) have small aircraft that fly between Islas Baltra, San Cristóbal and Isabela.

BOAT

Lanchas (speedboats) head daily to the islands of Isabela ($30, two to 2¼ hours) and San Cristóbal ($30, two hours). Both depart at 7am and 2pm. There's also boat service to Floreana ($30, 1¾ hours) at 8am, but service is irregular so it is best to find out the schedule from an operator in Puerto Ayora and then plan your trip accordingly. The rides can be rough and unpleasant for some. Advance reservations aren't required, but it's wise to purchase tickets a day in advance. A string of offices near the pier sell boat tickets to the islands of San Cristóbal, Isabela and Floreana.

Interisland Boat Pier Catch boats to other islands here – be sure to arrive 30 minutes before departure.

Interisland Boats Book speedboat tickets from one of the several offices near the pier.

Getting Around

Hotels, travel agencies, tour agencies and some cafes rent out bicycles (per hour from $2). To reach boats docked in the harbor, or one of the several hotels or sites southwest of town, take a **water taxi** (Av Charles Darwin). From 6am to 7pm water taxis costs per person $0.60, from 7pm to 6am it's $1.

TO/FROM THE AIRPORT

The airport is on Isla Baltra, a small island practically touching the far northern edge of Isla Santa Cruz. If you're booked on a prearranged tour, you will be met by a boat representative upon arrival, and ushered onto a bus for the 10-minute drive to the channel (separating Baltra from Santa Cruz) and the boat dock.

If you're traveling independently, take the public bus signed 'Muelle' to the dock (a free 10-minute ride) for the ferry to Isla Santa Cruz. A 10-minute ferry ride ($1) will take you across to Santa Cruz, where you will be met by a CITTEG bus to take you to Puerto Ayora, about 45 minutes to an hour away ($2). This drive (on a paved road) provides a good look at the interior and the highlands of Santa Cruz.

Buses ($2) from Puerto Ayora to Isla Baltra (via the ferry) leave every morning at 6:30am, 7:15am, 8am and 8:30am (schedules change, so verify before showing up) from the **CITTEG bus station** (Av Baltra) around 2km north of the harbor; a taxi to the station costs $1. If you're going to the airport to make a flight, it's a good idea to allow 1½ hours or more for the entire journey from town.

Taxis between town and the Santa Cruz side of the channel are $18 (35 to 40 minutes).

BUSES & TAXIS

Buses from the **CITTEG bus station** in Puerto Ayora leave for Santa Rosa (about $2) four times a day from Monday to Saturday, and less often on Sunday.

The most convenient way of seeing the interior (as it ensures you don't get stuck) is to hire a taxi for the day with a group of other travelers.

All taxis are pickups, so you can toss your bike in the back if you want to return to Puerto Ayora by pedal power. To Bellavista by taxi is around $4 and to Santa Rosa is around $6 – both one way. Hail one anywhere along Avenida Darwin.

AROUND ISLA SANTA CRUZ

Islas Seymour & Mosquera

Isla Seymour is a 1.9-sq-km island with a dry landing. A rocky 2.5km trail encircles some of the largest, most active seabird-breeding colonies in the islands. Frigates and blue-footed boobies are the main attractions and there is always some kind of courtship, mating, nesting or chick-rearing to observe. You can get close to the nests – there is always at least one pair of silly boobies that builds their nest in the middle of the trail. Sea lions and land and marine iguanas are common; occasional fur seals, lava lizards and Galápagos snakes are seen, too.

Mosquera is a tiny island (about 120m by 600m) between Baltra and Seymour. There's no trail, but visitors land on the beach to see (or swim with) the sea lions. Keep your distance – males are territorial and may charge or swim into you if you get too close to females or young.

Islas Plazas

These two small islands, just off the east coast of Santa Cruz, can be visited on a day trip from Puerto Ayora. They were formed by uplift due to faulting. Boats anchor between them, and visitors can land on **South Plaza** (the larger of the islands), which is only about 0.13 sq km in area. A dry landing on a jetty brings you to an opuntia cactus forest, which is home to many land iguanas. A 1km trail circuit leads visitors through sea-lion colonies and along a cliff-top walk where swallow-tailed gulls and other species nest. The 25m-high cliffs offer a superb vantage point from which to watch various seabirds such as red-billed tropic birds, frigate birds, pelicans and Audubon's shearwaters. Snorkeling with the sea lions is a possibility.

Islas Daphne

These two islands of volcanic origin are roughly 10km west of Seymour. **Daphne Minor** is much eroded, while **Daphne Major** retains most of its typically volcanic shape (called a tuff cone). A short but steep trail leads to the 120m-high summit of this tiny island.

There are two small craters at the top of the cone, and they contain hundreds of blue-footed booby nests. Nazca boobies nest on the crater rims, and a few red-billed tropicbirds nest in rocky crevices in the steep sides of the islands.

The island is difficult to visit because of the acrobatic landing – visitors have to jump from a moving *panga* on to a vertical cliff and scramble their way up the rocks. Special permission is required to visit.

Isla Santa Fé (Barrington)

This 24-sq-km island, about 20km southeast of Santa Cruz, is a popular destination for day trips. There is a good anchorage in an attractive bay on the northeast coast, and a wet landing gives the visitor a choice of two trails. A 300m trail takes you to one of the tallest stands of opuntia cacti on the islands, some over 10m high. A somewhat more strenuous 1.5km rough trail goes into the highlands, where the **Santa Fé land iguana** (found nowhere else in the world) may be seen, if you're lucky. Other attractions include a sea-lion colony, excellent snorkeling, marine iguanas and, of course, birds.

ISLA SAN CRISTÓBAL (CHATHAM)

Some local boosters say that San Cristóbal is the capital of paradise – and, technically, it is, because its port town of Puerto Baquerizo Moreno is the political seat of the Galápagos. It's the only island with fresh water and an airport in town, and it has several easily accessible visitor sites, all of which means that its tourism profile is second only to Santa Cruz. San Cristóbal is the fifth-largest island in the archipelago and has the second-largest population. The Chatham mockingbird, common throughout the island, is found nowhere else.

History

Though San Cristóbal was first settled in 1880, it was the establishment of a sugar factory by Manuel J Cobos in 1891 that signaled the start of a significant human presence on the island. Cobos recruited jailed mainlanders to work in his factory at El Progreso; imported train cars; and minted his own money, called the *cobo*. The experimental utopian project lasted for 13 years until the workers revolted and killed him in 1904; his son took over but was not very successful. The site is now a small village, where you can see the factory ruins and the site where Cobos is buried.

Sights & Activities

Southern San Cristóbal

You can plan your own DIY adventure in the south, by hiring a pick-up taxi to take you to El Junco Lagoon, Galapaguera and Puerto Chino. Drivers charge around $60 for the whole return trip from Puerto Baquerizo Moreno.

★ **León Dormido** ISLAND

About an hour's boat ride northeast of Puerto Baquerizo Moreno is León Dormido (Kicker Rock), so named because of its resemblance to a sleeping lion. León Dormido is an imposing, vertical, sheer-walled tuff cone that has been eroded in half; smaller

Isla San Cristóbal

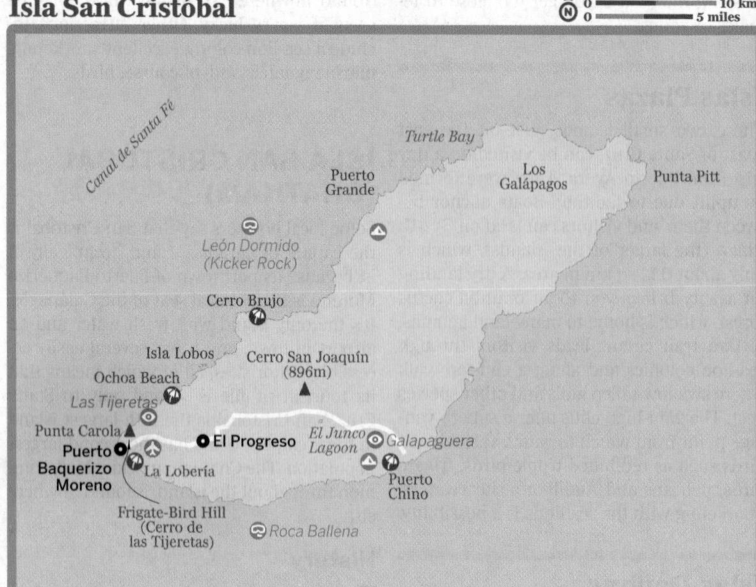

boats can sail between the two rocks. Because there's no place to land, this site is usually seen by snorkelers, passing boats or from the top of Cerro de las Tijeretas outside of Puerto Baquerizo Moreno, often to dramatic effect when the sun is setting. Day trips from Puerto Boquerizo Moreno here are around $80.

El Junco Lagoon — LAKE

Around 10km east of El Progreso along the main road, you'll find El Junco Lagoon – a freshwater lake some 700m above sea level. It's one of the few permanent freshwater bodies in the Galápagos. Here you can see frigate birds shower in the freshwater to remove salt from their feathers; white-cheeked pintails and common gallinules; and the typical highland miconia vegetation and endemic tree ferns. The weather is often misty or rainy. A return taxi costs in and around $30.

Cerro Brujo — BEACH

Possibly one of the nicest beaches in the Galápagos, Cerro Brujo is a huge white expanse found on the west side of the island. The sand here feels like powdered sugar. A colony of sea lions and blue-footed boobies call Cerro Brujo home, and behind the beach is a lagoon where you'll find great egrets and great blue herons. There's also good snorkeling in the turquoise waters.

Ochoa Beach — BEACH

On the western side of the island you'll find this horseshoe-shaped cove with a white sandy beach and shallow water that's good for snorkeling. Sea lions, frigate birds, pelicans and blue-footed boobies can be found frolicking here; however, it's only accessible by boat and usually with a guide. Kayaks are a possibility.

Galapaguera — WILDLIFE RESERVE

Galapaguera is part of the national park on the southeastern part of San Cristóbal, where giant tortoises live in semi-natural conditions. A taxi can take you there and back from Puerto Baquerizo Moreno for around $35.

El Progreso — VILLAGE

A road leads from the capital to the village of El Progreso, about 6km to the east and at the base of the 896m-high Cerro San Joaquín, the highest point on San Cristóbal. It's a sleepy, ramshackle village with nothing much to see. Buses go here several times a day from Puerto Baquerizo Moreno or you can hop in a taxi for around $3.50.

Near the town entrance, the **Casa del Ceibo** (☎099-934-1524; admission $2, climb $3.50, r per person $25; ⊙9am-12:30pm & 1:30-5:30pm) scores high on novelty. Halfway up an enormous ceiba tree (reached by narrow swinging bridge) is a tiny shed where you can bunk for the night. You can also climb up the outside or simply enjoy a cool drink in the snack bar below.

Puerto Chino BEACH

The road to El Junco continues across the island to the isolated beach of Puerto Chino. This is one of the better places for beginner surfers, since this is a beach break. Camping is allowed with prior permission.

Isla Lobos ISLAND

A half-hour northeast of Puerto Baquerizo Moreno by boat is the tiny, rocky Isla Lobos, with the main sea-lion and blue-footed booby colonies for visitors to San Cristóbal, and a 300m-long trail where lava lizards are often spotted. Both the boat crossing and the trail tend to be rough, and there are better wildlife colonies elsewhere.

Northern San Cristóbal

Los Galápagos WILDLIFE RESERVE

At the northern end of San Cristóbal is Los Galápagos, where you can often see giant **Galápagos tortoises** in the wild, although it does takes some effort to reach the highland area where they live.

One way to reach Los Galápagos is to land in a bay at the north end of the island and then hike up – it takes about two hours to get to the tortoise area following the trail. Some visitors report seeing many tortoises, while others see none.

Puerto Grande BEACH

Smaller than its name suggests, Puerto Grande is a well-protected little cove on San Cristóbal's northwestern coast. There is a good, sandy beach suitable for swimming, and various seabirds can be seen. It's reachable by kayak, and camping is allowed with prior permission.

Turtle Bay WILDLIFE RESERVE

You can see flamingos, turtles and other wildlife here; both Turtle Bay and Cerro Brujo can be visited as part of a trip to Punta Pitt and Los Galápagos.

Punta Pitt BIRDWATCHING, SNORKELING

The northeasternmost point of the island is Punta Pitt, where volcanic tuff formations are of interest to geologists (and attractive in their own right), but the unique feature of the site is that it's the only one where you can see all of the Galápagos booby species nesting. The walk is a little strenuous, but rewarding.

Getting There & Away

Inter-island flights operate Monday through Saturday between San Cristóbal, Balta and Isabela. Speedboats run daily between Puerto Ayora and Puerto Baquerizo Moreno ($30, 2¼ hours).

Puerto Baquerizo Moreno

☎05 / POP 7000

Despite its abundance of restaurants and hotels, Puerto Baquerizo Moreno retains its sleepy, time-stands-still fishing-village feel. And though an increasing number of trips begin or end here, it remains under the shadow of Puerto Ayora, its larger and higher-profile sister city in the Galápagos. The surfing is world class, and you can explore many places on the island from here on your own.

Sights

Interpretation Center MUSEUM

(☎05-252-0358; Av Alsacio Northia; ⊙8am-5pm) FREE This modern and easily digestible center explains the history and significance of the Galápagos better than anywhere else in the country. Exhibits deal with the biology, geology and human history of the islands – it deserves a visit even if you've been inundated with facts from boat guides. From the center there are also many well-marked trails that wind around the cacti and scrub of Cerro de las Tijeretas (Frigate-Bird Hill).

Cerro de las Tijeretas HILL

(Frigate-Bird Hill) About 1.7km northeast of Puerto Baquerizo Moreno, Cerro de las Tijeretas provides good views and can be reached on a trail. You'll pass a national park information office en route, and there's excellent snorkeling on the ocean side.

La Lobería BEACH

Southwest of town, a road leads 2.5km (about a 30-minute walk) to La Lobería, a rocky beach with a lazy sea-lion colony. It's good for year-round surfing, and there are lots of iguanas along the trail leading past the beach. Bring lots of water and sun protection. Taxis charge about $3 to take you out here and you can walk back. Once there,

Puerto Baquerizo Moreno

Puerto Baquerizo Moreno

Activities, Courses & Tours
- 1 Cañon Point A3
- 2 Chalo Tours C2
- 3 Dive & Surf Club C2
- Galakiwi .... (see 13)
- 4 Sharksky Tours B2

Sleeping
- 5 Casa Blanca C2
- 6 Casa de Laura Hostal A4
- 7 Casa de Nelly D1
- 8 Casa Iguana Mar y Sol D1
- 9 Casa Opuntia C2
- 10 Hostal León Dormido B3
- 11 Hostal San Francisco B2
- 12 Hotel Mar Azul B4
- 13 Miconia C2

Eating
- 14 Cabaña Mi Grande B2
- 15 Calypso Restaurant A3
- Casa Blanca Cafe .... (see 5)
- 16 Cuencan Taste C2
- 17 El Descanso Marinero C2
- La Zayapa .... (see 13)
- 18 Lucky's B3
- Miconia .... (see 13)
- 19 Rosita B3
- Supermercado Galamaxi .... (see 21)

Drinking & Nightlife
- 20 El Barquero B4
- 21 Iguana Rock C4

a cliffside path takes you past marine iguanas, lava lizards and soaring frigate birds. To get here on foot, take Av Alsacio Northia toward the airport, turn left after the stadium (look for the murals) and then take the first right.

Activities

Diving

There are several good spots for diving nearby. Eagle rays, sea turtles, sea lions, and hammerhead and white-tip sharks can be found at León Dormido (Kicker Rock). Schools of jacks, eagle rays, stingrays and sea horses are seen around Stephanie's Rock. Roca Ballena is a cave at about 23m to 24m down with corals, parrotfish and rays; strong currents mean it's for experienced divers only. There are also several wreck dives, including the *Caragua*, a 100m-long cargo ship near the site of the *Jessica* oil spill. Several companies in town offer diving.

Dive & Surf Club DIVING
(☎08-587-7122; www.divesurfclub.com; cnr Hernán Melville & Ignacio Hernández) PADI-registered Dive & Surf Club offers diving and surfing lessons, and can also arrange camping and horseback tours.

Surfing

Hands down, Baquerizo Moreno has the best surfing in the Galápagos. From December to March a northern swell brings world-class waves and more than a hundred surfers, especially Brazilians, head here around January. Waves are rideable year-round, but the best time is December to April. High-quality reef breaks near town are **El Cañon** and **Tongo Reef**, both of which are accessed by walking through the military zone. If you're carrying a board and show identification (your passport), the guard will sign you through. La Lobería (p321) and **Punta Carola** are also excellent spots with reef breaks. **Cañon Point** (Av de la Armada; bike per half-/full day $15/25; ⏲8am-7pm Mon-Thu & Sun, to 10pm Fri & Sat) rents out boards (per day $20) and provides half-day lessons ($50 per person or $45 each in groups of two or more).

Cycling & Kayaking

If you're a cyclist and in good shape, you can take on the steep uphill climb to El Junco, 16km east (and 700m up) from Puerto Baquerizo Moreno. It's a further 10km from El Junco downhill to Puerto Chino. If attempting both, you'll need to be fit and to start very early. Another option is to hire a truck taxi to take you one way and cycle back. Several agencies in town hire bikes. The best maintained are at Cañon Point.

To get out on the water, stop by Cabañas Don Jorge (p324), where you can hire a two-person kayak for $20 (for four hours), and go for a paddle off nearby Playa Mann.

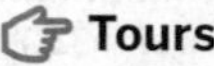

Tours

Sharksky Tours SNORKELING, DIVING
(☎05-252-1188; www.sharksky.com; Av Darwin; ⏲8am-6pm Mon-Sat & 8am-12pm Sun) This company offers island-hopping adventure-sports tours that range from four to eight days. It can also arrange longer cruises on many of the Galápagos expedition vessels.

Chalo Tours DIVING
(☎05-252-0953; chalotours@hotmail.com; Av Alsacio Northia) Offers day and overnight scuba trips, as well as day trips on San Cristóbal and to nearby islands; it also rents out snorkeling and biking equipment.

Galakiwi GROUP TOURS
(☎05-252-1770; www.galakiwi.com; Av Darwin; ⏲9am-5pm) Founded by a pair of New Zealanders, Galakiwi offers six- and 10-day adventure tours, with activities including kayaking, biking, yoga, paddleboarding and snorkeling.

Sleeping

Waterfront

★**Casa Blanca** HOTEL $$
(☎05-252-0392; www.casablancagalapagos.com; Av Darwin; s/d incl breakfast from $70/90; ❄📶) There's really no better place to base yourself in town: not only does this whitewashed adobe building have charmingly decorated rooms and tile floors, but it sits on the *malecón* directly across from the passenger pier, meaning rooms with sea-facing balconies have great views. There's even a top-floor cupola suite, with its own private balcony.

Hostal León Dormido HOSTAL $$
(☎05-252-0169; www.leondormidogalapagos.com.ec; Av Villamil; s/d $25/40; ❄📶) A half-block off the *malecón*, the friendly León Dormido has clean rooms with a cheery yellow color scheme and tile floors. Most have windows facing onto the interior patio (although No 7 has an exterior window – lean out and you'll see the sea). Below are bike hire and a tour outfitter.

Hostal San Francisco HOSTAL $$
(☎05-252-0304; Av Darwin; s/d per person $15/30; 📶) The best of several cheapies on

WORTH A TRIP

CERRO DE LAS TIJERETAS

From the **Interpretation Center** (p321), there are various well-marked and paved trails that wind around the scrub-covered **Cerro de las Tijeretas** (p321). One trail leads over the hill to the small Las Tijeretas bay, which has excellent **snorkeling**; there's no beach here – just step in from the rocks. Other paths lead to **viewing points** with breathtaking panoramas, and there's also a path down to scenic **Playa Baquerizo** (2km one-way from the viewing point); the last half is strewn with large, sharp rocks, so wear good shoes.

Directly in front of the Interpretation Center is **Playa Mann**, a small beach popular with locals and tourists alike, especially for lovely sunsets and on weekends. The large building across the street houses the Galápagos Academic Institute for the Arts & Sciences, which hosts semester-abroad international students and special marine-ecology and volunteer programs.

From the end of the dirt road that passes in front of the Interpretation Center, there's a short trail to **Playa Punta Carola**, a narrow beach nicknamed 'Playa del Amor' (Beach of Love) because the sheltering mangrove trees are favorite make-out spots (the sea lions here show little interest in the goings on). Surfing off the nearby point is excellent.

the waterfront, Hostal San Francisco has simple but clean rooms with hot-water bathrooms and friendly owners who also run the shop below.

Casa Opuntia HOTEL $$$
(☎02-604-6800; www.opuntiahotels.com; s/d incl breakfast from $175/200; ❄📶🏊) This whitewashed villa anchoring one end of the *malecón* has airy and sparsely decorated rooms, some with wicker and island knickknacks. Some rooms open onto balconies facing the pool in back; others have views of the sea, overlooking the pleasant front courtyard, which has hammocks.

Miconia HOTEL $$$
(Av Darwin; s/d from $95/165; ❄📶🏊) Near the east end of the waterfront, Miconia has a range of rooms. The best are the seven suites in the original building, with big windows, arched ceilings and contemporary decor. The small patio in back and the pool add to the appeal.

Inland

★**Casa de Laura Hostal** HOSTEL $
(☎05-252-0173; hostalcasadelaura@hotmail.com; Av de la Armada; r per person $20; ❄@📶) This friendly, family-owned hideaway is one of the best-value places in town. Located in a two-story adobe building with modern hot-water rooms, there's a nicely landscaped courtyard, and hammocks in the tiny cactus garden in front. It's just off the western end of Av Darwin.

Casa de Nelly GUESTHOUSE $$
(☎05-252-0112; www.casadenellygalapagos.com.ec; Av Alsacio Northía near Manuel Agama; s/d from $50/70; ❄📶) This friendly three-story guesthouse can be found just outside town on the way to Playa Mann. The best rooms are bright and airy with fine waterfront views. There's a small patio amid a few palm trees at the entrance.

Cabañas Don Jorge CABIN $$
(☎05-252-0208; eco.donjorge@gmail.com; Av Alsacio Northia; s/d per person $25/35; ❄📶) Looking very much like a wilderness ranger station, this is a hodgepodge of rustic aging cabins. Kitchens are fully stocked and good for self-catering, and it has bikes for guest use. It's on your right on the way to Playa Mann.

Hotel Mar Azul HOTEL $$
(☎05-252-0139; galapagosmarazul@gmail.com; Av Alsacio Northia & Esmeraldas; s/d $50/75; ❄@) A surprisingly good choice, considering the Mar Azul looks like a 1970s-era school building. Your best bet is one of the rooms that opens onto a small, sunny courtyard with a hammock. All rooms are comfortable and modern with hot water and cable TV, although you should avoid the handful of rooms that open directly onto the street because noise can be an issue. Wi-fi is available in theory, but the service is spotty.

★**Casa Iguana Mar y Sol** HOTEL $$
(☎05-252-1788; www.casaiguanamarysol.com; $135-285; ❄) Everything in this five-room ho

tel, only minutes from the *malecón* toward Playa Mann, is lovingly and painstakingly handcrafted – from the railings to the iguana carved into the front door. Each room is a large, boutique-quality suite with surprising flourishes. There's a sylish ground-floor lounge/bar/breakfast area, and the rooftop deck is ideal for a sundowner.

Cabañas Pimampiro HOTEL **$$$**
(05-252-0323; www.hotelcabañaspimampiro.com; Av Quito & Tulcan; s/d incl breakfast $61/95;) It's a long (1km) uphill trudge to this small walled-off complex overlooking town. If that isn't a problem, Pimampiro's spacious villa-style cabins with stone walls and hammock-strung porches are an excellent choice. The pool is a fine place in which to cool off on a hot day.

Eating

Casa Blanca Cafe INTERNATIONAL **$**
(Av Darwin; mains $5-12; 8am-1pm daily & 4:30-10pm Mon-Sat) Steps from the pier, this open-air cafe is one of the most popular spots in town. Stop in for tuna or chicken sandwiches, burgers, empanadas, cappuccinos and other snacks.

Cuencan Taste BAKERY **$**
(Av Alsacio Northia; snacks from $0.50; 6am-10pm) Join afternoon crowds for fresh-baked magnificence: chocolate or cinnamon bread, empanadas, pastries, and fruit and custard tarts.

La Zayapa CAFE **$**
(099-482-0384; www.lazayapahotel.com; Av Darwin; snacks $4-10; 9am-8:30pm) The laid-back La Zayapa cafe has the best wi-fi on the waterfront; sit at one of the outdoor tables nursing an iced coffee, a sandwich or a dessert. There's also a good-value guesthouse in back (per person $40 to $50).

Cabaña Mi Grande CAFE **$**
(Villamil; mains $4; 6am-3pm & 6-10pm) This 2nd-floor perch whips up tasty smoothies, plus burgers, toasted sandwiches and good breakfasts including granola with fruit and yogurt.

Lucky's ECUADORIAN **$**
(cnr Villamil & Hernández; mains $4; noon-2pm daily, 6-8pm Mon-Fri) Casual local favorite offering set lunches or dinners at low prices.

Supermercado Galamaxi SUPERMARKET **$**
(cnr Flores & Av Quito; 7:30am-9pm Mon-Fri, to 6pm Sat & Sun) The best supermarket in town.

Calypso Restaurant ECUADORIAN, INTERNATIONAL **$$**
(Av Darwin; mains $9-20; 9:30am-11pm) The Calypso does good seafood dishes (such as the *festival calypso*, a mixed seafood plate in coconut and ginger sauce), as well as burgers, pizzas and salads. It's an informal place with outdoor seating, and it's equally good for a coffee, a juice or a delicious slice of chocolate cake.

Rosita ECUADORIAN **$$**
(cnr Hernández & Villamil; mains $6-12; 8am-8pm) Rosita serves up popular set lunches ($6) in an appealing open-sided eatery with wood details and curious decorations (football jerseys hanging from the rafters, mounted fish, surfboards).

Miconia INTERNATIONAL, ECUADORIAN **$$**
(Av Darwin; mains $15-20) Occupying the 2nd floor of the hotel of the same name, this open-sided restaurant has a fine setting, though the food (seafood, meat, pastas, pizzas) receives mixed reviews.

El Descanso Marinero SEAFOOD **$$$**
(Av Alsacio Northia; mains $15-18; 9am-9pm Tue-Sun) Ceviche, lobster and other fresh-caught seafood is served up in a lovely outdoor garden with picnic tables.

Drinking & Nightlife

Iguana Rock BAR
(cnr Flores & Quito; 8pm-midnight Mon-Thu, to 3am Fri & Sat;) Iguana Rock draws a festive, dance-loving crowd on weekends, and remains a laid-back spot during the week. It has a pool table, salsa beats and even gets an off-island band or two.

El Barquero BAR
(Hernández; 9pm-3am Mon-Sat) El Barquero has an appealing, laid-back vibe with outdoor tables set on a small front patio. It has a pool table and American grooves. Order a *cerveza grande*, kick up your heels in the lava-rock gravel and take in the whimsical murals scattered around.

Information

INTERNET ACCESS

Iguana Rock Wi-fi by night.

La Zayapa Wi-fi by day.

MONEY

Banco del Pacifico (cnr Melville & Hernández; 8am-4pm Mon-Fri) Has an ATM, just a short stroll from the pier.

POST

Post Office (Av Darwin & Cobos)

TOURIST INFORMATION

Municipal Tourism Office (☎05-252-0119; www.turismosancristobal.com; Avs Darwin & 12 de Febrero; ⏰7:30am-12:30pm & 2-5pm Mon-Fri) Maps, accommodation and transportation information.

Getting There & Away

AIR

The airport is 700m from town – a 10-minute walk or a $1.50 taxi ride (taxis are white pickup cabs). Regardless of the airline, you should check your luggage at least two hours in advance; you can always return to town to spend your final hours in the islands more comfortably. Avianca, Emetebe, Lan and Tame all have desks at the airport.

Fly Galápagos (p342) Offers inter-island flights and charter tours.

BOAT

Boats head daily to Puerto Ayora at 7am and 3pm ($30, 2¼ hours). Most tour operators around Puerto Baquerizo Moreno book these boats. You must arrive at the **dock** 30 minutes before departure.

Getting Around

In Puerto Baquerizo Moreno, **Cooperativa de Transporte Terrestre** (☎05-252-0477) pickup-truck taxis hang out along the *malecón*. One-way rates include La Lobería ($3), El Progreso ($3.50), El Junco Lagoon ($15) and Puerto Chino ($30). You can also negotiate for day trips where the driver will take you to multiple sites. A half-day tour to El Junco, Galapaguera and El Chino is $60.

ISLA ISABELA (ALBEMARLE)

Isabela is the largest island in the archipelago at 4588 sq km, but despite its size and imposing skyline of active volcanoes, it's the delicate sights like frigates flying as high as the clouds or penguins making their way tentatively along the cliffs that really reward visitors.

It's a relatively young island and consists of a chain of five intermittently active volcanoes, including Volcán Sierra Negra, which erupted in late 2005 and sent up a 20km-high smoke column. One of the island's volcanoes, Volcán Wolf, is the highest point in the Galápagos at 1707m (some sources claim 1646m). There's also a small, older volcano, Volcán Ecuador (610m).

In response to an ecosystem-wide threat and a dwindling tortoise population on Isabela and especially around Volcán Alcedo (1097m), the Charles Darwin Research Station and Galápagos National Park Service successfully eradicated tens of thousands of feral goats by means of ground and aerial hunting.

Sights

Volcán Sierra Negra — VOLCANO

Northwest of the tiny settlement of Tomás de Berlanga lies the massive Volcán Sierra Negra (1490m), which last erupted in late 2005. An 8km trail leads around the east side of the volcano. It's possible to walk all the way around the caldera, but the trail peters out.

Galápagos hawks, short-eared owls, finches and flycatchers are among the birds commonly seen on this trip. The summit is often foggy (especially during the colder, drier *garúa* season, which extends from June to December) and it is easy to get lost. There are spectacular views from nearby Volcán Chico, a subcrater where you can see fumaroles. Several agencies in towns offer all-day tours (per person $35). These include transport up to the volcano, followed by an 11km walk. Bring a rain jacket, water and snacks (a sack lunch is provided).

Make sure you go only in a closed vehicle (and wear your seat belt); do *not* go in an open-sided *chiva*. A tragic accident in 2014 left several tourists on this outing gravely injured, when the driver of their *chiva* lost control coming down the mountain.

★Volcán Alcedo — VOLCANO

The summit of this volcano (1097m) is famous for its 7km-wide caldera and steaming fumaroles. Hundreds of giant tortoises can be seen here, especially from June to December, and juvenile hawks soar on thermal updrafts. The view is fantastic. Permits are required to hike this long, steep and waterless trail and to camp near the summit (two days required).

Darwin Lake — LAKE

A dry landing deposits you at the beginning of a 2km-long trail that brings you past this postcard-perfect saltwater lagoon. It has twice the salinity of the ocean, and is a tuff cone, like a chimney from the main volca-

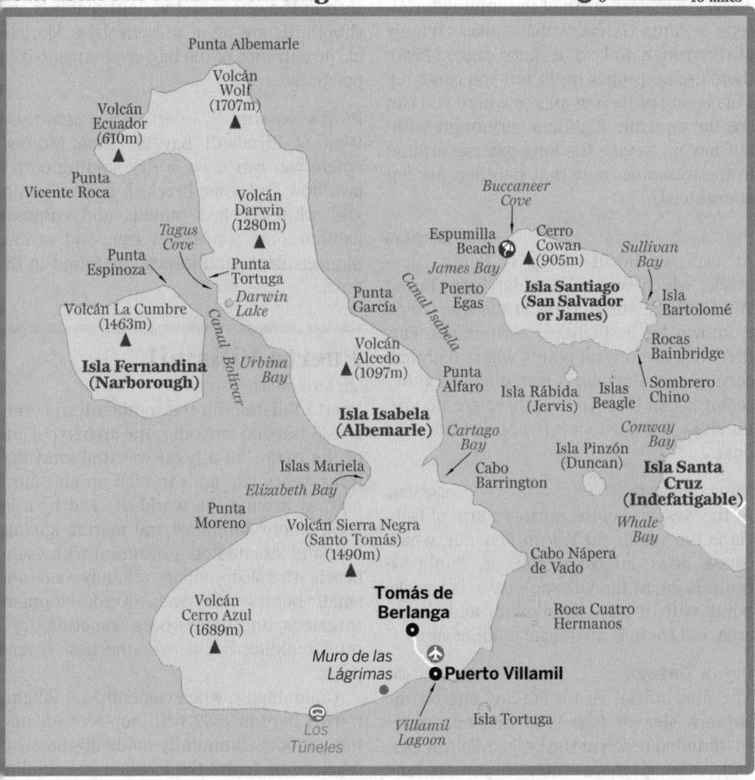

o. The trail leads to the lower lava slopes of Volcán Darwin (1280m), where various volcanic formations and stunning views of surrounding slopes can be observed. There are some steep sections on this trail. A *panga* ride along the cliffs to Tagus Cove will enable you to see the historical graffiti and various seabirds, usually including Galápagos penguins and flightless cormorants. There are snorkeling opportunities in the cove.

Tagus Cove HISTORIC SITE

Just south of Punta Tortuga is this cove where early sailors frequently anchored and scratched the names of their vessels into the cliffs. It's a strange sight to behold graffiti, the oldest from 1836, in an otherwise pristine environment, next to where sea lions lazily roam.

Volcán Wolf VOLCANO

Not only is Isla Isabela the largest Galápagos island, but its imposing skyline of grumbling volcanoes makes it the most striking. Volcán Wolf, at the northern tip of the island, is the highest point in the Galápagos, standing at 1707m (5600ft), and is one of the most active volcanoes in the archipelago – young lava covers the caldera floor. Ten eruptions have occurred between 1797 and 1982. The 1982 eruption saw fountains of lava emanating from vents before rising over the rim.

Activities

★ Los Túneles SNORKELING

Around a 30- to 40-minute boat ride from Puerto Villamil is this outstanding spot for snorkeling, formed by convoluted lava formations standing between mangroves and the open sea. Look out for white-tipped sharks, manta rays, eagle rays, sea lions, turtles and even sea horses in the shallows. Tour operators in Puerto Villamil run daily five-hour trips here for around $75.

Punta García BIRDWATCHING

A few kilometers north of the landing for Alcedo is Punta García, which consists mainly of very rough *aa* lava (a sharp, jagged lava); there are no proper trails, but you can land. This is one of the few places where you can see the endemic flightless cormorant without having to take the long passage around to the west side (note that sightings are not guaranteed).

Punta Albemarle BIRDWATCHING

At Isabela's northern tip is Punta Albemarle, which was a US radar base during WWII. There are no trails at the site, which is known for its flightless cormorants. Further west are several points where flightless cormorants, Galápagos penguins and other seabirds can be seen, but there are no visitor sites. You must view the birds from your boat.

Punta Vicente Roca SNORKELING

At the west end of the northern arm of Isabela is the small, old Volcán Ecuador, which comes down almost to the sea. Punta Vicente Roca, at the volcano's base, is a rocky point with a good snorkeling and diving area, but there is no official landing site.

Punta Tortuga BIRDWATCHING

The first official visitor-landing site on the western side of Isabela is this mangrove-surrounded beach at the base of Volcán Darwin. Although there is no trail, you can land on the beach and explore the mangroves for the mangrove finch – it's present here but not always easy to see. This finch is found only on Islas Isabela and Fernandina.

Urbina Bay BIRDWATCHING, WALKING

This bay lies around the middle of the western shore of Isabela and is a flat area formed by an uplift from the sea in 1954. Evidence of the uplift includes a coral reef on the land. Flightless cormorants, pelicans, giant tortoises and land and marine iguanas can be observed on land, and rays and turtles can be seen in the bay. A wet landing onto a beach brings you to a 1km trail that leads to the corals. There is a good view of Volcán Alcedo.

Elizabeth Bay WILDLIFE WATCHING

Near where the western shoreline of Isabela bends sharply toward the lower arm of the island, there's a visitor site that's known for its marine life. Elizabeth Bay is best visited by a *panga* ride, as there are no landing sites. Marine turtles and rays can usually be seen in the water, and various seabirds and shorebirds are often present. Islas Mariela, at the entrance of the bay, are frequented by penguins.

Punta Moreno BIRDWATCHING

West of Elizabeth Bay is Punta Moreno where you can make a dry landing onto a lava flow and some brackish pools. Flamingos, white-cheeked pintails and common gallinules are sometimes seen, and various pioneer plants and insects are found in the area.

Puerto Villamil

05 / POP 2600

Puerto Villamil (on the southeastern corner of Isla Isabela) embodies the archetypal end of the road – in a good way, the kind that lures weary city folks to pick up and move halfway around the world. Backed by a lagoon where flamingos and marine iguanas live, and situated on a beautiful white-sand beach, it's a sleepy village of sandy roads and small homes. However, overdevelopment threatens, and there's been something of a mini building boom over the past several years.

Undoubtedly, when General José Villamil moved here in 1832 with hopes of organizing a model community made up mostly of whalers, he found the location as beguiling as do today's visitors. Unfortunately, the draftees' peaceful inclinations proved to be more utopian than real, and they ended up destroying the colony. Villamil later introduced cows, horses and donkeys, which quickly reproduced, threatening the island's delicate ecosystem.

Arriving at the passenger *muelle* (pier), it's a 1km walk (or $2 taxi ride) to the town center. Avenida Antonio Gil is the main street where many hotels, restaurants and the central plaza are. The beachfront (*malecón*) is just one block south.

Sights

Muro de las Lágrimas HISTORIC SITE

Some 7km west of Puerto Villamil is the Muro de las Lágrimas (Wall of Tears), a 100m-long wall of lava rocks built by convicts under harsh and abusive conditions. The penal colony closed in 1959, but the wall stands as a monument to an infamous chapter in the island's history. The best way ou here is by bike, as there are other intriguing stops (mangroves, beaches, overlooks) along the way. Bring water and sun protection, as there's little shade on the way. A taxi here costs around $10.

Pozo Villamil WILDLIFE RESERVE

(trail 6am-6pm) Behind and to the west of the village is this lagoon, known for its marine iguanas and migrant birds, especially waders – more than 20 species have been reported here. A trail a little over 1km long begins just past the Iguana Crossing Hotel. The wooden boardwalk takes you over the lagoon, passing through mangroves and dense vegetation, eventually ending in the **Centro de Crianza de Tortugas** (Giant Tortoise Breeding Center).

Volunteers here can explain the work being done to help restore the population of this species on Isabela. Pickups from town ($1) can drop you at the entrance on the road to the highlands. After the breeding center, keep walking up the main road (north 400m) to reach a small lagoon where pink flamingos are commonly spotted.

Iglesia Cristo Salvador CHURCH

(Las Fragatas) Looming above the central square, this church boasts uniquely Galápagos iconography. Note the stained-glass windows of native wildlife (marine iguana, booby, penguin, flamingo), while the mural beside the altar shows Jesus ascending above Puerto Villamil while frigate birds, a marine iguana and blue-footed boobies look on. A giant tortoise keeps a watchful eye from the pulpit.

Pozo Salinas LAGOON

Around the corner from the main square, this small lagoon has a boardwalk along the edge, which makes a fine viewing spot for taking in the pink flamingos and stilts that sometimes feed here.

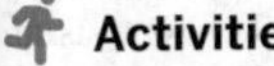

Activities

Snorkeling

There are several outstanding snorkeling sights near Puerto Villamil. Aside from Los Túneles (p327) and Los Tintoreras, you can snorkel in the small bay around Concha de Perla, where penguins are sometimes spotted. It's accessible by a boardwalk through the mangroves near the port.

★ **Los Tintoreras** SNORKELING

A five-minute boat ride from town is the wonderful Los Tintoreras snorkeling spot, a small volcanic island with marine iguanas, penguins, boobies and other birdlife, rays, marine turtles and the occasional white-tipped reef shark. It's especially fun to swim through the narrow fissures in the rocks, which are like underwater hallways decorated with plant and coral life. Tour operators charge $40 for the 2½-hour outing.

Surfing

There are a handful of good surf breaks for experienced surfers near town, some only reached by boat. Stop by **Isabela Discovery** (05-252-9303; jacibruns@hotmail.com; Av Conocarpus; 9am-7pm or by appointment) to rent a board.

Biking

Several operators in town hire bikes. The beaches east of town and the Muro de Lágrimas are popular biking destinations.

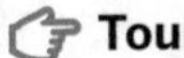

Tours

Many accommodations offer tours, as do a few agencies. Some standard trips are half-day Sierra Negra tours (walking $35, by horse $60), Los Túneles snorkeling ($60) and Los Tintoreras snorkeling ($25).

Sleeping

Some of the best beachfront hotels and guesthouses in the Galápagos can be found in Puerto Villamil. Further from the shore, there are several modest properties tucked among the town's sleepy streets.

Beachfront

Brisas del Mar GUESTHOUSE $

(05-301-6800; Av Conocarpus; r per person with fan/air-con $15/20) A few blocks from the central plaza, this good-value cheapie has bright, tile-floored rooms with sizeable windows, hot water and TVs (with one channel only). You can lounge in the shaded hammocks in the backyard.

Caleta Iguana HOSTEL $$

(Casa Rosada; 05-252-9405; claudiahodari@gmail.com; Av Antonio Gil; per person $40) Lay your head here for quick access to a lively, laid-back social scene. The beachfront bar, Casa Rosada, has hammocks, bonfires, live music and a sea-facing deck. It's on the beach at the western edge of town.

Isabela Beach House GUESTHOUSE $$$

(05-252-9303; theisabelabeachhouse@gmail.com; Av Vía Al Embarcadero; r from $99;)

This small beachfront house has a handful of bright and attractive rooms with an all-wood design, and the two upstairs rooms open onto a shared balcony with delightful ocean views. The owners offer a range of tours, and also rent out a full house next door. It's a welcoming, ecofriendly spot with solar panels on the roof.

Hotel Albemarle HOTEL $$$

(☎02-252-9489; www.hotelalbemarle.com; Malecón; r incl breakfast from $220;) Hotel Albemarle occupies a prime stretch of beachfront property in the center of Puerto Villamil. This two-story Mediterranean-style villa has stylish rooms with high ceilings and upmarket stone bathrooms (featuring dual sinks), plus some nice added touches like in-room water coolers and TVs with DVD players (with free movies to rent). The priciest rooms have balconies with ocean views.

Iguana Crossing Boutique Hotel LUXURY HOTEL $$$

(☎05-252-9484; www.iguanacrossing.com.ec; Av Antonio Gil; r incl breakfast $278-531;) Isabela's most upscale hotel has attractive rooms with lovely wooden decks (overlooking either the lagoon or the ocean). Think glossy design-magazine furnishings and taste throughout; there's a pool, a hot tub and a restaurant that serves some of the best food on the island. It's located across the sandy street from the beach at the edge of town.

La Casa de Marita INN $$$

(☎05-252-9301; www.casamaritagalapagos.com; s/d incl breakfast from $110/125, r with seaview from $170;) This beautiful property, the last to occupy beachfront space on the way to the harbor, has attractively decorated rooms, each trimmed with artwork and boasting a unique color scheme (some also have kitchenettes). The Casa de Marita also has an upstairs restaurant with views and a lovely seafront patio with hammocks and lounge chairs overlooking the surf.

Volcano Hotel HOTEL $$$

(☎098-831-8842; www.neotropicexpeditions.com; cnr Avs Antonio Gil & Los Flamingos; r incl breakfast $129-243;) Set in an attractive building with wood and stone details, this well-located hotel offers clean, bright and airy rooms and a kitchen for guests. The best rooms have sea views.

La Casita de la Playa HOTEL $$$

(☎05-252-9103; www.neotropicexpeditions.com; Malecón; r incl breakfast $130-188;) On the beach near the town center, this white adobe building with orange accents has tidy red, tile-floored rooms. The best rooms have ocean views; some have only internal windows (meaning they're very poor value). There are lounge chairs and a hammock on the small palm-fringed lawn facing the sea.

Sierra Negra HOTEL $$$

(☎05-252-9046; Malecón; d from $150;) Directly on the beach only a few blocks from the central square, this unadorned and modern building's lack of character is more than compensated for by the large windows in the oceanfront rooms. Pop them open for front-row sunset views. Large beds and quality showers.

In Town

La Posada del Caminante HOSTEL $

(☎05-252-9407; www.posadadelcaminante.com; Cormoran; r per person $20-25;) One of the best-value budget options (cash-only) is this friendly family-run place a few blocks behind Poza Salinas and west of the intersection of Avenidas 16 de Marzo and Cormoran. A handful of rooms surround a narrow courtyard with several hammocks; there are bananas and other fruit for the picking.

Coral Blanco Hotel HOSTERÍA $$

(☎05-252-9125; www.coralblanco.com.ec; Av Antonio Gil; s/d per person incl breakfast $40;) Features small, basic rooms a few blocks from the central plaza and across the road from the beach. All manner of tours offered.

Wooden House LODGE $$$

(☎05-252-9235; www.thewoodenhouselodge.com; Av Vía Al Embarcadero; r incl breakfast $105-140;) Located off the dusty road between the pier and town, this meticulously all-wood (almost Balinese-like) home is an excellent choice if beachfront location isn't a priority. Besides the tastefully decorated, cozy rooms with rainwater showerheads, it has a palm-fringed front garden set with hammocks and a small pool.

La Laguna de Galápagos HOTEL $$$

(☎02-244-0241; www.lalagunagalapagoshotel.com; Av Los Flamingos; s/d $61/102) Overlooking the Pozo Salinas lagoon, this place has pleasant rooms with tall ceilings, contemporary furnishings and modern bathrooms. The best rooms have large balconies overlooking the lagoon. There's a top-floor terrace with a hot tub heated by solar panels.

Hotel San Vicente HOTEL **$$$**
(☎02-244-0241; www.hotelsanvicentegalapagos.com; cnr Escalecias & Cormoran; r $91-153; ❄📶) This efficiently run hotel is found several blocks north of the central plaza (far from the beach). There are big, bright white stucco rooms and an attractive front yard with a hot tub.

Out of Town

Campo Duro CAMPGROUND **$$$**
(☎05-545-3045, 05-301-6604; www.campoduroecolodge.com.ec; per person incl breakfast $60) Campo Duro is a full-service campsite run by Puerto Ayora's Red Mangrove. Rates include transport to and from Puerto Villamil.

Eating

There are several restaurants located along Avenida Antonio Gil. Seafood mains here run from $10 to $20.

Shawerma Hot MIDDLE EASTERN **$**
(Av Antonio Gil; mains $7-12; ⏲10am-11pm; 🖉) A short stroll east of the main square, a rustic, thatch-roofed hut whips up tasty chicken shawermas, falafel wraps and *salchipapas* (potatoes and sausage).

Panaderia Fragatas BAKERY **$**
(Av Antonio Gil; snacks $1; ⏲6:30-10am & 4:30-7:30pm) Just past the main plaza, you'll find a tiny bakery selling banana bread, *orejas* (big cookies) and other treats.

Restaurante El Cafetal ECUADORIAN, INTERNATIONAL **$$**
(☎05-301-6775; Las Fragatas; mains $8-16; ⏲24hr) This contemporary little spot on the central plaza has creative, carefully prepared dishes with a changing menu of hits including *ceviches* (there's also a vegetarian version), grilled fish, chicken with mushrooms and *cazuela* (seafood stew). You can also stop in for good desserts and espresso drinks.

★**Coco Surf** SEAFOOD **$$$**
(☎05-252-9465; Avs Antonio Gil & 16 de Marzo; mains $15-24; ⏲noon-9:30pm) This sidewalk cafe serves up some of the tastiest seafood dishes in all of the Galápagos, and you'll hardly notice the high price points once the live band starts jamming out to jazzy island tunes. The tuna tartare and *patanachos mar y terra* (appetizer platter with an assortment of seafood and meat) are highly recommended.

Oasis SEAFOOD **$$$**
(☎05-252-9054; cnr Cormoran & Escalecias; mains $15-35; ⏲dinner by appointment) Esmeraldas native Geanny Bennett Valencia cooks up some of the best dishes in town. Mouth-watering *encocados* (coconut stews) are the favorite, served in versions like *camarones* (shrimp), *langosta* (lobster) or *pescado* (fish). The catch: the restaurant only opens by reservation; call ahead or stop by during the day.

Drinking & Nightlife

Casa Rosada BAR
(☎05-252-9405; claudiahodari@gmail.com; Av Antonio Gil; ⏲6:30am-midnight) The highlight of Isabela's nightlife is this laid-back, dig-your-feet-in-the-sand beach bar next door to Caleta Iguana Hotel & Surf Camp. A youthful crowd gathers around the outdoor tables (or the firepit as night falls), listening to tropical grooves or diving in the sand during regular volleyball games. It also has food for breakfast, lunch and dinner, plus occasional live music.

Iguana Point Bar BAR
(☎05-301-6801; Málecon; ⏲4-7pm & 8pm-2am) This is an atmospheric and fun place for a bite and sunset drinks. It's close to the main square, right on the *málecon*.

Information

There is no ATM that accepts foreign cards, so bring all the cash you'll need.

A few *lavanderías* (laundries) on the main street do wash and dry.

Getting There & Away

Isabela's volcanoes dominate the westward view during passages to the western part of Isla Santa Cruz, but the island itself is not frequently visited by smaller boats – only a handful of live-aboard cruises navigate its shores. This is because most of the best visitor sites are on the west side of the island, reached only after a long passage (over 200km) from Santa Cruz. Independent travelers who wish to visit Isabela for a series of day tours can take speedboats or flights from Puerto Ayora and Puerto Baquerizo Moreno to Puerto Villamil.

AIR

Emetebe (☎ in Guayaquil 04-230-1277; www.emetebe.com.ec; cnr Av Antonio Gil & Las Fragatas; ⏲ 8am-noon & 2-6pm Mon-Fri, to 1pm Sat) and **Fly Galápagos** (p342) connect Isabela to San Cristóbal and Baltra. One-way flights cost $135 ($270 return). You must pay a $10 fee on arrival at the airport in Puerto Villamil.

BOAT

There are daily 6am boats to Santa Cruz ($30, 2¼ hours) from Puerto Villamil. From Santa Cruz, boats leave at 2pm. Tickets can be purchased at the dock or from **Transmartisa** (☎ 05-252-9066; www.transmartisa.com.ec; cnr Av Antonio Gil & Las Fragatas), near the main plaza. When arriving at the passenger pier east of town you have to pay a $5 fee.

Getting Around

The entirety of Puerto Villamil can be walked in about an hour. Taxis can be hailed around the main square; fare to the airport or harbor is $5.

ISLA FERNANDINA (NARBOROUGH)

Even by Galápagos standards, Fernandina is unique. It's home to thousands of lethargic marine iguanas, and for the volcanically minded, it's the island on which you're most likely to witness an eruption – the most recent was in September 2017. At 642 sq km, Fernandina is the third largest, as well as the westernmost and youngest, of the main islands. Unlike other parts of the Galápagos, no introduced species have taken root here – the island's endemic residents include a contingent of marine iguanas, Galápagos penguins, sea lions and flightless cormorants.

The one visitor site at **Punta Espinoza**, just across from Tagus Cove on Isabela, is a memorable one. Marine iguanas, too many to count, can be seen sunning themselves on the black-lava formations, a dramatic sight that looks like a museum diorama on dinosaurs come to life. Flightless cormorants nest nearby, hawks soar overhead and Galápagos penguins, turtles and sea lions sometimes frolic in an admirable display of multispecies tolerance in the lagoon near the landing.

A dry landing brings you to two trails: a 250m trail to the point and a 750m trail to recently formed lava fields. Here you can see various pioneer plants, such as the *Brachycereus* cactus as well as *pahoehoe* and *aa* lava formations. Several movies, most famously *Master and Commander,* filmed scenes here in front of a now-iconic white-mangrove tree.

ISLA SANTIAGO (SAN SALVADOR OR JAMES)

Once a hideout for British buccaneers and one of the stops on Darwin's itinerary, Isla San Santiago is the fourth largest of the islands. Its terrain of rough lava fields is an example of the island's challenging beauty. It's a frequent stop on boat tours because of its variety of wildlife and there are several interesting visitor sites, including **Puerto Egas**, named after the owner of what was once the country's only salt mine.

Sullivan Bay is on Santiago's east coast. Here, a huge, black, century-old lava flow has solidified into a sheet that reaches to the edge of the sea. A dry landing enables visitors to step onto the flow and follow a trail of white posts in a 2km circuit on the lava. Volcanology or geology junkies will rejoice at the sight of uneroded volcanic formations such as *pahoehoe* lava, lava bubbles and tree-trunk molds in the surface.

One of the most popular sites in all the islands is **Puerto Egas** (on James Bay), on James Bay on the west side of Isla Santiago. It was named after Dario Egas, the owner of a salt mine on the island that was once, as a result of presidential patronage, the only producer of salt in all the country. Here, there is a long, flat, black-lava shoreline where eroded shapes form lava pools, caves and inlets that house a great variety of wildlife. This is a fabulous place to see colonies of marine iguanas basking in the sun. The tide pools contain hundreds of red Sally Lightfoot crabs, which attract hunting herons of all the commonly found species.

The inlets are favorite haunts of the Galápagos fur seals, and this is really a great opportunity to snorkel with these surprisingly agile animals as well as with many species of tropical fish, moray eels, sharks and octopuses.

Just behind the black-lava shoreline is Sugarloaf Volcano, which can be reached via a 2km path. Lava lizards, Darwin's finches and Galápagos doves are often seen on this path. It peters out near the top of the 395m summit, but from here the views are stupendous. There is an extinct crater in which feral goats are often seen (wild goats are a major problem on Santiago), and Galápagos hawks often hover a few meters above the top of the volcano. North of the volcano is a crater where the salt mine used to be; its remains can be visited by walking along a 3km trail from the coast.

At the north end of James Bay, about 5km from Puerto Egas, is the brown-sand Espumilla Beach, which can be reached with a wet landing. The swimming is good here, and by the small lagoon behind the beach you can see various wading birds including, at times, flamingos. A 2km trail leads inland through transitional vegetation, where there are various finches and the Galápagos flycatcher.

At the northwestern end of Santiago, another site that is normally visited by boat is Buccaneer Cove, so called because it was a popular place for 17th- and 18th-century buccaneers to careen their vessels. The cliffs and pinnacles, which are used as nesting areas by several species of seabirds, are the main attraction these days.

AROUND ISLA SANTIAGO

Isla Bartolomé

Panoramic views and frisky penguins make this tiny island, just off Sullivan Bay on Isla Santiago, a common stop for boat tours. A path from a jetty (for a dry landing) leads up to the wind-whipped 114m summit of the island, where the dramatic views make it de rigueur for group photos. This trail leads through a wild and unearthly looking lava landscape, where a wooden boardwalk and stairs have been built to aid visitors and to protect the trail from erosion.

The other visitor site is a small, sandy beach in a cove (wet landing), from where you can don your snorkeling gear and swim with the speedy Galápagos penguins that frequent this cove. Marine turtles and a gaudy variety of tropical fish are also frequently seen.

The best way to photograph the penguins on Bartolomé is by taking a *panga* ride close to the rocks on either side of the cove, particularly around the aptly named Pinnacle Rock, which is to the right of the cove from the seaward side. You can often get within a few meters of these fascinating birds – this is the closest point to Puerto Ayora where you can do so. Other penguin colonies are on the western side of Isla Isabela.

From the beach, a 100m trail leads across the narrowest part of Bartolomé to another sandy beach on the opposite side of the island. Marine turtles may nest here between January and March.

Isla Sombrero Chino

This tiny island, just off the southeastern tip of Isla Santiago, is less than a quarter of 1 sq km in size and is a fairly recent volcanic cone. The accuracy of its descriptive name, translated as 'Chinese Hat,' is best appreciated from the north. There is a small sea-lion cove on the northern shore, where you can anchor and land at the visitor site. Opposite Sombrero Chino, on the rocky shoreline of nearby Isla Santiago, penguins are often seen.

A 400m trail goes around the cove, where there are snorkeling and swimming opportunities, and through a sea-lion colony. Marine iguanas scurry everywhere.

Isla Rábida (Jervis)

This approximately 5-sq-km island, also known as Jervis, lies 5km south of Isla Santiago. There is a wet landing onto a dark-red beach, where sea lions haul out and pelicans nest. A 750m trail offers good views of the island's 367m volcanic peak, which is covered with palo santo trees and prickly pear cacti. There's a great snorkeling spot at the end of the trail.

SOUTHERN ISLANDS

Isla Floreana (Santa María or Charles)

This, the sixth largest of the islands, is known as much for the mysterious history of its first residents – a small contingent of European settlers who became entangled in power struggles, peculiar disappearances and alleged murders – as it is for its intensely pink flamingos and top-flight snorkeling sites.

Many Santa Cruz tour operators sell Floreana as a day trip. If you're considering this, know that on a day trip, almost none of your money goes to the community, and you will be subjected to over four hours of exhausting speedboat travel. Instead it's well worth staying overnight, as the village of Puerto Velasco Ibarra has appealing lodging options, and this is a fascinating area to explore for those willing to make the effort.

Tiny Puerto Velasco Ibarra, the only settlement on Floreana, is set on a black-sand beach on a sheltered bay. Travelers find it quite peaceful and a perfect ending to an action-filled trip around the islands. This is the Galápagos of 40 years ago, of narrow dirt lanes, car-free living and wildlife-watching without the crowds.

Sights & Activities

Post Office Bay HISTORIC SITE

Most groups spend several perfunctory minutes on the north coast at Post Office Bay, where scraps of wood covered in graffiti surround a a few gone-to-seed barrels. Although a functioning mailbox for American and British whalers from the late 18th century, these days it's tourists who leave postcards, hoping they will find their way, like a message in a bottle. Actually, it's more prosaic than that: visitors are asked to grab a few to post when they return to their home countries.

About 300m behind the barrels is a lava cave that can be descended with the aid of a short rope and flashlight. The path is slippery and involves sloshing through some chilly water. Nearby is a pleasant swimming beach and the remains of a canning factory; a wet landing is necessary.

★Devil's Crown SNORKELING

This ragged semicircle of rocks, poking up out of the ocean a few hundred meters from Punta Cormorant, is one of the most outstanding marine sites in all of the Galápagos. A strong current sweeps snorkelers briskly past thousands of bright tropical fish, a small coral formation, sea lions, marine turtles and the occasional shark. A *panga* ride around the semisubmerged volcanic cone will give views of red-billed tropicbirds, pelicans, herons and lava gulls nesting on the rocks.

Lagoon BIRDWATCHING

Between the two beaches you'll find a lagoon where several dozen **flamingos** are normally seen. This is also a good place to watch for other wading birds such as black-necked stilts, oystercatchers, willets and whimbrels. You must stop at the wooden rail on the edge of the lagoon – be sure to bring binoculars and your longest zoom lens, otherwise the flamingos will just be indistinct blurs on the horizon. White-cheeked pintail ducks are often seen in the lagoon and Galápagos hawks wheel overhead. It's an especially dramatic tableau when the dark shadows, cast from the setting sun, suggest a stillness that has lasted for eons.

Sleeping & Eating

Floreana is a regular stop on southerly cruise routes, so most visitors here sleep on the ship. For independent travelers there are a handful of accommodations options in the town of Puerto Velasco Ibarra.

The eating options on Floreana are limited to a few restaurants in Puerto Velasco Ibarra.

Getting There & Away

Most people visit Floreana as part of a liveaboard cruise. It's possible to get there independently by speedboat from Puerto Ayora ($30, 1¾ hours), but service runs irregularly and timetables change frequently. Check with an operator in Puerto Ayora to see if any boats have scheduled transfers to Floreana at any point during your stay in the Galápagos – it's best to do this at the beginning of your trip so you can plan accordingly.

Isla Española (Hood)

Certainly one of the more dramatically beautiful islands in the Galápagos, the 61-sq-km Española is also the most southerly. Because it's about 90km southeast of Santa Cruz, captains of some of the smaller boats may be reluctant to go this far.

Española is especially worth visiting from late March to December because it has the only colony of the waved albatross, one of the most spectacular Galápagos seabirds, plus swallow-tailed gulls, oystercatchers, three species of finches and the Hood mockingbird, which is found nowhere else in the world.

The opuntia cactus and giant tortoise population, virtually extinct in the 1960s due to introduced goats and hunting, have rebounded thanks to an aggressive restoration program – tortoises rely on the cacti for food, water and protection.

A wet landing at **Punta Suárez**, on the western end of the island, leads to a rocky

2km-long trail that takes visitors through masked and blue-footed booby colonies, a beach full of marine iguanas and, maybe most uniquely, a waved albatross colony (late March to early December, when much of the world's albatross population comes here to breed). Even at a few months old, these enormous birds are spectacular to behold, their long, curved yellow beak, fluffy molting hair and aware eyes make them seem more vulnerable than they are. Equally breathtaking are the views from the wave-battered cliffs to the south – blow holes in the rocky shore below shoot water high into the air. Seabirds, especially the red-billed tropicbirds, perform their aerial acrobatics and their clumsy take offs and landings.

Other birds to look out for are the Hood mockingbird, swallow-tailed gulls and oystercatchers. There are three species of finches: large cactus, small ground, and warbler. They're all part of the Darwin's finch family and may hop along after you hoping to get at some of your fresh water. The large cactus finch is found on few other islands.

Reached with a wet landing at the northeast end of Isla Española is **Gardner Bay**, a beautiful white-sand beach with good swimming and a large sea-lion colony. It's a little like walking through a minefield (albeit one that moves occasionally), and it's certainly a good idea to give the large male bulls a wide berth lest they interpret your curiosity as a challenge to their dominance. Marine iguanas and Sally Lightfoot crabs can be found on the rocks at the eastern end of the beach. An island a short distance offshore provides good, but sometimes rough, snorkeling and scuba diving – there's one rock that often has white-tipped reef sharks basking under it, and hammerheads, marine turtles, rays, sea stars and red-lipped batfish are often seen.

NORTHERN ISLANDS

Isla Genovesa (Tower)

Whatever you call it – Isla Genovesa, Tower Island or even Booby Island – lovers of the sometimes goofy- and cuddly-looking booby won't want to miss this. Watch your feet, since it's quite easy to miss a fluffy little baby booby or a camouflaged iguana while you're scanning the horizon for distant sperm whales or the hard-to-sight Galápagos owl.

The most northeastern of the Galápagos Islands, Isla Genovesa covers only 14 sq km and is the only regularly visited island that lies entirely north of the equator (the northernmost part of Isabela pokes above the line). Therefore, this often creates an opportunity for a little shipboard humorous advice to 'hold tight as we pass over the bump.' Because it's an outlying island, Isla Genovesa is infrequently included on shorter itineraries.

Genovesa is the best place to see a red-footed booby colony, and it provides visitors with the opportunity to visit colonies of great frigate birds, red-billed tropicbirds, swallow-tailed gulls, Nazca boobies and many thousands of storm petrels. Other bird attractions include Galápagos doves and short-eared owls. Sea lions and fur seals are present, and there's the chance to snorkel with groups of hammerhead sharks. The island is fairly flat and round, with a large, almost landlocked cove named Darwin Bay on the south side.

There are two visitor sites, both on Darwin Bay. **Prince Philip's Steps** take you up a steep and rocky path to the top of 25m-high cliffs, and nesting red-footed and masked boobies are often found right on the narrow path.

At the top of the cliffs, the 1km-long trail leads inland, past dry-forest vegetation and various seabird colonies to a cracked expanse of lava, where thousands of storm petrels make their nests and wheel overhead. Short-eared owls are sometimes seen here.

The second visitor site, **Darwin Bay Beach**, is a coral beach that passes through red-footed booby colonies and several tide pools, and ends at a viewpoint over the cliffs.

Islas Marchena (Bindloe) & Pinta (Abington)

Isla Marchena, at 130 sq km, is the seventh-largest island in the archipelago and the largest to have no official visitor sites. There are some good scuba-diving sites, however, so you may get to see the island up close if on a dive trip. The 343m-high volcano in the middle of the island was very active during 1991 – ask your guide about its current degree of activity.

Isla Pinta is the original home of the tortoise Lonesome George, the sole surviving member of a subspecies decimated by whalers and pirates. Just two centuries ago, the tortoises numbered an estimated 5000 to 10,000. In 2010, 39 tortoises of a hybrid species (they were sterilized, as repopulation is not the goal) raised in captivity were released into the wild on Pinta.

Marchena is further north than any of the bigger islands. There are landing sites, but both islands have no visitor sites, and researchers require a permit to visit.

Isla Wolf (Wenman) & Isla Darwin (Culpepper)

The northernmost islands are the twin islands of Isla Wolf and Isla Darwin, about 100km northwest of the rest of the archipelago. They are seldom visited except on scuba-diving trips (no snorkeling at either). Both have nearly vertical cliffs that make landing difficult. Frigates, boobies, tropicbirds and gulls nest on these islands by the thousands. Isla Darwin was first visited in 1964, when a helicopter expedition landed on the summit.

UNDERSTAND THE GALÁPAGOS ISLANDS

History

The Galápagos archipelago was discovered by accident in 1535, when Tomás de Berlanga, the first Bishop of Panama, drifted off course while sailing from Panama to Peru. The bishop reported his discovery to King Charles V of Spain and included in his report a description of the giant Galápagos tortoises, from which the islands received their name, and an amusing note about the islands' birds that any visitor today can appreciate: '...so silly that they didn't know how to flee and many were caught by hand.'

It is possible that the indigenous inhabitants of South America were aware of the islands' existence before 1535, but there are no definite records of this, and the islands don't appear on a world map until 1570, when they are identified as the 'island of the tortoises.' In 1953 Norwegian explorer Thor Heyerdahl discovered pottery shards that he thought to be pre-Columbian, but the evidence seems inconclusive. The first rough charts of the archipelago were made by buccaneers in the late 17th century, and scientific exploration began in the late 18th century.

For more than three centuries after their discovery, the Galápagos were used as a base by a succession of buccaneers, sealers and whalers. The islands provided sheltered anchorage, firewood, water and an abundance of fresh food in the form of the giant Galápagos tortoises, which were caught by the thousands and stacked, alive, in the ships' holds. More than 100,000 are estimated to have been taken between 1811 and 1844. The tortoises could survive for a year or more and thus provided fresh meat for the sailors long after they had left the islands. The fur seal population was also decimated, with thousands killed for their valuable pelts.

The first resident of the islands was Patrick Watkins, an Irishman who was marooned on Isla Santa María in 1807 and spent two years living there, growing vegetables and trading his produce for rum with passing boats. The story goes that he managed to remain drunk for most of his stay, then stole a ship's boat and set out for Guayaquil accompanied by five slaves. No one knows what happened to the slaves – only Watkins reached the mainland.

Ecuador officially claimed the Galápagos Archipelago in 1832 and General Villamil was named the first governor – basically in charge of a single colony of ex-rebel soldiers on Floreana. For roughly one century thereafter, the islands were inhabited by only a few settlers and were used as penal colonies, the last of which, on Isla Isabela, was closed in 1959.

The Galápagos' most famous visitor was Charles Darwin, who arrived in 1835 aboard the British naval vessel the *Beagle*. Darwin stayed for five weeks, 19 days of which were spent on four of the larger islands, making notes and collecting specimens that provided important evidence for his theory of evolution. It was not until decades later that he formulated and published his evidence. He spent the most time on Isla San Salvador observing and, for that matter, eating tortoises. Darwin devoted as much of his attention to geology and botany as he did to the animals and marine life of the Galápagos.

Some islands were declared wildlife sanctuaries in 1934, and 97% of the archipelago officially became a national park in 1959. Organized tourism began in the late 1960s and

CHARLES DARWIN: THE MAN BEHIND THE MYTH

In the general public's mind, the life and work of Charles Darwin is so closely connected with the Galápagos Islands that many people assume he spent a significant amount of time here. They also assume that the inspiration for ideas he sketches out in the *Origin of Species* came to him in a 'Eureka!' moment while touring the islands. Neither assumption is true.

Darwin spent only five weeks in the Galápagos, at first primarily interested in geology rather than biology. His later observations of pigeons and the methods of dog breeders in England were both much more influential than the finches that have become poster children for the shorthand of evolutionary theory.

Darwin lived in London for five years after he returned from the Galápagos, and then retreated to an estate in the countryside. From then on he hardly traveled and was confined to a sedentary lifestyle, in part because of chronic health concerns.

From an early age he was inspired more by free-thinking religious figures than secular atheists and was never motivated to disprove the role of a divine figure. After he spent 22 years trying to prove his theory, he renounced Christianity in his middle age and described himself as an agnostic.

Originally sent to Cambridge to be a clergyman, Darwin instead became inspired by the botany lessons of his mentor, JS Henslow. He collected beetles as a hobby and formed a club organized around the eating of animals that were unknown to the European kitchen. It was only after his uncle Josiah Wedgwood intervened that Darwin's father allowed him to go on a voyage at the age of 22. Darwin slept in a hammock on the *Beagle,* rode on top of Galápagos turtles and, in what is a violation of modern-day park rules, dined on their meat.

From 1831 to 1836, the *Beagle*'s task was to survey the South American coastline and chart harbors for the British navy, stopping in Brazil, the Falklands, Argentina and Chile before the Galápagos. Darwin returned with more than 1500 specimens, though for many of those from the Galápagos he neglected to label where each was found.

By the time the boat reached Bahía, Brazil, in 1836, Darwin was ready to return, writing in his journal, 'I loathe, I abhor the sea and all ships which sail on it.' In 1859 the *Origin of Species* sold out on its first day in print. Only 1% of the book refers to the Galápagos Islands.

in 1986 the government formed the Marine Resources Reserve.

Geology

The oldest of the islands visible today were formed roughly four to five million years ago by underwater volcanoes erupting and rising above the ocean's surface (the islands were never connected to the mainland). The Galápagos region is volcanically very active – more than 50 eruptions have been recorded since their discovery in 1535. The most recent was the February 2009 Volcán La Cumbre eruption on Fernandina, overall probably the most active island. Thus, the formation of the islands is an ongoing process; geologically speaking, the archipelago is quite young.

Geologists generally agree that two relatively new geological theories explain the islands' formation. The theory of plate tectonics holds that the earth's crust consists of several rigid plates that, over geological time, move relative to one another over the surface of the earth. The Galápagos lie on the northern edge of the Nazca Plate, close to its junction with the Cocos Plate. These two plates are spreading apart at a rate of about 1km every 14,000 years, which is pretty fast by plate-tectonic standards.

The hot-spot theory states that deep within the earth (below the moving tectonic plates) are certain superheated areas that remain stationary. At frequent intervals (measured in geological time), the heat from these hot spots increases enough to melt the earth's crust. This produces a volcanic eruption of sufficient magnitude to cause molten lava to rise above the ocean floor and, eventually, above the ocean's surface.

The Galápagos are moving slowly to the southeast over a stationary hot spot, so it makes sense that the southeastern islands were formed first and the northwestern islands were formed most recently. The most ancient rocks yet discovered on the islands are about 3.25 million years old and come from Isla Española in the southeast. In comparison, the oldest rocks on the islands of Isla Fernandina and Isla Isabela are less than 750,000 years old. The northwestern islands are still in the process of formation and contain active volcanoes, particularly Isabela and Fernandina. In addition to the gradual southeastern drift of the Nazca Plate, the northern drift of the Cocos Plate complicates the matter, meaning the islands do not get uniformly older from northwest to southeast.

Most of the Galápagos are surrounded by very deep ocean. Less than 20km off the coasts of the western islands, the ocean is over 3000m deep. When visitors cruise around the islands, they can see only about the top third of the volcanoes – the rest is underwater. Some of the oldest volcanoes in the area are, in fact, completely underwater. The Carnegie Ridge, a submerged mountain range stretching to the east of the Galápagos, includes the remnants of previous volcanic islands, some of which were as much as nine million years old. These have been completely eroded away; they now lie 2000m beneath the ocean's surface and stretch about half the distance between the Galápagos and the mainland.

Most of the volcanic rock forming the Galápagos Islands is basalt. Molten basalt is more fluid than other types of volcanic rock, so when an eruption occurs, basalt tends to

EVOLUTION IN ACTION

When the Galápagos Islands were formed, they were barren volcanic islands, devoid of all life. Because the islands were never connected to the mainland, it's most likely that all species now present must have somehow crossed 1000km of open ocean. Those that could fly or swim long distances had the best chance of reaching the islands, but other methods of colonization were also possible.

Small mammals, land birds and reptiles, as well as plants and insects, may have been ferried across on floating vegetation. For those animals that survived the trip, plant seeds or insect eggs and larvae may have been brought over in their stomachs, or attached to the feathers or feet of birds.

When the first migrating species arrived millions of years ago, they found there were few other species to compete with. Some animals were able to survive, breed and produce offspring. The young were the same species as their parents, but some had subtle differences.

A classic Galápagos example of this is a bird that produces a chick with a bill that is slightly different from those of its parents or siblings. In the different environment of the islands, some chicks with slightly different bills are more able to take advantage of the surroundings. These birds are said to be better adapted and are more likely to survive and raise a brood of their own.

These better-adapted survivors may pass on favorable genetic traits (in this case, a slightly better-adapted bill) to their offspring, and thus, over many generations, certain favorable traits are selected 'for' and other less-favorable traits are selected 'against'. Eventually, the difference between the original colonizers and their distant descendants is so great that the descendants can be considered a different species altogether. This is the essence of Darwin's theory of evolution by natural selection.

With a variety of islands and habitats, various types of bills could confer adaptive advantages to birds in different ecological niches. One ancestral species could therefore give rise to several modern species, which is called adaptive radiation. This explains the presence in the Galápagos of 13 similar, endemic species of finches called 'Darwin's finches.'

For many years, evolutionary biologists puzzled over how so many unique species could have evolved in the Galápagos over the relatively short period of about four million years (the age of the oldest islands). The answer was provided by geologists and oceanographers who found nine-million-year-old remnants of islands under the ocean to the east of the existing islands. Presumably, the ancestors of the present wildlife once lived on these lost islands, and therefore had at least nine million years to evolve – a span of time that evolutionary biologists find feasible.

erupt in the form of lava flows rather than in the form of explosions. Hence, the Galápagos Islands have gently rounded shield volcanoes rather than the cone-shaped variety that most people associate with volcanic formations.

Ecology & Environment

Every plant and animal species in the Galápagos arrived from somewhere else after journeying hundreds to thousands of kilometers on fortuitous wind, air and sea currents, mostly from South America and the Caribbean. Some flora and fauna arrived later less naturally, brought by settlers and others visiting the islands by ships and planes. There are no large terrestrial mammals, though the islands' wildlife is fascinating.

Concern about the islands' environment is not new. Even as early as the beginning of the 1900s, several scientific organizations were already alarmed. In 1934 the Ecuadorian government set aside some of the islands as wildlife sanctuaries, but it was not until 1959, the centenary of the publication of the *Origin of Species,* that the Galápagos were officially declared a national park (Unesco declared it a World Heritage Site in 1978). The construction of the Charles Darwin Research Station on Isla Santa Cruz began soon after, and the station began operating in 1964 as an international nongovernmental organization (NGO) dedicated to conservation. The Galápagos National Park Service (GNPS) began operating in 1968 and is the key institution of the Ecuadorian government responsible for the park. Both entities work together to manage the islands. In 1986 the Ecuadorian government granted more protection to the islands by creating the 133,000 sq km Galápagos Marine Resources Reserve. A law that was passed in 1998 enables the park and reserve to protect and conserve the islands and surrounding ocean; it also encourages educational and scientific research while allowing sustainable development of the islands as an Ecuadorian province.

Invasive Species

The introduction of domestic animals on every one of the main islands, except Fernandina, is one of the major challenges the archipelago faces. Feral goats and pigs and introduced rats decimated (or caused the extinction of) native species in just a few years – the goats themselves are thought to be responsible for the extinction of four to five species. It took over 127 years to eliminate the feral pig population on the island of San Salvador.

Cattle, cats, dogs, donkeys, frogs and rats are other threats to the survival of endemic flora and fauna; hundreds of insect species have been introduced, including a wasp species feared to be the cause of a declining number of caterpillar larvae, an important food for finches. Nearly 800 plant species have been introduced to the islands; blackberry is considered one of the worst because it reduces biodiversity by as much as 50%.

Overfishing

A major problem in all the world's seas, overfishing is a continuing source of tension in the islands. There have been periodic protests, and several quite serious incidents, organized by fishers unhappy with the restrictions on various fisheries – the protests are primarily over the fishing of sea cucumbers and lobster, two of the more lucrative catches. Coastal no-take zones have been established and large-scale commercial fishing has been banned since 1998; however, the laws are regularly flouted by both Ecuadorian and foreign-flagged ships. Most damaging are the longliners (hundreds or thousands of baited hooks hanging from a single line that's often miles long).

Although sea-cucumber fishing became illegal back in 1994, hundreds of thousands are exported illegally every year, chiefly for their purported aphrodisiac properties. Other illegal fishing activities include taking shark fins for shark-fin soup, killing sea lions for bait, and overfishing lobster to feed tourists and locals.

Only 'artisanal' fishing in small boats is permitted. However, this regulation has been controversially interpreted to allow sport fishing for tourists. Encouraged for a short time, then banned in 2005, it is once again permitted – although the handful of licensed operators is highly regulated.

Other Issues

Some islanders see the national park as a barrier to making a living in agriculture. They argue that if more food is cultivated locally, less food will need to be imported, resulting in a far cheaper cost of living for residents (with fewer concomitant environmental costs). Thus, there's an effort to promote the production of high-quality, organic foodstuffs in the islands. Of course, agriculture leads to habitat loss and the alteration of landscapes. An added complication is scarce water resources – springs have mostly run dry, coastal groundwater can be polluted and the little water there is to be found in the highlands is difficult to direct efficiently.

After an Ecuadorian oil tanker ran aground near Puerto Baquerizo Moreno on San Cristóbal in 2001, the government, along with the World Wildlife Fund (WWF), worked to modernize and rebuild the main fuel depot facility on Baltra so that it meets the highest environmental standards. More recently, in partnership with the UN and some of the world's largest utilities, the Ecuadorian government has pledged to wean the islands off fossil fuels completely by 2020 through the use of solar and wind power; a large-scale wind-turbine project already exists on San Cristóbal.

Certain species, most notably Galápagos penguins, green sea turtles and marine iguanas (the only sea-going lizard in the world), are vulnerable to the rising sea temperatures and sea levels associated with global warming. Increasingly protracted and severe El Niño years (when devastating rainfall pummels South America) – 1998 was the worst in a half-century – have disrupted various Galápagos ecosystems.

Conservation Efforts

More than 50% of flora and fauna species are threatened or endangered (no Galápagos bird species has been declared extinct), including the Floreana mockingbird and the Galápagos petrel. Despite these alarming numbers, more than 95% of the species inhabiting the islands before human contact still exist and the only wild extinct species are the giant land tortoise of Pinta and San Salvador land iguanas. Large-scale culling of non-native and invasive species through hunting, breeding and repatriation programs, nest protection, protective fencing and reforestation are some of the primary strategies of conservationists working in the islands.

Tour operator Metropolitan Touring's Fundacion Galápagos (www.metropolitan-touring.com/informacion-general-de-galapagos/fundacion-galapagos) partnered with various corporations and travel companies to build a recycling plant in Puerto Ayora, and now every home in the islands is supposed to have three color-coded bins for recycling. The foundation also runs volunteer coastal clean-up programs and pays local fishermen to collect trash at sea.

There are various solutions to the problems facing the Galápagos Islands. These include an emphasis on sustainable tourism over the extraction of limited underwater and underground resources, because the extractions could alter the environment irreparably. One extreme view is to prohibit all colonization and tourism – an option that appeals to few. Many colonists – there are around 30,000 full-time residents – act responsibly and actively oppose the disruptive and threatening behavior of some. They also provide the labor for the booming tourism industry.

That being said, the government periodically expels Ecuadorian nationals living in the islands who don't have residency or work permits. There are only three ways Ecuadorians are able to establish permanent residency in the Galápagos: they lived there for five years prior to 1998 or, from that point on, they were born there or married another permanent resident. Many find this strategy discriminatory, asking, 'why not reduce the number of relatively wealthy tourists allowed, instead?' However, the tourism industry is important for Ecuador's economy, accounting for over $200 million a year – a quarter of which ends up in local coffers. The majority of stakeholders believe the best solution to be a combination of environmental education for residents and visitors and a program of responsible and sustainable tourism, which may necessarily involve measures to reduce or cap tourist visits.

PARK RULES

Regulations regarding cruising itineraries were overhauled in early 2012. This was done in an attempt to reduce the number of stops at the most-visited sites; to reduce the total number of visitors; and to relieve pressure on the Baltra airport.

By law, tour boats must be accompanied by certified naturalist guides that have been trained by the National Park Service. However, in reality, guides on less-expensive boats may lack any kind of certification and there is only a limited number of Naturalist III Guides (the most qualified, usually multilingual, university-educated biologists intent on preserving and explaining wildlife).

Visitors to the islands are restricted to the official visitor sites (70 land and 79 marine sites). Important park rules protect wildlife and the environment, and they're mostly a matter of courtesy and common sense: don't feed or touch the animals; don't litter; don't remove any natural object (living or not); don't bring pets; and don't buy objects made from plants or animals. You are not allowed to enter the visitor sites after dark or without a qualified guide, and a guide will accompany every boat. On all shore trips, the guide will be there to answer your questions and also to ensure that you follow park rules.

Tourism

Until the mid-1960s, few tourists visited the islands, other than tycoons and princes on their private yachts or the extremely intrepid who were willing to bed down with livestock on a cargo ship. After the research station opened and charter flights began operating, organized tourism was inaugurated with a trickle of a little over 1000 visitors a year. This figure soon increased dramatically. By 1971 there were six small boats and one large cruise ship operating in the islands. In less than two decades the number of visitors had increased tenfold; back in the early 1990s an estimated 60,000 visited annually. Current figures indicate that around 203,000 tourists visited the islands in 2013, including foreign visitors (132,000) and Ecuadorian residents (72,000). There are around 85 boats (with sleeping accommodations) carrying four to 96 passengers; the majority carry fewer than 20.

While this is good for the economy of Ecuador, environmental problems have resulted. The Ecuadorian government and environmental organizations are aware of these issues and are working to reverse, or at the very least halt, the direction of development (including stopping the building of high-rises and reducing cruise-ship demand) to protect the flora, fauna and people of the Galápagos.

READING LIST

- *Floreana* by Margret Wittmer
- *Galápagos* by Kurt Vonnegut
- *Galápagos: World's End* by William Beebe
- *My Father's Island* by Johanna Angermeyer
- *The Beak of the Finch: A Story of Evolution in Our Time* by Jonathan Weiner
- *The Galapagos Affair* by John Treherne
- *Origin of Species* by Charles Darwin
- *Voyage of the Beagle* by Charles Darwin

Survival Guide

FEES & TAXES

The Galápagos national park fee is $100. It must be paid in cash at one of the airports after you arrive, or in advance through a pre-booked tour. You will not be allowed to leave the airport until you pay. In addition, a transit control fee of $20 must be paid at the Instituto Nacional Galápagos window next to the ticket counter in either the Quito or Guayaquil airports; the charge is already included in the price of many prearranged boat tours. When flying to Isla Isabela, tourists must pay a $10 fee on arrival.

MONEY

Compared to the mainland, you get much less bang for your buck in the Gålapagos. Cash is preferred for most transactions – many restaurants and shops don't accept cards and some accommodations may not, either.

- Bring cash with you from the mainland in case your credit card isn't accepted or the ATMs run out of bills.
- ATMs can be found in Puerto Ayora and Puerto Baquerizo Moreno only – make withdrawals before heading to Isabela or Floreana.
- Small bills are best – $5s and $10s are ideal; most places won't take any over $20.
- MasterCard and Visa are the most accepted credit cards, few businesses take American Express; note that some establishments may charge a 5% to 10% fee.
- Traveler's checks aren't widely accepted, so stick to cash and credit cards.

GETTING THERE & AWAY

Air

Flights from the mainland arrive at two airports: Isla Baltra just north of Santa Cruz, and Isla San Cristóbal. There are almost an equal number of flights to Baltra and San Cristóbal.

The three airlines flying to the Galápagos Islands are Tame (www.tame.com.ec), Avianca (www.avianca.com) and LAN (www.latam.com). All operate two morning flights daily from Quito via Guayaquil to the Isla Baltra airport (two hours), which is just over an hour away from

Puerto Ayora by public transportation. They also provide one or two daily morning flights to the San Cristóbal airport (1½ hours). Return flights are in the early afternoons of the same days.

Round-trip flights from Guayaquil start at $400, and round trips from Quito start around $490; the latter trips include a layover in Guayaquil, although you don't have to get off the plane. It's also possible to fly from Quito and return to Guayaquil or vice versa; it's often more convenient to fly into Baltra and out of San Cristóbal (or vice versa). If you're booked on a boat through an agency, it will likely make the arrangements for you. There is a limit of 20kg for checked luggage (per person) on the flight to the Galápagos.

GETTING AROUND

Most people get around the islands by organized boat tour, but it's very easy to visit the inhabited islands independently. Islas Santa Cruz, San Cristóbal, Isabela and Floreana all have accommodations and daily inter-island boat service (one way $30). There are also pricier inter-island flights between Santa Cruz, San Cristóbal and Isabela.

Air

Emetebe (☎ 05-252-4978; Av Darwin) and **Fly Galápagos** (☎ 05-301-6579; www.flygalapagos.net; cnr Hernandez & Villamil) offer daily flights on five-passenger aircraft between Baltra (Santa Cruz) and Isla Isabela (35 minutes), between Baltra and San Cristóbal (35 minutes), and between San Cristóbal and Isla Isabela (45 minutes). On average, fares are around $150 one way; you'll pay a little extra if you're over the 11kg baggage limit per person.

Boat

Private speedboats known as *lanchas* offer daily passenger ferry services between Santa Cruz and San Cristóbal; Santa Cruz and Isabela; and Santa Cruz and Floreana. Each one-way route takes approximately 2½ hours. Fares are $30 on any passage and are purchased either the day before departure, or the day of, from agencies near the port in each town. On arrival to the port, it's customary to take a small water taxi directly from the speedboat to the passenger dock ($1, paid directly to the boat driver).

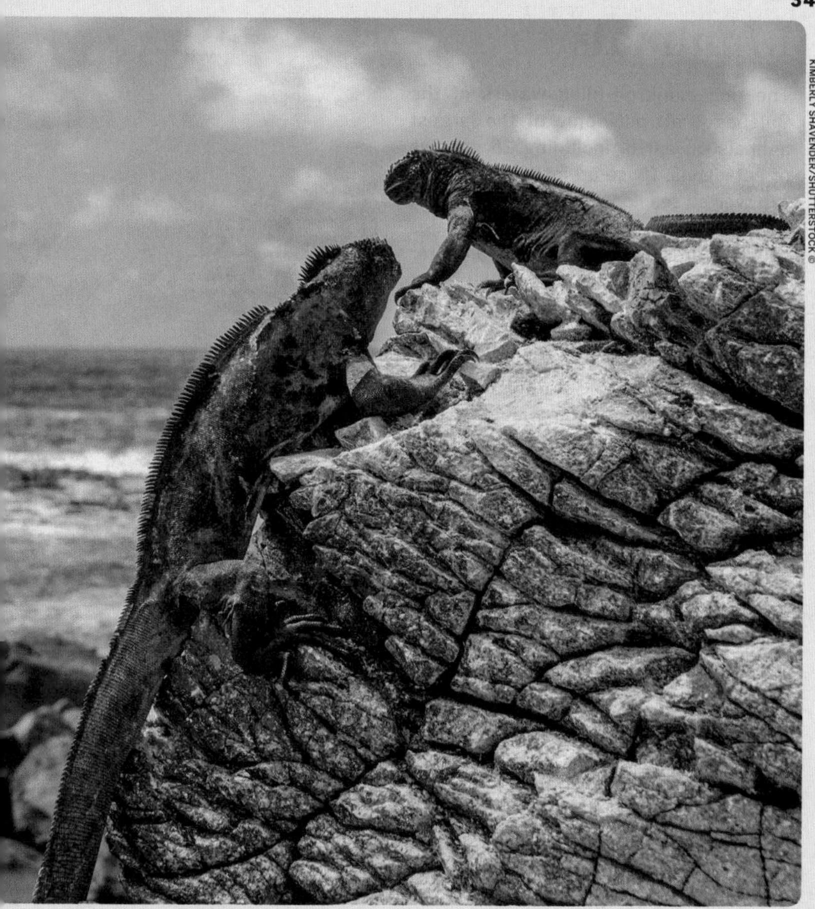
KIMBERLY SHAVENDER/SHUTTERSTOCK ©

Ecuador's famed archipelago was known to early explorers as Las Islas Encantadas (The Enchanted Isles). Although the name has changed, the Galápagos Islands have lost none of their power to captivate. This remote, seemingly barren chain of volcanic islands is home to an astounding variety of wildlife – including many species found nowhere else on earth. It remains one of the world's best places for interacting with animals in the wild at close range, both above and below the sea.

Galápagos Wildlife Guide

Above Marine iguanas

Mammals

The rich plankton-filled waters of the Galápagos attract some of the largest animals on earth, including 25 species of cetaceans. Close-up interactions with extroverted sea lions, dolphins riding your boat's bow wave or breaching whales could occur in any stretch of ocean here.

Killer Whale

Truly spectacular to see in the wild, the killer whale (orca) is actually a species of dolphin. It is a ferocious hunter (but no threat to humans), traveling at up to 55km per hour, while preying on fish or other whales. **Where to see:** Canal Bolívar.

Galápagos Sea Lion

Nearly everyone's favorite island mammal is the widespread Galápagos sea lion, which numbers about 50,000 and is found on every island. These delightful animals often lounge about on sandy beaches and will often swim with snorkelers and bathers. **Where to see:** Everywhere.

1. Galápagos fur seal **2.** Galápagos sea lions **3.** Bottlenose dolphin

Galápagos Fur Seal

More introverted than its sea lion cousin, the endemic Galápagos fur seal has a dense, luxuriant, insulating layer of fur. Although it was nearly hunted to extinction in the 19th century, it has made a remarkable comeback and numbers some 30,000 animals. **Where to see:** Isla Santiago (Puerto Egas, p332), Isla Genovesa (p335).

Bottlenose Dolphin

The most commonly sighted cetacean in Galápagos waters is the bottlenose dolphin, which has a playful and inquisitive nature. They typically feed cooperatively in pods of 20 to 30 individuals and have a varied diet, diving up to 500m offshore. **Where to see:** Everywhere.

2

FOTOS593/SHUTTERSTOCK ©

A. L. HOLMES/SHUTTERSTOCK ©

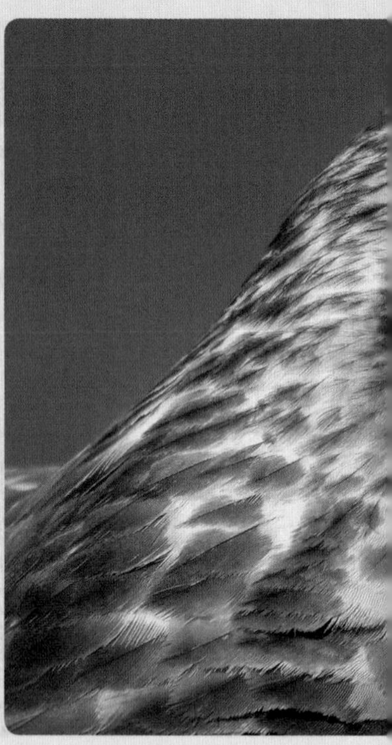

1. Short-eared owl **2.** Galápagos hawk **3.** Galápagos flamingos **4.** Mockingbird

AXEL FASSIO / GETTY IMAGES ©

Land Birds

From powerful predators to flittering songsters – you don't have to be an ornithologist to enjoy bird-watching in the Galápagos. Look for yellow warblers, mockingbirds and Darwin's finches – made famous by the great naturalist himself.

Galápagos Hawk

A generalist hunter, the endemic Galápagos hawk preys on creatures as small as insects and as large as small goats. **Where to see:** Isla Española (p334), Isla Santa Fé (p319), Isla Fernandina (Punta Espinoza, p332).

Darwin's Finches

All of the islands' finches are believed to be descendants of a common ancestor, and evolved into 13 unusual species, including the blood-sucking vampire finch. **Where to see:** Isla Santa Cruz (Los Gemelos, p309; Media Luna, p309), Isla Española (Punta Suárez, p334), Isla Genovesa (p335).

Galápagos Flamingo

These striking birds are one of the largest of the world's five species of flamingo. They're spread in small groups among the islands' shallow, brackish lagoons and number no more than 500. **Where to see:** Isla Floreana (Punta Cormorant, p334), Isla Rábida (p333), Isla Isabela (Puerto Villamil, p328).

Short-Eared Owl

Unlike most, this subspecies of owl hunts during the day as well as night. You can spot these regal-looking birds quartering their prey with slow, deep wing beats. **Where to see:** Isla Genovesa (p335), Isla Santa Cruz (Media Luna, p309).

Mockingbirds

These thrush-sized birds are actually fine songsters and are often the first birds to investigate visitors at beach landings, poking around in bags and perching on hats. **Where to see:** Isla Santa Cruz (p308), Isla Santa Fé (p319), Isla Genovesa (p335).

TRISTAN BROWN/GETTY IMAGES ©

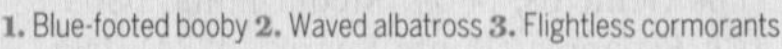

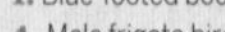

1. Blue-footed booby **2.** Waved albatross **3.** Flightless cormorants
4. Male frigate bird

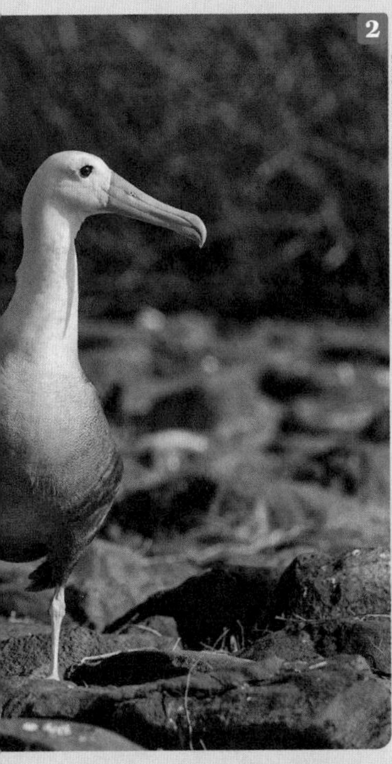
CHRISTIAN HANDL/GETTY IMAGES ©

Seabirds

Oceanic wanderers, such as the waved albatross and the flightless cormorant, call the islands home. The surprisingly agile Galápagos penguin, the comical blue-footed booby and the supremely maneuverable frigate birds join the amazing array of species.

Blue-Footed Booby

These boobies, one of four booby species on the islands, perform an enchanting, if rather clownish, display during courtship. **Where to see:** Isla Española (Punta Suárez, p334), Isla Genovesa (p335), Isla San Cristóbal (Punta Pitt, p321).

Waved Albatross

The waved albatross is helpless in calm weather, relying utterly on southeast trade winds to transport it to feeding areas. The archipelago's largest bird (weighing 5kg, with a 2.4m wingspan) is the only albatross species that breeds at the equator. **Where to see:** Isla Española (Punta Suárez, p334).

Frigate Birds

Dazzling fliers, frigates ride high on thermals above coastal cliffs, sometimes harassing smaller seabirds into dropping their catch and then swooping to snag the booty in midair. **Where to see:** North Seymour (p314), Isla Genovesa (p335), Isla San Cristóbal (Punta Pitt, p321).

Galápagos Penguin

Today the Galápagos penguin is the most northerly penguin in the world and the only species that lives in the tropics. **Where to see:** Isla Isabela (p326), Isla Fernandina (p332), Isla Bartolomé (p333).

Flightless Cormorant

Apart from penguins, the flightless cormorant is the only flightless seabird in the world, and it is endemic to the Galápagos. About 700 pairs remain. **Where to see:** Isla Fernandina (Punta Espinoza, p332), Isla Isabela (Tagus Cove, p327; Urbina Bay, p328).

Reptiles

Giant, prehistoric-looking tortoises and fearsome-looking land iguanas can be observed and photographed on land, while snorkelers can glimpse the bizarre seagoing iguana and graceful sea turtles in the water.

Giant Tortoise

The archipelago's most famous reptile is the giant tortoise, or Galápagos ('saddle' in Spanish), after which the islands are named. They can live for several hundred years. **Where to see:** Isla Santa Cruz (highlands, p308), Isla Isabela (Urbina Bay, p328), Isla San Cristóbal (Galapaguera, p320).

Galápagos Land Iguana

Despite their large size and fearsome appearance, land iguanas are harmless vegetarians. Mature males are territorial, engaging in head-butting contests to defend their terrain. **Where to see:** South Plaza (p319), Isla Isabela (p326), Isla Santa Cruz (Cerro Dragón, p310), Isla Fernandina (p332), Baltra and North Seymour (p314).

Lava Lizards

The most commonly seen reptiles on the islands are the various species of lava lizard, which are frequently seen scurrying across rocks or even perched on the backs of iguanas. **Where to see:** Everywhere.

Marine Iguana

The remarkable marine iguana is the world's only seagoing lizard. Its size and coloration vary between islands, with the largest specimens growing up to 1.5m. **Where to see:** Everywhere.

Green Sea Turtle

Adult green sea turtles can reach 150kg in weight and 1m in length. They can be seen readily surfacing for air at many anchorages in calm water and are often encountered by snorkelers. **Where to see:** Isla Santa Cruz (Black Turtle Cove, p310), Isla Fernandina (Punta Espinoza, p332), Isla Santiago (Espumilla Beach, p333), abundant elsewhere.

1

3

1. Land iguana 2. Giant tortoise 3. Green sea turtle
4. Lava lizard

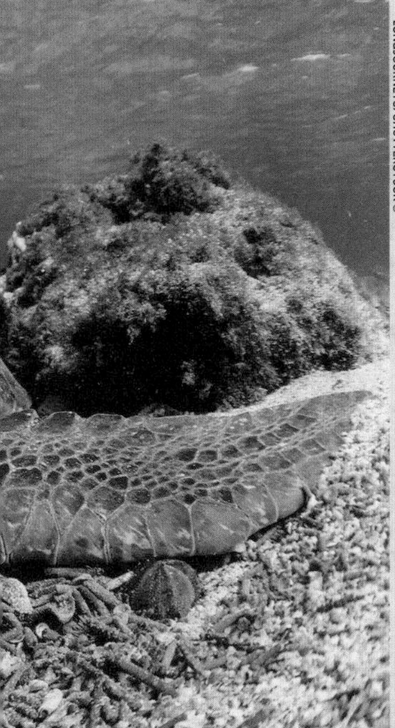

LONGJOURNEYS/SHUTTERSTOCK ©

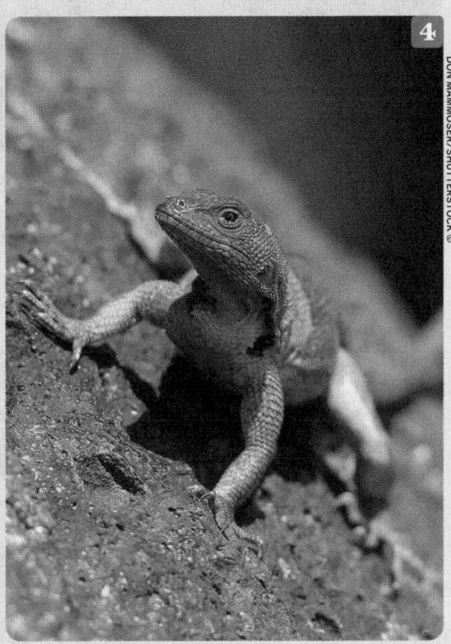

DON MAMMOSER/SHUTTERSTOCK ©

1

2

Sea Life

The archipelago is home to a wide range of marine life. There are many thousands of aquatic species in all shapes and sizes, including 25 species of dolphin and whale, and 400 species of fish.

MICHELE WESTMORLAND/GETTY IMAGES ©

. Hammerhead shark **2.** Sally Lightfoot crab **3.** Blue ırgeonfish

Tropical Fish

More than 400 fish species have been recorded in Galápagos waters, including some 50 endemic species. Some commonly sighted species while snorkeling are blue-eyed damselfish, white-banded angelfish, yellow-tailed surgeonfish, Moorish idols, blue parrotfish and concentric puffers. **Where to see:** Everywhere.

Hammerhead Sharks

You don't need to scuba dive to spot schools of this intimidating and bizarre-looking species of shark (though of course it heightens the experience). **Where to see:** North Seymour (p314), Isla Santa Cruz (Gordon Rocks, p313), Isla Floreana (Devil's Crown, p334), Isla Santa Fé (p319), Isla Genovesa (p335), Isla Wolf (p336), Isla Darwin (p336).

Sally Lightfoot Crab

This abundant marine animal is blessed with spectacular coloration. Sally Lightfoot crabs (named by English seafarers) adorn the rocks on every island and are extremely agile. They can jump from rock to rock and even appear to walk on water. **Where to see:** Everywhere.

Manta Ray

Of the 15 species of ray inhabiting Galápagos waters, the magnificent manta ray is the largest of the bunch – and one of the world's largest fish. Some giants reportedly stretch 9m across the 'wings', although 4m adults are more common. **Where to see:** Canal Bolívar, deep channels elsewhere.

Habitats

The entire archipelago is volcanic in origin, with the main islands just the tips of vast submarine volcanoes. In the relatively short span of geological time since the islands were formed, they have been transformed from sterile lava flows into complex vegetation communities with many unique species.

Coastline

Ever-eroding lava flows make up the rocky shoreline, providing habitat for sea lions, marine iguanas and Sally Lightfoot crabs. Mangroves provide breeding and nesting sites, as well as protective and shaded refuges for birds, sea lions and turtles.

Highlands Zone

The high peaks of several islands have eroded into rich volcanic soil, which along with occasional rainfall, support dense tropical vegetation. Fascinating species flourish here, such as the 15m-high scalesia (tree daisy), whose trunk and branches are covered in epiphytes: dripping mosses, ferns, orchids and bromeliads.

Arid Zone

Poor volcanic soils cover much of the islands, with bristling cacti towering above the surrounding vegetation. Despite the challenging environment, diverse species thrive here, including the endemic lava cactus, which takes root in the cracks in barren lava flows.

Ocean

Highly productive currents bathe the islands in a year-round supply of nutrients. Plankton drift on the sunlit surface, sustaining fish, their predators further up the food chain and some of the world's largest animals – the great whales.

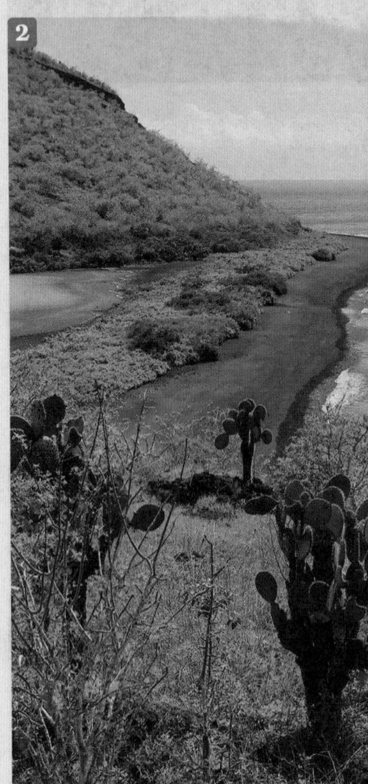

1. Isla Santa Fé (p319) **2.** Red beach, Isla Rábida (p333)

Understand Ecuador

Ecuador Today

Once an economic basket case, Ecuador, under the leadership of charismatic ex-president Rafael Correa, invested in new roads, hospitals, schools, and social programs. However, the high prices of crude oil and Ecuador's vast oil and mineral wealth played a pivotal role. When oil prices crashed in 2008, Correa borrowed heavily to maintain momentum, and the country is paying the price today in oil and mineral concessions to the lender nations, specifically China, to whom it owes billions.

Best in Print

The Farm on the River of Emeralds (Moritz Thomsen; 1978) Compelling memoir about living on the Ecuadorian coast.

The Villagers (Jorge Icaza; 1934) A portrait of the hardships of Andean indigenous life.

Savages (Joe Kane; 1995) Hilarious, eye-opening account of the Huaoranis vs the oil industry.

The Old Man Who Read Love Stories (Luis Sepúlveda; 1992) Moving story of love and loss in Ecuadorian Amazonia.

Plumas: Aves in Ecuador (Murray Cooper & Rudy Geis; 2006) Every avian picture tells a story in this stunning coffee-table book.

Best on Film

Qué tan lejos (2006) Road movie about two young women on a journey of self-discovery in the Andean highlands.

Ratas, Ratones, Rateros (1999) Award-winning film about two petty thieves on the run in Quito and Guayaquil.

Under Rich Earth (Bajos Suelos Ricos) (2008) A must-see documentary on the locally led struggle against destructive mining practices in the Intag Valley.

Boom Days

The 'Citizens Revolution' is how President Correa described the big changes that swept across Ecuador, and despite the hyperbole, it's hard to deny the enormous gains many citizens made during Correa's administration. He nearly doubled government spending on public investment (from 21% in 2006 to over 40% by 2014), pouring money into healthcare and education. The result: infant mortality rates are down, and with the building of new schools and universities, more students have access to education than ever before.

Big infrastructure projects sprung up across the nation, including new hydroelectric dams, brand-new highways and bridges and the opening of Quito's Mariscal Sucre airport. Other projects are underway, including a 23km metro system in the capital.

Given all this, it's not surprising that Correa enjoyed widespread popularity during his first term. He was one of the most popular leaders in Latin America, and probably the most popular president in the nation's history.

But Correa also amassed some enemies over the years. His opponents characterized him as a semi-authoritarian ruler who undermined democracy by expanding presidential power, weakening the independence of the courts and antagonizing those who disagreed with him. Organizations such as Human Rights Watch also cited the sweeping powers enacted to silence his perceived enemies.

Lenín Moreno, formerly Correa's vice president, was elected in May 2017. Upon assuming office, Moreno took a stand against Correa's free-spending ways, leading to a bitter dispute between the former allies.

Black Gold

Ecuador is particularly well endowed when it comes to petroleum; it's home to the third-largest oil reserves in South America after Venezuela and Brazil, accounting for more than 30% of government revenue and half of all export earnings. But while oil has undoubtedly lined the nation's coffers, it has also brought greater threats to Ecuador's ecology.

Parque Nacional Yasuní, a pristine area of the Amazon, holds one of Ecuador's largest reserves – thought to contain 846 million barrels (worth an estimated $7 billion). It also contains some of the greatest biodiversity on the planet, and is home to isolated indigenous groups. Attempts by environmental groups to hold a referendum on oil exploitation in the park were rejected by the government, and the state oil company Petroamazonas began drilling in this UNESCO World Heritage Site in early 2016. The building of access roads and pipelines – not to mention the possibility of oil spills – could be devastating for Yasuní.

Three indigenous leaders of the Shuar tribe have been killed in the struggle for sovereignty over the Amazon's resources.

Life After Correa

Ultimately Correa's legacy will be a mixed one. While he united the country with new roads and communication lines, he accomplished much of this by borrowing billions of dollars after the price of petroleum plummeted in 2008. The outstanding lender, the Chinese government, is calling in these loans by demanding rights to Ecuador's vast mineral and other resources, beginning with a massive hydroelectric project near coastal Manta which will dry up the nation's highest waterfall for a few months per year. As in other nations, China brings its own workers for these projects, and it is reported there is an unhealthy relationship between the Ecuadorian and Chinese laborers, sometimes to the point of violence.

Correa's legacy may also be tainted by a corruption scandal that began playing itself out a few months after he left office. In September 2017 his former vice president Jorge Glas (former oil minister and until then, also VP under Lenín Moreno) was jailed after being implicated in a huge bribery scandal concerning the Brazilian company Odebrecht, which was involved in many of Ecuador's massive infrastructure projects. Glas had been stripped of all his vice presidential powers the previous month by Moreno. The scandal, in fact, stretches across South America.

Tourism has been hit hard by the after-effects of the great earthquake of April 2016, which caused massive destruction along the coast (its epicenter was in Muisne) and resulted in nearly 700 deaths and thousands of injuries. Even more damaging, in the long term, was the sense of the nation as an international tourist destination, just one year after it poured millions into a 30-second Super Bowl ad aimed at that market. The quake, and misplaced fears about the ZIKA virus, had a negative impact on tourism.

POPULATION: **16.4 MILLION**

GDP GROWTH RATE: **1%**

GDP PER CAPITA: **$5,820**

UNEMPLOYMENT: **6.5%**

POVERTY RATE: **22.5%**

ADULT LITERACY RATE: **94%**

if Ecuador were 100 people

93 would speak Spanish
4 would speak Quechua
1 would speak other indigenous languages
2 would speak foreign languages

belief systems

(% of population)

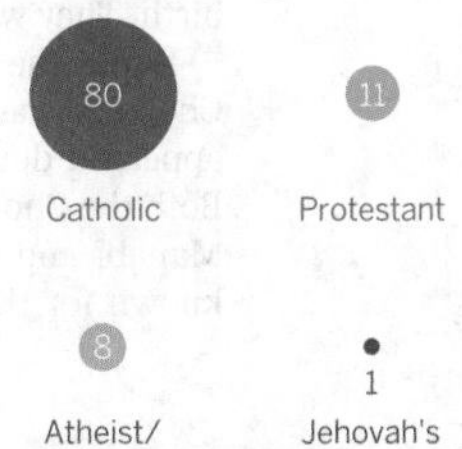

population per sq km

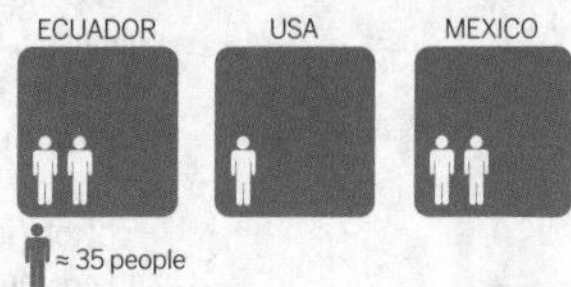

History

The land of fire and ice certainly has a tumultuous history. Since becoming an independent nation in 1830, Ecuador has gone through nearly 100 changes in government and 20 constitutions – the most recent drafted in 2008. Fueling the nation's volatility are rivalries both internal (conservative, church-backed Quito versus liberal, secular Guayaquil) and external (border disputes with Peru). For scholars, the unsung heroes are Ecuador's resilient indigenous groups, descendants of some of the great cultures that once flourished in the Americas.

Early Cultures

Although the majority of indigenous people today live in the highlands and the Oriente, in pre-Spanish (and pre-Inca) times the coastline supported the densest concentration of peoples. The coastal cultures of La Tolita, Bahía, Manta, Valdivia and Machalilla are paramount to Ecuadorian identity, their importance in many ways even eclipsing the Inca, who didn't arrive in present-day Ecuador until a half century before the Spanish.

At the height of its empire, the Inca ruled more than 12 million people across some 1 million sq km.

It's now generally accepted that Ecuador was populated by people migrating west from Brazil, who were drawn to the habitable landscapes along the shore. Ecuador's first permanent sedentary culture was the Valdivia, which developed along the Santa Elena Peninsula more than 5500 years ago. One of the oldest settled cultures in the Americas, the Valdivia are famous for their finely wrought pottery, particularly the 'Venus of Valdivia.' These were feminine ceramic figurines with exaggerated breasts and genitalia, depicted in various stages of pregnancy and childbirth. They were likely used in fertility rituals.

While the Valdivia was the first of Ecuador's settled cultures, the Chorrera was the most widespread and influential of the groups that appeared during this so-called Formative Period (4000 BC to 300 BC). Both the Chorrera and the Machalilla culture (which inhabited southern Manabí and the Santa Elena Peninsula from 1500 BC to 800 BC) are known for the practice of skull deformation. As a form of status, they

TIMELINE

3200 BC

Ecuador's first sedentary culture develops around Santa Elena Peninsula. Fishers and farmers, the Valdivia cultivate maize, yuca, beans, squash and cotton (for clothing), and are famed for their earthenware pottery.

600 BC

Indigenous societies become more stratified. Tribes are headed by an elite caste of shamans and merchants who conduct long-distance maritime trade – reaching as far north as Central America.

AD 800

Different cultures begin to merge, creating more hierarchical societies. Emergent powers include Manteños, Huancavilcas and Caras on the coast; and Quitus, Puruhá and Cañari in the Sierra.

used stones to slowly elongate and flatten their craniums, and they often removed two front teeth to further enhance their appearance.

Beginning sometime around 600 BC, societies became more stratified: they were ruled by an elite caste of shamans and merchants who conducted highly valued long-distance trade. These included the Bahía, Jama-Coaque, Guangala and La Tolita cultures on the coast and the Panzaleo in the highlands. It is likely the Panzaleo was the first culture to practice the technique of *tzantza* (shrinking heads) for which the Shuar of the southern Oriente are much more famous (they practiced it until the mid-20th century).

Slowly, beginning probably around AD 800, cultures became integrated into larger, more hierarchical societies. These included the Manteños, the Huancavilcas and the Caras on the coast; the Quitus (from which the city of Quito takes its name) of the northern highlands; the Puruhá of the central highlands; and the Cañari of the area around present-day Cuenca. Around the end of the 1st century AD, the expansionist Caras of the coast conquered the peaceful Quitus of the highlands and the combined cultures became collectively known as the Quitu-Caras, or the Shyris. They were the dominant force in the Ecuadorian highlands until about the 1300s, when the Puruhá of the central highlands became increasingly powerful. The third important culture was the Cañari, further south. These were the cultures the Inca Empire encountered when it began its expansion into the north.

Pre-Columbian Wonders

Ingapirca (p188), southern highlands

Museo Nacional (p63), Quito

Casa Museo Guayasamín (p63), Quito

Museo del Banco Central 'Pumapungo' (p175), Cuenca

Museo Arqueológico del Banco Central (p267), Manta

The Inca Empire

Until the early 15th century the Inca Empire was concentrated around Cuzco in Peru. That changed dramatically during the rule of Pachacuti Inca Yupanqui, whose expansionist policies set into motion the creation of the vast Inca Empire, Tahuantinsuyo, meaning 'Land of the Four Quarters' in Quechua. By the time the Inca reached Ecuador they were under the rule of Tupac Yupanqui, Pachacuti's successor, and were met with fierce resistance.

The Cañari put up a resolute defense against the Inca, and it took some years for Tupac Yupanqui to subdue them and turn his attention to the north, where he was met with even greater resistance. At one point, the Cañari drove the invading army all the way back to Saraguro.

The subjugation of the north took many years, during which the Inca Tupac fathered a son with a Cañari princess. The son, Huayna Capac, grew up in Ecuador and succeeded his father to the Inca throne. He spent years traveling throughout his empire, from Bolivia to Ecuador, constantly suppressing uprisings from all sides. Bloody battles continued. In the north, the Inca massacred thousands of Caranqui and

Inca ruler Huayna Capac had a third son, Manco Capac. He was the last Inca ruler and staged one of the greatest revolts against the Spanish. He was killed by a Spaniard whose life he had saved.

1463

The Inca, under the leadership of Pachacuti Inca Yupanqui, begin the conquest of Ecuador. His son Tupac leads the attack, facing down surprising resistance along the way.

1500

Tupac's son Huayna Capac conquers the Cañari (around modern-day Cuenca); the Caras (in the north); and the Quitus (around modern-day Quito). Ecuador becomes part of the vast Inca Empire.

1526

Inca ruler Huayna Capac dies suddenly (probably from smallpox or measles) and leaves the Inca Empire to his two sons, Atahualpa and Huáscar. A bitter power struggle ensues.

1532

Spanish conquistador Francisco Pizarro arrives with 180 men in present-day Ecuador. Hearing of fabled Inca riches, he plans to conquer the country for the Spanish crown.

dumped them into a lake near Otavalo, which supposedly turned the waters red and gave the lake its name, Laguna Yahuarcocha (Lake of Blood).

Wherever possible, he strengthened his position by marriage and in the process produced two sons: Atahualpa, who grew up in Quito, and Huáscar, who was raised in Cuzco.

When Huayna Capac died in 1526 he left his empire not to one son, as was traditional, but to two. Thus the Inca Empire was divided for the first time – an event that fatefully coincided with the mystifying appearance of a group of bearded men on horseback in present-day Esmeraldas province. They were the first Spaniards in Ecuador, led south by the pilot Bartolomé Ruiz de Andrade on an exploratory mission for Francisco Pizarro, who remained, for the time being, further north.

Meanwhile, the rivalry between Huayna Capac's two sons worsened, and the Inca nation broke into civil war. After several years of fighting, Atahualpa finally defeated Huáscar near Ambato and was thus the sole

LIFE UNDER THE INCA

The Inca arrived in Ecuador a short time before the Spanish conquistadors overthrew them, but they had a lasting effect on the indigenous peoples of the area. Agriculture, social organization and land ownership saw pronounced changes. The Inca introduced new crops, including cocoa, sweet potatoes and peanuts, and new farming methods using llamas and irrigation. Private land ownership was abolished, with land collectively held by the *ayllu*, newly established agrarian communities. Each family was allotted a small plot of arable land within the *ayllu*. The state and high priests also held sizable plots of land, upon which the emperor's subjects labored as part of their required public service.

The Inca state was highly organized. It introduced the Quechua language, levied taxes and built an extensive network of roads (later used with disastrous success by the horse-riding conquistadors). A system of runners relayed messages, allowing important news to travel hundreds of miles a day. The Incas spread their religion, whose pantheon of gods included Inti (the sun god) and Viracocha (the creator god). Local populations were required to worship the sun god, but their native beliefs were tolerated.

The economy was entirely based on farming, with maize and potatoes chief among the crops. They also raised *cuy* (guinea pigs), ducks, dogs, and llamas and alpacas, whose wool was spun for clothes. Cotton was also grown.

The Inca for their part grew quite fond of Ecuador. Emperor Huayna Capac made Quito a secondary capital of the Inca Empire and lived there until his death in 1526. Locals were largely left alone as long as they paid tribute and acknowledged his divinity. Those who opposed him were exiled to far reaches of the kingdom, with other colonists brought in to take their place. This forced migration of peoples also helped to spread Quechua (Kichwa in Ecuador), the language of the empire.

1533

The Inca ruler Atahualpa is killed by the Spanish, effectively decapitating the Inca Empire. Pizarro heads south to Cuzco (in present-day Peru) and plunders the once great capital of Tahuantinsuyo.

1542

While searching for gold, Francisco de Orellana spends eight months exploring the Amazon, becoming the first European to sail its length (vividly described in Buddy Levy's *River of Darkness*).

1563

The Spanish crown declares Ecuador the Audiencia de Quito, shifting political administration away from Lima, Peru. The territory extends from from Cali (Colombia) to Paita (Peru).

1600

The Quito School of Art (Escuela Quiteña) emerges, with indigenous artists and artisans producing some of the finest religious art in the Americas. Masterful, syncretic works appear over the next 150 years.

ruler of the weakened and still-divided Inca Empire when Pizarro arrived in 1532 with plans to conquer it.

The Spanish Conquest

Pizarro's advance was rapid and dramatic. His horseback-riding, armor-wearing, cannon-firing conquistadors were believed to be godlike, and although they were few in number, they spread terror among the local people. In late 1532 a summit meeting was arranged between Pizarro and Atahualpa. Although Atahualpa was prepared to negotiate with the Spaniards, Pizarro had other ideas. When the Inca arrived at the prearranged meeting place (Cajamarca, in Peru) on November 16, the conquistadors captured him and massacred most of his poorly armed guards.

Atahualpa was held for ransom, and incalculable quantities of gold, silver and other valuables poured into Cajamarca. Instead of being released when the ransom was paid, however, the Inca was put through a sham trial and sentenced to death. Atahualpa was charged with incest (marrying one's sister was traditional in the Inca culture), polygamy, worship of false gods and crimes against the king, and he was executed on August 29, 1533. His death effectively brought the Inca Empire to an end.

When Atahualpa was executed, his war-general Rumiñahui was supposedly on his way to Cajamarca with large quantities of gold and treasure as ransom for the Inca. Legend has it that, upon hearing of Atahualpa's death, Rumiñahui stashed the treasure in the impenetrable mountains of present-day Parque Nacional Llanganates; it has never been found.

Rumiñahui then continued to fight against the Spaniards for two more years. The general was so fierce that according to legend he dealt with a Spanish collaborator (and possible heir to Atahualpa's throne) by murdering him, breaking all the bones in his body to bits, extracting them through a hole, and stretching the body – with head and appendages intact – into a drum. By the time Pizarro's lieutenant, Sebastián de Benalcázar, had finally battled his way to Quito in late 1534, he found the city razed to the ground by Rumiñahui, who preferred to destroy the city rather than leave it in the hands of the conquistadors. Quito was refounded on December 6, 1534, and Rumiñahui was finally captured, tortured and executed in January 1535.

Despite the Inca's short presence in Ecuador (just over 100 years), they left an indelible mark on the country. Quechua (known as Kichwa in Ecuador) was imposed on the population and is still spoken today by a quarter of all Ecuadorians. The Inca built a vast system of roads that connected Cuzco in the south with Quito in the north, and part of the 'royal highway' – the Inca trail to Ingapirca – can still be hiked today.

Incas & Conquistadors: Top Reads

The Conquest of the Incas (1973), John Hemming

River of Darkness: Francisco Orellana's Legendary Voyage of Death and Discovery Down the Amazon (2011), Buddy Levy

The Last Days of the Incas (2007), Kim MacQuarrie

Written in the 16th century, Bartolomé de las Casas' *A Short Account of the Destruction of the Indies* is a searing and readable account of the Spaniards' abuse of the native population during colonization.

1690
An epidemic of smallpox and diphtheria rages throughout Ecuador, killing one third of the population. The native population (estimated at one million at the time of conquest) declines dramatically.

1767
King Charles III expels the Jesuits from the Spanish Empire. Missions in the Oriente are abandoned, while some of colonial Ecuador's best schools and haciendas fall into decline.

1790
Following a century of economic mismanagement by Spain, the Ecuadorian economy suffers a severe depression. Its cities are in ruins, with the elite reduced to poverty.

1791
Early independence advocate Eugenio de Santa Cruz y Espejo becomes director of the 'patriotic society,' aimed at civic improvement. His writings land him in prison, where he dies in 1795.

Ingapirca itself is Ecuador's most important Inca archaeological site and has splendid examples of the Inca's mortarless stonework.

The Colonial Era

From 1535 the colonial era proceeded with no major uprisings by indigenous Ecuadorians. Francisco Pizarro made his brother Gonzalo the governor of Quito in 1540.

During the first centuries of colonial rule, Lima, Peru, was the seat of Ecuador's political administration. Originally a *gobernación* (province), in 1563 Ecuador became the Audiencia de Quito (a more important political division), which in 1739 was transferred from the viceroyalty of Peru to the viceroyalty of Colombia (then known as Nueva Grenada).

Ecuador remained a peaceful colony throughout this period, and agriculture and the arts flourished. New products such as cattle and bananas were introduced from Europe, which remain important in Ecuador today. Churches and monasteries were constructed atop every sacred indigenous site and were decorated with unique carvings and paintings that blended Spanish and indigenous artistic influences. This so-called Escuela Quiteña (Quito School of Art), still admired by visitors today, left an indelible stamp on the colonial buildings of the time and Ecuador's unique art history.

Life was comfortable for the ruling colonialists, but the indigenous people (and later the mestizos, people of mixed Spanish and indigenous descent) were treated abysmally under their rule. A system of forced labor was not only tolerated but encouraged, and by the 18th century there were several indigenous uprisings against the Spanish ruling classes. Social unrest, as well as the introduction of cocoa and sugar plantations in the northwest, prompted landowners to import African slave laborers. Much of the rich Afro-Ecuadorian culture found in Esmeraldas province today is a legacy of this period.

Colonial Masterpieces

Iglesia de la Compañía de Jesús (p56), Quito

Monastery of San Francisco (p70), Quito

Haciendas of Laguna de San Pablo (p108), northern highlands

El Sagrario ('old cathedral'; p175, Cuenca

Numa Pompilio Llona (p273), Guayaquil

Hacienda Guachalá (p100), Cayambe

Independence

The first serious attempt to liberate Ecuador from Spanish rule was by a partisan group led by Juan Pío Montúfar on August 10, 1809. The group managed to take Quito and install a government, which lasted only 24 days before royalist troops (loyal to Spain) regained control.

Independence was finally achieved by Simón Bolívar, the Venezuelan liberator who marched southward from Caracas, freed Colombia in 1819 and supported the people of Guayaquil when they claimed independence on October 9, 1820. It took almost two years before Ecuador was entirely liberated from Spanish rule. The decisive battle was fought on May 24, 1822, when one of Bolívar's finest officers, Mariscal (Field Marshal)

1822 Two years after Guayaquil declares independence from Spain, António Jose de Sucre defeats Spanish royalists at the Battle of Pichincha. Ecuador becomes part of Gran Colombia.

1830 Ecuador leaves Gran Colombia and becomes an independent nation. A group of Quito notables draws up a constitution, placing General Flores in charge of military and political matters.

1835 A young naturalist named Charles Darwin spends five weeks exploring the Galápagos Islands – an experience that would prove pivotal for his groundbreaking theory of evolution years later.

1851 General José Maria Urbina frees the nation's slaves. His successor, General Francisco Robles, puts an end to 300 years of required annual payments by the indigenous.

THE MYTHICAL AMAZON

One of the most significant events of the early colonial period was the epic journey of Francisco de Orellana along the Río Napo. Orellana set off in December 1541 to search for food to bring relief to a hungry contingent of Gonzalo Pizarro's men following a rigorous crossing of the Cordillera Oriental. Once Orellana caught sight of the lush promise of dense jungle lining the riverbanks, however, he quickly abandoned his original mission and set off in search of gold. These were the days when Spanish conquistadors spoke of legendary lost cities of gold, and Orellana was obsessed with finding El Dorado. 'Having eaten our shoes and saddles boiled with a few herbs,' Orellana wrote, 'we set out to reach the Kingdom of Gold.' It was a grueling journey that would leave half of his comrades dead.

On June 5, 1542, some five months after setting sail, Orellana's boats reached a large village decorated with carvings of 'fierce lions' (probably jaguars). One of the villagers said that the carvings represented the tribe's mistress and their ruler. When his boat later came under ferocious attack (following several raids by his own men on other riverside settlements), Orellana was convinced that female warriors were leading the onslaught. He later named the river after the Amazons, the mythical all-female warriors of ancient Greece. By the time he reached the Atlantic Ocean – some eight months after he began – he had given up his quest for gold. He became the first European to travel the length of the Amazon River, a feat not to be repeated for another 100 years. The event is still commemorated in Ecuador during the annual Aniversario del Descubrimiento del Río Amazonas (Discovery of the Amazon River), celebrated on February 12.

Werner Herzog's 1972 film, *Aguirre, the Wrath of God*, was inspired by Orellana's fruitless quest and its subsequent documentation by chronicler Gaspar de Carvajal, although it borrowed from both Orellana's and Aguirre's separate voyages.

Antonio José de Sucre, defeated the royalists at the Battle of Pichincha and took Quito. This battle is commemorated at a stunningly situated monument on the flanks of Volcán Pichincha, overlooking the capital.

Bolívar's idealistic dream was to form a united South America, and he began by amalgamating Venezuela, Colombia and Ecuador into the independent nation of Gran Colombia. This lasted only eight years, with Ecuador becoming fully independent in 1830. In the same year a treaty was signed with Peru, drawing up a boundary between the two nations; this boundary is the one shown on all Ecuadorian maps prior to 1999. The border had been redrawn in 1942 after a war between Ecuador and Peru, but was not officially acknowledged by Ecuadorian authorities until a peace treaty was signed with Peru in late 1998.

1859

García Moreno comes to power. Decried by opponents as a dictator, he nevertheless makes vital contributions in education, public welfare and economic development. He is assassinated in 1875.

1895

José Eloy Alfaro Delgado takes power. A champion of liberalism, he strips the Church of power, legalizes civil marriage and divorce, and establishes freedom of speech and religion.

1920

Economic problems cripple Ecuador. A fungal disease and declining demand destroy the cacao industry. The working class protest rocketing inflation and deteriorating living standards. Strikes are brutally suppressed.

1930s

Following a period of reform in the late 1920s (including pensions for state workers), the Ecuadorian economy crashes. Unemployment soars and political instability rocks the government.

Political Development

Following independence from Spain, Ecuador's history unfolded with unbridled political warfare between liberals and conservatives. The turmoil frequently escalated to violence. In 1875 the church-backed, conservative dictator President García Moreno (who attempted to make Catholicism a requisite for citizenship) was hacked to death with a machete outside Quito's presidential palace. In 1912 liberal President Eloy Alfaro, who attempted to undo much of García Moreno's legacy, was murdered and burned by a conservative mob in Quito (ironically, Alfaro was transported to Quito via the Pacific Coast train line he helped pioneer). Rivalries between these factions continue to this day, albeit less violently. Quito remains the main center for the church-backed conservatives, while Guayaquil stands, as it has for centuries, on the side of more liberal and sometimes socialist beliefs.

Robert McCracken Peck's *Headhunters and Hummingbirds* is a quick, rip-roaring 108-page read of a 1984 scientific expedition into the Cutucu Mountains, Shuar territory, eating monkeys, chopping up tarantulas, and netting hummingbirds.

Throughout much of the 20th century Ecuador's political sphere remained volatile, though the country never experienced the bloodshed or brutal military dictatorships suffered by other Latin American countries. That's not to say the military never took the reins of power, with the 20th century seeing almost as many periods of military rule as civilian rule. One president, José María Velasco Ibarra, was elected five times between 1934 and 1972 and was ousted by the military before he could complete any one of his terms. Ibarra wasn't alone: in the 10 years between 1930 and 1940, 17 different presidents took a shot at leading Ecuador, not one of whom completed a term.

Part Mark Twain, part *Gulliver's Travels*, Albert Franklin's 1943 *Ecuador: Portrait of a People*, is just that, an outsider's look at the regional differences among the country's populations. It includes witty and candid observations from familiar places such as the Park America in Guayaquil and Otavalo's famed marketplace. Funny, interesting, and very old-school.

Yellow Gold to Black Gold

Until the 1970s Ecuador was the archetypal 'banana republic,' and the fruit was the country's single most important export. In fact, Ecuador exported more bananas than any country in the world. Although bananas are a staple of the country's economy today, they ceased being Ecuador's sole export after the discovery of oil in the Oriente in 1967. By 1973 oil exports had risen to first place, and by the early 1980s they accounted for well over half of total export earnings. Oil undoubtedly boosted the economy, though politicians from the left, allied with indigenous-rights groups, say much of the largesse remained in the hands of a few controlling interests with little benefit to the many. The statistics support this claim, with the majority of the rural population at an equal – or lower – living standard than they experienced in the 1970s.

After oil was discovered, Ecuador began to borrow money, with the belief that profits from oil exports would enable the country to repay its foreign debts. But this proved impossible in the mid-1980s due to the sharp decline in Ecuador's oil exports; world oil prices slumped in 1986,

1941

Tensions rise over disputed Amazon territories, and Peru invades Ecuador with 13,000 troops. Following peace accords, Ecuador cedes over half its territories, but doesn't acknowledge its new borders.

1948

Galo Plaza is elected president, marking an era of progress and prosperity. He slows inflation, balances the budget and invests in schools, roads and other infrastructure.

1948–52

As disease plagues plantations in Central America, Ecuador becomes one of the world's top banana producers, with exports growing from $2 million to $20 million between 1948 and 1952.

1955

Ecuadorian officials seize two US fishing boats, charging them with fishing inside Ecuador's 200-nautical-mile territory. It was the opening salvo in what was later known as 'the tuna wars.'

and in 1987 a disastrous earthquake wiped out about 40km of oil pipeline, severely damaging both the environment and the economy. The discovery of oil also opened up vast tracts of Ecuador's Amazon Basin to exploration, affecting both the rainforest and the local indigenous tribes – some of whom had never before encountered outsiders.

Ecuador continues to rely on oil as its economic mainstay, but reserves are not as large as had been anticipated. Over-reliance on oil revenues has also wreaked havoc on the economy when the world price of oil collapses (as it did most recently in 2008).

The granting of mining concessions to foreign companies (Japan, Canada, China and Chile) has brought much controversy in recent years, as these concessions have most often been granted without a public discussion period. Groups such as DECOIN have rallied against these concessions, made possible by a loophole in the constitution which allows the president to open park lands to development.

Tom Miller went to Ecuador in the early 1980s to explore the origins of the nation's most famous export. *The Panama Hat Trail* is a funny investigation into a product which ended up being named for a different country entirely, but it also explores the general challenges of bathrooms and buses in a foreign land.

Return to Democracy

The 1980s and early '90s were a continuing struggle between conservatives and liberals, with corruption scandals weakening public confidence in the ruling elites. The contenders in the 1996 election were two firebrand politicians from Guayaquil, both known for their brashness. The candidate who won, Abdala Bucaram, was nicknamed 'El Loco' (The Madman) for his fiery, curse-laden style of oration and his penchant for performing at rock concerts as part of his campaign. Bucaram promised cheap public housing, lower prices for food staples and free medicine; but instead he promptly devalued Ecuador's currency, the sucre, and increased living costs, and was often spotted carousing in nightclubs by Quito residents.

Within a few months massive strikes led by trade unions and the Confederation of Indigenous Nationalities of Ecuador (CONAIE) paralyzed the country. Congress declared Bucaram 'mentally unfit' and terminated his presidency, and Bucaram fled to Panama.

After Bucaram was ousted, his vice president, Rosalía Arteaga, became Ecuador's first female president, albeit for fewer than two days. Congress voted overwhelmingly to replace her with Fabián Alarcón, the head of congress. He led the government until 1998, when *quiteño* Jamil Mahuad of the Popular Democracy party was elected president.

Mahuad had his political savvy put to the test. The effects of a nasty El Niño weather pattern and the sagging oil market of 1997–98 sent the economy into a tailspin in 1999, the same year that shrimp exports dropped by 80% following devastating shrimp diseases. When inflation topped 60% – making Ecuador's the worst in Latin America – the embattled president took drastic measures: he pinned Ecuador's economic

Former president Abdala Bucaram (aka 'The Madman') recorded a CD titled *El Loco Que Ama (Madman in Love)*. The 18-track album featured a photo of him on the cover in presidential sash, with his signature Chaplin-esque moustache.

1959

Ecuador designates the Galápagos Islands the country's first national park, protecting 97% of the archipelago as a reserve. In 1979 Unesco declares the islands a World Heritage Site.

1970s

Following the discovery of oil in the Oriente, Ecuador undergoes profound changes. The government budget, exports and per-capita income increase 500%, and a small middle-class begins to emerge.

1992

Thousands of indigenous protesters seeking land reform march in Quito on the 500th anniversary of Columbus' arrival. In ensuing negotiations they are granted title to 2.5 million acres in Amazonia.

1995

Ecuador and Peru have another short but intense border dispute that leaves 400 dead. A 1998 peace treaty resolves hostilities, with both sides dedicated to removing thousands of land mines.

survival on dollarization, a process whereby Ecuador's unstable national currency would be replaced by the US dollar.

Dollarization

John Perkin's *Confessions of an Economic Hitman* is an insider's exposé in which the author claims the US government played a key role in Ecuador's acceptance of huge development loans, and in ensuring the lucrative projects were contracted to US corporations.

Dollarization has been used successfully in a few other struggling countries, including nearby Panama (where the US dollar is called a balboa). But when President Mahuad declared his plan to dump the national currency, the country erupted in strikes, protests and road closures. On January 21, 2000, marches shut down the capital, and protesters took over the legislative palace, forcing Mahuad to resign.

The protesters were led by Antonio Vargas, Colonel Lucio Gutiérrez and former supreme court president Carlos Solorzano, who then formed a brief ruling triumvirate. Two days later – and largely due to the international pressure that followed Latin America's first military coup in two decades – the triumvirate turned the presidency over to Vice President Gustavo Noboa.

Noboa went ahead with dollarization, and in September 2000 the US dollar became the official currency. Although only one year earlier 6000 sucres bought one dollar, people were forced to exchange their sucres at the dramatically inflated year 2000 rate of 25,000 to $1. Their losses were severe.

The 21st Century

Along with dollarizing the economy, Noboa also implemented austerity measures to obtain $2 billion in aid from the International Monetary Fund (IMF) and other international lenders. At the end of 2000, gas and cooking-fuel prices sky-rocketed (largely because of dollarization) and the new year saw frequent strikes and protests by unions and indigenous groups. The economy finally stabilized, and Noboa left office on somewhat favorable terms.

O Hugo Benavides' *Making Ecuadorian Histories: Four Centuries of Defining Power* is an excellent if scholarly exploration of nation-building, gender, race and sexuality as it relates to the corridors of power inside Ecuador.

After Noboa, former coup leader Lucio Gutiérrez, elected president in 2002, promised a populist agenda but instead implemented IMF austerity measures to finance the country's massive debt. Protests erupted in the capital, and in 2005 congress voted overwhelmingly to remove Gutiérrez (the third Ecuadorian president ousted in eight years), replacing him with Vice President Alfredo Palacio.

A political newcomer who referred to himself as a 'simple doctor,' Palacio soon turned his attention to the social problems his predecessor had abandoned. In order to fund health and education programs and kick-start the economy, Palacio announced he would redirect oil profits earmarked for paying the foreign debt. An essential partner in this endeavor was Rafael Correa, a US-educated economist, whom Palacio appointed as his finance minister and who later carried out even more

2000

Facing spiraling inflation and contracting GDP, Ecuador dumps the sucre (the national currency) for the US dollar. The economy makes a modest recovery, although many Ecuadorians slip into poverty.

2008

In a nationwide referendum, Ecuadorians approve a new constitution, which expands the president's powers while increasing spending on social welfare and enshrining rights for indigenous people and the environment.

2010

A new law increases government control over Ecuador's oil industry. It stipulates that Ecuador will own 100% of all oil and gas produced in the country.

2011

Following an 18-year court case, the US oil giant Chevron is ordered to pay $18 billion to clean up decades of petro-contamination in the northeast Oriente. Chevron appealed, and in 2017 the decision was reversed.

aggressive social reforms – while also consolidating power – after becoming president in 2006.

Correa described himself as a humanist, a fervent Catholic of the left and a proponent of 21st-century socialism. After taking the reins, he ushered in a series of large-scale changes. A new constitution in 2008, approved by referendum, laid the groundwork for a new social archetype that increased spending on healthcare and the poor, gave more rights to indigenous groups, accorded new protections to the environment and even allowed civil unions for gay couples.

One of Correa's biggest targets was the oil industry: he called for increased taxes on oil revenue to be spent on the Ecuadorian poor, and accused foreign oil companies operating in Ecuador of failing to meet current environmental regulations. He also criticized his predecessor Mahuad for adopting the US dollar as the national currency, and suggested Ecuador would return to the sucre when economically feasible. More recently Correa focused on creating a digital currency, but few entered the market. Supporters applauded Correa's attention to the poor and his focus on economic reform.

Meanwhile, critics described Correa as an aspiring version of the late Hugo Chávez, Venezuela's controversial left-wing president, who nationalized major industries such as telecommunications, and attempted to stay president in perpetuity (following a Venezuelan referendum removing term limits for public officials). Others said he was reneging on his promises to protect the environment, particularly when drilling for oil began in 2016 in Parque Nacional Yasuní, a region of staggering biodiversity in the Amazon.

Lenín Moreno, formerly Correa's vice president, was elected in May 2017. In an historic moment, Moreno became the only global head of state in a wheelchair, having been paralyzed in an armed robbery in 1998. He had done much for the disabled in Ecuador during his time as vice president, increasing spending on disabled services 50-fold, and was even nominated for the Nobel Prize in 2012.

Science and history buffs and those after a good (real-life) adventure story should check out Larrie D Ferreiro's *Measure of the Earth: The Enlightenment Expedition That Reshaped Our World* (2011). It describes the fascinating 18th-century European scientific expedition to Quito to determine the true shape of our planet.

2014

Permits are granted to allow drilling for oil in Yasuni National Park. New roads, development and the danger of oil spills bring grave threats to this biologically rich reserve.

2014

After spending more than $280 million, Ecuador rebuilds its rail network and begins running tourist-oriented passenger trains along spectacular routes between Quito and Guayaquil.

2016

A devastating 7.8 magnitude earthquake rocks the Pacific coast of the nation, resulting in widespread destruction, nearly 700 deaths, and thousands of injuries.

2017

Lenín Boltaire Moreno, former vice president, is elected president in a runoff with Guillermo Lasso. Moreno became the only current global head of state in a wheelchair, having been paralyzed in a shooting in 1998.

Indigenous Ecuador

Ecuador's diverse indigenous population is made up of nearly four million people, roughly 25% of Ecuadorians (another 65% of the population are mestizos, with mixed indigenous and European ancestry). There are more than a dozen distinct groups in Ecuador, speaking some 20 different languages. Historically, Ecuador's native peoples suffered heavy discrimination and abuse from early Europeans, and today's groups face equally daunting challenges – particularly from the loss of lands owing to deforestation.

Present-Day Challenges

Ecuador's indigenous people have suffered from centuries of discrimination and remain at the bottom of the country's highly stratified social-class structure. It's a well-known truth that if you're indigenous in Ecuador, you're more likely to be poor, have fewer years of education and have less access to basic healthcare. According to a report by the World Bank, poverty among Ecuadorian indigenous people is about 87% and reaches 96% in the rural highlands. To make matters worse, oil drilling, mining and logging has led to the widespread displacement of indigenous groups or to the polluting of their natural environment – the $18 billion lawsuit against Texaco (which is now owned by Chevron) for the heavy petro-contamination of the Amazon is but one high-profile example.

For insights into the customs and cosmology of the Shuar, read *Spirit of the Shuar* (2001) by John Perkins and Shakaim Chumpi. Through interviews with members of the Amazonian tribe, Perkins explores Shuar warrior culture, healing and sexual practices, spiritual beliefs and challenges in the face of ever-encroaching development.

Despite enormous hardships, indigenous people have made some strides on the political front. Through marches and popular uprisings, the Confederation of Indigenous Nationalities of Ecuador (CONAIE) has lobbied for greater autonomy and land reform – protesting, in particular, the expropriation of indigenous lands to multinational companies. Since its founding in the 1980s, CONAIE's political power has grown, and the government has made a few concessions – granting 16,000 sq km of land to indigenous groups in 1992 and giving them greater autonomy and recognition in the new constitution, drafted in 2008.

Kichwa

The country's largest indigenous ethnic group, the Kichwa number well over two million. They live in both the Sierra and the Amazon, and vary considerably in customs and lifestyles. Those in the mountains subsist on small plots of farmland, raising sheep and cattle, and their fine textiles and weavings are an essential source of income.

One of the best-known groups within the Kichwa community are the *otavaleños*. Like other indigenous groups, they have a unique dress that sets them apart from other groups. For men, this consists of a blue poncho, a fedora, white calf-length socks, and a *shimba* (a long braid that hangs down nearly to the waist). Wearing the hair in this fashion probably dates back to pre-Inca times, and is an established and deeply rooted tradition. The women's dress may be the closest to Inca costume worn anywhere in the Andes. White blouses, blue skirts, shawls and jewelry are all ways of outwardly expressing their ethnicity.

LOVE & WAR AMONG THE SHUAR

One of the most studied Amazonian groups, the Shuar were once feared as 'headhunters' and had a reputation for being fierce warriors – in fact, they were never conquered by the Spanish. Up until the mid-20th century they were famous for the elaborate process of *tzantza,* shrinking the heads of slain opponents. Shuar believed the *muisak* (soul) of the victim remained inside the head and that keeping the *tzantza* would bring the warrior good fortune and please the spirits of his ancestors.

Shuar men take one or two wives, and girls are often married between the ages of 12 and 14. Unlike in some other societies, women are given autonomy in the marriage; those that are dissatisfied with their husbands can leave and return to their families. The men, however, cannot abandon their wives (those that run off will be brought back by the wife's family!). Outside marriage, some Shuar take lovers, which may or may not be tolerated by the spouse. Older wives sometimes take it upon themselves to teach young unmarried men the arts of lovemaking, and having multiple partners is not necessarily frowned upon. Nevertheless, misunderstandings are not uncommon, and bloody, long-standing family feuds have sometimes resulted from such infidelities.

Huaoranis

Short in stature (men average 1.5m or about 5ft tall), the Huaoranis are an Amazonian tribe living between the Río Napo and the Río Curaray in the Oriente. They number no more than 4000 and remain one of Ecuador's most isolated indigenous groups. They have a reputation for being warriors, defending their territory against outsiders – whether rival tribes or oil developers. They have a complex cosmology – making no distinction between the physical and spiritual worlds – and an intimate understanding of the rainforest in cultivating medicine, poisons for defense and hallucinogens for spiritual rites. Some still refer to them as the Aucas, meaning 'savage' in Kichwa, which the Huaoranis find extremely offensive.

One of the more unusual Amazonian leaders is the 50-something 'Gringo Chief' Randy Borman. Born to American missionaries living in the Amazon, he has become one of the Cofán's most influential chiefs. He speaks flawless Cofán and has helped the tribe win major land concessions. You can read his blog at www.cofan.org.

Shuar

Until the 1950s the Shuar, from the Amazonian lowlands, were a society of male hunters and female gardeners. To preserve their culture and lands, the Shuar (who today number 40,000) formed the first ethnic federation in Ecuadorian Amazonia in 1964. Traditionally, they were seminomadic, practicing small-scale slash-and-burn agriculture, planting crops (such as yuca and sweet potato) and moving on before the soil was depleted. Like other Amazonian groups, Shuar shamans administer *ayahuasca,* a psychoactive infusion, to reach higher planes of consciousness in spiritual practices.

Chachi

The Chachi originally lived in Ecuador's highlands, but fled to the Pacific coast (in present-day Esmeraldas province) in the wake of Inca and Spanish conquests. With a population of around 4000, they live in homes made of palm fronds, travel by canoe through a watery landscape and cultivate cocoa and tropical fruits. They are highly skilled artisans, particularly known for their hammocks.

Cofán

Straddling the Ecuador-Colombia border in the northeast, the Cofán number about 1200, half of whom live in Ecuador. Like other Amazonian groups they have seen a significant loss and degradation of their environment, largely due to oil drilling. However, in recent years they have waged a successful campaign for land rights, and are presently in control of 4000 sq km of rainforest (a seemingly broad expanse, but only a fraction of the 30,000 sq km originally belonging to the group).

Arts & Music

Poncho-wearing, flute-playing Andean groups are a staple in nearly every large city across the globe. The musical and artistic traditions of this culturally rich nation, however, are far more complex. You'll find stunning colonial architecture, powerful artworks by celebrated Ecuadorian painters and rich folkloric song traditions that tap into the nation's African and indigenous roots.

Architecture

When it comes to colonial architecture, two cities stand high above the rest: Quito and Cuenca. Both have historical centers so stunning they've been declared Unesco World Heritage Sites (Quito in 1978 and Cuenca in 1999). Quito's churches are some of the richest, most spectacular colonial buildings in all of South America. Bearing testament to the fact that Spain was under the rule of the Moors for centuries, many of Quito's churches have striking Moorish (Arabic) influences known as mudéjar.

Many of Quito's churches were built atop sacred indigenous sights, adding yet another layer to the cultural mix. The overall appearance of the city's colonial churches is overpoweringly ornamental and almost cloyingly opulent.

The biopic *Julio Jaramillo: Ruisenor de America* (1996) does an excellent job of capturing the brilliance and decadence of the Latin American music legend. Throughout a 20-plus-year career, he recorded over 4000 songs, living an alcohol-fueled bohemian life and leaving behind a string of lovers (and dozens of illegitimate children).

Painting & Sculpture

Ecuador's most significant artistic contribution is the Quito School of Art, which reached its zenith between 1600 and 1765. The Quito School died out following independence, largely because the style was associated with the Spanish regime. The 19th century brought the Republican period, during which favorite subjects were heroes of the revolution, florid landscapes and important members of the new republic's high society.

The 20th century saw the rise of the *indigenista* (indigenous-led) movement, whose unifying theme was the oppression and burdens of Ecuador's indigenous inhabitants. The pioneer of the *indigenista* movement was Camilo Egas (1899–1962), who, along with painter Eduardo Kingman (1913–98), placed Ecuadorian modern art on the international map. The country's most famous *indigenista* painter, however, is Oswaldo Guayasamín (1919–99), whose evocative and haunting works tackle such themes as torture, poverty and loss. His pieces hang in galleries all over the world, although the best place to see his work is in Quito.

No discussion of Ecuadorian painting is complete without mentioning *tigua*, an intricate, colorful painting style generally depicting Andean indigenous groups. The art form's major progenitor is the internationally known Alfredo Toaquiza.

Literature

Ecuador has several notable literary figures, although none have become household names outside the country. Juan Montalvo (1832–89) was a prolific essayist from Ambato who frequently attacked the dictatorial political figures of his time. His best-known work is the book *Siete tratados* (*Seven Treatises*; 1882), which includes a comparison between Simón

Bolívar and George Washington. Juan León Mera (1832–94), also from Ambato, is famous for his novel *Cumandá* (1891), which describes indigenous life in the 19th century.

Perhaps the most notable Ecuadorian writer of the 20th century is *quiteño* Jorge Icaza (1906–79), who was profoundly influenced by the *indigenista* movement. His most famous novel, *Huasipungo* (1934; translated as *The Villagers* in 1973) is a brutal story about indigenous Ecuadorians, the seizure of their land and the savage massacre of those who protested.

A good introduction to Ecuadorian literature is *Diez cuentistas ecuatorianos* (1990), an anthology of short stories by 10 Ecuadorian writers born in the 1940s. The stories are written in Spanish with English translations.

Música Folklórica

One of the most recognizable tunes of traditional Andean *música folklórica* (folk music) is Simon and Garfunkel's version of 'El Cóndor Pasa (If I Could)'. This was already a classic Andean tune (written by Peruvian composer Daniel Alomía Robles in 1913) before the popular duo got their hands on it.

Andean songs like this one typically have a breathy, mournful quality courtesy of the panpipes – which in Ecuador is known as the *rondador,* a single row of bamboo pipes in a pentatonic (five-note) scale. It's considered Ecuador's national instrument and varies from other Andean instruments such as the *zampoña* (two rows of cane pipes, originating in the highlands area around Lake Titicaca) and the *quena* and *pingullo* (large and small bamboo flutes). Other traditional instruments include the *charango,* a mandolin-like instrument with 10 strings and a sounding box that was originally made with an armadillo shell.

Pasillo

Although most people associate Ecuador with *folklórica,* the country's most popular national music is *pasillo,* which is rooted in the waltz. *Pasillo's* origins date back to the 19th century when Ecuador (along with Colombia, Venezuela and Panama) was part of Gran Colombia. These poignant songs with their melancholic melodies often touch on themes of disillusionment, lost love and unquenchable longing for the past. Less commonly, the lyrics celebrate the beauty of the Ecuadorian landscape (or its women), the valor of its men (indeed, *pasillo* was popular during the Ecuadorian War of Independence) or the charm of its towns and cities.

THE QUITO SCHOOL OF ART

The beauty of the Escuela Quiteña lies in its fascinating blend of indigenous concepts and styles and European art forms. The beliefs and artistic heritages of the artisans crept into their work. If you look closely at paintings in Quito's many religious museums and churches, you'll see a lot of non-European themes: Christ eating a plate of *cuy* (roast guinea pig), or the 12 apostles dining on *humitas* (a type of corn dumpling). Religious figures are often depicted with darker skin or stouter builds that reflect indigenous Ecuadorian body types. Inside churches, sun motifs and planetary symbols appear on ceilings that are decorated in what appear to be Moorish patterns.

The Escuela Quiteña became renowned for its mastery of the realistic. By the 18th century, artisans were using glass eyes and real hair and eyelashes in their sculptures. They added moving joints, inserted tiny mirrors into mouths to mimic saliva, and their accomplished polychrome painting (the use of multiple colors) became famous. Some sculptures, particularly those of the 18th-century carver Manuel Chili (nicknamed 'Caspicara'), are so realistic they almost seem to be alive. Notable painters of the Escuela Quiteña include Miguel de Santiago (whose huge canvases grace the walls of Quito's Monastery of San Agustín), Manuel Samaniego, Nicolás Goríbar and Bernardo Rodríguez. Caspicara's work can be seen in Quito's Monastery of San Francisco.

Pasillo's most famous voice was that of Julio Jaramillo, known affectionately as 'JJ' (pronounced 'jota jota' in Spanish). Born in 1935, this handsome singer from Guayaquil popularized the genre throughout Latin America with his lyrical songs. Unfortunately, hard living led to his early death (from cirrhosis of the liver) at the age of 42. At the time of his death, he had become a legend, and some 250,000 mourners came out for his funeral.

Afro-Ecuadorian Music

Northwest Ecuador, particularly Esmeraldas province, is the heart of the country's Afro-Ecuadorian population. Here – and in Afro-Colombian communities of neighboring Colombia – you can find musical traditions quite distinct from those in other parts of Ecuador.

The iconic instrument here is the marimba (a percussion instrument laid out like a xylophone but with wooden bars), which produces a range of bright but mellow sounds. It's accompanied by the conga-drum-like *cunuco,* the bigger bomba (large sheepskin drum) and the maraca-like guasá. Big West African–style beats back the simple choral arrangements; traditional dances like the stylized bambuco sometimes accompany the music.

In addition to the north coast, in the Chota Valley there's also an Afro-Ecuadorian community, the only population of its kind found anywhere in the highlands. The music there blends more indigenous elements (including pan flutes) to African rhythms and is called *bomba,* named after the large drum that lays down the heavy beats.

Among the more popular Afro-Ecuadorian music and dance groups is Azúcar, which is named in honor of the group's early ancestors, who labored on sugarcane plantations. The outstanding Esmeraldas-based Grupo Bambuco add a horn section to the driving, highly danceable beats.

Top Songs

- 'A Mi Lindo Ecuador' – Pueblo Nuevo
- 'Algo Así' – Fausto Miño
- 'Andarele' – Grupo Bambuco
- 'Ayayay!' – Tomback
- 'Caderona' – Papá Rincón
- 'Codominio de Cartón' – Rocola Bacalao
- 'De Mis Manos' – Manolo Criollo
- 'Homenaje a Mis Viejos' – Raíces Negras
- 'Entiendo Lo Que Hice Para Ti' – Fausto Miño

Other Styles

Musical hybrids have flourished in Ecuador over the last 200 years, creating new genres from traditional Spanish styles shaped by indigenous influences.

The *sanjuanito* (which means 'little St John') is a joyful dance and music style (though it too has melancholic undertones) with traditional Andean rhythms and instrumentation. Its origin dates back to religious celebrations held on June 24 – an important day to both Catholics (St John's Day) and the indigenous (Inti Raymi or the Inca Festival of the Sun).

Born in the early 20th century, the *pasacalle* is a distant relative of the Spanish *pasodoble,* the march-like music typically played at bullfights. The Ecuadorian variant is equally fast-paced with dramatic elements and a clean 2/4 beat.

If there's one inescapable music in this Andean country, it's *cumbia,* whose rhythm resembles that of a trotting three-legged horse. Originally from Colombia, Ecuadorian *cumbia* has a rawer (almost amateur), melancholic sound, and is dominated by the electronic keyboard. Bus drivers love the stuff, perhaps because it so strangely complements those backroad journeys through the Andes (and hopefully it keeps them awake at the wheel).

The Natural World

Despite its diminutive size, Ecuador has some of the world's most varied geography. Crammed into a nation roughly the size of the UK, you'll find Andean peaks, Amazonian rainforest and misty cloud forests – not to mention those spectacular volcanic islands 1000km offshore. Among such diverse landscapes, Ecuador harbors an extraordinary variety of wildlife. From the tiny American pygmy kingfisher to the regal jaguar, Ecuador is home to a jaw-dropping menagerie of creatures great and small.

The Land

Ecuador straddles the equator on the Pacific coast of South America, and is bordered by Colombia to the north and Peru to the south and east. The country can be divided into three regions: the Andes form the backbone of Ecuador; the coastal lowlands lie west of the mountains; and the Oriente, to the east, comprises the jungles of the upper Amazon Basin.

In only 200km as the condor flies, you can climb from the coast to snowcaps and then descend to the jungle on the country's eastern side. The Galápagos Islands lie on the equator, 1000km west of Ecuador's coast, and constitute one of the country's 21 provinces.

The Andes (known in Ecuador as the highlands) stretch high above the landscape, with Volcán Chimborazo, Ecuador's highest peak, topping out at 6310m. The central highlands contain two parallel volcanic mountain ranges, each about 400km long. The valley nestled between them was appropriately dubbed 'the Avenue of the Volcanoes' by the German explorer Alexander von Humboldt, who visited the country in 1802. Quito lies within this valley and, at 2850m, is the world's second-highest national capital, second only to La Paz in Bolivia. The central highlands are also home to countless towns and tiny villages well known for their indigenous markets and fiestas. This region has the highest population density in the country.

The Doldrums was the name sailors gave to the windless belt around the equator. It is caused by intense heating along the equator, causing air to rise rather than blow, spelling disaster for sailing ships. The word later entered common usage to mean a period of boredom, inactivity or despondency.

The western coastal lowlands were once heavily forested, but encroaching agriculture has meant the replacement of forest with fruit plantations and the clear-cutting of mangroves for shrimp farming. The beaches are blessed with warm water year-round and provide decent surfing, but are not as pretty as the beaches of the Caribbean.

The eastern lowlands of the Oriente still retain much of their virgin rainforest, but colonization and oil drilling have damaged this delicate habitat. The population of the Oriente has more than tripled since the late 1970s.

Wildlife

Ecologists have labeled Ecuador one of the world's 'megadiversity hotspots.' The tiny nation is one of the most species-rich countries on the planet. Ecuador's astounding biodiversity is due to the great number of habitats within its borders, with dramatically different fauna in the Andes, the tropical rainforests, the coastal regions and the numerous transitional zones. The result is a wealth of habitats, ecosystems and wildlife.

Birds

Bird-watchers from all over the world flock to Ecuador for one simple reason: the country is home to more than 1600 bird species – twice the number found in the continents of Europe and North America combined (and fourth, in number, in the world, behind Brazil, Colombia, and Peru). It's impossible to give a precise number because formerly unobserved species are often reported, and very occasionally a new species is discovered – an incredibly rare event in the world of birds.

Bird-watching is outstanding year-round and every part of the country offers unique habitats. Mindo remains a favorite and often records the most species during Audubon's annual 'Christmas Count.' A local favorite there is the Andean Cock-of-the-Rock, which makes both stunning visual and vocal displays.

Hummingbirds beat their wings up to 80 times per second in a figure-eight pattern that allows them to hover in place or even to fly backward.

For many visitors, the diminutive hummingbirds found throughout Ecuador are the most delightful birds to observe. Around 130 species have been recorded in Ecuador, and their exquisite beauty is matched by extravagant names such as green-tailed goldenthroat, spangled coquette, fawn-breasted brilliant and amethyst-throated sunangel.

Mammals

Some 300 species of mammals have been recorded in Ecuador. These range from monkeys in the Amazonian lowlands to the rare Andean spectacled bear in the highlands.

For many, the most amusing mammals to spy upon are monkeys. Ecuadorian species include howler monkeys, spider monkeys, woolly monkeys, titi monkeys, capuchin monkeys, squirrel monkeys, tamarins and marmosets. The best places to see them in their natural habitat include

FINE & FEATHERED: ECUADOR'S GREATS

Ecuador's unique and diverse habitats are home to a wondrous variety of bird species both great and small. A few perennial favorites include the following:

Andean Condor Ecuador's emblematic bird with its 3m wingspan is one of the largest flying birds in the world. In 1880 the British mountaineer Edward Whymper noted that he commonly saw a dozen condors on the wing at the same time. Today there are only a few hundred pairs left in the Ecuadorian highlands, so sighting one is a thrilling experience.

Scarlet Macaws These brilliantly colored birds, with blue, red and yellow feathers, are a magnificent sight and one of more than 40 parrot species found in Ecuador. They often travel in pairs and have lifespans of 40-plus years.

Harpy Eagle One of the world's largest birds of prey, with a wingspan of up to 2m and weighing up to 10kg, this apex predator has powerful claws capable of carrying off coatis, sloths, monkeys and other tree-dwelling mammals.

Plate-Billed Mountain Toucans Among the best-known Latin American birds, toucans have huge (but mostly hollow) beaks perfectly suited for nibbling ripe fruit off the ends of branches. This particular species, with its black and ivory bill, is found on the west Andean slopes and makes quite a racket with loud vocalizations heard up to 1km away.

American Pygmy Kingfisher Weighing just 18 grams and topping out around 12cm, this diminutive bird has a classic kingfisher appearance (long bill and short tail), but is often mistaken for a hummingbird as it flits past.

Andean Cock-of-the-Rock A must-see on many birders' life lists, this red-headed, parrot-sized bird is a visual and vocal star, with more than 20 known songs (most quite loud) and striking plumage. Males gather in 'leks' of 10 to 20 individuals in order to wow potential mates – good guides will know where to find them.

Reserva Producción Faunística Cuyabeno, Parque Nacional Yasuní in the Amazonian lowlands, and the rarely visited lowlands sector of Reserva Ecológica Cotacachi-Cayapas, near the coast. A group of marvelously mischievous capuchin monkeys has taken over the central plaza in the Oriente town of Misahuallí, where you're guaranteed an up-close (and sometimes too personal) experience. In the Oriente you may hear howler monkeys well before you see them; the males' eerie roars carry great distances and can sound like anything from a baby crying to wind moaning through the trees.

In two excellent (but cumbersome) volumes, *The Birds of Ecuador*, by Robert Ridgely and Paul Greenfield, is the most authoritative bird-watching tome available. A more practical field guide is the (much smaller) *Fieldbook of the Birds of Ecuador*, by Miles McMullan and Lelis Navarrete.

Other tropical specialties include two species of sloth: the diurnal three-toed sloth and the nocturnal two-toed sloth. It's very possible to spot the former while hiking in the Amazon. They are usually found hanging motionless from tree limbs or progressing at a painfully slow speed along a branch toward a particularly succulent bunch of leaves, which are their primary food source.

There are far fewer species of mammals in the highlands than in the lowlands, but they include commonly seen deer and rabbits and the more rarely sighted Andean fox. One of the icons of the Andes is the llama, which is domesticated and used primarily as a pack animal. Its wild relative, the lovely vicuña, has been reintroduced to the Chimborazo area – you're almost guaranteed to see them as you drive, bus or walk through the park.

Other possible mammal sightings include anteaters, armadillos, agoutis (large rodents), capybaras (even larger rodents, some weighing up to 65kg), peccaries (wild pigs) and otters. River dolphins are occasionally sighted in Amazonian tributaries.

Other exotic mammals, such as ocelots, jaguars, tapirs, pumas and the Andean spectacled bear, are very rarely seen. The first recorded *olinguito*, a racoon-like mammal new to scientific observers, was recorded at Bellavista Lodge, between Quito and Mindo, in 2013. It was the first new mammal 'discovered' in 35 years.

Amphibians & Reptiles

The majority of Ecuador's approximately 460 species of amphibians are frogs. There are tree frogs that spend their entire lives in trees and lay their eggs in water trapped inside bromeliads (a type of epiphytic plant). The ominously named poison-dart frog is among the most brightly colored species of frogs anywhere. Its colors run the spectrum from bright red-orange with jet-black spots to neon green with black wavy lines. Some poison-dart frogs have skin glands exuding toxins that can cause paralysis and death in animals and humans.

No one knows for sure why the sloth engages in its fastidious toilet habits: climbing down its tree once a week, digging a hole into which it will defecate and then covering it afterwards. This exposes the sloth to predators, though the tree surely appreciates the nutrient-rich deposit!

Two new frog species in the past decade have made a case for further investigation into the Intag Valley: the Prince Charles Stream Tree Frog and the Longnose Harlequin Frog, a beauty in yellow-and-black. Meanwhile, Reserva Jama-Coaque, near Canoa, has reported more than 40 new frog species since 2009. There's much to be discovered yet, apparently.

Of Ecuador's reptiles, four really make an impression on visitors. Three of them – the land tortoise, the land iguana and the marine iguana – live in the Galápagos and are easy to see. The fourth is the caiman, which inhabits lagoons in the Oriente. With a little patience and a good canoe guide, you'll spot these spooky creatures as well.

Snakes, which are much talked about but seldom seen, make up a large portion of Ecuador's reptiles. They usually slither away into the undergrowth at the sound of approaching humans, so only a few fortunate visitors get to see them. Perhaps Ecuador's most feared snake is the fer-de-lance, which is extremely poisonous. Visitors are rarely bitten,

UNSEEN BOUNTY OF THE RAINFOREST

Home to poisonous snakes, toxic plants and flesh-eating fish (not to mention predatorial caiman and jaguars), the Amazon rainforest may not seem like the world's most inviting habitat. But for the indigenous people who have always lived there, the rainforest has everything needed for survival; it functions as their supermarket, pharmacy, hardware store and cathedral.

For those of us that couldn't imagine living without Western medicine, it's perhaps most fascinating to read about life in the Oriente, where village shamans still serve as healers, harnessing the powerful extractions of the rainforest for all manner of ailments. There are remedies for headaches, fevers, insect bites, constipation, muscular aches, nervous disorders, diarrhea, asthma, epilepsy, ulcers and intestinal parasites – and plants are even used as contraceptives. In addition to medicinal use, rainforest plants and animals serve many other purposes. The tiny but extremely lethal poison-dart frogs – one of which has enough toxicity to kill about a dozen humans – play a key role in hunting; the psychotropic plant *ayahuasca* is a powerful hallucinogen used in spiritual ceremonies.

but it is wise to take precautions. If you do see a snake, keep a respectful distance and avoid provoking it.

Habitats

Some 25,000 species of vascular plants reside in Ecuador's diverse habitats (compared to 17,000 species in North America), and new species are being discovered every year. Cloud forests, rainforests, *páramo* (high-altitude Andean grasslands) and mangrove swamps all set the stage for discovering Ecuador's photogenic natural wonders.

Rainforests

The Oriente is Ecuador's slice of the Amazon, the greatest rainforest habitat in the world. It is home to an astounding variety of plants and animals, located in much denser concentrations than in temperate forests.

The largest ant in the South American rainforest is the Conga or 'bullet' ant, so nicknamed because its extremely painful sting is likened to being shot. The paralyzing neurotoxic venom produces severe pain that can last up to 24 hours.

Lianas (thick dangling vines) hang from high up in the canopy, and the massive roots of strangler figs engulf other trees, slowly choking them of light and life. Spread across the forest floor are the buttressed roots of tropical hardwoods, which are sometimes so massive you can just about disappear inside their weblike supports. Equally impressive are the forest's giant leaves, which are thick and waxy and have pointed 'drip tips,' which facilitate water runoff during downpours.

Much of the rainforest's plant and animal life is up in the canopy rather than on the forest floor, which can appear surprisingly empty to the first-time visitor. If you're staying in a jungle lodge, find out if it has a canopy tower; climbing above the treetops provides spectacular views.

Tropical Cloud Forests

One of Ecuador's most enchanting habitats is the tropical cloud forest *(bosque nebludo)*. These moist environments are found at higher elevations and earn their name from the clouds they trap (and help create), which drench the forest in a fine mist. This continual moisture allows particularly delicate forms of plant life to survive. Dense, small-leaved canopies and moss-covered branches set the scene for a host of plant life within, including orchids, ferns and bromeliads. The dense vegetation at all levels of this forest gives it a mysterious and delicate fairy-tale appearance. Some people find it even more beautiful than the rainforest since many of the plants grow closer to the forest floor. This creates a far more luxuriant environment where the diverse fauna thrives – and remains easier to spot.

Páramo

Above the cloud forests lie the Andes' high-altitude grasslands and scrublands, known as the *páramo*. The *páramo* is characterized by a harsh climate, high levels of ultraviolet light and wet, peaty soils. It is an extremely specialized habitat unique to the neotropics (tropical America) and is found only in the area between the highlands of Costa Rica and northern Peru.

The *páramo* is dominated by cushion plants, hard grasses and small herbaceous plants that have adapted well to the harsh highland environment. Most plants up here are small and compact and grow close to the ground. An exception is the giant *Espeletia,* one of the *páramo*'s strangest sights. These bizarre-looking plants stand as high as a person, and have earned the local nickname *frailejones* (gray friars). They are an unmistakable feature of the northern Ecuadorian *páramo,* particularly in the El Ángel region, high above Ibarra.

The *páramo* is also characterized by dense thickets of small trees, often of the *Polylepis* species that, along with Himalayan pines, are the highest-growing trees in the world. They were once extensive, but fire and grazing have pushed them back into small pockets.

NATIONAL PARKS

NAME OF PARK	FEATURES	ACTIVITIES	BEST TIME TO VISIT
Cajas (p377)	*páramo,* lakes, small *Polylepis,* forests	hiking, fishing, bird-watching	year-round
Cayambe-Coca (p377)	*páramo,* lakes, cloud forest, hot springs, Andean condors, tapirs, indigenous communities	hiking, hot springs, camping	year-round
Cotopaxi (p377)	*páramo,* Volcán Cotopaxi, Andean condors, deer, rabbits	hiking, climbing	year-round
Galápagos (p377)	volcanically formed islands, seabirds, iguanas, turtles, rich underwater life	wildlife-watching, snorkeling, diving	Nov–Jun
Llanganates (p377)	*páramo,* cloud forest, lowland forest, deer, tapirs, jaguars, spectacled bears	hiking	year-round (access difficult)
Machalilla (p377)	coastal dry forest, beaches, islands, whales, seabirds, monkeys, reptiles	hiking, wildlife-watching	year-round
Podocarpus (p377)	*páramo,* cloud forest, tropical humid forest, spectacled bears, tapirs, deer, birds	hiking, bird-watching	year-round
Sumaco-Galeras (p377)	Volcán Sumaco, subtropical forest, cloud forest	off-trail hiking	year-round (access difficult)
Sangay (p377)	volcanoes, *páramo,* cloud forest, lowland forest, spectacled bears, tapirs, pumas, ocelots	hiking, climbing	year-round
Yacuri	evergreen forest, high plains, cloud forest, lakes, spectacled bears, tapirs	hiking, climbing	year-round
Yasuní (p377)	rainforest, rivers, lagoons, monkeys, birds, sloths, jaguars, pumas, tapirs	hiking, wildlife-watching	year-round

Mangrove Swamps

Mangroves are trees that have evolved with the remarkable ability to grow in salt water. The red mangrove is the most common in Ecuador, and like other mangroves it has a broadly spreading system of intertwining stilt roots to support the tree in the unstable soils of the shoreline. These roots trap sediments and build up rich organic soil, which creates a protected habitat for many plants and fish, as well as mollusks, crustaceans and other invertebrates. The branches provide nesting areas for seabirds, such as pelicans and frigate birds. Extensive mangrove areas on Ecuador's coastline have been cleared for shrimp farms, and most are now found in the far northern and southern coastal regions. The tallest mangroves in the world are inside the Reserva Ecológica de Manglares Cayapas Mataje.

Caterpillars are masters of disguise, some mimicking twigs, others the head of a viper, even a pile of bird droppings – all in the name of defense.

Tropical Dry Forests

This fascinating habitat is fast disappearing and is found primarily in the hot coastal areas near Parque Nacional Machalilla and in southwest Loja Province en route to Macará. Its definitive plant species is the majestic bottle-trunk ceiba (also known as kapok), a glorious tree with a massively bulging trunk and seasonal white flowers that dangle like lightbulbs from the bare branches.

Regardless of your scientific background (or lack of it), the entertaining and highly readable classic *Tropical Nature*, by Adrian Forsyth and Kenneth Miyata, is an excellent read before or during any trip to the rainforest.

National Parks & Reserves

Ecuador has more than 30 government-protected parks and reserves (of which nine carry the title of 'national park') as well as numerous privately administered nature reserves. A total of 18% of the country lies within protected areas. Yet despite their protected status, many of these areas continue to be susceptible to oil drilling, logging, mining, ranching and colonization.

Many parks are inhabited by indigenous groups, whose connection to the area long precedes modern park or reserve status. In the case of the Oriente parks, the indigenous people maintain traditional hunting rights, which also affect the ecology. The question of how to protect the national parks from damage by heavy industry (oil, timber and mining) while recognizing the rights of indigenous peoples – all in the context of keeping the nation financially solvent – remains a hot-button topic in Ecuador.

Ecuadorian Cuisine

Ecuadorian cuisine benefits from the country's rich geographic diversity, with tropical fruits, fresh seafood and classic recipes from the *campo* (countryside) all contributing to the bounty of the Andean table. Many dishes have evolved over the years, blending Spanish and indigenous influences. And while it's little known outside the country's borders, Ecuadorian cooking offers some outstanding opportunities for food-minded adventures, with wildly different recipes and techniques varying from region to region.

Highland Hits

It's impossible to consider food from the highlands without discussing the once highly revered crop, *maíz* (corn). In its numerous varieties, corn has been the staple of the Andean diet for a millennium, and today it forms the basis of countless highland specialties. Kernels are toasted into *tostada* (toasted corn), popped into *cangil* (popcorn), boiled and treated to make *mote* (hominy) and milled into cornmeal. The latter is flavored or filled and wrapped in corn husks or dark green achira leaves and steamed. The results are some of the tastiest treats in the highlands, including *tamales* (similar to Mexican tamales), *humitas* (similar to tamales) and *quimbolitos* (sweeter, more cakelike corn dumplings).

Potatoes, of course, originated in the Andes, and are another important highland staple. Besides a vast array of tiny colorful potatoes, you'll find creations such as *llapingachos*, fried potato-and-cheese pancakes that are often served as a side dish with fried eggs. Quinoa is an extremely protein-rich grain that forms a staple of the highland indigenous diet and has made its way into contemporary dishes throughout Ecuador.

During the week leading up to Good Friday, Ecuadorians feast on a delicious and hearty soup called *fanesca*. The best *fanesca* is made with salt cod and at least a dozen types of grains and is quite labor intensive. Seek it out, if you're around then!

One of the highlands' most famous dishes is *cuy* (roasted guinea pig). *Cuy* is an indigenous specialty that dates back to Inca times and is supposedly high in protein and low in cholesterol. They're usually roasted whole on spits, and the sight of the little paws and teeth sticking out can be a bit unnerving, but for meat eaters it's well worth sampling. Cuenca and Loja are both good places to try it.

Another eye-catching specialty is whole roasted pig. Known as *hornado* (literally, 'roasted'), this is one of the highland's most popular dishes. In the markets, the juicy meat is pulled right off the golden-brown carcass when you order it. *Hornado* is almost as popular as *fritada*, fried chunks of pork that are almost invariably served with *mote*. Latacunga has a famous take on this dish known as the *chugchucara*, which makes for a great (if not terribly healthy) weekend feast.

An old Ecuadorian adage affirms that '*Amor sin besos es como chocolate sin queso*' (love without kisses is like chocolate without cheese). Based on the old Ecuadorian snack favorite.

As throughout Ecuador, soups are an important part of the highland diet and come in countless varieties, including *caldos* (brothy soups), *sopas* (thicker broth-based soups), *locros* (creamier and generally heartier soups), *sancochos* (stewlike soups) and *secos* (stews that are usually served over rice). *Seco de chivo* (goat stew) is an Ecuadorian classic that's popular across the country. If you're not keen on goat, look for *seco de pollo*, the same dish made with chicken. For a belly-warming treat on a misty highland day, try *locro de papas*, a smooth potato soup served with avocado and cheese.

BANANA REPUBLIC

Bananas play a vital role in Ecuador. They keep the economy humming along (Ecuador exports five million tons a year, making it the world's largest banana exporter), and provide the basis for countless recipes. Bananas are even a part of pop culture. In the coastal city of Machala, the biggest annual event is the Feira Mundial del Banana (World Banana Festival), which culminates in one lucky girl being crowned *reina del banano* (banana queen).

You'll come across bananas and plantains in many forms and shapes while traveling here, so keep an eye out for these popular dishes:

Chifles Dried, salted plantain chips; a great snack or accompaniment to soups and ceviches.

Empanadas de verde Pasties made from green plantain dough and often stuffed with cheese.

Majado de verde Mashed plantains, peppers and cheese, often topped with a fried egg. Popular at breakfast.

Patacones Thickly sliced, smashed green plantains fried into chewy fritters.

Bolones de verde Mashed and fried plantain balls often stuffed with cheese or meat.

Tigrillo A filling plantain mash served with eggs and cheese and often sausage or beef.

Coastal Cooking

The coast is where Ecuadorian food really shines. It's blessed with culinary riches, and it's easy to eat delicious, healthy food there. The cooking of the Manabí province in particular rates among the country's best, and it is a big reason so many Ecuadorian expats long for home.

The staple of coastal cuisine, of course, is seafood, with the great fruits of the sea arriving fresh from the fishing boat at ports across the country. The most widely found seafood dish is *corvina*, which literally means 'sea bass', but is usually just whatever white fish happens to be available that day. When it's really *corvina*, it's worth seeking out.

For mouth-watering Ecuadorian recipes and background on culinary traditions, check out the beautifully photographed site www.laylita.com, created by Vilcabamba native Layla Pujol. She lives in the Pacific Northwest of the US, but keeps Ecuador close to her heart (and stove).

Ceviche is superb in Ecuador. This delicious dish consists of uncooked seafood marinated in lemon juice and seasoned with thinly sliced onion and herbs. It's served cold and, on a hot afternoon, goes down divinely with popcorn and a cold beer. Ceviche is prepared with *pescado* (fish), *camarones* (shrimp), *calamares* (squid), *concha* (conch), *cangrejo* (crab) or some combination *(mixto)*. Only shrimp is cooked before being marinated.

Esmeraldas province, which has a large Afro-Ecuadorian population, is home to some delicious African-influenced specialties including the sublime *encocado*, shrimp or fish cooked in a rich, spiced coconut sauce. Guayas province, and especially the town of Playas, is famous for its crab, which is cooked whole and served in piles as big as your appetite, along with a wooden hammer for cracking open the shells. It's one of the most pleasurable (and messy!) culinary experiences in the country.

Plantains and bananas play a huge role in coastal cooking. One tasty and intriguing dish is *sopa de bolas de verde*, a thick peanut-based soup with seasoned, mashed-plantain balls floating in it. As you're busing along the northern coast, kids often board selling *corviche* (a delicious plantain dumpling stuffed with seafood or shrimp) from big baskets.

Seafood soups are often outstanding. One of the most popular (and cheap) is *encebollado*, a brothy fish and onion soup poured over yuca and served with *chifles* (fried banana chips) and popcorn. It's usually eaten in the morning or for an early lunch. Another fabulous soup is *sopa marinera*, a fine broth – which can range from clear to thick and peanuty – loaded with fish, shellfish, shrimp and sometimes crab.

Survival Guide

Directory A–Z

Accommodations

Ecuador has a wide range of accommodations, from wooden shacks in the mangroves to jungle lodges in the Amazon. There's no need to book ahead, apart from during major fiestas or before market days.

B&Bs A tried-and-true option in Ecuador.

Hotels From the more basic to luxury top-end options.

Hostels Limited hostels, though Quito is packed with them.

Lodges Immerse yourself in Ecuador's wildlife.

Haciendas & Hosterías Refurbished historic family ranches.

Homestays Allow travelers to interact with a local family.

Camping Allowed in much of the countryside.

B&Bs

Bed and breakfasts are especially popular in tourist destinations such as Quito, Baños, Cuenca and Otavalo. Once you're out in the countryside, there's a fine line between B&Bs and *hosterías* (small hotels).

Camping

Camping is allowed on the grounds of a few rural hotels, and in the countryside and most national parks. There are no campgrounds in towns. There are climbers' *refugios* (mountain refuges) on some of the major mountains, in some national parks, but you'll need to bring a sleeping bag.

Haciendas & Hosterías

The Ecuadorian highlands have some fabulous haciendas (historic family ranches that have been refurbished to accept tourists). They usually fall into the top-end price bracket, but the price may include home-cooked meals and activities such as horseback riding or fishing. The best-known haciendas are in the northern and central highlands.

Hosterías are similar, but are often smaller and more intimate. *Hosterías* regularly have rates that include full board and/or activities.

Homestays

Spanish-language schools can often arrange homestays, where you can stay overnight, eat meals and interact with a local family. Homestays are available in Quito and Cuenca, but are difficult to find elsewhere.

In some rural communities, where there are no hotels, you can ask around and often find a local family willing to let you spend the night. This happens only in the most off-the-beaten-track places, and you should always offer payment (although it may not be accepted).

Hotels

Budget hotels range from $10 to $40 per person and may be basic, with just a bed and four walls. They can nevertheless be well looked after, very clean and excellent value. The cheapest rooms have communal bathrooms, but you can often find deals with a private bathroom for not much more.

Midrange hotels run to about $40 to $90 for a double and usually offer greater charm and more amenities – cable TV, reliably hot water and a better location – than their budget cousins.

Top-end hotels are found in larger cities and resort areas. They generally offer a bit more luxury – spacious, design-strong or heritage rooms, great views, top-notch service and the like.

No matter where you stay, make sure to always peek at a room before committing.

BOOK YOUR STAY ONLINE

For more accommodations reviews by Lonely Planet authors, check out http://lonelyplanet.com/hotels/. You'll find independent reviews, as well as recommendations on the best places to stay. Best of all, you can book online.

Lodges

Ecolodges and jungle lodges provide a fantastic way to experience Ecuador's wildlife. Lodges are most popular in the Oriente and in the cloud forests of the western Andean slopes. The lodges in the Oriente are generally only available as part of a three- to five-day package, but this usually includes meals and activities. The lodge will arrange any river or jungle transportation, but you may have to get to the nearest departure town on your own.

Prices

Room rates are highest throughout Ecuador around Christmas and New Year's Eve, around Semana Santa (Easter week) and during July and August. They also peak during local fiestas. Hotels along the coast sometimes charge higher rates (and certainly draw bigger crowds) on weekends. Hotels are required to charge 12% sales tax (called IVA), though it's often already included in the quoted rate. Better hotels often tack on an additional 10% to 15% service charge, so be sure to check whether the rate you're quoted includes this.

Also look out for rates listed per person in many hotels.

Reservations

Most hotels accept reservations without a credit card number. If you haven't prepaid, however, always confirm your reservation if you're arriving late in the day, to avoid it being given to someone else or the reception closing and you struggling to get into your room. Pricier hotels may request prepayment.

Booking Services

Columbus Ecuador (www.columbusecuador.com) For help in booking a range of guesthouses all over Ecuador.

Ecuador for All (www.ecuadorforall.com) For help booking accommodation suitable for disabled travelers.

Lonely Planet (www.lonelyplanet.com/ecuador/hotels) Recommended guesthouses.

True Ecuador Travel (www.true-ecuador-travel.org) Educational Travel Specialists.

Sleeping Price Ranges

The following price ranges refer to a double room in high season. Room prices include bathroom. Exceptions are noted in specific listings.

$ less than $40

$$ $40–$90

$$$ more than $90

Children

Foreigners traveling with children are still a curiosity in Ecuador (especially if they are gringos), and a crying or laughing child at your side can quickly break down barriers between you and locals. Parents will likely be met with extra-friendly attention. As is the case throughout the world, people in Ecuador love children. Lonely Planet's *Travel with Children* is an excellent resource.

Practicalities

Children pay full fare on buses if they occupy a seat, but they often ride for free if they sit on a parent's lap. The fare for children under 12 years is halved for domestic flights (and they get a seat), while infants under two cost 10% of the fare (but they don't get a seat). In hotels, the general rule is simply to bargain.

While kids' meals are not normally offered in restaurants, it is perfectly acceptable to order a meal to split between two children or an adult and a child.

Changing facilities are rarities in all but the best restaurants. Breastfeeding is acceptable in public. Formula foods can be difficult to come by outside the large big-city supermarkets, but disposable diapers are sold at most markets.

Safety seats are generally hard to come by in rental cars (be sure to arrange one ahead of time), and in taxis they're unheard of. This is, after all, a country where a family of four can blaze across town on a motorcycle.

Electricity

Embassies & Consulates

Hours are short and change regularly, so it's a good idea to call ahead. New Zealand does not have an embassy or consulate in Ecuador.

Australian Consulate (☎04-601-7529; ausconsulate@unidas.com.ec; SBC Office Centre Bldg Office 1-14, 1st fl, Samborondon)

Canadian Embassy (☎02-245-5499; www.canadainternational.gc.ca/ecuador-equateur; Av Amazonas 4153 near Unión de Periodistas, 3rd fl, Quito; ⏱9am-noon Mon-Fri)

Canadian Consulate (☎04-263-1109; www.canadainternational.gc.ca; Av Francisco de Orellana 234, 6th fl, Guayaquil)

Colombian Embassy (☎02-333-0268; http://quito.consulado.gov.co/; Catalina Aldaz N34-131 near Portugal, 2nd fl, Quito; ⏱8am-1:30pm Mon-Sat)

Colombian Consulate (☎04-263-0674; Francisco de Orellana 111, World Trade Center, Tower B, 11th fl, Guayaquil)

French Embassy (☎02-294-3800; www.ambafrance-ec.org; cnr Leonidas Plaza 127 & Av Patria, Quito; ⏱9am-noon Mon-Fri)

French Consulate (☎04-232-8442; cnr José Mascote 909 & Hurtado)

German Embassy (☎02-297-0820; www.quito.diplo.de; Naciones Unidas E10-44 near República de El Salvador, Edificio Citiplaza, 12th fl, Quito; ⏱8am-1pm & 2-4pm Mon-Thu, 8-1pm Fri)

Irish Honorary Consul (☎02-380-1345; www.dfa.ie; Calle del Establo 50, tower III, office 104, Urb Santa Lucia Alta, Cumbaya, Quito; ⏱10am-1pm)

Peruvian Consulate (☎04-228-0114, 04-228-0135, 04-228-0183; Av Francisco de Orellana 501, 14th fl, Guayaquil)

UK Embassy (☎02-397-2200; www.gov.uk/world/ecuador; cnr Naciones Unidas & El Salvador, Edificio Citiplaza, 14th fl, Quito; ⏱9-11am Mon-Fri)

US Embassy (☎02-398-5000; https://ec.usembassy.gov/; Av Avigiras E12-170 near Eloy Alfaro, Quito; ⏱8-12:30pm & 1:30-5pm Mon-Fri)

US Consulate (☎04-371-7000; http://guayaquil.usconsulate.gov; Santa Ana near Av José Rodriguez Bonin, Guayaquil)

Food

Ecuador has eating options for most palates, especially in Guayaquil and Quito, where international cuisine, fast food and most styles of South American dishes can be found. Ecuadorian specialties vary depending on which region you find yourself in, but one thing's for sure – the whole country loves plantain. Typical plates include meat or fish, with a choice of carbs plus vegetables or salad. It's common to be served double carbs (commonly rice, with beans, lentils, plantain or potatoes) with most meals.

EATING PRICE RANGES

Ecuador has a rich and diverse cuisine (p379). We've used the following price ranges, based on the cost of a standard main course. Fancier places usually add on tax (12%) and service charge (10%) to the bill.

$ less than $8

$$ $8–$15

$$$ more than $15

Health

Medical care is usually available in major cities, but may be quite difficult to find in rural areas. Pharmacies in Ecuador are known as *farmacias*. It can be challenging to find imported pharmaceutical items; bring essential health and hygiene supplies since these generally cost more in Ecuador.

Availability & Cost of Health Care

Public health care is free for everyone in Ecuador, visitors included, although the quality of services varies.

Private medical services are quite inexpensive compared to the US, and in larger cities such as Quito, Guayaquil and Cuenca, it's possible to find foreign-trained, English-speaking physicians.

Typically, patients must pay at the time of treatment. Contact your embassy or consulate for recommendations of quality providers should you require serious medical attention.

Environmental Hazards

ALTITUDE SICKNESS

Altitude sickness may develop in travelers who ascend rapidly to altitudes greater than 2500m, including those flying directly to Quito. Symptoms may include headaches, nausea, vomiting, dizziness, malaise, insomnia and loss of appetite. Severe cases may be complicated by fluid in the lungs (high-altitude pulmonary edema) or swelling of the brain (high-altitude cerebral edema). The most common cause of death related to high altitude is high-altitude pulmonary edema.

To lessen the chance of getting altitude sickness, ascend gradually to higher altitudes, avoid overexertion, eat light meals and steer clear of alcohol.

Infectious Diseases

CHOLERA

This is the worst of the watery diarrheas, and medical help should be sought. Outbreaks of cholera are generally widely reported, so you can avoid problem areas. Fluid replacement is the most vital treatment – the risk of dehydration is severe, as you may lose up to 20L a day. If there is a delay in getting to a hospital, then begin taking tetracycline. The adult dose is 250mg four times daily.

DENGUE FEVER

Unlike the malaria mosquito, the *Aedes aegypti* mosquito, which transmits the dengue virus, is most active during the day and is found mainly in urban areas, in and around human dwellings.

Symptoms of dengue fever include a sudden onset of high fever, headache, joint and muscle pains (hence its old name, 'breakbone fever'), and nausea and vomiting. Seek medical attention as soon as possible.

MALARIA

Malaria is transmitted by mosquito bites, usually between dusk and dawn. The main symptom is high-spiking fevers, often accompanied by chills, sweats, headache, body aches, weakness, vomiting or diarrhea. Severe cases may involve the central nervous system and lead to seizures, confusion, coma and death.

Taking malaria pills is recommended for all rural areas below 1500m. Risk is highest along the northernmost coast and in the northern Oriente. There is no malaria risk in the highlands.

TYPHOID

A dangerous gut infection, typhoid fever is caused by contaminated water and food. Medical help must be sought.

In its early stages, sufferers may feel they have a bad cold or flu on the way, as initial symptoms are a headache, body aches and a fever that rises a little each day until it is around 40°C (104°F) or more. The victim's pulse is often slow relative to the degree of fever present – unlike a normal fever, during which the pulse increases. There may also be vomiting, abdominal pain, diarrhea or constipation.

YELLOW FEVER

This viral disease is endemic in South America and is transmitted by mosquitoes. The initial symptoms are fever, headache, abdominal pain and vomiting. Seek medical care urgently and drink lots of fluids.

Insurance

In addition to health insurance and car insurance, a policy that protects baggage and valuables, such as cameras and camcorders, is a good idea. Keep your insurance records separate from other possessions in case you have to make a claim.

Worldwide travel insurance is available at www.lonelyplanet.com/travel-insurance. You can buy, extend and claim online anytime – even if you're already on the road.

Internet Access

Wi-fi is widespread, with guesthouses across the country offering access (usually free). The wi-fi symbol in this book indicates where it is available.

Internet cafes are disappearing in Ecuador, though most larger towns have a few. These cost around $1.50 an hour. Some hotels also have a computer or two for guest use. Accommodations options in this book that have a computer for internet access are labeled with an internet symbol.

Language Courses

Ecuador is one of the best places to study Spanish in South America. Ecuadorian Spanish is clear and precise, and similar to Mexican and Central American Spanish, and rates are cheap. Quito (p68) and Cuenca (p179) are the best places to study, and both have a plethora of language schools. Expect to pay around $10 per hour for private lessons. Accommodations with local families can be arranged. There are also schools in Baños (p155) and Otavalo (p103) if you want a more small-town experience.

Legal Matters

Ecuador has recently implemented a zero-tolerance policy for possession of illegal drugs of any amount. Previously, possession of up to 10 grams of cannabis and up to two grams of cocaine did not result in criminal charges, but this is no longer the case – the use or trafficking of drugs is a punishable offense that could result in imprisonment; and a scale is used to differentiate between drug users, micro-traffickers and large-scale traffickers when handing down prison sentences.

Drivers should carry their passport, as well as their driver's license. In the event of an accident, unless it's extremely minor, the vehicles should stay where they are until the police arrive and make a report. This is essential for all insurance claims. If the accident results in injury and you are unhurt, you should take the victim to obtain medical help, particularly in the case of a pedestrian accident. You are legally responsible for a pedestrian's injuries and will be jailed unless you pay, even if the accident was not your fault. Drive defensively.

LGBT Travelers

Same-sex couples traveling in Ecuador should be wary of showing affection when in public. All same-sex civil unions were recently enshrined in the new 2008 constitution, and for most Ecuadorians gay rights remains a non-issue in a political context. But homosexuality was technically illegal until 1998, and anti-gay bias still exists.

Several fiestas in Ecuador have parades with men cross-dressing as women. This is all meant in fun, rather than as an open acceptance of sexual alternatives, but it does provide the public at large (both gay and straight) with a popular cultural situation in which to enjoy themselves in an accepting environment.

Useful Websites & Organizations

Gay Guide to Quito (www.quitogay.net)

FEDAEPS (☎02-255-9999; www.fedaeps.org; Av 12 de Octubre N18-24, oficina 203) A community center for lesbian, gay, bisexual and transsexual people, as well as an AIDS-activist organization.

Zenith Travel (☎02-252-9993; www.galapagosgay.com; cnr Juan Leon Mera N24-264 & Luis Cordero, Quito) Specializes in gay and lesbian tours.

Money

Ecuador's official currency is the US dollar. Aside from euros, Peruvian soles and Colombian nuevos soles, it's very difficult to change foreign currencies in Ecuador.

ATMs

ATMs are the easiest way of getting cash. They're found in most cities and even in smaller towns, though they are occasionally out of order. Make sure you have a four-digit Personal Identification Number (PIN); many Ecuadorian ATMs don't recognize longer ones.

Cash

US dollars are the official currency; they are identical to those issued in the USA. Coins of one, five, 10, 25 and 50 cents are identical in shape, size and color to their US equivalents, but bear images of famous Ecuadorians. Both US and Ecuadorian coins are used in Ecuador. The $1 coin is widely used.

Credit Cards

Credit cards are great as backup. Visa, MasterCard and Diners Club are the most widely accepted cards. First-class restaurants, hotels, souvenir shops and travel agencies usually accept MasterCard or Visa. Small hotels, restaurants and stores don't. Even if an establishment has a credit-card sticker in the window, don't assume that credit cards are accepted. In Ecuador, merchants accepting credit cards will often add between 5% and 10% to the bill. Paying cash is often better value.

Money-changers

It is best to change money in the major cities of Quito, Guayaquil and Cuenca, where rates are best. Because banks have limited hours, *casas de cambio* (currency-exchange bureaus) are sometimes the only option for changing money. They are usually open 9am to 6pm Monday to Friday and until at least noon on Saturday.

Tipping

Restaurants Better restaurants add a 10% service charge to the bill. Add another 5% for great service, handing it to the server directly.

Taxis Not usually tipped; always appreciated.

Guides Tips expected on guided tours. For groups, tip top-notch guides about $5 per person per day; tip the driver about half that. For private guides, tip about $10 per day.

Galápagos cruises Tip $10 to $20 per client per day.

Opening Hours

Opening hours are provided when they differ from the following standard hours:

Restaurants 10:30am to 11pm Monday to Saturday

Bars 6pm to midnight Monday to Thursday, to 2am Friday and Saturday

Shops 9am to 7pm Monday to Friday, 9am to noon Saturday

Banks 8am to 2pm or 4pm Monday to Friday

Post offices 8am to 6pm Monday to Friday, 8am to 1pm Saturday

Telephone call centers 8am to 10pm daily

Post

Ecuador's postal service is reliable. Allow one to two weeks for a letter or package to reach its destination. Courier services including FedEx, DHL and UPS are readily available in sizable towns, but the service is costly.

Public Holidays

On major holidays, banks, offices and other services close. Transportation gets crowded, so buy bus tickets in advance. Major holidays are sometimes celebrated for several days around the actual date. If an official public holiday falls on a weekend, offices may be closed on the nearest Friday or Monday.

New Year's Day January 1

Epiphany January 6

Semana Santa (Easter Week) March/April

Labor Day May 1

Battle of Pichincha May 24

Simón Bolívar's Birthday July 24

Quito Independence Day August 10

Guayaquil Independence Day October 9

Columbus Day/Día de la Raza October 12

All Saints' Day November 1

Day of the Dead (All Souls' Day) November 2

Cuenca Independence Day November 3

Christmas Eve December 24

Christmas Day December 25

Safe Travel

Don't be paranoid; most unpleasant incidents can be avoided by using common sense. But no matter where you travel, it's wise to get some travel insurance.

Drugging

Be prudent about accepting food or drinks from strangers. Keep in mind that these could be laced with something, and you could be unwittingly drugged and robbed.

Kidnapping

While highly unlikely, there are occasional incidents of express kidnapping (*secuestro exprés*) in urban areas. This is when armed thieves (usually operating an unlicensed taxi) force you to withdraw money from an ATM, then abandon you on the outskirts of town. To avoid this happening, have a hotel or restaurant call a taxi for you. You can also use the Easy Taxi app to hail one.

Taxis now are supposed to have emergency GPS-connected panic buttons on the side armrest in back that automatically alert police and start video and audio recording. Look for the '*transporte seguro*' label on taxis.

Robbery

If it can be avoided, do not carry valuables on day hikes, especially in areas commonly visited by tourists.

Hotel rooms near bus stations will often save you a couple of bucks, but can be dangerous and often double as brothels.

If you are driving a car in Ecuador, never park it unattended. Never leave valuables in sight in the car – even attended cars can have their windows smashed by hit-and-run merchants.

On the off chance you are robbed, you should file a police report as soon as possible. This is a requirement for any insurance claim, although it is unlikely that the police will be able to recover the property.

Theft

Armed robbery is rare in Ecuador, although parts of Quito and some coastal areas are dangerous. Specific information is given in the appropriate regional chapters of this book.

Sneak theft is more common, and you should always watch your back (and back pockets) in busy bus stations, on crowded city buses and in bustling markets. Theft on buses is common, especially on nighttime trips and journeys between Quito, Latacunga, Baños and Riobamba in the central highlands. All of these places are worked by bag-slashers and pickpockets. But there are ways you can avoid becoming victim to them by being smart.

It's wise to carry a wallet with a small amount of spending money in your front pocket and keep the important stuff hidden in your money pouch beneath your clothes.

Leaving money in the hotel safe deposit boxes is usually reliable, but make sure that it is in a sealed, taped envelope. A few readers have reported a loss of money from deposit boxes in the cheaper hotels.

Trouble Spots

Due to occasional armed conflict in neighboring Colombia, areas along the Colombian border (particularly in the northern Oriente) can be dangerous. Tours into the Oriente are generally safe, but there have been a few isolated incidents of armed robbery.

PRACTICALITIES

Addresses In Ecuadorian addresses, the term 's/n' refers to '*sin numero*' (without number), meaning the address has no street number.

Weights & Measures Ecuador uses the metric system.

Newspapers Quito's biggest newspaper is *El Comercio* (www.elcomercio.com). Guayaquil's papers are *El Telégrafo* (www.eltelegrafo.com.ec) and *El Universo* (www.eluniverso.com). Ecuador's best-known news magazine is *Vistazo* (www.vistazo.com). International newspapers, including a locally published edition of the *Miami Herald*, can be found in Quito.

Magazines For travel inspiration, pick up a copy of the beautifully produced bilingual magazine *Ñan* (www.nanmagazine.com), at airport kiosks, bookshops or some larger supermarkets.

DVDs Ecuador uses Region 4, common throughout Latin America as well as Australia and Oceania.

Smoking Banned in any enclosed public spaces and on public transportation, although the law is unregulated and smoking is commonly accepted in bars and clubs.

Telephone

In a country where mobile phone use is commonplace, pay phones and call centers are rapidly disappearing from the landscape. If you're without a mobile phone and you need to make a call, using Skype where wi-fi is available may be your best bet. Or if you lack a computer, there are still a few internet cafes in most towns.

In regards to public street phones, some use phonecards, which are sold in convenient places such as newsagents. Others accept only coins. All but the most basic hotels will allow you to make local city calls.

Hotels that provide international phone connections very often surcharge extremely heavily.

All telephone numbers in Ecuador have seven digits (after the area code) – except for cellular phone numbers, which have 10 digits including the initial 0.

Cell Phones

Cellular (mobile) numbers in Ecuador are preceded by 09. Bring your own phone and purchase a SIM card (called a 'chip', costing around $5 to $10) from one of several local networks. Add credit at convenience stores, supermarkets and pharmacies.

Phone Codes

Two-digit area codes beginning with '0' are used throughout Ecuador. Area codes are not dialed if calling from within that area code, unless dialing from a cellular phone.

Ecuador's country code is 593. To call a number in Ecuador from abroad, call your international access code, Ecuador's country code, the area code *without* the 0, and the seven-digit local telephone number (or the nine-digit mobile number – again without the initial 0).

Time

The Ecuadorian mainland is five hours behind Greenwich Mean Time, and the Galápagos are six hours behind. Mainland time here is equivalent to Eastern Standard Time in North America. When it's noon in Quito, it's noon in New York, 5pm in London and 4am (daylight-saving time) in Melbourne. Because of Ecuador's location on the equator, days and nights are of equal length year-round, and there's no daylight-saving time.

Toilets

As throughout South America, Ecuadorian plumbing has very low pressure, and putting toilet paper into the bowl is a serious no-no anywhere except in the fanciest hotels and in Quito airport. Always put your used toilet paper in the basket (it's better than a clogged and overflowing toilet!). A well-run cheap hotel will ensure that the receptacle is emptied and the toilet cleaned daily.

Public toilets are limited mainly to bus terminals, airports and restaurants. Lavatories are called *servicios higiénicos* and are usually marked 'SS.HH.' – there's often an attendant, whom you will pay about $0.10 or $0.15, for which you will receive a ration of toilet paper. You can simply ask to use the *baño* (bathroom) in a restaurant. Toilet paper is not always available, so the experienced traveler always carries a personal supply. Remember 'M' on the door means *mujeres* (women) not 'men' – though it might also be 'D' for *damas* (ladies). Men's toilets are signed with an 'H' for *hombres* (men) or a 'C' for *caballeros* (gentlemen).

Tourist Information

The system of government-run tourist offices in Ecuador is hit or miss, but is getting better. Tourist information in Quito and Cuenca is of excellent quality.

Many towns have some form of municipal or provincial tourist office; most of the time, the staff are good at answering the majority of questions.

Ministerio de Turismo (http://ecuador.travel) Responsible for tourist information at the national level.

Travelers with Disabilities

Unfortunately, Ecuador's infrastructure for disabled travelers is virtually nonexistent. Wheelchair ramps are few and far between, and sidewalks are often badly potholed and cracked. Bathrooms and toilets are often too small for wheelchairs. Signs in braille or telephones for the hearing impaired are practically unheard of.

GOVERNMENT TRAVEL ADVICE

The following government websites offer travel advisories and information on current hot spots.

Australia Department of Foreign Affairs (www.smartraveller.gov.au)

British Foreign Office (www.gov.uk/foreign-travel-advice)

Canadian Department of Foreign Affairs (www.dfait-maeci.gc.ca/)

US State Department (http://travel.state.gov)

Nevertheless, Ecuadorians with disabilities get around, mainly through the help of others. It's not particularly unusual to see travelers with disabilities being carried onto a bus, for example. Buses are (legally) supposed to carry travelers with disabilities for free. Local city buses, which are already overcrowded, won't do that, but long-distance buses sometimes do. Travelers with disabilities are also eligible for 50% discounts on domestic airfares.

When it comes to hotels, the only truly accessible rooms are found at the international chain hotels in Quito and Guayaquil.

Download Lonely Planet's free Accessible Travel guides from http://lptravel.to/AccessibleTravel.

Visas

Visitors from most countries don't need visas for stays of less than 90 days. Residents from a handful of African and Asian countries (including China) require visas.

Stay Extensions

New regulations mean it's a real headache getting visa extensions. Unless you're from an Andean Pact country, tourist visas are not extendable. If you wish to stay longer than 90 days, you'll need to apply for a 12-IX Visa; you can also do this while in Ecuador, though it's more time-consuming than doing it in advance through an Ecuadorian consulate in your home country. Pick up the necessary paperwork for the 12-IX Visa, and pay the $230 fee at the **Ministerio de Relaciones Exteriores y Movilidad Humana** (☎02-299-3200; www.cancilleria.gob.ec; Carrión E1-76 & Av 10 de Agosto, Quito). For step-by-step instructions on applying for the visa, check out the excellent post on one Canadian traveler's blog: roamaholic.com/tourist-visa-ecuador.

No matter what, don't wait until your visa has expired to sort out your paperwork, as the fine for overstaying can be hefty – $200 to $2000.

Volunteering

Numerous organizations look for the services of volunteers; however, the vast majority require at least a minimal grasp of Spanish, a minimum commitment of several weeks or months, as well as fees (anywhere from $10 per day to $700 per month) to cover the costs of room and board. Volunteers can work in conservation programs, help street kids, teach, build nature trails, construct websites, do medical or agricultural work – the possibilities are endless. Many jungle lodges also accept volunteers for long-term stays. To keep your volunteer costs down, your best bet is to look when you get to Ecuador.

The classifieds section on Ecuador Explorer (www.ecuadorexplorer.com) has a long list of organizations seeking volunteers.

AmaZOOnico (www.selvaviva.ec/en/amazoonico) Accepts volunteers for the animal-rehabilitation sector.

Andean Bear Conservation Project (www.andeanbear.org) The Andean Bear Conservation Project trains volunteers as bear trackers. Hike through remote cloud forest to track the elusive spectacled bear, whose predilection for sweet corn is altering its wild behavior. Other jobs here include maintaining trails and working with local farmers to replenish cornfields ravaged by bears (to discourage bear hunting). Volunteers can come for as little as a week, but a month ($700) is recommended.

Bosque Nublado Santa Lucia (www.santaluciaecuador.com) Community-based ecotourism project in the cloud forests of northwest Ecuador. It regularly contracts volunteers to work in reforestation, trail maintenance, construction, teaching English and more.

FEVI (www.fevi.org) The Fund for Intercultural Education & Community Volunteer Service works with children, the elderly, women's groups and indigenous communities throughout Ecuador.

Inti Sisa (www.intisisa.org) In Guamote, this hostel has info on volunteer opportunities in early-childhood education.

Jatun Sacha Foundation (www.jatunsacha.org) This foundation has four biological research stations in four zones of Ecuador: the coast, highlands, Amazonía and the Galápagos. They accept volunteers at each one, with a minimum commitment of two weeks.

Junto con los Niños (www.juconi.org.ec) Organization that works with street kids in the slum areas of Guayaquil. One-month minimum preferred.

Merazonia (www.merazonia.org) A central highlands refuge for injured animals.

New Era Galápagos Foundation (www.neweragalapagos.org) Nonprofit offering volunteerships focused on community empowerment and sustainable tourism in the Galápagos. Volunteers live and work on Isla San Cristóbal.

Progreso Verde (www.progresoverde.org) Accepts volunteers for reforestation, organic farming, teaching and other areas.

Reserva Biológica Los Cedros (www.reservaloscedros.org) This biological reserve in the cloud forests of the western Andean slopes often needs volunteers.

Río Muchacho Organic Farm (☎05-302-0487; www.riomuchacho.com; via Canoa Jama Km 10, Troncal del Pacifico, northeast of Canoa) Guests and locals get their hands dirty learning about sustainable farming practices. There are short programs from one to three days, plus one-week-to-month-long courses ($300 to $1200). You can volunteer here for $300 per month. Most people come here on a three-day, two-night tour costing $172 per person, with discounts for larger groups.

On the accommodation front, cabins are Thoreau-approved-rustic, with shared showers and composting toilets. The coveted spot is a tree-house bunk. Lying along the river of the same name, this tropical organic farm is reached by a 7km rough, unpaved road branching inland from the road north of Canoa.

Siempre Verde (☎ext 1460 in the US 404-262-3032; www.siempreverde.org; N 0 22' 18) Get off the road just before Santa Rosa for the two-hour walk into Siempre Verde, a small community-run research station supporting tropical-conservation education with excellent hiking and bird-watching. Students and researchers are welcome with prior arrangement.

Yanapuma Foundation (Map p56; ☎02-228-7084; www.yanapuma.org; Guayaquil E9-59 near Oriente, Quito) Offers a number of ways for volunteers to get involved: teaching English, building houses in remote communities, helping with reforestation projects or taking part in coastal clean-ups. Stop by its Quito headquarters and language school for more information.

Women Travelers

Generally, women travelers will find Ecuador safe and pleasant, despite the fact that machismo is alive and well. Ecuadorian men often make flirtatious comments and whistle at single women, both Ecuadorian and foreigners. The best strategy is to ignore them.

On the coast, come-ons are more predatory, and solo female travelers should take precautions such as staying away from bars and discos where they'll obviously get hit on, and opting for taxis over walking etc. Do not accept drinks from strangers, and don't leave your drink unattended – there are occasional reports of drugging.

Lonely Planet has received warnings in the past from women who were molested while on organized tours. If you're traveling solo, it's essential to do some research before committing to a tour: find out who's leading the tour, what other tourists will be on the outing and so on. Women-only travel groups or guides are available in a few situations.

Work

Although Ecuador has a low unemployment rate, the underemployment rate is high (above 50%), so finding work isn't easy. Officially, you need a worker's visa to be allowed to work in Ecuador. Aside from the occasional position at a tourist lodge or expat bar, there is little opportunity for paid work. The one exception is teaching English.

Most paid English-teaching job openings are in Quito and Guayaquil. Schools sometimes advertise for teachers on the bulletin boards of hotels and restaurants. Pay is just enough to live on unless you've acquired a full-time position from home. If you have a bona fide teaching credential, so much the better. Schools such as the American School in Quito will often hire teachers of mathematics, biology and other subjects, and may help you get a work visa. They also pay much better than the language schools. Check ads in local hotels and newspapers. One of the best online English-teaching resources, complete with job boards, is Dave's ESL Cafe (www.eslcafe.com).

Transportation

GETTING THERE & AWAY

Entering the Country

Entering the country is straightforward, and border officials, especially at the airports, efficiently whisk you through. At land borders, officers may take a little more time examining your passport, if only to kill time. Officially, you need proof of onward travel and evidence of sufficient funds for your stay, but this is rarely requested. Proof of $20 per day or a credit card is usually evidence of sufficient funds. However, international airlines flying to Quito may require a round-trip or onward ticket or a residence visa before they let you on the plane; you should be prepared for this possibility, though it's unlikely. Though it's not law, you may be required to show proof of vaccination against yellow fever if you are entering Ecuador from an infected area.

Flights, tours and rail tickets can all be booked online at www.lonelyplanet.com/bookings.

Passport

All nationals entering as tourists need a passport that is valid for at least six months after arrival. You are legally required to have your passport on you at all times. Many people carry only a copy when they're hanging around a town, though this is not an officially acceptable form of ID.

Air

Airports & Airlines

Ecuador has two international airports.

Aeropuerto Internacional Mariscal Sucre (☎02-395-4200; www.aeropuertoquito.aero) Quito's airport is located about 38km east of the center.

Aeropuerto José Joaquín de Olmedo (GYE; Map p281; ☎04-216-9000; www.tagsa.aero; Av de las Américas) Guayaquil's airport is just a few kilometers from downtown.

TAME (☎1-700-500-800; www.tame.com.ec) Ecuador's main airline; it has had a good safety record in recent years, with a modern fleet of Boeing, Airbus and Embraer aircraft as well as several turboprop ATRs.

LATAM (☎1-800-000-527; www.latam.com) Flies internationally to New York and various cities in Peru, Argentina, Chile, Brazil and Bolivia.

Tickets

Ticket prices are highest during tourist high seasons: mid-June through early September, and December through mid-January. Working with a travel agent that deals specifically in Latin American travel is usually an advantage.

CLIMATE CHANGE & TRAVEL

Every form of transport that relies on carbon-based fuel generates CO_2, the main cause of human-induced climate change. Modern travel is dependent on airplanes, which might use less fuel per kilometer per person than most cars but travel much greater distances. The altitude at which aircraft emit gases (including CO_2) and particles also contributes to their climate change impact. Many websites offer 'carbon calculators' that allow people to estimate the carbon emissions generated by their journey and, for those who wish to do so, to offset the impact of the greenhouse gases emitted with contributions to portfolios of climate-friendly initiatives throughout the world. Lonely Planet offsets the carbon footprint of all staff and author travel.

Land

Border Crossings

Peru and Colombia are the only countries sharing borders with Ecuador. If you are entering or leaving Ecuador, border formalities are straightforward if you have your documents in order. No taxes are levied on tourists when entering or exiting overland.

If you've overstayed the allowed amount of time on your T3 visa (90 days – consecutive or not – per year, beginning on your stamped entry date), you'll have to pay a hefty fine or you will be sent back to Quito. If you don't have an *entrada* (entrance) stamp, you will also be sent back.

COLOMBIA

The main border crossing to Colombia is via Tulcán in the northern highlands, currently the only safe place to cross into Colombia. The border crossing north of Lago Agrio in the Oriente is unsafe due to smuggling and conflict in Colombia.

PERU

There are three important border posts connecting Ecuador and Peru.

Huaquillas This crossing, south of Machala, gets most of the international traffic between the two countries. It consists of side-by-side border posts on the highway a few kilometers north of town. Buses to Huaquillas don't stop at this border post, though international buses (Ecuador–Peru) do stop there and wait for everyone to complete the formalities. Another option is simply hiring a taxi from Huaquillas to take you out to the border post and back.

Macará Increasingly popular because it's more relaxed than the Huaquillas crossing, and the journey from Loja in the southern highlands is beautiful. Direct buses run between Loja and Piura, Peru (eight hours) via Macará, and wait for you at the border while you take care of formalities; it's easy.

La Balsa at Zumba South of Vilcabamba, this little-used crossing is remote and interesting and gets little traffic. People often hang out in Vilcabamba for a few days before heading to Zumba and Peru.

Bus

Busing into Ecuador from Colombia or Peru is straightforward and usually requires walking across one of the international borders and catching another bus once you're across (this is more complicated in Huaquillas, though). Some international bus companies offer direct, long-haul services from major cities such as Lima and Bogotá.

Car & Motorcycle

Driving a private vehicle into Ecuador can be a huge hassle, depending largely upon the mood of the official who stops you at the border. To bring your car into Ecuador, you are officially required to have a Carnet de Passage en Douane (CPD), an internationally recognized customs document that allows you to temporarily 'import' a vehicle into Ecuador without paying an import tax. The document is issued through an automobile club in the country where the car is registered, and you are strongly advised to obtain one well in advance of travel. Motorcycles seem to present fewer hassles at the border.

> **DEPARTURE TAX**
>
> Departure tax is now included in ticket prices rather than payable at the airport.

River

It is possible but time-consuming to travel down the Río Napo from Ecuador to Peru, joining the Amazon near Iquitos. The border facilities are minimal, and the boats doing the journey are infrequent. It is also geographically possible to travel down Río Putumayo into Colombia and Peru, but this is a dangerous region because of drug smuggling and terrorism, and is not recommended.

GETTING AROUND

Air

Airlines in Ecuador

With the exception of flying to the Galápagos Islands, internal flights are generally fairly cheap, rarely exceeding $125 for a one-way ticket. All mainland flights are under an hour and often provide you with incredible views over the Andes.

Flights to most destinations originate in Quito or Guayaquil only. The following are Ecuador's passenger airlines:

Avianca (☎1-800-003-434; www.avianca.com) Serves Quito, Guayaquil, Cuenca, Isla Baltra (Galápagos), Isla San Cristóbal (Galápagos), Manta and Coca.

Emetebe (☎in Guayaquil 04-230-1277; www.emetebe.com.ec) Galápagos-based airline that flies between Isla Baltra, Isla Santa Cruz, Isla San Cristóbal and Isla Isabela.

LATAM (☎1-800-000-527; www.latam.com) Flies from Quito to Cuenca, Guayaquil and the Galápagos (Isla San Cristóbal and Isla Baltra), plus New York and various cities in Peru, Argentina, Chile, Brazil and Bolivia.

TAME (☎1-700-500-800; www.tame.com.ec) Serves Coca, Cuenca, Esmeraldas, Isla Baltra (Galápagos), Isla San Cristóbal

Internal Air Services

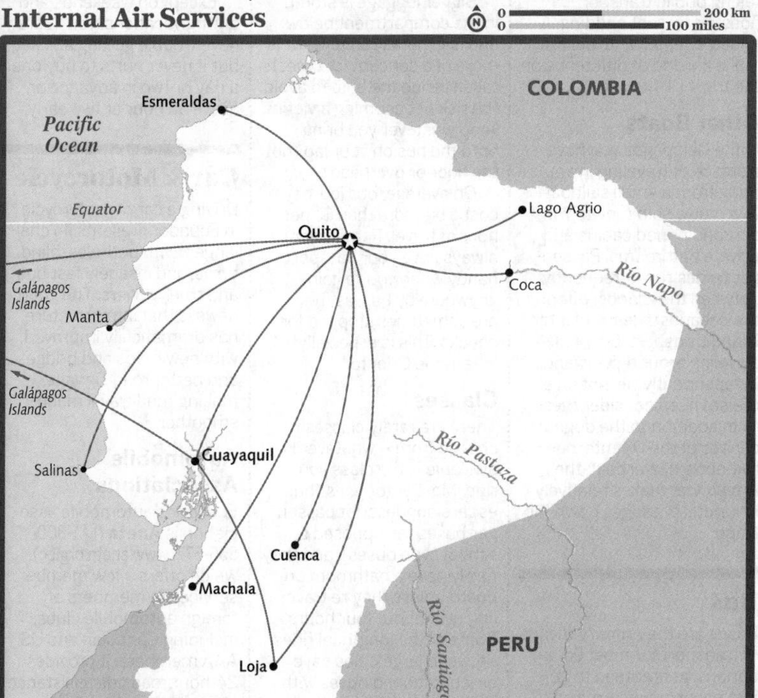

(Galápagos), Guayaquil, Lago Agrio, Loja, Manta, Quito, Salinas, plus Bogotá and Cali (Colombia), Lima (Peru), New York and Fort Lauderdale (USA) and Caracas (Venezuela).

Bicycle

Cycling in the Andes is strenuous, not only because of hill climbs but because of the altitudes. Road rules are few, and there are not many bike lanes around the country. But, after major investments in infrastructure, the roads are in good shape in Ecuador, and many larger cities have signed *ciclovias* (bike paths), some of which are closed to vehicle traffic on Sundays, notably in Quito.

Bike shops are scarce outside of Quito, and those that do exist usually have a very limited selection of parts. Bring all important spare parts and tools from home. The country's best mountain-bike tour operators are in Quito and Riobamba.

Hire

Renting bikes is mainly for short tours, mostly from Quito, Riobamba, Cuenca and Baños.

Boat

Boat transportation is common in some parts of Ecuador and can be divided into several types.

Canoe

The most common boat is the motorized canoe, which acts as a water taxi or bus along the major rivers of the Oriente (especially on the Río Napo) and parts of the northern coast. Most people experience this novel form of transport during a tour in the Amazon, as motorized canoes are often the only way to a rainforest lodge.

These canoes often carry as many as three dozen passengers. Generally, they're long in shape and short on comfort. Seating is normally on hard, low wooden benches which accommodate two people each. Most river lodges provide bench cushions on their boats. If you're taking public transport canoes: bring seat padding. A folded sweater or towel will make a world of difference on the trip.

Other Boats

In the Galápagos you have a choice of traveling in anything from a small sailboat to a cruise ship replete with air-conditioned cabins and private bathrooms. Passenger ferries run infrequently between the islands, offering the cheapest means of inter-island transport. Only folks traveling around the islands independently (ie, not on a cruise) need consider these.

In addition to the dugout canoes of the Oriente, one live-aboard riverboat, the *Anakonda,* makes relatively luxurious passages down Río Napo.

Bus

Buses are the primary means of transport for most Ecuadorians, guaranteed to go just about anywhere. They can be exciting, cramped, comfy, smelly, fun, scary, sociable and grueling, depending on your state of mind, where you're going and who's driving.

There have also been some tragic bus accidents in recent years. Most buses lack seat belts, but if you're on one that has them, do use them.

Most major cities have a main *terminal terrestre* (bus terminal), although some towns have a host of private terminals – and you'll have to go to the right one to catch the bus going where you need to go. Most stations are within walking distance or a short cab ride of the town's center. Smaller towns are occasionally served by passing buses, in which case you have to walk from the highway into town, usually only a short walk since only the smallest towns lack terminals.

Bigger luggage is stored in the compartment below and is generally safe. Theft is more of a concern for objects taken inside the bus. To avoid the risk of becoming a victim, keep whatever you bring onto the bus on your lap (not the floor or overhead).

On average, bus journeys cost a bit more than $1 per hour of travel. Remember to always have your passport handy when you're going anywhere by bus, as they are sometimes stopped for checks. This is especially true in the Oriente.

Classes

There are rarely classes to choose from – whatever is available is the class you ride. Most *autobuses* (buses) are nondescript passenger buses (as opposed to school-type buses), and they rarely have a bathroom on board unless they're traveling over about four hours. Some of the long-haul rides between large cities have air-conditioned buses with on-board toilets, but they are few and far between.

Long-Distance Buses

These usually stop for a 20-minute meal break at the appropriate times. The food in terminal restaurants may be somewhat basic, so if you have dietary restrictions or are a picky eater, you should bring food with you.

Reservations & Schedules

Most bus companies have scheduled departure times, but these change often and may not always be adhered to. If a bus is full, it might leave early. Conversely, an almost empty bus may spend half an hour *dando vueltas* (driving around), with the driver's assistant yelling out of the door in the hope of attracting more passengers.

The larger terminals often have information booths that can advise you about routes, fares and times.

Except on weekends and during vacations, you'll rarely have trouble getting a ticket, but it never hurts to buy one a day or two in advance or arrive an hour or two early.

Car & Motorcycle

Driving a car or motorcycle in Ecuador presents its challenges, with potholes, blind turns, and insanely fast bus and truck drivers. The good news is that infrastructure has dramatically improved, with new roads and bridges, and better road signage, making road travel much smoother.

Automobile Associations

Ecuador's automobile association is **Aneta** (☎1-800-556-677; www.aneta.org.ec), which offers a few member services to members of foreign automobile clubs, including Canadian and US AAA members. It provides 24-hour roadside assistance to Aneta members.

Driver's License

You are required to have a driver's license from your home country and a passport whenever you're driving. The international driver's license can also come in handy when renting a car (though it's not officially required).

Fuel

There are two octane ratings for gasoline in Ecuador: 'Extra' (82 octane) and 'Super' (92 octane). Gasoline is sold by the gallon and costs about $1.90 per gallon for Extra and about $2.25 per gallon for Super; note that the latter is not always available in rural areas and prices can vary.

Hire

Few people rent cars in Ecuador, mainly because public transport makes getting around so easy. Most of the international car-rental companies, including **Avis** (www.

avis.com), **Budget** (www.budget.com), **Hertz** (www.hertz.com) and **Localiza** (www.localiza.com), have outlets in Ecuador, but it is difficult to find any agency outside of Quito, Guayaquil or Cuenca.

To rent a car, you must be at least 25 years old and have a credit card, a valid driver's license and a passport. Occasionally a company will rent to someone between 21 and 25 years old, though it may require a higher deposit. Typical rates start at around $40 per day for a compact car, but can go over $100 for a 4WD vehicle (high clearance can be a life saver during ventures off the beaten track). Be sure to ask if the quoted rate includes *seguro* (insurance), *kilometraje libre* (unlimited kilometers) and IVA (tax) – most likely it won't.

The best place to hire a motorcycle is in Quito. In the Mariscal, **Freedom Bike** (☎02-250-4339; www.freedombikerental.com; Finlandia N35-06 near Suecia) rents touring and off-road bikes with gear as well as scooters and bicycles.

You can also hire motorbikes in Baños, where 250cc Enduro-type motorcycles are available for about $10 per hour or $40 per day. Riders with their own machines will find helpful information at **Horizons Unlimited** (www.horizonsunlimited.com).

Insurance

Car-rental companies offer insurance policies on their vehicles, but they can carry a hefty deductible – anywhere between $1000 and $3500, depending on the company – so be sure you read the fine print. Even if an accident is not your fault, you will likely be responsible for the deductible in the event of a collision.

Road Hazards

Hazards in Ecuador include potholes, blind turns and, most obvious of all, bus and truck drivers who pass other buses and trucks at seemingly impossible moments. Always be alert for stopped vehicles, sudden road blocks and occasional livestock on the road. Signage in Ecuador is poor.

Hitchhiking

Hitchhiking is never entirely safe in any country, and we don't recommend it. Travelers who decide to hitchhike should understand that they are taking a small but potentially serious risk. People who do choose to hitchhike will be safer if they travel in pairs and let someone know where they are planning to go.

Hitching is not very practical in Ecuador for three reasons: there are few private cars, public transportation is relatively cheap and trucks are used as public transportation in remote areas, so trying to hitch a free ride on one is the same as trying to hitch a free ride on a bus. Many drivers of *any* vehicle will pick you up, but will also expect payment, usually minimal.

Local Transportation

Bus

Local buses are usually slow and crowded, but they are also very cheap. You can get around most towns for $0.25. Local buses often travel to nearby villages, and riding along is a good, inexpensive way to see the area.

Outside of Quito the concept of a fixed bus stop is pretty much nonexistent. Buses stop (or at least come to a slow roll) when people flag them down. When you want to get off a local bus, yell '*¡Baja!*,' which means 'Down!' (as in 'the passenger is getting down'). Another favorite way of getting the driver to stop is by yelling '*¡Gracias!*' ('Thank you!'), which is unmistakably polite.

Taxi

Ecuadorian taxis come in a variety of shapes and sizes, but they are all yellow. Most taxis have a lit 'taxi' sign on top or a 'taxi' sticker on the windshield. In Quito and other bigger cities, licensed taxis have an orange or orange-striped license plate, with ID numbers clearly marked on the sides.

Always ask the fare beforehand, or you may be overcharged. Meters are rarely seen, except in Quito, Guayaquil and Cuenca. A long ride in these cities should rarely go over $5 (unless traveling to Quito's bus terminals, which are quite distant from the center). The minimum fare nearly everywhere is $1.25, and you'll be required to pay $1 in Quito even if the meter only says $0.80. On weekends and at night, fares are always about 25% to 50% higher.

You can hire a taxi for a day for about $40 to $60. Hiring a taxi for a few days is comparable to renting a car, except that you don't have to drive. But you will have to pay for the driver's food and room. Some tour companies in Quito rent 4WD vehicles with experienced drivers.

In less urban areas, you're also likely to see ecotaxis (a three-wheeled bicycle with a small covered carriage in back that fits two people) as well as *taxis ecológicos* (motorcycle taxis with a two-seater carriage in back).

Tours

If you're short on time, the best place to organize a tour is either Quito or Guayaquil. A plethora of operators for every budget offer trips including Galápagos cruises, climbing and hiking tours, horseback-riding, jungle tours, mountain-biking tours, hacienda tours and more.

Tour costs vary tremendously depending on what your requirements are. The cheapest city tours start from around $65 per person; a banana and cocoa trail tour starts from $98 per person per day, while a two-night Amazon camping tour starts at $68 (per person based on two or more people). Meanwhile, the most expensive lodges can exceed $200 per person per night including meals and tours. Volcano national park hiking tours start around $95 per day per person, and start from $190 for a two-day volcano summit hike. Many tour prices reduce the more people you have in your group. Galápagos boat cruises range from $3,000 up to $7,000 per week excluding airfare, taxes and entrance fees.

Train

Much to the delight of train enthusiasts, Ecuador's rail system has finally been restored. Unfortunately, it's not useful for travel, as the routes are used for day trips designed exclusively for tourists. The trains run along short routes, typically on weekends, sometimes with return service by bus. The most famous line is the dramatic descent from Alausí along La Nariz del Diablo (The Devil's Nose), a spectacular section of train track that was one of the world's greatest feats of railroad engineering. The second is the weekend train excursion between Quito and the Area Nacional de Recreación El Boliche, near Cotopaxi.

Other routes run from Durán (near Guayaquil), Ibarra, Ambato, Riobamba and El Tambo (near Ingapirca).

For departure times, ticket prices and itinerary information, visit Tren Ecuador (www.trenecuador.com).

Truck (Ranchera & Missionary)

In certain towns, especially in rural areas where there are many dirt roads, *camionetas* (pickup trucks) act as taxis. If you need to get to a national park, a climbers refuge or a trailhead from a town, often the best way to do so is by hiring a pickup, which is usually as easy as asking around.

In remote areas, trucks often double as buses. Sometimes these are large, flatbed trucks with a tin roof, open wooden sides and uncomfortable wooden-plank seats. These curious-looking 'buses' are called *rancheras* or *chivas*, and are seen on the coast and in the Oriente.

In the remote parts of the highlands, *camionetas* (ordinary trucks or pickups) are used to carry passengers; you just climb in the back. If the weather is good, you get fabulous views and the refreshing sensation of Andean wind in your face. If the weather is bad, you hunker down beneath a tarpaulin with the other passengers.

Payment is usually determined by the driver and is a standard fare depending on the distance. You can ask other passengers how much they are paying; trucks typically charge about the same as buses.

Language

Latin American Spanish pronunciation is easy, as most sounds have equivalents in English. Also, Spanish spelling is phonetically consistent, meaning that there's a clear and consistent relationship between what you see in writing and how it's pronounced. Read our coloured pronunciation guides as if they were English, and you'll be understood. Note that kh is a throaty sound (like the 'ch' in the Scottish *loch*), v and b are like a soft English 'v' (between a 'v' and a 'b'), and r is strongly rolled.

There are some variations in spoken Spanish across Latin America, the most notable being the pronunciation of the letters *ll* and *y* – depending on where you are on the continent, you'll hear them pronounced like the 'y' in 'yes', 'lli' in 'million', the 's' in 'measure', the 'sh' in 'shut' or the 'dg' in 'judge'. In our pronunciation guides in this chapter they are represented with y because they are pronounced as the 'y' in 'yes' in Ecuador (as in many other parts of Latin America).

The stressed syllables are indicated with an acute accent in written Spanish (eg *días*) and with italics in our pronunciation guides.

The polite form is used in this chapter; where both polite and informal options are given, they are indicated by the abbreviations 'pol' and 'inf'. Where necessary, both masculine and feminine forms of words are included, separated by a slash and with the masculine form first, eg *perdido/a* (m/f).

BASICS

Hello.	*Hola.*	o·la
Goodbye.	*Adiós.*	a·*dyos*
How are you?	*¿Qué tal?*	ke tal
Fine, thanks.	*Bien, gracias.*	byen *gra*·syas
Excuse me.	*Perdón.*	per·*don*
Sorry.	*Lo siento.*	lo *syen*·to
Please.	*Por favor.*	por fa·*vor*
Thank you.	*Gracias.*	*gra*·syas
You're welcome.	*De nada.*	de *na*·da
Yes.	*Sí.*	see
No.	*No.*	no

My name is ...
Me llamo ... — me *ya*·mo ...

What's your name?
¿Cómo se llama Usted? — *ko*·mo se *ya*·ma oo·*ste* (pol)
¿Cómo te llamas? — *ko*·mo te *ya*·mas (inf)

Do you speak English?
¿Habla inglés? — *a*·bla een·*gles* (pol)
¿Hablas inglés? — *a*·blas een·*gles* (inf)

I don't understand.
Yo no entiendo. — yo no en·*tyen*·do

ACCOMMODATIONS

I'd like a ... room.	*Quisiera una habitación ...*	kee·*sye*·ra *oo*·na a·bee·ta·*syon* ...
single	*individual*	een·dee·vee·*dwal*
double	*doble*	*do*·ble

How much is it per night/person?
¿Cuánto cuesta por noche/persona? — *kwan*·to *kwes*·ta por *no*·che/per·*so*·na

Does it include breakfast?
¿Incluye el desayuno? — een·*kloo*·ye el de·sa·*yoo*·no

campsite	*terreno de cámping*	te·*re*·no de *kam*·peeng
hotel	*hotel*	o·*tel*
guesthouse	*pensión*	pen·*syon*
(small) hotel/ country inn	*hostal/ hostería*	os·*tal*/ os·te·*ree*·a
youth hostel	*albergue juvenil*	al·*ber*·ge khoo·ve·*neel*
air-con	*aire acondicionado*	*ai*·re a·kon·dee·syo·*na*·do

KICHWA

Most indigenous groups are bilingual, with Kichwa as their mother tongue and Spanish as second language. The Kichwa spoken in Ecuador is quite different from that of Peru and Bolivia.

The following phrases could be useful in areas where Ecuadorian Kichwa is spoken. Pronounce them as you would a Spanish word. The apostrophe (') represents a glottal stop, ie the sound that occurs in the middle of 'uh-oh'.

Hello.	*Napaykullayki.*
Please.	*Allichu.*
Thank you.	*Yusulipayki.*
Yes./No.	*Ari./Mana.*
How do you say ...?	*Imainata nincha chaita ...?*
It is called ...	*Chaipa'g sutin'ha ...*
Please repeat.	*Ua'manta niway.*
How much?	*Maik'ata'g?*
father	*tayta*
food	*mikiuy*
mother	*mama*
river	*mayu*
snowy peak	*riti-orko*
water	*yacu*
1	*u'*
2	*iskai*
3	*quinsa*
4	*tahua*
5	*phiska*
6	*so'gta*
7	*khanchis*
8	*pusa'g*
9	*iskon*
10	*chunca*

bathroom	*baño*	ba·nyo
bed	*cama*	ka·ma
window	*ventana*	ven·ta·na

DIRECTIONS

Where's ...?
¿Dónde está ...? don·de es·ta ...

What's the address?
¿Cuál es la dirección? kwal es la dee·rek·syon

Could you please write it down?
¿Puede escribirlo, por favor? pwe·de es·kree·beer·lo por fa·vor

Can you show me (on the map)?
¿Me lo puede indicar (en el mapa)? me lo pwe·de een·dee·kar (en el ma·pa)

at the corner	*en la esquina*	en la es·kee·na
at the traffic lights	*en el semáforo*	en el se·ma·fo·ro
behind ...	*detrás de ...*	de·tras de ...
far	*lejos*	le·khos
in front of ...	*enfrente de ...*	en·fren·te de ...
left	*izquierda*	ees·kyer·da
near	*cerca*	ser·ka
next to ...	*al lado de ...*	al la·do de ...
opposite ...	*frente a ...*	fren·te a ...
right	*derecha*	de·re·cha
straight ahead	*todo recto*	to·do rek·to

EATING & DRINKING

Can I see the menu, please?
¿Puedo ver el menú, por favor? pwe·do ver el me·noo por fa·vor

What would you recommend?
¿Qué recomienda? ke re·ko·myen·da

Do you have vegetarian food?
¿Tienen comida vegetariana? tye·nen ko·mee·da ve·khe·ta·rya·na

I don't eat (red meat).
No como (carne roja). no ko·mo (kar·ne ro·kha)

That was delicious!
¡Estaba buenísimo! es·ta·ba bwe·nee·see·mo

Cheers!
¡Salud! sa·loo

The bill, please.
La cuenta, por favor. la kwen·ta por fa·vor

I'd like a table for ...	*Quisiera una mesa para ...*	kee·sye·ra oo·na me·sa pa·ra ...
(eight) o'clock	*las (ocho)*	las (o·cho)
(two) people	*(dos) personas*	(dos) per·so·nas

Key Words

bottle	*botella*	bo·te·ya
bowl	*bol*	bol
breakfast	*desayuno*	de·sa·yoo·no
children's menu	*menú infantil*	me·noo een·fan·teel
(too) cold	*(muy) frío*	(mooy) free·o
dinner	*cena*	se·na

fork	*tenedor*	te·ne·*dor*
glass	*vaso*	*va*·so
highchair	*trona*	*tro*·na
hot (warm)	*caliente*	kal·*yen*·te
knife	*cuchillo*	koo·*chee*·yo
lunch	*almuerzo*	al·*mwer*·so
plate	*plato*	*pla*·to
restaurant	*restaurante*	res·tow·*ran*·te
spoon	*cuchara*	koo·*cha*·ra
with/without	*con/sin*	kon/seen

Meat & Fish

beef	*carne de vaca*	*kar*·ne de *va*·ka
chicken	*pollo*	*po*·yo
fish	*pescado*	pes·*ka*·do
lamb	*cordero*	kor·*de*·ro
pork	*cerdo*	*ser*·do
turkey	*pavo*	*pa*·vo
veal	*ternera*	ter·*ne*·ra

Fruit & Vegetables

apple	*manzana*	man·*sa*·na
apricot	*damasco*	da·*mas*·ko
artichoke	*alcaucil*	al·*kow*·seel
asparagus	*espárragos*	es·*pa*·ra·gos
banana	*banana*	ba·*na*·na
beans	*chauchas*	*chow*·chas
beetroot	*remolacha*	re·mo·*la*·cha
cabbage	*repollo*	re·*po*·yo
carrot	*zanahoria*	sa·na·*o*·rya
celery	*apio*	*a*·pyo
cherry	*cereza*	se·*re*·sa
corn	*choclo*	*cho*·klo
cucumber	*pepino*	pe·*pee*·no
fruit	*fruta*	*froo*·ta
grape	*uvas*	*oo*·vas
lemon	*limón*	lee·*mon*
lentils	*lentejas*	len·*te*·khas
lettuce	*lechuga*	le·*choo*·ga
mushroom	*champiñón*	cham·pee·*nyon*
nuts	*nueces*	*nwe*·ses
onion	*cebolla*	se·*bo*·ya
orange	*naranja*	na·*ran*·kha
peach	*melocotón*	me·lo·ko·*ton*
peas	*arvejas*	ar·*ve*·khas
(red/green) pepper	*pimiento (rojo/verde)*	pee·*myen*·to (*ro*·kho/*ver*·de)
pineapple	*ananá*	a·na·*na*
plum	*ciruela*	seer·*we*·la
potato	*papa*	*pa*·pa
pumpkin	*zapallo*	sa·*pa*·yo
spinach	*espinacas*	es·pee·*na*·kas
strawberry	*frutilla*	froo·*tee*·ya
tomato	*tomate*	to·*ma*·te
vegetable	*verdura*	ver·*doo*·ra
watermelon	*sandía*	san·*dee*·a

Other

bread	*pan*	pan
butter	*manteca*	man·*te*·ka
cheese	*queso*	*ke*·so
egg	*huevo*	*we*·vo
honey	*miel*	myel
jam	*mermelada*	mer·me·*la*·da
oil	*aceite*	a·*sey*·te
pepper	*pimienta*	pee·*myen*·ta
rice	*arroz*	a·*ros*
salt	*sal*	sal
sugar	*azúcar*	a·*soo*·kar
vinegar	*vinagre*	vee·*na*·gre

Drinks

beer	*cerveza*	ser·*ve*·sa
coffee	*café*	ka·*fe*
(orange) juice	*jugo (de naranja)*	*khoo*·go (de na·*ran*·kha)
milk	*leche*	*le*·che
tea	*té*	te
(mineral) water	*agua (mineral)*	*a*·gwa (mee·ne·*ral*)
(red/white) wine	*vino (tinto/ blanco)*	*vee*·no (*teen*·to/ *blan*·ko)

SIGNS

Abierto	Open
Cerrado	Closed
Entrada	Entrance
Hombres/Varones	Men
Mujeres/Damas	Women
Prohibido	Prohibited
Salida	Exit
Servicios/Baños	Toilets

EMERGENCIES

Help!	*¡Socorro!*	so·ko·ro
Go away!	*¡Vete!*	ve·te

Call ...!	*¡Llame a ...!*	*ya*·me a ...
a doctor	*un médico*	oon *me*·dee·ko
the police	*la policía*	la po·lee·*see*·a

I'm lost.
Estoy perdido/a. es·*toy* per·*dee*·do/a (m/f)

I'm ill.
Estoy enfermo/a. es·*toy* en·*fer*·mo/a (m/f)

It hurts here.
Me duele aquí. me *dwe*·le a·*kee*

I'm allergic to (antibiotics).
Soy alérgico/a a (los antibióticos). soy a·*ler*·khee·ko/a a (los an·tee·*byo*·tee·kos) (m/f)

Where are the toilets?
¿Dónde están los baños? *don*·de es·*tan* los *ba*·nyos

SHOPPING & SERVICES

I'd like to buy ...
Quisiera comprar ... kee·*sye*·ra kom·*prar* ...

I'm just looking.
Sólo estoy mirando. *so*·lo es·*toy* mee·*ran*·do

NUMBERS

1	*uno*	*oo*·no
2	*dos*	dos
3	*tres*	tres
4	*cuatro*	*kwa*·tro
5	*cinco*	*seen*·ko
6	*seis*	seys
7	*siete*	*sye*·te
8	*ocho*	*o*·cho
9	*nueve*	*nwe*·ve
10	*diez*	dyes
20	*veinte*	*veyn*·te
30	*treinta*	*treyn*·ta
40	*cuarenta*	kwa·*ren*·ta
50	*cincuenta*	seen·*kwen*·ta
60	*sesenta*	se·*sen*·ta
70	*setenta*	se·*ten*·ta
80	*ochenta*	o·*chen*·ta
90	*noventa*	no·*ven*·ta
100	*cien*	syen
1000	*mil*	meel

Can I look at it?
¿Puedo verlo? *pwe*·do *ver*·lo

I don't like it.
No me gusta. no me *goos*·ta

How much is it?
¿Cuánto cuesta? *kwan*·to *kwes*·ta

That's too expensive.
Es muy caro. es mooy *ka*·ro

Can you lower the price?
¿Podría bajar un poco el precio? po·*dree*·a ba·*khar* oon *po*·ko el *pre*·syo

There's a mistake in the bill.
Hay un error en la cuenta. ai oon e·*ror* en la *kwen*·ta

ATM	*cajero automático*	ka·*khe*·ro ow·to·*ma*·tee·ko
credit card	*tarjeta de crédito*	tar·*khe*·ta de *kre*·dee·to
internet cafe	*cibercafé*	see·ber·ka·*fe*
market	*mercado*	mer·*ka*·do
post office	*correos*	ko·*re*·os
tourist office	*oficina de turismo*	o·fee·*see*·na de too·*rees*·mo

TIME & DATES

What time is it?	*¿Qué hora es?*	ke *o*·ra es
It's (10) o'clock.	*Son (las diez).*	son (las dyes)
Half past ...	*... y media.*	... ee *me*·dya
morning	*mañana*	ma·*nya*·na
afternoon	*tarde*	*tar*·de
evening	*noche*	*no*·che
yesterday	*ayer*	a·*yer*
today	*hoy*	oy
tomorrow	*mañana*	ma·*nya*·na

Monday	*lunes*	*loo*·nes
Tuesday	*martes*	*mar*·tes
Wednesday	*miércoles*	*myer*·ko·les
Thursday	*jueves*	*khwe*·ves
Friday	*viernes*	*vyer*·nes
Saturday	*sábado*	*sa*·ba·do
Sunday	*domingo*	do·*meen*·go

January	*enero*	e·*ne*·ro
February	*febrero*	fe·*bre*·ro
March	*marzo*	*mar*·so
April	*abril*	a·*breel*
May	*mayo*	*ma*·yo
June	*junio*	*khoon*·yo
July	*julio*	*khool*·yo
August	*agosto*	a·*gos*·to
September	*septiembre*	sep·*tyem*·bre
October	*octubre*	ok·*too*·bre

November	*noviembre*	no·*vyem*·bre
December	*diciembre*	dee·*syem*·bre

TRANSPORTATION

boat	*barco*	*bar*·ko
bus	*autobús*	ow·to·*boos*
(basic) bus	*chiva/ ranchera*	*chee*·va/ ran·*che*·ra
plane	*avión*	a·*vyon*
(shared) taxi	*colectivo*	ko·lek·*tee*·vo
train	*tren*	tren
truck/pickup	*camioneta*	ka·myo·*ne*·ta
first	*primero*	pree·*me*·ro
last	*último*	*ool*·tee·mo
next	*próximo*	*prok*·see·mo
A ... ticket, please.	*Un boleto de ..., por favor.*	oon bo·*le*·to de ... por fa·*vor*
1st-class	*primera clase*	pree·*me*·ra *kla*·se
2nd-class	*segunda clase*	se·*goon*·da *kla*·se
one-way	*ida*	*ee*·da
return	*ida y vuelta*	*ee*·da ee *vwel*·ta

I want to go to ...
Quisiera ir a ... kee·*sye*·ra eer a ...

Does it stop at ...?
¿Para en ...? *pa*·ra en ...

What stop is this?
¿Cuál es esta parada? kwal es *es*·ta pa·*ra*·da

What time does it arrive/leave?
¿A qué hora llega/sale? a ke *o*·ra *ye*·ga/*sa*·le

Please tell me when we get to ...
¿Puede avisarme cuando lleguemos a ...? *pwe*·de a·vee·*sar*·me *kwan*·do ye·*ge*·mos a ...

I want to get off here.
Quiero bajarme aquí. *kye*·ro ba·*khar*·me a·*kee*

airport	*aeropuerto*	a·e·ro·*pwer*·to
aisle seat	*asiento de pasillo*	a·*syen*·to de pa·*see*·yo
bus stop	*parada de autobuses*	pa·*ra*·da de ow·to·*boo*·ses
bus station	*terminal terrestre*	ter·mee·*nal* te·*res*·tre
cancelled	*cancelado*	kan·se·*la*·do
delayed	*retrasado*	re·tra·*sa*·do
platform	*plataforma*	pla·ta·*for*·ma
ticket office	*taquilla*	ta·*kee*·ya
timetable	*horario*	o·*ra*·ryo
train station	*estación de trenes*	es·ta·*syon* de *tre*·nes
window seat	*asiento junto a la ventana*	a·*syen*·to *khoon*·to a la ven·*ta*·na

QUESTION WORDS

How?	*¿Cómo?*	*ko*·mo
What?	*¿Qué?*	ke
When?	*¿Cuándo?*	*kwan*·do
Where?	*¿Dónde?*	*don*·de
Who?	*¿Quién?*	kyen
Why?	*¿Por qué?*	por ke

I'd like to hire a ...	*Quisiera alquilar ...*	kee·*sye*·ra al·kee·*lar* ...
4WD	*un todo-terreno*	oon to·do·te·*re*·no
bicycle	*una bicicleta*	*oo*·na bee·see·*kle*·ta
car	*un coche*	oon *ko*·che
motorcycle	*una moto*	*oo*·na *mo*·to
child seat	*asiento de seguridad para niños*	a·*syen*·to de se·goo·ree·*da* *pa*·ra *nee*·nyos
diesel	*petróleo*	pet·*ro*·le·o
helmet	*casco*	*kas*·ko
hitchhike	*hacer botella*	a·*ser* bo·*te*·ya
mechanic	*mecánico*	me·*ka*·nee·ko
petrol/gas	*gasolina*	ga·so·*lee*·na
service station	*gasolinera*	ga·so·lee·*ne*·ra
truck	*camion*	ka·*myon*

Is this the road to ...?
¿Se va a ... por esta carretera? se va a ... por *es*·ta ka·re·*te*·ra

(How long) Can I park here?
¿(Cuánto tiempo) Puedo aparcar aquí? (*kwan*·to *tyem*·po) *pwe*·do a·par·*kar* a·*kee*

The car has broken down (at ...).
El coche se ha averiado (en ...). el *ko*·che se a a·ve·*rya*·do (en ...)

I had an accident.
He tenido un accidente. e te·*nee*·do oon ak·see·*den*·te

I've run out of petrol.
Me he quedado sin gasolina. me e ke·*da*·do seen ga·so·*lee*·na

I have a flat tyre.
Se me pinchó una rueda. se me peen·*cho* *oo*·na *rwe*·da

GLOSSARY

AGAR – Asociación de Guías de Águas Rápidas del Ecuador (Ecuadorian White-Water Guides Association)
aguardiente – sugarcane alcohol
ASEGUIM – Asociación Ecuatoriana de Guías de Montaña (Ecuadorian Mountain Guides Association)

balneario – literally 'spa', but any place where you can swim or soak

cabaña – cabin, found both on the coast and in the Oriente
camioneta – pickup or light truck
campesino – peasant
capitanía – port captain
casa de cambio – currency-exchange bureau
centro comercial – shopping center; often abbreviated to 'CC'
chifa – Chinese restaurant
chiva – open-sided bus, or truck mounted with uncomfortably narrow bench seats; also called *ranchera*
colectivo – shared taxi
comedore – cheap restaurant
comida típica – traditional Ecuadorian food
cuencano – person from Cuenca
curandero – medicine man

ejecutivo – 1st class, on buses

folklórica – traditional Andean folk music
guayaquileño – person from Guayaquil
hostal – small and reasonably priced hotel; not a youth hostel
hostería – small hotel, which tends to be a midpriced country inn; often, but not always, found in rural areas

IGM – Instituto Geográfico Militar, the Ecuadorian government agency that produces topographic and other maps
indígena – indigenous person

lavandería – laundry

malecón – waterfront
mestizo – person of mixed indigenous and Spanish descent

otavaleño – person from Otavalo

paja toquilla – straw from the *toquilla* (a small palm), used in crafts and hat making
Panamericana – Pan-American Hwy, which is the main route joining Latin American countries to one another; known as the Interamericana in some countries
panga – small boat used to ferry passengers, especially in the Galápagos Islands, but also on the rivers and lakes of the Oriente and along the coast
páramo – high-altitude Andean grasslands of Ecuador, which continue north into Colombia with relicts in the highest parts of Costa Rica
parque nacional – national park
pasillo – Ecuador's national music
peña – bar or club featuring live folkloric music
playa – beach
puente – bridge

quinta – fine house or villa found in the countryside
quiteño – person from Quito

ranchera – see *chiva*
refugio – simple mountain shelters for spending the night
residencial – cheap hotel
río – river

salsateca – (also *salsoteca*) nightclub where dancing to salsa music is the main attraction
serranos – people from the highlands
shigra – small string bag

tagua nut – from a palm tree grown in local forest; the 'nuts' are actually hard seeds, which are carved into a variety of ornaments
terminal terrestre – central bus terminal for many different companies
tzantza – shrunken head

Behind the Scenes

SEND US YOUR FEEDBACK

We love to hear from travelers – your comments keep us on our toes and help make our books better. Our well-traveled team reads every word on what you loved or loathed about this book. Although we cannot reply individually to your submissions, we always guarantee that your feedback goes straight to the appropriate authors, in time for the next edition. Each person who sends us information is thanked in the next edition – the most useful submissions are rewarded with a selection of digital PDF chapters.

Visit **lonelyplanet.com/contact** to submit your updates and suggestions or to ask for help. Our award-winning website also features inspirational travel stories, news and discussions.

Note: We may edit, reproduce and incorporate your comments in Lonely Planet products such as guidebooks, websites and digital products, so let us know if you don't want your comments reproduced or your name acknowledged. For a copy of our privacy policy visit lonelyplanet.com/privacy.

OUR READERS

Many thanks to the travelers who used the last edition and wrote to us with helpful hints, useful advice and interesting anecdotes:

Alfredo Martí Albiol, Bert Waslander, Carlos Manrique de Lara Cadiñanos, Christopher Shingleton, Claudia Baldwin, Eize & Geeske Siegersma, Elise van Vliet, Esther Kalabis, Eva Franc, Geoff Goodwin, Ginny Sutcliffe, Heather Scott, Heather Utteridge, Ingrid Astfalk, Linda E Bayless, Manuela Casanova, Mark White, Maya Wodnicka , Michael Ten Bhomer, Ned Cresswell, Oliver Hiller, Renata Kolar, Sarah Astfalk, Shanelle Reilly, Theresa Astfalk, Tim Urban, Yolanda Guaman

WRITER THANKS

Isabel Albiston

Many thanks to everyone I met along the road who made my research trip so enjoyable, especially Jamie Mitchell and her family, Galo Brito and Carlos at Pro Bici, Luis at Julio Verne, Anibal Tenemasa, Joaquín Andino, Belén Arellano, Jazmín Arellano, Jesús Alcalá, Anita Hughes and Fernando Vallejo. Thanks also to MaSovaida Morgan and my co-writers.

Jade Bremner

Gracias to Destination Editor MaSovaida Morgan for this project and being so helpful along the way. Thanks also to local expert Mario Xavier for his outstanding knowledge and passion for Ecuador, plus his tips and recommendations, and last but not least, thanks to everyone working hard behind the scenes – including Cheree Broughton and Neill Coen.

Brian Kluepfel

Thanks to MaSovaida Morgan, Sandra Patiño, Cesar 'La Tortuga' Soledispa (best *taxista* ever), Ingo, Carlos Zorrilla, Sandra Statz, Polivio Perez, Diana and Vlady, Ignacio de la Torre at La Roulotte, Goyon Benchwick, and my amazing wife, Paula Zorrilla, who lets me go on these amazing adventures as long as I bring back cool presents from the airports.

MaSovaida Morgan

Deepest thanks to the countless kind souls who helped me navigate this magical place – in particular, Jaci Bruns, Regis St Louis, Jackie Vazquez, Erick Ortiz, Luis Jaramillo and the Galaven crew. Thanks also to my co-writers for a smooth project while I wore two hats, Simon Williamson for showing mercy, and Evan Godt for pulling strings with the quickness. As always, gratitude and love to Ny, Ty and Haj for always carrying me.

Wendy Yanagihara

Many thanks to Jerry, Edgar, Carlos, and Gennaro in Cuenca; Lauro in Saraguro; Rodrigo in Baeza; and all of my fantastic guides in Amazonía: Andrés, Gabriel, Fabricio, Livio, Victor, Carlos, and Sergio. I am grateful most of all to Luis Hernández and Fernando Vaca for their invaluable logistics help and expertise. Thanks also to Laura, Victoria, and John, my support crew at home.

ACKNOWLEDGEMENTS

Climate map data adapted from Peel MC, Finlayson BL & McMahon TA (2007) 'Updated World Map of the Köppen-Geiger Climate Classification', Hydrology and Earth System Sciences, 11, 163344.

Cover photograph: Baby sea lion on Isla Santiago, Galápagos Islands, MindStorm/Shutterstock©

THIS BOOK

This 11th edition of Lonely Planet's *Ecuador & the Galápagos Islands* guidebook was researched and written by Isabel Albiston, Jade Bremner, Brian Kluepfel, MaSovaida Morgan and Wendy Yanagihara, and curated by Isabel. The previous edition was written by Regis St Louis, Greg Benchwick, Michael Grosberg and Luke Waterson. This guidebook was produced by the following:

Destination Editors MaSovaida Morgan

Product Editor Sandie Kestell

Senior Cartographer Corey Hutchison

Book Designer Gwen Cotter

Assisting Editors Katie Connolly, Samantha Forge, Lou McGregor, Sarah Reid, Sarah Stewart, Sam Wheeler, Simon Williamson

Assisting Cartographer James Leversha

Cover Researcher Naomi Parker

Thanks to Jessica Ryan, Saralinda Turner

Index

Map Pages **000**
Photo Pages **000**

D

E

F

Map Pages **000**
Photo Pages **000**

Map Pages **000**
Photo Pages **000**

Map Legend

Sights

- Beach
- Bird Sanctuary
- Buddhist
- Castle/Palace
- Christian
- Confucian
- Hindu
- Islamic
- Jain
- Jewish
- Monument
- Museum/Gallery/Historic Building
- Ruin
- Shinto
- Sikh
- Taoist
- Winery/Vineyard
- Zoo/Wildlife Sanctuary
- Other Sight

Activities, Courses & Tours

- Bodysurfing
- Diving
- Canoeing/Kayaking
- Course/Tour
- Sento Hot Baths/Onsen
- Skiing
- Snorkeling
- Surfing
- Swimming/Pool
- Walking
- Windsurfing
- Other Activity

Sleeping

- Sleeping
- Camping
- Hut/Shelter

Eating

- Eating

Drinking & Nightlife

- Drinking & Nightlife
- Cafe

Entertainment

- Entertainment

Shopping

- Shopping

Information

- Bank
- Embassy/Consulate
- Hospital/Medical
- Internet
- Police
- Post Office
- Telephone
- Toilet
- Tourist Information
- Other Information

Geographic

- Beach
- Gate
- Hut/Shelter
- Lighthouse
- Lookout
- Mountain/Volcano
- Oasis
- Park
- Pass
- Picnic Area
- Waterfall

Population

- Capital (National)
- Capital (State/Province)
- City/Large Town
- Town/Village

Transport

- Airport
- Border crossing
- Bus
- Cable car/Funicular
- Cycling
- Ferry
- Metro station
- Monorail
- Parking
- Petrol station
- Subway/Subte station
- Taxi
- Train station/Railway
- Tram
- Underground station
- Other Transport

Routes

- Tollway
- Freeway
- Primary
- Secondary
- Tertiary
- Lane
- Unsealed road
- Road under construction
- Plaza/Mall
- Steps
- Tunnel
- Pedestrian overpass
- Walking Tour
- Walking Tour detour
- Path/Walking Trail

Boundaries

- International
- State/Province
- Disputed
- Regional/Suburb
- Marine Park
- Cliff
- Wall

Hydrography

- River, Creek
- Intermittent River
- Canal
- Water
- Dry/Salt/Intermittent Lake
- Reef

Areas

- Airport/Runway
- Beach/Desert
- Cemetery (Christian)
- Cemetery (Other)
- Glacier
- Mudflat
- Park/Forest
- Sight (Building)
- Sportsground
- Swamp/Mangrove

Note: Not all symbols displayed above appear on the maps in this book

Wendy Yanagihara

Cuenca & the Southern Highlands, The Oriente Wendy serendipitously landed her dream job of writing for Lonely Planet in 2003, and has spent the intervening years contributing to titles including *Southeast Asia on a Shoestring, Vietnam, Japan, Mexico, Costa Rica, Indonesia,* and *Grand Canyon National Park*. In the name of research, she has hiked remote valleys of West Papua, explored tiny nooks and alleys of Tokyo sprawl, trekked on a Patagonian glacier, and rafted Colorado River whitewater. Wendy has also written for *BBC Travel,* the *Guardian, Lonely Planet Magazine,* lonelyplanet.com, and intermittently freelances as a graphic designer, illustrator, and visual artist. Wendy also wrote the Survival Guide section of this book.

OUR STORY

A beat-up old car, a few dollars in the pocket and a sense of adventure. In 1972 that's all Tony and Maureen Wheeler needed for the trip of a lifetime – across Europe and Asia overland to Australia. It took several months, and at the end – broke but inspired – they sat at their kitchen table writing and stapling together their first travel guide, *Across Asia on the Cheap*. Within a week they'd sold 1500 copies. Lonely Planet was born.

Today, Lonely Planet has offices in Franklin, London, Melbourne, Oakland, Dublin, Beijing and Delhi, with more than 600 staff and writers. We share Tony's belief that 'a great guidebook should do three things: inform, educate and amuse'.

OUR WRITERS

Isabel Albiston

Quito, Central Highlands After six years working for the *Daily Telegraph* in London, Isabel left to spend more time on the road. A job as writer for a magazine in Sydney, Australia, was followed by a four-month overland trip across Asia and five years living and working in Buenos Aires, Argentina. Isabel started writing for Lonely Planet in 2014 and has contributed to 10 guidebooks. She's currently based in Madrid, Spain. Isabel also wrote the Plan section of this book.

Jade Bremner

South Coast Jade has been a journalist for more than a decade. She has lived in and reported on four different regions. Wherever she goes she finds action sports to try, the weirder the better, and it's no coincidence many of her favorite places have some of the best waves in the world. Jade has edited travel magazines and sections for *Time Out* and *Radio Times* and has contributed to the *Times*, *CNN* and the *Independent*. She feels privileged to share tales from this wonderful planet we call home and is always looking for her next adventure.

Brian Kluepfel

North Coast & Lowlands, Northern Highlands Brian had lived in three states and seven different residences by the time he was nine, and he's just kept moving ever since, making stops in Berkeley, Bolivia, the Bronx and the 'burbs further down the line. His journalistic work across the Americas has ranged from the Copa America soccer tournament in Paraguay to an accordion festival in Quebec. He has contributed to Lonely Planet titles including *Venezuela, Costa Rica, Belize & Guatemala*, and *Bolivia*. Brian is an avid birder and musician and dabbles in both on the road; his singing has been tolerated at open mics from Sámara, Costa Rica, to Beijing, China. Brian also wrote the Understand section of this book.

MaSovaida Morgan

The Galápagos Islands After nearly four years as Lonely Planet's Destination Editor for South America and Antarctica, a last-minute research trip to the Galápagos Islands for this edition prompted MaSovaida to hang up her editor hat for good. As a newly minted guidebook writer, she's also written about her hometown of Savannah, Georgia, and Korea for Lonely Planet. Learn more about her at www.masovaida.com, and follow her on Instagram, Twitter, and everywhere else on the internet @MaSovaida.

Published by Lonely Planet Global Limited
CRN 554153
11th edition – Aug 2018
ISBN 978 1 78657 062 8

10 9 8 7 6 5 4 3 2 1
Printed in China